SMALL SCALE APPROACH ORGANIC LABORATORY TECHNIQUES

CHEM 241L

Donald L. Pavia | Gary M. Lampman | George S. Kriz | Randall G. Engel

Australia • Brazil • Japan • Korea • Mexico • Singapore • Spain • United Kingdom • United States

SMALL SCALE APPROACH ORGANIC LABORATORY TECHNIQUES: CHEM 241L

Introduction to Organic Laboratory Techniques: A Small-Scale Approach, 2nd Edition
Donald L. Pavia | Gary M. Lampman | George S. Kriz | Randall G. Engel

Executive Editors:
Maureen Staudt
Michael Stranz

Senior Project Development Manager:
Linda deStefano

Marketing Specialist:
Courtney Sheldon

Senior Production/Manufacturing Manager:
Donna M. Brown

PreMedia Manager:
Joel Brennecke

Sr. Rights Acquisition Account Manager:
Todd Osborne

Cover Image:
Getty Images*

*Unless otherwise noted, all cover images used by Custom Solutions, a part of Cengage Learning, have been supplied courtesy of Getty Images with the exception of the Earthview cover image, which has been supplied by the National Aeronautics and Space Administration (NASA).

ISBN-13: 978-1-111-46475-2

ISBN-10: 1-111-46475-8

Cengage Learning
5191 Natorp Boulevard
Mason, Ohio 45040
USA

Cengage Learning is a leading provider of customized learning solutions with office locations around the globe, including Singapore, the United Kingdom, Australia, Mexico, Brazil, and Japan. Locate your local office at: **international.cengage.com/region.**

Cengage Learning products are represented in Canada by Nelson Education, Ltd.
For your lifelong learning solutions, visit **www.cengage.com/custom.**
Visit our corporate website at **www.cengage.com.**

Printed in the United States of America

PREFACE

When we set out to write the first edition of *Introduction to Organic Laboratory Techniques: A Small-Scale Approach,* we initially saw it as a "fourth edition" of our successful "macroscale" organic laboratory textbook. During this same period, we had gathered experience with microscale techniques in the organic laboratory through the development of experiments for the microscale versions of our laboratory textbook. That experience taught us that students *can* learn to do careful work in the organic laboratory on a small scale. They do not have to consume large quantities of chemicals, and they do not have to work in very large flasks to learn the standard techniques. At the same time, we recognized that many instructors do not wish to abandon the traditional-scale approach to their course, and many colleges and universities cannot afford to convert all of their glassware to microscale. Some instructors prefer to use equipment that more closely resembles research-style equipment. As a result, we recast our "macroscale" textbook as a **small-scale** approach to the laboratory. This second edition of *Introduction to Organic Laboratory Techniques: A Small-Scale Approach* develops these ideas further.

In the traditional approach to teaching this subject (called **macroscale**), the quantities of chemicals used were on the order to 5–100 grams. The approach used in this textbook, a **small-scale** approach, differs from the traditional laboratory in that nearly all of the experiments use smaller amounts of chemicals (1–10 grams). However, the glassware and methods used in small-scale experiments are identical to the glassware and methods used in standard-scale experiments.

The advantages of the small-scale approach include improved safety in the laboratory, reduced risk of fire and explosion, and reduced exposure to hazardous vapors. This approach decreases the need for hazardous waste disposal, leading to reduced contamination of the environment.

Another approach, a **microscale** approach, is used at many colleges and universities and differs from the traditional laboratory in that the experiments use *very* small amounts of chemicals (0.050–1.000 gram). Some of the microscale glassware is very different from standard-scale glassware, and there are a few special techniques that are unique to the microscale laboratory. Because of the widespread use of microscale methods, some reference to microscale techniques will be made in the technique chapters of this book. In fact, a few experiments in this textbook will feature microscale methods. However, these experiments have been designed to use ordinary glassware; they do not require specialized microscale equipment.

In preparing the first edition, therefore, we focused on converting our earlier experiments to a small scale. Along with these changes, we also devoted considerable effort toward improving the safety of all of the experiments. Technique Chapter 1, "Laboratory Safety," places strong emphasis on the safe use and disposal of hazardous chemicals. Information describing Material Safety Data Sheets and Right-to-Know laws is included. We have continued to update and improve instructions for the handling of waste products that are produced in the experiments. In this textbook we recommend that virtually all waste, including aqueous solutions, should be placed into appropriate waste containers.

NEW TO THIS EDITION

We have not included stand-alone technique experiments in previous editions of our "macroscale" textbooks. However, we are aware of many schools that use our textbook supplemented with their own technique experiments. Because of this, and because our teaching philosophy has evolved for the past twenty-five years, we have included five new technique experiments in this book: "Crystallization," "Extraction," "Chromatography," "Distillation," and "Infrared Spectroscopy and Boiling-Point Determination" (Experiments 2–6). We have also included an introductory experiment on solubility (Experiment 1), because solubility principles form the basis for several of the basic techniques. These six experiments emphasize understanding of and proficiency in performing the techniques. To further their understanding and to encourage students to think critically, we have included a number of "Critical Thinking Applications" at the end of several of these experiments. These are short exercises in which students must provide experimentally determined solutions to problems related to the techniques and the underlying principles.

For those instructors who want to continue to teach techniques within the context of relevant experiments, we recommend skipping the introductory technique experiments and using this book, starting with Experiment 7.

There is a new section (Part Five) in this textbook titled "Project-Based Experiments." In all these experiments, students must either solve a significant problem or they must generate all or part of a procedure. These experiments are intended to require considerable critical thinking and to challenge the students. By adding "open-ended" experiments such as these, we hope to demonstrate to students something of the intellectual approach that is part of scientific research or the practice of chemistry in industry.

New experiments, besides the introductory experiments in Part One, that have been added to this edition of the textbook include:

Experiment 32	Nitration of Aromatic Compounds Using a Recyclable Catalyst
Experiment 57	A Separation and Purification Scheme
Experiment 60	The Analysis of Antihistamine Drugs by Gas Chromatography-Mass Spectrometry
Experiment 62	The Aldehyde Enigma
Experiment 63	Synthesis of Substituted Chalcones: A Guided-Inquiry Experience
Experiment 66	An Oxidation Puzzle

Experiment 31 ("Chiral Reduction of Ethyl Acetoacetate: Optical Purity Determination") has been revised extensively. The organic qualitative analysis experiment (Experiment 55, "Identification of Unknowns") has been improved. The list of possible unknowns has been expanded significantly, and new exercises involving molecular modeling and computational chemistry have been added to several experiments.

A new essay, "Green Chemistry," has been added, and several of the experiments have been modified to make them "greener." We believe that an important future trend in the organic laboratory will be the introduction of environmentally responsible methods of performing laboratory experiments. These changes represent our initial endeavors in that direction.

Part Six of this book contains the chapters on techniques. These chapters have been reorganized from the first edition of the small-scale book. The technique chapters have been written to focus on traditional-scale laboratory techniques; however, because the use of microscale methods is increasing in popularity, we have included a discussion of the corresponding microscale methods as well.

We would also like to point out that an instructor's manual is available for persons who use our textbook. The instructor's manual contains complete instructions for the preparation of reagents and equipment for each experiment, as well as answers to each of the questions. Other comments that should prove helpful to the instructor are also included in the instructor's manual. We strongly recommend that instructors obtain access to this manual. The instructor's manual is an on-line document and may be viewed at http://chemistry.brookscole.com/smallscale2e. The password to gain access to the on-line instructor's manual is available for qualified instructors from your local Thomson Learning or Brooks/Cole field representative.

We owe our sincere thanks to the many colleagues who have used our textbooks and who have offered their suggestions for changes and improvements in our laboratory procedures. Although we cannot mention everyone who has made valuable contributions, we must make special mention of Frank Deering and Jim Patterson. We have also received a great deal of important assistance from people who work on our own campus. We especially thank James Vyvyan and Charles Wandler. Production of this textbook was capably handled by Brooks/Cole Publishers and G & S Typesetters. We thank all who contributed, with special thanks to our editor, Peter McGahey, and to Jamie Armstrong at G & S Typesetters.

We are especially grateful to the students and friends who have volunteered to participate in the development of experiments or who offered their help and criticism. We thank Carolyn Agasinski, Kathleen Barry, Roxana Blythe, Jessica Brooks, Steve Chrisman, Sky Countryman, Kathleen Holt, Laura Hooper, Matthew Hovde, Peter Kasselman, Erika Larson, Rachel Meyer, and Dawn Wagner.

If you wish to contact us with comments, questions, or suggestions, we have a special electronic mail address for this purpose (plke@chem.wwu.edu). We encourage you to visit our home page at http://lightning.chem.wwu.edu/dept/staff/org/plkhome.html. You may also wish to visit the Brooks/Cole Web site at http://www.brookscole.com.

Finally, we must thank our families and special friends, especially Neva-Jean Pavia, Marian Lampman, Carolyn Kriz, and Tawny for their encouragement, support, and patience.

Donald L. Pavia
Gary M. Lampman
George S. Kriz
Randall G. Engel
December 2003

CONTENTS ■

FALL

SPRING

Experiments & Techniques

WELCOME TO ORGANIC CHEMISTRY!

Organic chemistry can be fun, and we hope to prove it to you. The work in this laboratory course will teach you a lot. The personal satisfaction that comes with performing a sophisticated experiment skillfully and successfully will be great.

To get the most out of the laboratory course, you should strive to do several things. First, you must review all relevant safety material. Second, you need to understand the organization of this laboratory manual and how to use it effectively. The manual is your guide to learning. Third, you must try to understand both the purpose and the principles behind each experiment you do. Finally, you must try to organize your time effectively before each laboratory period.

LABORATORY SAFETY

Before undertaking any laboratory work, it is essential that you familiarize yourself with the appropriate safety procedures and that you understand what precautions you should take. We strongly urge you to read Technique 1, "Laboratory Safety" (pp. 558–575), before starting any laboratory experiments. It is your responsibility to know how to perform the experiments safely and how to understand and evaluate the risks that are associated with laboratory experiments. Knowing what to do and what not to do in the laboratory is of paramount importance, because the laboratory has many potential hazards associated with it.

ORGANIZATION OF THE TEXTBOOK

Consider briefly how this textbook is organized. After this introduction, the textbook is divided into six parts. Part One consists of 17 experiments that introduce you to most of the important basic laboratory techniques in organic chemistry. Part Two contains 2 experiments that introduce you to the modern, computer-based techniques of molecular modeling and computational chemistry. Part Three consists of 35 experiments that may be assigned as part of your laboratory course. Your instructor will choose a set of these experiments.

Part Four is devoted to the identification of organic compounds and contains 1 experiment that provides experience in the analytical aspects of organic chemistry. Interspersed within these first four parts of the textbook are numerous covering essays that provide background information related to the experiments and that place the experiments into a larger, overall context, showing how the experiments and compounds can be applied to areas of everyday concern and interest. Part Five contains 11 project-based experiments that require you to develop important critical thinking skills. Many of these experiments have a result that is not easily predicted in advance. To arrive at an appropriate conclusion, you may have to use many of the thought processes that are important in research. Part Six is composed of a series of detailed instructions and explanations dealing with the techniques of organic chemistry.

The techniques are extensively developed and used, and you will become familiar with them in the context of the experiments. The techniques chapters include infrared spectroscopy, nuclear magnetic resonance, ^{13}C nuclear magnetic resonance, and mass spectrometry. Many of the experiments included in Parts One through Five utilize these spectroscopic techniques, and your instructor may choose to add them to other experiments. Within each experiment, you will find the section "Required Reading," which indicates which techniques you should study to do that experiment. Extensive cross-referencing to the techniques chapters in Part Six is included in the experiments. Many experiments also contain a section called "Special Instructions," which lists special safety precautions and specific instructions to you, the student. Finally, most experiments contain a section entitled "Suggested Waste Disposal," which provides instruction on the correct means of disposing of the reagents and materials used during the experiment.

ADVANCE PREPARATION

It is essential to plan carefully for each laboratory period so that you will be able to keep abreast of the material you will learn in your organic chemistry laboratory course. You should not treat these experiments as a novice cook would treat *The Good Housekeeping Cookbook.* You should come to the laboratory with a plan for the use of your time and some understanding of what you are about to do. A really good cook does not follow the recipe line by line with a finger, nor does a good mechanic fix your car with the instruction manual in one hand and a wrench in the other. In addition, it is unlikely that you will learn much if you try to follow the instructions blindly, without understanding them. We can't emphasize strongly enough that you should come to the lab *prepared.*

If there are items or techniques that you do not understand, you should not hesitate to ask questions. You will learn more, however, if you figure things out on your own. Don't rely on others to do your thinking for you.

You should read Technique 2, "The Laboratory Notebook, Calculations, and Laboratory Records" right away. Although your instructor will undoubtedly have a preferred format for keeping records, much of the material here will help you learn to think constructively about laboratory experiments in advance. It would also save time if, as soon as possible, you read the first nine techniques chapters in Part Six. These techniques are basic to all experiments in this textbook. The laboratory class will begin with experiments almost immediately, and a thorough familiarity with this particular material will save you much valuable laboratory time.

BUDGETING TIME

As just mentioned in "Advance Preparation," you should read several techniques chapters of this book even before your first laboratory class meeting. You should also read the assigned experiment carefully before every class meeting. Having read the experiment will allow you to schedule your time wisely. Often you will be doing more than one experiment at a time. Experiments such as the fermentation of sugar or the chiral reduction of ethyl acetoacetate require a few minutes of advance preparation several days ahead of the actual experiment. At other times you will have to catch up on some unfinished details of a previous experiment. For instance, usually it is not possible to determine a yield accurately or a melting point of a product immediately after you first obtain the product. Products must be free of solvent to give an accurate weight or melting point range; they have to be "dried." Usually, this drying is done by leaving the product in an open container on your desk or in your locker. Then, when you have a pause in your schedule during the subsequent experiment, you can determine these missing data using a sample that is dry. Through careful planning you can set aside the time required to perform these miscellaneous experimental details.

PURPOSE

The main purpose of an organic laboratory course is to teach you the techniques necessary for a person dealing with organic chemicals. You will also learn the techniques needed for separating and purifying organic compounds. If the appropriate experiments are included in your course, you may also learn how to identify unknown compounds. The experiments themselves are only the vehicles for learning these techniques. The techniques chapters in Part Six are the heart of this textbook, and you should learn these techniques thoroughly. Your instructor may provide laboratory lectures and demonstrations explaining the techniques, but the burden is on you to master them by familiarizing yourself with the chapters in Part Six.

Besides good laboratory technique and the methods of carrying out basic laboratory procedures, other things you will learn from this laboratory course are

1. How to take data carefully
2. How to record relevant observations
3. How to use your time effectively
4. How to assess the efficiency of your experimental method
5. How to plan for the isolation and purification of the substance you prepare
6. How to work safely
7. How to solve problems and think like a chemist

In choosing experiments, we have tried whenever possible to make them relevant and, more important, interesting. To that end, we have tried to make them a learning experiment of a different kind. Most experiments are prefaced by a background essay to place things in context and to provide you with some new information. We hope to show you that organic chemistry pervades your lives (drugs, foods, plastics, perfumes, and so on). Furthermore, you should leave your course well trained in organic laboratory techniques. We are enthusiastic about our subject and hope you will receive it with the same spirit.

This textbook discusses the important laboratory techniques of organic chemistry and illustrates many important reactions and concepts. In the traditional approach to teaching this subject (called **macroscale**), the quantities of chemicals used were on the order of 5–100 grams. The approach used in this textbook, a **small-scale** approach, differs from the traditional laboratory in that nearly all of the experiments use smaller amounts of chemicals (1–10 grams). However, the glassware and methods used in small-scale experiments are identical to the glassware and methods used in macroscale experiments.

The advantages of the small-scale approach include improved safety in the laboratory, reduced risk of fire and explosion, and reduced exposure to hazardous vapors. This approach decreases the need for hazardous waste disposal, leading to reduced contamination of the environment.

Another approach, a **microscale** approach, differs from the traditional laboratory in that the experiments use very small amounts of chemicals (0.050–1.000 grams). Some microscale glassware is very different from macroscale scale glassware, and there are a few techniques that are unique to the microscale laboratory. Because of the widespread use of microscale methods, some reference to microscale techniques will be made in the techniques chapters. A few experiments in this textbook feature microscale methods. These experiments have been designed to use ordinary glassware; they do not require specialized microscale equipment.

TECHNIQUE 1

Laboratory Safety

In any laboratory course, familiarity with the fundamentals of laboratory safety is critical. Any chemistry laboratory, particularly an organic chemistry laboratory, can be a dangerous place in which to work. Understanding potential hazards will serve you well in minimizing that danger. It is ultimately your responsibility, along with your laboratory instructor's, to make sure that all laboratory work is carried out in a safe manner.

1.1 SAFETY GUIDELINES

It is vital that you take necessary precautions in the organic chemistry laboratory. Your laboratory instructor will advise you of specific rules for the laboratory in which you work. The following list of safety guidelines should be observed in all organic chemistry laboratories.

A. Eye Safety

Always Wear Approved Safety Glasses or Goggles. It is essential to wear eye protection whenever you are in the laboratory. Even if you are not actually carrying out an experiment, a person near you might have an accident that could endanger your eyes. Even dish washing can be hazardous. We know of cases in which a person has been cleaning glassware only to have an undetected piece of reactive material explode, throwing fragments into the person's eyes. To avoid such accidents, wear your safety glasses or goggles at all times.

Learn the Location of Eyewash Facilities. If there are eyewash fountains in your laboratory, determine which one is nearest to you before you start to work. If any chemical enters your eyes, go immediately to the eyewash fountain and flush your eyes and face with large amounts of water. If an eyewash fountain is not available, the laboratory will usually have at least one sink fitted with a piece of flexible hose. When the water is turned on, this hose can be aimed upward, and the water can be directed into the face, working much as an eyewash fountain does. To avoid damaging the eyes, the water flow rate should not be set too high, and the water temperature should be slightly warm.

B. Fires

Use Care with Open Flames in the Laboratory. Because an organic chemistry laboratory course deals with flammable organic solvents, the danger of fire is frequently present. Because of this danger, DO NOT SMOKE IN THE LABORATORY. Furthermore, use extreme caution when you light matches or use any open flame. Always check to see whether your neighbors on either side, across the bench, and behind you are using flammable solvents. If so, either wait or move to a safe location, such as a fume hood, to use your open flame. Many flammable organic substances are the source of dense vapors that can travel for some distance down a bench. These vapors present a fire danger, and you should be careful, because the source of those vapors may be far away from you. Do not use the bench sinks to dispose of flammable solvents. If your bench has a trough running along it, pour only *water* (no flammable solvents!) into it. The troughs and sinks are designed to carry water—not flammable materials—from the condenser hoses and aspirators.

Learn the Location of Fire Extinguishers, Fire Showers, and Fire Blankets. For your own protection in case of a fire, you should immediately determine the location of the nearest fire extinguisher, fire shower, and fire blanket. You should learn how to operate these safety devices, particularly the fire extinguisher. Your instructor can demonstrate this.

If there is a fire, the best advice is to get away from it and let the instructor or laboratory assistant take care of it. DON'T PANIC! Time spent in thought before action is never wasted. If it is a small fire in a container, it can usually be extinguished quickly by placing a wire-gauze screen with a ceramic fiber center or, possibly, a watch glass over the mouth of the container. It is good practice to have a wire screen or watch glass handy whenever you are using a flame. If this method does not extinguish the fire and if help from an experienced person is not readily available, then extinguish the fire yourself with a fire extinguisher.

Should your clothing catch on fire, DO NOT RUN. Walk *purposefully* toward the fire shower station or the nearest fire blanket. Running will fan the flames and intensify them.

C. Organic Solvents: Their Hazards

Avoid Contact with Organic Solvents. It is essential to remember that most organic solvents are flammable and will burn if they are exposed to an open flame or a match. Remember also that on repeated or excessive exposure, some organic solvents may be toxic, carcinogenic (cancer causing), or both. For example, many chlorocarbon solvents, when accumulated in the body, result in liver deterioration similar to cirrhosis caused by excessive use of ethanol. The body does not easily rid itself of chlorocarbons nor does it detoxify them; they build up over time and may cause future illness. Some chlorocarbons are also suspected of being carcinogens. MINIMIZE YOUR EXPOSURE. Long-term exposure to benzene may cause a form of leukemia. Do not sniff benzene and avoid spilling it on yourself. Many other solvents, such as chloroform and ether, are good anesthetics and will put you to sleep if you breathe too much of them. They subsequently cause nausea. Many of these solvents have a synergistic effect with ethanol, meaning that they enhance its effect. Pyridine causes temporary impotence. In other words, organic solvents are just as dangerous as corrosive chemicals, such as sulfuric acid, but manifest their hazardous nature in other, more subtle ways.

If you are pregnant, you may want to consider taking this course at a later time. Some exposure to organic fumes is inevitable, and any possible risk to an unborn baby should be avoided.

Minimize any direct exposure to solvents and treat them with respect. The laboratory room should be well ventilated. Normal cautious handling of solvents should not result in any health problem. If you are trying to evaporate a solution in an open container, you must do the evaporation in the hood. Excess solvents should be discarded in a container specifically intended for waste solvents, rather than down the drain at the laboratory bench.

A sensible precaution is to wear gloves when working with solvents. Gloves made from polyethylene are inexpensive and provide good protection. The disadvantage of polyethylene gloves is that they are slippery. Disposable surgical gloves provide a better grip on glassware and other equipment, but they do not offer as much protection as polyethylene gloves. Nitrile gloves offer better protection (see p. 563).

Do Not Breathe Solvent Vapors. In checking the odor of a substance, be careful not to inhale very much of the material. The technique for smelling flowers is not advisable here; you could inhale dangerous amounts of the compound. Rather, a technique for smelling minute amounts of a substance is used. Pass a stopper or spatula moistened with the substance (if it is a liquid) under your nose. Or hold the substance away from you and waft the vapors toward you with your hand. But *never* hold your nose over the container and inhale deeply!

The hazards associated with organic solvents you are likely to encounter in the organic laboratory are discussed in detail beginning on page 571. If you use proper safety precautions, your exposure to harmful organic vapors will be minimized and should present no health risk.

Safe Transportation of Chemicals. When transporting chemicals from one location to another, particularly from one room to another, it is always best to usc some form of **secondary containment.** This means that the bottle or flask is carried inside another, larger container. This outer container serves to contain the contents of the inner vessel in case a leak or breakage should occur. Scientific suppliers offer a variety of chemical-resistant carriers for this purpose.

D. Waste Disposal

Do Not Place Any Liquid or Solid Waste in Sinks; Use Appropriate Waste Containers. Many substances are toxic, flammable, and difficult to degrade; it is neither legal nor advisable to dispose of organic solvents or other liquid or solid reagents by pouring them down the sink.

The correct disposal method for wastes is to put them in appropriately labeled waste containers. These containers should be placed in the hoods in the laboratory. The waste containers will be disposed of safely by qualified persons using approved protocols.

Specific guidelines for disposing of waste will be determined by the people in charge of your particular laboratory and by local regulations. Two alternative systems for handling waste disposal are presented here. For each experiment that you are assigned, you will be instructed to dispose of all wastes according to the system that is in operation in your laboratory.

In one model of waste collection, a separate waste container for each experiment is placed in the laboratory. In some cases, more than one container, each labeled according to the type of waste that is anticipated, is set out. The containers will be labeled with a list that details each substance that is present in the container. In this model, it is common practice to use separate waste containers for aqueous solutions, organic halogenated solvents, and other organic nonhalogenated materials. At the end of the laboratory class period, the waste containers are transported to a central hazardous materials storage location. These wastes may be later consolidated and poured into large drums for shipping. Complete labeling, detailing each chemical contained in the waste, is required at each stage of this waste-handling process, even when the waste is consolidated into drums.

In a second model of waste collection, you will be instructed to dispose of all wastes in one of the following ways:

Nonhazardous solids. Nonhazardous solids such as paper and cork can be placed in an ordinary wastebasket.

Broken glassware. Broken glassware should be put into a container specifically designated for broken glassware.

Organic solids. Solid products that are not turned in or any other organic solids should be disposed of in the container designated for organic solids.

Inorganic solids. Solids such as alumina and silica gel should be put in a container specifically designated for them.

Nonhalogenated organic solvents. Organic solvents such as diethyl ether, hexane, and toluene, or any solvent that does not contain a halogen atom, should be disposed of in the container designated for nonhalogenated organic solvents.

Halogenated solvents. Methylene chloride (dichloromethane), chloroform, and carbon tetrachloride are examples of common halogenated organic solvents. Dispose of all halogenated solvents in the container designated for them.

Strong inorganic acids and bases. Strong acids such as hydrochloric, sulfuric, and nitric acid will be collected in specially marked containers. Strong bases such as sodium hydroxide and potassium hydroxide will also be collected in specially designated containers.

Aqueous solutions. Aqueous solutions will be collected in a specially marked waste container. It is not necessary to separate each type of aqueous solution (unless the solution contains heavy metals); rather, unless otherwise instructed, you may combine all aqueous solutions into the same waste container. Although many types of solutions (aqueous sodium bicarbonate, aqueous sodium chloride, and so on) may seem innocuous and it may seem that their disposal down the sink drain is not likely to cause harm, many communities are becoming increasingly restrictive about what substances they will permit to enter municipal sewage-treatment systems. In light of this trend toward greater caution, it is important to develop good laboratory habits regarding the disposal of *all* chemicals.

Heavy metals. Many heavy metal ions such as mercury and chromium are highly toxic and should be disposed of in specifically designated waste containers.

Whichever method is used, the waste containers must eventually be labeled with a complete list of each substance that is present in the waste. Individual waste containers are collected, and their contents are consolidated and placed into drums for transport to the waste-disposal site. Even these drums must bear labels that detail each of the substances contained in the waste.

In either waste-handling method, certain principles will always apply:

- Aqueous solutions should not be mixed with organic liquids.
- Concentrated acids should be stored in separate containers; certainly they must *never* be allowed to come into contact with organic waste.

- Organic materials that contain halogen atoms (fluorine, chlorine, bromine, or iodine) should be stored in separate containers from those used to store materials that do not contain halogen atoms.

In each experiment in this textbook, we have suggested a method of collecting and storing wastes. Your instructor may opt to use another method for collecting wastes.

E. Use of Flames

Even though organic solvents are frequently flammable (for example, hexane, diethyl ether, methanol, acetone, and petroleum ether), there are certain laboratory procedures for which a flame must be used. Most often, these procedures involve an aqueous solution. In fact, as a general rule, use a flame to heat only aqueous solutions. Heating methods that do not use a flame are discussed in detail in Technique 6, starting on page 612. Most organic solvents boil below 100°C, and an aluminum block, heating mantle, sand bath, or water bath may be used to heat these solvents safely. Common organic solvents are listed in Technique 10, Table 10.3, page 676. Solvents marked in the table with boldface type will burn. Diethyl ether, pentane, and hexane are especially dangerous, because in combination with the correct amount of air, they may explode.

Some commonsense rules apply to using a flame in the presence of flammable solvents. Again, we stress that you should check to see whether anyone in your vicinity is using flammable solvents before you ignite any open flame. If someone is using a flammable solvent, move to a safer location before you light your flame. Your laboratory should have an area set aside for using a burner to prepare micropipets or other pieces of glassware.

The drainage troughs or sinks should never be used to dispose of flammable organic solvents. They will vaporize if they are low boiling and may encounter a flame farther down the bench on their way to the sink.

F. Inadvertently Mixed Chemicals

To avoid unnecessary hazards of fire and explosion, never pour any reagent back into a stock bottle. There is always the chance that you may accidentally pour back some foreign substance that will react explosively with the chemical in the stock bottle. Of course, by pouring reagents back into the stock bottles, you may introduce impurities that could spoil the experiment for the person using the stock reagent after you. Pouring things back into bottles is not only a dangerous practice but an inconsiderate one. Thus, you should not take more chemicals than you need.

G. Unauthorized Experiments

Never undertake any unauthorized experiments. The risk of an accident is high, particularly if the experiment has not been completely checked to reduce hazards. Never work alone in the laboratory. The laboratory instructor or supervisor must always be present.

H. Food in the Laboratory

Because all chemicals are potentially toxic, avoid accidentally ingesting any toxic substance; therefore, never eat or drink any food while in the laboratory. There is always the possibility that whatever you are eating or drinking may become contaminated with a potentially hazardous material.

I. Clothing

Always wear closed shoes in the laboratory; open-toed shoes or sandals offer inadequate protection against spilled chemicals or broken glass. Do not wear your best clothing in the laboratory because some chemicals can make holes in or permanent stains on your clothing. To protect yourself and your clothing, it is advisable to wear a full-length laboratory apron or coat.

When working with chemicals that are very toxic, wear some type of gloves. Disposable gloves are inexpensive, offer good protection, provide acceptable "feel," and can be bought in many departmental stockrooms and college bookstores. Disposable latex surgical or polyethylene gloves are the least expensive type of glove; they are satisfactory when working with inorganic reagents and solutions. Better protection is afforded by disposable nitrile gloves. This type of glove provides good protection against organic chemicals and solvents. Heavier nitrile gloves are also available.

Finally, hair that is shoulder length or longer should be tied back. This precaution is especially important if you are working with a burner.

J. First Aid: Cuts, Minor Burns, and Acid or Base Burns

If any chemical enters your eyes, immediately irrigate the eyes with copious quantities of water. Tempered (slightly warm) water, if available, is preferable. Be sure that the eyelids are kept open. Continue flushing the eyes in this way for 15 minutes.

In case of a cut, wash the wound well with water unless you are specifically instructed to do otherwise. If necessary, apply pressure to the wound to stop the flow of blood.

Minor burns caused by flames or contact with hot objects may be soothed by immediately immersing the burned area in cold water or cracked ice until you no longer feel a burning sensation. Applying salves to burns is discouraged. Severe burns must be examined and treated by a physician. For chemical acid or base burns, rinse the burned area with copious quantities of water for at least 15 minutes.

If you accidentally ingest a chemical, call the local poison control center for instructions. Do not drink anything until you have been told to do so. It is important that the examining physician be informed of the exact nature of the substance ingested.

1.2 RIGHT-TO-KNOW LAWS

The federal government and most state governments now require that employers provide their employees with complete information about hazards in the workplace. These regulations are often referred to as **Right-to-Know Laws.** At the federal level, the Occupational Safety and Health Administration (OSHA) is charged with enforcing these regulations.

In 1990, the federal government extended the Hazard Communication Act, which established the Right-to-Know Laws, to include a provision that requires the establishment of a Chemical Hygiene Plan at all academic laboratories. Every college and university chemistry department should have a Chemical Hygiene Plan. Having this plan means that all the safety regulations and laboratory safety procedures should be written in a manual. The plan also provides for the training of all employees in laboratory safety. Your laboratory instructor and assistants should have this training.

One of the components of Right-to-Know Laws is that employees and students have access to information about the hazards of any chemicals with which they are working. Your instructor will alert you to dangers to which you need to pay particular attention. However, you may want to seek additional information. Two excellent sources of information are labels on the bottles that come from a chemical manufacturer and **Material Safety Data Sheets** (MSDSs). The MSDSs are also provided by the manufacturer and must be kept available for all chemicals used at educational institutions.

A. Material Safety Data Sheets

Reading an MSDS for a chemical can be a daunting experience, even for an experienced chemist. MSDSs contain a wealth of information, some of which must be decoded to understand. The MSDS for methanol is shown on pages 565–569. Only the information that might be of interest to you is described in the paragraphs that follow.

Section 1. The first part of Section 1 identifies the substance by name, formula, and various numbers and codes. Most organic compounds have more than one name. In this case, the systematic (or International Union of Pure and Applied Chemistry [IUPAC]) name is methanol, and the other names are common names or are from an older system of nomenclature. The Chemical Abstract Service Number (CAS No.) is often used to identify a substance, and it may be used to access extensive information about a substance found in many computer databases or in the library.

Section 3. The Baker SAF-T-DATA System is found on all MSDSs and bottle labels for chemicals supplied by J. T. Baker, Inc. For each category listed, the number indicates the degree of hazard. The lowest number is 0 (very low hazard), and the highest number is 4 (extreme hazard). The Health category refers to damage involved when the substance is inhaled, ingested, or absorbed. Flammability indicates the tendency of a substance to burn. Reactivity refers to how reactive a substance is with air, water, or other substances. The last category, Contact, refers to how hazardous a substance is when it comes in contact with external parts of the body. Note that this rating scale is applicable only to Baker MSDSs and labels; other rating scales with different meanings are also in common use.

Section 4. This section provides helpful information for emergency and first aid procedures.

Section 6. This part of the MSDS deals with procedures for handling spills and disposal. The information could be very helpful, particularly if a large amount of the chemical was spilled. More information about disposal is also given in Section 13.

Section 8. Much valuable information is found in Section 8. To help you understand this material, some of the more important terms used in this section are defined:

> ***Threshold Limit Value (TLV).*** The American Conference of Governmental Industrial Hygienists (ACGIH) developed the TLV: This is the maximum concentration of a substance in air that a person should be exposed to on a regular basis. It is usually expressed in ppm or mg/m^3. Note that this value assumes that a person is exposed to the substance 40 hours per week, on a long-term basis. This value may not be particularly

MSDS Number: M2015 | Effective Date: 12/8/96

Material Safety Data Sheet

From: Mallinckrodt Baker, Inc.
222 Red School Lane
Phillipsburg, NJ 08865

24 Hour Emergency Telephone: 908-859-2151
CHEMTREC: 1-800-424-9300

National Response in Canada
CANUTEC: 613-996-6666

Outside U.S. and Canada
Chemtrec: 202-483-7616

NOTE: CHEMTREC, CANUTEC and National Response Center emergency numbers to be used only in the event of chemical emergencies involving a spill, leak, fire, exposure or accident involving chemicals.

All non-emergency questions should be directed to Customer Service (1-800-582-2537) for assistance.

METHYL ALCOHOL

1. Product Identification

Synonyms: Wood alcohol; methanol; carbinol
CAS No: 67-56-1
Molecular Weight: 32.04
Chemical Formula: CH_3OH
Product Codes: **J.T. Baker:**
5217, 5370, 5794, 5807, 5811, 5842, 5869, 9049, 9063, 9066, 9067, 9069, 9070, 9071, 9073, 9075, 9076, 9077, 9091, 9093, 9096, 9097, 9098, 9263, 9893
Mallinckrodt:
3004, 3006, 3016, 3017, 3018, 3024, 3041, 3701, 4295, 5160, 8814, H080, H488, H603, V079, V571

2. Composition/Information on Ingredients

Ingredient	CAS No.	Percent	Hazardous
Methyl Alcohol	67-56-1	100%	Yes

3. Hazards Identification

Emergency Overview

POISON! DANGER! VAPOR HARMFUL. MAY BE FATAL OR CAUSE BLINDNESS IF SWALLOWED. HARMFUL IF INHALED OR ABSORBED THROUGH SKIN. CANNOT BE MADE NONPOISONOUS. FLAMMABLE LIQUID AND VAPOR. CAUSES IRRITATION TO SKIN, EYES AND RESPIRATORY TRACT. AFFECTS THE LIVER.

J.T. Baker SAF-T-DATA(tm) Ratings

(Provided here for your convenience)

Health:	Flammability:	Reactivity:	Contact:
3 - Severe (Poison)	4 - Extreme (Flammable)	1 - Slight	1 - Slight

Lab Protection Equip: GOGGLES & SHIELD; LAB COAT & APRON; VENT HOOD; PROPER GLOVES; CLASS B EXTINGUISHER

Storage Color Code: Red (Flammable)

Potential Health Effects

Inhalation:

A slight irritant to the mucous membranes. Toxic effects exerted upon nervous system, particularly the optic nerve. Once absorbed into the body, it is very slowly eliminated. Symptoms of overexposure may include headache, drowsiness, nausea, vomiting, blurred vision, blindness, coma, and death. A person may get better but then worse again up to 30 hours later.

Ingestion:

Toxic. Symptoms parallel inhalation. Can intoxicate and cause blindness. Usual fatal dose: 100-125 milliliters.

Skin Contact:

Methyl alcohol is a defatting agent and may cause skin to become dry and cracked. Skin absorption can occur; symptoms may parallel inhalation exposure.

Eye Contact:

Irritant. Continued exposure may cause eye lesions.

Chronic Exposure:

Marked impairment of vision and enlargement of the liver has been reported. Repeated or prolonged exposure may cause skin irritation.

Aggravation of Pre-existing Conditions:

Persons with pre-existing skin disorders or eye problems or impaired liver or kidney function may be more susceptible to the effects of the substance.

4. First Aid Measures

Inhalation:

Remove to fresh air. If not breathing, give artificial respiration. If breathing is difficult, give oxygen. Call a physician.

Ingestion:

Induce vomiting immediately as directed by medical personnel. Never give anything by mouth to an unconscious person.

Skin Contact:

Remove any contaminated clothing. Wash skin with soap or mild detergent and water for at least 15 minutes. Get medical attention if irritation develops or persists.

Eye Contact:

Immediately flush eyes with plenty of water for at least 15 minutes, lifting lower and upper eyelids occasionally. Get medical attention immediately.

5. Fire Fighting Measures

Fire:

Flash point: 12°C (54°F) CC
Autoignition temperature: 464°C (867°F)
Flammable limits in air % by volume:
lel: 7.3; uel: 36
Flammable.

Explosion:

Above flash point, vapor-air mixtures are explosive within flammable limits noted above. Moderate explosion hazard and dangerous fire hazard when exposed to heat, sparks or flames. Sensitive to static discharge.

Fire Extinguishing Media:

Water spray, dry chemical, alcohol foam, or carbon dioxide.

Special Information:

In the event of a fire, wear full protective clothing and NIOSH-approved self-contained breathing apparatus with full facepiece operated in the pressure demand or other positive pressure mode. Use water spray to blanket fire, cool fire exposed containers, and to flush non-ignited spills or vapors away from fire. Vapors can flow along surfaces to distant ignition source and flash back.

6. Accidental Release Measures

Ventilate area of leak or spill. Remove all sources of ignition. Wear appropriate personal protective equipment as specified in Section 8. Isolate hazard area. Keep unnecessary and unprotected personnel from entering. Contain and recover liquid when possible. Use non-sparking tools and equipment. Collect liquid in an appropriate container or absorb with an inert material (e. g., vermiculite, dry sand, earth), and place in a chemical waste container. Do not use combustible materials, such as saw dust. Do not flush to sewer!
J. T. Baker SOLUSORB® solvent adsorbent is recommended for spills of this product.

7. Handling and Storage

Protect against physical damage. Store in a cool, dry well-ventilated location, away from any area where the fire hazard may be acute. Outside or detached storage is preferred. Separate from incompatibles. Containers should be bonded and grounded for transfers to avoid static sparks. Storage and use areas should be No Smoking areas. Use non-sparking type tools and equipment, including explosion proof ventilation. Containers of this material may be hazardous when empty since they retain product residues (vapors, liquid); observe all warnings and precautions listed for the product.

8. Exposure Controls/Personal Protection

Airborne Exposure Limits:

For Methyl Alcohol:
- OSHA Permissible Exposure Limit (PEL):
  200 ppm (TWA)
- ACGIH Threshold Limit Value (TLV):
  200 ppm (TWA), 250 ppm (STEL) skin

Ventilation System:

A system of local and/or general exhaust is recommended to keep employee exposures below the Airborne Exposure Limits. Local exhaust ventilation is generally preferred because it can control the emissions of the contaminant at its source, preventing dispersion of it into the general work area. Please refer to the ACGIH document, "Industrial Ventilation, A Manual of Recommended Practices", most recent edition, for details.

Personal Respirator (NIOSH Approved)

If the exposure limit is exceeded, wear a supplied air, full-facepiece respirator, airlined hood, or full-facepiece self-contained breathing apparatus.

Skin Protection:

Rubber or neoprene gloves and additional protection including impervious boots, apron, or coveralls, as needed in areas of unusual exposure.

Eye Protection:

Use chemical safety goggles. Maintain eye wash fountain and quick-drench facilities in work area.

9. Physical and Chemical Properties

Appearance:
Clear, colorless liquid.

Odor:
Characteristic odor.

Solubility:
Miscible in water.

Specific Gravity:
0.8

pH:
No information found.

% Volatiles by volume @ 21°C (70°F):
100

Boiling Point:
64.5°C (147°F)

Melting Point:
-98°C (-144°F)

Vapor Density (Air=1):
1.1

Vapor Pressure (mm Hg):
97 @ 20°C (68°F)

Evaporation Rate (BuAc=1):
5.9

10. Stability and Reactivity

Stability:

Stable under ordinary conditions of use and storage.

Hazardous Decomposition Products:

May form carbon dioxide, carbon monoxide, and formaldehyde when heated to decomposition.

Hazardous Polymerization:

Will not occur.

Incompatabilities:

Strong oxidizing agents such as nitrates, perchlorates or sulfuric acid. Will attack some forms of plastics, rubber, and coatings. May react with metallic aluminum and generate hydrogen gas.

Conditions to Avoid:

Heat, flames, ignition sources and incompatibles.

11. Toxicological Information

Methyl Alcohol (Methanol) Oral rat LD50: 5628 mg/kg; inhalation rat LC50: 64000 ppm/4H; skin rabbit LD50: 15800 mg/kg; Irritation data-standard Draize test: skin, rabbit: 20mg/24 hr. Moderate; eye, rabbit: 100 mg/24 hr. Moderate; Investigated as a mutagen, reproductive effector.

Cancer Lists

	—NTP Carcinogen—		
Ingredient	**Known**	**Anticipated**	**IARC Category**
Methyl Alcohol (67-56-1)	No	No	None

12. Ecological Information

Environmental Fate:

When released into the soil, this material is expected to readily biodegrade. When released into the soil, this material is expected to leach into groundwater. When released into the soil, this material is expected to quickly evaporate. When released into the water, this material is expected to have a half-life between 1 and 10 days. When released into water, this material is expected to readily biodegrade. When released into the air, this material is expected to exist in the aerosol phase with a short half-life. When released into the air, this material is expected to be readily degraded by reaction with photochemically produced hydroxyl radicals. When released into air, this material is expected to have a half-life between 10 and 30 days. When released into the air, this material is expected to be readily removed from the atmosphere by wet deposition.

Environmental Toxicity:

This material is expected to be slightly toxic to aquatic life.

13. Disposal Considerations

Whatever cannot be saved for recovery or recycling should be handled as hazardous waste and sent to a RCRA approved incinerator or disposed in a RCRA approved waste facility. Processing, use or contamination of this product may change the waste management options. State and local disposal regulations may differ from federal disposal regulations.

Dispose of container and unused contents in accordance with federal, state and local requirements.

14. Transport Information

Domestic (Land, D.O.T.)

Proper Shipping Name:	METHANOL		
Hazard Class:	3		
UN/NA:	UN1230	**Packing Group:**	II

Information reported for product/size: 350LB

International (Water, I.M.O.)

Proper Shipping Name: METHANOL
Hazard Class: 3.2, 6.1
UN/NA: UN1230 **Packing Group:** II
Information reported for product/size: 350LB

15. Regulatory Information

Chemical Inventory Status

Ingredient	TSCA	EC	Japan	Australia	Korea	---Canada--- DSL	NDSL	Phil.
Methyl Alcohol (67-56-1)	Yes	Yes	Yes	Yes	Yes	Yes	No	Yes

Federal, State & International Regulations

	---SARA 302---		---------SARA 313---------			-RCRA-	-TSCA-
Ingredient	RQ	TPQ	List	Chemical Catg.	CERCLA	261.33	8(d)
Methyl Alcohol (67-56-1)	No	No	Yes	No	5000	U154	No

Chemical Weapons Convention: No **TSCA 12(b):** No **CDTA:** No
SARA 311/312: Acute: Yes Chronic: Yes Fire: Yes Pressure: No Reactivity: No (Pure / Liquid)

Australian Hazchem Code: 2PE **Australian Poison Schedule:** S6
WHMIS: This MSDS has been prepared according to the hazard criteria of the Controlled Products Regulations (CPR) and the MSDS contains all of the information required by the CPR.

16. Other Information

NFPA Ratings:

Health: 1 Flammability: 3 Reactivity: 0

Label Hazard Warning:

POISON! DANGER! VAPOR HARMFUL. MAY BE FATAL OR CAUSE BLINDNESS IF SWALLOWED. HARMFUL IF INHALED OR ABSORBED THROUGH SKIN. CANNOT BE MADE NONPOISONOUS. FLAMMABLE LIQUID AND VAPOR. CAUSES IRRITATION TO SKIN, EYES AND RESPIRATORY TRACT. AFFECTS THE LIVER.

Label Precautions:

Keep away from heat, sparks and flame.
Keep container closed.
Use only with adequate ventilation.
Wash thoroughly after handling.
Avoid breathing vapor.
Avoid contact with eyes, skin and clothing.

Label First Aid:

If swallowed, induce vomiting immediately as directed by medical personnel. Never give anything by mouth to an unconscious person. In case of contact, immediately flush eyes or skin with plenty of water for at least 15 minutes while removing contaminated clothing and shoes. Wash clothing before reuse. If inhaled, remove to fresh air. If not breathing give artificial respiration. If breathing is difficult, give oxygen. In all cases get medical attention immediately.

Product Use:

Laboratory Reagent.

Revision Information:

New 16 section MSDS format, all sections have been revised.

Disclaimer:

Mallinckrodt Baker, Inc. provides the information contained herein in good faith but makes no representation as to its comprehensiveness or accuracy. This document is intended only as a guide to the appropriate precautionary handling of the material by a properly trained person using this product. Individuals receiving the information must exercise their independent judgment in determining its appropriateness for a particular purpose. MALLINCKRODT BAKER, INC. MAKES NO REPRESENTATIONS OR WARRANTIES, EITHER EXPRESS OR IMPLIED, INCLUDING WITHOUT LIMITATION ANY WARRANTIES OR MERCHANTABILITY, FITNESS FOR A PARTICULAR PURPOSE WITH RESPECT TO THE INFORMATION SET FORTH HEREIN OR THE PRODUCT TO WHICH THE INFORMATION REFERS. ACCORDINGLY, MALLINCKRODT BAKER, INC. WILL NOT BE RESPONSIBLE FOR DAMAGES RESULTING FROM USE OF OR RELIANCE UPON THIS INFORMATION.

Prepared By: Strategic Services Division
Phone Number: (314) 539-1600 (U.S.A.)

applicable in the case of a student performing an experiment in a single laboratory period.

Permissible Exposure Limit (PEL). This has the same meaning as TLV; however, PELs were developed by OSHA. Note that for methanol, the TLV and PEL are both 200 ppm.

Section 10. The information contained in Section 10 refers to the stability of the compound and the hazards associated with mixing of chemicals. It is important to consider this information before carrying out an experiment not previously done.

Section 11. More information about the toxicity is given in this section. Another important term must first be defined:

Lethal Dose, 50% Mortality (LD_{50}). This is the dose of a substance that will kill 50% of the animals administered a single dose. Different means of administration are used, such as oral, intraperitoneal (injected into the lining of the abdominal cavity), subcutaneous (injected under the skin), and application to the surface of the skin. The LD_{50} is usually expressed in milligrams (mg) of substance per kilogram (kg) of animal weight. The lower the value of LD_{50}, the more toxic the substance. It is assumed that the toxicity in humans will be similar.

Unless you have considerably more knowledge about chemical toxicity, the information in Sections 8 and 11 is most useful for comparing the toxicity of one substance with another. For example, the TLV for methanol is 200 ppm, whereas the TLV for benzene is 10 ppm. Clearly, performing an experiment involving benzene would require much more stringent precautions than an experiment involving methanol. One of the LD_{50} values for methanol is 5628 mg/kg. The comparable LD_{50} value of aniline is 250 mg/kg. Clearly, aniline is much more toxic, and because it is easily absorbed through the skin, it presents a significant hazard. It should also be mentioned that both TLV and PEL ratings assume that the worker comes in contact with a substance on a repeated and long-term basis. Thus, even if a chemical has a relatively low TLV or PEL, it does not mean that using it for one experiment will present a danger to you. Furthermore, by performing experiments using small amounts of chemicals and with proper safety precautions, your exposure to organic chemicals in this course will be minimal.

Section 16. Section 16 contains the National Fire Protection Association (NFPA) rating. This is similar to the Baker SAF-T-DATA (discussed in Section 3), except that the number represents the hazards when a fire is present. The order here is Health, Flammability, and Reactivity. Often, this is presented in graphic form on a label (see figure). The small diamonds are often color coded: blue for Health, red for Flammability, and yellow for Reactivity. The bottom diamond (white) is sometimes used to display graphic symbols denoting unusual reactivity, hazards, or special precautions to be taken.

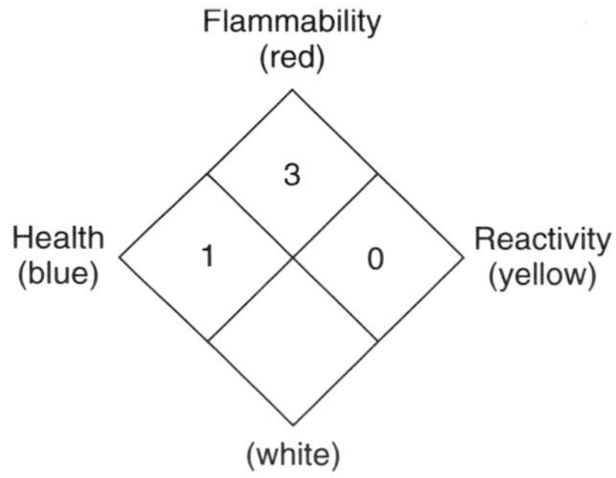

B. Bottle Labels

Reading the label on a bottle can be a very helpful way of learning about the hazards of a chemical. The amount of information varies greatly, depending on which company supplied the chemical.

Apply some common sense when you read MSDSs and bottle labels. Using these chemicals does not mean you will experience the consequences that can potentially result from exposure to each chemical. For example, an MSDS for sodium chloride states, "Exposure to this product may have serious adverse health effects." Despite the apparent severity of this cautionary statement, it would not be reasonable to expect people to stop using sodium chloride in a chemistry experiment or to stop sprinkling a small amount of it (as table salt) on eggs to enhance their flavor. In many cases, the consequences described in MSDSs from exposure to chemicals are somewhat overstated, particularly for students using these chemicals to perform a laboratory experiment.

1.3 COMMON SOLVENTS

Most organic chemistry experiments involve an organic solvent at some step in the procedure. A list of common organic solvents follows, with a discussion of toxicity, possible carcinogenic properties, and precautions that you should use when handling these solvents. A tabulation of the compounds currently suspected of being carcinogens appears at the end of Technique 1.

Acetic Acid. Glacial acetic acid is corrosive enough to cause serious acid burns on the skin. Its vapors can irritate the eyes and nasal passages. Care should be exercised not to breathe the vapors and not to allow them to escape into the laboratory.

Acetone. Relative to other organic solvents, acetone is not very toxic. It is flammable, however. Do not use acetone near open flames.

Benzene. Benzene can damage bone marrow, it causes various blood disorders, and its effects may lead to leukemia. Benzene is considered a serious carcinogenic hazard. It is absorbed rapidly through the skin and also poisons the liver and kidneys. In addition, benzene is flammable. Because of its toxicity and its carcinogenic properties, benzene should not be used in the laboratory; you should use some less dangerous solvent instead. Toluene is considered a safer alternative solvent in procedures that specify benzene.

Carbon Tetrachloride. Carbon tetrachloride can cause serious liver and kidney damage as well as skin irritation and other problems. It is absorbed rapidly through the skin. In high concentrations, it can cause death as a result of respiratory failure. Moreover, carbon tetrachloride is suspected of being a carcinogenic material. Although this solvent has the advantage of being nonflammable (in the past, it was used on occasion as a fire extinguisher), it causes health problems, so it should not be used routinely in the laboratory. If no reasonable substitute exists, however, it must be used in small quantities, as in preparing samples for infrared (IR) and nuclear magnetic resonance (NMR) spectroscopy. In such cases, you must use it in a hood.

Chloroform. Chloroform is similar to carbon tetrachloride in its toxicity. It has been used as an anesthetic. However, chloroform is currently on the list of suspected carcinogens. Because of this, do not use chloroform routinely as a solvent in the laboratory. If it is occasionally necessary to use chloroform as a solvent for special samples, then you must use it in a hood. Methylene chloride is usually found to be a safer substitute in procedures that specify chloroform as a solvent. Deuterochloroform, $CDCl_3$, is a common solvent for NMR spectroscopy. Caution dictates that you should treat it with the same respect as chloroform.

1,2-Dimethoxyethane (Ethylene Glycol Dimethyl Ether or Monoglyme). Because it is miscible with water, 1,2-dimethoxyethane is a useful alternative to solvents such as dioxane and tetrahydrofuran, which may be more hazardous. 1,2-Dimethoxyethane is flammable and should not be handled near an open flame. On long exposure of 1,2-dimethoxyethane to light and oxygen, explosive peroxides may form. 1,2-Dimethoxyethane is a possible reproductive toxin.

Dioxane. Dioxane has been used widely because it is a convenient, water-miscible solvent. It is now suspected, however, of being carcinogenic. It is also toxic, affecting the central nervous system, liver, kidneys, skin, lungs, and mucous membranes. Dioxane is also flammable and tends to form explosive peroxides when it is exposed to light and air. Because of its carcinogenic properties, it is no longer used in the laboratory unless absolutely necessary. Either 1,2-dimethoxyethane or tetrahydrofuran is a suitable, water-miscible alternative solvent.

Ethanol. Ethanol has well-known properties as an intoxicant. In the laboratory, the principal danger arises from fires, because ethanol is a flammable solvent. When using ethanol, take care to work where there are no open flames.

Ether (diethyl ether). The principal hazard associated with diethyl ether is fire or explosion. Ether is probably the most flammable solvent found in the laboratory. Because ether vapors are much denser than air, they may travel along a laboratory bench for a considerable distance from their source before being ignited. Before using ether, it is very important to be sure that no one is working with matches or any open flame. Ether is not a particularly toxic solvent, although in high enough concentrations it can cause drowsiness and perhaps nausea. It has been used as a general anesthetic. Ether can form highly explosive peroxides when exposed to air. Consequently, you should never distill it to dryness.

Hexane. Hexane may be irritating to the respiratory tract. It can also act as an intoxicant and a depressant of the central nervous system. It can cause skin irritation because it is an excellent solvent for skin oils. The most serious hazard, however, comes from its flammability. The precautions recommended for using diethyl ether in the presence of open flames apply equally to hexane.

Ligroin. See Hexane.

Methanol. Much of the material outlining the hazards of ethanol applies to methanol. Methanol is more toxic than ethanol; ingestion can cause blindness and even death. Because methanol is more volatile, the danger of fires is more acute.

Methylene Chloride (Dichloromethane). Methylene chloride is not flammable. Unlike other members of the class of chlorocarbons, it is not currently considered a serious carcinogenic hazard. Recently, however, it has been the subject of much serious investigation, and there have been proposals to regulate it in industrial situations in which workers have high levels of exposure on a day-to-day basis. Methylene chloride is less toxic than chloroform and carbon tetrachloride. It can cause liver damage when ingested, however, and its vapors may cause drowsiness or nausea.

Pentane. See Hexane.

Petroleum Ether. See Hexane.

Pyridine. Some fire hazard is associated with pyridine. However, the most serious hazard arises from its toxicity. Pyridine may depress the central nervous system; irritate the skin and respiratory tract; damage the liver, kidneys, and gastrointestinal system; and even cause temporary sterility. You should treat pyridine as a highly toxic solvent and handle it only in the fume hood.

Tetrahydrofuran. Tetrahydrofuran may cause irritation of the skin, eyes, and respiratory tract. It should never be distilled to dryness because it tends to form potentially explosive peroxides on exposure to air. Tetrahydrofuran does present a fire hazard.

Toluene. Unlike benzene, toluene is not considered a carcinogen. However, it is at least as toxic as benzene. It can act as an anesthetic and damage the central nervous system. If benzene is present as an impurity in toluene, expect the usual hazards associated with benzene. Toluene is also a flammable solvent, and the usual precautions about working near open flames should be applied.

You should not use certain solvents in the laboratory because of their carcinogenic properties. Benzene, carbon tetrachloride, chloroform, and dioxane are among these solvents. For certain applications, however, notably as solvents for infrared or NMR spectroscopy, there may be no suitable alternative. When it is necessary to use one of these solvents, use safety precautions and refer to the discussions in Techniques 25–28.

Because relatively large amounts of solvents may be used in a large organic laboratory class, your laboratory supervisor must take care to store these substances safely. Only the amount of solvent needed for a particular experiment should be kept in the laboratory. The preferred location for bottles of solvents being used during a class period is in a hood. When the solvents are not being used, they should be stored in a fireproof storage cabinet for solvents. If possible, this cabinet should be ventilated into the fume hood system.

1.4 CARCINOGENIC SUBSTANCES

A **carcinogen** is a substance that causes cancer in living tissue. The usual procedures for determining whether a substance is carcinogenic is to expose laboratory animals to high dosages over a long period. It is not clear whether short-term exposure to these chemicals carries a comparable risk, but it is prudent to use these substances with special precautions.

Many regulatory agencies have compiled lists of carcinogenic substances or substances suspected of being carcinogenic. Because these lists are inconsistent, compiling a definitive list of carcinogenic substances is difficult. The following common substances are included in many of these lists.

Acetamide	4-Methyl-2-oxetanone (β-butyrolactone)
Acrylonitrile	1-Naphthylamine
Asbestos	2-Naphthylamine
Benzene	*N*-Nitroso compounds
Benzidine	2-Oxetanone (β-propiolactone)
Carbon tetrachloride	Phenacetin
Chloroform	Phenylhydrazine and its salts
Chromic oxide	Polychlorinated biphenyl (PCB)

Coumarin	Progesterone
Diazomethane	Styrene oxide
1,2-Dibromoethane	Tannins
Dimethyl sulfate	Testosterone
p-Dioxane	Thioacetamide
Ethylene oxide	Thiourea
Formaldehyde	*o*-Toluidine
Hydrazine and its salts	Trichloroethylene
Lead (II) acetate	Vinyl chloride

REFERENCES

Aldrich Catalog and Handbook of Fine Chemicals. Milwaukee, WI: Aldrich Chemical Co., current edition.

Armour, M. A., *Pollution Prevention and Waste Minimization in Laboratories.* Edited by Peter A. Reinhardt, K. Leigh Leonard, Peter C. Ashbrook. Boca Raton, Florida: Lewis Publishers, 1996.

Fire Protection Guide on Hazardous Materials, 10th ed. Quincy, MA: National Fire Protection Association, 1991.

Flinn Chemical Catalog Reference Manual. Batavia, IL: Flinn Scientific, current edition.

Gosselin, R. E., Smith, R. P., and Hodge, H. C. *Clinical Toxicology of Commercial Products,* 5th ed. Baltimore, MD: Williams & Wilkins, 1984.

Lenga, R. E., ed. *The Sigma-Aldrich Library of Chemical Safety Data.* Milwaukee, WI: Sigma-Aldrich, 1985.

Lewis, R. J. *Carcinogenically Active Chemicals: A Reference Guide.* New York: Van Nostrand Reinhold, 1990.

Lewis, R. J., *Sax's Dangerous Properties of Industrial Materials,* 8th edition, New York: Van Nostrand Reinhold, 1992.

The Merck Index, 13th ed. Rahway, NJ: Merck and Co., 2001.

Prudent Practices in the Laboratory: Handling and Disposal of Chemicals. Washington, DC: Committee on Prudent Practices for Handling, Storage, and Disposal of Chemicals in Laboratories, Board on Chemical Sciences and Technology, Commission on Physical Sciences, Mathematics, and Applications, National Research Council, National Academy Press, 1995.

Renfrew, M. M., ed. *Safety in the Chemical Laboratory.* Easton, PA: Division of Chemical Education, American Chemical Society, 1967–1991.

Safety in Academic Chemistry Laboratories, 4th ed. Washington, DC: Committee on Chemical Safety, American Chemical Society, 1985.

Sax, N. I., and Lewis, R. J. *Dangerous Properties of Industrial Materials,* 7th ed. New York: Van Nostrand Reinhold, 1988.

Sax, N. I., and Lewis, R. J., eds. *Rapid Guide to Hazardous Chemicals in the Work Place,* 2nd ed. New York: Van Nostrand Reinhold, 1990.

Useful Safety-Related Internet Addresses

Interactive Learning Paradigms, Inc.
http://www.ilpi.com/msds/
This is an excellent general site for MSDS sheets. The site lists chemical manufacturers and suppliers. Selecting a company will take you directly to the appropriate place to obtain an MSDS sheet. Many of the sites listed require you to register in order to obtain a MSDS sheet for a particular chemical. Ask your departmental or college safety supervisor to obtain the information for you.

Acros chemicals and Fisher Scientific
https://www1.fishersci.com/

Alfa Aesar
http://www.alfa.com/alf/index.htm

Cornell University, Department of Environmental Health and Safety
http://msds.pdc.cornell.edu/msdssrch.asp
This is an excellent searchable database of more than 325,000 MSDS files. No registration is required.

Eastman Kodak
http://msds.kodak.com/ehswww/external/index.jsp

EMD Chemicals (formerly EM Science) and Merck
http://www.emdchemicals.com/corporate/emd_corporate.asp

J. T. Baker and Mallinckrodt Laboratory Chemicals
http://www.jtbaker.com/asp/Catalog.asp

National Institute for Occupational Safety and Health (NIOSH) has an excellent website that includes databases and information resources, including links:
http://www.cdc.gov/niosh/topics/chemical-safety/default.html

Sigma, Aldrich and Fluka
http://www.sigmaaldrich.com/Area_of_Interest/The_Americas/United_States.html

VWR Scientific Products
http://www.vwrsp.com/search/index.cgi?tmpl=msds

TECHNIQUE 2

The Laboratory Notebook, Calculations, and Laboratory Records

In the Introduction to this book, we mentioned the importance of advance preparation for laboratory work. Presented here are some suggestions about what specific information you should try to obtain in your advance studying. Because much of this information must be obtained while preparing your laboratory notebook, the two subjects, advance study and notebook preparation, are developed simultaneously.

An important part of any laboratory experience is learning to maintain very complete records of every experiment undertaken and every item of data obtained. Far too often, careless recording of data and observations has resulted in mistakes, frustration, and lost time due to needless repetition of experiments. If reports are required, you will find that proper collection and recording of data can make your report writing much easier.

Because organic reactions are seldom quantitative, special problems result. Frequently, reagents must be used in large excess to increase the amount of product. Some reagents are expensive, and, therefore, care must be used in measuring the amounts of these substances. Very often, many more reactions take place than you desire. These extra reactions, or **side reactions,** may form products other than the desired product. These are called **side products.** For all these reasons, you must plan your experimental procedure carefully before undertaking the actual experiment.

2.1 THE NOTEBOOK

For recording data and observations during experiments, use a *bound notebook.* The notebook should have consecutively numbered pages. If it does not, number the pages immediately. A spiral-bound notebook or any other notebook from which the pages can be removed easily is not acceptable, because the possibility of losing the pages is great.

All data and observations must be recorded in the notebook. Paper towels, napkins, toilet tissue, or scratch paper tend to become lost or destroyed. It is bad laboratory practice to record information on such random and perishable pieces of paper. All entries must be recorded in *permanent ink.* It can be frustrating to have important information disappear from the notebook because it was recorded in washable ink or pencil and could not survive a flood caused by the student at the next position on the bench. Because you will be using your notebook in the laboratory, the book will probably become soiled or stained by chemicals, filled with scratched-out entries, or even slightly burned. That is expected and is a normal part of laboratory work.

Your instructor may check your notebook at any time, so you should always have it up to date. If your instructor requires reports, you can prepare them quickly from the material recorded in the laboratory notebook.

2.2 NOTEBOOK FORMAT

A. Advance Preparation

Individual instructors vary greatly in the type of notebook format they prefer; such variation stems from differences in philosophies and experience. You must obtain specific directions from your own instructor for preparing a notebook. Certain features, however, are common to most notebook formats. The following discussion indicates what might be included in a typical notebook.

It will be very helpful and you can save much time in the laboratory if for each experiment you know the main reactions, the potential side reactions, the mechanism, and the stoichiometry and you understand fully the procedure and the theory underlying it before you come to the laboratory. Understanding the procedure by which the desired product is to be separated from undesired materials is also very important. If you examine each of these topics before coming to class, you will be prepared to do the experiment efficiently. You will have your equipment and reagents already prepared when they are to be used. Your reference material will be at hand when you need it. Finally, with your time efficiently organized, you will be able to take advantage of long reaction or reflux periods to perform other tasks, such as doing shorter experiments or finishing previous ones.

For experiments in which a compound is synthesized from other reagents, that is, **preparative experiments,** it is essential to know the main reaction. To perform stoichiometric calculations, you should balance the equation for the main reaction. Therefore, before you begin the experiment, your notebook should contain the balanced equation for the pertinent reaction. Using the preparation of isopentyl acetate, or banana oil, as an example, you should write the following:

$$CH_3-\overset{\overset{\displaystyle O}{\|}}{C}-OH + CH_3-\overset{\overset{\displaystyle CH_3}{|}}{CH}-CH_2-CH_2-OH \xrightarrow{H^+}$$

Acetic acid Isopentyl alcohol

$$CH_3-\overset{\overset{\displaystyle O}{\|}}{C}-O-CH_2-CH_2-\overset{\overset{\displaystyle CH_3}{|}}{CH}-CH_3 + H_2O$$

Isopentyl acetate

Also enter in the notebook the possible side reactions that divert reagents into contaminants (side products), before beginning the experiment. You will have to separate these side products from the major product during purification.

You should list physical constants such as melting points, boiling points, densities, and molecular weights in the notebook when this information is needed to perform an experiment or to do calculations. These data are located in sources such as the *CRC Handbook of Chemistry and Physics, The Merck Index, Lange's Handbook of Chemistry,* or *Aldrich Handbook of Fine Chemicals.* Write physical constants required for an experiment in your notebook before you come to class.

Advance preparation may also include examining some subjects, information not necessarily recorded in the notebook, that should prove useful in understanding the experiment. Included among these subjects are an understanding of the mechanism of the reaction, an examination of other methods by which the same compound might be prepared, and a detailed study of the experimental procedure. Many students find that an outline of the procedure, prepared *before* they come to class, helps them use their time more efficiently once they begin the experiment. Such an outline could very well be prepared on some loose sheet of paper rather than in the notebook itself.

Once the reaction has been completed, the desired product does not magically appear as purified material; it must be isolated from a frequently complex mixture of side products, unreacted starting materials, solvents, and catalysts. You should try to outline a **separation scheme** in your notebook for isolating the product from its contaminants. At each stage, you should try to understand the reason for the particular instruction given in the experimental procedure. This not only will familiarize you with the basic separation and purification techniques used in organic chemistry but also will help you understand when to use these techniques. Such an outline might take the form of a flowchart. For example, see the separation scheme for isopentyl acetate (Figure 2.1). Careful attention to understanding the separation, besides familiarizing you with the procedure by which the desired product is separated from impurities in your particular experiments, may prepare you for original research in which no experimental procedure exists.

In designing a separation scheme, note that the scheme outlines those steps undertaken once the reaction period has been concluded. For this reason, the represented scheme does not include steps such as the addition of the reactants (isopentyl alcohol and acetic acid) and the catalyst (sulfuric acid) or the heating of the reaction mixture.

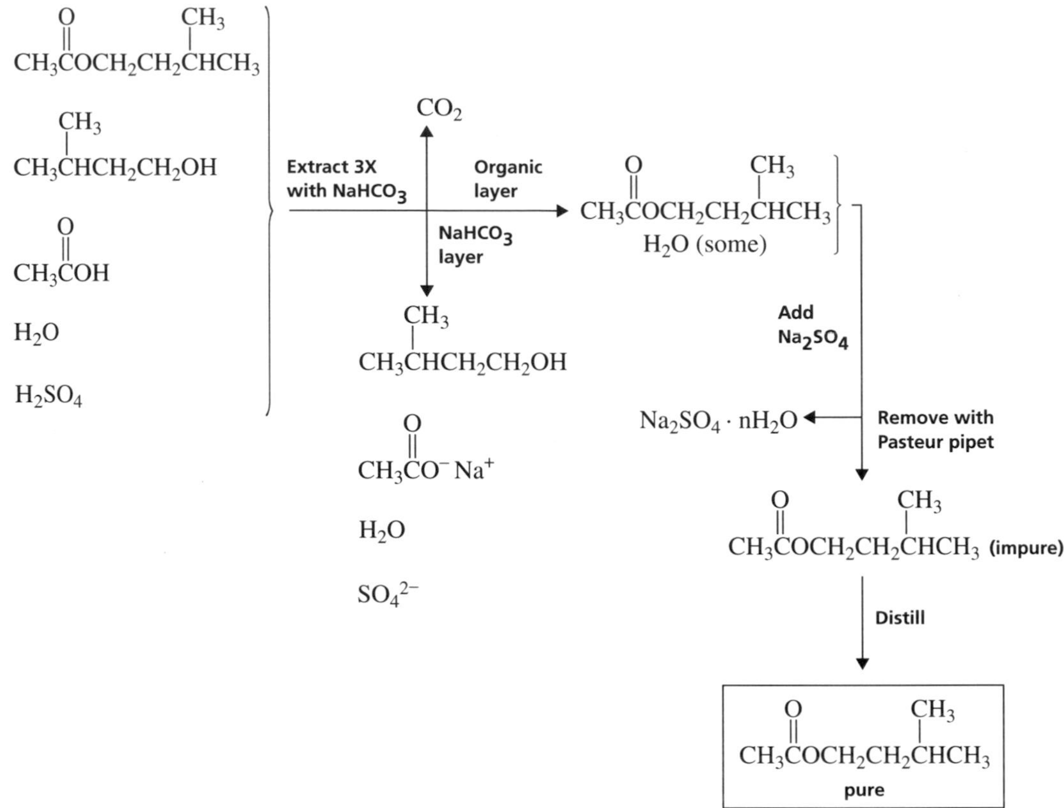

Figure 2.1 Separation scheme for isopentyl acetate.

For experiments in which a compound is isolated from a particular source and is not prepared from other reagents, some information described in this section will not be applicable. Such experiments are called **isolation experiments.** A typical isolation experiment involves isolating a pure compound from a natural source. Examples include isolating caffeine from tea or isolating cinnamaldehyde from cinnamon. Although isolation experiments require somewhat different advance preparation, this advance study may include looking up physical constants for the compound isolated and outlining the isolation procedure. A detailed examination of the separation scheme is very important here because it is the heart of such an experiment.

B. Laboratory Records

When you begin the actual experiment, keep your notebook nearby so you will be able to record those operations you perform. When working in the laboratory, the notebook serves as a place in which to record a rough transcript of your experimental method. Data from actual weighings, volume measurements, and determinations of physical constants are also noted. This section of your notebook should *not* be prepared in advance. The purpose is not to write a recipe but rather to record what you *did* and what you *observed.* These observations will help you write reports without resorting to memory. They will also help you or other workers repeat the experiment in as nearly as possible the same way. The sample notebook pages found in Figures 2.2 and 2.3 illustrate the type of data and observations that should be written in your notebook.

When your product has been prepared and purified, or isolated if it is an isolation experiment, record pertinent data such as the melting point or boiling point of the substance, its density, its index of refraction, and the conditions under which spectra were determined.

C. Calculations

A chemical equation for the overall conversion of the starting materials to products is written on the assumption of simple ideal stoichiometry. Actually, this assumption is seldom realized. Side reactions or competing reactions will also occur, giving other products. For some synthetic reactions, an equilibrium state will be reached in which an appreciable amount of starting material is still present and can be recovered. Some of the reactant may also remain if it is present in excess or if the reaction was incomplete. A reaction involving an expensive reagent illustrates another reason for needing to know how far a particular type of reaction converts reactants to products. In such a case, it is preferable to use the most efficient method for this conversion. Thus, information about the efficiency of conversion for various reactions is of interest to the person contemplating the use of these reactions.

The quantitative expression for the efficiency of a reaction is found by calculating the **yield** for the reaction. The **theoretical yield** is the number of grams of the product expected from the reaction on the basis of ideal stoichiometry, with side reactions, reversibility, and losses ignored. To calculate the theoretical yield, it is first necessary to determine the **limiting reagent.** The limiting reagent is the reagent that is not present in excess and on which the overall yield of product depends. The method for determining the limiting reagent in the isopentyl acetate experiment is illustrated in the sample notebook pages shown in Figures 2.2 and 2.3. You should consult your general chemistry textbook for more complicated examples. The theoretical yield is then calculated from the expression

$$\text{Theoretical yield} = (\text{moles of limiting reagent})(\text{ratio})(\text{molecular weight of product})$$

The ratio here is the stoichiometric ratio of product to limiting reagent. In preparing isopentyl acetate, that ratio is 1:1. One mole of isopentyl alcohol, under ideal circumstances, should yield 1 mole of isopentyl acetate.

The **actual yield** is simply the number of grams of desired product obtained. The **percentage yield** describes the efficiency of the reaction and is determined by

$$\text{Percentage yield} = \frac{\text{Actual yield}}{\text{Theoretical yield}} \times 100$$

Calculation of the theoretical yield and percentage yield can be illustrated using hypothetical data for the isopentyl acetate preparation:

$$\text{Theoretical yield} = (6.94 \times 10^{-2}\ \cancel{\text{mol isopentyl alcohol}})\left(\frac{1\ \cancel{\text{mol isopentyl acetate}}}{1\ \cancel{\text{mol isopentyl alcohol}}}\right)$$

$$\times \left(\frac{130.2\ \text{g isopentyl acetate}}{1\ \cancel{\text{mol isopentyl acetate}}}\right) = 9.03\ \text{g isopentyl acetate}$$

THE PREPARATION OF ISOPENTYL ACETATE (BANANA OIL)

Main Reaction

$$\underset{\text{Acetic acid}}{CH_3-\overset{\overset{O}{\|}}{C}-OH} + \underset{\text{Isopentyl alcohol}}{CH_3-\overset{\overset{CH_3}{|}}{CH}-CH_2-CH_2-OH} \xrightarrow{H^+} \underset{\text{Isopentyl acetate}}{CH_3-\overset{\overset{O}{\|}}{C}-O-CH_2-CH_2-\overset{\overset{CH_3}{|}}{CH}-CH_3} + H_2O$$

Table of Physical Constants

	MW	BP	Density
Isopentyl alcohol	88.2	132°C	0.813 g/ml
Acetic acid	60.1	118	1.06
Isopentyl acetate	130.2	142	0.876

Separation Scheme

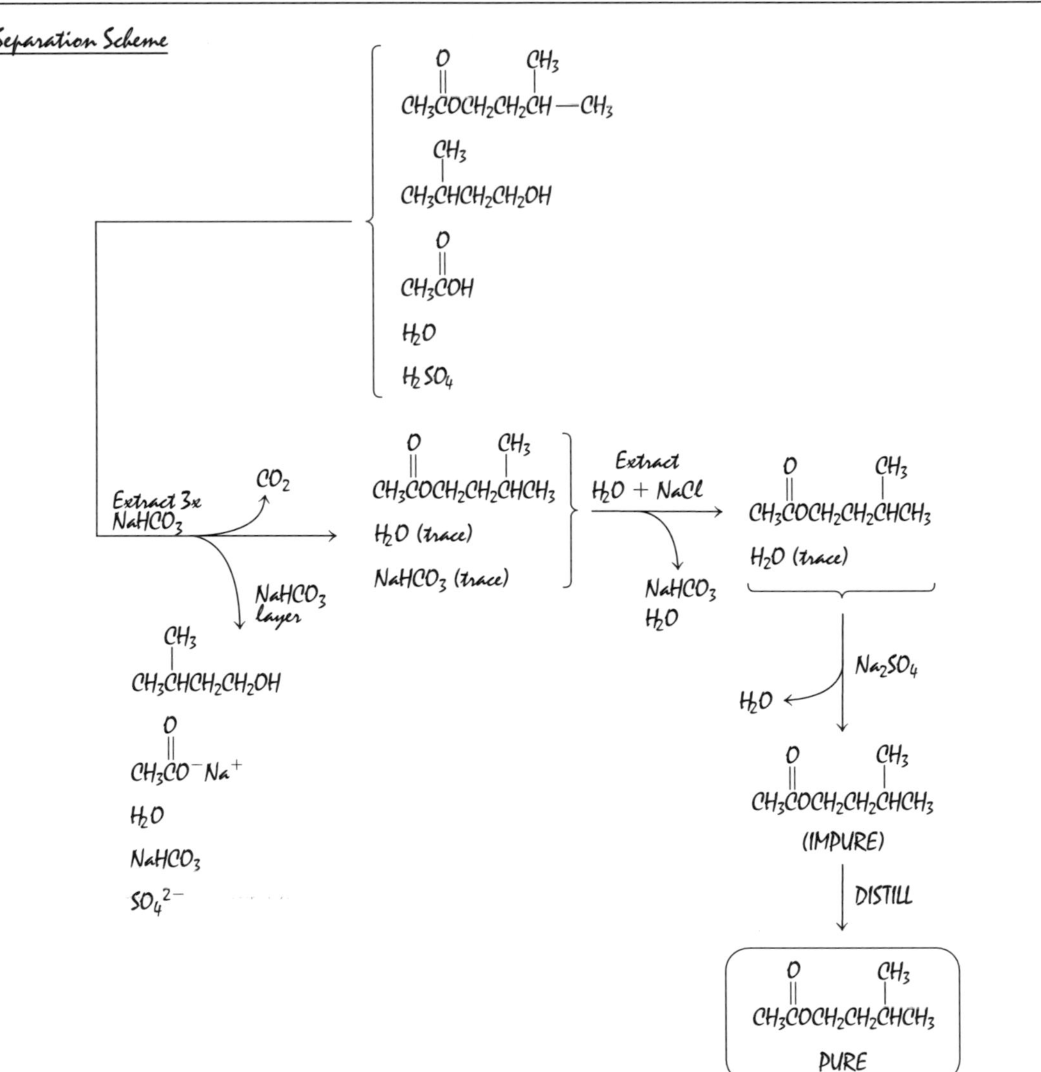

Figure 2.2 A sample notebook, page 1.

Data and Observations

7.5 mL of isopentyl alcohol was added to a pre-weighed 50-mL round-bottomed flask:

Flask + alcohol	139.75 g
Flask	133.63 g
	6.12 g isopentyl alcohol

Glacial acetic acid (10 mL) and 2 mL of concentrated sulfuric acid were also added to the flask, with swirling, along with several boiling stones. A water-cooled condenser was attached to the flask. The reaction was allowed to boil, using a heating mantle, for about one hour. The color of the reaction mixture was brownish-yellow.

After the reaction mixture had cooled to room temperature, the boiling stones were removed, and the reaction mixture was poured into a separatory funnel. About 30 mL of cold water was added to the separatory funnel. The reaction flask was rinsed with 5 mL of cold water, and the water was also added to the separatory funnel. The separatory funnel was shaken, and the lower aqueous layer was removed and discarded. The organic layer was extracted twice with two 10–15-mL portions of 5% aqueous sodium bicarbonate. During the first extraction, much CO_2 was given off, but the amount of gas evolved was markedly diminished during the second extraction. The organic layer was a light yellow in color. After the second extraction, the aqueous layer turned red litmus blue. The bicarbonate layers were discarded, and the organic layer was extracted with a 10–15-mL portion of water. A 2–3 mL portion of saturated sodium chloride solution was added during this extraction. When the aqueous layer had been removed, the upper, organic phase was transferred to a 15-mL Erlenmeyer flask. 2 g of anhydrous magnesium sulfate was added. The flask was stoppered, swirled gently, and allowed to stand for 15 mins.

The product was transferred to a 25-mL round-bottomed flask, and it was distilled by simple distillation. The distillation continued until no liquid could be observed dripping into the collection flask. After the distillation, the ester was transferred to a pre-weighed sample vial.

Sample vial + product	9.92 g
Sample vial	6.11 g
	3.81 g isopentyl acetate

The product was colorless and clear. The observed boiling point obtained during the distillation, was 140°C. An IR spectrum was obtained of the product.

Calculations

Determine limiting reagent:

$$\text{isopentyl alcohol } 6.12\,\cancel{g}\left(\frac{1 \text{ mol isopentyl alcohol}}{88.2\,\cancel{g}}\right) = 6.94 \times 10^{-2} \text{ mol}$$

$$\text{acetic acid: } (10\,\cancel{mL})\left(\frac{1.06\,\cancel{g}}{\cancel{mL}}\right)\left(\frac{1 \text{ mol acetic acid}}{60.1\,\cancel{g}}\right) = 1.76 \times 10^{-1} \text{ mol}$$

Since they react in a 1:1 ratio, isopentyl alcohol is the limiting reagent. Theoretical yield:

$$(6.94 \times 10^{-2}\ \cancel{\text{mol isopentyl alcohol}})\left(\frac{1\ \cancel{\text{mol isopentyl acetate}}}{1\ \cancel{\text{mol isopentyl alcohol}}}\right)\left(\frac{130.2 \text{ g isopentyl acetate}}{1\ \cancel{\text{mol isopentyl acetate}}}\right)$$

$$= 9.03 \text{ g isopentyl acetate}$$

$$\text{Percentage yield} = \frac{3.81 \text{ g}}{9.03 \text{ g}} \times 100 = 42.2\%$$

Figure 2.3 A sample notebook, page 2.

$$\text{Actual yield} = 3.81 \text{ g isopentyl acetate}$$

$$\text{Percentage yield} = \frac{3.81 \text{ g}}{9.03 \text{ g}} \times 100 = 42.2\%$$

For experiments that have the principal objective of isolating a substance such as a natural product rather than preparing and purifying some reaction product, the **weight percentage recovery** and not the percentage yield is calculated. This value is determined by

$$\text{Weight percentage recovery} = \frac{\text{Weight of substance isolated}}{\text{Weight of original material}} \times 100$$

Thus, for instance, if 0.014 g of caffeine was obtained from 2.3 g of tea, the weight percentage recovery of caffeine would be

$$\text{Weight percentage recovery} = \frac{0.014 \text{ g caffeine}}{2.3 \text{ g tea}} \times 100 = 0.61\%$$

2.3 LABORATORY REPORTS

Various formats for reporting the results of the laboratory experiments may be used. You may write the report directly in your notebook in a format similar to the sample notebook pages included in this section. Alternatively, your instructor may require a more formal report that is not written in your notebook. When you do original research, these reports should include a detailed description of all the experimental steps undertaken. Frequently, the style used in scientific periodicals such as *Journal of the American Chemical Society* is applied to writing laboratory reports. Your instructor is likely to have his or her own requirements for laboratory reports and should describe the requirements to you.

2.4 SUBMISSION OF SAMPLES

In all preparative experiments and in some isolation experiments, you will be required to submit to your instructor the sample of the substance you prepared or isolated. How this sample is labeled is very important. Again, learning a correct method of labeling bottles and vials can save time in the laboratory, because fewer mistakes will be made. More important, learning to label properly can decrease the danger inherent in having samples of material that cannot be identified correctly at a later date.

Solid materials should be stored and submitted in containers that permit the substance to be removed easily. For this reason, narrow-mouthed bottles or vials are not used for solid substances. Liquids should be stored in containers that will not let them escape through leakage. Be careful not to store volatile liquids in containers that have plastic caps, unless the cap is lined with an inert material such as Teflon. Otherwise, the vapors from the liquid are likely to contact the plastic and dissolve some of it, thus contaminating the substance being stored.

On the label, print the name of the substance, its melting or boiling point, the actual and percentage yields, and your name. An illustration of a properly prepared label follows:

Isopentyl Acetate
BP 140°C
Yield 3.81 g (42.2%)
Joe Schmedlock

TECHNIQUE 3

Laboratory Glassware: Care and Cleaning

Because your glassware is expensive and you are responsible for it, you will want to give it proper care and respect. If you read this section carefully and follow the procedures presented here, you may be able to avoid some unnecessary expense. You may also save time, because cleaning problems and replacing broken glassware are time consuming.

If you are unfamiliar with the equipment found in an organic chemistry laboratory or are uncertain about how such equipment should be treated, this section provides some useful information, such as cleaning glassware and caring for glassware when using corrosive or caustic reagents. At the end of this section are illustrations that show and name most of the equipment you are likely to find in your drawer or locker.

3.1 CLEANING GLASSWARE

Glassware can be cleaned easily if you clean it immediately after use. It is good practice to do your "dish washing" right away. With time, organic tarry materials left in a container begin to attack the surface of the glass. The longer you wait to clean glassware, the more extensively this interaction will have progressed. If you wait, cleaning is more difficult, because water will no longer wet the surface of the glass as effectively. If you cannot wash your glassware immediately after use, soak the dirty pieces of glassware in soapy water. A half-gallon plastic container is convenient for soaking and washing glassware. Using a plastic container also helps prevent the loss of small pieces of equipment.

Various soaps and detergents are available for washing glassware. They should be tried first when washing dirty glassware. Organic solvents can also be used, because the residue remaining in dirty glassware is likely to be soluble. After the solvent has been used, the glass item probably will have to be washed with soap and water to remove the residual solvent. When you use solvents to clean glassware, use caution, because the solvents are hazardous (see Technique 1). Use fairly small amounts of a solvent for cleaning purposes. Usually less than 5 mL (or 1–2 mL for microscale glassware) will be sufficient. Acetone is commonly used, but it is expensive. Your **wash acetone** can be used effectively several times before it is "spent." Once your acetone is spent, dispose of it as your instructor directs. If acetone does not work, other organic solvents such as methylene chloride or toluene can be used.

Caution: Acetone is very flammable. Do not use it around flames.

For troublesome stains and residues that adhere to the glass despite your best efforts, use a mixture of sulfuric acid and nitric acid. Cautiously add about 20 drops of concentrated sulfuric acid and 5 drops of concentrated nitric acid to the flask or vial.

Caution: You must wear safety glasses when you are using a cleaning solution made from sulfuric acid and nitric acid. Do not allow the solution to come into contact with your skin or clothing. It will cause severe burns on your skin and create holes in your clothing. The acids may also react with the residue in the container.

Swirl the acid mixture in the container for a few minutes. If necessary, place the glassware in a warm water bath and heat it cautiously to accelerate the cleaning process. Continue heating the glassware until any sign of a reaction ceases. When the cleaning procedure is completed, decant the mixture into an appropriate waste container.

Caution: Do not pour the acid solution into a waste container that is intended for organic wastes.

Rinse the piece of glassware thoroughly with water and then wash it with soap and water. For most common organic chemistry applications, any stains that survive this treatment are not likely to cause difficulty in subsequent laboratory procedures.

If the glassware is contaminated with stopcock grease, rinse the glassware with a small amount (1–2 mL) of methylene chloride. Discard the rinse solution into an appropriate waste container. Once the grease is removed, wash the glassware with soap or detergent and water.

3.2 DRYING GLASSWARE

The easiest way to dry glassware is to let it stand overnight. Store vials, flasks, and beakers upside down on a piece of paper towel to permit the water to drain from them. Drying ovens can be used to dry glassware if they are available and if they are not being used for other purposes. Rapid drying can be achieved by rinsing the glassware with acetone and air drying it or placing it in an oven. First, thoroughly drain the glassware of water. Then rinse it with one or two *small* portions (1–2 mL) of acetone. Do not use any more acetone than is suggested here. Return the used acetone to an acetone waste container for recycling. After you rinse the glassware with acetone, dry it by placing it in a drying oven for a few minutes or allow it to air dry at room temperature. The acetone can also be removed by aspirator suction. In some laboratories, it may be possible to dry the glassware by blowing a *gentle* stream of dry air into the container. (Your laboratory instructor will indicate if you should do this.) Before drying the glassware with air, make sure that the air line is not filled with oil. Otherwise, the oil will be blown into the container, and you will have to clean it again. It is not necessary to blast the acetone out of the glassware with a wide-open stream of air; a gentle stream of air is just as effective and will not startle other people in the room.

Do not dry your glassware with a paper towel unless the towel is lint free. Most paper will leave lint on the glass that can interfere with subsequent procedures. Sometimes it is not necessary to dry a piece of equipment thoroughly. For example, if you are going to place water or an aqueous solution in a container, it does not need to be completely dry.

3.3 GROUND-GLASS JOINTS

It is likely that the glassware in your organic kit has **standard-taper ground-glass joints.** For example, the Claisen head in Figure 3.1 consists of an inner (male) ground-glass joint at the bottom and two outer (female) joints at the top. Each end is ground to a precise size, which is designated by the symbol ₮ followed by two numbers. A common joint size in many macroscale organic glassware kits is ₮ 19/22. The first number indicates the diameter (in millimeters) of the joint at its widest point, and the second number refers to its length (see Figure 3.1). One advantage of standard-taper joints is that the pieces fit together snugly and form a good seal. In addition, standard-taper joints allow all glassware components with the same joint size to be connected, thus permitting the assembly of a wide variety of apparatuses. One disadvantage of glassware with ground-glass joints, however, is that it is expensive.

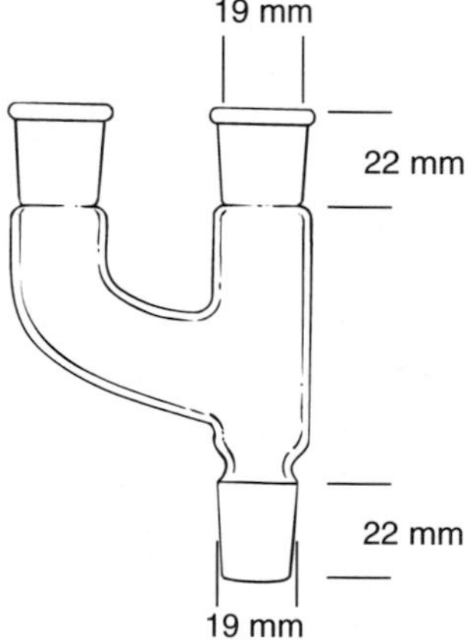

Figure 3.1 Illustration of inner and outer joints, showing dimensions. A Claisen head with ₮ 19/22 joints.

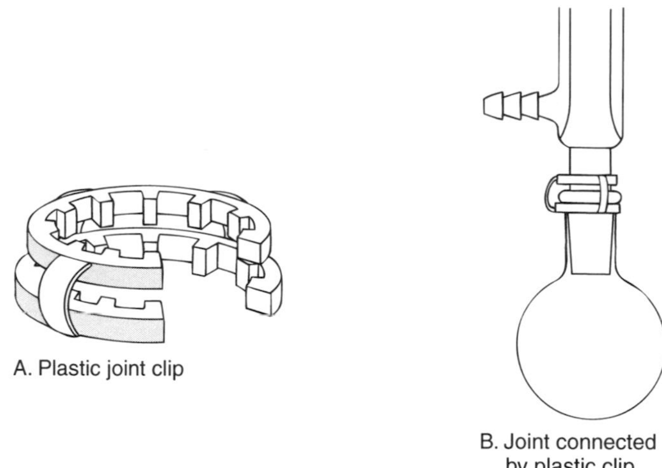

Figure 3.2 Connection of ground-glass joints. The use of a plastic clip (A) is also shown (B).

3.4 CONNECTING GROUND-GLASS JOINTS

It is a simple matter to connect pieces of macroscale glassware using standard-taper ground-glass joints. Figure 3.2B illustrates the connection of a condenser to a round-bottom flask. At times, however, it may be difficult to secure the connection so that it does not come apart unexpectedly. Figure 3.2A shows a plastic clip that serves to secure the connection. Methods to secure ground-glass connections with macroscale apparatus, including the use of plastic clips, are covered in Technique 7.

It is important to make sure no solid or liquid is on the joint surfaces. Either of these will decrease the efficiency of the seal, and the joints may leak. With microscale glassware, the presence of solid particles could cause the ground-glass joints to break when the plastic cap is tightened. Also, if the apparatus is to be heated, material caught between the joint surfaces will increase the tendency for the joints to stick. If the joint surfaces are coated with liquid or adhering solid, you should wipe the surfaces with a cloth or a lint-free paper towel before assembling.

3.5 CAPPING FLASKS, CONICAL VIALS, AND OPENINGS

The sidearms in two-necked or three-necked round-bottom flasks can be capped using the ₸ 19/22 ground-glass stoppers that are part of a normal macroscale organic kit. Figure 3.3 shows such a stopper being used to cap the sidearm of a three-necked flask.

3.6 SEPARATING GROUND-GLASS JOINTS

When ground-glass joints become "frozen" or stuck together, you are faced with the often vexing problem of separating them. The techniques for separating ground-glass

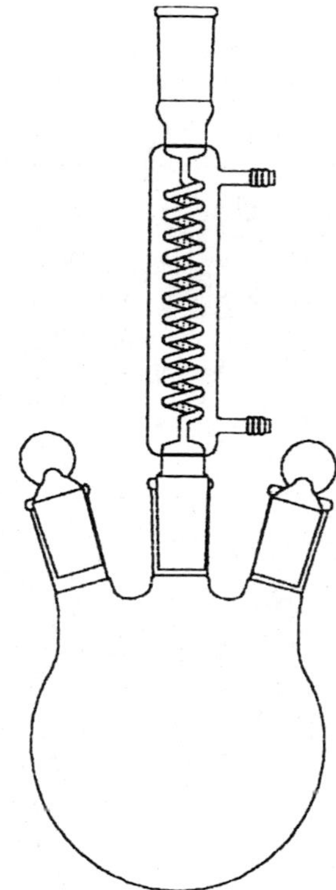

Figure 3.3 Capping a sidearm with a ₮ 19/22 stopper.

joints, or for removing stoppers that are stuck in the openings of flasks and vials, are the same for both macroscale and microscale glassware.

The most important thing you can do to prevent ground-glass joints from becoming frozen is to disassemble the glassware as soon as possible after a procedure is completed. Even when this precaution is followed, ground-glass joints may become stuck tightly together. The same is true of glass stoppers in bottles or conical vials. Because certain items of microscale glassware may be small and very fragile, it is relatively easy to break a piece of glassware when trying to pull two pieces apart. If the pieces do not separate easily, you must be careful when you try to pull them apart. The best way is to hold the two pieces, with both hands touching, as close as possible to the joint. With a firm grasp, try to loosen the joint with a slight twisting motion (do not twist very hard). If this does not work, try to pull your hands apart without pushing sideways on the glassware.

If it is not possible to pull the pieces apart, the following methods may help. A frozen joint can sometimes be loosened if you tap it *gently* with the wooden handle of a spatula. Then try to pull it apart as already described. If this procedure fails, you may try heating the joint in hot water or a steam bath. If heating fails, the instructor may be able to advise you. As a last resort, you may try heating the joint in a flame. You should not try this unless the apparatus is hopelessly stuck, because heating by flame often causes the joint to expand rapidly and crack or break. If you use a flame, make sure the joint is clean and dry. Heat the outer part of the joint slowly, in the yellow portion of a low flame, until it expands and separates from the inner section. Heat the joint very slowly and carefully, or it may break.

3.7 ETCHING GLASSWARE

Glassware that has been used for reactions involving strong bases such as sodium hydroxide or sodium alkoxides must be cleaned thoroughly *immediately* after use. If these caustic materials are allowed to remain in contact with the glass, they will etch the glass permanently. The etching makes later cleaning more difficult, because dirt particles may become trapped within the microscopic surface irregularities of the etched glass. Furthermore, the glass is weakened, so the lifetime of the glassware is shortened. If caustic materials are allowed to come into contact with ground-glass joints without being removed promptly, the joints will become fused or "frozen." It is extremely difficult to separate fused joints without breaking them.

3.8 ATTACHING RUBBER TUBING TO EQUIPMENT

When you attach rubber tubing to the glass apparatus or when you insert glass tubing into rubber stoppers, first lubricate the rubber tubing or the rubber stopper with either water or glycerin. Without such lubrication, it can be difficult to attach rubber tubing to the sidearms of items of glassware such as condensers and filter flasks. Furthermore, glass tubing may break when it is inserted into rubber stoppers. Water is a good lubricant for most purposes. Do not use water as a lubricant when it might contaminate the reaction. Glycerin is a better lubricant than water and should be used when there is considerable friction between the glass and rubber. If glycerin is the lubricant, be careful not to use too much.

3.9 DESCRIPTION OF EQUIPMENT

Figures 3.4 and 3.5 include examples of glassware and equipment that are commonly used in the organic laboratory. Your glassware and equipment may vary slightly from the pieces shown on pages 589–591.

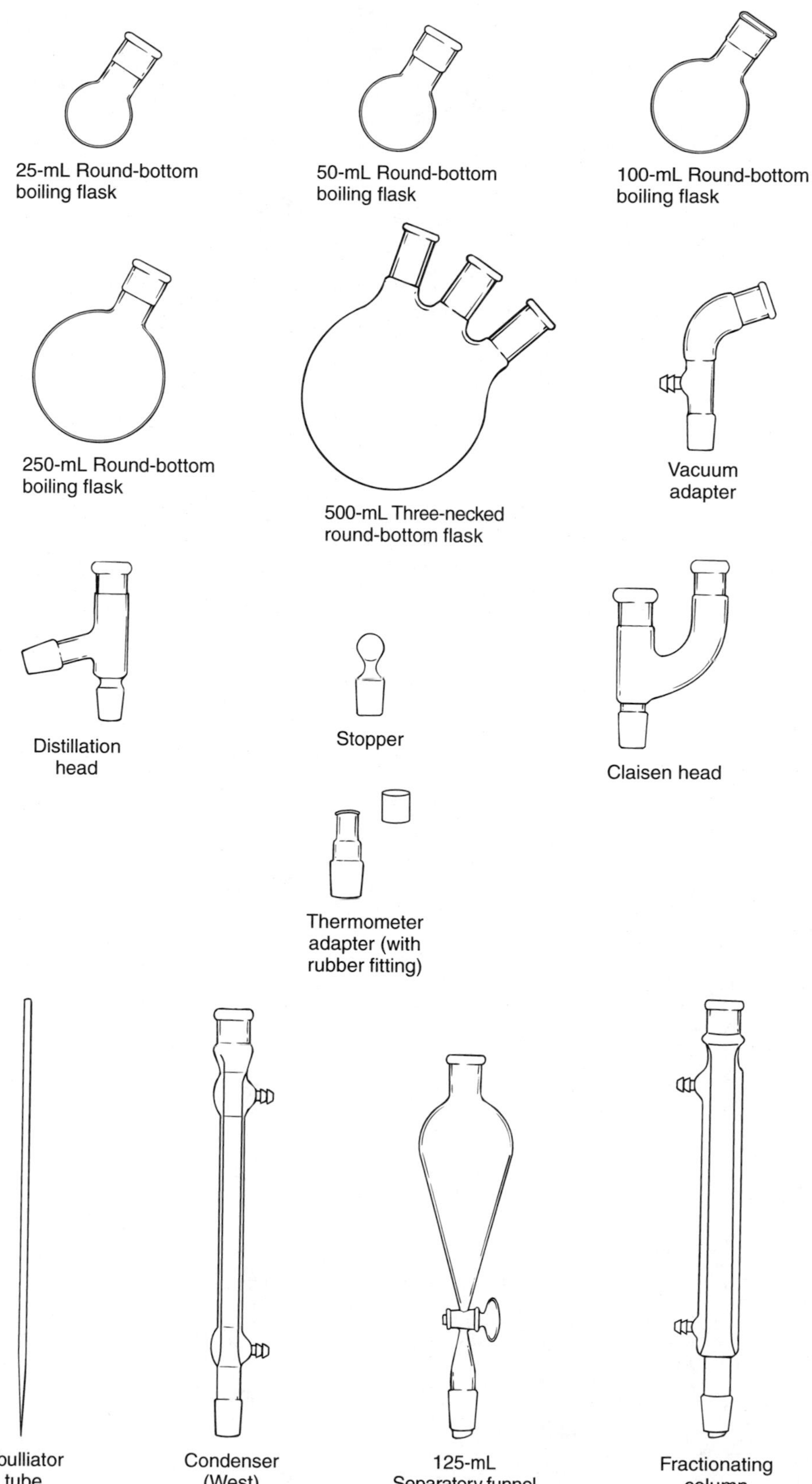

Figure 3.4 Components of the macroscale organic laboratory kit.

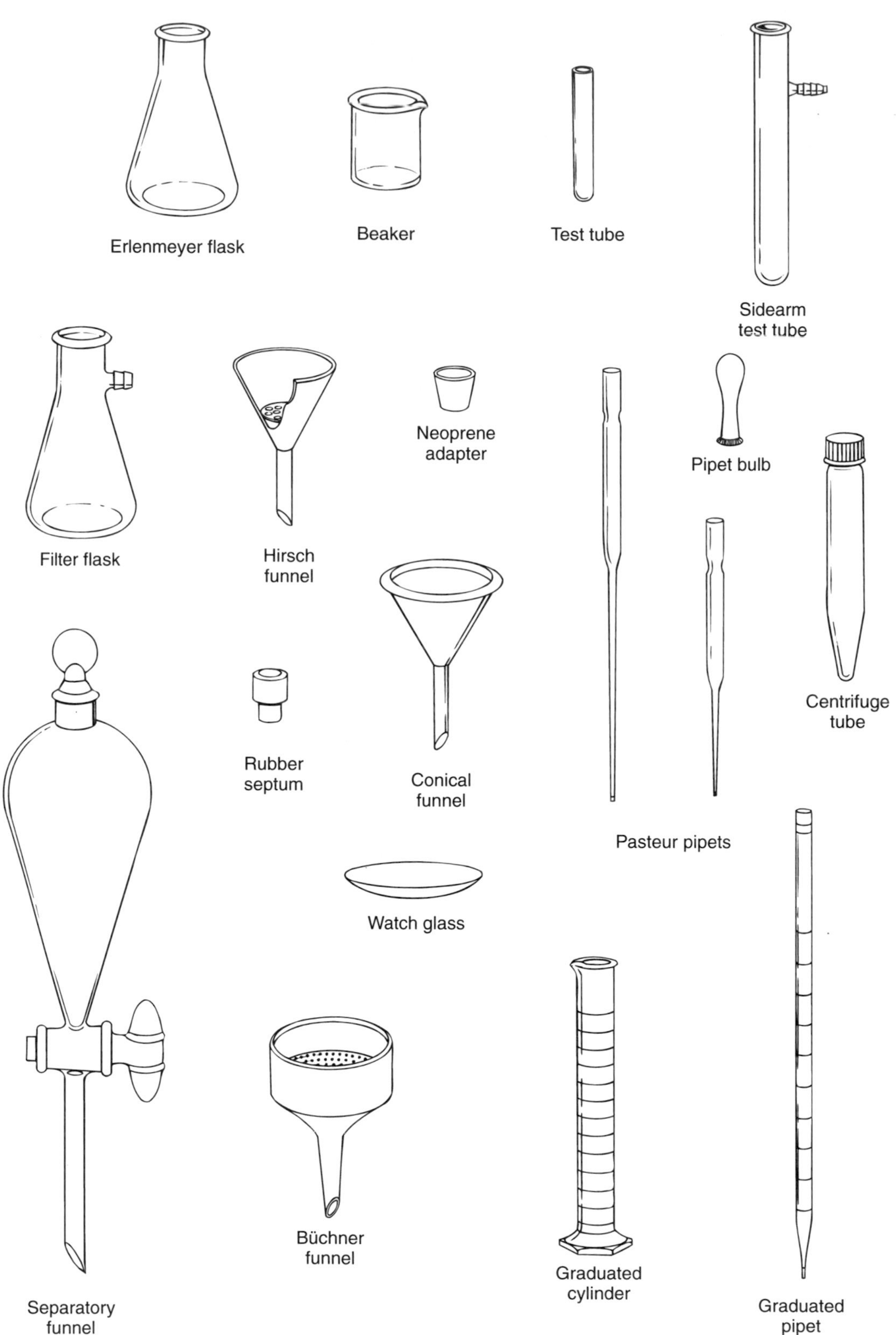

Figure 3.5 Equipment commonly used in the organic chemistry laboratory.

Test tube brush

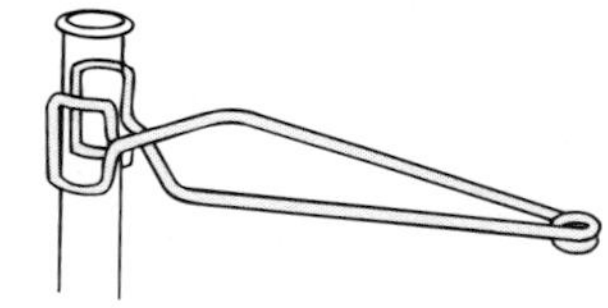

Test tube holder

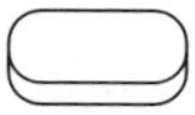

Spin Bar

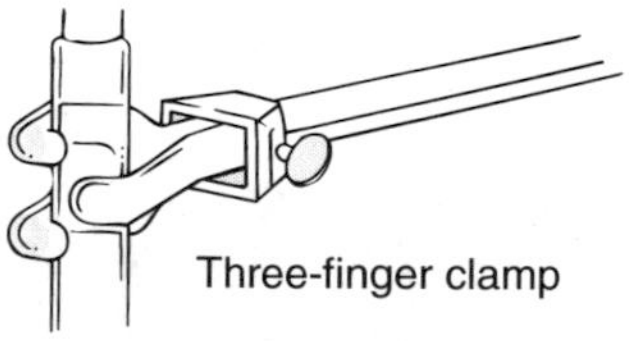

Forceps

Three-finger clamp

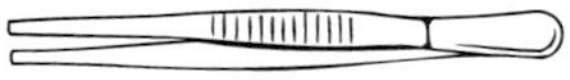

Syringe

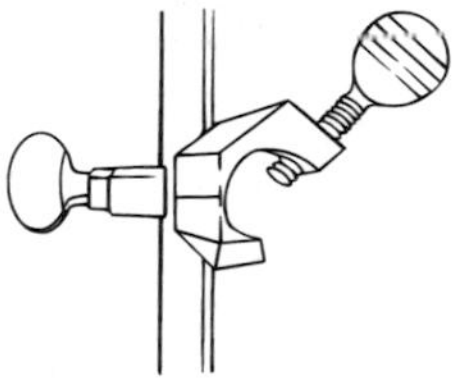

Spatula

Clamp holder

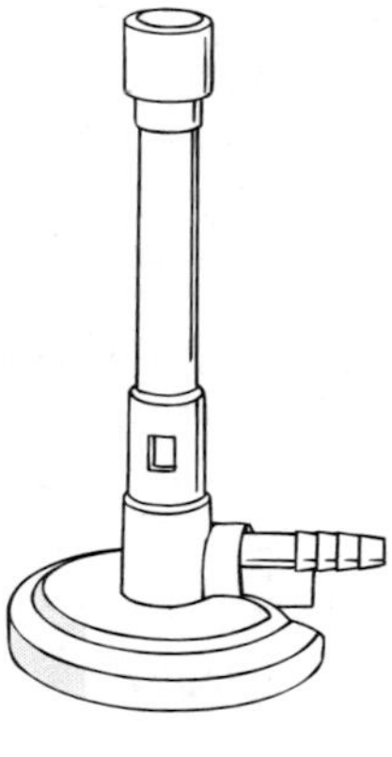

Microburner

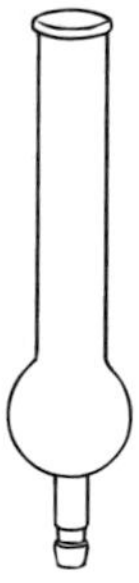

Drying tube

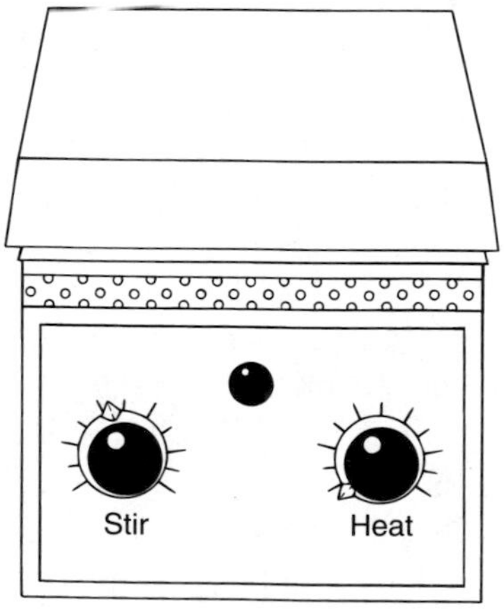

Stir

Heat

Hot plate / Stirrer

ESSAY

Identification of Drugs

Frequently, a chemist is called on to identify a particular unknown substance. If there is no prior information to work from, this can be a formidable task. There are several million known compounds, both inorganic and organic. For a completely unknown substance, the chemist must often use every available method. If the unknown substance is a mixture, then the mixture must be separated into its components and each component identified separately. A pure compound can often be identified from its physical properties (melting point, boiling point, density, refractive index, and so on) and a knowledge of its functional groups. These can be identified by the reactions that the compound is observed to undergo or by spectroscopy (infrared, ultraviolet, nuclear magnetic resonance, and mass spectroscopy). The techniques necessary for this type of identification are introduced in a later section.

A somewhat simpler situation often arises in drug identification. The scope of drug identification is more limited, and the chemist working in a hospital trying to identify the source of a drug overdose or the law enforcement officer trying to identify a suspected illicit drug or a poison usually has some prior clues to work from. So does the medicinal chemist working for a pharmaceutical manufacturer who might be trying to discover why a competitor's product may be better.

Consider a drug overdose case as an example. The patient is brought into the emergency ward of a hospital. This person may be in a coma or a hyperexcited state, have an allergic rash, or clearly be hallucinating. These physiological symptoms are themselves a clue to the nature of the drug. Samples of the drug may be found in the patient's possession. Correct medical treatment may require a rapid and accurate identification of a drug powder or capsule. If the patient is conscious, the necessary information can be elicited orally; if not, the drug must be examined. If the drug is a tablet or a capsule, the process is often simple, because many drugs are coded by a manufacturer's trademark or logo, by shape (round, oval, bullet shape), by formulation (tablet, gelatin capsule, time-release microcapsules), and by color. Some drugs bear an imprinted number or code.

It is more difficult to identify a powder, but under some circumstances such identification may be easy. Plant drugs are often easily identified because they contain microscopic bits and pieces of the plant from which they are obtained. This cellular debris is often characteristic for certain types of drugs, and they can be identified on this basis alone. A microscope is all that is needed. Sometimes chemical color tests can be used as confirmation. Certain drugs give rise to characteristic colors when treated with special reagents. Other drugs form crystalline precipitates of characteristic color and crystal structure when treated with appropriate reagents.

If the drug itself is not available and the patient is unconscious (or dead), identification may be more difficult. It may be necessary to pump the stomach or bladder contents of the patient (or corpse) or to obtain a blood sample and work on these. These samples of stomach fluid, urine, or blood would be extracted with an appropriate organic solvent, and the extract would be analyzed.

Often the final identification of a drug, as an extract of urine, serum, or stomach fluid, hinges on some type of **chromatography.** Thin-layer chromatography (TLC) is often used.

Under specified conditions, many drug substances can be identified by their R_f values and by the colors that their TLC spots turn when treated with various reagents or when they are observed under certain visualization methods. In the experiment that follows, TLC is applied to the analysis of an unknown analgesic drug.

REFERENCES

Keller, E. "Origin of Modern Criminology." *Chemistry, 42* (1969): 8.

Keller, E. "Forensic Toxicology: Poison Detection and Homicide." *Chemistry, 43* (1970): 14.

Lieu, V. T. "Analysis of APC Tablets." *Journal of Chemical Education, 48* (1971): 478.

Neman, R. L. "Thin Layer Chromatography of Drugs." *Journal of Chemical Education, 49* (1972): 834.

Rodgers, S. S. "Some Analytical Methods Used in Crime Laboratories." *Chemistry, 42* (1969): 29.

Tietz, N. W. *Fundamentals of Clinical Chemistry.* Philadelphia: W. B. Saunders, 1970.

Walls, H. J. *Forensic Science.* New York: Praeger, 1968.

A collection of articles on forensic chemistry can be found in

Berry, K., and Outlaw, H. E., eds. "Forensic Chemistry—A Symposium Collection." *Journal of Chemical Education, 62* (December 1985): 1043–1065.

EXPERIMENT 10

TLC Analysis of Analgesic Drugs

Thin-layer chromatography

In this experiment, thin-layer chromatography (TLC) will be used to determine the composition of various over-the-counter analgesics. If the instructor chooses, you may also be required to identify the components and actual identity (trade name) of an unknown analgesic. You will be given either two or three commercially prepared TLC plates with a flexible backing and a silica gel coating with a fluorescent indicator. On the first TLC plate, a reference plate, you will spot five standard compounds often used in analgesic formulations. In addition, a standard reference mixture containing four of these same compounds will be spotted. Ibuprofen is omitted from this standard mixture because it would overlap with salicylamide after the plate is developed. If your instructor wishes, you will spot five additional reference substances on a second reference plate, including the newest analgesic drugs. On the final plate (the sample plate) you will spot several commercial analgesic preparations in order to determine their composition. At your instructor's option, one or more of these may be an unknown.

The standard compounds will all be available as solutions of 1 g of each dissolved in 20 mL of a 50:50 mixture of methylene chloride and ethanol. The purpose of the first reference plate is to determine the order of elution (R_f values) of the known substances and to index the standard reference mixture. On the second reference plate (optional), several of

Reference Plate 1		Reference Plate 2 (optional)		Sample Plate
Acetaminophen	(Ac)	Aspirin	(Asp)	Five commercial preparations (or unknowns) plus the reference mixture
Aspirin	(Asp)	Ibuprofen	(Ibu)	
Caffeine	(Cf)	Ketoprofen	(Kpf)	
Ibuprofen	(Ibu)	Naproxen sodium	(Nap)	
Salicylamide	(Sal)	Salicylamide	(Sal)	
Reference mixture 1	(Ref-1)	Reference mixture 2	(Ref-2)	

the substances have similar R_f values, but you will note a different behavior for each spot with the visualization methods. On the sample plate, the standard reference mixture will be spotted, along with several solutions that you will prepare from commercial analgesic tablets. These tablets will each be crushed and dissolved in a 50:50 methylene chloride–ethanol mixture for spotting.

Two methods of visualization will be used to observe the positions of the spots on the developed TLC plates. First, the plates will be observed while under illumination from a short-wavelength ultraviolet (UV) lamp. This is done best in a darkened room or in a fume hood that has been darkened by taping butcher paper or aluminum foil over the lowered glass cover. Under these conditions, some of the spots will appear as dark areas on the plate, while others will fluoresce brightly. This difference in appearance under UV illumination will help to distinguish the substances from one another. You will find it convenient to outline very lightly in *pencil* the spots observed and to place a small **x** inside those spots that fluoresce. For a second means of visualization, iodine vapor will be used. Not all the spots will become visible when treated with iodine, but some will develop yellow, tan, or deep brown colors. The differences in the behaviors of the various spots with iodine can be used to further differentiate among them.

It is possible to use several developing solvents for this experiment, but ethyl acetate with 0.5% glacial acetic acid added is preferred. The small amount of glacial acetic acid supplies protons and suppresses ionization of aspirin, ibuprofen, naproxen sodium, and ketoprofen, allowing them to travel upward on the plates in their protonated form. Without the acid, these compounds do not move.

In some analgesics, you may find ingredients besides the five mentioned previously. Some include an antihistamine and some, a mild sedative. For instance, Midol contains N-cinnamylephedrine (cinnamedrine), an antihistamine, and Excedrin PM contains the sedative methapyrilene hydrochloride. Cope contains the related sedative methapyrilene fumarate. Some tablets may be colored with a chemical dye.

Required Reading

Review:	Essay	Analgesics
New:	Technique 19	Column Chromatography, Sections 19.1–19.3
	Technique 20	Thin-Layer Chromatography
	Essay	Identification of Drugs

Special Instructions

You must examine the developed plates under ultraviolet light first. After comparisons of *all* plates have been made with UV light, iodine vapor can be used. The iodine permanently affects some of the spots, making it impossible to go back and repeat the UV visualization. Take special care to notice those substances that have similar R_f values; these spots each have a different appearance when viewed under UV illumination or a different staining color with iodine, allowing you to distinguish among them.

Aspirin presents some special problems because it is present in a large amount in many of the analgesics and because it hydrolyzes easily. For these reasons, the aspirin spots often show excessive tailing.

Suggested Waste Disposal

Dispose of all development solvent in the container for nonhalogenated organic solvents. Dispose of the ethanol–methylene chloride mixture in the container for halogenated organic solvents. The micropipets used for spotting the solution should be placed in a special container labeled for that purpose. The TLC plates should be stapled in your lab notebook.

Notes to the Instructor

If you wish, students may work in pairs on this experiment, each one preparing one of the two reference plates and then cooperating on the third plate. Alternatively, especially if students are to work alone, you may wish to omit plate 2 and forgo identifying the two newest analgesics (ketoprofen and naproxen sodium).

Perform the thin-layer chromatography with flexible Silica Gel 60 F-254 plates (EM Science, No. 5554-7). If the TLC plates have not been purchased recently, you should place them in an oven at 100°C for 30 minutes and store them in a desiccator until used. If you use different thin-layer plates, try out the experiment before using them with a class. Other plates may not resolve all five substances.

Ibuprofen and salicylamide have approximately the same R_f value, but they show up differently under the detection methods. For reasons that are not yet clear, ibuprofen sometimes gives two or even three spots. Naproxen sodium and ketoprofen have approximately the same R_f as aspirin. Once again, however, they show up differently under the detection methods. Fortunately, none of the new drugs appears in combination, either together, or with aspirin or ibuprofen, in any current commercial product.

Procedure

Initial Preparations. You will need at least 12 capillary micropipets (18 if both reference plates are prepared) to spot the plates. The preparation of these pipets is described and illustrated in Technique 20, Section 20.4, page 822. A common error is

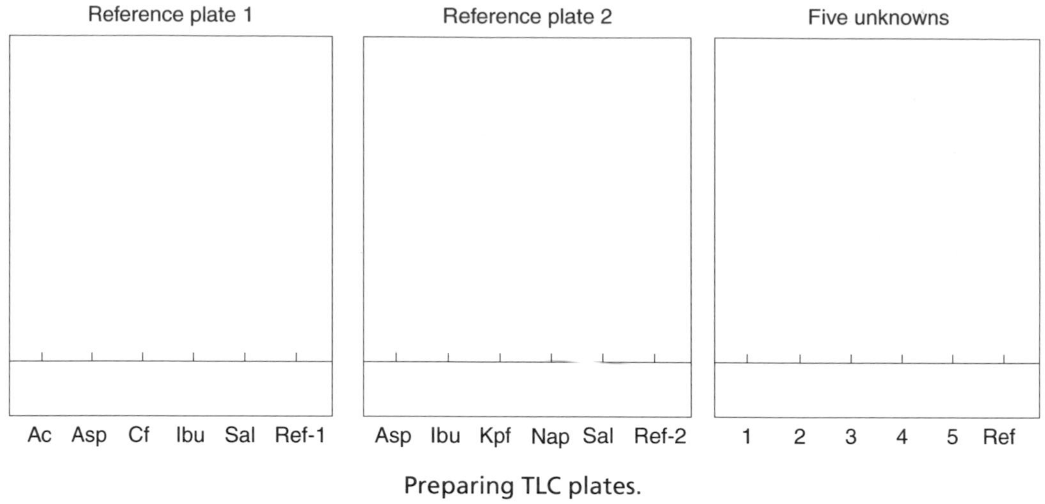

Preparing TLC plates.

to pull the center section out too far when making these pipets, with the result that too little sample is applied to the plate. If this happens, you won't see *any* spots. Follow the directions carefully.

After preparing the micropipets, obtain two (or three) 10-cm × 6.6-cm TLC plates (EM Science Silica Gel 60 F-254, No. 5554-7) from your instructor. These plates have a flexible backing, but they should not be bent excessively. Handle them carefully or the adsorbent may flake off. Also, you should handle them only by the edges; the surface should not be touched. Using a lead pencil (not a pen), *lightly* draw a line across the plates (short dimension) about l cm from the bottom. Using a centimeter ruler, move its index about 0.6 cm in from the edge of the plate and lightly mark off six 1-cm intervals on the line (see figure). These are the points at which the samples will be spotted. If you are preparing two reference plates, it would be a good idea to mark a small number **1** or **2** in the upper right-hand corner of each plate to allow easy identification.

Spotting the First Reference Plate. On the first plate (marked 1), starting from left to right, spot acetaminophen, then aspirin, caffeine, ibuprofen, and salicylamide. This order is alphabetic and will avoid any further memory problems or confusion. Solutions of these compounds will be found in small bottles on the side shelf. The standard reference mixture (Ref-1), also found on the side shelf, is spotted in the last position. The correct method of spotting a TLC plate is described in Technique 20, Section 20.4, page 822. It is important that the spots be made as small as possible, but not too small. With too much sample, the spots will tail and will overlap one another after development. With too little sample, no spots will be observed after development. The optimum applied spot should be about 1–2 mm (1/16 in.) in diameter. If scrap pieces of the TLC plates are available, it would be a good idea to practice spotting on these before preparing the actual sample plates.

Spotting the Second Reference Plate (Optional). On the second plate (marked 2), starting from left to right, spot aspirin, ibuprofen, ketoprofen, naproxen sodium, salicylamide, and the reference mixture (Ref-2). Follow the same procedure and take the precautions noted above for the first plate.

Preparing the Development Chamber. When the reference plate (or plates) has been spotted, obtain a 16-oz wide-mouth, screw-cap jar (or other suitable container) for use as a development chamber. The preparation of a development chamber is described in Technique 20, Section 20.5, page 823. Because the backing on the TLC plates is very thin, if they touch the filter paper liner of the development chamber *at any point,* solvent will begin to diffuse onto the absorbent surface at that point. To avoid this, you may either omit the liner or make the following modification.

If you wish to use a liner, use a very narrow strip of filter paper (approximately 5 cm wide). Fold it into an L shape that is long enough to traverse the bottom of the jar and extend up the side to the top of the jar. TLC plates placed in the jar for development should *straddle* this liner strip but not touch it.

When the development chamber has been prepared, obtain a small amount of the development solvent (0.5% glacial acetic acid in ethyl acetate). Your instructor should prepare this mixture; it contains such a small amount of acetic acid that small individual portions are difficult to prepare. Fill the chamber with the development solvent to a depth of about 0.5–0.7 cm. If you are using a liner, be sure it is saturated with the solvent. Recall that the solvent level must not be above the spots on the plate or the samples will dissolve off the plate into the reservoir instead of developing.

Development of the Reference TLC Plates. Place the spotted plate (or plates) in the chamber (straddling the liner if one is present) and allow the spots to develop. If you are doing two reference plates, both plates may be placed in the same development jar. Be sure the plates are placed in the developing jar so that their bottom edge is parallel to the bottom of the jar (straight, not tilted); if not, the solvent front will not advance evenly, increasing the difficulty of making good comparisons. The plates should face each other and slant or lean back in opposite directions. When the solvent has risen to a level about 0.5 cm from the top of the plate, remove each plate from the chamber (in the hood) and, using a lead pencil, mark the position of the solvent front. Set the plate on a piece of paper towel to dry. It may be helpful to place a small object under one end to allow optimum air flow around the drying plate.

UV Visualization of the Reference Plates. When the plates are dry, observe them under a short-wavelength UV lamp, preferably in a darkened hood or a darkened room. Lightly outline all of the observed spots with a pencil. Carefully notice any differences in behavior between the spotted substances, especially those on plate 2. Several compounds have similar R_f values, but the spots have a different appearance under UV illumination or iodine staining. Currently, there are no commercial analgesic preparations containing any compounds that have the same R_f values, but you will need to be able to distinguish them from one another to identify which one is present. Before proceeding, make a sketch of the plates in your notebook and note the differences in appearance that you observed. Using a ruler marked in millimeters, measure the distance that each spot has traveled relative to the solvent front. Calculate R_f values for each spot (Technique 20, Section 20.9, p. 827).

Analysis of Commercial Analgesics or Unknowns (Sample Plate). Next, obtain half a tablet of each of the analgesics to be analyzed on the final TLC plate. If you were issued an unknown, you may analyze four other analgesics of your choice; if not, you may analyze five. The experiment will be most interesting if you make your choices in a way that gives a wide spectrum of results. Try to pick at least one analgesic each containing aspirin, acetaminophen, ibuprofen, a newer analgesic, and, if available, salicylamide. If you have a favorite analgesic, you may wish to include it among your samples. Take each analgesic half-tablet, place it on a smooth piece of notebook paper, and crush it well with a spatula. Transfer each crushed half-tablet to a labeled test tube or a small Erlenmeyer flask. Using a graduated cylinder, mix 15 mL of absolute ethanol and 15 mL of methylene chloride. Mix the solution well. Add 5 mL of this solvent to each of the crushed half-tablets and then heat each of them *gently* for a few minutes on a steam bath or sand bath at about 100°C. Not all the tablet will dissolve, because the analgesics usually contain an insoluble binder. In addition, many of them contain inorganic buffering agents or coatings that are insoluble in this solvent mixture. After heating the samples, allow them to settle and then spot the clear liquid extracts on the sample plate. At the sixth position, spot the standard reference solution (Ref-1 or Ref-2). Develop the plate in 0.5% glacial acetic acid–ethyl acetate as before. Observe the plate under UV illumination and mark the visible spots as you did for the first plate. Sketch the plate in your notebook and record your conclusions about the contents of each tablet. This can be done by directly comparing your plate to the reference plate(s)—they can all be placed under the UV light at the same time. If you were issued an unknown, try to determine its identity (trade name).

Iodine Analysis. Do not perform this step until UV comparisons of all the plates are complete. When ready, place the plates in a jar containing a few iodine crystals, cap the jar, and warm it gently on a steam bath or warm hot plate until the spots begin to appear. Notice which spots become visible and note their relative colors. You can directly compare colors of the reference spots to those on the unknown plate(s). Remove the plates from the jar and record your observations in your notebook.

QUESTIONS

1. What happens if the spots are made too large when preparing a TLC plate for development?
2. What happens if the spots are made too small when preparing a TLC plate for development?
3. Why must the spots be above the level of the development solvent in the developing chamber?
4. What would happen if the spotting line and positions were marked on the plate with a ballpoint pen?
5. Is it possible to distinguish two spots that have the same R_f value but represent different compounds? Give two different methods.
6. Name some advantages of using acetaminophen (Tylenol) instead of aspirin as an analgesic.

TECHNIQUE 20

Thin-Layer Chromatography

Thin-layer chromatography (TLC) is a very important technique for the rapid separation and qualitative analysis of small amounts of material. It is ideally suited for the analysis of mixtures and reaction products in both macroscale and microscale experiments. The technique is closely related to column chromatography. In fact, TLC can be considered column chromatography *in reverse,* with the solvent ascending the adsorbent rather than descending. Because of this close relationship to column chromatography and because the principles governing the two techniques are similar, Technique 19, on column chromatography, should be read first.

20.1 PRINCIPLES OF THIN-LAYER CHROMATOGRAPHY

Like column chromatography, TLC is a solid–liquid partitioning technique. However, the moving liquid phase is not allowed to percolate down the adsorbent; it is caused to *ascend* a thin layer of adsorbent coated onto a backing support. The most typical backing is a plastic material, but other materials are also used. A thin layer of the adsorbent is spread onto the plate and allowed to dry. A coated and dried plate is called a **thin-layer plate** or a **thin-layer slide.** (Microscope slides were often used to prepare small thin-layer plates, thus the reference to *slide.*) When a thin-layer plate is placed upright in a vessel that contains a shallow layer of solvent, the solvent ascends the layer of adsorbent on the plate by capillary action.

In TLC, the sample is applied to the plate before the solvent is allowed to ascend the adsorbent layer. The sample is usually applied as a small spot near the base of the plate; this technique is often referred to as **spotting.** The plate is spotted by repeated applications of a sample solution from a small capillary pipet. When the filled pipet touches the plate, capillary action delivers its contents to the plate, and a small spot is formed.

As the solvent ascends the plate, the sample is partitioned between the moving liquid phase and the stationary solid phase. During this process, you are **developing,** or **running,** the thin-layer plate. In development, the various components in the applied mixture are separated. The separation is based on the many equilibrations the solutes experience between the moving and the stationary phases. (The nature of these equilibrations was thoroughly discussed in Technique 19, Sections 19.2 and 19.3, pp. 795–798.) As in column chromatography, the least polar substances advance faster than the most polar substances. A separation results from the differences in the rates at which the individual components of the mixture advance upward on the plate. When many substances are present in a mixture, each has its own characteristic solubility and adsorptivity properties, depending on the functional groups in its structure. In general, the stationary phase is strongly polar and strongly binds polar substances. The moving liquid phase is usually less polar than the adsorbent and most easily dissolves substances that are less polar or even nonpolar. Thus, the most polar substances travel slowly upward, or not at all, and nonpolar substances travel more rapidly if the solvent is sufficiently nonpolar.

When the thin-layer plate has been developed, it is removed from the developing tank and allowed to dry until it is free of solvent. If the mixture that was originally spotted on the plate was separated, there will be a vertical series of spots on the plate. Each spot corresponds to a separate component or compound from the original mixture. If the components of the mixture are colored substances, the various spots will be clearly visible after development. More often, however, the "spots" will not be visible because they correspond to colorless substances. If spots are not apparent, they can be made visible only if a **visualization method** is used. Often, spots can be seen when the thin-layer plate is held under ultraviolet light; the ultraviolet lamp is a common visualization method. Also common is the use of iodine vapor. The plates are placed in a chamber containing iodine crystals and left to stand for a short time. The iodine reacts with the various compounds adsorbed on the plate to give colored complexes that are clearly visible. Because iodine often changes the compounds by reaction, the components of the mixture cannot be recovered from the plate when the iodine method is used. (Other methods of visualization are discussed in Section 20.7.)

20.2 COMMERCIALLY PREPARED TLC PLATES

The most convenient type of TLC plate is prepared commercially and sold in a ready-to-use form. Many manufacturers supply glass plates precoated with a durable layer of silica gel or alumina. More conveniently, plates are also available that have either a flexible plastic backing or an aluminum backing. The most common types of commercial TLC plates are composed of plastic sheets that are coated with silica gel and polyacrylic acid, which serves as a binder. A fluorescent indicator may be mixed with the silica gel. Due to the presence of compounds in the sample, the indicator renders the spots visible under ultraviolet light (see Section 20.7). Although these plates are relatively expensive compared with plates prepared in the laboratory, they are far more convenient to use, and they provide more consistent results. The plates are manufactured quite uniformly. Because the plastic backing is flexible, an additional advantage is that the coating does not flake off the plates easily. The plastic sheets (usually 8 in. $\times$ 8 in. square) can also be cut with a pair of scissors or paper cutter to whatever size may be required.

If the package of commercially prepared TLC plates has been opened previously or if the plates have not been purchased recently, they should be dried before use. Dry the plates by placing them in an oven at 100°C for 30 minutes and store them in a desiccator until they are to be used.

20.3 PREPARATION OF THIN-LAYER SLIDES AND PLATES

Commercially prepared plates (Section 20.2) are the most convenient to use, and we recommend their use for most applications. If you must prepare your own slides or plates, this section provides directions for doing so. The two adsorbent materials used most often for TLC are alumina G (aluminum oxide) and silica gel G (silicic acid). The G designation stands for gypsum (calcium sulfate). Calcined gypsum $CaSO_4 \cdot \frac{1}{2}H_2O$ is better known as plaster of paris. When exposed to water or moisture, gypsum sets in a rigid mass $CaSO_4 \cdot 2H_2O$, which binds the adsorbent together and to the glass plates used as a backing support. In the adsorbents used for TLC, about 10–13% by weight of gypsum is added as a binder. The adsorbent materials are otherwise similar to those used in column chromatography; the adsorbents used in column chromatography have a larger particle size, however. The material for thin-layer work is a fine powder. The small particle size, along with the added gypsum, makes it impossible to use silica gel G or alumina G for column work. In a column, these adsorbents generally set so rigidly that solvent virtually stops flowing through the column.

For separations involving large amounts of material or for difficult separations, it may be necessary to use larger thin-layer plates. Under these circumstances, you may have to prepare your own plates. Plates with dimensions up to 200–250 cm^2 are common. With larger plates, it is desirable to have a somewhat durable coating, and a water slurry of the adsorbent should be used to prepare them. If silica gel is used, the slurry should be prepared in the ratio of about 1 g silica gel G to each 2 mL of water. The glass plate used for the thin-layer plate should be washed, dried, and placed on a sheet of newspaper. Place two strips of masking tape along two edges of the plate. Use more than one layer of masking tape if a thicker coating is desired on the plate. A slurry is prepared, shaken well, and poured along one of the untaped edges of the plate.

Caution: Avoid breathing silica dust or methylene chloride, prepare and use the slurry in a hood, and avoid getting methylene chloride or the slurry mixture on your skin. Perform the coating operation under a hood.

A heavy piece of glass rod, long enough to span the taped edges, is used to level and spread the slurry over the plate. While the rod is resting on the tape, it is pushed along the plate from the end at which the slurry was poured toward the opposite end of the plate. This is illustrated in Figure 20.1. After the slurry is spread, the masking tape strips are removed, and the plates are dried in a 110°C oven for about 1 hour. Plates of 200–250 cm^2 are easily prepared by this method. Larger plates present more difficulties. Many laboratories have a commercially manufactured spreading machine that makes the entire operation simpler.

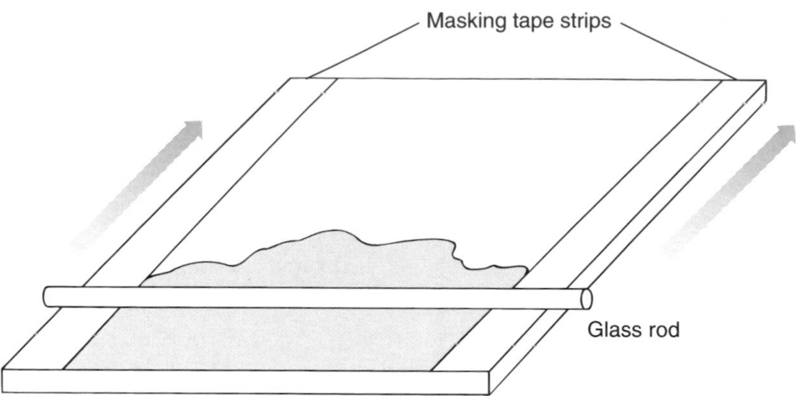

Figure 20.1 Preparing a large thin-layer chromatography plate.

20.4 SAMPLE APPLICATION: SPOTTING THE PLATES

A. Preparing a Micropipet

To apply the sample that is to be separated to the thin-layer plate, use a micropipet. A micropipet is easily made from a short length of thin-walled capillary tubing such as that used for melting-point determinations, but open at both ends. The capillary tubing is heated at its midpoint with a microburner and rotated until it is soft. When the tubing is soft, the heated portion of the tubing is drawn out until a constricted portion of tubing 4–5 cm long is formed. After cooling, the constricted portion of tubing is scored at its center with a file or scorer and broken. The two halves yield two capillary micropipets. Try to make a clean break without jagged or sharp edges. Figure 20.2 shows how to make such pipets.

B. Spotting the Plate

To apply a sample to the plate, begin by placing about 1 mg of a solid test substance or 1 drop of a liquid test substance in a small container such as a watch glass or a test tube. Dissolve the sample in a few drops of a volatile solvent. Acetone or methylene chloride is usually a suitable solvent. If a solution is to be tested, it can often be used directly (undiluted). The small capillary pipet, prepared as described, is filled by dipping the pulled end into the solution to be examined. Capillary action fills the pipet. Empty the pipet by touching it lightly to the thin-layer plate at a point about 1 cm from the bottom (Figure 20.3). The spot must be high enough so that it does not dissolve in the developing solvent. It is important to touch the plate very lightly and not to gouge a hole in the adsorbent. When the pipet touches the plate, the solution is transferred to the plate as a small spot. The pipet should be touched to the plate very briefly and then removed. If the pipet is held to the plate, its entire contents will be delivered to the plate. Only a small amount of material is needed. It is often helpful to blow gently on the plate as the sample is applied. This helps keep the spot small by evaporating the solvent before it can spread out on the plate. The smaller the spot formed, the better the separation obtainable. If needed, additional material can be applied to the plate by repeating the spotting procedure. You should repeat the procedure with several small amounts rather than apply one large amount. The solvent should be allowed to evaporate between ap-

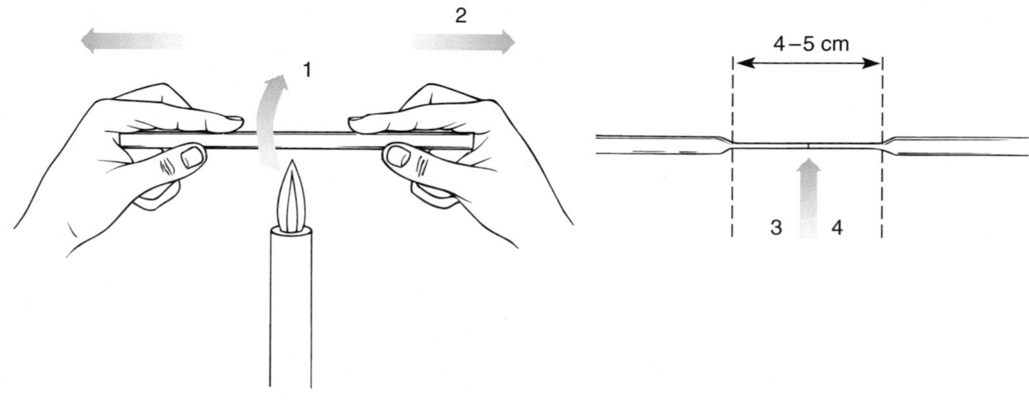
2
1
4–5 cm
3
4
① Rotate in flame until soft.
② Remove from flame and pull.
③ Score lightly in center of pulled section.
④ Break in half to give two pipets.

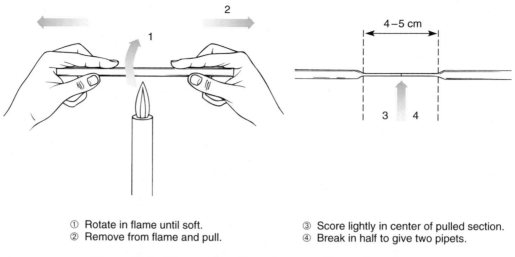

Figure 20.2 The construction of two capillary micropipets.

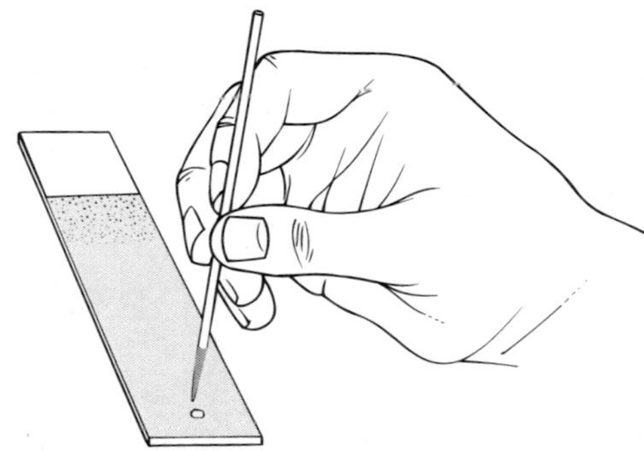

Figure 20.3 Spotting the thin-layer chromatography plate with a drawn capillary pipet.

plications. If the spot is not small (about 2 mm in diameter), a new plate should be prepared. The capillary pipet may be used several times if it is rinsed between uses. It is repeatedly dipped into a small portion of solvent to rinse it and touched to a paper towel to empty it.

As many as three different spots may be applied to a 1-inch-wide TLC plate. Each spot should be about 1 cm from the bottom of the plate, and all spots should be evenly spaced, with one spot in the center of the plate. Due to diffusion, spots often increase in diameter as the plate is developed. To keep spots containing different materials from merging and to avoid confusing the samples, do not place more than three spots on a single plate. Larger plates can accommodate many more samples.

20.5 DEVELOPING (RUNNING) TLC PLATES

A. Preparing a Development Chamber

A convenient development chamber for TLC plates can be made from a 4-oz wide-mouth jar. An alternative development chamber can be constructed from a beaker, using alu-

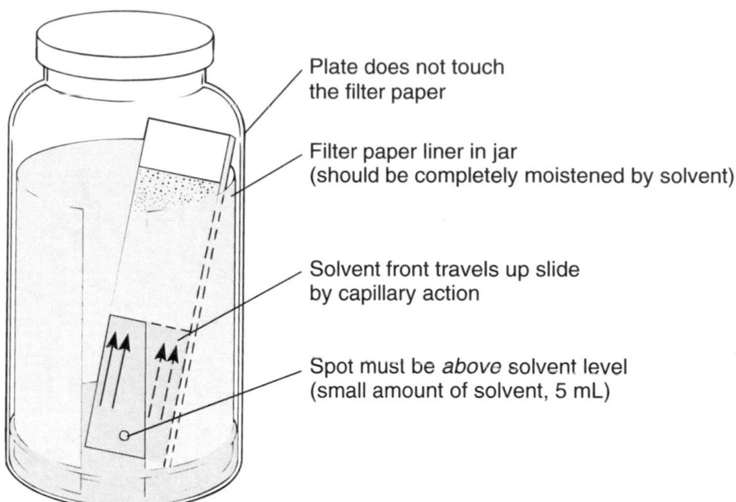

Figure 20.4 A development chamber with a thin-layer chromatography plate undergoing development.

minum foil to cover the opening. The inside of the jar or beaker should be lined with a piece of filter paper, cut so that it does not quite extend around the inside of the jar. A small vertical opening (2–3 cm) should be left in the filter paper so the development can be observed. Before development, the filter paper inside the jar or beaker should be thoroughly moistened with the development solvent. The solvent-saturated liner helps to keep the chamber saturated with solvent vapors, thereby speeding the development. Once the liner is saturated, the level of solvent in the bottom of the development chamber is adjusted to a depth of about 5 mm, and the chamber is capped (or covered with aluminum foil) and set aside until it is to be used. A correctly prepared development chamber (with TLC plate in place) is shown in Figure 20.4.

B. Developing the TLC Plate

Once the spot has been applied to the thin-layer plate and the solvent has been selected (see Section 20.6), the plate is placed in the chamber for development. The plate must be placed in the chamber carefully so that no part of the plate touches the filter paper liner. In addition, the solvent level in the bottom of the chamber must not be above the spot that was applied to the plate, or the spotted material will dissolve in the pool of solvent instead of undergoing chromatography. Once the plate has been placed correctly, replace the cap on the developing chamber and wait for the solvent to advance up the plate by capillary action. This generally occurs rapidly, and you should watch carefully. As the solvent rises, the plate becomes visibly moist. When the solvent has advanced to within 5 mm of the end of the coated surface, the plate should be removed, and the position of the solvent front should be marked immediately by scoring the plate along the solvent line with a pencil. The solvent front must not be allowed to travel beyond the end of the coated surface. The plate should be removed before this happens. The solvent will not actually advance beyond the end of the plate, but spots allowed to stand on a completely moistened plate on which the solvent is not in motion expand by diffusion. Once the plate has dried, any visible spots should be outlined on the plate with a pencil. If no spots are apparent, a visualization method (Section 20.7) may be needed.

20.6 CHOOSING A SOLVENT FOR DEVELOPMENT

The development solvent used depends on the materials to be separated. You may have to try several solvents before a satisfactory separation is achieved. Because small TLC plates can be prepared and developed rapidly, an empirical choice is usually not hard to make. A solvent that causes all the spotted material to move with the solvent front is too polar. One that does not cause any of the material in the spot to move is not polar enough. As a guide to the relative polarity of solvents, consult Table 19.2 in Technique 19 (p. 801).

Methylene chloride and toluene are solvents of intermediate polarity and good choices for a wide variety of functional groups to be separated. For hydrocarbon materials, good first choices are hexane, petroleum ether (ligroin), or toluene. Hexane or petroleum ether with varying proportions of toluene or ether gives solvent mixtures of moderate polarity that are useful for many common functional groups. Polar materials may require ethyl acetate, acetone, or methanol.

A rapid way to determine a good solvent is to apply several sample spots to a single plate. The spots should be placed a minimum of 1 cm apart. A capillary pipet is filled with a solvent and gently touched to one of the spots. The solvent expands outward in a circle. The solvent front should be marked with a pencil. A different solvent is applied to each spot. As the solvents expand outward, the spots expand as concentric rings. From the appearance of the rings, you can judge approximately the suitability of the solvent. Several types of behavior experienced with this method of testing are shown in Figure 20.5.

20.7 VISUALIZATION METHODS

It is fortunate when the compounds separated by TLC are colored because the separation can be followed visually. More often than not, however, the compounds are colorless. In that case, some reagent or some method must be used to make the separated materials visible. Reagents that give rise to colored spots are called **visualization reagents.** Methods of viewing that make the spots apparent are **visualization methods.**

The most common method of visualization is by an ultraviolet (UV) lamp. Under UV

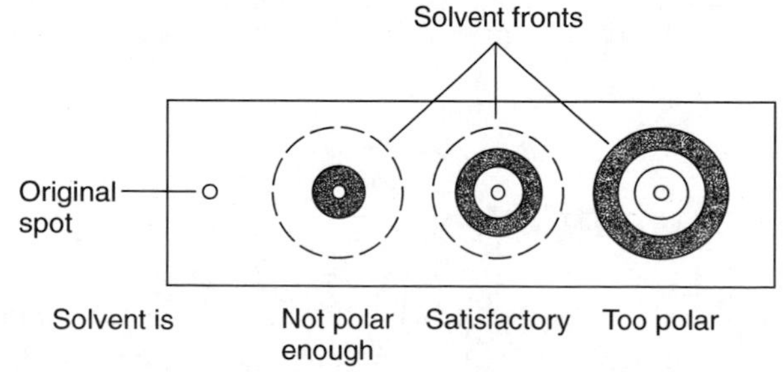

Figure 20.5 The concentric ring method of testing solvents.

light, compounds often look like bright spots on the plate. This often suggests the structure of the compound. Certain types of compounds shine very brightly under UV light because they fluoresce.

Plates can be purchased with a fluorescent indicator added to the adsorbent. A mixture of zinc and cadmium sulfides is often used. When treated in this way and held under UV light, the entire plate fluoresces. However, dark spots appear on the plate where the separated compounds are seen to quench this fluorescence.

Iodine is also used to visualize plates. Iodine reacts with many organic materials to form complexes that are either brown or yellow. In this visualization method, the developed and dried TLC plate is placed in a 4-oz wide-mouth, screw-cap jar along with a few crystals of iodine. The jar is capped and gently warmed on a steam bath or a hot plate at low heat. The jar fills with iodine vapors, and the spots begin to appear. When the spots are sufficiently intense, the plate is removed from the jar, and the spots are outlined with a pencil. The spots are not permanent. Their appearance results from the formation of complexes the iodine makes with the organic substances. As the iodine sublimes off the plate, the spots fade. Hence, they should be marked immediately. Nearly all compounds except saturated hydrocarbons and alkyl halides form complexes with iodine. The intensities of the spots do not accurately indicate the amount of material present, except in the crudest way.

In addition to the preceding methods, several chemical methods are available that either destroy or permanently alter the separated compounds through reaction. Many of these methods are specific for particular functional groups.

Alkyl halides can be visualized if a dilute solution of silver nitrate is sprayed on the plates. Silver halides are formed. These halides decompose if exposed to light, giving rise to dark spots (free silver) on the TLC plate.

Most organic functional groups can be made visible if they are charred with sulfuric acid. Concentrated sulfuric acid is sprayed on the plate, which is then heated in an oven at 110°C to complete the charring. Permanent spots are thus created.

Colored compounds can be prepared from colorless compounds by making derivatives before spotting them on the plate. An example of this is the preparation of 2,4-dinitrophenylhydrazones from aldehydes and ketones to produce yellow and orange compounds. You may also spray the 2,4-dinitrophenylhydrazine reagent on the plate after the ketones or aldehydes have separated. Red and yellow spots form where the compounds are located. Other examples of this method are the use of ferric chloride to visualize phenols and the use of bromocresol green to detect carboxylic acids. Chromium trioxide, potassium dichromate, and potassium permanganate can be used to visualize compounds that are easily oxidized. *p*-Dimethylaminobenzaldehyde easily detects amines. Ninhydrin reacts with amino acids to make them visible. Numerous other methods and reagents available from various supply outlets are specific for certain types of functional groups. These visualize only the class of compounds of interest.

20.8 PREPARATIVE PLATES

If you use large plates (Section 20.3), materials can be separated, and the separated components can be recovered individually from the plates. Plates used in this way are called **preparative plates.** For preparative plates, a thick layer of adsorbent is generally used. Instead of being applied as a spot or a series of spots, the mixture to be separated is applied as a line of material about 1 cm from the bottom of the plate. As the plate is developed, the separated materials form bands. After development, you can observe the separated bands, usually by UV light, and outline the zones in pencil. If the method of visualization is destructive, most of the plate is covered with paper to protect it, and the reagent is applied only at the extreme edge of the plate.

Once the zones have been identified, the adsorbent in those bands is scraped from the plate and extracted with solvent to remove the adsorbed material. Filtration removes the adsorbent, and evaporation of the solvent gives the recovered component from the mixture.

20.9 THE R_f VALUE

Thin-layer chromatography conditions include

1. Solvent system
2. Adsorbent
3. Thickness of the adsorbent layer
4. Relative amount of material spotted

Under an established set of such conditions, a given compound always travels a fixed distance relative to the distance the solvent front travels. This ratio of the distance the compound travels to the distance the solvent travels is called the **R_f value.** The symbol R_f stands for "retardation factor," or "ratio to front," and it is expressed as a decimal fraction:

$$R_f = \frac{\text{distance traveled by substance}}{\text{distance traveled by solvent front}}$$

When the conditions of measurement are completely specified, the R_f value is constant for any given compound, and it corresponds to a physical property of that compound.

The R_f value can be used to identify an unknown compound, but like any other identification based on a single piece of data, the R_f value is best confirmed with some additional data. Many compounds can have the same R_f value, just as many compounds have the same melting point.

It is not always possible, in measuring an R_f value, to duplicate exactly the conditions of measurement another researcher has used. Therefore, R_f values tend to be of more use to a single researcher in one laboratory than they are to researchers in different laboratories. The only exception to this occurs when two researchers use TLC plates from the same source, as in commercial plates, or know the exact details of how the plates were prepared. Nevertheless, the R_f value can be a useful guide. If exact values cannot be relied on, the relative values can provide another researcher with useful information about what to expect. Anyone using published R_f values will find it a good idea to check them by comparing them with standard substances whose identity and R_f values are known.

To calculate the R_f value for a given compound, measure the distance that the compound has traveled from the point at which it was originally spotted. For spots that are not too large, measure to the center of the migrated spot. For large spots, the measurement should be repeated on a new plate, using less material. For spots that show tailing, the measurement is made to the "center of gravity" of the spot. This first distance measurement is

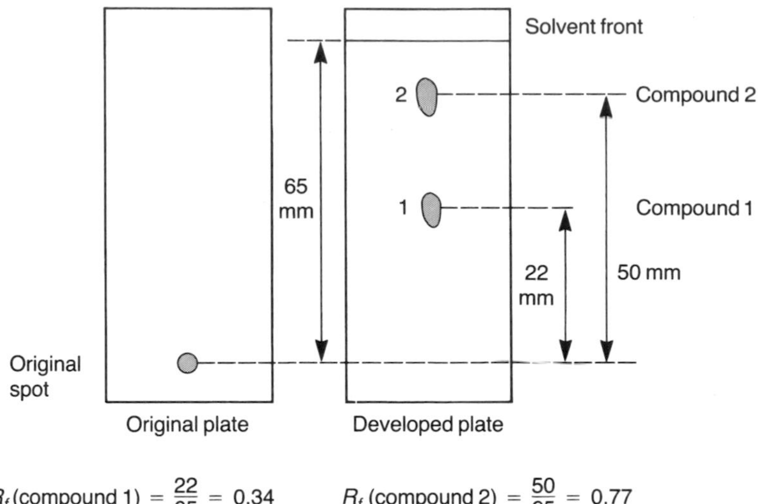

$R_f\text{(compound 1)} = \frac{22}{65} = 0.34 \qquad R_f\text{(compound 2)} = \frac{50}{65} = 0.77$

Figure 20.6 Sample calculation of R_f values.

then divided by the distance the solvent front has traveled from the same original spot. A sample calculation of the R_f values of two compounds is illustrated in Figure 20.6.

20.10 THIN-LAYER CHROMATOGRAPHY APPLIED IN ORGANIC CHEMISTRY

Thin-layer chromatography has several important uses in organic chemistry. It can be used in the following applications:

1. To establish that two compounds are identical
2. To determine the number of components in a mixture
3. To determine the appropriate solvent for a column-chromatographic separation
4. To monitor a column-chromatographic separation
5. To check the effectiveness of a separation achieved on a column, by crystallization or by extraction
6. To monitor the progress of a reaction

In all these applications, TLC has the advantage that only small amounts of material are necessary. Material is not wasted. With many of the visualization methods, less than a tenth of a microgram (10^{-7} g) of material can be detected. On the other hand, samples as large as a milligram may be used. With preparative plates that are large (about 9 inches on a side) and have a relatively thick coating of adsorbent ($> 500\ \mu m$), it is often possible to separate from 0.2 g to 0.5 g of material at one time. The main disadvantage of TLC is that volatile materials cannot be used because they evaporate from the plates.

Thin-layer chromatography can establish that two compounds suspected to be identical are in fact identical. Simply spot both compounds side by side on a single plate and develop the plate. If both compounds travel the same distance on the plate (have the same R_f value), they are probably identical. If the spot positions are not the same, the compounds are definitely not identical. It is important to spot compounds *on the same plate.* This is especially important with slides and plates that you prepare yourself. Because plates vary widely from one sample to another, no two plates have exactly the same thickness of adsorbent. If you use commercial plates, this precaution is not necessary, although it is nevertheless strongly recommended.

Thin-layer chromatography can establish whether a sample is a single substance or a mixture. A single substance gives a single spot no matter which solvent is used to develop the plate. However, the number of components in a mixture can be established by trying various solvents on a mixture. A word of caution should be given. It may be difficult, in dealing with compounds of very similar properties, such as isomers, to find a solvent that will separate the mixture. Inability to achieve a separation is not absolute proof that a sample is a single pure substance. Many compounds can be separated only by *multiple developments* of the TLC slide with a fairly nonpolar solvent. In this method, you remove the plate after the first development and allow it to dry. After being dried, it is placed in the chamber again and developed once more. This effectively doubles the length of the slide. At times, several developments may be necessary.

When a mixture is to be separated, you can use TLC to choose the best solvent to separate it if column chromatography is contemplated. You can try various solvents on a plate coated with the same adsorbent as will be used in the column. The solvent that resolves the components best will probably work well on the column. These small-scale experiments are quick, use very little material, and save time that would be wasted by attempting to separate the entire mixture on the column. Similarly, TLC plates can *monitor* a column. A hypothetical situation is shown in Figure 20.7. A solvent was found that would separate the mixture into four components (A–D). A column was run using this solvent, and 11 fractions of 15 mL each were collected. Thin-layer analysis of the various fractions showed that fractions 1–3 contained component A; fractions 4–7, component B; fractions 8–9, component C; and fractions 10–11, component D. A small amount of cross-contamination was observed in fractions 3, 4, 7, and 9.

In another TLC example, a researcher found a product from a reaction to be a mix-

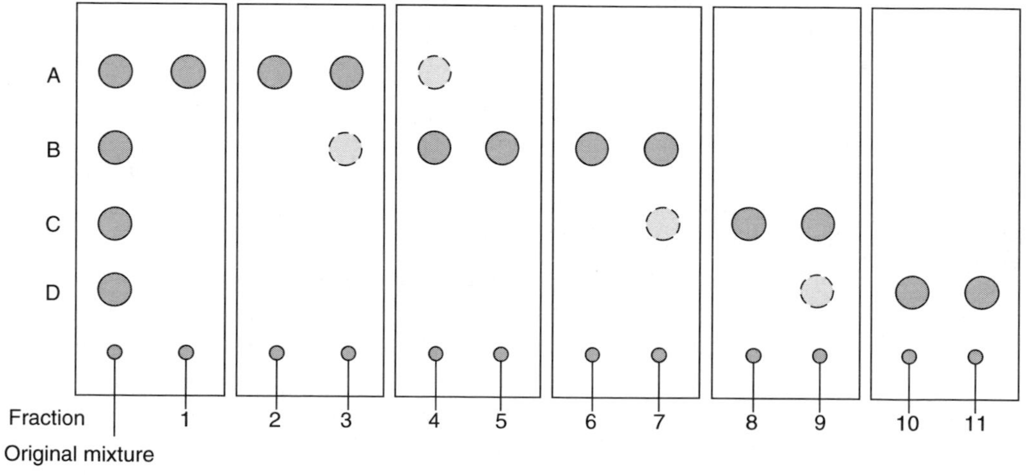

Figure 20.7 Monitoring column chromatography with TLC plates.

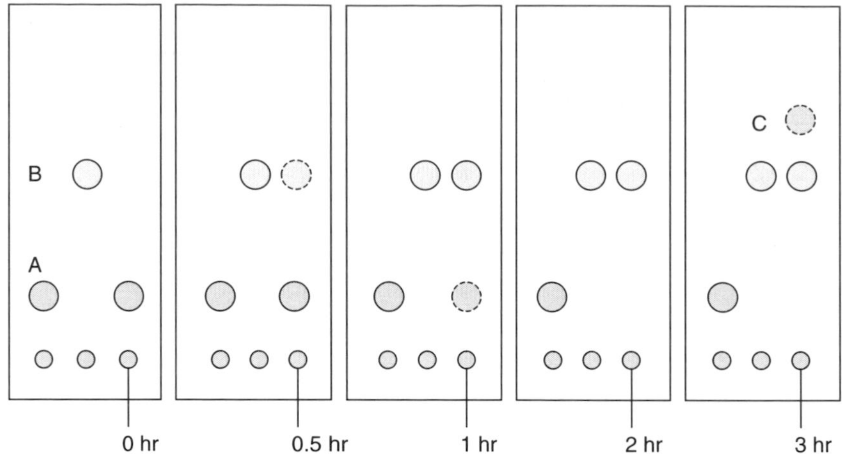

Figure 20.8 Monitoring a reaction with TLC plates.

ture. It gave two spots, A and B, on a TLC plate. After the product was crystallized, the crystals were found by TLC to be pure A, whereas the mother liquor was found to have a mixture of A and B. The crystallization was judged to have purified A satisfactorily.

Finally, it is often possible to monitor the progress of a reaction by TLC. At various points during a reaction, samples of the reaction mixture are taken and subjected to TLC analysis. An example is given in Figure 20.8. In this case, the desired reaction was the conversion of A to B. At the beginning of the reaction (0 hour), a TLC plate was prepared that was spotted with pure A, pure B, and the reaction mixture. Similar plates were prepared at 0.5, 1, 2, and 3 hours after the start of the reaction. The plates showed that the reaction was complete in 2 hours. When the reaction was run longer than 2 hours, a new compound, side product C, began to appear. Thus, the optimum reaction time was judged to be 2 hours.

20.11 PAPER CHROMATOGRAPHY

Paper chromatography is often considered to be related to thin-layer chromatography. The experimental techniques are somewhat like those of TLC, but the principles are more closely related to those of extraction. Paper chromatography is actually a liquid–liquid partitioning technique rather than a solid–liquid technique. For paper chromatography, a spot is placed near the bottom of a piece of high-grade filter paper (Whatman No. 1 is often used). Then the paper is placed in a developing chamber. The development solvent ascends the paper by capillary action and moves the components of the spotted mixture upward at differing rates. Although paper consists mainly of pure cellulose, the cellulose itself does not function as the stationary phase. Rather, the cellulose absorbs water from the atmosphere, especially from an atmosphere saturated with water vapor. Cellulose can absorb up to about 22% of water. It is this water adsorbed on the cellulose that functions as the stationary phase. To ensure that the cellulose is kept saturated with water, many development solvents used in paper chromatography contain water as a component. As the solvent ascends the paper, the compounds are partitioned between the stationary water phase and the moving solvent. Because the water phase is stationary, the components in a mixture that are most highly water soluble, or those that have the greatest hydrogen-bonding capacity, are the ones that are held back and move most slowly. Paper chromatography applies mostly to highly polar compounds or to compounds that are polyfunctional. The most common use of paper chromatography is for sugars, amino acids, and natural pigments. Because filter paper is manufactured consistently, R_f values can often be relied on in paper chromatographic work. However, R_f values are customarily measured from the leading edge (top) of the spot—not from its center, as is customary in TLC.

PROBLEMS

1. A student spots an unknown sample on a TLC plate and develops it in dichloromethane solvent. Only one spot, for which the R_f value is 0.95, is observed. Does this indicate that the unknown material is a pure compound? What can be done to verify the purity of the sample using thin-layer chromatography?

2. You and another student were each given an unknown compound. Both samples contained colorless material. You each used the same brand of commercially prepared TLC plate and developed the plates using the same solvent. Each of you obtained a single spot of $R_f = 0.75$. Were the two samples necessarily the same substances? How could you prove unambiguously that they were identical using TLC?

3. Each of the solvents given should effectively separate one of the following mixtures by TLC. Match the appropriate solvent with the mixture that you would expect to separate well with that solvent. Select your solvent from the following: hexane, methylene chloride, or acetone. You may need to look up the structures of the solvents and compounds in a handbook.

- **a.** 2-Phenylethanol and acetophenone
- **b.** Bromobenzene and *p*-xylene
- **c.** Benzoic acid, 2,4-dinitrobenzoic acid, and 2,4,6-trinitrobenzoic acid

4. Consider a sample that is a mixture composed of biphenyl, benzoic acid, and benzyl alcohol. The sample is spotted on a TLC plate and developed in a dichloromethane–cyclohexane solvent mixture. Predict the relative R_f values for the three components in the sample. (*Hint:* See Table 19.3.)

5. Consider the following errors that could be made when running TLC. Indicate what should be done to correct the error.

- **a.** A two-component mixture containing 1-octene and 1,4-dimethylbenzene gave only one spot with an R_f value of 0.95. The solvent used was acetone.
- **b.** A two-component mixture containing a dicarboxylic acid and a tricarboxylic acid gave only one spot with an R_f value of 0.05. The solvent used was hexane.
- **c.** When a TLC plate was developed, the solvent front ran off the top of the plate.

6. Calculate the R_f value of a spot that travels 5.7 cm, with a solvent front that travels 13 cm.

7. A student spots an unknown sample on a TLC plate and develops it in pentane solvent. Only one spot, for which the R_f value is 0.05, is observed. Is the unknown material a pure compound? What can be done to verify the purity of the sample using thin-layer chromatography?

8. A colorless unknown substance is spotted on a TLC plate and developed in the correct solvent. The spots do not appear when visualization with a UV lamp or iodine vapors is attempted. What could you do to visualize the spots if the compound is the following?

- **a.** An alkyl halide
- **b.** A ketone
- **c.** An amino acid
- **d.** A sugar

TECHNIQUE 14

Simple Distillation

Distillation is the process of vaporizing a liquid, condensing the vapor, and collecting the condensate in another container. This technique is very useful for separating a liquid mixture when the components have different boiling points or when one of the components will not distill. It is one of the principal methods of purifying a liquid. Four basic distillation methods are available to the chemist: simple distillation, fractional distillation, vacuum distillation (distillation at reduced pressure), and steam distillation. Fractional distillation will be discussed in Technique 15; vacuum distillation, in Technique 16; and steam distillation, in Technique 18.

A typical modern distillation apparatus is shown in Figure 14.1. The liquid to be distilled is placed in the distilling flask and heated, usually by a heating mantle. The heated liquid vaporizes and is forced upward past the thermometer and into the condenser. The vapor is condensed to liquid in the cooling condenser, and the liquid flows downward through the vacuum adapter (no vacuum is used) and into the receiving flask.

14.1 THE EVOLUTION OF DISTILLATION EQUIPMENT

There are probably more types and styles of distillation apparatus than exist for any other technique in chemistry. Over the centuries, chemists have devised just about every conceivable design. The earliest known types of distillation apparatus were the **alembic** and the **retort** (Figure 14.2). They were used by alchemists in the Middle Ages and the Renaissance, and probably even earlier by Arabic chemists. Most other distillation equipment has evolved as variations on these designs.

Figure 14.2 shows several stages in the evolution of distillation equipment as it relates to the organic laboratory. It is not intended to be a complete history; rather, it is representative. Up until recent years, equipment based on the retort design was common in the laboratory. Although the retort itself was still in use early in the last century, it had evolved by that time into the distillation flask and water-cooled condenser combination. This early

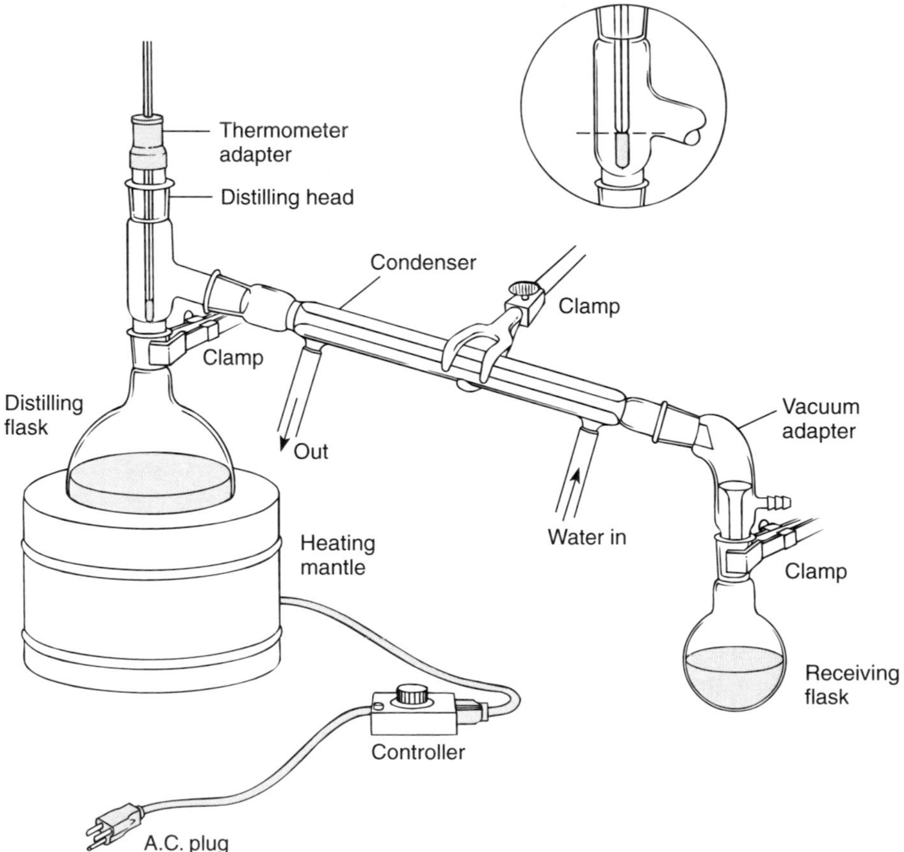

Figure 14.1 Distillation with the standard macroscale lab kit.

equipment was connected with drilled corks. By 1958, most introductory laboratories were beginning to use "organic lab kits" that included glassware connected by standard-taper glass joints. The original lab kits contained large ₸ 24/40 joints. Within a short time, they became smaller with ₸ 19/22 and even ₸ 14/20 joints. These later kits are still being used today in many "macroscale" laboratory courses such as yours.

In the 1960s, researchers developed even smaller versions of these kits for working at the "microscale" level (in Figure 14.2, see the box labeled "Research use only"), but this glassware is generally too expensive to use in an introductory laboratory. However, in the mid-1980s, several groups developed a different style of microscale distillation equipment based on the alembic design (see the box labeled "Modern microscale organic lab kit"). This new microscale equipment has ₸ 14/10 standard-taper joints, threaded outer joints with screw-cap connectors, and an internal O-ring for a compression seal. Microscale equipment similar to this is now used in many introductory courses. The advantages of this glassware are that there is less material used (lower cost), lower personal exposure to chemicals, and less waste generated. Because both types of equipment are in use today, after we describe macroscale equipment, we will also show the equivalent microscale distillation apparatus.

14.2 DISTILLATION THEORY

In the traditional distillation of a pure substance, vapor rises from the distillation flask and comes into contact with a thermometer that records its temperature. The vapor then passes through a condenser, which reliquefies the vapor and passes it into the receiving flask. The temperature observed during the distillation of a **pure substance** remains constant throughout the distillation so long as both vapor *and* liquid are present in the system (see Figure 14.3A). When a **liquid mixture** is distilled, often the temperature does not remain constant but increases throughout the distillation. The reason for this is that the composition of the vapor that is distilling varies continuously during the distillation (see Figure 14.3B).

For a liquid mixture, the composition of the vapor in equilibrium with the heated solution is different from the composition of the solution itself. This is shown in Figure 14.4, which is a phase diagram of the typical vapor–liquid relation for a two-component system (A + B).

In this diagram, horizontal lines represent constant temperatures. The upper curve represents vapor composition, and the lower curve represents liquid composition. For any horizontal line (constant temperature), such as that shown at *t,* the intersections of the line with the curves give the compositions of the liquid and the vapor that are in equilibrium with each other at that temperature. In the diagram, at temperature *t,* the intersection of the curve at *x* indicates that liquid of composition *w* will be in equilibrium with vapor of composition *z,* which corresponds to the intersection at *y.* Composition is given as a mole percentage of A and B in the mixture. Pure A, which boils at temperature t_A, is represented at the left. Pure B, which boils at temperature t_B, is represented at the right. For either pure A or pure B, the vapor and liquid curves meet at the boiling point. Thus, either pure A or pure B will distill at a constant temperature (t_A or t_B). Both the vapor and the liquid must have the same composition in either of these cases. This is not the case for mixtures of A and B.

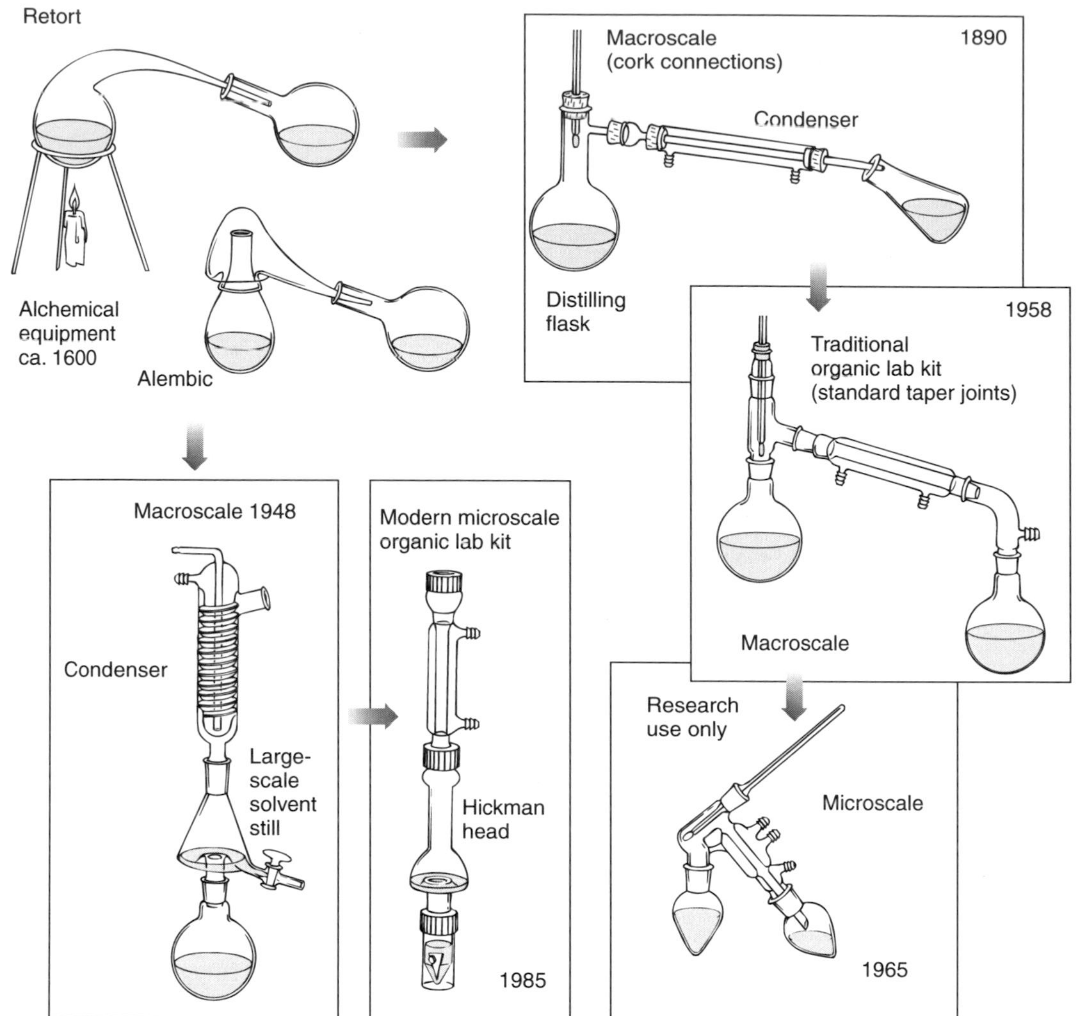

Figure 14.2 Some stages in the evolution of distillation equipment from alchemical equipment (dates represent approximate time of use).

A mixture of A and B of composition *w* will have the following behavior when heated. The temperature of the liquid mixture will increase until the boiling point of the mixture is reached. This corresponds to following line *wx* from *w* to *x*, the boiling point of the mixture *t*. At temperature *t* the liquid begins to vaporize, which corresponds to line *xy*. The vapor has the composition corresponding to *z*. In other words, the first vapor obtained in distilling a mixture of A and B does not consist of pure A. It is richer in A than the original mixture but still contains a significant amount of the higher-boiling component B, *even from the very beginning of the distillation.* The result is that it is never possible to separate a mixture completely by a simple distillation. However, in two cases it is possible to get an acceptable separation into relatively pure components. In the first case, if the boiling points of A and B differ by a large amount ($> 100°$) and if the distillation is carried out carefully, it will be possible to get a fair separation of A and B. In the second case, if A contains a fairly small amount of B ($< 10\%$), a reasonable separation of A from B can be achieved.

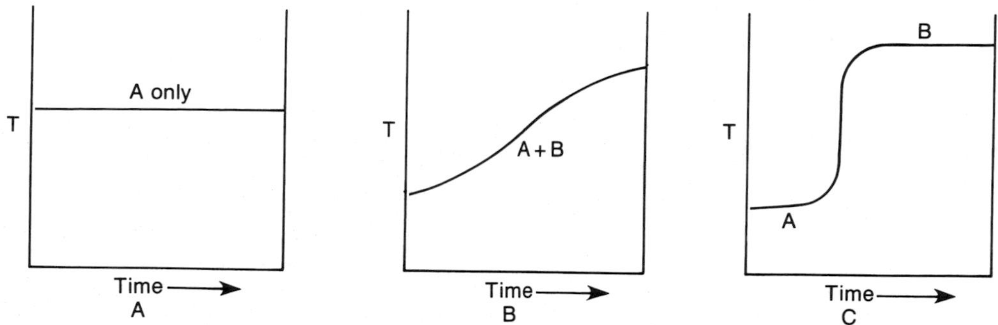

Figure 14.3 Three types of temperature behavior during a simple distillation. (A) A single pure component. (B) Two components of similar boiling points. (C) Two components with widely differing boiling points. Good separations are achieved in A and C.

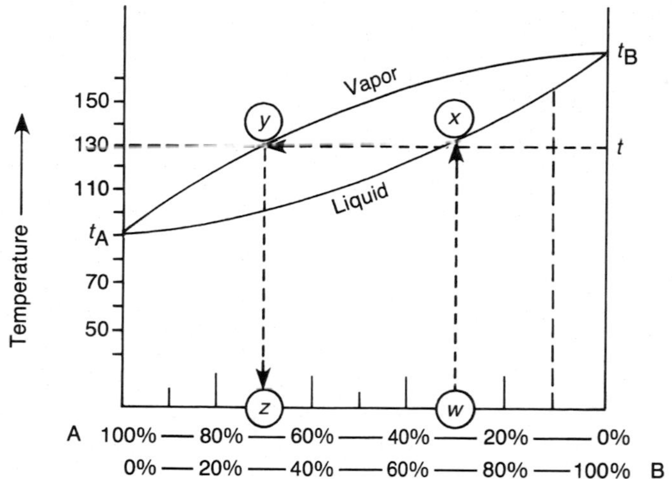

Figure 14.4 Phase diagram for a typical liquid mixture of two components.

When the boiling-point differences are not large and when highly pure components are desired, it is necessary to perform a **fractional distillation.** Fractional distillation is described in Technique 15, where the behavior during a simple distillation is also considered in detail. Note that only as vapor distills from the mixture of composition *w* (Figure 14.4), is it richer in A than is the solution. Thus, the composition of the material left behind in the distillation becomes richer in B (moves to the right from *w* toward pure B in the graph). A mixture of 90% B (dotted line on the right side in Figure 14.4) has a higher boiling point than at *w*. Hence, the temperature of the liquid in the distillation flask will increase during the distillation, and the composition of the distillate will change (as is shown in Figure 14.3B).

When two components that have a large boiling-point difference are distilled, the temperature remains constant while the first component distills. If the temperature remains constant, a relatively pure substance is being distilled. After the first substance distills, the temperature of the vapors rises, and the second component distills, again at a constant temperature. This is shown in Figure 14.3C. A typical application of this type of distillation might be an instance of a reaction mixture containing the desired component A (bp 140°C) contaminated with a small amount of undesired component B (bp 250°C) and mixed with a solvent such as diethyl ether (bp 36°C). The ether is removed easily at low temperature. Pure A is removed at a higher temperature and collected in a separate receiver. Component B can then be distilled, but it usually is left as a residue and not distilled. This separation is not difficult and represents a case where simple distillation might be used to advantage.

14.3 SIMPLE DISTILLATION—STANDARD APPARATUS

For a simple distillation, the apparatus shown in Figure 14.1 is used. Six pieces of specialized glassware are used:

1. Distilling flask
2. Distillation head
3. Thermometer adapter
4. Water condenser
5. Vacuum adapter
6. Receiving flask

The apparatus is usually heated electrically, using a heating mantle. The distilling flask, condenser, and vacuum adapter should be clamped. Two different methods of clamping this apparatus were shown in Technique 7 (Figure 7.2, p. 625 and Figure 7.4, p. 626). The receiving flask should be supported by removable wooden blocks or a wire gauze on an iron ring attached to a ring stand. The various components are each discussed in the following sections, along with some other important points.

Distilling Flask. The distilling flask should be a round-bottom flask. This type of flask is designed to withstand the required input of heat and to accommodate the boiling action. It gives a maximized heating surface. The size of the distilling flask should be chosen so that it is never filled more than two-thirds full. When the flask is filled beyond this point, the neck constricts and "chokes" the boiling action, resulting in bumping. The surface area of the boiling liquid should be kept as large as possible. However, too large a distilling flask should also be avoided. With too large a flask, the **holdup** is excessive; the holdup is the amount of material that cannot distill because some vapor must fill the empty flask. When you cool the apparatus at the end, this material drops back into the distilling flask.

Boiling Stones. A boiling stone (Technique 7, Section 7.4, p. 631) should be used during distillation to prevent bumping. As an alternative, the liquid being distilled may be rapidly stirred using a magnetic stirrer and stir bar (Technique 7, Section 7.3, p. 630). If you forget a boiling stone, cool the mixture before adding it. If you add a boiling stone to a hot superheated liquid, it may "erupt" into vigorous boiling, breaking your apparatus and spilling hot solvent everywhere.

Grease. In most cases, it is unnecessary to grease standard-taper joints for a simple distillation. The grease makes cleanup more difficult, and it may contaminate your product.

Distillation Head. The distillation head directs the distilling vapors into the condenser and allows the connection of a thermometer via the thermometer adapter. The thermometer should be positioned in the distillation head so that the thermometer is directly in the stream of vapor that is distilling. This can be accomplished if the entire bulb of the thermometer is positioned *below* the sidearm of the distilling head (see the circular inset in Figure 14.1). The entire bulb must be immersed in the vapor to achieve an accurate temperature reading. When distilling, you should be able to see a reflux ring (Technique 7, Section 7.2, p. 628) positioned well above both the thermometer bulb and the bottom of the sidearm.

Thermometer Adapter. The thermometer adapter connects to the top of the distillation head (see Figure 14.1). There are two parts to the thermometer adapter: a glass joint with an open rolled edge on the top, and a rubber adapter that fits over the rolled edge and holds the thermometer. The thermometer fits in a hole in the top of the rubber adapter and can be adjusted upward and downward by sliding it in the hole. Adjust the bulb to a point below the sidearm. The distillation temperature can be monitored most accurately by using a partial immersion mercury thermometer (see Technique 13, Section 13.4, p. 729).

Water Condenser. The joint between the distillation head and the water condenser is the joint most prone to leak in this entire apparatus. Because the distilling liquid is both hot and vaporized when it reaches this joint, it will leak out of any small opening between the two joint surfaces. The odd angle of the joint, neither vertical or horizontal, also makes a good connection more difficult. Be sure this joint is well sealed. If possible, use one of the plastic joint clips described in Technique 7, Figure 7.3, p. 626. Otherwise, adjust your clamps to be sure that the joint surfaces are pressed together and not pulled apart.

The condenser will remain full of cooling water only if the water flows *upward,* not downward. The water input hose should be connected to the lower opening in the jacket, and the exit hose should be attached to the upper opening. Place the other end of the exit hose in a sink. A moderate water flow will perform a good deal of cooling. A high rate of water flow may cause the tubing to pop off the joints and cause a flood. If you hold the exit hose horizontally and point the end into a sink, the flow rate is correct if the water stream continues horizontally for about two inches before bending downward.

If a distillation apparatus is to be left untended for a period of time, it is a good idea to wrap copper wire around the ends of the tubing and twist it tight. This will help to prevent the hoses from popping off of the connectors if there is an unexpected water-pressure change.

Vacuum Adapter. In a simple distillation, the vacuum adapter is not connected to a vacuum but is left open. It is merely an opening to the outside air so that pressure does not build up in the distillation system. If you plug this opening, you will have a **closed system** (no outlet). It is always dangerous to heat a closed system. Enough pressure can build up in the closed system to cause an explosion. The vacuum adapter, in this case, merely directs the distillate into the receiving, or collection, flask.

If the substance you are distilling is water sensitive, you can attach a calcium chloride drying tube to the vacuum connection to protect the freshly distilled liquid from atmospheric water vapor. Air that enters the apparatus will have to pass through the calcium chloride and be dried. Depending on the severity of the problem, drying agents other than calcium chloride may also be used.

The vacuum adapter has a disturbing tendency to obey the laws of Newtonian physics and fall off the slanted condenser onto the desk and break. If plastic joint clips are available, it is a good idea to use them on both ends of this piece. The top clip will secure the vacuum adapter to the condenser, and the bottom clip will secure the receiving flask, preventing it from falling.

Rate of Heating. The rate of heating for the distillation can be adjusted to the proper rate of **takeoff,** the rate at which distillate leaves the condenser, by watching drops of liquid emerge from the bottom of the vacuum adapter. A rate of from one to three drops per second is considered a proper rate of takeoff for most applications. At a greater rate, equilibrium is not established within the distillation apparatus, and the separation may be poor. A slower rate of takeoff is also unsatisfactory because the temperature recorded on the thermometer is not maintained by a constant vapor stream, thus leading to an inaccurate low boiling point.

Receiving Flask. The receiving flask, which is usually a round-bottom flask, collects the distilled liquid. If the liquid you are distilling is extremely volatile and there is danger of losing some of it to evaporation, it is sometimes advisable to cool the receiving flask in an ice-water bath.

Fractions. The material being distilled is called the **distillate.** Frequently, a distillate is collected in contiguous portions, called **fractions.** This is accomplished by replacing the collection flask with a clean one at regular intervals. If a small amount of liquid is collected at the beginning of a distillation and not saved or used further, it is called a **forerun.** Subsequent fractions will have higher boiling ranges, and each fraction should be labeled with its correct boiling range when the fraction is taken. For a simple distillation of a pure material, most of the material will be collected in a single, large **midrun** fraction, with only a small forerun. In some small-scale distillations, the volume of the forerun will be so small that you will not be able to collect it separately from the midrun fraction. The material left behind is called the **residue.** It is usually advised that you discontinue a distillation before the distilling flask becomes empty. Typically, the residue becomes increasingly dark in color during distillation, and it frequently contains thermal decomposition products. In addition, a dry residue may explode on overheating, or the flask may melt or crack when it becomes dry. Don't distill until the distilling flask is completely dry!

14.4 MICROSCALE AND SEMI-MICROSCALE EQUIPMENT

When you wish to distill quantities that are smaller than 4–5 mL, different equipment is required. What you use depends on how small a quantity you wish to distill.

A. Semi-Microscale

One possibility is to use equipment identical in style to that used with conventional macroscale procedures, but to "downsize" it using ₸ 14/10 joints. The major manufacturers do make distillation heads and vacuum takeoff adapters with ₸ 14/10 joints. This equipment will allow you to handle quantities of 5–15 mL. An example of such a "semi-microscale" apparatus is given in Figure 14.5. Although the manufacturers make ₸ 14/10 condensers, the condenser has been left out in this example. This can be done if the material to be distilled is not extremely volatile or is high boiling. It is also possible to omit the condenser if you not have a large amount of material and can cool the receiving flask in an ice-water bath as shown in the figure.

B. Microscale—Student Equipment

Figure 14.6 shows the typical distillation setup for those students who are taking a microscale laboratory course. Instead of a distillation head, condenser, and vacuum

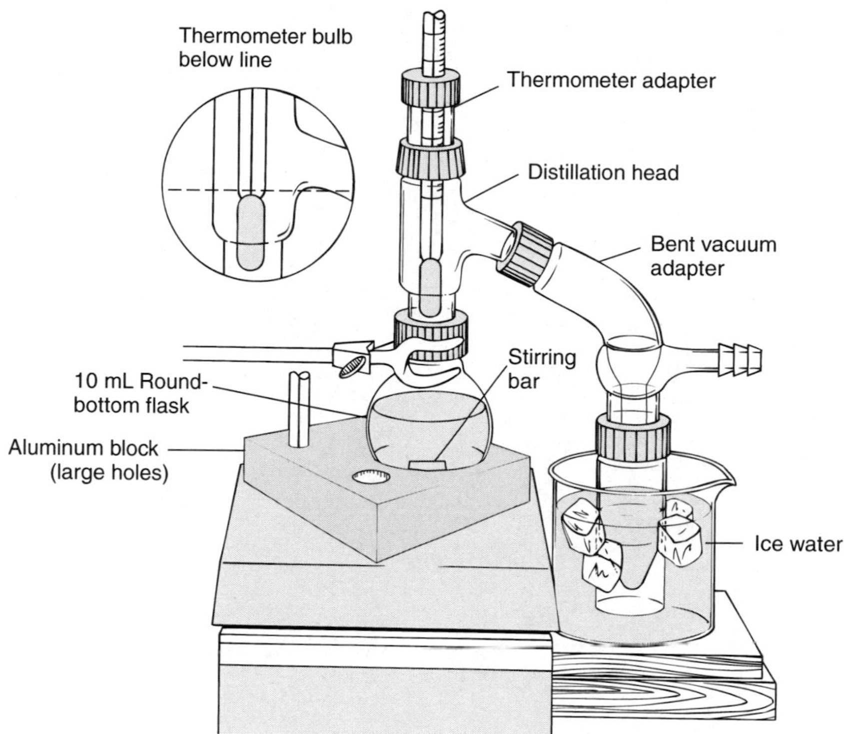

Figure 14.5 Semi-microscale distillation.

takeoff, this equipment uses a single piece of glassware called a **Hickman head.** The Hickman head provides a "short path" for the distilled liquid to travel before it is collected. The liquid is boiled, moves upward through the central stem of the Hickman head, condenses on the walls of the "chimney," and then runs down the sides into the circular well surrounding the stem. With very volatile liquids, a condenser can be placed on top of the Hickman head to improve its efficiency. The apparatus shown uses a 5-mL conical vial as the distilling flask, meaning that this apparatus can distill 1–3 mL of liquid. Unfortunately, the well in most Hickman heads holds only about 0.5–1.0 mL. Thus, the well must be emptied several times using a disposable Pasteur pipet, as shown in Figure 14.7. The figure shows two different styles of Hickman head. The one with the side port makes removal of the distillate easier.

C. Microscale—Research Equipment

Figure 14.8 shows a very well designed research-style, short-path distillation head. Note how the equipment has been "unitized," eliminating several joints and decreasing the holdup.

PROBLEMS

1. Using Figure 14.4, answer the following questions.
   a. What is the molar composition of the vapor in equilibrium with a boiling liquid that has a composition of 60% A and 40% B?

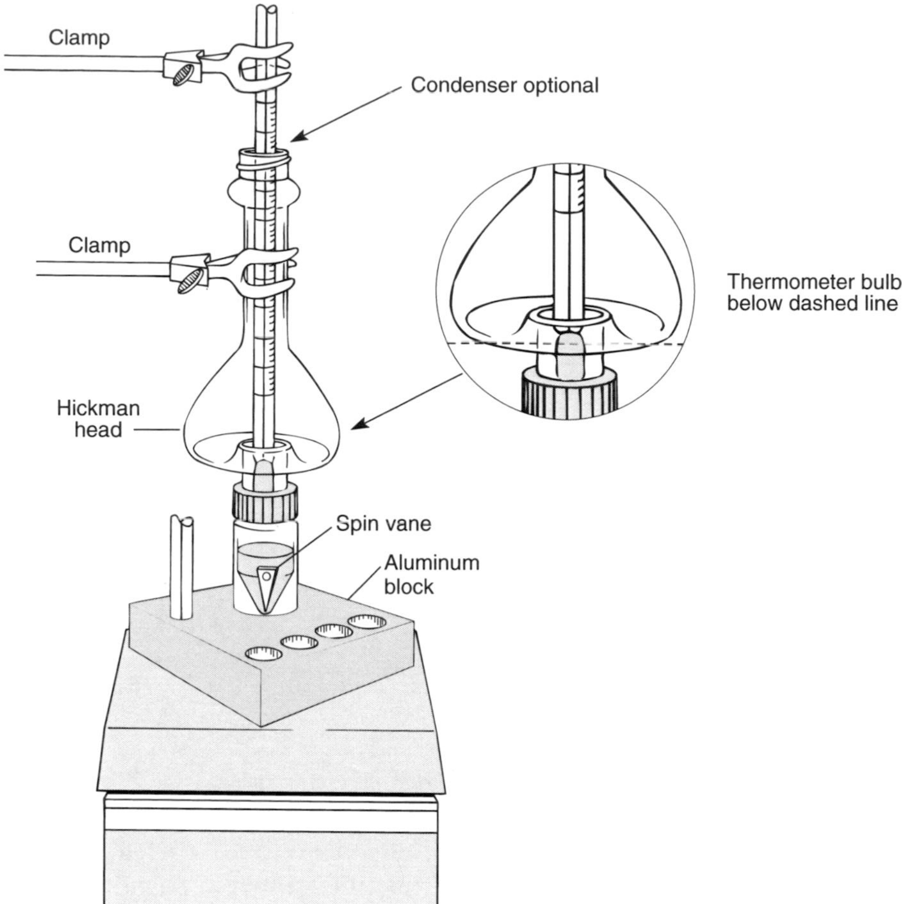

Figure 14.6 Basic microscale distillation.

b. A sample of vapor has the composition 50% A and 50% B. What is the composition of the boiling liquid that produced this vapor?

2. Use an apparatus similar to that shown in Figure 14.1 and assume that the round-bottom flask holds 100 mL and the distilling head has an internal volume of 12 mL in the vertical section. At the end of a distillation, vapor would fill this volume, but it could not be forced through the system. No liquid would remain in the distillation flask. Assuming this holdup volume of 112 mL, use the ideal gas law and assume a boiling point of 100°C (760 mmHg) to calculate the number of milliliters of liquid (d = 0.9 g/mL, MW = 200) that would recondense into the distillation flask upon cooling.

3. Explain the significance of a horizontal line connecting a point on the lower curve with a point on the upper curve (such as line xy) in Figure 14.4.

4. Using Figure 14.4, determine the boiling point of a liquid having a molar composition of 50% A and 50% B.

5. Where should the thermometer bulb be located in the following setups:

a. A microscale distillation apparatus using a Hickman head

b. A macroscale distillation apparatus using a distilling head, condenser, and vacuum takeoff adapter

6. Under what conditions can a good separation be achieved with a simple distillation?

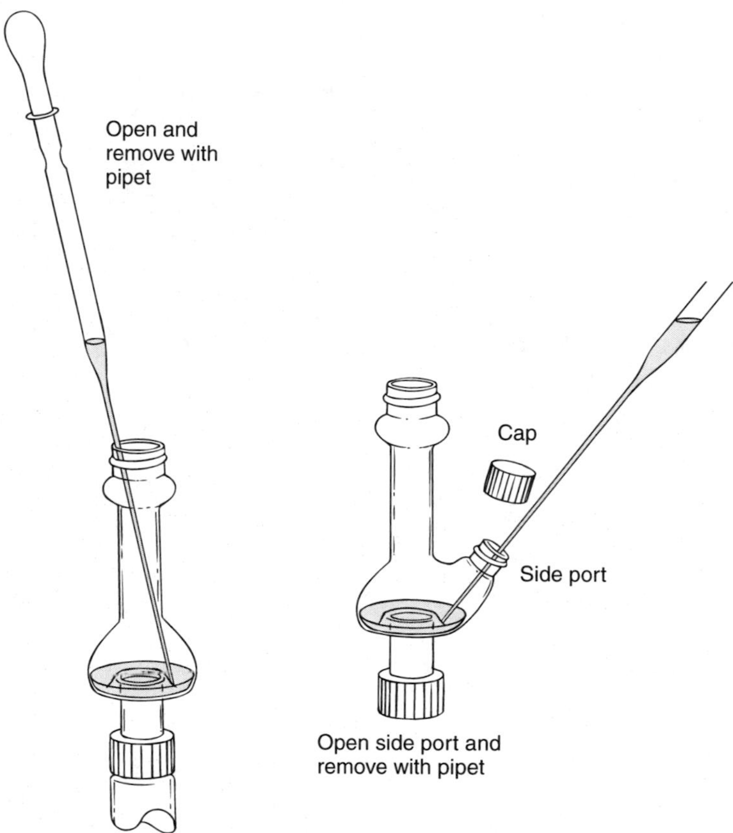

Figure 14.7 Two styles of Hickman head.

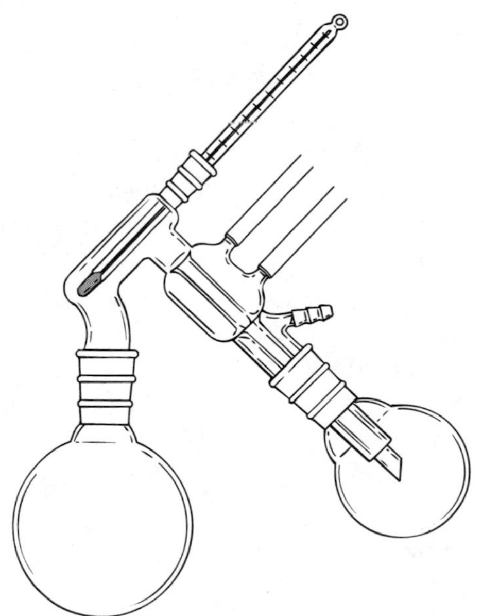

Figure 14.8 A research-style short-path distillation apparatus.

TECHNIQUE 15

Fractional Distillation, Azeotropes

Simple distillation, described in Technique 14, works well for most routine separation and purification procedures for organic liquids. When the boiling-point differences of the components to be separated are not large, however, fractional distillation must be used to achieve a good separation.

A typical fractional distillation apparatus is shown in Figure 15.2 in Section 15.1, where the differences between simple and fractional distillation are discussed in detail. This apparatus differs from that for simple distillation by the insertion of a **fractionating column** between the distilling flask and the distillation head. The fractionating column is filled with a **packing,** a material that causes the liquid to condense and revaporize repeatedly as it passes through the column. With a good fractionating column, better separations are possible, and liquids with small boiling-point differences may be separated by using this technique.

Part A. Fractional Distillation

15.1 DIFFERENCES BETWEEN SIMPLE AND FRACTIONAL DISTILLATION

When an ideal solution of two liquids, such as benzene (bp 80°C) and toluene (bp 110°C), is distilled by simple distillation, the first vapor produced will be enriched in the lower-boiling component (benzene). However, when that initial vapor is condensed and analyzed, the distillate will not be pure benzene. The boiling point difference of benzene and toluene (30°C) is too small to achieve a complete separation by simple distillation. Following the principles outlined in Technique 14, Section 14.2 (pp. 735–738), and using the vapor-liquid composition curve given in Figure 15.1, you can see what would happen if you started with an equimolar mixture of benzene and toluene.

Following the dashed lines shows that an equimolar mixture (50 mole percent benzene) would begin to boil at about 91°C and, far from being 100% benzene, the distillate would contain about 74 mole percent benzene and 26 mole percent toluene. As the distillation continued, the composition of the undistilled liquid would move in the direction of A′ (there would be increased toluene due to removal of more benzene than toluene), and the corresponding vapor would contain a progressively smaller amount of benzene. In effect, the temperature of the distillation would continue to increase throughout the distillation (as in Figure 14.3B, p. 737), and it would be impossible to obtain any fraction that consisted of pure benzene.

Suppose, however, that we are able to collect a small quantity of the first distillate that was 74 mole percent benzene and redistill it. Using Figure 15.1, we can see that this liquid would begin to boil at about 84°C and would give an initial distillate containing 90 mole percent of benzene. If we were experimentally able to continue taking small fractions at the

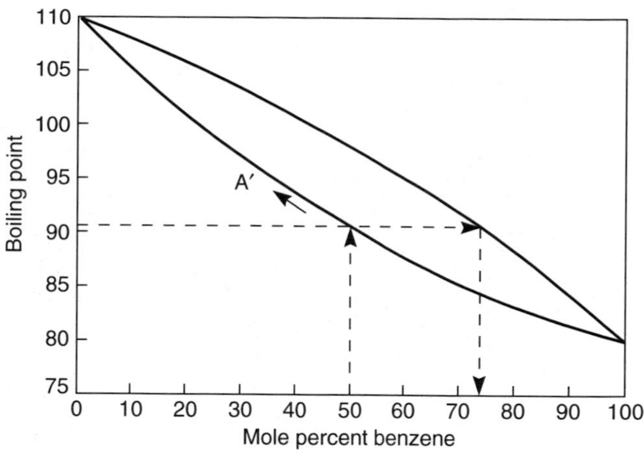

Figure 15.1 The vapor-liquid composition curve for mixtures of benzene and toluene.

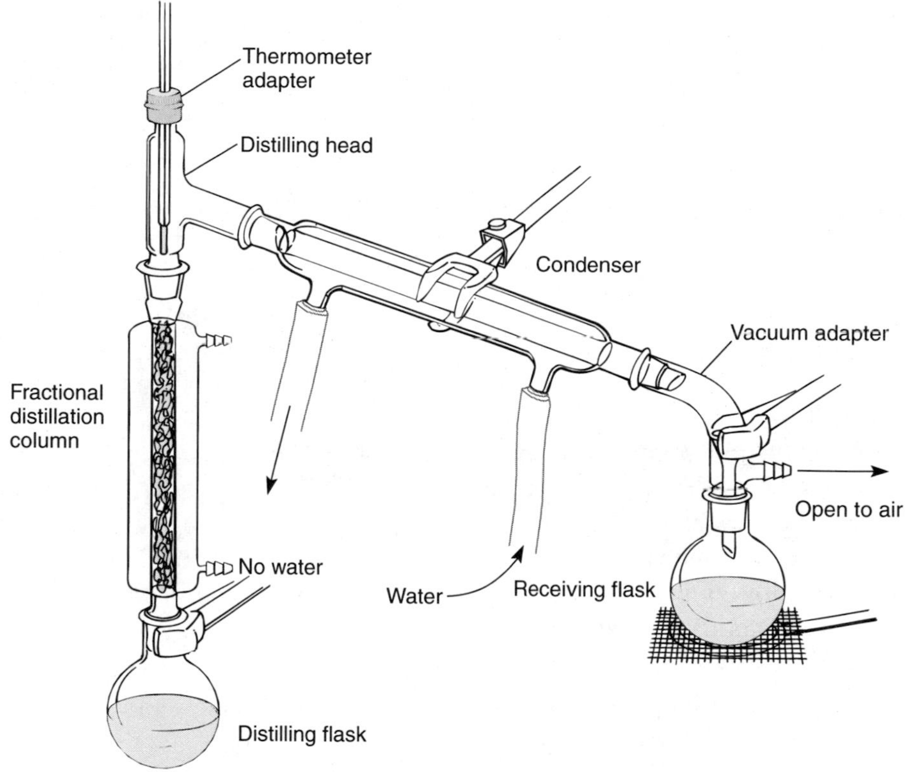

Figure 15.2 Fractional distillation apparatus.

beginning of each distillation and redistill them, we would eventually reach a liquid with a composition of nearly 100 mole percent benzene. However, since we took only a small amount of material at the beginning of each distillation, we would have lost most of the material we started with. To recapture a reasonable amount of benzene, we would have to process each of the fractions left behind in the same way as our early fractions. As each of them was partially distilled, the material advanced would become progressively richer in benzene, and that left behind would become progressively richer in toluene. It would require thousands (maybe millions) of such microdistillations to separate benzene from toluene.

Obviously, the procedure just described would be very tedious; fortunately, it need not be performed in usual laboratory practice. **Fractional distillation** accomplishes the same result. You simply have to use a column inserted between the distillation flask and the distilling head, as shown in Figure 15.2. This **fractionating column** is filled, or **packed,** with a suitable material, such as a stainless steel sponge. This packing allows a mixture of benzene and toluene to be subjected continuously to many vaporization–condensation cycles as the material moves up the column. With each cycle within the column, the composition of the vapor is progressively enriched in the lower-boiling component (benzene). Nearly pure benzene (bp 80°C) finally emerges from the top of the column, condenses, and passes into the receiving head or flask. This process continues until all the benzene is removed. The distillation must be carried out slowly to ensure that numerous vaporization–condensation cycles occur. When nearly all the benzene has been removed, the temperature begins to rise, and a small amount of a second fraction, which contains some benzene and toluene, may be collected. When the temperature reaches 110°C, the boiling point of pure toluene, the vapor is condensed and collected as the third fraction. A plot of boiling point versus volume of condensate (distillate) would resemble Figure 14.3C (p. 737). This separation would be much better than that achieved by simple distillation (Figure 14.3B, p. 737).

15.2 VAPOR–LIQUID COMPOSITION DIAGRAMS

A vapor–liquid composition phase diagram like the one in Figure 15.3 can be used to explain the operation of a fractionating column with an **ideal solution** of two liquids, A and B. An ideal solution is one in which the two liquids are chemically similar, are miscible (mutually soluble) in all proportions, and do not interact. Ideal solutions obey **Raoult's Law.** Raoult's Law is explained in detail in Section 15.3.

The phase diagram relates the compositions of the boiling liquid (lower curve) and its vapor (upper curve) as a function of temperature. Any horizontal line drawn across the diagram (a constant-temperature line) intersects the diagram in two places. These intersections relate the vapor composition to the composition of the boiling liquid that produces that vapor. By convention, composition is expressed either in **mole fraction** or in **mole percentage.** The mole fraction is defined as follows:

$$\text{Mole fraction A} = N_A = \frac{\text{Moles A}}{\text{Moles A} + \text{Moles B}}$$

$$\text{Mole fraction B} = N_B = \frac{\text{Moles B}}{\text{Moles A} + \text{Moles B}}$$

$$N_A + N_B = 1$$

$$\text{Mole percentage A} = N_A \times 100$$

$$\text{Mole percentage B} = N_B \times 100$$

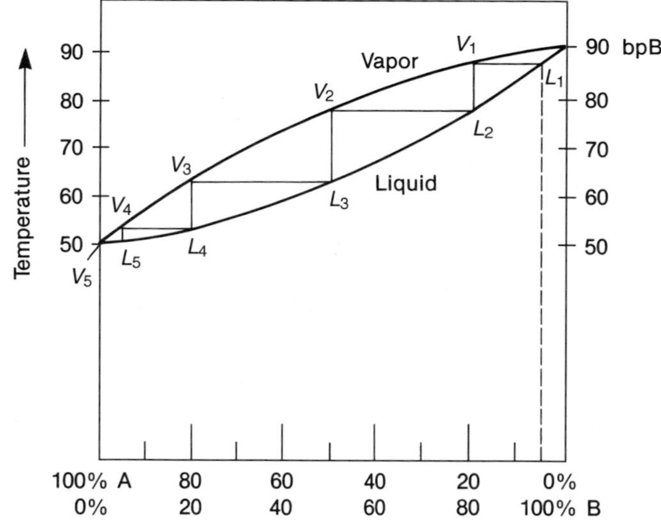

Figure 15.3 Phase diagram for a fractional distillation of an ideal two-component system.

The horizontal and vertical lines shown in Figure 15.3 represent the processes that occur during a fractional distillation. Each of the **horizontal lines** (L_1V_1, L_2V_2, and so on) represents both the **vaporization** step of a given vaporization–condensation cycle and the composition of the vapor in equilibrium with liquid at a given temperature. For example, at 63°C a liquid with a composition of 50% A (L_3 on the diagram) would yield vapor of composition 80% A (V_3 on diagram) at equilibrium. The vapor is richer in the lower-boiling component A than the original liquid was.

Each of the **vertical lines** (V_1L_2, V_2L_3, and so on) represents the **condensation** step of a given vaporization–condensation cycle. The composition does not change as the temperature drops on condensation. The vapor at V_3, for example, condenses to give a liquid (L_4 on the diagram) of composition 80% A with a drop in temperature from 63° to 53°C.

In the example shown in Figure 15.3, pure A boils at 50°C, and pure B boils at 90°C. These two boiling points are represented at the left- and right-hand edges of the diagram, respectively. Now consider a solution that contains only 5% of A but 95% of B. (Remember that these are *mole* percentages.) This solution is heated (following the dashed line) until it is observed to boil at L_1 (87°C). The resulting vapor has composition V_1 (20% A, 80% B). The vapor is richer in A than the original liquid was, but it is by no means pure A. In a simple distillation apparatus, this vapor would be condensed and passed into the receiver in a very impure state. However, with a fractionating column in place, the vapor is condensed in the **column** to give liquid L_2 (20% A, 80% B). Liquid L_2 is immediately revaporized (bp 78°C) to give a vapor of composition V_2 (50% A, 50% B), which is condensed to give liquid L_3. Liquid L_3 is revaporized (bp 63°C) to give vapor of composition V_3 (80% A, 20% B), which is condensed to give liquid L_4. Liquid L_4 is revaporized (bp 53°C) to give vapor of composition V_4 (95% A, 5% B). This process continues to V_5, which condenses to give nearly pure liquid A. The fractionating process follows the stepped lines in the figure downward and to the left.

As this process continues, all of liquid A is removed from the distillation flask or vial, leaving nearly pure B behind. If the temperature is raised, liquid B may be distilled as a

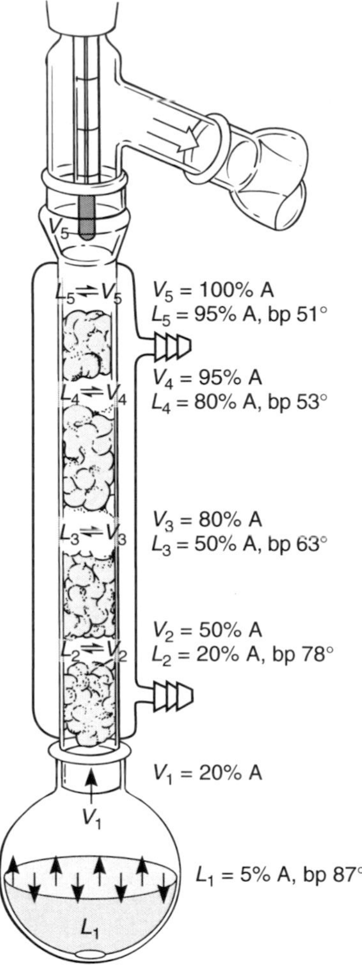

Figure 15.4 Vaporization–condensation in a fractionation column.

nearly pure fraction. Fractional distillation will have achieved a separation of A and B, a separation that would have been nearly impossible with simple distillation. Notice that the boiling point of the liquid becomes lower each time it vaporizes. Because the temperature at the bottom of a column is normally higher than the temperature at the top, successive vaporizations occur higher and higher in the column as the composition of the distillate approaches that of pure A. This process is illustrated in Figure 15.4, where the composition of the liquids, their boiling points, and the composition of the vapors present are shown alongside the fractionating column.

15.3 RAOULT'S LAW

Two liquids (A and B) that are miscible and that do not interact form an **ideal solution** and follow Raoult's Law. The law states that the partial vapor pressure of component A in the solution (P_A) equals the vapor pressure of pure A (P_A^0) times its mole fraction (N_A)

(equation 1). A similar expression can be written for component B (equation 2). The mole fractions N_A and N_B were defined in Section 15.2.

$$\text{Partial vapor pressure of A in solution} = P_A = (P_A^0)(N_A) \tag{1}$$

$$\text{Partial vapor pressure of B in solution} = P_B = (P_B^0)(N_B) \tag{2}$$

P_A^0 is the vapor pressure of pure A, independent of B. P_B^0 is the vapor pressure of B, independent of A. In a mixture of A and B, the partial vapor pressures are added to give the total vapor pressure above the solution (equation 3). When the total pressure (sum of the partial pressures) equals the applied pressure, the solution boils.

$$P_{\text{total}} = P_A + P_B = P_A^0 N_A + P_B^0 N_B \tag{3}$$

The composition of A and B in the vapor produced is given by equations 4 and 5.

$$N_A\ (\text{vapor}) = \frac{P_A}{P_{\text{total}}} \tag{4}$$

$$N_B\ (\text{vapor}) = \frac{P_B}{P_{\text{total}}} \tag{5}$$

Several exercises involving applications of Raoult's Law are illustrated in Table 15.1. Note, particularly in the result from equation 4, that the vapor is richer ($N_A = 0.67$) in the lower-boiling (higher vapor pressure) component A than it was before vaporization ($N_A = 0.50$). This proves mathematically what was described in Section 15.2.

The consequences of Raoult's Law for distillations are shown schematically in Figure 15.5. In Part A the boiling points are identical (vapor pressures the same), and no separation is attained regardless of how the distillation is conducted. In Part B a fractional distillation is required, while in Part C a simple distillation provides an adequate separation.

When a solid B (rather than another liquid) is dissolved in a liquid A, the boiling point is increased. In this extreme case, the vapor pressure of B is negligible, and the vapor will be pure A no matter how much solid B is added. Consider a solution of salt in water.

$$P_{\text{total}} = P^0_{\text{water}} N_{\text{water}} + P^0_{\text{salt}} N_{\text{salt}}$$

$$P^0_{\text{salt}} = 0$$

$$P_{\text{total}} = P^0_{\text{water}} N_{\text{water}}$$

A solution whose mole fraction of water is 0.7 will not boil at 100°C, because $P_{\text{total}} = (760)(0.7) = 532$ mmHg and is less than atmospheric pressure. If the solution is heated to 110°C, it will boil because $P_{\text{total}} = (1085)(0.7) = 760$ mmHg. Although the solution must be heated at 110°C to boil it, the vapor is pure water and has a boiling-point temperature of 100°C. (The vapor pressure of water at 110°C can be looked up in a handbook; it is 1085 mmHg.)

TABLE 15.1 Sample Calculations with Raoult's Law

Consider a solution at 100°C where $N_A = 0.5$ and $N_B = 0.5$.

1. What is the partial vapor pressure of A in the solution if the vapor pressure of pure A at 100°C is 1020 mmHg?

   Answer: $P_A = P_A^0 N_A = (1020)(0.5) = 510$ mmHg

2. What is the partial vapor pressure of B in the solution if the vapor pressure of pure B at 100°C is 500 mmHg?

   Answer: $P_B = P_B^0 N_B = (500)(0.5) = 250$ mmHg

3. Would the solution boil at 100°C if the applied pressure were 760 mmHg?

   Answer: Yes. $P_{total} = P_A + P_B = (510 + 250) = 760$ mmHg

4. What is the composition of the vapor at the boiling point?

   Answer: The boiling point is 100°C.

$$N_A\,(\text{vapor}) = \frac{P_A}{P_{total}} = 510/760 = 0.67$$

$$N_B\,(\text{vapor}) = \frac{P_B}{P_{total}} = 250/760 = 0.33$$

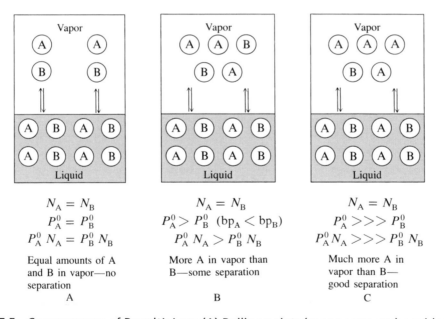

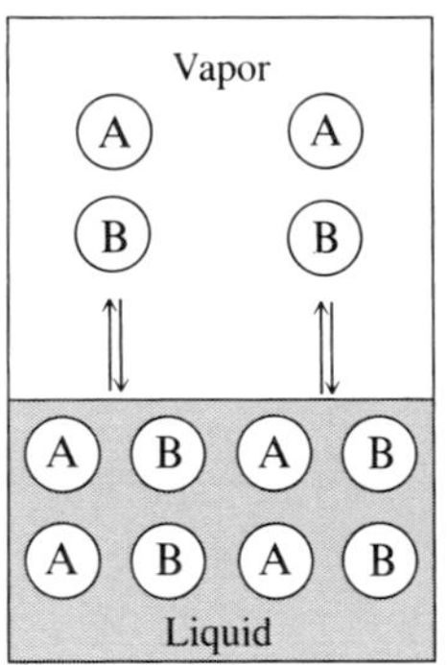

$N_A = N_B$

$P_A^0 = P_B^0$

$P_A^0\,N_A = P_B^0\,N_B$

Equal amounts of A and B in vapor—no separation

A

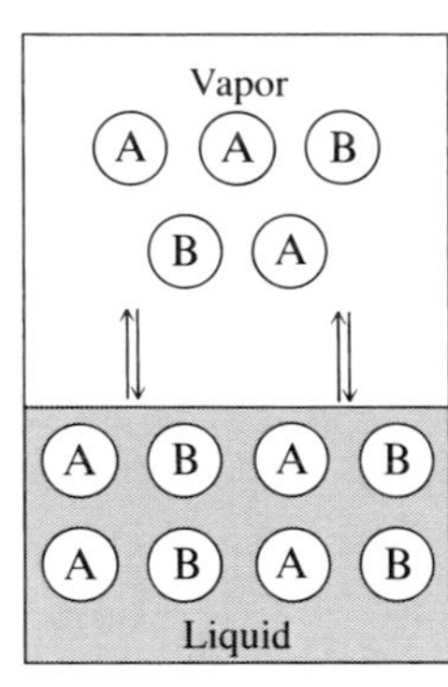

$N_A = N_B$

$P_A^0 > P_B^0$ ($bp_A < bp_B$)

$P_A^0\,N_A > P_B^0\,N_B$

More A in vapor than B—some separation

B

Vapor

A A A

B A

A B A B

A B A B

Liquid

$N_A = N_B$

$P_A^0 >>> P_B^0$

$P_A^0\,N_A >>> P_B^0\,N_B$

Much more A in vapor than B—good separation

C

Figure 15.5 Consequences of Raoult's Law. (A) Boiling points (vapor pressures) are identical—no separation. (B) Boiling points somewhat less for A than for B—requires fractional distillation. (C) Boiling points much less for A than for B—simple distillation will suffice.

15.4 COLUMN EFFICIENCY

A common measure of the efficiency of a column is given by its number of **theoretical plates.** The number of theoretical plates in a column is related to the number of vaporization–condensation cycles that occur as a liquid mixture travels through it. Using the example mixture in Figure 15.3, if the first distillate (condensed vapor) had the composition at L_2 when starting with liquid of composition L_1, the column would be said to have *one theoretical plate.* This would correspond to a simple distillation, or one vaporization–condensation cycle. A column would have two theoretical plates if the first distillate had the composition at L_3. The two-theoretical-plate column essentially carries out "two simple distillations." According to Figure 15.3, *five theoretical plates* would be required to separate the mixture that started with composition L_1. Notice that this corresponds to the number of "steps" that need to be drawn in the figure to arrive at a composition of 100% A.

Most columns do not allow distillation in discrete steps, as indicated in Figure 15.3. Instead, the process is *continuous,* allowing the vapors to be continuously in contact with liquid of changing composition as they pass through the column. Any material can be used to pack the column as long as it can be wetted by the liquid and does not pack so tightly that vapor cannot pass.

The approximate relationship between the number of theoretical plates needed to separate an ideal two-component mixture and the difference in boiling points is given in Table 15.2. Notice that more theoretical plates are required as the boiling-point differences between the components decrease. For instance, a mixture of A (bp 130°C) and B (bp 166°C) with a boiling-point difference of 36°C would be expected to require a column with a minimum of five theoretical plates.

TABLE 15.2 Theoretical Plates Required to Separate Mixtures, Based on Boiling-Point Differences of Components

Boiling-Point Difference	Number of Theoretical Plates
108	1
72	2
54	3
43	4
36	5
20	10
10	20
7	30
4	50
2	100

15.5 TYPES OF FRACTIONATING COLUMNS AND PACKINGS

Several types of fractionating columns are shown in Figure 15.6. The Vigreux column (A), has indentations that incline downward at angles of 45° and are in pairs on opposites sides of the column. The projections into the column provide increased possibilities for condensation and for the vapor to equilibrate with the liquid. Vigreux columns are popular in cases where only a small number of theoretical plates are required. They are not very efficient (a 20-cm column might have only 2.5 theoretical plates), but they allow for rapid distillation and have a small **holdup** (the amount of liquid retained by the column). A column packed with a stainless steel sponge is a more effective fractionating column than a Vigreux column, but not by a large margin. Glass beads or glass helices can also be used as a packing material, and they have even a slightly greater efficiency. The air condenser or the water condenser can be used as an improvised column if an actual fractionating column is unavailable. If a condenser is packed with glass beads, glass helices, or sections of glass tubing, the packing must be held in place by inserting a small plug of stainless steel sponge into the bottom of the condenser.

The most effective type of column is the **spinning-band column.** In the most elegant form of this device, a tightly fitting, twisted platinum screen or a Teflon rod with helical threads is rotated rapidly inside the bore of the column (Figure 15.7). A spinning-band column that is available for microscale work is shown in Figure 15.8. This spinning-band column has a band about 2–3 cm in length and provides four or five theoretical plates. It can separate 1–2 mL of a mixture with a 30°C boiling-point difference. Larger research models of this spinning-band column can provide as many as 20

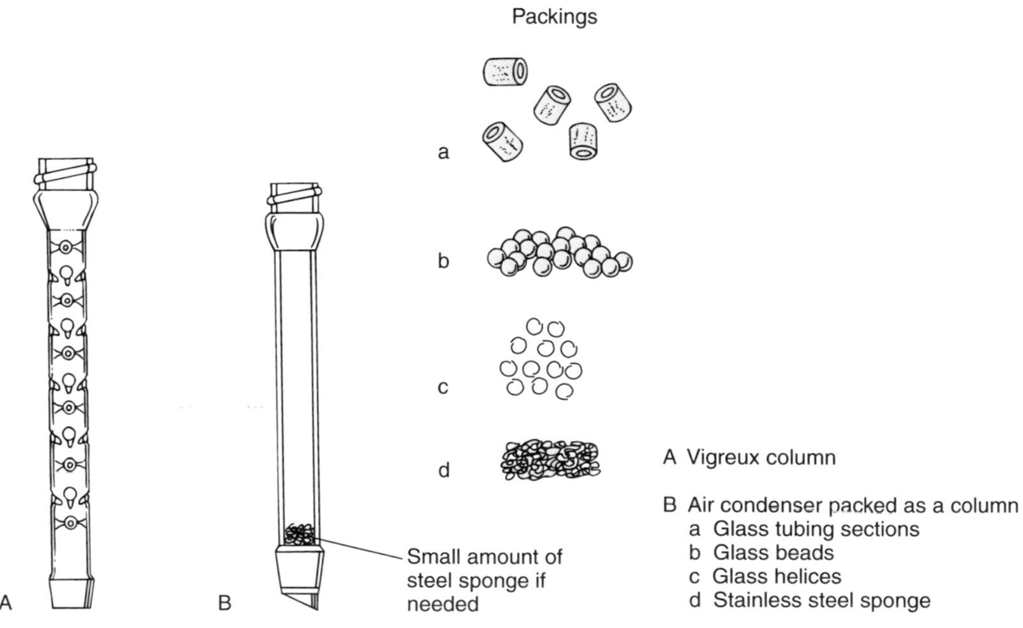

Figure 15.6 Columns for fractional distillation.

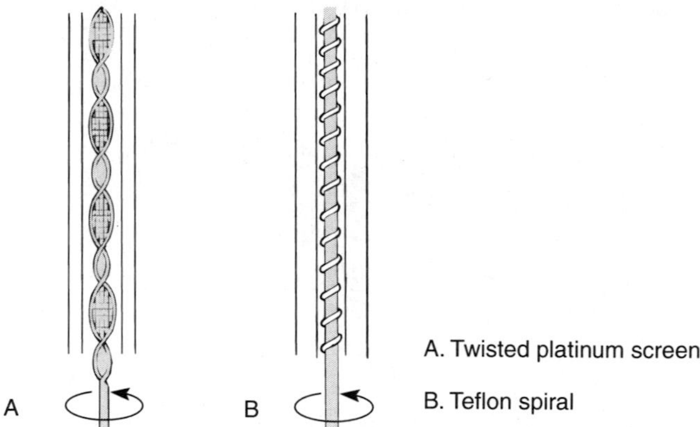

Figure 15.7 Bands for spinning-band columns.

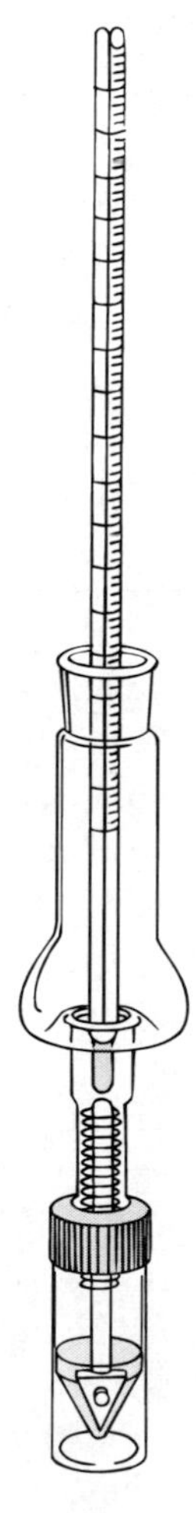

Figure 15.8 A commercially available microscale spinning-band column.

or 30 theoretical plates and can separate mixtures with a boiling-point difference of as little as 5–10°C.

Manufacturers of fractionating columns often offer them in a variety of lengths. Because the efficiency of a column is a function of its length, longer columns have more theoretical plates than shorter ones do. It is common to express efficiency of a column in a unit called **HETP,** the **H**eight of a column that is **E**quivalent to one **T**heoretical **P**late. HETP is usually expressed in units of cm/plate. When the height of the column (in centimeters) is divided by this value, the total number of theoretical plates is specified.

Fractionating columns must be insulated so that temperature equilibrium is maintained at all times. External temperature fluctuations will interfere with a good separation. Many fractionating columns are jacketed as a condenser is, but instead of water passing through the outer jacket, the jacket is evacuated and sealed. A vacuum jacket provides very good insulation of the inner column from the outside air temperature. In most student macroscale kits, the fractionating column is not evacuated but does have a jacket for insulation. This jacket, even though not evacuated, is usually sufficient for the demands of the introductory laboratory. The fractionating column looks very much like a water condenser; however, it has a larger diameter both for the inner tube and for the jacket. Be sure to take care to distinguish the larger-diameter fractionating column from the smaller-diameter water condenser.

15.6 FRACTIONAL DISTILLATION: METHODS AND PRACTICE

Many fractionating columns must be insulated so that temperature equilibrium is maintained at all times. Additional insulation will not be required for columns that have an outer jacket, but those that do not can benefit from being wrapped in insulation.

Cotton and aluminum foil (shiny side in) are often used for insulation. You can wrap the column with cotton and then use a wrapping of the aluminum foil to keep it in place. Another version of this method, which is especially effective, is to make an insulation blanket by placing a layer of cotton between two rectangles of aluminum foil, placed shiny side in. The sandwich is bound together with duct tape. This blanket, which is reusable, can be wrapped around the column and held in place with twist ties or tape.

The **reflux ratio** is defined as the ratio of the number of drops of distillate that return to the distillation flask compared to the number of drops of distillate collected. In an efficient column, the reflux ratio should equal or exceed the number of theoretical plates. A high reflux ratio ensures that the column will achieve temperature equilibrium and achieve its maximum efficiency. This ratio is not easy to determine; in fact, it is impossible to determine when using a Hickman head, and it should not concern a beginning student. In some cases, the **throughput,** or **rate of takeoff,** of a column may be specified. This is expressed as the number of milliliters of distillate that can be collected per unit of time, usually as mL/min.

Macroscale Apparatus. Figure 15.2 illustrates a fractional distillation assembly that can be used for larger-scale distillations. It has a glass-jacketed column that is packed with a stainless steel sponge. This apparatus would be common in situations where quantities of liquid in excess of 10 mL were to be distilled.

In a fractional distillation, the column should be clamped in a vertical position. The distilling flask would normally be heated by a heating mantle, which allows a precise adjustment of the temperature. A proper rate of distillation is extremely important. The distillation should be conducted as slowly as possible to allow as many vaporization–condensation cycles as possible to occur as the vapor passes through the column. However, the rate of distillation must be steady enough to produce a constant temperature reading at the thermometer. A rate that is too fast will cause the column to "flood" or "choke." In this instance, there is so much condensing liquid flowing downward in the column that the vapor cannot rise upward, and the column fills with liquid. Flooding can also occur if the column is not well insulated and has a large temperature difference from bottom to top. This situation can be remedied by employing one of the insulation methods that uses cotton or aluminum foil, as described in Section 15.5. It may also be necessary to insulate the distilling head at the top of the column. If the distilling head is cold, it will stop the progress of the distilling vapor. The distillation temperature can be monitored most accurately by using a partial immersion mercury thermometer (see Technique 13, Section 13.4, page 729.)

Microscale Apparatus. The apparatus shown in Figure 15.9 is the one you are most likely to use in the microscale laboratory. If your laboratory is one of the better equipped ones, you may have access to spinning-band columns like the one shown in Figure 15.8.

Part B. Azeotropes

15.7 NONIDEAL SOLUTIONS: AZEOTROPES

Some mixtures of liquids, because of attractions or repulsions between the molecules, do not behave ideally; they do not follow Raoult's Law. There are two types of vapor–liquid composition diagrams that result from this nonideal behavior: **minimum-boiling-point** and **maximum-boiling-point** diagrams. The minimum or maximum points in these diagrams correspond to a constant-boiling mixture called an **azeotrope.** An azeotrope is a mixture with a fixed composition that cannot be altered by either simple or fractional distillation. An azeotrope behaves as if it were a pure compound, and it distills from the beginning to the end of its distillation at a constant temperature, giving a distillate of constant (azeotropic) composition. The vapor in equilibrium with an azeotropic liquid has the same composition as the azeotrope. Because of this, an azeotrope is represented as a *point* on a vapor–liquid composition diagram.

A. Minimum-Boiling-Point Diagrams

A minimum-boiling-point azeotrope results from a slight incompatibility (repulsion) between the liquids being mixed. This incompatibility leads to a higher-than-expected combined vapor pressure from the solution. This higher combined vapor pressure brings about a lower boiling point for the mixture than is observed for the pure components. The most common two-component mixture that gives a minimum-boiling-point azeotrope is the ethanol–water system shown in Figure 15.10. The azeotrope at V_3 has a composition of 96% ethanol–4% water and a boiling point of 78.1°C. This boiling point is not much lower than

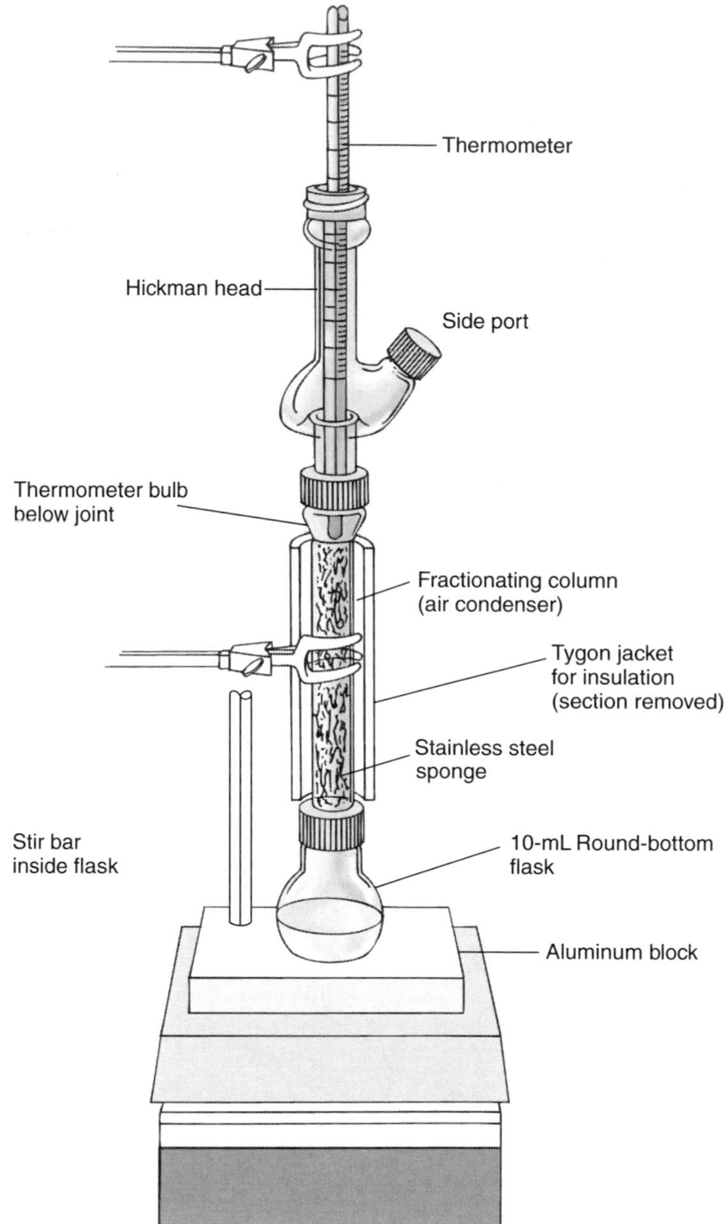

Figure 15.9 Microscale apparatus for fractional distillation.

that of pure ethanol (78.3°C), but it means that it is impossible to obtain pure ethanol from the distillation of any ethanol–water mixture that contains more than 4% water. Even with the best fractionating column, you cannot obtain 100% ethanol. The remaining 4% of water can be removed by adding benzene and removing a different azeotrope, the ternary benzene–water–ethanol azeotrope (bp 65°C). Once the water is removed, the excess benzene is removed as an ethanol–benzene azeotrope (bp 68°C). The resulting material is free of water and is called "absolute" ethanol.

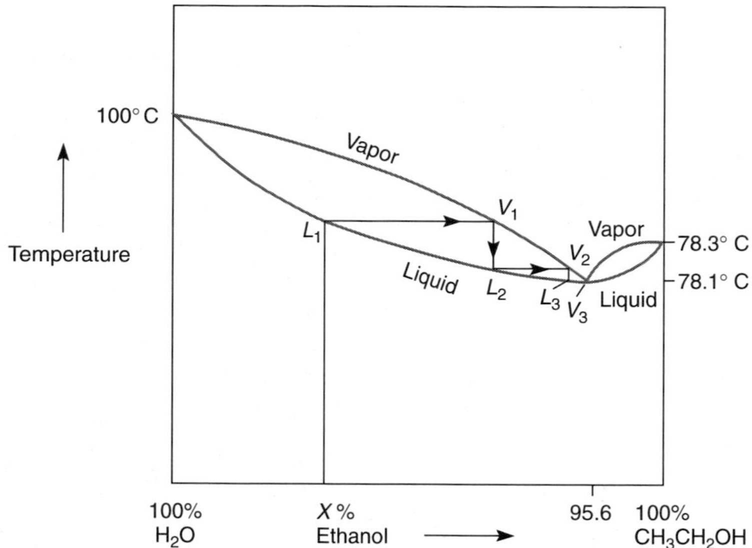

Figure 15.10 Ethanol–water minimum-boiling-point phase diagram.

The fractional distillation of an ethanol–water mixture of composition X can be described as follows. The mixture is heated (follow line XL_1) until it is observed to boil at L_1. The resulting vapor at V_1 will be richer in the lower-boiling component, ethanol, than the original mixture was.[1] The condensate at L_2 is vaporized to give V_2. The process continues, following the lines to the right, until the azeotrope is obtained at V_3. The liquid that distills is not pure ethanol, but it has the azeotropic composition of 96% ethanol and 4% water, and it distills at 78.1°C. The azeotrope, which is richer in ethanol than the original mixture was, continues to distill. As it distills, the percentage of water left behind in the distillation flask continues to increase. When all the ethanol has been distilled (as the azeotrope), pure water remains behind in the distillation flask, and it distills at 100°C.

If the azeotrope obtained by the preceding procedure is redistilled, it distills from the beginning to the end of the distillation at a constant temperature of 78.1°C as if it were a pure substance. There is no change in the composition of the vapor during the distillation.

Some common minimum-boiling-point azeotropes are given in Table 15.3. Numerous other azeotropes are formed in two- and three-component systems; such azeotropes are common. Water forms azeotropes with many substances; therefore, water must be carefully removed with **drying agents** whenever possible before compounds are distilled. Extensive azeotropic data are available in references such as the *CRC Handbook of Chemistry and Physics*.[2]

B. Maximum-Boiling-Point Diagrams

A maximum-boiling-point azeotrope results from a slight attraction between the component molecules. This attraction leads to lower combined vapor pressure than expected in

[1] Keep in mind that this distillate is not pure ethanol but is an ethanol–water mixture.

[2] More examples of azeotropes, with their compositions and boiling points, can be found in the *CRC Handbook of Chemistry and Physics;* also in L. H. Horsley, ed., *Advances in Chemistry Series,* No. 116, Azeotropic Data, III (Washington, DC: American Chemical Society, 1973).

TABLE 15.3 Common Minimum-Boiling-Point Azeotropes

Azeotrope	Composition (weight percentage)	Boiling Point (°C)
Ethanol–water	95.6% C_2H_5OH, 4.4% H_2O	78.17
Benzene–water	91.1% C_6H_6, 8.9% H_2O	69.4
Benzene–water–ethanol	74.1% C_6H_6, 7.4% H_2O, 18.5% C_2H_5OH	64.9
Methanol–carbon tetrachloride	20.6% CH_3OH, 79.4% CCl_4	55.7
Ethanol–benzene	32.4% C_2H_5OH, 67.6% C_6H_6	67.8
Methanol–toluene	72.4% CH_3OH, 27.6% $C_6H_5CH_3$	63.7
Methanol–benzene	39.5% CH_3OH, 60.5% C_6H_6	58.3
Cyclohexane–ethanol	69.5% C_6H_{12}, 30.5% C_2H_5OH	64.9
2-Propanol–water	87.8% $(CH_3)_2CHOH$, 12.2% H_2O	80.4
Butyl acetate–water	72.9% $CH_3COOC_4H_9$, 27.1% H_2O	90.7
Phenol–water	9.2% C_6H_5OH, 90.8% H_2O	99.5

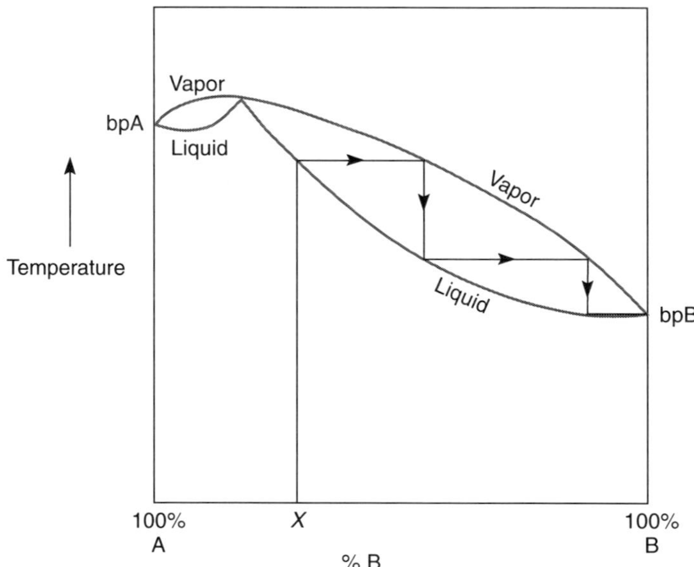

Figure 15.11 A maximum-boiling-point phase diagram.

the solution. The lower combined vapor pressures cause a higher boiling point than what would be characteristic for the components. A two-component maximum-boiling-point azeotrope is illustrated in Figure 15.11. Because the azeotrope has a higher boiling point than any of the components, it will be concentrated in the distillation flask as the distillate (pure B) is removed. The distillation of a solution of composition *X* would follow to the right along the lines in Figure 15.11. Once the composition of the material remaining in the flask has reached that of the azeotrope, the temperature will rise, and the azeotrope will be-

TABLE 15.4 Maximum-Boiling-Point Azeotropes

Azeotrope	Composition (weight percentage)	Boiling Point (°C)
Acetone–chloroform	20.0% CH_3COCH_3, 80.0% $CHCl_3$	64.7
Chloroform–methyl ethyl ketone	17.0% $CHCl_3$, 83.0% $CH_3COCH_2CH_3$	79.9
Hydrochloric acid	20.2% HCl, 79.8% H_2O	108.6
Acetic acid–dioxane	77.0% CH_3COCH, 23.0% $C_4H_8O_2$	119.5
Benzaldehyde–phenol	49.0% C_6H_5CHO, 51.0% C_6H_5OH	185.6

gin to distill. The azeotrope will continue to distill until all the material in the distillation flask has been exhausted.

Some maximum-boiling-point azeotropes are listed in Table 15.4. They are not nearly as common as minimum-boiling-point azeotropes.[3]

C. Generalizations

There are some generalizations that can be made about azeotropic behavior. They are presented here without explanation, but you should be able to verify them by thinking through each case using the phase diagrams given. (Note that pure A is always to the left of the azeotrope in these diagrams, and pure B is to the right of the azeotrope.)

Minimum-Boiling-Point Azeotropes

Initial Composition	Experimental Result
To left of azeotrope	Azeotrope distills first, pure A second
Azeotrope	Unseparable
To right of azeotrope	Azeotrope distills first, pure B second

Maximum-Boiling-Point Azeotropes

Initial Composition	Experimental Result
To left of azeotrope	Pure A distills first, azeotrope second
Azeotrope	Unseparable
To right of azeotrope	Pure B distills first, azeotrope second

[3] See footnote 2.

TECHNIQUE 11

Crystallization: Purification of Solids

In most organic chemistry experiments, the desired product is first isolated in an impure form. If this product is a solid, the most common method of purification is crystallization. The general technique involves dissolving the material to be crystallized in a *hot* solvent (or solvent mixture) and cooling the solution slowly. The dissolved material has a decreased solubility at lower temperatures and will separate from the solution as it is cooled. This phenomenon is called either **crystallization,** if the crystal growth is relatively slow and selective, or **precipitation,** if the process is rapid and nonselective. Crystallization is an equilibrium process and produces very pure material. A small seed crystal is formed initially, and it then grows layer by layer in a reversible manner. In a sense, the crystal "selects" the correct molecules from the solution. In precipitation, the crystal lattice is formed so rapidly that impurities are trapped within the lattice. Therefore, any attempt at purification with too rapid a process should be avoided. Because the impurities are usually present in much smaller amounts than the compound being crystallized, most of the impurities will remain in the solvent even when it is cooled. The purified substance can then be separated from the solvent and from the impurities by filtration.

The method of crystallization described here is called **macroscale crystallization.** This technique, which is carried out with an Erlenmeyer flask to dissolve the material and a Büchner funnel to filter the crystals, is normally used when the weight of solid to be crystallized is more than 0.1 g. Another method, which is performed with a Craig tube, is used with smaller amounts of solid. Referred to as **microscale crystallization,** this technique is discussed briefly in Section 11.4.

When the macroscale crystallization procedure described in Section 11.3 is used with a Hirsch funnel, the procedure is sometimes referred to as a **semi-microscale crystallization.** This procedure is commonly used in microscale work when the amount of solid is greater than 0.1 g or in macroscale work when the amount of solid is less than about 0.5 g.

Part A. Theory

11.1 SOLUBILITY

The first problem in performing a crystallization is selecting a solvent in which the material to be crystallized shows the desired solubility behavior. In an ideal case, the material should be sparingly soluble at room temperature and yet quite soluble at the boiling point of the solvent selected. The solubility curve should be steep, as can be seen in line A of Figure 11.1. A curve with a low slope (line B) would not cause significant crys-

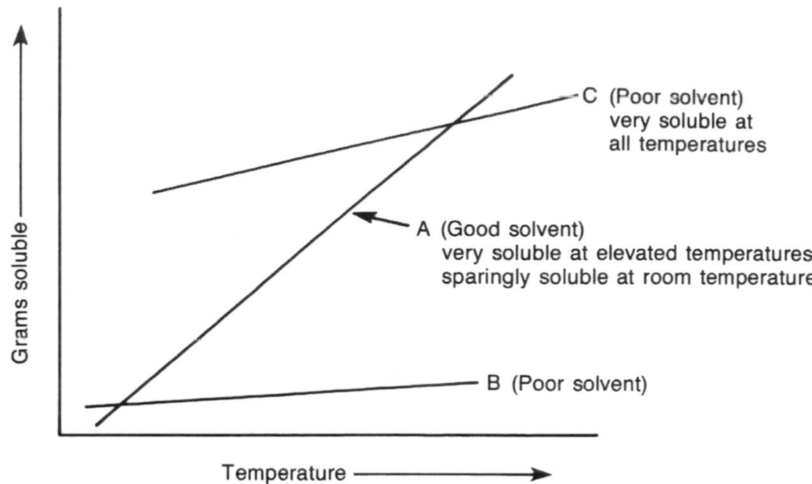

Figure 11.1 Graph of solubility vs. temperature.

tallization when the temperature of the solution was lowered. A solvent in which the material is very soluble at all temperatures (line C) also would not be a suitable crystallization solvent. The basic problem in performing a crystallization is to select a solvent (or mixed solvent) that provides a steep solubility-vs.-temperature curve for the material to be crystallized. A solvent that allows the behavior shown in line A is an ideal crystallization solvent. It should also be mentioned that solubility curves are not always linear, as they are depicted in Figure 11.1. This figure represents an idealized form of solubility behavior. The solubility curve for sulfanilamide in 95% ethyl alcohol, shown in Figure 11.2, is typical of many organic compounds and shows what solubility behavior might look like for a real substance.

The solubility of organic compounds is a function of the polarities of both the solvent and the **solute** (dissolved material). A general rule is "Like dissolves like." If the solute is very polar, a very polar solvent is needed to dissolve it; if the solute is nonpolar, a nonpolar solvent is needed. Applications of this rule are discussed extensively in Technique 10, Section 10.2, page 670 and in Section 11.5, page 689.

11.2 THEORY OF CRYSTALLIZATION

A successful crystallization depends on a large difference between the solubility of a material in a hot solvent and its solubility in the same solvent when it is cold. When the impurities in a substance are equally soluble in both the hot and the cold solvent, an effective purification is not easily achieved through crystallization. A material can be purified by crystallization when both the desired substance and the impurity have similar solubilities, but only when the impurity represents a small fraction of the total solid. The desired substance will crystallize on cooling, but the impurities will not.

For example, consider a case in which the solubilities of substance A and its impurity B are both 1 g/100 mL of solvent at 20°C and 10 g/100 mL of solvent at 100°C. In the impure sample of A, the composition is 9 g of A and 2 g of B. In the calculations for this example, it is assumed that the solubilities of both A and B are unaffected by the presence of the other substance. To make the calculations easier to understand, 100 mL of solvent are

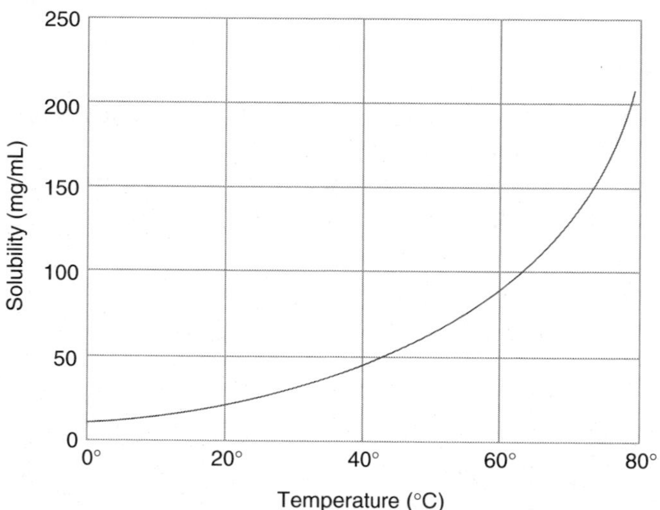

Figure 11.2 Solubility of sulfanilamide in 95% ethyl alcohol.

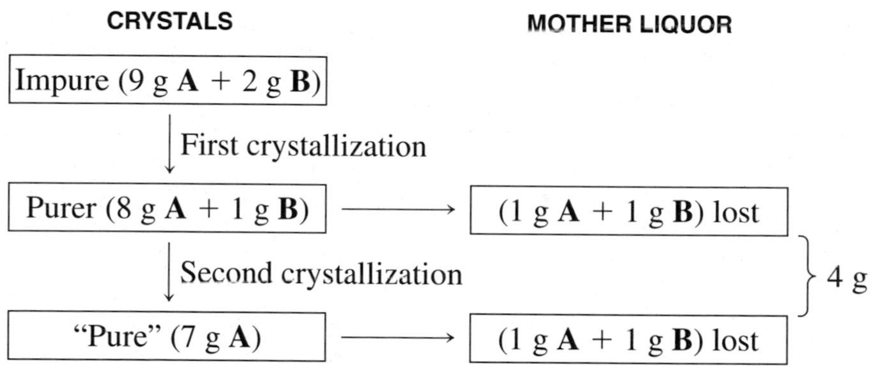

Figure 11.3 Purification of a mixture by crystallization.

used in each crystallization. Normally, the minimum amount of solvent required to dissolve the solid would be used.

At 20°C, this total amount of material will not dissolve in 100 mL of solvent. However, if the solvent is heated to 100°C, all 11 g dissolve. The solvent has the capacity to dissolve 10 g of A *and* 10 g of B at this temperature. If the solution is cooled to 20°C, only 1 g of each solute can remain dissolved, so 8 g of A and 1 g of B crystallize, leaving 2 g of material in the solution. This crystallization is shown in Figure 11.3. The solution that remains after a crystallization is called the **mother liquor.** If the process is now repeated by treating the crystals with 100 mL of fresh solvent, 7 g of A will crystallize again, leaving 1 g of A and 1 g of B in the mother liquor. As a result of these operations, 7 g of pure A are obtained, but with the loss of 4 g of material (2 g of A plus 2 g of B). Again, this second crystallization step is illustrated in Figure 11.3. The final result illustrates an important aspect of crystallization—it is wasteful. Nothing can be done to prevent this waste; some A must be lost along with the impurity B for the method to be successful. Of course, if the impurity B were *more* soluble than A in the solvent, the losses would be reduced. Losses could also be reduced if the impurity were present in *much smaller* amounts than the desired material.

Note that in the preceding case, the method operated successfully because A was present in substantially larger quantity than its impurity B. If there had been a 50-50 mixture of A and B initially, no separation would have been achieved. In general, a crystallization is successful only if there is a *small* amount of impurity. As the amount of impurity increases, the loss of material must also increase. Two substances with nearly equal solubility behavior, present in equal amounts, cannot be separated. If the solubility behavior of two components present in equal amounts is different, however, a separation or purification is frequently possible.

In the preceding example, two crystallization procedures were performed. Normally, this is not necessary; however, when it is, the second crystallization is more appropriately called **recrystallization.** As illustrated in this example, a second crystallization results in purer crystals, but the yield is lower.

In some experiments, you will be instructed to cool the crystallizing mixture in an ice-water bath before collecting the crystals by filtration. Cooling the mixture increases the yield by decreasing the solubility of the substance; however, even at this reduced temperature, some of the product will be soluble in the solvent. It is not possible to recover all your product in a crystallization procedure even when the mixture is cooled in an ice-water bath. A good example of this is illustrated by the solubility curve for sulfanilamide shown in Figure 11.2. The solubility of sulfanilamide at 0°C is still significant, 14 mg/mL.

Part B. Macroscale Crystallization

11.3 MACROSCALE CRYSTALLIZATION

The crystallization technique described in this section is used when the weight of solid to be crystallized is more than 0.1 g. There are four main steps in a macroscale crystallization:

1. Dissolving the solid
2. Removing insoluble impurities (when necessary)
3. Crystallizing
4. Collecting and drying

These steps are illustrated in Figure 11.4. An Erlenmeyer flask of an appropriate size must be chosen. It should be pointed out that a microscale crystallization with a Craig tube involves the same four steps, although the apparatus and procedures are somewhat different (see Section 11.4).

A. Dissolving the Solid

To minimize losses of material to the mother liquor, it is desirable to *saturate* the boiling solvent with solute. This solution, when cooled, will return the maximum possible amount of solute as crystals. To achieve this high return, the solvent is brought to its boiling point, and the solute is dissolved in the *minimum amount* (!) *of boiling solvent.* For this procedure, it is advisable to maintain a container of boiling solvent (on a hot plate). From

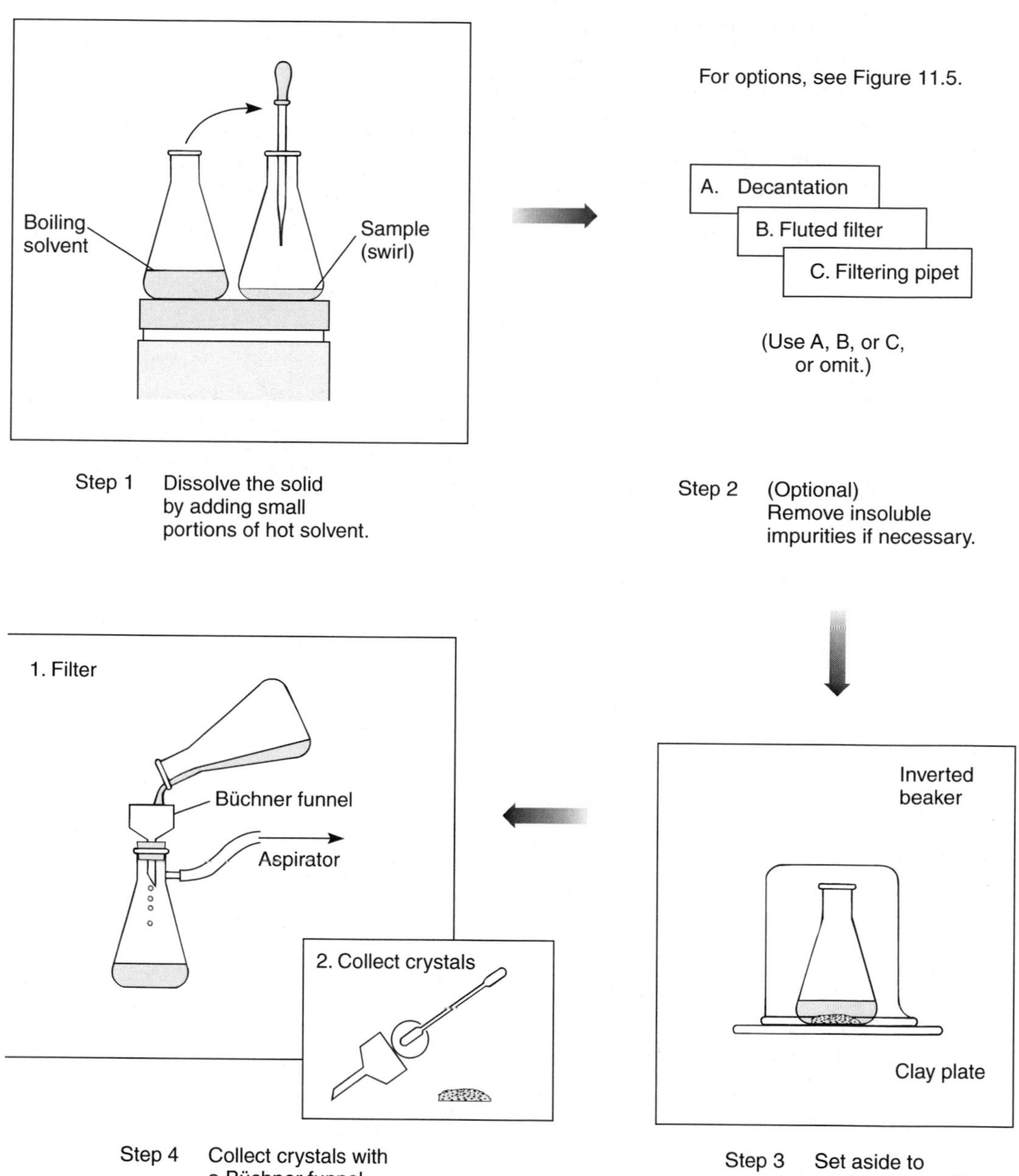

Boiling solvent
Sample (swirl)
Step 1 Dissolve the solid by adding small portions of hot solvent.
For options, see Figure 11.5.
A. Decantation
B. Fluted filter
C. Filtering pipet
(Use A, B, or C, or omit.)
Step 2 (Optional) Remove insoluble impurities if necessary.
Inverted beaker
Clay plate
Step 3 Set aside to cool and crystallize.
1. Filter
Büchner funnel
Aspirator
2. Collect crystals
Step 4 Collect crystals with a Büchner funnel.

Figure 11.4 Steps in a macroscale crystallization (no decolorization).

this container, a small portion (about 1–2 mL) of the solvent is added to the Erlenmeyer flask containing the solid to be crystallized, and this mixture is heated while swirling occasionally until it resumes boiling.

> **Caution:** Do not heat the flask containing the solid until after you have added the first portion of solvent.

If the solid does not dissolve in the first portion of boiling solvent, then another small portion of boiling solvent is added to the flask. The mixture is swirled and heated again until it resumes boiling. If the solid dissolves, no more solvent is added. But if the solid has not dissolved, another portion of boiling solvent is added, as before, and the process is repeated until the solid dissolves. It is important to stress that the portions of solvent added each time are small, so only the *minimum* amount of solvent necessary for dissolving the solid is added. It is also important to emphasize that the procedure requires the addition of solvent to solid. You must never add portions of solid to a fixed quantity of boiling solvent. By this latter method, it may be impossible to determine when saturation has been achieved. This entire procedure should be performed fairly rapidly, or you may lose solvent through evaporation nearly as quickly as you are adding it, and this procedure will then take a very long time. This is most likely to happen when using highly volatile solvents such as methyl alcohol or ethyl alcohol. The time from the first addition of solvent until the solid dissolves completely should not be longer than 15–20 minutes.

Comments on This Procedure for Dissolving the Solid

1. One of the most common mistakes is to add too much solvent. This can happen most easily if the solvent is not hot enough or if the mixture is not stirred sufficiently. If too much solvent is added, the percentage recovery will be reduced; it is even possible that no crystals will form when the solution is cooled. If too much solvent is added, you must evaporate the excess by heating the mixture. A nitrogen or air stream directed into the container will accelerate the evaporation process (see Technique 7, Section 7.10, p. 639).
2. It is very important not to heat the solid until you have added some solvent. Otherwise, the solid may melt and possibly form an oil or decompose, and it may not crystallize easily (see p. 691).
3. It is also important to use an Erlenmeyer flask rather than a beaker for performing the crystallization. A beaker should not be used because the large opening allows the solvent to evaporate too rapidly and allows dust particles to get in too easily.
4. In some experiments, a specified amount of solvent for a given weight of solid will be recommended. In these cases, you should use the amount specified rather than the minimum amount of solvent necessary to dissolve the solid. The amount of solvent recommended has been selected to provide the optimum conditions for good crystal formation.
5. Occasionally, you may encounter an impure solid that contains small particles of insoluble impurities, pieces of dust, or paper fibers that will not dissolve in the hot crystallizing solvent. A common error is to add too much of the hot solvent in an attempt to dissolve these small particles, not realizing that they are insoluble. In such cases, you must be careful not to add too much solvent.
6. It is sometimes necessary to decolorize the solution by adding activated charcoal or by passing the solution through a column containing alumina or silica gel (see Section 11.7 and Technique 19, Section 19.15, p. 814). A decolorization step should be performed only if the mixture is *highly* colored and it is clear that the color is due to impurities and not to the actual color of the substance being crys-

tallized. If decolorization is necessary, it should be accomplished before the following filtration step.

B. Removing Insoluble Impurities

It is necessary to use one of the following three methods only if insoluble material remains in the hot solution or if decolorizing charcoal has been used.

> **Caution:** Indiscriminate use of the procedure can lead to needless loss of your product.

Decantation is the easiest method of removing solid impurities and should be considered first. If filtration is required, a filtering pipet is used when the volume of liquid to be filtered is less than 10 mL (see Technique 8, Section 8.1C, p. 649), and you should use gravity filtration through a fluted filter when the volume is 10 mL or greater (see Technique 8, Section 8.1B, p. 646). These three methods are illustrated in Figure 11.5, and each is discussed below.

Decantation. If the solid particles are relatively large in size or they easily settle to the bottom of the flask, it may be possible to separate the hot solution from the impurities by carefully pouring off the liquid, leaving the solid behind. This is accomplished most easily by holding a glass stirring rod along the top of the flask and tilting the flask so that the liquid pours out along one end of the glass rod into another container. A technique similar in principle to decantation, which may be easier to perform with smaller amounts of liquid, is to use a **preheated Pasteur pipet** to remove the hot solution. With this method, it may be helpful to place the tip of the pipet against the bottom of the flask when removing the last portion of solution. The small space between the tip of the pipet and the inside surface of the flask prevents solid material from being drawn into the pipet. An easy way to preheat the pipet is to draw up a small portion of hot *solvent* (not the *solution* being transferred) into the pipet and expel the liquid. Repeat this process several times.

Fluted Filter. This method is the most effective way to remove solid impurities when the volume of liquid is greater than 10 mL or when decolorizing charcoal has been used (see Technique 8, Section 8.1B, p. 646 and Section 11.7). You should first add a small amount of extra solvent to the hot mixture. This action helps prevent crystal formation in the filter paper or the stem of the funnel during the filtration. The funnel is then fitted with a fluted filter and installed at the top of the Erlenmeyer flask to be used for the actual filtration. It is advisable to place a small piece of wire between the funnel and the mouth of the flask to relieve any increase in pressure caused by hot filtrate.

The Erlenmeyer flask containing the funnel and fluted paper is placed on top of a hot plate (low setting). The liquid to be filtered is brought to its boiling point and poured through the filter in portions. (If the volume of the mixture is less than 10 mL, it may be more convenient to transfer the mixture to the filter with a preheated Pasteur pipet.) It is necessary to keep the solutions in both flasks at their boiling temperatures to prevent premature crystallization. The refluxing action of the filtrate keeps the funnel warm and reduces the chance that the filter will clog with crystals that may have formed during the filtration.

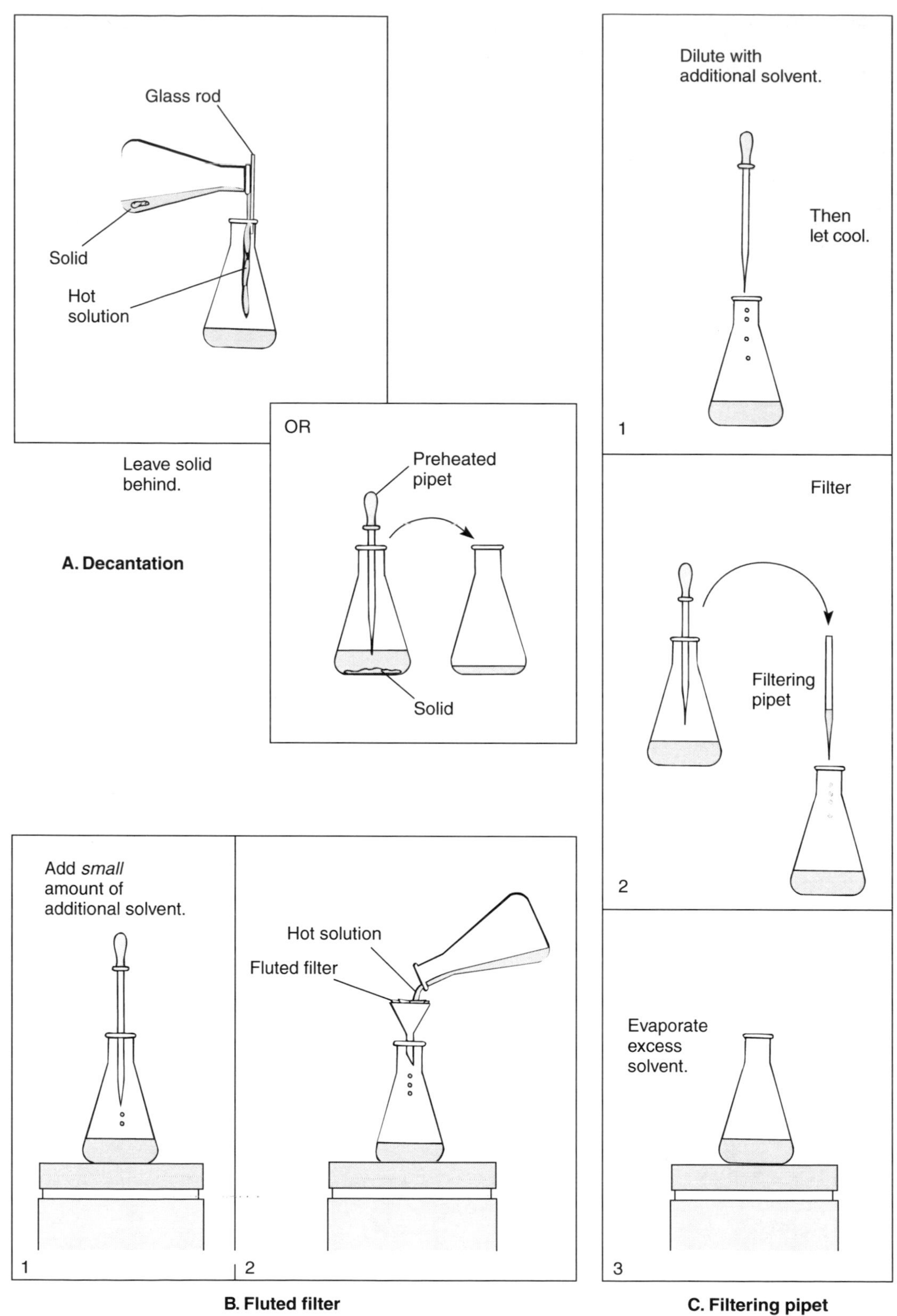

Figure 11.5 Methods for removing insoluble impurities in a macroscale crystallization.

With low-boiling solvents, be aware that some solvent may be lost through evaporation. Consequently, extra solvent must be added to make up for this loss. If crystals begin to form in the filter during filtration, a minimum amount of boiling solvent is added to redissolve the crystals and to allow the solution to pass through the funnel. If the volume of liquid being filtered is less than 10 mL, a small amount of hot solvent should be used to rinse the filter after all the filtrate has been collected. The rinse solvent is then combined with the original filtrate.

After the filtration, it may be necessary to remove extra solvent by evaporation until the solution is once again saturated at the boiling point of the solvent (see Technique 7, Section 7.10, p. 639).

Filtering Pipet. If the volume of solution after dissolving the solid in hot solvent is less than 10 mL, gravity filtration with a filtering pipet may be used to remove solid impurities. However, using a filtering pipet to filter a hot solution saturated with solute can be difficult without premature crystallization. The best way to prevent this from occurring is to add enough solvent to dissolve the desired product at room temperature (be sure not to add too much solvent) and perform the filtration at room temperature, as described in Technique 8, Section 8.1C, p. 649. After filtration, the excess solvent is evaporated by boiling until the solution is saturated at the boiling point of the mixture (see Technique 7, Section 7.10, p. 639). If powdered decolorizing charcoal was used, it will probably be necessary to perform two filtrations with a filtering pipet to remove all of the charcoal, or a fluted filter can be used.

C. Crystallizing

An Erlenmeyer flask, not a beaker, should be used for crystallization. The large open top of a beaker makes it an excellent dust catcher. The narrow opening of the Erlenmeyer flask reduces contamination by dust and allows the flask to be stoppered if it is to be set aside for a long period. Mixtures set aside for long periods must be stoppered after cooling to room temperature to prevent evaporation of solvent. If all the solvent evaporates, no purification is achieved, and the crystals originally formed become coated with the dried contents of the mother liquor. Even if the time required for crystallization to occur is relatively short, it is advisable to cover the top of the Erlenmeyer flask with a small watch glass or inverted beaker to prevent evaporation of solvent while the solution is cooling to room temperature.

The chances of obtaining pure crystals are improved if the solution cools to room temperature slowly. When the volume of solution is 10 mL or less, the solution is likely to cool more rapidly than is desired. This can be prevented by placing the flask on a surface that is a poor heat conductor and covering the flask with a beaker to provide a layer of insulating air. Appropriate surfaces include a clay plate or several pieces of filter paper on top of the laboratory bench. It may also be helpful to use a clay plate that has been warmed slightly on a hot plate or in an oven.

After crystallization has occurred, it is sometimes desirable to cool the flask in an ice-water bath. Because the solute is less soluble at lower temperatures, this will increase the yield of crystals.

If a cooled solution does not crystallize, it will be necessary to induce crystallization. Several techniques are described in Section 11.8A.

D. Collecting and Drying

After the flask has been cooled, the crystals are collected by vacuum filtration through a Büchner (or Hirsch) funnel (see Technique 8, Section 8.3, p. 651, and Figure 8.5). The crystals should be washed with a small amount of *cold* solvent to remove any mother liquor adhering to their surface. Hot or warm solvent will dissolve some of the crystals. The crystals should then be left for a short time (usually 5–10 minutes) in the funnel, where air, as it passes, will dry them free of most of the solvent. It is often wise to cover the Büchner funnel with an oversized filter paper or towel during this air drying. This precaution prevents accumulation of dust in the crystals. When the crystals are nearly dry, they should be gently scraped off the filter paper (so paper fibers are not removed with the crystals) onto a watch glass or clay plate for further drying (see Section 11.9).

The four steps in a macroscale crystallization are summarized in Table 11.1.

TABLE 11.1 Steps in a Macroscale Crystallization

A. Dissolving the Solid

1. Find a solvent with a steep solubility-vs.-temperature characteristic (done by trial and error using small amounts of material or by consulting a handbook).
2. Heat the desired solvent to its builing point.
3. Dissolve the solid in a **minimum** of boiling solvent in a flask.
4. If necessary, add decolorizing charcoal or decolorize the solution on a silica gel or alumina column.

B. Removing Insoluble Impurities

1. Decant or remove the solution with a Pasteur pipet.
2. Alternatively, filter the hot solution through a fluted filter, a filtering pipet, or a filter-tip pipet to remove insoluble impurities or charcoal.

> **Note:** If no decolorizing charcoal has been added or if there are no undissolved particles, Part B should be omitted.

C. Crystallizing

1. Allow the solution to cool.
2. If crystals appear, cool the mixture in an ice-water bath (if desired) and go to Part D. If crystals do not appear, go to the next step.
3. Inducing crystallization
  a. Scratch the flask with a glass rod.
  b. Seed the solution with original solid, if available.
  c. Cool the solution in an ice-water bath.
  d. Evaporate excess solvent and allow the solution to cool again.

D. Collecting and Drying

1. Collect crystals by vacuum filtration using a Büchner funnel.
2. Rinse crystals with a small portion of **cold** solvent.
3. Continue suction until crystals are nearly dry.
4. Drying (three options)
  a. Air-dry the crystals.
  b. Place the crystals in a drying oven.
  c. Dry the crystals under a vacuum.

Part C. Microscale Crystallization

11.4 MICROSCALE CRYSTALLIZATION

In many microscale experiments, the amount of solid to be crystallized is small enough (generally less than 0.1 g) that a **Craig tube** (see Technique 8, Figure 8.10, p. 657) is the preferred method for crystallization. The main advantage of the Craig tube is that it minimizes the number of transfers of solid material, thus resulting in a greater yield of crystals. Also, the separation of the crystals from the mother liquor with the Craig tube is very efficient, and little time is required for drying the crystals. The steps involved are, in principle, the same as those performed when a crystallization is accomplished with an Erlenmeyer flask and a Büchner funnel.

The solid is transferred to the Craig tube, and small portions of hot solvent are added to the tube while the mixture is stirred with a spatula and heated. If there are any insoluble impurities present, they can be removed with a filter-tip pipet. The inner plug is then inserted into the Craig tube and the hot solution is cooled slowly to room temperature. When the crystals have formed, the Craig tube is placed into a centrifuge tube, and the crystals are separated from the mother liquor by centrifugation (see Technique 8, Section 8.7, p. 656). The crystals are then scraped off the end of the inner plug or from inside the Craig tube onto a watch glass or piece of paper. Minimal drying will be necessary (see Section 11.9).

Part D. Additional Experimental Considerations: Macroscale and Microscale

11.5 SELECTING A SOLVENT

A solvent that dissolves little of the material to be crystallized when it is cold but a great deal of the material when it is hot is a good solvent for crystallization. Quite often, correct crystallization solvents are indicated in the experimental procedures that you will be following. When a solvent is not specified in a procedure, you can determine a good crystallization solvent by consulting a handbook or making an educated guess based on polarities, both discussed in this section. A third approach, involving experimentation, is discussed in Section 11.6.

With compounds that are well known, the correct crystallization solvent has already been determined through the experiments of earlier researchers. In such cases, the chemical literature can be consulted to determine which solvent should be used. Sources such as *The Merck Index* or the *CRC Handbook of Chemistry and Physics* may provide this information.

For example, consider naphthalene, which is found in *The Merck Index*. It states under the entry for naphthalene: "Monoclinic prismatic plates from ether." This statement means that naphthalene can be crystallized from ether. It also gives the type of crystal structure. Unfortunately, the crystal structure may be given without reference to the solvent. Another way to determine the best solvent is by looking at solubility-vs.-temperature data. When this is given, a good solvent is one in which the solubility of the compound increases significantly as the temperature increases. Sometimes, the solubility data will be given for only cold solvent and boiling solvent. This should provide enough information to determine whether this would be a good solvent for crystallization.

In most cases, however, the handbooks will state only whether a compound is soluble or not in a given solvent, usually at room temperature. Determining a good solvent for crystallization from this information can be somewhat difficult. The solvent in which the compound is soluble may or may not be an appropriate solvent for crystallization. Sometimes, the compound may be too soluble in the solvent at all temperatures, and you would recover very little of your product if this solvent were used for crystallization. It is possible that an appropriate solvent would be the one in which the compound is nearly insoluble at room temperature because the solubility-vs.-temperature curve is very steep. Although the solubility information may give you some ideas about what solvents to try, you will most likely need to determine a good crystallizing solvent by experimentation as described in Section 11.6.

When using *The Merck Index* or *Handbook of Chemistry and Physics,* you should be aware that alcohol is frequently listed as a solvent. This generally refers to 95% or 100% ethyl alcohol. Because 100% (absolute) ethyl alcohol is more expensive than 95% ethyl alcohol, the cheaper grade is usually used in the chemistry laboratory. Another solvent frequently listed is benzene. Benzene is a known carcinogen, so it is rarely used in student laboratories. Toluene is a suitable substitute; the solubility behavior of a substance in benzene and toluene is so similar that you may assume any statement made about benzene also applies to toluene.

Another way to identify a solvent for crystallization is to consider the polarities of the compound and the solvents. Generally, you would look for a solvent that has a polarity somewhat similar to that of the compound to be crystallized. Consider the compound sulfanilamide, shown in the figure. There are several polar bonds in sulfanilamide, the NH and

Sulfanilamide

NH_2

O=S=O

NH_2

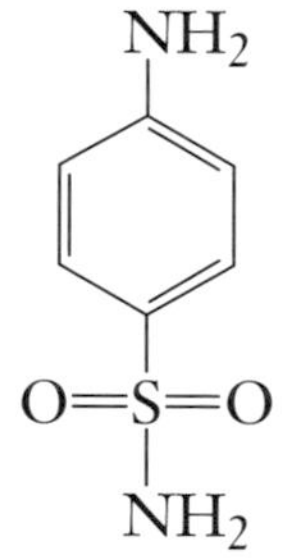

the SO bonds. In addition, the NH_2 groups and the oxygen atoms in sulfanilamide can form hydrogen bonds. Although the benzene ring portion of sulfanilamide is nonpolar, sulfanilamide has an intermediate polarity because of the polar groups. A common organic solvent of intermediate polarity is 95% ethyl alcohol. Therefore, it is likely that sulfanilamide would be soluble in 95% ethyl alcohol because they have similar polarities. (Note that the other 5% in 95% ethyl alcohol is usually a substance such as water or isopropyl alcohol, which does not alter the overall polarity of the solvent.) Although this kind of analysis is a good first step in determining an appropriate solvent for crystallization, without more information it is not enough to predict the shape of the solubility curve for the temperature-vs.-solubility data (see Figure 11.1, p. 680). Therefore, knowing that sulfanilamide is soluble in 95% ethyl alcohol does not necessarily mean that this is a good solvent for crystallizing sulfanilamide. You would still need to test the solvent to see if it is appropriate. The solubility curve for sulfanilamide (see Figure 11.2, page 681) indicates that 95% ethyl alcohol is a good solvent for crystallizing this substance.

When choosing a crystallization solvent, do not select one whose boiling point is higher than the melting point of the substance (solute) to be crystallized. If the boiling point of the solvent is too high, the substance may come out of solution as a liquid rather than a crystalline solid. In such a case, the solid may **oil out.** Oiling out occurs when on cooling the solution to induce crystallization, the solute begins to come out of solution at a temperature above its melting point. The solute will then come out of solution as a liquid. Furthermore, as cooling continues, the substance may still not crystallize; rather, it will become a supercooled liquid. Oils may eventually solidify if the temperature is lowered, but often they will not actually crystallize. Instead, the solidified oil will be an amorphous solid or a hardened mass. In this case, purification of the substance will not have occurred as it does when the solid is crystalline. It can be very difficult to deal with oils when trying to obtain a pure substance. You must try to redissolve them and hope that the substance will crystallize with slow, careful cooling. During the cooling period, it may be helpful to scratch the glass container where the oil is present with a glass stirring rod that has not been fire polished. Seeding the oil as it cools with a small sample of the original solid is another technique that is sometimes helpful in working with difficult oils. Other methods of inducing crystallization are discussed in Section 11.8.

One additional criterion for selecting the correct crystallization solvent is the **volatility** of that solvent. Volatile solvents have low boiling points or evaporate easily. A solvent with a low boiling point may be removed from the crystals through evaporation without much difficulty. It will be difficult to remove a solvent with a high boiling point from the crystals without heating them under vacuum.

Table 11.2 lists common crystallization solvents. The solvents used most commonly are listed in the table first.

11.6 TESTING SOLVENTS FOR CRYSTALLIZATION

When the appropriate solvent is not known, select a solvent for crystallization by experimenting with various solvents and a very small amount of the material to be crystallized. Experiments are conducted on a small test tube scale before the entire quantity of material is committed to a particular solvent. Such trial-and-error methods are common when trying to purify a solid material that has not been previously studied.

Procedure

1. Place about 0.05 g of the sample in a test tube.
2. Add about 0.5 mL of solvent at room temperature and stir the mixture by rapidly twirling a microspatula between your fingers. If all (or almost all) of the solid dissolves at room temperature, then your solid is *probably* too soluble in this solvent and little compound would be recovered if this solvent were used. Select another solvent.
3. If none (or very little) of the solid dissolves at room temperature, heat the tube carefully and stir with a spatula. (A hot water bath is perhaps better than an alu-

TABLE 11.2 Common Solvents for Crystallization

	Boils (°C)	Freezes (°C)	Soluble in H_2O	Flammability
Water	100	0	+	−
Methanol	65	*	+	+
95% Ethanol	78	*	+	+
Ligroin	60–90	*	−	+
Toluene	111	*	−	+
Chloroform**	61	*	−	−
Acetic acid	118	17	+	+
Dioxane**	101	11	+	+
Acetone	56	*	+	+
Dicthyl cthcr	35	*	Slightly	++
Petroleum ether	30–60	*	−	++
Methylene chloride	41	*	−	−
Carbon tetrachloride**	77	*	−	−

*Lower than 0°C (ice temperature).

**Suspected carcinogen.

minum block because you can more easily control the temperature of the hot water bath. The temperature of the hot water bath should be slightly higher than the boiling point of the solvent.) Add more solvent dropwise, while continuing to heat and stir. Continue adding solvent until the solid dissolves, but do not add more than about 1.5 mL (total) of solvent. If all the solid dissolves, go to step 4. If all the solid has not dissolved by the time you have added 1.5 mL of solvent, this is probably not a good solvent. However, if most of the solid has dissolved at this point, you might try adding a little more solvent. Remember to heat and stir at all times during this step.

4. If the solid dissolves in about 1.5 mL or less of boiling solvent, then remove the test tube from the heat source, stopper the tube, and allow it to cool to room temperature. Then place it in an ice-water bath. If a lot of crystals come out, this is most likely a good solvent. If crystals do not come out, scratch the sides of the tube with a glass stirring rod to induce crystallization. If crystals still do not form, this is probably not a good solvent.

Comments about This Procedure

1. Selecting a good solvent is something of an art. There is no perfect procedure that can be used in all cases. You must think about what you are doing and use some common sense in deciding whether to use a particular solvent.
2. Do not heat the mixture above the melting point of your solid. This can occur most easily when the boiling point of the solvent is higher than the melting point of the solid. Normally, do not select a solvent that has a higher boiling point than the melt-

ing point of the substance. If you do, make certain that you do not heat the mixture beyond the melting point of your solid.

11.7 DECOLORIZATION

Small amounts of highly colored impurities may make the original crystallization solution appear colored; this color can often be removed by **decolorization,** either by using activated charcoal (often called Norit) or by passing the solution through a column packed with alumina or silica gel. A decolorizing step should be performed only if the color is due to impurities, not to the color of the desired product, and if the color is significant. Small amounts of colored impurities will remain in solution during crystallization, making the decolorizing step unnecessary. The use of activated charcoal is described separately for macroscale and microscale crystallizations, and then the column technique, which can be used with both crystallization techniques, is described.

A. Macroscale—Powdered Charcoal

As soon as the solute is dissolved in the minimum amount of boiling solvent, the solution is allowed to cool slightly, and a small amount of Norit (powdered charcoal) is added to the mixture. The Norit adsorbs the impurities. When performing a crystallization in which the filtration is performed with a fluted filter, you should add powdered Norit because it has a larger surface area and can remove impurities more effectively. A reasonable amount of Norit is what could be held on the end of a microspatula, or about 0.01–0.02 g. If too much Norit is used, it will adsorb product as well as impurities. A small amount of Norit should be used, and its use should be repeated if necessary. (It is difficult to determine if the initial amount added is sufficient until after the solution is filtered, because the suspended particles of charcoal will obscure the color of the liquid.) Caution should be exercised so that the solution does not froth or erupt when the finely divided charcoal is added. The mixture is boiled with the Norit for several minutes and then filtered by gravity, using a fluted filter (see Section 11.3 and Technique 8, Section 8.1B, p. 646), and the crystallization is carried forward as described in Section 11.3.

The Norit preferentially adsorbs the colored impurities and removes them from the solution. The technique seems to be most effective with hydroxylic solvents. In using Norit, be careful not to breathe the dust. Normally, small quantities are used so that little risk of lung irritation exists.

B. Microscale—Pelletized Norit

If the crystallization is being performed in a Craig tube, it is advisable to use pelletized Norit. Although this is not as effective in removing impurities as powdered Norit, it is easier to remove, and the amount of pelletized Norit required is more easily determined because you can see the solution as it is being decolorized. Again, the Norit is added to the hot solution (the solution should not be boiling) after the solid has dissolved. This should be performed in a test tube rather than in a Craig tube. About 0.02 g is added, and the mixture is boiled for a minute or so to see if more Norit is required. More Norit is added, if necessary, and the liquid is boiled again. It is important not to add too much pelletized Norit because the Norit will also adsorb some of the desired material, and it is possible that not all the color can be removed no matter how much is added. The decolorized solution is then removed with a preheated filter-tip pipet (see Technique 8, Section 8.6, p. 655) to filter the mixture and transferred to a Craig tube for crystallization as described in Section 11.4.

C. Decolorization on a Column

The other method for decolorizing a solution is to pass the solution through a column containing alumina or silica gel. The adsorbent removes the colored impurities while allowing the desired material to pass through (see Technique 8, Figure 8.6, p. 654, and Technique 19, Section 19.15, p. 814). If this technique is used, it will be necessary to dilute the solution with additional solvent to prevent crystallization from occurring during the process. The excess solvent must be evaporated after the solution is passed through the column (Technique 7, Section 7.10, p. 639) and the crystallization procedure is continued as described in Sections 11.3 or 11.4.

11.8 INDUCING CRYSTALLIZATION

If a cooled solution does not crystallize, several techniques may be used to induce crystallization. Although identical in principle, the actual procedures vary slightly when performing macroscale and microscale crystallizations.

A. Macroscale

In the first technique, you should try scratching the inside surface of the flask vigorously with a glass rod that *has not been* fire polished. The motion of the rod should be vertical (in and out of the solution) and should be vigorous enough to produce an audible scratching. Such scratching often induces crystallization, although the effect is not well understood. The high-frequency vibrations may have something to do with initiating crystallization; or perhaps—a more likely possibility—small amounts of solution dry by evaporation on the side of the flask, and the dried solute is pushed into the solution. These small amounts of material provide "seed crystals," or nuclei, on which crystallization may begin.

A second technique that can be used to induce crystallization is to cool the solution in an ice bath. This method decreases the solubility of the solute.

A third technique is useful when small amounts of the original material to be crystallized are saved. The saved material can be used to "seed" the cooled solution. A small crystal dropped into the cooled flask often will start the crystallization—this is called **seeding.**

If all these measures fail to induce crystallization, it is likely that too much solvent was added. The excess solvent must then be evaporated (Technique 7, Section 7.10, p. 639) and the solution allowed to cool.

B. Microscale

The strategy is basically the same as described for macroscale crystallizations. Scratching vigorously with a glass rod *should be avoided,* however, because the Craig tube is fragile and expensive. Scratching *gently* is allowed.

Another measure is to dip a spatula or glass stirring rod into the solution and allow the solvent to evaporate so that a small amount of solid will form on the surface of the spatula or glass rod. When placed back into the solution, the solid will seed the solution. A small amount of the original material, if some was saved, may also be used to seed the solution.

A third technique is to cool the Craig tube in an ice-water bath. This method may also be combined with either of the previous suggestions.

If none of these measures is successful, it is possible that too much solvent is present, and it may be necessary to evaporate some of the solvent (Technique 7, Section 7.10, p. 639) and allow the solution to cool again.

11.9 DRYING CRYSTALS

The most common method of drying crystals involves allowing them to dry in air. Several different methods are illustrated in Figure 11.6, below. In all three methods, the crystals must be covered to prevent accumulation of dust particles. Note that in each method, the spout on the beaker provides an opening so that solvent vapor can escape from the system. The advantage of this method is that heat is not required, thus reducing the danger of decomposition or melting; however, exposure to atmospheric moisture may cause the hydration of strongly hygroscopic materials. A **hygroscopic** substance is a substance that absorbs moisture from the air.

Another method of drying crystals is to place the crystals on a watch glass, a clay plate, or a piece of absorbent paper in an oven. Although this method is simple, some possible difficulties deserve mention. Crystals that sublime readily should not be dried in an oven because they might vaporize and disappear. Care should be taken that the temperature of the oven does not exceed the melting point of the crystals. Remember that the melting point of crystals is lowered by the presence of solvent; allow for this melting-point depression when selecting a suitable oven temperature. Some materials decompose on exposure to heat, and they should not be dried in an oven. Finally, when many different samples are being dried in the same oven, crystals might be lost due to confusion or reac-

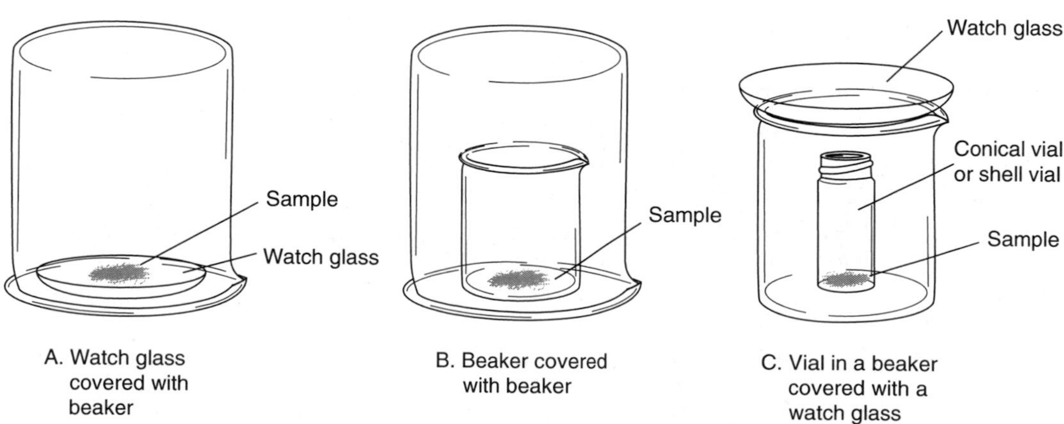

Figure 11.6 Methods for drying crystals in air.

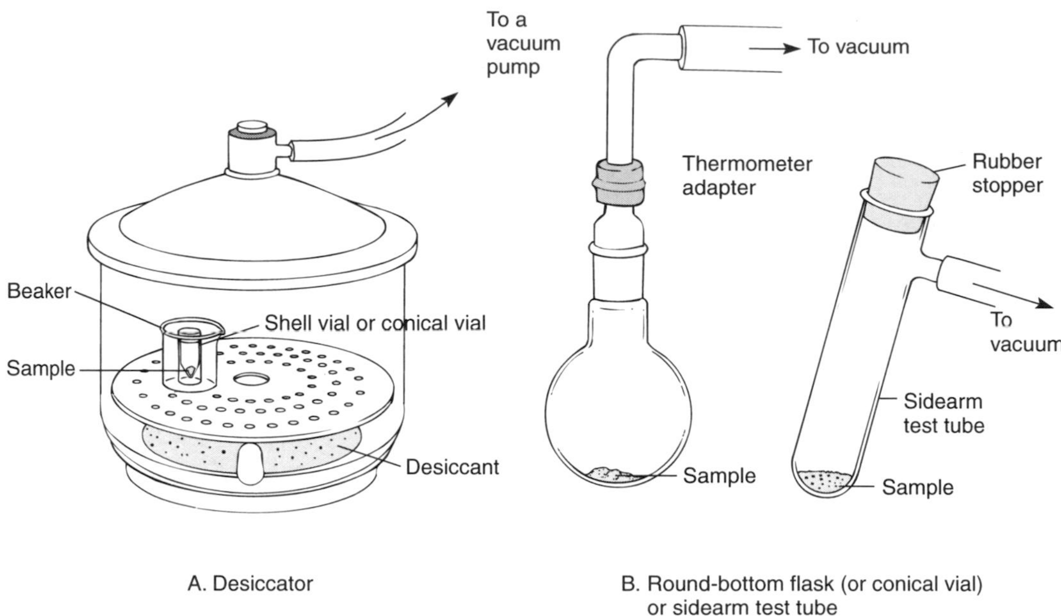

Figure 11.7 Methods for drying crystals in a vacuum.

tion with another person's sample. It is important to label the crystals when they are placed in the oven.

A third method, which requires neither heat nor exposure to atmospheric moisture, is drying *in vacuo.* Two procedures are illustrated in Figure 11.7.

Procedure A. In this method, a desiccator is used. The sample is placed under vacuum in the presence of a drying agent. Two potential problems must be noted. The first deals with samples that sublime readily. Under vacuum, the likelihood of sublimation is increased. The second problem deals with the vacuum desiccator itself. Because the surface area of glass that is under vacuum is large, there is some danger that the desiccator could implode. A vacuum desiccator should never be used unless it has been placed within a protective metal container (cage). If a cage is not available, the desiccator can be wrapped with electrical or duct tape. If you use an aspirator as a source of vacuum, you should use a water trap (see Figure 8.5, p. 652).

Procedure B. This method can be accomplished with a round-bottom flask and a thermometer adapter equipped with a short piece of glass tubing, as illustrated in Figure 11.7B. In microscale work, the apparatus with the round-bottom flask can be modified by replacing the round-bottom flask with a conical vial. The glass tubing is connected by vacuum tubing to either an aspirator or a vacuum pump. A convenient alternative, using a sidearm test tube, is also shown in Figure 11.7B. With either apparatus, install a water trap when an aspirator is used.

11.10 MIXED SOLVENTS

Often, the desired solubility characteristics for a particular compound are not found in a single solvent. In these cases, a mixed solvent may be used. You simply select a first

TABLE 11.3 Common Solvent Pairs for Crystallization

Methanol–water	Ether–acetone
Ethanol–water	Ether–petroleum ether
Acetic acid–water	Toluene–ligroin
Acetone–water	Methylene chloride–methanol
Ether–methanol	Dioxane[a]–water

[a] Suspected carcinogen.

solvent in which the solute is soluble and a second solvent, miscible with the first, in which the solute is relatively insoluble. The compound is dissolved in a minimum amount of the boiling solvent in which it is soluble. Following this, the second hot solvent is added to the boiling mixture, dropwise, until the mixture barely becomes cloudy. The cloudiness indicates precipitation. At this point, more of the first solvent should be added. Just enough is added to clear the cloudy mixture. At that point, the solution is saturated, and as it cools, crystals should separate. Common solvent mixtures are listed in Table 11.3.

It is important not to add an excess of the second solvent or to cool the solution too rapidly. Either of these actions may cause the solute to oil out, or separate as a viscous liquid. If this happens, reheat the solution and add more of the first solvent.

PROBLEMS

1. Listed below are solubility-vs.-temperature data for an organic substance A dissolved in water.

Temperature (°C)	Solubility of A in 100 mL of Water (g)
0	1.5
20	3.0
40	6.5
60	11.0
80	17.0

a. Graph the solubility of A vs. temperature. Use the data given in the table. Connect the data points with a smooth curve.
b. Suppose 0.1 g of A and 1.0 mL of water were mixed and heated to 80°C. Would all the substance A dissolve?
c. The solution prepared in (b) is cooled. At what temperature will crystals of A appear?
d. Suppose the cooling described in (c) were continued to 0°C. How many grams of A would come out of solution? Explain how you obtained your answer.

2. What would likely happen if a hot saturated solution were filtered by vacuum filtration using a Büchner funnel? (*Hint:* The mixture will cool as it comes in contact with the Büchner funnel.)

3. A compound you have prepared is reported in the literature to have a pale yellow color. When the substance is dissolved in hot solvent to purify it by crystallization, the resulting solution is yellow. Should you use decolorizing charcoal before allowing the hot solution to cool? Explain your answer.

4. While performing a crystallization, you obtain a light tan solution after dissolving your crude product in hot solvent. A decolorizing step is determined to be unnecessary, and there are no solid impurities present. Should you perform a filtration to remove impurities before allowing the solution to cool? Why or why not?

5. a. Draw a graph of a cooling curve (temperature vs. time) for a solution of a solid substance that shows no supercooling effects. Assume that the solvent does not freeze.

b. Repeat the instructions in (a) for a solution for a solid substance that shows some supercooling behavior but eventually yields crystals if the solution is cooled sufficiently.

6. A solid substance A is soluble in water to the extent of 10 mg/mL of water at 25°C and 100 mg/mL of water at 100°C. You have a sample that contains 100 mg of A and an impurity B.

a. Assuming that 2 mg of B are present along with 100 mg of A, describe how you can purify A if B is completely insoluble in water. Your description should include the volume of solvent required.

b. Assuming that 2 mg of the impurity B are present along with 100 mg of A, describe how you can purify A if B has the same solubility behavior as A. Will one crystallization produce pure A? (Assume that the solubilities of both A and B are unaffected by the presence of the other substance.)

c. Assume that 25 mg of the impurity B are present along with 100 mg of A. Describe how you can purify A if B has the same solubility behavior as A. Each time, use the minimum amount of water to just dissolve the solid. Will one crystallization produce absolutely pure A? How many crystallizations would be needed to produce pure A? How much A will have been recovered when the crystallizations have been completed?

7. An organic chemistry student dissolved 0.30 g of a crude product in 10.5 mL (the minimum amount required) of ethanol at 25°C. He cooled the solution in an ice-water bath for 15 minutes and obtained beautiful crystals. He filtered the crystals on a Hirsch funnel and rinsed them with about 2.0 mL of ice-cold ethanol. After drying, the weight of the crystals was found to be 0.015 g. Why was the recovery so low?

TECHNIQUE 9

Physical Constants of Solids: The Melting Point

9.1 PHYSICAL PROPERTIES

The physical properties of a compound are those properties that are intrinsic to a given compound when it is pure. A compound may often be identified simply by determining a number of its physical properties. The most commonly recognized physical properties of a compound include its color, melting point, boiling point, density, refractive index, molecular weight, and optical rotation. Modern chemists would include the various types of spectra (infrared, nuclear magnetic resonance, mass, and ultraviolet-visible) among the physical properties of a compound. A compound's spectra do not vary from one pure sample to another. Here, we look at methods of determining the melting point. Boiling point and density of compounds are covered in Technique 13. Refractive index, optical rotation, and spectra are also considered separately.

Many reference books list the physical properties of substances. You should consult Technique 4 for a complete discussion on how to find data for specific compounds. The works most useful for finding lists of values for the nonspectroscopic physical properties include

The Merck Index

The CRC Handbook of Chemistry and Physics

Lange's Handbook of Chemistry

Aldrich Handbook of Fine Chemicals

Complete citations for these references can be found in Technique 29 (p. 984). Although the *CRC Handbook* has very good tables, it adheres strictly to IUPAC nomenclature. For this reason, it may be easier to use one of the other references, particularly *The Merck Index* or the *Aldrich Handbook of Fine Chemicals,* in your first attempt to locate information (see Technique 4).

9.2 THE MELTING POINT

The melting point of a compound is used by the organic chemist not only to identify the compound, but also to establish its purity. A small amount of material is heated *slowly* in a special apparatus equipped with a thermometer or thermocouple, a heating bath or heating coil, and a magnifying eyepiece for observing the sample. Two temperatures are noted. The first is the point at which the first drop of liquid forms among the crystals; the second is the point at which the whole mass of crystals turns to a *clear* liquid. The melting point is recorded by giving this range of melting. You might say, for example, that the melting point of a substance is 51–54°C. That is, the substance melted over a 3-degree range.

The melting point indicates purity in two ways. First, the purer the material, the higher its melting point. Second, the purer the material, the narrower its melting-point range. Adding successive amounts of an impurity to a pure substance generally causes its melting point to decrease in proportion to the amount of impurity. Looking at it another way, adding impurities lowers the freezing point. The freezing point, a colligative property, is simply the melting point (solid → liquid) approached from the opposite direction (liquid → solid).

Figure 9.1 is a graph of the usual melting-point behavior of mixtures of two substances, A and B. The two extremes of the melting range (the low and high temperature) are shown for various mixtures of the two. The upper curves indicate the temperatures at which all the sample has melted. The lower curves indicate the temperature at which melting is observed to begin. With pure compounds, melting is sharp and without any range. This is shown at the left- and right-hand edges of the graph. If you begin with pure A, the melting point decreases as impurity B is added. At some point, a minimum temperature, or **eutectic,** is reached, and the melting point begins to increase to that of substance B. The vertical distance between the lower and upper curves represents the melting range. Notice that for mixtures that contain relatively small amounts of impurity ($< 15\%$) and are not close to the eutectic, the melting range increases as the sample becomes less pure. The range indicated by the lines in Figure 9.1 represents the typical behavior.

We can generalize the behavior shown in Figure 9.1. Pure substances melt with a narrow range of melting. With impure substances, the melting range becomes wider, and the entire melting range is lowered. Be careful to note, however, that at the minimum point of the melting-point–composition curves, the mixture often forms a eutectic, which also melts sharply. Not all binary mixtures form eutectics, and some caution must be exercised in assuming that every binary mixture follows the previously described behavior. Some mixtures may form more than one eutectic; others might not form even one. In spite of these variations, both the melting point and its range are useful indications of purity, and they are easily determined by simple experimental methods.

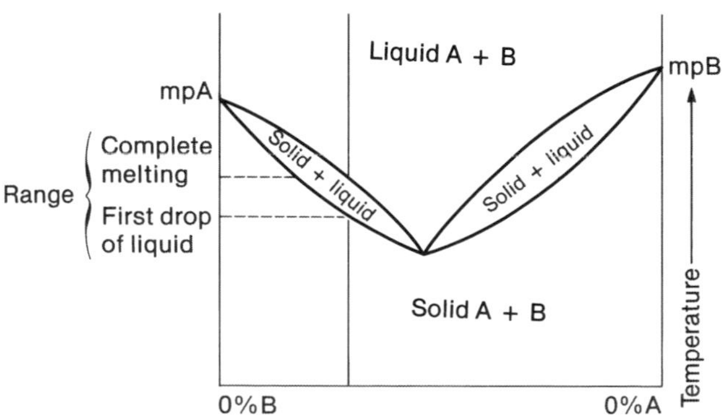

Figure 9.1 A melting-point–composition curve.

9.3 MELTING-POINT THEORY

Figure 9.2 is a phase diagram describing the usual behavior of a two-component mixture (A + B) on melting. The behavior on melting depends on the relative amounts of A and B in the mixture. If A is a pure substance (no B), then A melts sharply at its melting point t_A. This is represented by point A on the left side of the diagram. When B is a pure substance, it melts at t_B; its melting point is represented by point B on the right side of the diagram. At either point A or point B, the pure solid passes cleanly, with a narrow range, from solid to liquid.

In mixtures of A and B, the behavior is different. Using Figure 9.2, consider a mixture of 80% A and 20% B on a mole-per-mole basis (that is, mole percentage). The melting point of this mixture is given by t_M at point M on the diagram. That is, adding B to A has lowered the melting point of A from t_A to t_M. It has also expanded the melting range. The temperature t_M corresponds to the **upper limit** of the melting range.

Lowering the melting point of A by adding impurity B comes about in the following way. Substance A has the lower melting point in the phase diagram shown, and if heated, it begins to melt first. As A begins to melt, solid B begins to dissolve in the liquid A that is formed. When solid B dissolves in liquid A, the melting point is depressed. To understand this, consider the melting point from the opposite direction. When a liquid at a high temperature cools, it reaches a point at which it solidifies, or "freezes." The temperature at which a liquid freezes is identical to its melting point. Recall that the freezing point of a liquid can be lowered by adding an impurity. Because the freezing point and the melting point are identical, lowering the freezing point corresponds to lowering the melting point. Therefore, as more impurity is added to a solid, its melting point becomes lower. There is, however, a limit to how far the melting point can be depressed. You cannot dissolve an infinite amount of the impurity substance in the liquid. At some point, the liquid will become saturated with the impurity substance. The solubility of B in A has an upper limit. In Figure 9.2, the solubility limit of B in liquid A is reached at point C, the **eutectic point.** The melting point of the mixture cannot be lowered below t_C, the melting temperature of the eutectic.

Now consider what happens when the melting point of a mixture of 80% A and 20% B is approached. As the temperature is increased, A begins to "melt." This is not really a

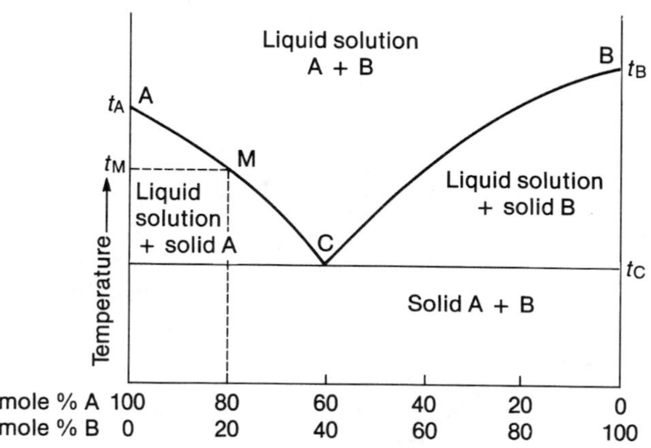

Figure 9.2 A phase diagram for melting in a two-component system.

visible phenomenon in the beginning stages; it happens before liquid is visible. It is a softening of the compound to a point at which it can begin to mix with the impurity. As A begins to soften, it dissolves B. As it dissolves B, the melting point is lowered. The lowering continues until all B is dissolved or until the eutectic composition (saturation) is reached. When the maximum possible amount of B has been dissolved, actual melting begins, and one can observe the first appearance of liquid. The initial temperature of melting will be below t_A. The amount below t_A at which melting begins is determined by the amount of B dissolved in A but will never be below t_C. Once all B has been dissolved, the melting point of the mixture begins to rise as more A begins to melt. As more A melts, the semisolid solution is diluted by more A, and its melting point rises. While all this is happening, you can observe *both* solid and liquid in the melting-point capillary. Once all A has begun to melt, the composition of the mixture M becomes uniform and will reach 80% A and 20% B. At this point, the mixture finally melts sharply, giving a clear solution. The maximum melting-point range will be $t_C - t_M$, because t_A is depressed by the impurity B that is present. The lower end of the melting range will always be t_C; however, melting will not always be observed at this temperature. An observable melting at t_C comes about only when a large amount of B is present. Otherwise, the amount of liquid formed at t_C will be too small to observe. Therefore, the melting behavior that is actually observed will have a smaller range, as shown in Figure 9.1.

9.4 MIXTURE MELTING POINTS

The melting point can be used as supporting evidence in identifying a compound in two different ways. Not only may the melting points of the two individual compounds be compared but a special procedure called a **mixture melting point** may also be performed. The mixture melting point requires that an authentic sample of the same compound be available from another source. In this procedure, the two compounds (authentic and suspected) are finely pulverized and mixed together in equal quantities. Then the melting point of the mixture is determined. If there is a melting-point depression or if the range of melting is expanded by a large amount compared to that of the individual substances, you may conclude that one compound has acted as an impurity toward the other and that they are not the same compound. If there is no lowering of the melting point for the mixture (the melting point is identical with those of pure A and pure B), then A and B are almost certainly the same compound.

9.5 PACKING THE MELTING-POINT TUBE

Melting points are usually determined by heating the sample in a piece of thin-walled capillary tubing (1 mm × 100 mm) that has been sealed at one end. To pack the tube, press the open end gently into a *pulverized* sample of the crystalline material. Crystals will stick in the open end of the tube. The amount of solid pressed into the tube should correspond to a column no more than 1–2 mm high. To transfer the crystals to the closed end of the tube, drop the capillary tube, closed end first, down a ⅔-m length of glass tubing, which is held upright on the desktop. When the capillary tube hits the desktop, the crystals will pack down into the bottom of the tube. This procedure is repeated if necessary. Tapping the capillary on the desktop with fingers is not recommended because it is easy to drive the small tubing into a finger if the tubing should break.

Some commercial melting-point instruments have a built-in vibrating device that is designed to pack capillary tubes. With these instruments, the sample is pressed into the open end of the capillary tube, and the tube is placed in the vibrator slot. The action of the vibrator will transfer the sample to the bottom of the tube and pack it tightly.

9.6 DETERMINING THE MELTING POINT—THE THIELE TUBE

There are two principal types of melting-point apparatus available: the Thiele tube and commercially available, electrically heated instruments. The Thiele tube, shown in Figure 9.3, is the simpler device and was once widely used. It is a glass tube designed to contain a heating oil (mineral oil or silicone oil) and a thermometer to which a capillary tube containing the sample is attached. The shape of the Thiele tube allows convection currents to form in the oil when it is heated. These currents maintain a uniform temperature distri-

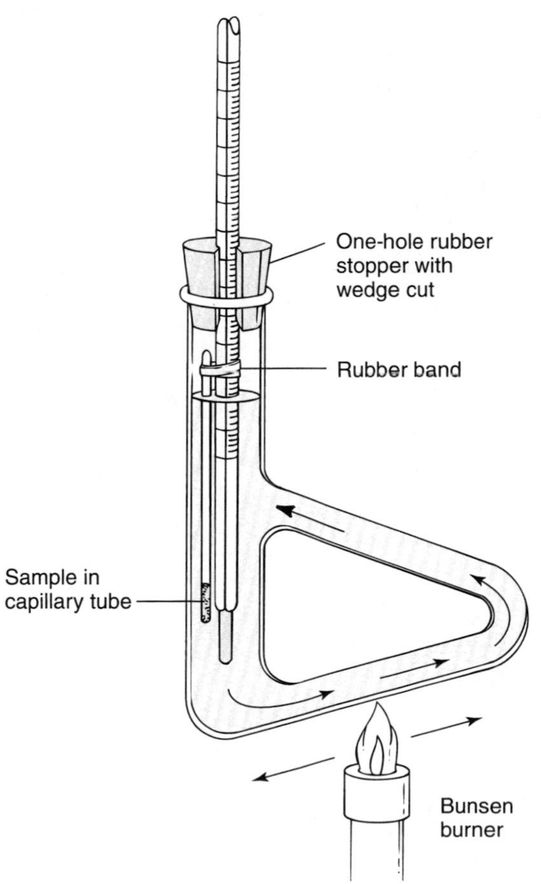

Figure 9.3 A Thiele tube.

bution through the oil in the tube. The sidearm of the tube is designed to generate these convection currents and thus transfer the heat from the flame evenly and rapidly throughout the oil. The sample, which is in a capillary tube attached to the thermometer, is held by a rubber band or a thin slice of rubber tubing. It is important that this rubber band be above the level of the oil (allowing for expansion of the oil on heating) so that the oil does not soften the rubber and allow the capillary tubing to fall into the oil. If a cork or a rubber stopper is used to hold the thermometer, a triangular wedge should be sliced in it to allow pressure equalization.

The Thiele tube is usually heated by a microburner. During the heating, the rate of temperature increase should be regulated. Hold the burner by its cool base and, using a low flame, move the burner slowly back and forth along the bottom of the arm of the Thiele tube. If the heating is too fast, remove the burner for a few seconds and then resume heating. The rate of heating should be *slow* near the melting point (about 1°C per minute) to ensure that the temperature increase is not faster than the rate at which heat can be transferred to the sample being observed. At the melting point, it is necessary that the mercury in the thermometer and the sample in the capillary tube be at temperature equilibrium.

9.7 DETERMINING THE MELTING POINT—ELECTRICAL INSTRUMENTS

Three types of electrically heated melting-point instruments are illustrated in Figure 9.4. In each case, the melting-point tube is filled as described in Section 9.5 and placed in a holder located just behind the magnifying eyepiece. The apparatus is operated by moving the switch to the ON position, adjusting the potentiometric control dial for the desired rate of heating, and observing the sample through the magnifying eyepiece. The temperature is read from a thermometer or, in the most modern instruments, from a digital display attached to a thermocouple. Your instructor will demonstrate and explain the type used in your laboratory.

Most electrically heated instruments do not heat or increase the temperature of the sample linearly. Although the rate of increase may be linear in the early stages of heating, it usually decreases and leads to a constant temperature at some upper limit. The upper-limit temperature is determined by the setting of the heating control. Thus, a family of heating curves is usually obtained for various control settings, as shown in Figure 9.5. The four hypothetical curves shown (1–4) might correspond to different control settings. For a compound melting at temperature t_1, the setting corresponding to curve 3 would be ideal. In the beginning of the curve, the temperature is increasing too rapidly to allow determination of an accurate melting point, but after the change in slope, the temperature increase will have slowed to a more usable rate.

If the melting point of the sample is unknown, you can often save time by preparing two samples for melting-point determination. With one sample, you can rapidly determine a crude melting-point value. Then repeat the experiment more carefully using the second sample. For the second determination, you already have an approximate idea of what the melting-point temperature should be, and a proper rate of heating can be chosen.

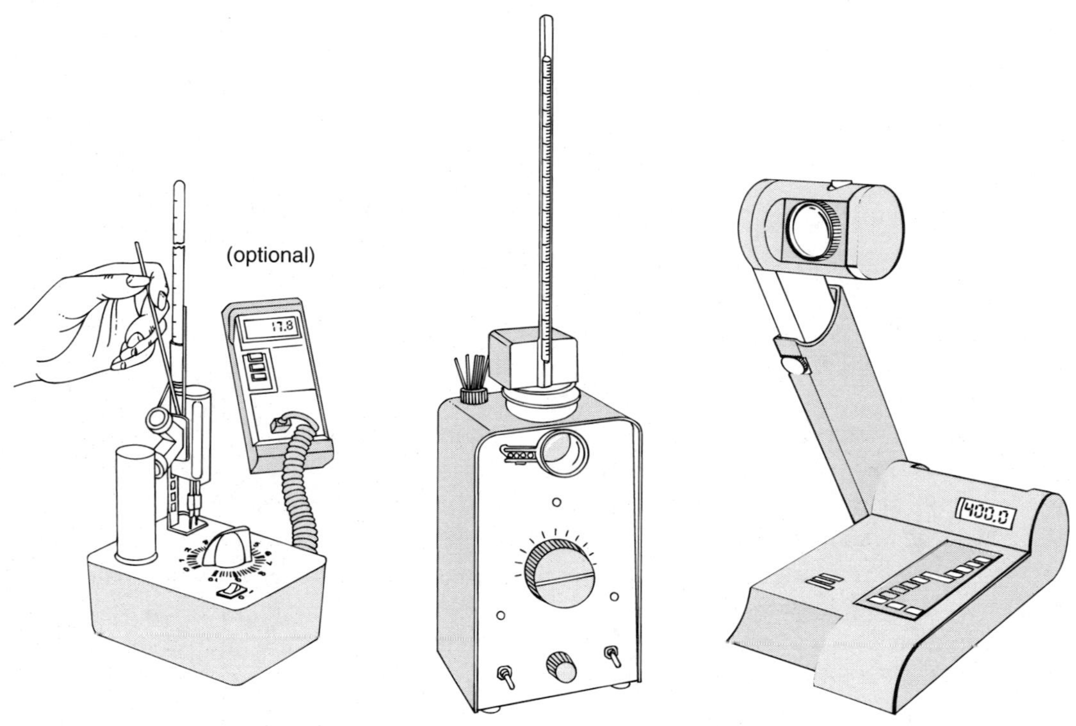

Figure 9.4 Melting-point apparatus.

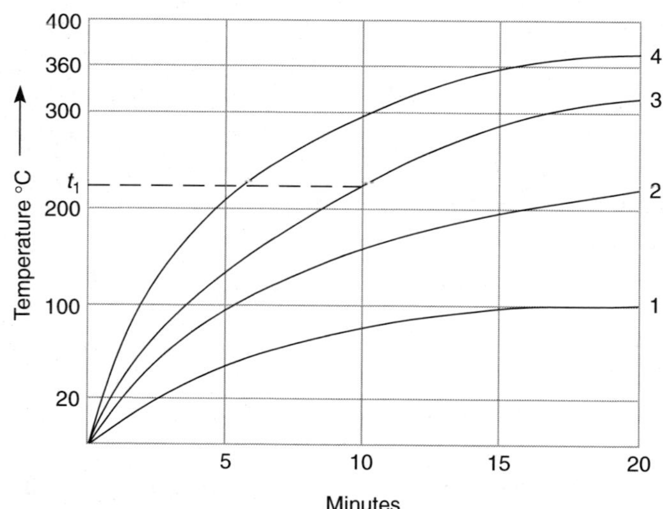

Figure 9.5 Heating-rate curves.

When measuring temperatures above 150°C, thermometer errors can become significant. For an accurate melting point with a high-melting solid, you may wish to apply a **stem correction** to the thermometer as described in Technique 13, Section 13.4. An even better solution is to calibrate the thermometer as described in Section 9.9.

9.8 DECOMPOSITION, DISCOLORATION, SOFTENING, SHRINKAGE, AND SUBLIMATION

Many solid substances undergo some degree of unusual behavior before melting. At times it may be difficult to distinguish these types of behavior from actual melting. You should learn, through experience, how to recognize melting and how to distinguish it from decomposition, discoloration, and particularly, softening and shrinkage.

Some compounds decompose on melting. This decomposition is usually evidenced by discoloration of the sample. Frequently, this decomposition point is a reliable physical property to be used in lieu of an actual melting point. Such decomposition points are indicated in tables of melting points by placing the symbol *d* immediately after the listed temperature. An example of a decomposition point is thiamine hydrochloride, whose melting point would be listed as 248°d, indicating that this substance melts with decomposition at 248°C. When decomposition is a result of reaction with the oxygen in air, it may be avoided by determining the melting point in a sealed, evacuated melting-point tube.

Figure 9.6 shows two simple methods of evacuating a packed tube. Method A uses an ordinary melting-point tube, and method B constructs the melting-point tube from a disposable Pasteur pipet. Before using method B, be sure to determine that the tip of the pipet will fit into the sample holder in your melting-point instrument.

Method A. In method A, a hole is punched through a rubber septum using a large pin or a small nail, and the capillary tube is inserted from the inside, sealed end first. The septum is placed over a piece of glass tubing connected to a vacuum line. After the tube is evacuated, the upper end of the tube may be sealed by heating and pulling it closed.

Method B. In method B, the thin section of a 9-inch Pasteur pipet is used to construct the melting-point tube. Carefully seal the tip of the pipet using a flame. Be sure to hold the tip *upward* as you seal it. This will prevent water vapor from condensing inside the pipet. When the sealed pipet has cooled, the sample may be added through the open end using a microspatula. A small wire may be used to compress the sample into the closed tip. (If your melting-point apparatus has a vibrator, it may be used in place of the wire to simplify the packing.) When the sample is in place, the pipet is connected to the vacuum line with tubing and evacuated. The evacuated sample tube is sealed by heating it with a flame and pulling it closed.

Some substances begin to decompose *below* their melting points. Thermally unstable substances may undergo elimination reactions or anhydride formation reactions during heating. The decomposition products formed represent impurities in the original sample, so the melting point of the substance may be lowered due to their presence.

It is normal for many compounds to soften or shrink immediately before melting. Such behavior represents not decomposition but a change in the crystal structure or a mixing with impurities. Some substances "sweat," or release solvent of crystallization, before melting. These changes do not indicate the beginning of melting. Actual melting begins

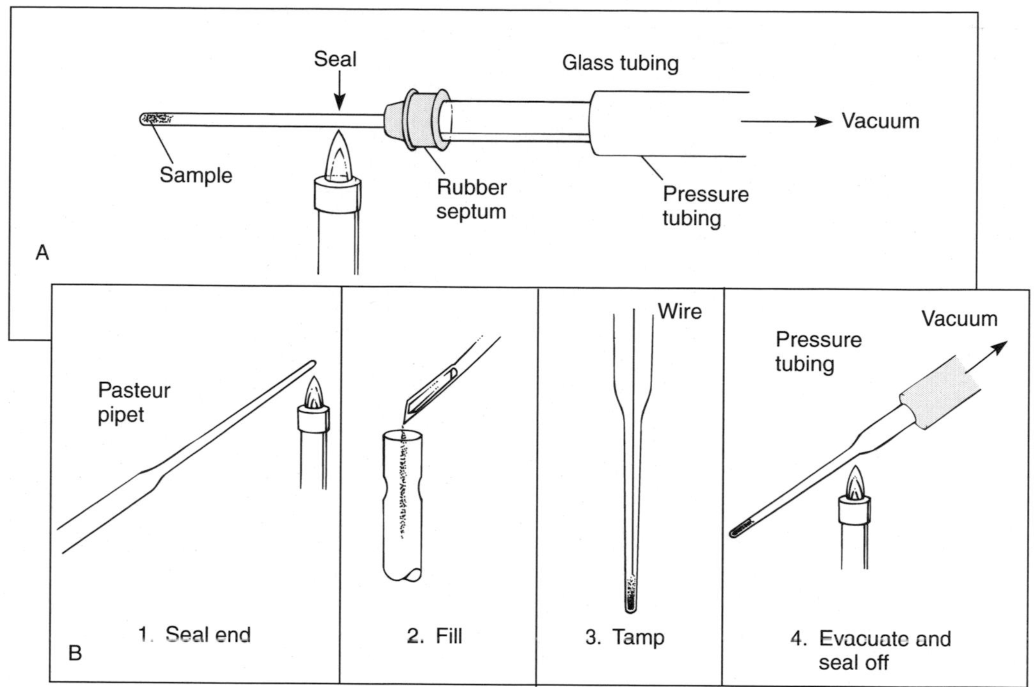

Figure 9.6 Evacuation and sealing of a melting-point capillary.

when the first drop of liquid becomes visible, and the melting range continues until the temperature is reached at which all the solid has been converted to the liquid state. With experience, you soon learn to distinguish between softening, or "sweating," and actual melting. If you wish, the temperature of the onset of softening or sweating may be reported as a part of your melting-point range: 211°C (softens), 223–225°C (melts).

Some solid substances have such a high vapor pressure that they sublime at or below their melting points. In many handbooks, the sublimation temperature is listed along with the melting point. The symbols *sub, subl,* and sometimes *s* are used to designate a substance that sublimes. In such cases, the melting-point determination must be performed in a sealed capillary tube to avoid loss of the sample. The simplest way to accomplish sealing a packed tube is to heat the open end of the tube in a flame and pull it closed with tweezers or forceps. A better way, although more difficult to master, is to heat the center of the tube in a small flame, rotating it about its axis, and keeping the tube straight, until the center collapses. If this is not done quickly, the sample may melt or sublime while you are working. With the smaller chamber, the sample will not be able to migrate to the cool top of the tube that may be above the viewing area. Figure 9.7 illustrates the method.

9.9 THERMOMETER CALIBRATION

When a melting-point or boiling-point determination has been completed, you expect to obtain a result that exactly duplicates the result recorded in a handbook or in the original literature. It is not unusual, however, to find a discrepancy of several degrees from the lit-

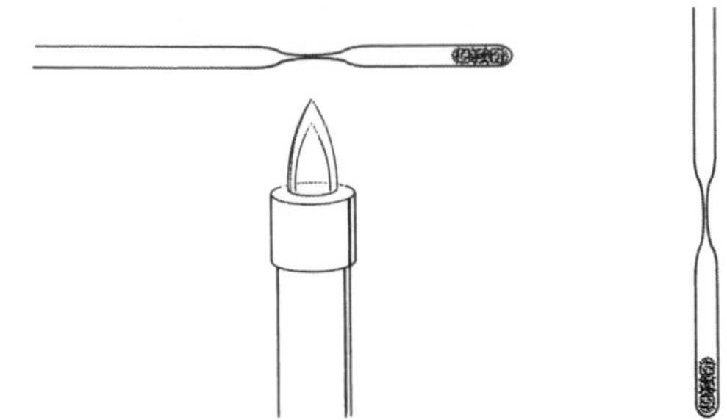

Figure 9.7 Sealing a tube for a substance that sublimes.

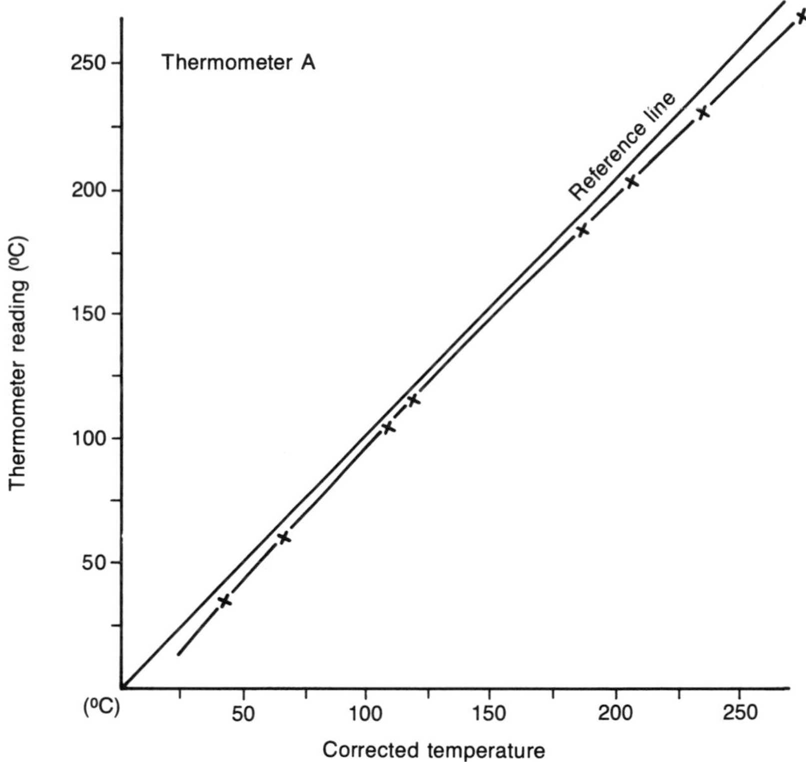

Figure 9.8 A thermometer-calibration curve.

erature value. Such a discrepancy does not necessarily indicate that the experiment was incorrectly performed or that the material is impure; rather, it may indicate that the thermometer used for the determination was slightly in error. Most thermometers do not measure the temperature with perfect accuracy.

To determine accurate values, you must calibrate the thermometer that is used. This calibration is done by determining the melting points of a variety of standard substances with the thermometer. A plot is drawn of the observed temperature vs. the published value of each standard substance. A smooth line is drawn through the points to complete the chart. A correction chart prepared in this way is shown in Figure 9.8. This chart is used to correct

TABLE 9.1 Melting-Point Standards

Compound	Melting Point (°C)
Ice (solid–liquid water)	0
Acetanilide	115
Benzamide	128
Urea	132
Succinic acid	189
3,5-Dinitrobenzoic acid	205

any melting point determined with that particular thermometer. Each thermometer requires its own calibration curve. A list of suitable standard substances for calibrating thermometers is provided in Table 9.1. The standard substances, of course, must be pure in order for the corrections to be valid.

PROBLEMS

1. Two substances, A and B, have the same melting point. How can you determine if they are the same without using any form of spectroscopy? Explain in detail.
2. Using Figure 9.5, determine which heating curve would be most appropriate for a substance with a melting point of about 150°C.
3. What steps can you take to determine the melting point of a substance that sublimes before it melts?
4. A compound melting at 134°C was suspected to be either aspirin (mp 135°C) or urea (mp 133°C). Explain how you could determine whether one of these two suspected compounds was identical to the unknown compound without using any form of spectroscopy.
5. An unknown compound gave a melting point of 230°C. When the molten liquid solidified, the melting point was redetermined and found to be 131°C. Give a possible explanation for this discrepancy.

TECHNIQUE 12

Extractions, Separations, and Drying Agents

Part A. Theory

12.1 EXTRACTION

Transferring a solute from one solvent into another is called **extraction,** or more precisely, liquid–liquid extraction. The solute is extracted from one solvent into the other because the solute is more soluble in the second solvent than in the first. The two solvents must not be **miscible** (mix freely), and they must form two separate **phases** or layers, in order for this procedure to work. Extraction is used in many ways in organic chemistry. Many **natural products** (organic chemicals that exist in nature) are present in animal and plant tissues having high water content. Extracting these tissues with a water-immiscible solvent is useful for isolating the natural products. Often, diethyl ether (commonly referred to as "ether") is used for this purpose. Sometimes, alternative water-immiscible solvents such as hexane, petroleum ether, ligroin, and methylene chloride are used. For instance, caffeine, a natural product, can be extracted from an aqueous tea solution by shaking the solution successively with several portions of methylene chloride.

A generalized extraction process, using a specialized piece of glassware called a **separatory funnel,** is illustrated in Figure 12.1. The first solvent contains a mixture of black-and-white molecules (Figure 12.1A). A second solvent that is not miscible with the first is added. After the separatory funnel is capped and shaken, the layers separate. In this example, the second solvent (shaded) is less dense than the first, so it becomes the top layer (Figure 12.1B). Because of differences in physical properties, the white molecules are more soluble in the second solvent, whereas the black molecules are more soluble in the first solvent. Most of the white molecules are in the upper layer, but there are some black molecules there, too. Likewise, most of the black molecules are in the lower layer. However, there are still a few white molecules in this lower phase. The lower phase may be separated from the upper phase by opening the stopcock at the bottom of the separatory funnel and allowing the lower layer to drain into a beaker (Figure 12.1C). In this example, notice that it was not possible to effect a complete separation of the two types of molecules with a single extraction. This is a common occurrence in organic chemistry.

Many substances are soluble in both water and organic solvents. Water can be used to

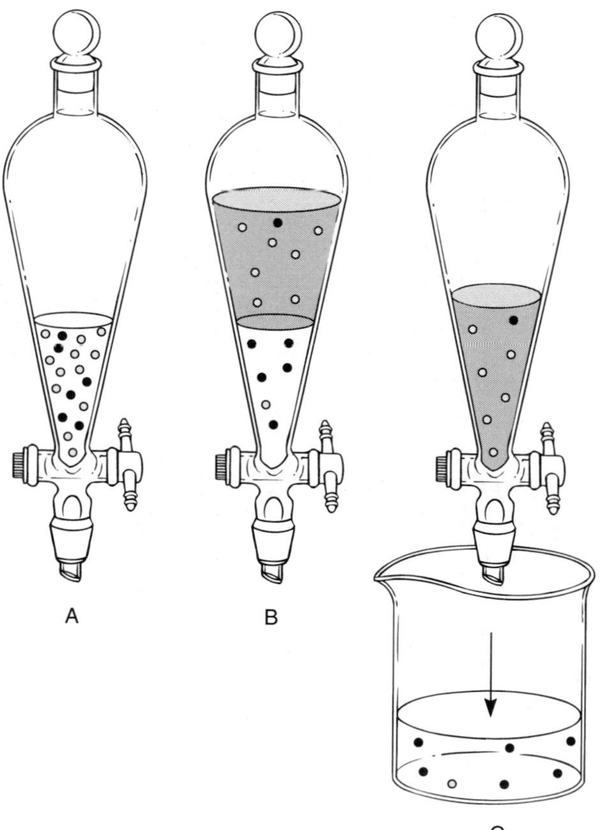

A. Solvent 1 contains a mixture of molecules (black and white).

B. After shaking with solvent 2 (shaded), most of the white molecules have been extracted into the new solvent. The white molecules are more soluble in the second solvent, whereas the black molecules are more soluble in the original solvent.

C. With removal of the lower phase, the black and white molecules have been partially separated.

Figure 12.1 The extraction process.

extract, or "wash," water-soluble impurities from an organic reaction mixture. To carry out a "washing" operation, you add water and an immiscible organic solvent to the reaction mixture contained in a separatory funnel. After stoppering the funnel and shaking it, you allow the organic layer and the aqueous (water) layer to separate. A water wash removes highly polar and water-soluble materials, such as sulfuric acid, hydrochloric acid, and sodium hydroxide, from the organic layer. The washing operation helps to purify the desired organic compound present in the original reaction mixture.

12.2 DISTRIBUTION COEFFICIENT

When a solution (solute A in solvent 1) is shaken with a second solvent (solvent 2) with which it is not miscible, the solute distributes itself between the two liquid phases. When the two phases have separated again into two distinct solvent layers, an equilibrium will have been achieved such that the ratio of the concentrations of the solute in each layer defines a constant. The constant, called the **distribution coefficient** (or partition coefficient) K, is defined by

$$K = \frac{C_2}{C_1}$$

where C_1 and C_2 are the concentrations at equilibrium, in grams per liter or milligrams per milliliter of solute A in solvent 1 and in solvent 2, respectively. This relationship is a ratio of two concentrations and is independent of the actual amounts of the two solvents mixed. The distribution coefficient has a constant value for each solute considered and depends on the nature of the solvents used in each case.

Not all the solute will be transferred to solvent 2 in a single extraction unless K is very large. Usually, it takes several extractions to remove all the solute from solvent 1. In extracting a solute from a solution, it is always better to use several small portions of the second solvent than to make a single extraction with a large portion. Suppose, as an illustration, a particular extraction proceeds with a distribution coefficient of 10. The system consists of 5.0 g of organic compound dissolved in 100 mL of water (solvent 1). In this illustration, the effectiveness of three 50-mL extractions with ether (solvent 2) is compared with one 150-mL extraction with ether. In the first 50-mL extraction, the amount extracted into the ether layer is given by the following calculation. The amount of compound remaining in the aqueous phase is given by x.

$$K = 10 = \frac{C_2}{C_1} = \frac{\left(\dfrac{5.0 - x}{50}\ \dfrac{\text{g}}{\text{mL ether}}\right)}{\left(\dfrac{x}{100}\ \dfrac{\text{g}}{\text{mL H}_2\text{O}}\right)}; \qquad 10 = \frac{(5.0 - x)(100)}{50x}$$

$$\begin{aligned} 500x &= 500 - 100x \\ 600x &= 500 \\ x &= 0.83 \text{ g remaining in the aqueous phase} \\ 5.0 - x &= 4.17 \text{ g in the ether layer} \end{aligned}$$

As a check on the calculation, it is possible to substitute the value 0.83 g for x in the original equation and demonstrate that the concentration in the ether layer divided by the concentration in the water layer equals the distribution coefficient.

$$\frac{\left(\dfrac{5.0 - x}{50} \dfrac{\text{g}}{\text{mL ether}}\right)}{\left(\dfrac{x}{100} \dfrac{\text{g}}{\text{mL H}_2\text{O}}\right)} = \frac{\dfrac{4.17}{50}}{\dfrac{0.83}{100}} = \frac{0.083 \text{ g/mL}}{0.0083 \text{ g/mL}} = 10 = K$$

The second extraction with another 50-mL portion of fresh ether is performed on the aqueous phase, which now contains 0.83 g of the solute. The amount of solute extracted is given by the calculation shown in Figure 12.2. Also shown in the figure is a calculation for a third extraction with another 50-mL portion of ether. This third extraction will transfer 0.12 g of solute into the ether layer, leaving 0.02 g of solute remaining in the water layer. A total of 4.98 g of solute will be extracted into the combined ether layers, and 0.02 g will remain in the aqueous phase.

Figure 12.3 shows the result of a *single* extraction with 150 mL of ether. As shown there, 4.69 g of solute were extracted into the ether layer, leaving 0.31 g of compound in

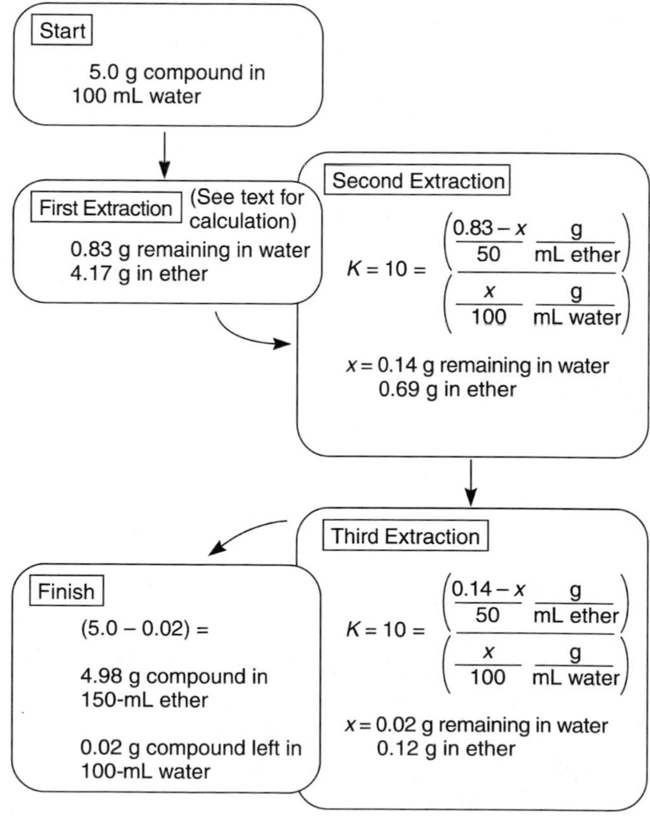

Figure 12.2 The result of extraction of 5.0 g of compound in 100 mL of water by three successive 50-mL portions of ether. Compare this result with that of Figure 12.3.

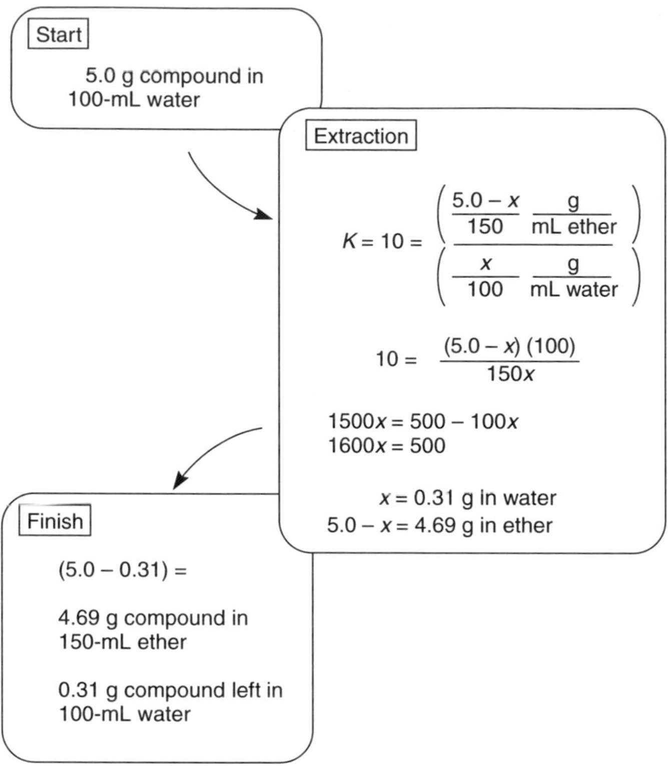

Figure 12.3 The result of extraction of 5.0 g of compound in 100 mL of water with one 150-mL portion of ether. Compare this result with that of Figure 12.2.

the aqueous phase. Three successive 50-mL ether extractions (Figure 12.2) succeeded in removing 0.29 g more solute from the aqueous phase than using one 150-mL portion of either (Figure 12.3). This differential represents 5.8% of the total material.

> **Note:** Several extractions with smaller amounts of solvent are more effective than one extraction with a larger amount of solvent.

12.3 CHOOSING AN EXTRACTION METHOD AND A SOLVENT

Three types of apparatus are used for extractions: conical vials, centrifuge tubes, and separatory funnels (Figure 12.4). Conical vials may be used with volumes of less than 4 mL; volumes of up to 10 mL may be handled in centrifuge tubes. A centrifuge tube equipped with a screw cap is particularly useful for extractions. Conical vials and centrifuge tubes are most often used in microscale experiments, although a centrifuge tube may also be used in some macroscale applications. The separatory funnel is used with larger volumes of liquid in macroscale experiments. The separatory funnel is discussed in Part B and the conical vial and centrifuge tube are discussed in Part C.

TABLE 12.1 Densities of Common Extraction Solvents

Solvent	Density (g/mL)
Ligroin	0.67–0.69
Diethyl ether	0.71
Toluene	0.87
Water	1.00
Methylene chloride	1.330

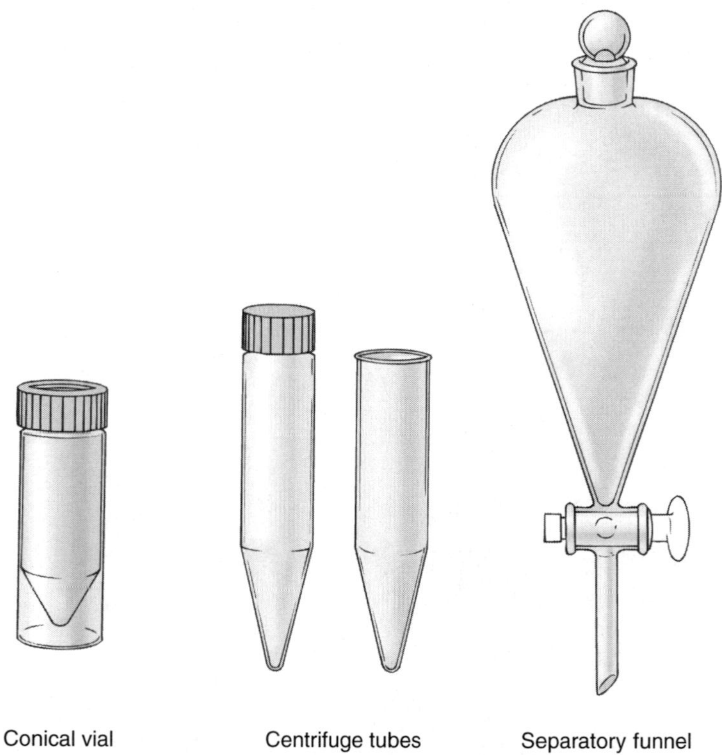

Figure 12.4 The apparatus used in extraction.

Most extractions consist of an aqueous phase and an organic phase. To extract a substance from an aqueous phase, you must use an organic solvent that is not miscible with water. Table 12.1 lists a number of the common organic solvents that are not miscible with water and are used for extractions.

Solvents that have a density less than that of water (1.00 g/mL) will separate as the top layer when shaken with water. Solvents that have a density greater than that of water will separate into the lower layer. For instance, diethyl ether ($d = 0.71$ g/mL) when shaken with water will form the upper layer, whereas methylene chloride ($d = 1.33$ g/mL) will form the lower layer. When an extraction is performed, slightly different methods are used to separate the lower layer (whether or not it is the aqueous layer or the organic layer) than to separate the upper layer.

Part B. Macroscale Extraction

12.4 THE SEPARATORY FUNNEL

A separatory funnel is illustrated in Figure 12.5. It is the piece of equipment used for carrying out extractions with medium to large quantities of material. To fill the separatory funnel, support it in an iron ring attached to a ring stand. Since it is easy to break a separa-

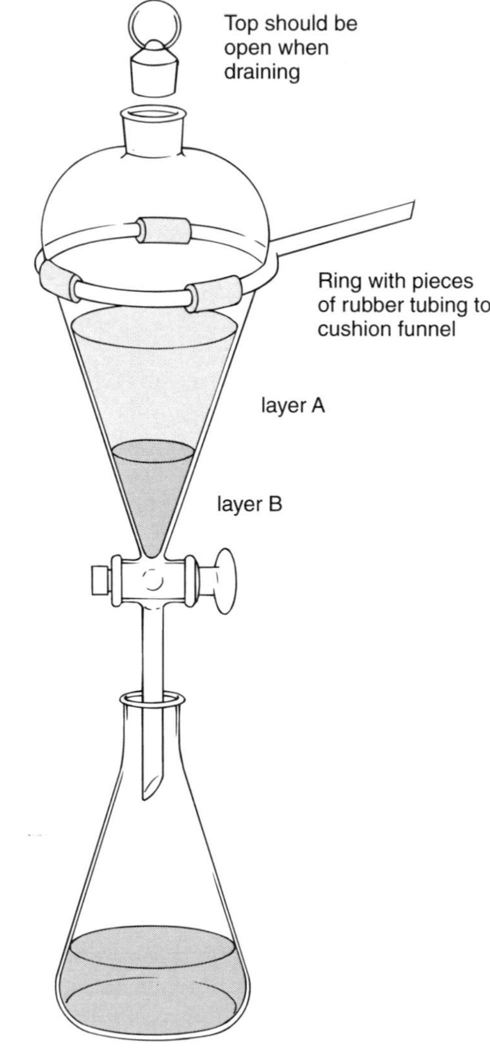

Figure 12.5 A separatory funnel.

tory funnel by "clanking" it against the metal ring, pieces of rubber tubing are often attached to the ring to cushion the funnel, as shown in Figure 12.5. These are short pieces of tubing cut to a length of about 3 cm and slit open along their length. When slipped over the inside of the ring, they cushion the funnel in its resting place.

When beginning an extraction, first close the stopcock. (Don't forget!) Using a powder funnel (wide bore) placed in the top of the separatory funnel, fill the funnel with both the solution to be extracted and the extraction solvent. Swirl the funnel gently by holding it by its upper neck and then stopper it. Pick up the separatory funnel with two hands and hold it as shown in Figure 12.6. Hold the stopper in place firmly because the two immiscible liquids will build pressure when they mix, and this pressure may force the stopper out of the separatory funnel. To release this pressure, vent the funnel by holding it upside down (hold the stopper securely) and slowly open the stopcock. Usually, the rush of vapors out of the opening can be heard. Continue shaking and venting until the "whoosh" is no longer audible. Now continue shaking the mixture gently for about 1 minute. This can be done by inverting the funnel in a rocking motion repeatedly or, if the formation of an emulsion is not a problem (see Section 12.10, p. 716), by shaking the funnel more vigorously for less time.

> **Note:** There is an art to shaking and venting a separatory funnel correctly, and it usually seems awkward to the beginner. The technique is best learned by observing a person, such as your instructor, who is thoroughly familiar with the separatory funnel's use.

Figure 12.6 The correct way of shaking and venting a separatory funnel.

When you have finished mixing the liquids, place the separatory funnel in the iron ring and remove the top stopper immediately. The two immiscible solvents separate into two layers after a short time, and they can be separated from one another by draining most of the lower layer through the stopcock.[1] Allow a few minutes to pass so that any of the lower phase adhering to the inner glass surfaces of the separatory funnel can drain down. Open the stopcock again and allow the remainder of the lower layer to drain until the interface between the upper and lower phases just begins to enter the bore of the stopcock. At this moment, close the stopcock and remove the remaining upper layer by pouring it from the top opening of the separatory funnel.

Note: To minimize contamination of the two layers, the lower layer should always be drained from the bottom of the separatory funnel and the upper layer poured out from the top of the funnel.

When methylene chloride is used as the extracting solvent with an aqueous phase, it will settle to the bottom and be removed through the stopcock. The aqueous layer remains in the funnel. A second extraction of the remaining aqueous layer with fresh methylene chloride may be needed.

With a diethyl ether (ether) extraction of an aqueous phase, the organic layer will form on top. Remove the lower aqueous layer through the stopcock and pour the upper ether layer from the top of the separatory funnel. Pour the aqueous phase back into the separatory funnel and extract it a second time with fresh ether. The combined organic phases must be dried using a suitable drying agent (Section 12.9) before the solvent is removed.

The usual macroscale procedure requires the use of a 125-mL or 250-mL separatory funnel. For microscale procedures, a 60-mL or 125-mL separatory funnel is recommended. Because of surface tension, water has a difficult time draining from the bore of smaller funnels.

Part C. Microscale Extraction

12.5 THE CONICAL VIAL—SEPARATING THE LOWER LAYER

Before using a conical vial for an extraction, make sure that the capped conical vial does not leak when shaken. To do this, place some water in the conical vial, place the Teflon liner in the cap, and screw the cap securely onto the conical vial. Shake the vial vigorously and check for leaks. Conical vials that are used for extractions must not be chipped on the edge of the vial or they will not seal adequately. If there is a leak, try tightening the cap or

[1] A common error is to try to drain the separatory funnel without removing the top stopper. Under this circumstance, the funnel will not drain because a partial vacuum is created in the space above the liquid.

replacing the Teflon liner with another one. Sometimes it helps to use the silicone rubber side of the liner to seal the conical vial. Some laboratories are supplied with Teflon stoppers that fit into the 5-mL conical vials. You may find that this stopper eliminates leakage.

When shaking the conical vial, do it gently at first in a rocking motion. When it is clear that an emulsion will not form (see Section 12.10, p. 716), you can shake it more vigorously.

In some cases, adequate mixing can be achieved by spinning your microspatula for at least 10 minutes in the conical vial. Another technique of mixing involves drawing the mixture up into a Pasteur pipet and squirting it rapidly back into the vial. Repeat this process for at least 5 minutes to obtain an adequate extraction.

The 5-mL conical vial is the most useful piece of equipment for carrying out extractions on a microscale level. In this section, we consider the method for removing the lower layer. A concrete example would be the extraction of a desired product from an aqueous layer using methylene chloride (d = 1.33 g/mL) as the extraction solvent. Methods for removal of the upper layer are discussed in the next section.

Note: Always place a conical vial in a small beaker to prevent the vial from falling over.

Removing the Lower Layer. Suppose that we extract an aqueous solution with methylene chloride. This solvent is denser than water and will settle to the bottom of the conical vial. Use the following procedure, which is illustrated in Figure 12.7, to remove the lower layer.

1. Place the aqueous phase containing the dissolved product into a 5-mL conical vial (Figure 12.7A).
2. Add about 1 mL of methylene chloride, cap the vial, and shake the mixture gently at first in a rocking motion and then more vigorously when it is clear that an emulsion will not form. Vent or unscrew the cap slightly to release the pressure in the vial. Allow the phases to separate completely so that you can detect two distinct layers in the vial. The organic phase will be the lower layer in the vial (Figure 12.7B). If necessary, tap the vial with your finger or stir the mixture gently if some of the organic phase is suspended in the aqueous layer.
3. Prepare a Pasteur filter-tip pipet (Technique 8, Section 8.6, p. 655) using a 5¾-inch pipet. Attach a 2-mL rubber bulb to the pipet, depress the bulb, and insert the pipet into the vial so that the tip touches the bottom (Figure 12.7C). The filter-tip pipet gives you better control in removing the lower layer. In some cases, however, you may be able to use a Pasteur pipet (no filter tip), but considerably more care must be taken to avoid losing liquid from the pipet during the transfer operation. With experience, you should be able to judge how much to squeeze the bulb to draw in the desired volume of liquid.
4. Slowly draw the lower layer (methylene chloride) into the pipet in such a way that you exclude the aqueous layer and any emulsion (Section 12.10) that might be at the interface between the layers (Figure 12.7D). Be sure to keep the tip of the pipet squarely in the V at the bottom of the vial.

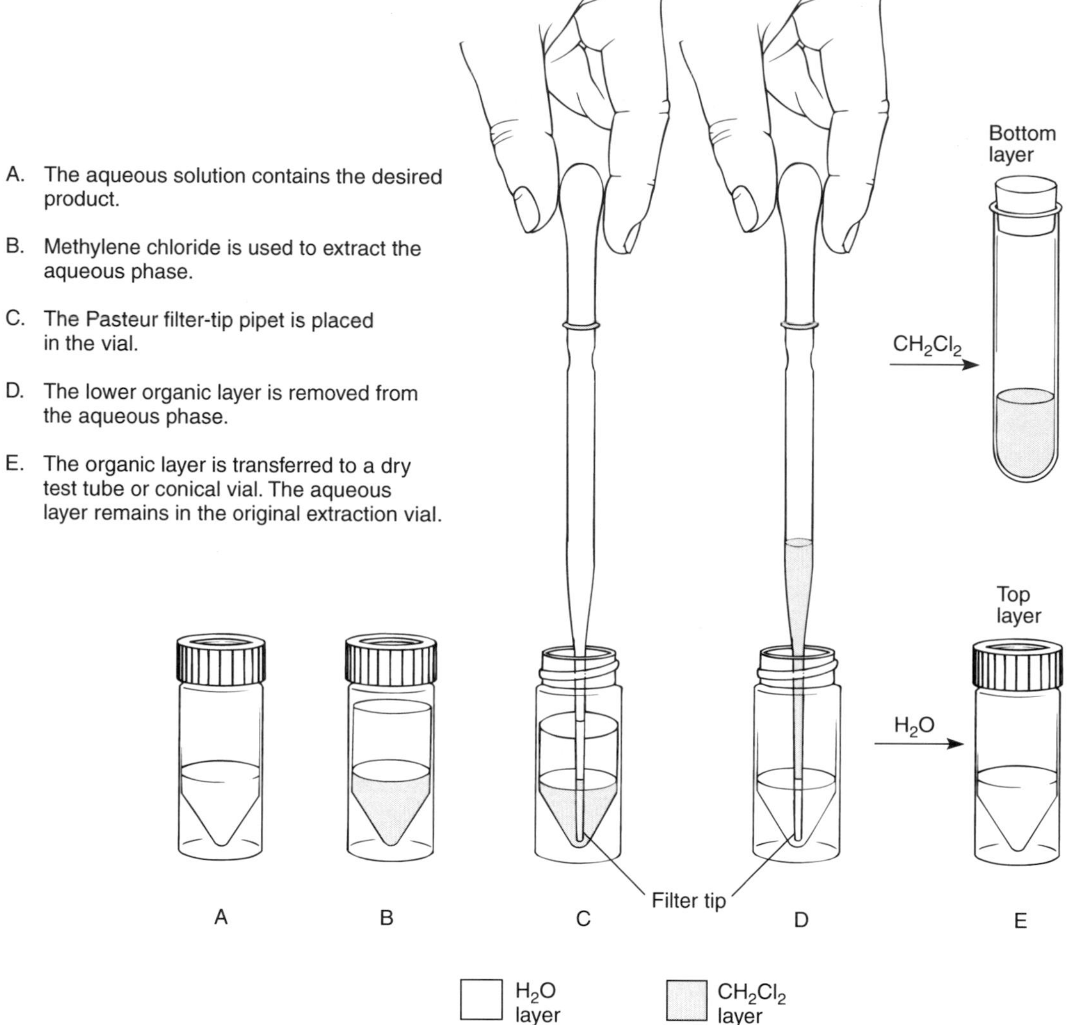

A. The aqueous solution contains the desired product.
B. Methylene chloride is used to extract the aqueous phase.
C. The Pasteur filter-tip pipet is placed in the vial.
D. The lower organic layer is removed from the aqueous phase.
E. The organic layer is transferred to a dry test tube or conical vial. The aqueous layer remains in the original extraction vial.
Bottom layer
CH_2Cl_2
Top layer
H_2O
Filter tip
A
B
C
D
E
H_2O layer
CH_2Cl_2 layer

Figure 12.7 Extraction of an aqueous solution using a solvent denser than water: methylene chloride.

5. Transfer the withdrawn organic phase into a *dry* test tube or another *dry* conical vial if one is available. It is best to have the test tube or vial located next to the extraction vial. Hold the vials in the same hand between your index finger and thumb, as shown in Figure 12.8. This avoids messy and disastrous transfers. The aqueous layer (upper layer) is left in the original conical vial (Figure 12.7E).

In performing an actual extraction in the laboratory, you would extract the aqueous phase with a second 1-mL portion of fresh methylene chloride to achieve a more complete extraction. Steps 2–5 would be repeated, and the organic layers from both extractions would be combined. In some cases, you may need to extract a third time with yet another 1-mL portion of methylene chloride. Again, the methylene chloride would be combined with the other extracts. The overall process would use three 1-mL portions of methylene chloride to transfer the product from the

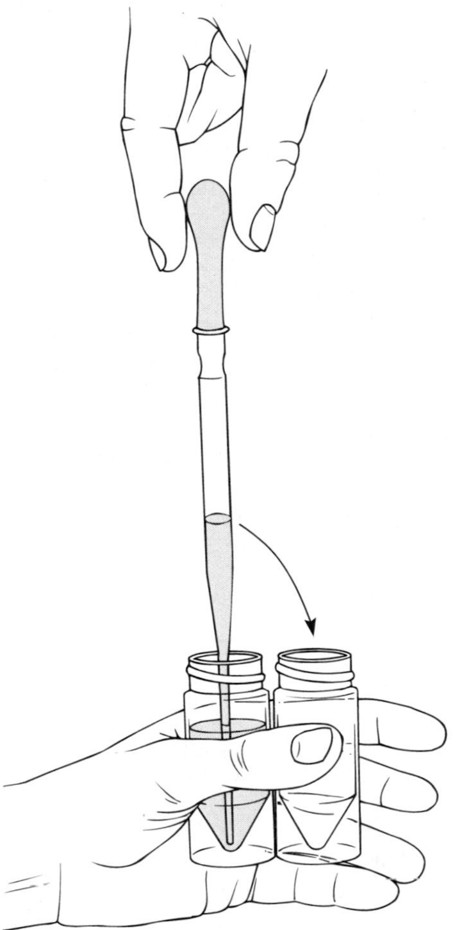

Figure 12.8 Method for holding vials while transferring liquids.

water layer into methylene chloride. Sometimes you will see the statement "extract the aqueous phase with three 1-mL portions of methylene chloride" in an experimental procedure. This statement describes in a shorter fashion the process described previously. Finally, the methylene chloride extracts will contain some water and must be dried with a drying agent as indicated in Section 12.9.

Note: If an organic solvent has been extracted with water, it should be dried with a drying agent (see Section 12.9) before proceeding.

In this example, we extracted water with the heavy solvent methylene chloride and removed it as the lower layer. If you were extracting a light solvent (for instance, diethyl ether) with water and you wished to keep the water layer, the water would be the lower layer and would be removed using the same procedure. You would not dry the water layer, however.

12.6 THE CONICAL VIAL—SEPARATING THE UPPER LAYER

In this section, we consider the method used when you wish to remove the upper layer. A concrete example would be the extraction of a desired product from an aqueous layer using diethyl ether ($d = 0.71$ g/mL) as the extraction solvent. Methods for removing the lower layer were discussed previously.

> **Note:** Always place a conical vial in a small beaker to prevent the vial from falling over.

Removing the Upper Layer. Suppose we extract an aqueous solution with diethyl ether (ether). This solvent is less dense than water and will rise to the top of the conical vial. Use the following procedure, which is illustrated in Figure 12.9, to remove the upper layer.

1. Place the aqueous phase containing the dissolved product in a 5-mL conical vial (Figure 12.9A).
2. Add about 1 mL of ether, cap the vial, and shake the mixture vigorously. Vent or unscrew the cap slightly to release the pressure in the vial. Allow the phases to separate completely so that you can detect two distinct layers in the vial. The ether phase will be the upper layer in the vial (Figure 12.9B).
3. Prepare a Pasteur filter-tip pipet (Technique 8, Section 8.6, p. 655) using a 5¾-inch pipet. Attach a 2-mL rubber bulb to the pipet, depress the bulb, and insert the pipet into the vial so that the tip touches the bottom. The filter-tip pipet gives you better control in removing the lower layer. In some cases, however, you may be able to use a Pasteur pipet (no filter tip), but considerably more care must be taken to avoid losing liquid from the pipet during the transfer operation. With experience, you should be able to judge how much to squeeze the bulb to draw in the desired volume of liquid. Slowly draw the lower *aqueous* layer into the pipet. Be sure to keep the tip of the pipet squarely in the V at the bottom of the vial (Figure 12.9C).
4. Transfer the withdrawn aqueous phase into a test tube or another conical vial for temporary storage. It is best to have the test tube or vial located next to the extraction vial. This avoids messy and disastrous transfers. Hold the vials in the same hand between your index finger and thumb, as shown in Figure 12.8. The ether layer is left behind in the conical vial (Figure 12.9D).
5. The ether phase remaining in the original conical vial should be transferred with a Pasteur pipet into a test tube for storage and the aqueous phase returned to the original conical vial (Figure 12.9E).

In performing an actual extraction, you would extract the aqueous phase with another 1-mL portion of fresh ether to achieve a more complete extraction. Steps 2–5 would be repeated, and the organic layers from both extractions would be combined in the test tube. In some cases, you may need to extract the aqueous layer a third time with yet another 1-mL portion of ether. Again, the ether would be combined with the other two layers. This over-

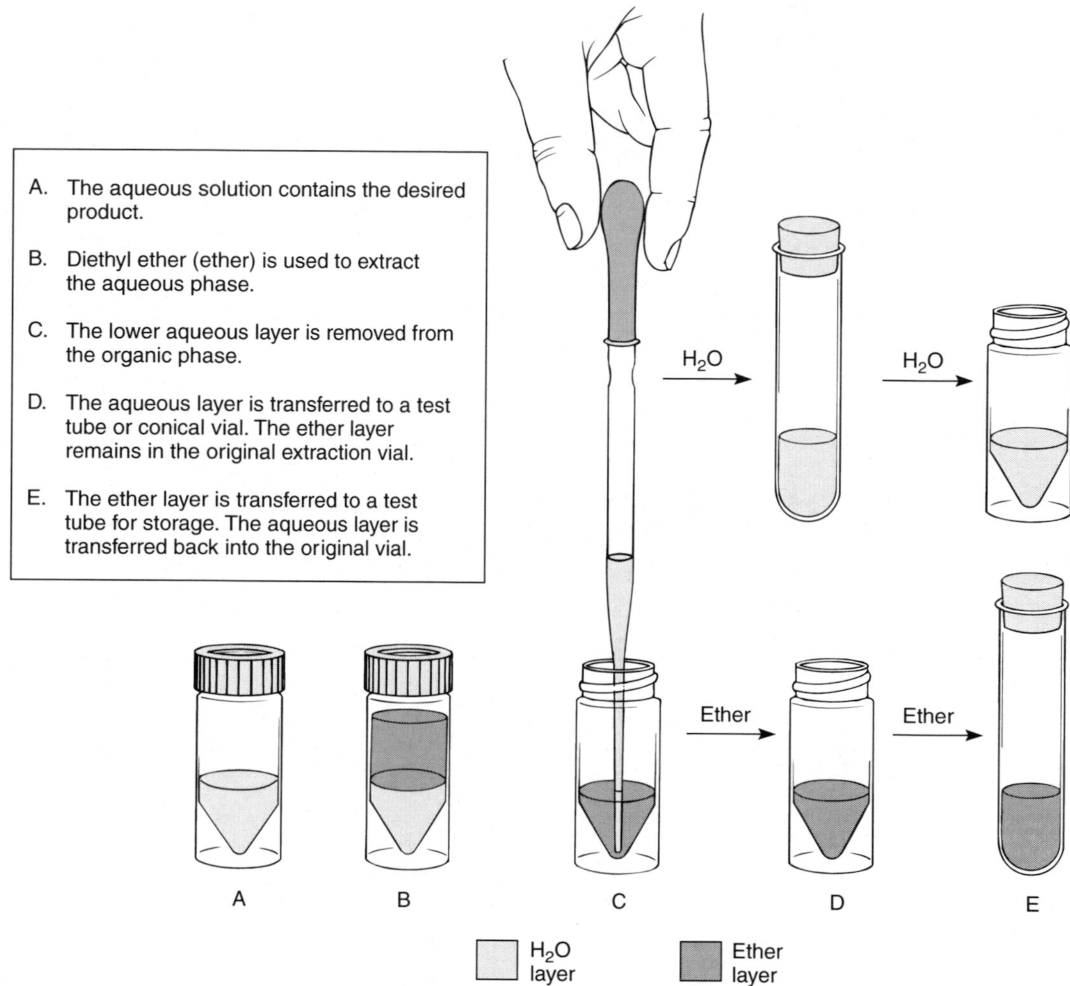

A. The aqueous solution contains the desired product.
B. Diethyl ether (ether) is used to extract the aqueous phase.
C. The lower aqueous layer is removed from the organic phase.
D. The aqueous layer is transferred to a test tube or conical vial. The ether layer remains in the original extraction vial.
E. The ether layer is transferred to a test tube for storage. The aqueous layer is transferred back into the original vial.
H_2O
H_2O
Ether
Ether
A
B
C
D
E
H_2O layer
Ether layer

Figure 12.9 Extraction of an aqueous solution using a solvent less dense than water: diethyl ether.

all process uses three 1-mL portions of ether to transfer the product from the water layer into ether. The ether extracts contain some water and must be dried with a drying agent as indicated in Section 12.9.

12.7 THE SCREW-CAP CENTRIFUGE TUBE

If you require an extraction that uses a larger volume than a conical vial can accommodate (about 4 mL), a centrifuge tube can often be used. A centrifuge tube can also be used instead of a separatory funnel for some macroscale applications in which the total volume of liquid is less than about 12 mL. A commonly available size of centrifuge tube has a volume of about 15 mL and is supplied with a screw cap. In performing an extraction with a screw-cap centrifuge tube, use the same procedures outlined for the conical vial (Sections 12.5 and 12.6). As is the case for a conical vial, the tapered bottom of the centrifuge tube makes it easy to withdraw the lower layer with a Pasteur pipet.

> **Note:** A centrifuge tube has a great advantage over other methods of extraction. If an emulsion (Section 12.10) forms, you can use a centrifuge to aid in the separation of the layers.

You should check the capped centrifuge tube for leaks by filling it with water and shaking it vigorously. If it leaks, try replacing the cap with a different one. A **vortex mixer,** if available, provides an alternative to shaking the tube. In fact, a vortex mixer works well with a variety of containers, including small flasks, test tubes, conical vials, and centrifuge tubes. You start the mixing action on a vortex mixer by holding the test tube or other container on one of the neoprene pads. The unit mixes the sample by high-frequency vibration.

Part D. Additional Experimental Considerations: Macroscale and Microscale

12.8 HOW DO YOU DETERMINE WHICH ONE IS THE ORGANIC LAYER?

A common problem encountered during an extraction is trying to determine which of the two layers is the organic layer and which is the aqueous (water) layer. The most common situation occurs when the aqueous layer is on the bottom in the presence of an upper organic layer consisting of ether, ligroin, petroleum ether, or hexane (see densities in Table 12.1). However, the aqueous layer will be on the top when you use methylene chloride as a solvent (again, see Table 12.1). Although a laboratory procedure may frequently identify the expected relative positions of the organic and aqueous layers, sometimes their actual positions are reversed. Surprises usually occur in situations in which the aqueous layer contains a high concentration of sulfuric acid or a dissolved ionic compound, such as sodium chloride. Dissolved substances greatly increase the density of the aqueous layer, which may lead to the aqueous layer being found on the bottom even when coexisting with a relatively dense organic layer such as methylene chloride.

> **Note:** Always keep both layers until you have actually isolated the desired compound or until you are certain where your desired substance is located.

To determine if a particular layer is the aqueous one, add a few drops of water to the layer. Observe closely as you add the water to see where it goes. If the layer is water, then the drops of added water will dissolve in the aqueous layer and increase its volume. If the added water forms droplets or a new layer, however, you can assume that the suspected aqueous layer is actually organic. You can use a similar procedure to identify a suspected organic layer. This time, try adding more of the solvent, such as methylene chloride. The organic layer should increase in size, without separation of a new layer, if the tested layer is actually organic.

When performing an extraction procedure on the microscale level, you can use the following approach to identify the layers. When both layers are present, it is always a good idea to think carefully about the volumes of materials that you have added to the conical vial. You can use the graduations on the vial to help determine the volumes of the layers in the vial. If, for example, you have 1 mL of methylene chloride in a vial and you add 2 mL of water, you should expect the water to be on top because it is less dense than methylene chloride. As you add the water, *watch to see where it goes.* By noting the relative volumes of the two layers, you should be able to tell which is the aqueous layer and which is the organic layer. This approach can also be used when performing an extraction procedure using a centrifuge tube. Of course, you can always test to see which layer is the aqueous layer by adding one or two drops of water, as described previously.

12.9 DRYING AGENTS

After an organic solvent has been shaken with an aqueous solution, it will be "wet"; that is, it will have dissolved some water even though its solubility with water is not great. The amount of water dissolved varies from solvent to solvent; diethyl ether represents a solvent in which a fairly large amount of water dissolves. To remove water from the organic layer, use a **drying agent.** A drying agent is an *anhydrous* inorganic salt that acquires waters of hydration when exposed to moist air or a wet solution:

$$\underset{\substack{\text{Anhydrous}\\\text{drying agent}}}{\overset{\text{Insoluble}}{Na_2SO_4(s)}} + \text{Wet Solution } (nH_2O) \longrightarrow \underset{\substack{\text{Hydrated}\\\text{drying agent}}}{\overset{\text{Insoluble}}{Na_2SO_4 \cdot nH_2O\ (s)}} + \text{Dry Solution}$$

The insoluble drying agent is placed directly into the solution, where it acquires water molecules and becomes hydrated. If enough drying agent is used, all of the water can be removed from a wet solution, making it "dry," or free of water.

The following anhydrous salts are commonly used: sodium sulfate, magnesium sulfate, calcium chloride, calcium sulfate (Drierite), and potassium carbonate. These salts vary in their properties and applications. For instance, not all will absorb the same amount of water for a given weight, nor will they dry the solution to the same extent. **Capacity** refers to the amount of water a drying agent absorbs per unit weight. Sodium and magnesium sulfates absorb a large amount of water (high capacity), but magnesium sulfate dries a solution more completely. **Completeness** refers to a compound's effectiveness in removing all the water from a solution by the time equilibrium has been reached. Magnesium ion, a strong Lewis acid, sometimes causes rearrangements of compounds such as epoxides. Calcium chloride is a good drying agent but cannot be used with many compounds containing oxygen or nitrogen because it forms complexes. Calcium chloride absorbs methanol and ethanol in addition to water, so it is useful for removing these materials when they are present as impurities. Potassium carbonate is a base and is used for drying solutions of basic substances, such as amines. Calcium sulfate dries a solution completely but has a low capacity.

Anhydrous sodium sulfate is the most widely used drying agent. The granular variety is recommended because it is easier to remove the dried solution from it than from the powdered variety. Sodium sulfate is mild and effective. It will remove water from most common solvents, with the possible exception of diethyl ether, in which case a prior drying with saturated salt solution may be advised (see p. 715). Sodium sulfate must be used at room temperature to be effective; it cannot be used with boiling solutions. Table 12.2 compares the various common drying agents.

Macroscale. An Erlenmeyer flask is the most convenient container for drying a large volume of an organic layer. Before attempting to dry an organic layer, check closely to see that there are no visible signs of water. If you see droplets of water in the organic layer or clinging to the sides of the flask, transfer the organic layer to a *dry* flask before adding any drying agent. If a puddle (water layer) is present, separate the layers, using a separatory funnel if necessary, and place the organic layer in a clean, dry flask. To dry a large amount of solution, you should add enough granular anhydrous sodium sulfate to give a 1–3-mm layer on the bottom of the flask, depending on the volume of the solution. Stop-

TABLE 12.2 Common Drying Agents

	Acidity	Hydrated	Capacity[a]	Completeness[b]	Rate[c]	Use
Magnesium sulfate	Neutral	$MgSO_4 \cdot 7H_2O$	High	Medium	Rapid	General
Sodium sulfate	Neutral	$Na_2SO_4 \cdot 7H_2O$ $Na_2SO_4 \cdot 10H_2O$	High	Low	Medium	General
Calcium chloride	Neutral	$CaCl_2 \cdot 2H_2O$ $CaCl_2 \cdot 6H_2O$	Low	High	Rapid	Hydrocarbons Halides
Calcium sulfate (Drierite)	Neutral	$CaSO_4 \cdot \frac{1}{2}H_2O$ $CaSO_4 \cdot 2H_2O$	Low	High	Rapid	General
Potassium carbonate	Basic	$K_2CO_3 \cdot 1\frac{1}{2}H_2O$ $K_2CO_3 \cdot 2H_2O$	Medium	Medium	Medium	Amines, esters, bases, ketones
Potassium hydroxide	Basic	—	—	—	Rapid	Amines only
Molecular sieves (3 or 4 Å)	Neutral	—	High	Extremely high	—	General

[a]Amount of water removed per given weight of drying agent.

[b]Refers to amount of H_2O still in solution at equilibrium with drying agent.

[c]Refers to rate of action (drying).

TABLE 12.3 Common Signs That Indicate a Solution Is Dry

1. There are no visible water droplets on the side of flask or suspended in solution.
2. There is not a separate layer of liquid or a "puddle."
3. The solution is clear, not cloudy. Cloudiness indicates water is present.
4. The drying agent (or a portion of it) flows freely on the bottom of the container when stirred or swirled and does not "clump" together as a solid mass.

per the flask and dry the solution for at least 15 minutes, occasionally swirling the flask. The mixture is dry if it appears clear and shows the common signs of a dry solution given in Table 12.3.

If the solution remains cloudy after treatment with the first batch of drying agent, add more drying agent and repeat the drying procedure. If the drying agent clumps badly, with no drying agent that will flow freely when the flask is swirled, you should transfer (decant) the solution to a clean, dry flask and add a fresh portion of drying agent. When the solution is dry, the drying agent should be removed by using decantation (pouring carefully to leave the drying agent behind). With granular sodium sulfate, decantation is quite easy to perform because of the size of the drying agent particles. If a powdered drying agent, such as magnesium sulfate, is used, it may be necessary to use gravity filtration (Technique 8, Section 8.1B, p. 646) to remove the drying agent. The solvent is removed by distillation (Technique 14, Section 14.3, p. 738) or evaporation (Technique 7, Section 7.10, p. 639).

Microscale. Before attempting to dry an organic layer, check closely to see that there are no visible signs of water. If you see droplets of water in the organic layer or water droplets clinging to the sides of the conical vial or test tube, transfer the organic layer with a *dry* Pasteur pipet to a *dry* container before adding any drying agent. Now add one spatulaful of granular anhydrous sodium sulfate (or other drying agent) from the V-grooved end of a microspatula into a solution contained in a conical vial or test tube. If all the drying agent "clumps," add another spatulaful of sodium sulfate. Dry the solution for at least 15 minutes. Stir the mixture occasionally with a spatula during that period. The mixture is dry if there are no visible signs of water and the drying agent flows freely in the container when stirred with a microspatula. The solution should not be cloudy. Add more drying agent if necessary. You should not add more drying agent if a "puddle" (water layer) forms or if drops of water are visible. Instead, you should transfer the organic layer to a dry container before adding fresh drying agent. When dry, use a *dry* Pasteur pipet or a *dry* filter-tip pipet (Technique 8, Section 8.6, p. 655) to remove the solution from the drying agent and transfer the solution to a *dry* conical vial. Rinse the drying agent with a small amount of fresh solvent and transfer this solvent to the vial containing the solution. Remove the solvent by evaporation using heat and a stream of air or nitrogen (Technique 7, Section 7.10, p. 639).

An alternative method of drying an organic phase is to pass it through a filtering pipet (Technique 8, Section 8.1C, p. 649) that has been packed with a small amount (ca. 2 cm) of drying agent. Again, the solvent is removed by evaporation.

Saturated Salt Solution. At room temperature, diethyl ether (ether) dissolves 1.5% by weight of water, and water dissolves 7.5% of ether. Ether, however, dissolves a much smaller amount of water from a saturated aqueous sodium chloride solution. Hence, the bulk of water in ether, or ether in water, can be removed by shaking it with a saturated aqueous sodium chloride solution. A solution of high ionic strength is usually not compatible with an organic solvent and forces separation of it from the aqueous layer. The water migrates into the concentrated salt solution. The ether phase (organic layer) will be on top, and the saturated sodium chloride solution will be on the bottom (d = 1.2 g/mL). After removing the organic phase from the aqueous sodium chloride, dry the organic layer completely with sodium sulfate or with one of the other drying agents listed in Table 12.2.

12.10 EMULSIONS

An **emulsion** is a colloidal suspension of one liquid in another. Minute droplets of an organic solvent are often held in suspension in an aqueous solution when the two are mixed or shaken vigorously; these droplets form an emulsion. This is especially true if any gummy or viscous material was present in the solution. Emulsions are often encountered in performing extractions. Emulsions may require a long time to separate into two layers and are a nuisance to the organic chemist.

Fortunately, several techniques may be used to break a difficult emulsion once it has formed.

1. Often an emulsion will break up if it is allowed to stand for some time. Patience is important here. Gently stirring with a stirring rod or spatula may also be useful.
2. If one of the solvents is water, adding a saturated aqueous sodium chloride solution will help destroy the emulsion. The water in the organic layer migrates into the concentrated salt solution.
3. If the total volume is less than 13 mL, the mixture may be transferred to a centrifuge tube. The emulsion will often break during centrifugation. Remember to place another tube filled with water on the opposite side of the centrifuge to balance it. Both tubes should weigh the same.
4. Adding a very small amount of a water-soluble detergent may also help. This method has been used in the past for combating oil spills. The detergent helps to solubilize the tightly bound oil droplets.
5. Gravity filtration (see Technique 8, Section 8.1, p. 645) may help to destroy an emulsion by removing gummy polymeric substances. With large volumes, you might try filtering the mixture through a fluted filter (Technique 8, Section 8.1B, p. 646) or a piece of cotton. With small-scale reactions, a filtering pipet may work (Technique 8, Section 8.1C, p. 649). In many cases, once the gum is removed, the emulsion breaks up rapidly.
6. If you are using a separatory funnel, you might try to use a gentle swirling action in the funnel to help break an emulsion. Gently stirring with a stirring rod may also be useful.

When you know through prior experience that a mixture may form a difficult emulsion, you should avoid shaking the mixture vigorously. When using conical vials for extractions, it may be better to use a magnetic spin vane for mixing and not shake the mixture at all. When using separatory funnels, extractions should be performed with gentle swirling instead of shaking or with several gentle inversions of the separatory funnel. Do not shake the separatory funnel vigorously in these cases. It is important to use a longer extraction period if the more gentle techniques described in this paragraph are being employed. Otherwise, you will not transfer all the material from the first phase to the second one.

12.11 PURIFICATION AND SEPARATION METHODS

In nearly all synthetic experiments undertaken in the organic laboratory, a series of operations involving extractions is used after the actual reaction has been concluded. These extractions form an important part of the purification. Using them, you separate the desired product from unreacted starting materials or from undesired side products in the reaction mixture. These extractions may be grouped into three categories, depending on the nature of the impurities they are designed to remove.

The first category involves extracting or "washing" an organic mixture with water. Water washes are designed to remove highly polar materials, such as inorganic salts, strong acids or bases, and low-molecular-weight, polar substances including alcohols, carboxylic acids, and amines. Many organic compounds containing fewer than five carbons are water soluble. Water extractions are also used immediately following extractions of a mixture with either acid or base to ensure that all traces of acid or base have been removed.

The second category concerns extraction of an organic mixture with a dilute acid, usually 1–2 *M* hydrochloric acid. Acid extractions are intended to remove basic impurities, especially such basic impurities as organic amines. The bases are converted to their corresponding cationic salts by the acid used in the extraction. If an amine is one of the reactants or if pyridine or another amine is a solvent, such an extraction might be used to remove any excess amine present at the end of a reaction.

$$RNH_2 + HCl \longrightarrow \underset{\text{(water-soluble ammonium salt)}}{RNH_3^+Cl^-}$$

Cationic ammonium salts are usually soluble in the aqueous solution, and they are thus extracted from the organic material. A water extraction may be used immediately following the acid extraction to ensure that all traces of the acid have been removed from the organic material.

The third category is extraction of an organic mixture with a dilute base, usually 1 *M* sodium bicarbonate, although extractions with dilute sodium hydroxide can also be used. Such basic extractions are intended to convert acidic impurities, such as organic acids, to their corresponding anionic salts. For example, in the preparation of an ester, a sodium bicarbonate extraction might be used to remove any excess carboxylic acid that is present.

$$\underset{(\mathrm{p}K_a \sim 5)}{RCOOH} + NaHCO_3 \longrightarrow \underset{\text{(water-soluble carboxylate salt)}}{RCOO^-Na^+} + H_2O + CO_2$$

Anionic carboxylate salts, being highly polar, are soluble in the aqueous phase. As a result, these acid impurities are extracted from the organic material into the basic solution. A water extraction may be used after the basic extraction to ensure that all the base has been removed from the organic material.

Occasionally, phenols may be present in a reaction mixture as impurities, and removing them by extraction may be desired. Because phenols, although they are acidic, are about 10^5 times less acidic than carboxylic acids, basic extractions may be used to separate phenols from carboxylic acids by a careful selection of the base. If sodium bicarbonate is used as a base, carboxylic acids are extracted into the aqueous base, but phenols are not. Phenols are not sufficiently acidic to be deprotonated by the weak base bicarbonate. Extraction with sodium hydroxide, on the other hand, extracts both carboxylic acids and phenols into the aqueous basic solution, because hydroxide ion is a sufficiently strong base to deprotonate phenols.

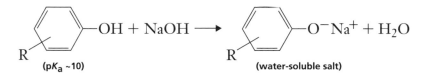

$$\text{R-C}_6\text{H}_4\text{-OH} + \text{NaOH} \longrightarrow \text{R-C}_6\text{H}_4\text{-O}^-\text{Na}^+ + \text{H}_2\text{O}$$

(pK_a ~10) **(water-soluble salt)**

Mixtures of acidic, basic, and neutral compounds are easily separated by extraction techniques. One such example is shown in Figure 12.10.

Organic acids or bases that have been extracted can be regenerated by neutralizing the extraction reagent. This would be done if the organic acid or base were a product of a reaction rather than an impurity. For example, if a carboxylic acid has been extracted with the aqueous base, the compound can be regenerated by acidifying the extract with 6 *M* HCl until the solution becomes *just* acidic, as indicated by litmus or pH paper. When the solution becomes acidic, the carboxylic acid will separate from the aqueous solution. If the acid is a solid at room temperature, it will precipitate and can be purified by filtration and crystallization. If the acid is a liquid, it will form a separate layer. In this case, it would usually be necessary to extract the mixture with ether or methylene chloride. After removing the organic layer and drying it, the solvent can be evaporated to yield the carboxylic acid.

In the example shown in Figure 12.10, you also need to perform a drying step at (3) before isolating the neutral compound. When the solvent is ether, you should first extract the ether solution with saturated aqueous sodium chloride to remove much of the water. The ether layer is then dried over a drying agent such as anhydrous sodium sulfate. If the solvent were methylene chloride, it would not be necessary to do the step with saturated sodium chloride.

When performing acid–base extractions, it is common practice to extract a mixture several times with the appropriate reagent. For example, if you were extracting a carboxylic acid from a mixture, you might extract the mixture three times with 2-mL portions of 1 *M* NaOH. In most published experiments, the procedure will specify the volume and concentration of extracting reagent and the number of times to do the extractions. If this information is not given, you must devise your own procedure. Using a carboxylic acid as an example, if you know the identity of the acid and the approximate amount present, you can actually calculate how much sodium hydroxide is needed. Because the carboxylic acid (assuming it is monoprotic) will react with sodium hydroxide in a 1:1 ratio, you would need the same number of moles of sodium hydroxide as there are moles of acid. To ensure that

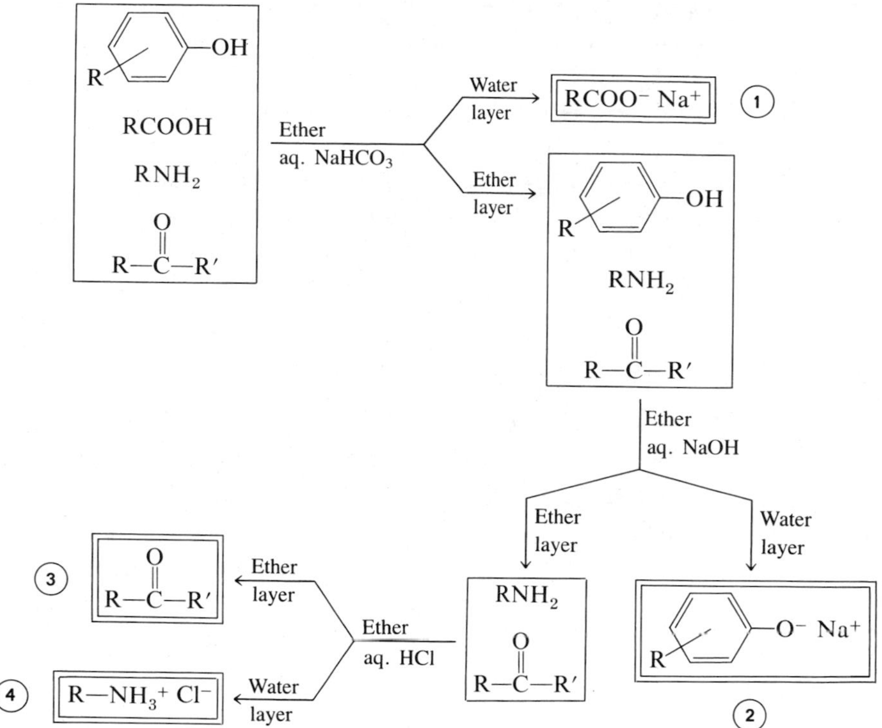

Figure 12.10 Separating a four-component mixture by extraction.

all the carboxylic acid is extracted, you should use about a *twofold* excess of the base. From this, you could calculate the number of milliliters of base needed. This should be divided into two or three equal portions, one portion for each extraction. In a similar fashion, you could calculate the amount of 5% sodium bicarbonate required to extract an acid or the amount of 1 *M* HCl required to extract a base. If the amount of organic acid or base is not known, then the situation is more difficult. A guideline that sometimes works is to do two or three extractions so that the total volume of the extracting reagent is approximately equal to the volume of the organic layer. To test this procedure, neutralize the aqueous layer from the last extraction. If a precipitate or cloudiness results, perform another extraction and test again. When no precipitate forms, you know that all the organic acid or base has been removed.

For some applications of acid–base extraction, an additional step, called **backwashing** or **back extraction,** is added to the scheme shown in Figure 12.10. Consider the first step, in which the carboxylic acid is extracted by sodium bicarbonate. This aqueous layer may contain some unwanted neutral organic material from the original mixture. To remove this contamination, backwash the aqueous layer with an organic solvent such as ether or methylene chloride. After shaking the mixture and allowing the layers to separate, remove and discard the organic layer. This technique may also be used when an amine is extracted with hydrochloric acid. The resulting aqueous layer is backwashed with an organic solvent to remove unwanted neutral material.

Part E. Continuous Extraction Methods

12.12 CONTINUOUS SOLID–LIQUID EXTRACTION

The technique of liquid–liquid extraction was described in Sections 12.1–12.8. In this section, solid–liquid extraction is described. Solid–liquid extraction is often used to extract a solid natural product from a natural source, such as a plant. A solvent is chosen that selectively dissolves the desired compound but that leaves behind the undesired insoluble solid. A continuous solid–liquid extraction apparatus, called a Soxhlet extractor, is commonly used in a research laboratory.

As shown in Figure 12.11, the solid to be extracted is placed in a thimble made from filter paper, and the thimble is inserted into the central chamber. A low-boiling solvent, such as diethyl ether, is placed in the round-bottom distilling flask and is heated to reflux. The vapor rises through the left sidearm into the condenser where it liquefies. The condensate (liquid) drips into the thimble containing the solid. The hot solvent begins to fill the thimble and extracts the desired compound from the solid. Once the thimble is filled with sol-

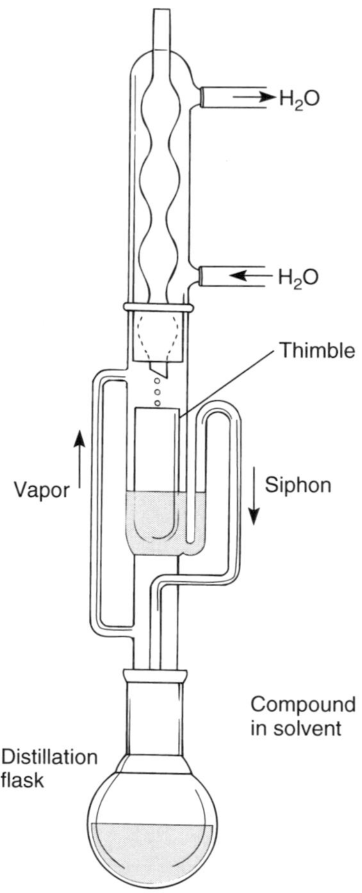

Figure 12.11 Continuous solid–liquid extraction using a Soxhlet extractor.

vent, the sidearm on the right acts as a siphon, and the solvent, which now contains the dissolved compound, drains back into the distillation flask. The vaporization–condensation–extraction–siphoning process is repeated hundreds of times, and the desired product is concentrated in the distillation flask. The product is concentrated in the flask because the product has a boiling point higher than that of the solvent or because it is a solid.

12.13 CONTINUOUS LIQUID–LIQUID EXTRACTION

When a product is very soluble in water, it is often difficult to extract using the techniques described in Sections 12.4–12.7 because of an unfavorable distribution coefficient. In this case, you need to extract the aqueous solution numerous times with fresh batches of an immiscible organic solvent to remove the desired product from water. A less labor-intensive technique involves the use of a continuous liquid–liquid extraction apparatus. One type of extractor, used with solvents that are less dense than water, is shown in Figure 12.12. Diethyl ether is usually the solvent of choice.

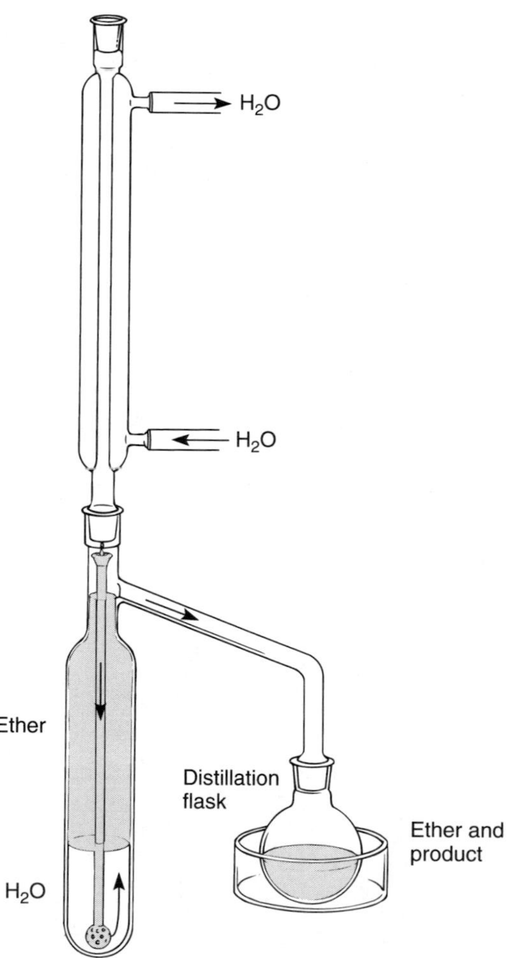

Figure 12.12 Continuous liquid–liquid extraction using a solvent less dense than water.

The aqueous phase is placed in the extractor, which is then filled with diethyl ether up to the sidearm. The round-bottom distillation flask is partially filled with ether. The ether is heated to reflux in the round-bottom flask, and the vapor is liquefied in the water-cooled condenser. The ether drips into the central tube, passes through the porous sintered glass tip, and flows through the aqueous layer. The solvent extracts the desired compound from the aqueous phase, and the ether is recycled back into the round-bottom flask. The product is concentrated in the flask. The extraction is rather inefficient and must be placed in operation for at least 24 hours to remove the compound from the aqueous phase.

PROBLEMS

1. Suppose solute A has a distribution coefficient of 1.0 between water and diethyl ether. Demonstrate that if 100 mL of a solution of 5.0 g of A in water were extracted with two 25-mL portions of ether, a smaller amount of A would remain in the water than if the solution were extracted with one 50-mL portion of ether.

2. Write an equation to show how you could recover the parent compounds from their respective salts (1, 2, and 4) shown in Figure 12.10.

3. Aqueous hydrochloric acid was used *after* the sodium bicarbonate and sodium hydroxide extractions in the separation scheme shown in Figure 12.10. Is it possible to use this reagent earlier in the separation scheme to achieve the same overall result? If so, explain where you would perform this extraction.

4. Using aqueous hydrochloric acid, sodium bicarbonate, or sodium hydroxide solutions, devise a separation scheme using the style shown in Figure 12.10 to separate the following two-component mixtures. All the substances are soluble in ether. Also indicate how you would recover each of the compounds from its respective salts.

a. Give two different methods for separating this mixture.

OH
Br
Br

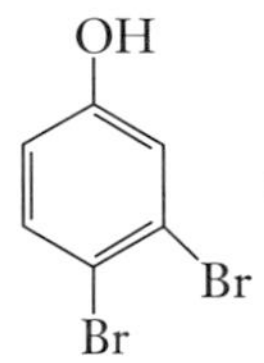

$(CH_3CH_2CH_2CH_2)_3N$

b. Give two different methods for separating this mixture.

O OH
C

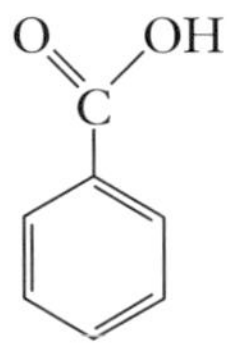

$CH_3CH_2CH_2CH_2CH_2CH_2OH$

c. Give one method for separating this mixture.

OH
Br
Br

O OH
C

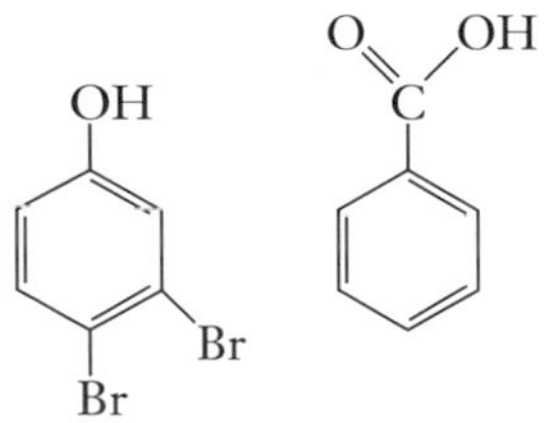

5. Solvents other than those in Table 12.1 may be used for extractions. Determine the relative positions of the organic layer and the aqueous layer in a conical vial or separatory funnel after shaking each of the following solvents with an aqueous phase. Find the densities for each of these solvents in a handbook (see Technique 4, p. 592).

a. 1,1,1-Trichloroethane

b. Hexane

6. A student prepares ethyl benzoate by the reaction of benzoic acid with ethanol using a sulfuric acid catalyst. The following compounds are found in the crude reaction mixture: ethyl benzoate (major component), benzoic acid, ethanol, and sulfuric acid. Using a handbook, obtain the solubility properties in water for each of these compounds (see Technique 4, p. 592). Indicate how you would remove benzoic acid, ethanol, and sulfuric acid from ethyl benzoate. At some point in the purification, you should also use an aqueous sodium bicarbonate solution.

7. Calculate the weight of water that could be removed from a wet organic phase using 50.0 mg of magnesium sulfate. Assume that it gives the hydrate listed in Table 12.2.

8. Explain exactly what you would do when performing the following laboratory instructions:

a. "Wash the organic layer with 5.0 mL of 1 *M* aqueous sodium bicarbonate."

b. "Extract the aqueous layer three times with 2-mL portions of methylene chloride."

9. Just prior to drying an organic layer with a drying agent, you notice water droplets in the organic layer. What should you do next?

10. What should you do if there is some question about which layer is the organic one during an extraction procedure?

11. Saturated aqueous sodium chloride (d = 1.2 g/mL) is added to the following mixtures in order to dry the organic layer. Which layer is likely to be on the bottom in each case?

a. Sodium chloride layer or a layer containing a high-density organic compound dissolved in methylene chloride (d = 1.4 g/mL)

b. Sodium chloride layer or a layer containing a low-density organic compound dissolved in methylene chloride (d = 1.1 g/mL)

ESSAY

Caffeine

The origins of coffee and tea as beverages are so old that they are lost in legend. Coffee is said to have been discovered by an Abyssinian goatherd who noticed an unusual friskiness in his goats when they consumed a certain little plant with red berries. He decided to try the berries himself and discovered coffee. The Arabs soon cultivated the coffee plant, and one of the earliest descriptions of its use is found in an Arabian medical book circa A.D. 900. The great systematic botanist Linnaeus named the tree *Coffea arabica.*

One legend of the discovery of tea—from the Orient, as you might expect—attributes the discovery to Daruma, the founder of Zen. Legend has it that he inadvertently fell asleep one day during his customary meditations. To be assured that this indiscretion would not recur, he cut off both eyelids. Where they fell to the ground, a new plant took root that had the power to keep a person awake. Although some experts assert that the medical use of tea was reported as early as 2737 B.C. in the pharmacopeia of Shen Nung, an emperor of China, the first indisputable reference is from the Chinese dictionary of Kuo P'o, which appeared in A.D. 350. The nonmedical, or popular, use of tea appears to have spread slowly. Not until about A.D. 700 was tea widely cultivated in China. Tea is native to upper Indochina and upper India, so it must have been cultivated in these places before its introduction to China. Linnaeus named the tea shrub *Thea sinensis;* however, tea is more properly a relative of the camellia, and botanists have renamed it *Camellia thea.*

The active ingredient that makes tea and coffee valuable to humans is **caffeine.** Caffeine is an **alkaloid,** a class of naturally occurring compounds containing nitrogen and having the properties of an organic amine base (alkaline, hence, *alkaloid*). Tea and coffee are not the only plant sources of caffeine. Others include kola nuts, maté leaves, guarana seeds, and in small amount, cocoa beans. The pure alkaloid was first isolated from coffee in 1821 by the French chemist Pierre Jean Robiquet.

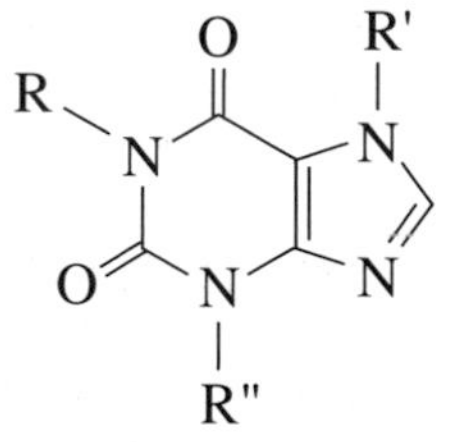

XANTHINES
Xanthine R = R' = R" = H
Caffeine R = R' = R" = CH_3
Theophylline R = R" = CH_3, R' = H
Theobromine R = H, R' = R" = CH_3

Caffeine belongs to a family of naturally occurring compounds called **xanthines.** The xanthines, in the form of their plant progenitors, are possibly the oldest known stimulants. They all, to varying extents, stimulate the central nervous system and the skeletal muscles. This stimulation results in an increased alertness, the ability to put off sleep, and an increased capacity for thinking. Caffeine is the most powerful xanthine in this respect. It is the main ingredient of the popular No-Doz keep-alert tablets. Although caffeine has a powerful effect on the central nervous system, not all xanthines are as effective. Thus, theobromine, the xanthine found in cocoa, has fewer central nervous system effects. It is, however, a strong **diuretic** (induces urination) and is useful to doctors in treating patients with severe water-retention problems. Theophylline, a second xanthine found in tea, also has fewer central nervous system effects but is a strong **myocardial** (heart muscle) stimulant; it **dilates** (relaxes) the coronary artery that supplies blood to the heart. Its most important use is in the treatment of bronchial asthma, because it has the properties of a **bronchodilator** (relaxes the bronchioles of the lungs). Because it is also a **vasodilator** (relaxes blood vessels), it is often used in treating hypertensive headaches. It is also used to alleviate and to reduce the frequency of attacks of **angina pectoris** (severe chest pain). In addition, it is a more powerful diuretic than theobromine.

One can develop both a tolerance for the xanthines and a dependence on them, particularly caffeine. The dependence is real, and a heavy user (> 5 cups of coffee per day) will experience lethargy, headache, and perhaps nausea after about 18 hours of abstinence. An excessive intake of caffeine may lead to restlessness, irritability, insomnia, and muscular tremor. Caffeine can be toxic, but to achieve a lethal dose of caffeine, one would have to drink about 100 cups of coffee over a relatively short period.

Caffeine is a natural constituent of coffee, tea, and kola nuts (*Kola nitida*). Theophylline is found as a minor constituent of tea. The chief constituent of cocoa is theobromine. The amount of caffeine in tea varies from 2% to 5%. In one analysis of black tea, the following compounds were found: caffeine, 2.5%; theobromine, 0.17%; theophylline, 0.013%; adenine, 0.014%; and guanine and xanthine, traces. Coffee beans can contain up to 5% by weight of caffeine, and cocoa contains around 5% theobromine. Commercial cola is a beverage based on a kola nut extract. We cannot easily get kola nuts in this country, but we can get the ubiquitous commercial extract as a syrup. The syrup can be converted into "cola." The syrup contains caffeine, tannins, pigments, and sugar. Phosphoric acid is added, and caramel is added to give the syrup a deep color. The final drink is prepared by adding water and carbon dioxide under pressure, to give the bubbly mixture. Before decaffeination, the Food and Drug Administration required a "cola" to contain some caffeine (about 0.2 mg per ounce). In 1990, when new nutrition labels were adopted, this requirement was dropped. The Food and Drug Administration currently requires that a "cola" contain *some* caffeine but limits this amount to a maximum of 5 milligrams per ounce. To achieve a regulated level of caffeine, most manufacturers remove all caffeine from the kola extract and then re-add the correct amount to the syrup. The caffeine content of various beverages is listed in the accompanying table.

With the recent popularity of gourmet coffee beans and espresso stands, it is interesting to consider the caffeine content of these specialty beverages. Gourmet coffee certainly has more flavor than the typical ground coffee you may find on any grocery store shelf, and the concentration of brewed gourmet coffee tends to be higher than ordinary drip-grind coffee. Brewed gourmet coffee probably contains something on the order of 20–25 mg of caffeine per ounce of liquid. Espresso coffee is a very concentrated, dark-brewed coffee. Although the darker roasted beans used for espresso actually contain less caffeine per gram than regularly roasted beans, the method of preparing espresso (extraction using pressurized steam) is more efficient, and a higher percentage of the total caffeine in the beans is extracted. The caffeine content per ounce of liquid, therefore, is substantially higher than in most brewed coffees. The serving size for espresso coffee, however, is much smaller than for ordinary coffee (about 1.5–2 oz per serving), so the total caffeine available in a serving of espresso turns out to be about the same as in a serving of ordinary coffee.

Amount of Caffeine (mg/oz) Found in Beverages

Brewed coffee	12–30	Tea	4–20
Instant coffee	8–20	Cocoa (but 20 mg/oz theobromine)	0.5–2
Espresso (1 serving = 1.5–2 oz)	50–70	Coca-Cola	3.75
Decaffeinated coffee	0.4–1.0		

Note: The average cup of coffee or tea contains about 5–7 oz of liquid. The average bottle of cola contains about 12 oz of liquid.

Because of the central nervous system effects from caffeine, many people prefer **decaffeinated** coffee. The caffeine is removed from coffee by extracting the whole beans with an organic solvent. Then the solvent is drained off, and the beans are steamed to remove any residual solvent. The beans are dried and roasted to bring out the flavor. Decaffeination reduces the caffeine content of coffee to the range of 0.03% to 1.2% caffeine. The extracted caffeine is used in various pharmaceutical products, such as APC tablets.

Among coffee lovers there is some controversy about the best method to remove the caffeine from coffee beans. **Direct contact** decaffeination uses an organic solvent (usually methylene chloride) to remove the caffeine from the beans. When the beans are subsequently roasted at 200°C, virtually all traces of the solvent are removed, because methylene chloride boils at 40°C. The advantage of direct contact decaffeination is that the method removes only the caffeine (and some waxes) but leaves the substances responsible for the flavor of the coffee intact in the bean. A disadvantage of this method is that all organic solvents are toxic to some extent.

Water process decaffeination is favored among many drinkers of decaffeinated coffee because it does not use organic solvents. In this method, hot water and steam are used to remove caffeine and other soluble substances from the coffee. The resulting solution is then passed through activated charcoal filters to remove the caffeine. Although this method does not use organic solvents, the disadvantage is that water is not a very selective decaffeinating agent. Many of the flavor oils in the coffee are removed at the same time, resulting in a coffee with a somewhat bland flavor.

A third method, the **carbon dioxide decaffeination process,** is being used with increasing frequency. The raw coffee beans are moistened with steam and water, and they are then placed into an extractor where they are treated with carbon dioxide gas under very high temperature and pressure. Under these conditions, the carbon dioxide gas is in a **supercritical** state, which means that it takes on the characteristics of both a liquid and a gas. The supercritical carbon dioxide acts as a selective solvent for caffeine, thus extracting it from the beans.

Caffeine has always been a controversial compound. Medically, its actions are suspect. It definitely has strong effects on the heart and blood vessels, causing an increase in blood pressure. It stimulates the central nervous system, making a person more alert but also more jittery. Many people consider caffeine to be a dangerous and addictive drug, and some religions forbid the use of beverages containing caffeine for this very reason.

Another problem, not related to caffeine but rather to the beverage tea, is that in some cases persons who consume high quantities of tea may show symptoms of Vitamin B_1 (thiamine) deficiency. It is suggested that the tannins in the tea may complex with the thiamine, rendering it unavailable for use. An alternative suggestion is that caffeine may reduce the levels of the enzyme transketolase, which depends on the presence of thiamine for its activity. Lowered levels of transketolase would produce the same symptoms as lowered levels of thiamine.

REFERENCES

Emboden, W. "The Stimulants." *Narcotic Plants,* rev. ed. New York: Macmillan, 1979.

Ray, O. S. "Caffeine." *Drugs, Society and Human Behavior,* 7th ed. St. Louis: C. V. Mosby, 1996.

Ritchie, J. M. "Central Nervous System Stimulants. II: The Xanthines." In L. S. Goodman and A. Gilman, *The Pharmacological Basis of Therapeutics,* 8th ed. New York: Macmillan, 1990.
Taylor, N. *Plant Drugs That Changed the World.* New York: Dodd, Mead, 1965. Pp. 54–56.
Taylor, N. "Three Habit-Forming Nondangerous Beverages." In *Narcotics—Nature's Dangerous Gifts.* New York: Dell, 1970. (Paperbound revision of Flight from Reality.)

EXPERIMENT 11

Isolation of Caffeine

Isolation of a natural product
Extraction
Sublimation

In this experiment, caffeine is isolated from tea leaves. The chief problem with the isolation is that caffeine does not exist alone in tea leaves but is accompanied by other natural substances from which it must be separated. The main component of tea leaves is cellulose, which is the principal structural material of all plant cells. Cellulose is a polymer of glucose. Because cellulose is virtually insoluble in water, it presents no problems in the isolation procedure. Caffeine, on the other hand, is water soluble and is one of the main substances extracted into the solution called tea. Caffeine constitutes as much as 5% by weight of the leaf material in tea plants.

Tannins also dissolve in the hot water used to extract tea leaves. The term **tannin** does not refer to a single homogeneous compound or even to substances that have similar chemical structure. It refers to a class of compounds that have certain properties in common. Tannins are phenolic compounds having molecular weights between 500 and 3000. They are widely used to tan leather. They precipitate alkaloids and proteins from aqueous solutions. Tannins are usually divided into two classes: those that can be **hydrolyzed** (react with water) and those that cannot. Tannins of the first type that are found in tea generally yield glucose and gallic acid when they are hydrolyzed. These tannins are esters of gallic acid and glucose. They represent structures in which some of the hydroxyl groups in glucose have been esterified by digalloyl groups. The nonhydrolyzable tannins found in tea are condensation polymers of catechin. These polymers are not uniform in structure; catechin molecules are usually linked at ring positions 4 and 8.

When tannins are extracted into hot water, some of these compounds are partially hydrolyzed to form free gallic acid. The tannins, because of their phenolic groups, and gallic acid, because of its carboxyl groups, are both acidic. If sodium carbonate, a base, is added to tea water, these acids are converted to their sodium salts, which are highly soluble in water.

Although caffeine is soluble in water, it is much more soluble in the organic solvent methylene chloride. Caffeine can be extracted from the basic tea solution with methylene chloride, but the sodium salts of gallic acid and the tannins remain in the aqueous layer.

The brown color of a tea solution is due to flavonoid pigments and chlorophylls and to their respective oxidation products. Although chlorophylls are soluble in methylene

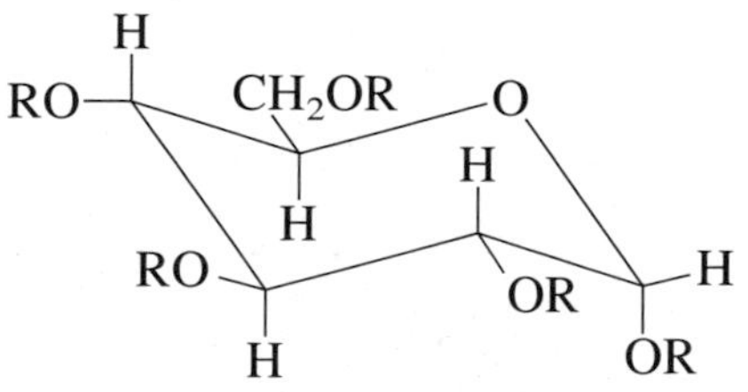

Glucose if R = H
A tannin if some R = digalloyl

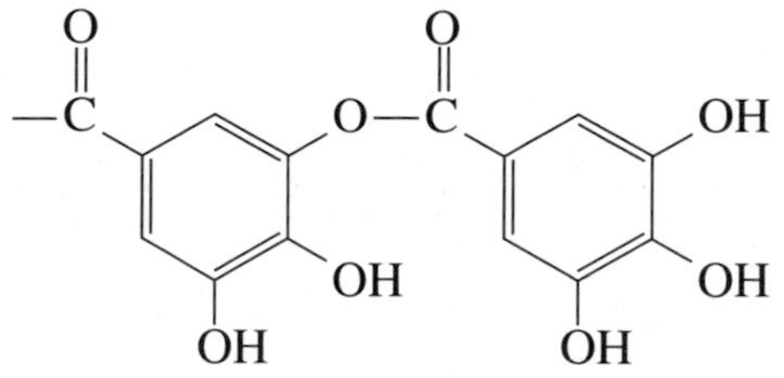

A digalloyl group

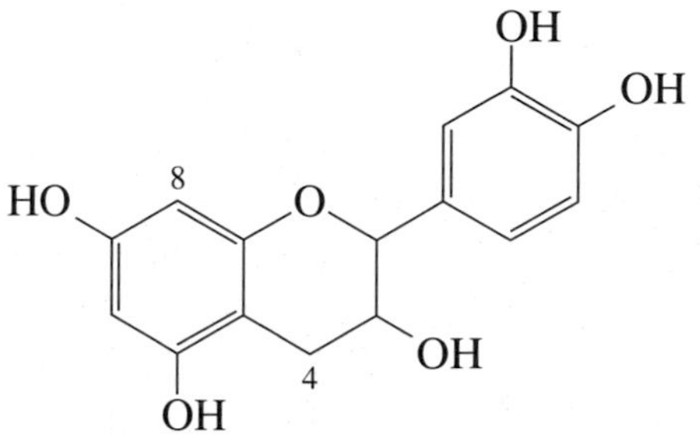

Catechin

chloride, most other substances in tea are not. Thus, the methylene chloride extraction of the basic tea solution removes nearly pure caffeine. The methylene chloride is easily removed by evaporation (bp 40°C) to leave the crude caffeine. The caffeine is then purified by sublimation.

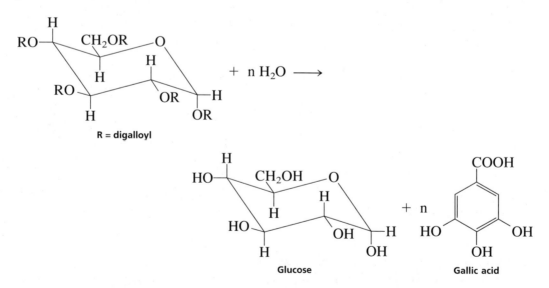

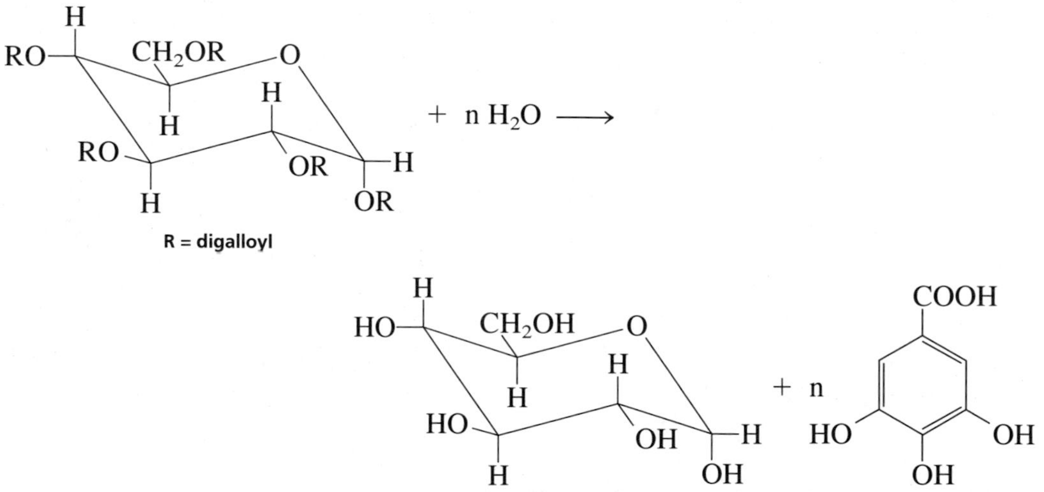

R = digalloyl $+ \; n\,H_2O \longrightarrow$

Glucose $+ \; n$ Gallic acid

Experiment 11A outlines the isolation of caffeine from tea using macroscale techniques. An optional procedure in Experiment 11A allows the student to convert caffeine to a **derivative.** A derivative of a compound is a second compound, of known melting point, formed from the original compound by a simple chemical reaction. In trying to make a positive identification of an organic compound, it is often necessary to convert it to a derivative. If the first compound, caffeine in this case, and its derivative have melting points that

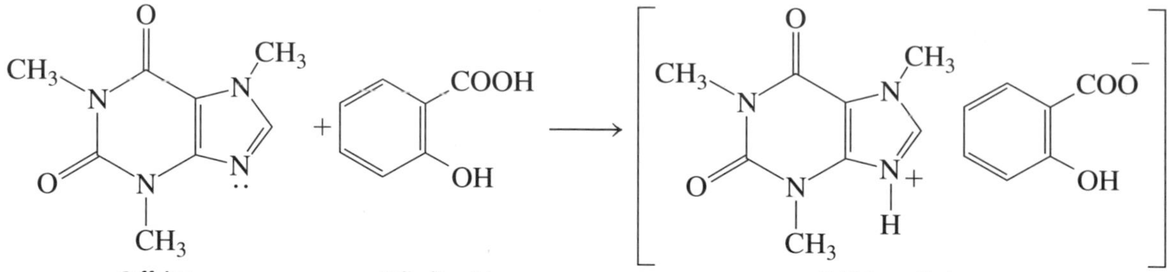

Caffeine + Salicylic acid ⟶ Caffeine salicylate

match those reported in the chemical literature (a handbook, for instance), it is assumed that there is no coincidence and that the identity of the first compound, caffeine, has been established conclusively.

Caffeine is a base and will react with an acid to give a salt. With salicylic acid, a derivative **salt** of caffeine, caffeine salicylate, can be made to establish the identity of the caffeine isolated from tea leaves.

In Experiment 11B, the isolation of caffeine is accomplished using microscale methods. In this experiment, you will be asked to isolate the caffeine from the tea contained in a single tea bag.

Required Reading

Review:	Techniques 5 and 6	
	Technique 7	Reaction Methods, Sections 7.2 and 7.10
	Technique 9	Physical Constants of Solids: The Melting Point
New:	Technique 12	Extractions, Separations, and Drying Agents, Sections 12.1–12.5, and 12.7–12.9
	Technique 17	Sublimation
	Essay	Caffeine

Special Instructions

Be careful when handling methylene chloride. It is a toxic solvent, and you should not breathe it excessively or spill it on yourself. In Experiment 11B, the extraction procedure with methylene chloride calls for two centrifuge tubes with screw caps. Corks can also be used to seal the tubes; however, the corks will absorb a small amount of the liquid. Rather than shake the centrifuge tube, you can conveniently accomplish agitation with a vortex mixer.

Suggested Waste Disposal

You must dispose of methylene chloride in a waste container marked for the disposal of halogenated organic waste. When you are discarding tea leaves, do not put them in the sink; they will clog the drain. Dispose of them in a waste container. Dispose of the tea bags in a waste container, not in the sink. The aqueous solutions obtained after the extraction steps must be disposed of in a waste container labeled for aqueous waste.

EXPERIMENT 11A

Isolation of Caffeine from Tea Leaves

Procedure

Preparing the Tea Solution. Place 5 g of tea leaves, 2 g of calcium carbonate powder, and 50 mL of water in a 100-mL round-bottom flask equipped with a condenser for reflux (Technique 7, Figure 7.6, p. 628). Heat the mixture under gentle reflux, being careful to prevent any bumping, for about 20 minutes. Use a heating mantle to heat the mixture. Shake the flask occasionally during this heating period. While the solution is still hot, vacuum filter it through a fast filter paper such as E&D No. 617 or S&S No. 595 (Technique 8, Section 8.3, p. 651). A 125-mL filter flask is appropriate for this step.

Extraction and Drying. Cool the filtrate (filtered liquid) to room temperature, and using a 125-mL separatory funnel, extract it (Technique 12, Section 12.4, p. 704) with a 10-mL portion of methylene chloride (dichloromethane). Shake the mixture vigorously for 1 minute. The layers should separate after standing for several minutes, although some emulsion will be present in the lower organic layer (Technique 12, Section 12.10, p. 716). The emulsion can be broken and the organic layer dried at the same time by passing the lower layer *slowly* through anhydrous magnesium sulfate, according to the following method. Place a small piece of cotton (not glass wool) in the neck of a conical funnel and add a 1-cm layer of anhydrous magnesium sulfate on top of the cotton. Pass the organic layer directly from the separatory funnel into the drying agent and collect the filtrate in a dry Erlenmeyer flask. Rinse the magnesium sulfate with 1 or 2 mL of fresh methylene chloride solvent. Repeat the extraction with another 10-mL portion of methylene chloride on the aqueous layer remaining in the separatory funnel, and repeat the drying, as described above, with a *fresh* portion of anhydrous magnesium sulfate. Collect the organic layer in the flask containing the first methylene chloride extract. These extracts should now be clear, showing no visible signs of water contamination. If some water should pass through the filter, repeat the drying, as described above, with a fresh portion of magnesium sulfate. Collect the dried extracts in a dry Erlenmeyer flask.

Distillation. Pour the dry organic extracts into a 50-mL round-bottom flask. Assemble an apparatus for simple distillation (Technique 14, Figure 14.1, p. 734), add a boiling stone, and remove the methylene chloride by distillation on a steam bath or heating mantle. The residue in the distillation flask contains the caffeine and is purified by crystallization and sublimation. Save the methylene chloride that was distilled; you may use some of it in the next step. The remaining methylene chloride must be placed in a waste container marked for halogenated waste; it must *not* be discarded in the sink.

Crystallization (Purification). Dissolve the residue from the methylene chloride extraction of the tea solution in about 5 mL of the methylene chloride that you saved from the distillation. You may have to heat the mixture on a steam bath or heating mantle to dissolve the solid. Transfer the solution to a 25-mL Erlenmeyer flask. Rinse the distillation flask with an additional 2–3 mL of methylene chloride and combine this solution with the contents of the Erlenmeyer flask. Add a boiling stone and evaporate the now light green solution to dryness by heating it on a steam bath or a hot plate *in the hood.*

The residue obtained on evaporation of the methylene chloride is next crystallized by the mixed-solvent method (Technique 11, Section 11.10, p. 696). Using a steam bath or hot plate, dissolve the residue in a small quantity (about 2 mL) of hot acetone and add dropwise just enough low-boiling (bp 30–60°C) petroleum ether to turn the solution faintly cloudy.[1] Cool the solution and collect the crystalline product by vacuum filtration, using a small Büchner funnel. A small amount of petroleum ether can be used to help in transferring the crystals to the Büchner funnel. A second crop of crystals can be obtained by concentrating the filtrate. Weigh the product (an analytical balance may be necessary). Calculate the weight percentage yield (see page 579) based on the 5 g of tea originally used and determine the melting point. The melting point of pure caffeine is 236°C. Note the color of the solid for comparison with the material obtained after sublimation.

Sublimation of Caffeine. Caffeine can be purified by sublimation (Technique 17, p. 799). Assemble a sublimation apparatus as shown in Figure 17.2C, page 784. If it is available, the apparatus shown in Figure 17.2A will give superior results. Insert a 15-mm × 125-mm test tube into a No. 2 neoprene adapter, using a *little* water as a lubricant, until the tube is fully inserted. Place the crude caffeine into a 20-mm × 150-mm sidearm test tube. Next place the 15-mm × 120-mm test tube into the sidearm test tube, making sure they fit together tightly. Turn on the aspirator or house vacuum and make sure a good seal is obtained. At the point at which a good seal has been achieved, you should hear or observe a change in the water velocity in the aspirator. At this time, also make sure that the central tube is centered in the sidearm test tube; this will allow for optimal collection of the purified caffeine. Once the vacuum has been established, place small chips of ice in the test tube to fill it.[2] When a good vacuum seal has been obtained and ice has been added to the inner test tube, heat the sample gently and carefully with a microburner to sublime the caffeine. Hold the burner in your hand (hold it at the *base,* not by the hot barrel) and apply heat by moving the flame back and forth under the outer tube and up the sides. If the sample begins to melt, remove the flame for a few seconds before you resume heating. When sublimation is complete, remove the burner and allow the apparatus to cool. As the

[1] If the residue does not dissolve in this quantity of acetone, magnesium sulfate may be present as an impurity (drying agent). Add additional acetone (up to about 5 mL), gravity-filter the mixture to remove the solid impurity, and reduce the volume of the filtrate to about 2 mL. Now add petroleum ether as indicated in the procedure.

[2] It is very important that ice not be added to the inner test tube until the vacuum has been established. If the ice is added before the vacuum is turned on, condensation on the outer walls of the inner tube will contaminate the sublimed caffeine.

apparatus is cooling, and before you disconnect the vacuum, remove the water and ice from the inner tube using a Pasteur pipet.

When the apparatus has cooled and the water has been removed from the tube, you may disconnect the vacuum. The vacuum should be removed carefully to avoid dislodging the crystals from the inner tube by the sudden rush of air into the apparatus. *Carefully* remove the inner tube of the sublimation apparatus. If this operation is done carelessly, the sublimed crystals may be dislodged from the inner tube and fall back into the residue. Scrape the sublimed caffeine onto weighing paper, using a small spatula. Determine the melting point of this purified caffeine and compare it in melting point and color with the caffeine obtained following crystallization. Submit the sample to the instructor in a labeled vial, or if the instructor directs, prepare the caffeine salicylate derivative.

THE DERIVATIVE (OPTIONAL)

The amounts given in this part, including solvents, should be adjusted to fit the quantity of caffeine you obtained. Use an analytical balance. Dissolve 25 mg of caffeine and 18 mg of salicylic acid in 2 mL of toluene in a small Erlenmeyer flask by warming the mixture on a steam bath or hot plate. Add about 0.5 mL (10 drops) of high-boiling (bp 60–90°C) petroleum ether or ligroin and allow the mixture to cool and crystallize. It may be necessary to cool the flask in an ice-water bath or to add a small amount of extra petroleum ether to induce crystallization. Collect the crystalline product by vacuum filtration, using a Hirsch funnel or a small Büchner funnel. Dry the product by allowing it to stand in the air and determine its melting point. Pure caffeine salicylate melts at 137°C. Submit the sample to the instructor in a labeled vial.

EXPERIMENT 11B

Isolation of Caffeine from a Tea Bag

Procedure

Preparing the Tea Solution. Place 20 mL of water in a 50-mL beaker. Cover the beaker with a watch glass and heat the water on a hot plate until the water is almost boiling. Place a tea bag into the hot water so that it lies flat on the bottom of the beaker and is covered as completely as possible with water.[3] Replace the watch glass and continue heating for about 15 minutes. During this heating period, it is important to push down *gently* on the tea bag with a test tube so that all the tea leaves are in constant contact with water. As the water evaporates during this heating step, replace it by adding water from a Pasteur pipet.

[3] The weight of tea in the bag will be given to you by your instructor. This can be determined by opening several bags of tea and determining the average weight. If this is done carefully, the tea can be returned to the bags, which can be restapled.

Using a Pasteur pipet, transfer the concentrated tea solution to two centrifuge tubes fitted with screw caps. Try to keep the liquid volume in each centrifuge tube approximately equal. To squeeze additional liquid out of the tea bag, hold the tea bag on the inside wall of the beaker and roll a test tube back and forth while exerting *gentle* pressure on the tea bag. Press out as much liquid as possible without breaking the bag. Combine this liquid with the solution in the centrifuge tubes. Place the tea bag on the bottom of the beaker again and pour 2 mL of hot water over the bag. Squeeze the liquid out, as just described, and transfer this liquid to the centrifuge tubes. Add 0.5 g of sodium carbonate to the hot liquid in each centrifuge tube. Cap the tubes and shake the mixture until the solid dissolves.

Extraction and Drying. Cool the tea solution to room temperature. Using a calibrated Pasteur pipet (p. 607), add 3 mL of methylene chloride to each centrifuge tube to extract the caffeine (Technique 12, Section 12.7, p. 711). Cap the centrifuge tubes and gently shake the mixture for several seconds. Vent the tubes to release the pressure, being careful that the liquid does not squirt out toward you. Shake the mixture for an additional 30 seconds with occasional venting. To separate the layers and break the emulsion (see Technique 12, Section 12.10, p. 716), centrifuge the mixture for several minutes (be sure to balance the centrifuge by placing the two centrifuge tubes on opposite sides). If an emulsion still remains (indicated by a green brown layer between the clear methylene chloride layer and the top aqueous layer), centrifuge the mixture again.

Remove the lower organic layer with a Pasteur pipet and transfer it to a test tube. Be sure to squeeze the bulb before placing the tip of the Pasteur pipet into the liquid, and try not to transfer any of the dark aqueous solution along with the methylene chloride layer. Add a fresh 3-mL portion of methylene chloride to the aqueous layer remaining in each centrifuge tube, cap the centrifuge tubes, and shake the mixture in order to carry out a second extraction. Separate the layers by centrifugation, as described previously. Combine the organic layers from each extraction into one test tube. If there are visible drops of the dark aqueous solution in the test tube, transfer the methylene chloride solution to another test tube using a clean, dry Pasteur pipet. If necessary, leave a small amount of the methylene chloride solution behind in order to avoid transferring any of the aqueous mixture. Add a small amount of granular anhydrous sodium sulfate to dry the organic layer (Technique 12, Section 12.9, p. 713). If all the sodium sulfate clumps together when the mixture is stirred with a spatula, add some additional drying agent. Allow the mixture to stand for 10–15 minutes. Stir occasionally with a spatula.

Evaporation. Transfer the dry methylene chloride solution with a Pasteur pipet to a dry, preweighed 25-mL Erlenmeyer flask, while leaving the drying agent behind. Evaporate the methylene chloride by heating the flask in a hot water bath (Technique 7, Section 7.10, p. 639). This should be done in a hood and can be accomplished more rapidly if a stream of dry air or nitrogen gas is directed at the surface of the liquid. When the solvent is evaporated, the crude caffeine will coat the bottom of the flask. Do not heat the flask after the solvent has evaporated, or you may sublime some of the caffeine. Weigh the flask and determine the weight of crude caffeine. Calculate the weight percentage recovery (see p. 582) of caffeine from tea leaves, using the weight of tea given to you by your instructor. You may store the caffeine by simply placing a stopper firmly into the flask.

Sublimation of Caffeine. Caffeine can be purified by sublimation (Technique 17, Section 17.5, p. 783). Follow the method described in Experiment 11A. Add approximately 0.5 mL of methylene chloride to the Erlenmeyer flask and transfer the solution to the sublimation apparatus using a clean, dry Pasteur pipet. Add a few more drops of methylene chloride to the flask in order to rinse the caffeine out completely. Transfer this liquid to the sublimation apparatus. Evaporate the methylene chloride from the outer tube of the sublimation apparatus by gentle heating in a warm water bath under a stream of dry air or nitrogen.

Assemble the apparatus as described in Experiment 11A or use the apparatus shown in Figure 17.2A on page 784, if it is available. Be sure that the inside of the assembled apparatus is clean and dry. If you are using an aspirator, install a trap between the aspirator and the sublimation apparatus. Turn on the vacuum and check to make sure that all joints in the apparatus are sealed tightly. Place *ice-cold* water in the inner tube of the apparatus. Heat the sample gently and carefully with a microburner to sublime the caffeine. Hold the burner in your hand (hold it at its base, not by the hot barrel) and apply the heat by moving the flame back and forth under the outer test tube and up the sides. If the sample begins to melt, remove the flame for a few seconds before you resume heating. When sublimation is complete, discontinue heating. Remove the cold water and remaining ice from the inner tube and allow the apparatus to cool while continuing to apply the vacuum.

When the apparatus is at room temperature, remove the vacuum and *carefully* remove the inner tube. If this operation is done carelessly, the sublimed crystals may be dislodged from the inner tube and fall back into the residue at the bottom of the outer test tube. Scrape the sublimed caffeine onto a tared piece of smooth paper and determine the weight of caffeine recovered. Calculate the weight percentage recovery (see p. 582) of caffeine after the sublimation. Compare this value to the percentage recovery determined after the evaporation step. Determine the melting point of the purified caffeine. The melting point of pure caffeine is 236°C; however, the observed melting point will be lower. Submit the sample to the instructor in a labeled vial.

QUESTIONS

1. Outline a separation scheme for isolating caffeine from tea (Experiment 11A or Experiment 11B). Use a flowchart similar in format to that shown in Technique 2 (see p. 578).

2. Why was the sodium carbonate added in Experiment 11B? Why was calcium carbonate added in Experiment 11A?

3. The crude caffeine isolated from tea has a green tinge. Why?

4. What are some possible explanations for why the melting point of your isolated caffeine was lower than the literature value (236°C)?

5. What would happen to the caffeine if the sublimation step were performed at atmospheric pressure?

TECHNIQUE 17

Sublimation

In Technique 13, the influence of temperature on the change in vapor pressure of a liquid was considered (see Figure 13.1, p. 724). It was shown that the vapor pressure of a liquid increases with temperature. Because the boiling point of a liquid occurs when its vapor pressure is equal to the applied pressure (normally atmospheric pressure), the vapor pressure of a liquid equals 760 mmHg at its boiling point. The vapor pressure of a solid also varies with temperature. Because of this behavior, some solids can pass directly into the vapor phase without going through a liquid phase. This process is called **sublimation.** Because the vapor can be resolidified, the overall vaporization–solidification cycle can be used as a purification method. The purification can be successful only if the impurities have significantly lower vapor pressures than the material being sublimed.

Part A. Theory

17.1 VAPOR PRESSURE BEHAVIOR OF SOLIDS AND LIQUIDS

In Figure 17.1, vapor pressure curves for solid and liquid phases for two different substances are shown. Along lines *AB* and *DF,* the sublimation curves, the solid and vapor are

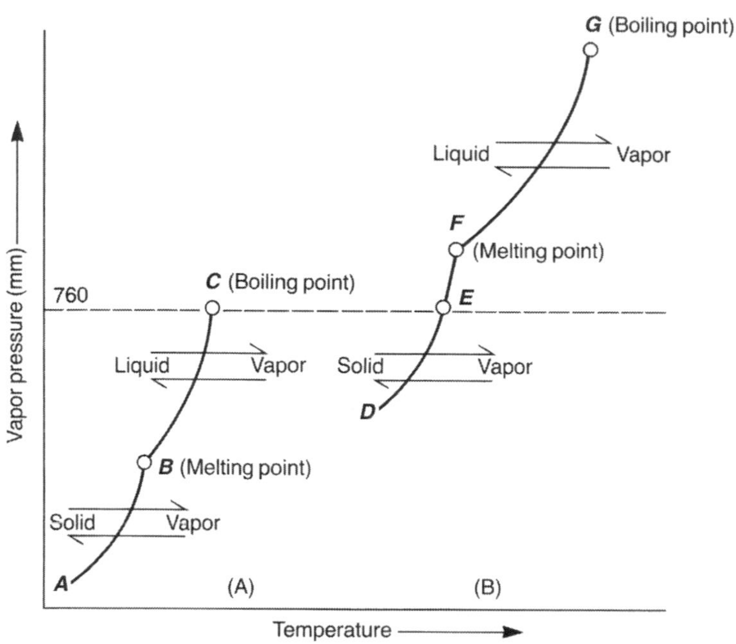

Figure 17.1 Vapor pressure curves for solids and liquids. (A) This substance shows normal solid-to-liquid-to-gas transitions at 760 mmHg pressure. (B) This substance shows a solid-to-gas transition at 760 mmHg pressure.

at equilibrium. To the left of these lines, the solid phase exists, and to the right of these lines, the vapor phase is present. Along lines *BC* and *FG,* the liquid and vapor are at equilibrium. To the left of these lines, the liquid phase exists, and to the right, the vapor is present. The two substances vary greatly in their physical properties, as shown in Figure 17.1.

In the first case (Figure 17.1A), the substance shows normal change-of-state behavior on being heated, going from solid to liquid to gas. The dashed line, which represents an atmospheric pressure of 760 mmHg, is located *above* the melting point *B* in Figure 17.1A. Thus, the applied pressure (760 mmHg) is *greater* than the vapor pressure of the solid–liquid phase at the melting point. Starting at *A,* as the temperature of the solid is raised, the vapor pressure increases along *AB* until the solid is observed to melt at *B.* At *B,* the vapor pressures of *both* the solid and liquid are identical. As the temperature continues to rise, the vapor pressure will increase along *BC* until the liquid is observed to boil at *C.* The description given is for the "normal" behavior expected for a solid substance. All three states (solid, liquid, and gas) are observed sequentially during the change in temperature.

In the second case (Figure 17.1B), the substance develops enough vapor pressure to vaporize completely at a temperature below its melting point. The substance shows a solid-to-gas transition only. The dashed line is now located *below* the melting point *F* of this substance. Thus, the applied pressure (760 mmHg) is *less* than the vapor pressure of the solid–liquid phase at the melting point. Starting at *D,* the vapor pressure of the solid rises as the temperature increases along line *DF.* However, the vapor pressure of the solid reaches atmospheric pressure (point *E*) *before* the melting point at *F* is attained. Therefore, sublimation occurs at *E.* No melting behavior will be observed at atmospheric pressure for this substance. For a melting point to be reached and the behavior along line *FG* to be observed, an

TABLE 17.1 Vapor Pressures of Solids at Their Melting Points

Compound	Vapor Pressure of Solid at MP (mmHg)	Melting Point (°C)
Carbon dioxide	3876 (5.1 atm)	−57
Perfluorocyclohexane	950	59
Hexachloroethane	780	186
Camphor	370	179
Iodine	90	114
Naphthalene	7	80
Benzoic acid	6	122
p-Nitrobenzaldehyde	0.009	106

applied pressure greater than the vapor pressure of the substance at point *F* would be required. This could be achieved by using a sealed pressure apparatus.

The sublimation behavior just described is relatively rare for substances at atmospheric pressure. Several compounds exhibiting this behavior—carbon dioxide, perfluorocyclohexane, and hexachloroethane—are listed in Table 17.1. Notice that these compounds have vapor pressures *above* 760 mmHg at their melting points. In other words, their vapor pressures reach 760 mmHg below their melting points, and they sublime rather than melt. Anyone trying to determine the melting point of hexachloroethane at atmospheric pressure will see vapor pouring from the end of the melting-point tube! Using a sealed capillary tube, you will observe the melting point of 186°C.

17.2 SUBLIMATION BEHAVIOR OF SOLIDS

Sublimation is usually a property of relatively nonpolar substances that also have highly symmetrical structures. Symmetrical compounds have relatively high melting points and high vapor pressures. The ease with which a substance can escape from the solid state is determined by the strength of intermolecular forces. Symmetrical molecular structures have a relatively uniform distribution of electron density and a small dipole moment. A smaller dipole moment means a higher vapor pressure because of lower electrostatic attractive forces in the crystal.

Solids sublime if their vapor pressures are greater than atmospheric pressure at their melting points. Some compounds with the vapor pressures at their melting points are listed in Table 17.1. The first three entries in the table were discussed in Section 17.1. At atmospheric pressure, they would sublime rather than melt, as shown in Figure 17.1B.

The next four entries in Table 17.1 (camphor, iodine, naphthalene, and benzoic acid) exhibit typical change-of-state behavior (solid, liquid, and gas) at atmospheric pressure, as shown in Figure 17.1A. These compounds sublime readily under reduced pressure, however. Vacuum sublimation is discussed in Section 17.3.

Compared with many other organic compounds, camphor, iodine, and naphthalene have relatively high vapor pressures at relatively low temperatures. For example, they have a vapor pressure of 1 mmHg at 42°C, 39°C, and 53°C, respectively. Although this vapor pressure does not seem very large, it is high enough to lead, after a time, to **evaporation** of the solid from an open container. Mothballs (naphthalene and 1,4-dichlorobenzene) show this behavior. When iodine stands in a closed container over a period of time, you can observe movement of crystals from one part of the container to another.

Although chemists often refer to any solid–vapor transition as sublimation, the process described for camphor, iodine, and naphthalene is really an **evaporation** of a solid. Strictly speaking, a sublimation point is like a melting point or a boiling point. It is defined as the point at which the vapor pressure of the solid *equals* the applied pressure. Many liquids readily evaporate at temperatures far below their boiling points. It is, however, much less common for solids to evaporate. Solids that readily sublime (evaporate) must be stored in sealed containers. When the melting point of such a solid is being determined, some of the solid may sublime and collect toward the open end of the melting-point tube while the rest of the sample melts. To solve the sublimation problem, seal the capillary tube or rapidly determine the melting point. It is possible to use the sublimation behavior to purify a substance. For example, at atmospheric pressure, camphor can be readily sublimed, just below its melting point at 175°C. At 175°C, the vapor pressure of camphor is 320 mmHg. The vapor solidifies on a cool surface.

17.3 VACUUM SUBLIMATION

Many organic compounds sublime readily under reduced pressure. When the vapor pressure of the solid equals the applied pressure, sublimation occurs, and the behavior is identical to that shown in Figure 17.1B. The solid phase passes directly into the vapor phase. From the data given in Table 17.1, you should expect camphor, naphthalene, and benzoic acid to sublime at or below the respective applied pressures of 370 mmHg, 7 mmHg, and 6 mmHg. In principle, you can sublime *p*-nitrobenzaldehyde (last entry in the table), but it would not be practical because of the low applied pressure required.

17.4 ADVANTAGES OF SUBLIMATION

One advantage of sublimation is that no solvent is used, and therefore none needs to be removed later. Sublimation also removes occluded material, such as molecules of solvent, from the sublimed substance. For instance, caffeine (sublimes at 178°C, melts at 236°C) absorbs water gradually from the atmosphere to form a hydrate. During sublimation, this water is lost, and anhydrous caffeine is obtained. If too much solvent is present in a sample to be sublimed, however, instead of becoming lost, it condenses on the cooled surface and thus interferes with the sublimation.

Sublimation is a faster method of purification than crystallization but not as selective. Similar vapor pressures are often a factor in dealing with solids that sublime; consequently, little separation can be achieved. For this reason, solids are far more often purified by crystallization. Sublimation is most effective in removing a volatile substance from a nonvolatile compound, particularly a salt or other inorganic material. Sublimation is also effective in removing highly volatile bicyclic or other symmetrical molecules from less volatile reaction products. Examples of volatile bicyclic compounds are borneol, camphor, and isoborneol.

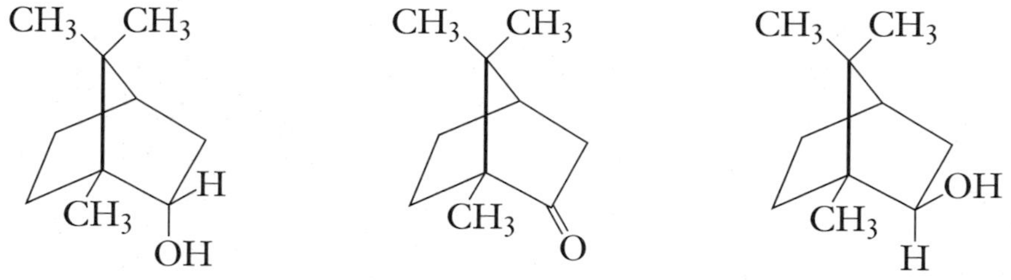

Borneol

Camphor

Isoborneol

Part B. Macroscale and Microscale Sublimation

17.5 SUBLIMATION—METHODS

Sublimation can be used to purify solids. The solid is warmed until its vapor pressure becomes high enough for it to vaporize and condense as a solid on a cooled surface placed closely above. Three types of apparatus are illustrated in Figure 17.2. Because all of the parts fit securely, they are all capable of holding a vacuum. Chemists usually perform vacuum sublimations because most solids undergo the solid-to-gas transition only at low pressures. Reduction of pressure also helps to prevent thermal decomposition of substances that would require high temperatures to sublime at ordinary pressures. One end of a piece of rubber pressure tubing is attached to the apparatus, and the other end is attached to an aspirator, to the house vacuum system, or to a vacuum pump.

A sublimation is probably best carried out using one of the pieces of microscale equipment shown in Figures 17.2A and B. It is recommended that the laboratory instructor make available either one type or the other to be used on a communal basis. Each apparatus shown employs a central tube (closed on one end) filled with ice-cold water that serves as a condensing surface. The tube is filled with ice chips and a minimum of water. If the cooling water becomes warm before the sublimation is completed, a Pasteur pipet can be used to remove the warm water. The tube is then refilled with more ice-cold water. Warm water is undesirable because the vapor will not condense efficiently to form a solid as readily on a warm surface as it would on a cold surface. A poor recovery of solid results.

The apparatus shown in Figure 17.2C can be constructed from a sidearm test tube, a neoprene adapter, and a piece of glass tubing sealed at one end. Alternatively, a 15-mm × 125-mm test tube may be used instead of the piece of glass tubing. The test tube is inserted into a No. 1 neoprene adapter using a little water as a lubricant. All pieces must fit securely to obtain a good vacuum and to avoid water being drawn into the sidearm test tube around the rubber adapter. To achieve an adequate seal, you may need to flare the sidearm test tube somewhat.

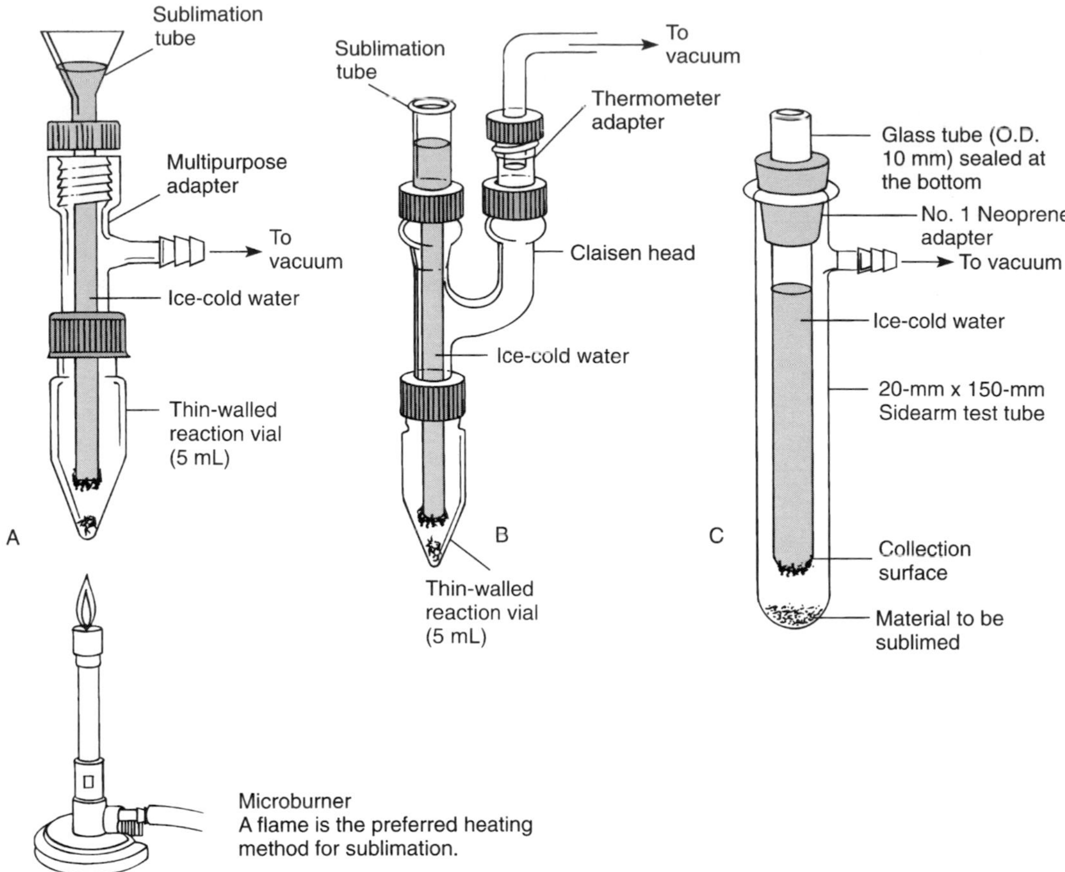

Figure 17.2 A sublimation apparatus.

A flame is the preferred heating device because the sublimation will occur more quickly than with other heating devices. The sublimation will be finished before the ice water warms significantly. The burner can be held by its cool base (not the hot barrel!) and moved up and down the sides of the outer tube to "chase" any solid that has formed on the sides toward the cold tube in the center. When using the apparatus shown in Figures 17.2A and B with a flame, you will need to use a thin-walled vial. Thicker glass can shatter when heated with a flame.

Remember that while performing a sublimation, it is important to keep the temperature below the melting point of the solid. After sublimation, the material that has collected on the cooled surface is recovered by removing the central tube (cold finger) from the apparatus. Take care in removing this tube to avoid dislodging the crystals that have collected. The deposit of crystals is scraped from the inner tube with a spatula. If reduced pressure has been used, the pressure must be released carefully to keep a blast of air from dislodging the crystals.

17.6 SUBLIMATION—SPECIFIC DIRECTIONS

A. Microscale Apparatus

Assemble a sublimation apparatus as shown in Figure 17.2A.[1] Place your impure compound in a small Erlenmeyer flask. Add approximately 0.5 mL of methylene chloride to the Erlenmeyer flask, swirl to dissolve the solid, and transfer the solution of your compound to a clean 5-mL, thin-walled, conical vial, using a clean, dry Pasteur pipet.[2] Add a few more drops of methylene chloride to the flask in order to rinse the compound out completely. Transfer this liquid to the conical vial. Evaporate the methylene chloride from the conical vial by gentle heating in a warm water bath under a stream of dry air or nitrogen.

Insert the cold finger into the sublimation apparatus. If you are using the sublimator with the multipurpose adapter, adjust it so that the tip of the cold finger will be positioned about 1 cm above the bottom of the conical vial. Be sure that the inside of the assembled apparatus is clean and dry. If you are using an aspirator, install a trap between the aspirator and the sublimation apparatus. Turn on the vacuum and check to make sure that all joints in the apparatus are sealed tightly. Place *ice-cold* water in the inner tube of the apparatus. Heat the sample gently and carefully with a microburner to sublime your compound. Hold the burner in your hand (hold it at its base, *not* by the hot barrel) and apply the heat by moving the flame back and forth under the conical vial and up the sides. If the sample begins to melt, remove the flame for a few seconds before you resume heating. When sublimation is complete, discontinue heating. Remove the cold water and remaining ice from the inner tube and allow the apparatus to cool while continuing to apply the vacuum.

When the apparatus is at room temperature, slowly vent the vacuum and *carefully* remove the inner tube. If this operation is done carelessly, the sublimed crystals may be dislodged from the inner tube and fall back into the conical vial. Scrape the sublimed compound onto a tared piece of smooth paper and determine the weight of your compound recovered.

B. Sidearm Test Tube Apparatus

Assemble a sublimation apparatus as shown in Figure 17.2C. Insert a 15-mm × 125-mm test tube into a No. 1 neoprene adapter, using a *little* water as a lubricant, until the tube is fully inserted. Place the crude compound into a 20-mm × 150-mm sidearm test tube. Next, place the 15-mm × 120-mm test tube into the sidearm test tube, making sure they fit together tightly. Turn on the aspirator or house vacuum and make sure a good seal is obtained. At the point at which a good seal has been achieved, you should hear or observe a change in the water velocity in the aspirator. At this time, also make sure that the central tube is centered in the sidearm test tube; this will allow for optimal collection of the purified compound. Once the vacuum has been established, place small chips of ice in the test tube to fill it.[3] When a good vacuum seal has been obtained and ice has been added to the inner

---

[1] If you are using another type of sublimation apparatus, your instructor will provide you with specific instructions on how to assemble it correctly.

[2] If your compound does not dissolve freely in methylene chloride, use some other appropriate low-boiling solvent, such as ether, acetone, or pentane.

[3] It is very important that ice not be added to the inner test tube until the vacuum has been established. If the ice is added before the vacuum is turned on, condensation on the outer walls of the inner tube will contaminate the sublimed compound.

test tube, heat the sample gently and carefully with a microburner to sublime your compound. Hold the burner in your hand (hold it at the *base,* not by the hot barrel) and apply heat by moving the flame back and forth under the outer tube and up the sides. If the sample begins to melt, remove the flame for a few seconds before you resume heating. When sublimation is complete, remove the burner and allow the apparatus to cool. As the apparatus is cooling and before you disconnect the vacuum, remove the water and ice from the inner tube using a Pasteur pipet.

When the apparatus has cooled and the water has been removed from the tube, you may disconnect the vacuum. The vacuum should be removed carefully to avoid dislodging the crystals from the inner tube by the sudden rush of air into the apparatus. *Carefully* remove the inner tube of the sublimation apparatus. If this operation is done carelessly, the sublimed crystals may be dislodged from the inner tube and fall back into the residue. Scrape the sublimed compound onto tared weighing paper, using a small spatula. Determine the weight of this purified compound.

PROBLEMS

1. Why is solid carbon dioxide called dry ice? How does it differ from solid water in behavior?
2. Under what conditions can you have *liquid* carbon dioxide?
3. A solid substance has a vapor pressure of 800 mmHg at its melting point (80°C). Describe how the solid behaves as the temperature is raised from room temperature to 80°C while the atmospheric pressure is held constant at 760 mmHg.
4. A solid substance has a vapor pressure of 100 mmHg at the melting point (100°C). Assuming an atmospheric pressure of 760 mmHg, describe the behavior of this solid as the temperature is raised from room temperature to its melting point.
5. A substance has a vapor pressure of 50 mmHg at the melting point (100°C). Describe how you would experimentally sublime this substance.

EXPERIMENT 55

Identification of Unknowns

Qualitative organic analysis, the identification and characterization of unknown compounds, is an important part of organic chemistry. Every chemist must learn the appropriate methods for establishing the identity of a compound. In this experiment, you will be issued an unknown compound and will be asked to identify it through chemical and spectroscopic methods. Your instructor may give you a general unknown or a specific unknown. With a **general unknown,** you must first determine the class of compound to which the unknown belongs, that is, identify its main functional group; then you must determine the specific compound in that class that corresponds to the unknown. With a **specific unknown,** you will know the class of compound (ketone, alcohol, amine, and so on) in advance, and it will be necessary to determine only whatever specific member of that class was issued to you as an unknown. This experiment is designed so that the instructor can issue several general unknowns or as many as six successive specific unknowns, each having a different main functional group.

Although there are well over a million organic compounds that an organic chemist might be called on to identify, the scope of this experiment is necessarily limited. In this textbook, about 500 compounds are included in the tables of possible unknowns given for the experiment (see Appendix 1). Your instructor may wish to expand the list of possible unknowns, however. In such a case, you will have to consult more extensive tables, such as those found in the work compiled by Rappoport (see References). In addition, the experiment is restricted to include only seven important functional groups:

Aldehydes	Amines
Ketones	Alcohols
Carboxylic acids	Esters
Phenols	

Even though this list of functional groups omits some of the important types of compounds (alkyl halides, alkenes, alkynes, aromatics, ethers, amides, mercaptans, nitriles, acid chlorides, acid anhydrides, nitro compounds, and so on), the methods introduced here can be applied equally well to other classes of compounds. The list is sufficiently broad to illustrate all the principles involved in identifying an unknown compound.

In addition, although many of the functional groups listed as being excluded will not appear as the major functional group in a compound, several of them will frequently appear as secondary, or subsidiary, functional groups. Three examples of this are presented here.

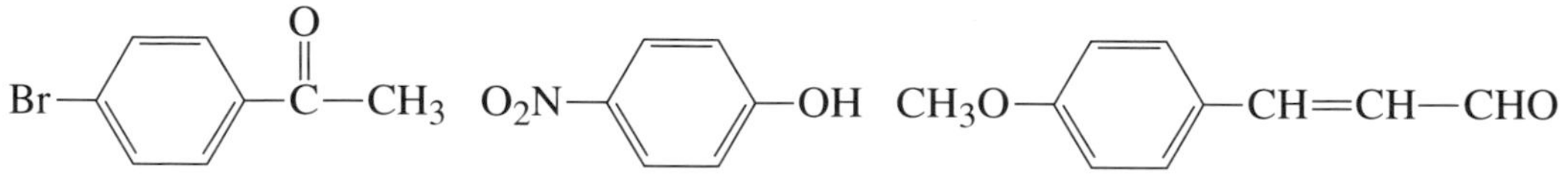

$$Br-C_6H_4-\overset{O}{\overset{\|}{C}}-CH_3 \qquad O_2N-C_6H_4-OH \qquad CH_3O-C_6H_4-CH{=}CH-CHO$$

MAJOR:	KETONE	PHENOL	ALDEHYDE
SUBSIDIARY:	Halide Aromatic	Nitro Aromatic	Alkene Aromatic Ether

The groups included that have subsidiary status are

—Cl	Chloro	$—NO_2$	Nitro	C=C	Double Bond
—Br	Bromo	—C≡N	Cyano	C≡C	Triple Bond
—I	Iodo	—OR	Alkoxy	⬡	Aromatic

The experiment presents all the chief chemical and spectroscopic methods of determining the main functional groups, and it includes methods for verifying the presence of the subsidiary functional groups as well. It will usually not be necessary to determine the presence of the subsidiary functional groups to identify the unknown compound correctly. Every piece of information helps the identification, however, and if these groups can be detected easily, you should not hesitate to determine them. Finally, complex bifunctional compounds are generally avoided in this experiment; only a few are included.

How to Proceed

Fortunately, we can detail a fairly straightforward procedure for determining all the necessary pieces of information. This procedure consists of the following steps:

Part One: Chemical Classification

1. Preliminary classification by physical state, color, and odor
2. Melting-point or boiling-point determination; other physical data
3. Purification, if necessary
4. Determination of solubility behavior in water and in acids and bases
5. Simple preliminary tests: Beilstein, ignition (combustion)
6. Application of relevant chemical classification tests
7. Inspection of tables for possible structure(s) of unknown; elimination of unlikely compounds

Part Two: Spectroscopy

8. Determination of infrared and NMR spectra

Part Three: Optional Procedures

9. Elemental analysis, if necessary
10. Preparation of derivatives, if required
11. Confirmation of identity

Each of these steps is discussed briefly in the following sections.

1. PRELIMINARY CLASSIFICATION

Note the physical characteristics of the unknown, including its color, its odor, and its physical state (liquid, solid, crystalline form). Many compounds have characteristic colors or odors, or they crystallize with a specific crystal structure. This information can often be found in a handbook and can be checked later. Compounds with a high degree of conjugation are frequently yellow to red. Amines often have a fishlike odor. Esters have a pleasant fruity or floral odor. Acids have a sharp and pungent odor. A part of the training of every good chemist includes cultivating the ability to recognize familiar or typical odors. As a note of caution, many compounds have distinctly unpleasant or nauseating odors. Some have corrosive vapors. Sniff any unknown substance with the greatest caution. As a first step, open the container, hold it away from you, and using your hand, carefully waft the vapors toward your nose. If you get past this stage, a closer inspection will be possible.

2. MELTING-POINT OR BOILING-POINT DETERMINATION

The single most useful piece of information to have for an unknown compound is its melting point or boiling point. Either piece of data will drastically limit the compounds that are possible. The electric melting-point apparatus gives a rapid and accurate measurement (see Technique 9, Sections 9.5 and 9.7). To save time, you can often determine two separate melting points. The first determination can be made rapidly to get an approximate value. Then you can determine the second melting point more carefully. Because some of the unknown solids contain traces of impurities, you may find that your observed melting point is lower than the values found in the tables in Appendix 1. This is especially true for low-melting compounds ($<50°C$). For these low-melting compounds, it is a good idea to look at compounds in the tables in Appendix 1 that have melting points above your observed melting-point range. The same advice may apply to other solid compounds issued to you as unknowns.

The boiling point is easily obtained by a simple distillation of the unknown (Technique 14, Section 14.3), by reflux (Technique 13, Section 13.2), or by a micro boiling-point determination (Technique 13, Section 13.3). The simple distillation has the advantage in that it also purifies the compound. The smallest distilling flask available should be used if a simple distillation is performed, and you should be sure that the thermometer bulb is fully immersed in the vapor of the distilling liquid. The liquid should be distilled rapidly to determine an accurate boiling-point value. The micro boiling-point method requires the least amount of unknown, but the refluxing method is more reliable and requires much less liquid than performing a distillation.

When inspecting the tables of unknowns in Appendix 1, you may find that the observed boiling point that you determined is lower than the value for the corresponding compound listed in the tables. This is especially true for compounds boiling above 200°C. It is less likely, but not impossible, that the observed boiling point of your unknown will be higher than the value given in the table. Thus, your strategy should be to look for boiling points of compounds in the tables that are nearly equal to or above the value you obtained, within a range of about $\pm$ 5°C. For high-boiling liquid compounds ($>200°C$), you may need to apply a thermometer correction (Technique 13, Section 13.4).

3. PURIFICATION

If the melting point of a solid has a wide range (about 5°C), the solid should be recrystallized and the melting point redetermined.

If a liquid was highly colored before distillation, if it yielded a wide boiling-point range, or if the temperature did not hold constant during the distillation, it should be redistilled to determine a new temperature range. A reduced-pressure distillation is in order for high-boiling liquids or for those that show any sign of decomposition on heating.

Occasionally, column chromatography may be necessary to purify solids that have large amounts of impurities and do not yield satisfactory results on crystallization.

Acidic or basic impurities that contaminate a neutral compound may often be removed by dissolving the compound in a low-boiling solvent, such as CH_2Cl_2 or ether, and extracting with 5% $NaHCO_3$ or 5% HCl, respectively. Conversely, acidic or basic compounds can be purified by dissolving them in 5% $NaHCO_3$ or 5% HCl, respectively, and extracting them with a low-boiling organic solvent to remove impurities. After the aqueous solution has been neutralized, the desired compound can be recovered by extraction.

4. SOLUBILITY BEHAVIOR

Tests on solubility are described fully in Experiment 55A. They are extremely important. Determine the solubility of small amounts of the unknown in water, 5% HCl, 5% $NaHCO_3$, 5% NaOH, concentrated H_2SO_4, and organic solvents. This information reveals whether a compound is an acid, a base, or a neutral substance. The sulfuric acid test reveals whether a neutral compound has a functional group that contains an oxygen, a nitrogen, or a sulfur atom that can be protonated. This information allows you to eliminate or to choose various functional-group possibilities. The solubility tests must be made on *all* unknowns.

5. PRELIMINARY TESTS

The two combustion tests, the Beilstein test (Experiment 55B) and the ignition test (Experiment 55C) can be performed easily and quickly, and they often give valuable information. It is recommended that they be performed on all unknowns.

6. CHEMICAL CLASSIFICATION TESTS

The solubility tests usually suggest or eliminate several possible functional groups. The chemical classification tests listed in Experiments 55D to 55I allow you to distinguish among the possible choices. Choose only those tests that the solubility tests suggest might be meaningful. Time will be wasted performing unnecessary tests. There is no substitute for a firsthand, thorough knowledge of these tests. Study each of the sections carefully until you understand the significance of each test. Also, it is essential to actually try the tests on *known* substances. In this way, it will be easier to recognize a positive test. Appropriate test compounds are listed for many of the tests. When you are performing a test that is new to you, it is always good practice to run the test separately on both a known substance and the unknown *at the same time.* This practice lets you compare results directly.

Do not perform the chemical tests either haphazardly or in a methodical, comprehensive sequence. Instead, use the tests selectively. Solubility tests automatically eliminate the need for some of the chemical tests. Each successive test will either eliminate the need for another test or dictate its use. You should also cxaminc thc tables of unknowns in Appendix 1 carefully. The boiling point or the melting point of the unknown may eliminate the need for many of the tests. For instance, the possible compounds may simply not include one with a double bond. *Efficiency* is the key word here. Do not waste time performing nonsensical or unnecessary tests. Many possibilities can be eliminated on the basis of logic alone.

How you proceed with the following steps may be limited by your instructor's wishes. Many instructors may restrict your access to infrared and NMR spectra until you have narrowed your choices to a few compounds *all within the same class.* Others may have you determine these data routinely. Some instructors may want students to perform elemental analysis on all unknowns; others may restrict it to only the most essential situations. Again, some instructors may require derivatives as a final confirmation of the compound's identity; others may not wish to use them at all.

7. INSPECTION OF TABLES FOR POSSIBLE STRUCTURES

Once the melting or boiling point, the solubilities, and the main chemical classification tests have been made, you should be able to identify the class of compound (aldehyde, ketone, and so on). At this stage, with the melting point or boiling point as a guide, you can compile a list of possible compounds from one of the appropriate tables in Appendix 1. It is very important to draw out the structures of compounds that fit the solubility, classification tests, and melting point or boiling point that were determined. If necessary, you can look up the structures in the *CRC Handbook, The Merck Index,* or the *Aldrich Handbook.* Remember that the boiling point or melting point recorded in the table may be higher than what you obtained in the laboratory (see Section 2 on page 470).

The short list that you developed by inspection of the tables in Appendix 1 and the structures drawn should suggest that some additional tests may be needed to distinguish among the possibilities. For instance, one compound may be a methyl ketone, and the other may not. The iodoform test is called for to distinguish the two possibilities. The tests for the subsidiary functional groups may also be required. These tests are described in Experiments 55B and 55C. These tests should also be studied carefully; there is no substitute for firsthand knowledge about these tests.

8. SPECTROSCOPY

Spectroscopy is probably the most powerful and modern tool available to the chemist for determining the structure of an unknown compound. It is often possible to determine structure through spectroscopy alone. On the other hand, there are also situations for which spectroscopy may not be of much help, and the traditional methods must be relied on. For this reason, you should not use spectroscopy to the exclusion of the more traditional tests but rather as a confirmation of those results. Nevertheless, the main functional groups and their immediate environmental features can be determined quickly and accurately with spectroscopy.

9. ELEMENTAL ANALYSIS

Elemental analysis—which allows you to determine the presence of nitrogen, sulfur, or a specific halogen atom (Cl, Br, I) in a compound—is often useful; however, other information may render these tests unnecessary. A compound identified as an amine by solubility tests obviously contains nitrogen. Many nitrogen-containing groups (for instance, nitro groups) can be identified by infrared spectroscopy. Finally, it is not usually necessary to identify a specific halogen. The simple information that the compound contains a halogen (any halogen) may be enough information to distinguish between two compounds. A simple Beilstein test provides this information.

10. DERIVATIVES

One of the principal tests for the correct identification of an unknown compound comes in trying to convert the compound by a chemical reaction to another known compound. This second compound is called a **derivative.** The best derivatives are solid compounds, because the melting point of a solid provides an accurate and reliable identification of most compounds. Solids are also easily purified through crystallization. The derivative provides a way of distinguishing two otherwise very similar compounds. Usually, they will have derivatives (both prepared by the same reaction) that have different melting points. Tables of unknowns and derivatives are listed in Appendix 1. Procedures for preparing derivatives are given in Appendix 2.

11. CONFIRMATION OF IDENTITY

A rigid and final test for identifying an unknown can be made if an "authentic" sample of the compound is available for comparison. One can compare infrared and NMR spectra of the unknown compound with the spectra of the known compound. If the spectra match, peak for peak, then the identity is probably certain. Other physical and chemical properties can also be compared. If the compound is a solid, a convenient test is the mixed melting point (Technique 9, Section 9.4). Thin-layer or gas-chromatographic comparisons may also be useful. For thin-layer analysis, however, it may be necessary to experiment with several different development solvents to reach a satisfactory conclusion about the identity of the substance in question.

Although we cannot be complete in this experiment in terms of the functional groups covered or the tests described, the experiment should provide a good introduction to the methods and the techniques chemists use to identify unknown compounds. Textbooks that cover the subject more thoroughly are listed in the References. You are encouraged to consult these for more information, including specific methods and classification tests.

REFERENCES

Comprehensive Textbooks

Cheronis, N. D., and Entrikin, J. B. *Identification of Organic Compounds.* New York: Wiley-Interscience, 1963.

Pasto, D. J., and Johnson, C. R. *Laboratory Text for Organic Chemistry.* Englewood Cliffs, NJ: Prentice-Hall, 1979.

Shriner, R. L., Hermann, C. K. F., Morrill, T. C., Curtin, D. Y., and Fuson, R. C. *The Systematic Identification of Organic Compounds,* 7th ed. New York: Wiley, 1997.

Spectroscopy

Bellamy, L. J. *The Infra-red Spectra of Complex Molecules,* 3rd ed. New York: Methuen, 1975.

Colthup, N. B., Daly, L. H., and Wiberly, S. E. *Introduction to Infrared and Raman Spectroscopy,* 3rd ed. San Diego, CA: Academic Press, 1990.

Lin-Vien, D., Colthup, N. B., Fateley, W. B., and Grasselli, J. G. *The Handbook of Infrared and Raman Characteristic Frequencies of Organic Molecules.* San Diego, CA: Academic Press, 1991.

Nakanishi, K. *Infrared Absorption Spectroscopy,* 2nd ed. San Francisco: Holden-Day, 1977.

Pavia, D. L., Lampman, G. M., and Kriz, G. S. *Introduction to Spectroscopy: A Guide for Students of Organic Chemistry,* 3rd ed. Fort Worth, TX: Harcourt, 2001.

Silverstein, R. M., and Webster, F. X. *Spectrometric Identification of Organic Compounds,* 6th ed. New York: Wiley, 1998.

Extensive Tables of Compounds and Derivatives

Rappoport, Z., ed. *Handbook of Tables for Organic Compound Identification,* 3rd ed. Boca Raton, FL: CRC Press, 1967.

EXPERIMENT 55A

Solubility Tests

Solubility tests should be performed on *every unknown.* They are extremely important in determining the nature of the main functional group of the unknown compound. The tests are very simple and require only small amounts of the unknown. In addition, solubility tests reveal whether the compound is a strong base (amine), a weak acid (phenol), a strong acid (carboxylic acid), or a neutral substance (aldehyde, ketone, alcohol, ester). The common solvents used to determine solubility types are

5% HCl	Concentrated H_2SO_4
5% $NaHCO_3$	Water
5% NaOH	Organic solvents

The solubility chart on page 475 indicates solvents in which compounds containing the various functional groups are likely to dissolve. The summary charts in Experiments 55D through 55I repeat this information for each functional group included in this experiment. In this section, the correct procedure for determining whether a compound is soluble in a test solvent is given. Also given is a series of explanations detailing the reasons that compounds having specific functional groups are soluble in only specific solvents. This is accomplished by indicating the type of chemistry or the type of chemical interaction that is possible in each solvent.

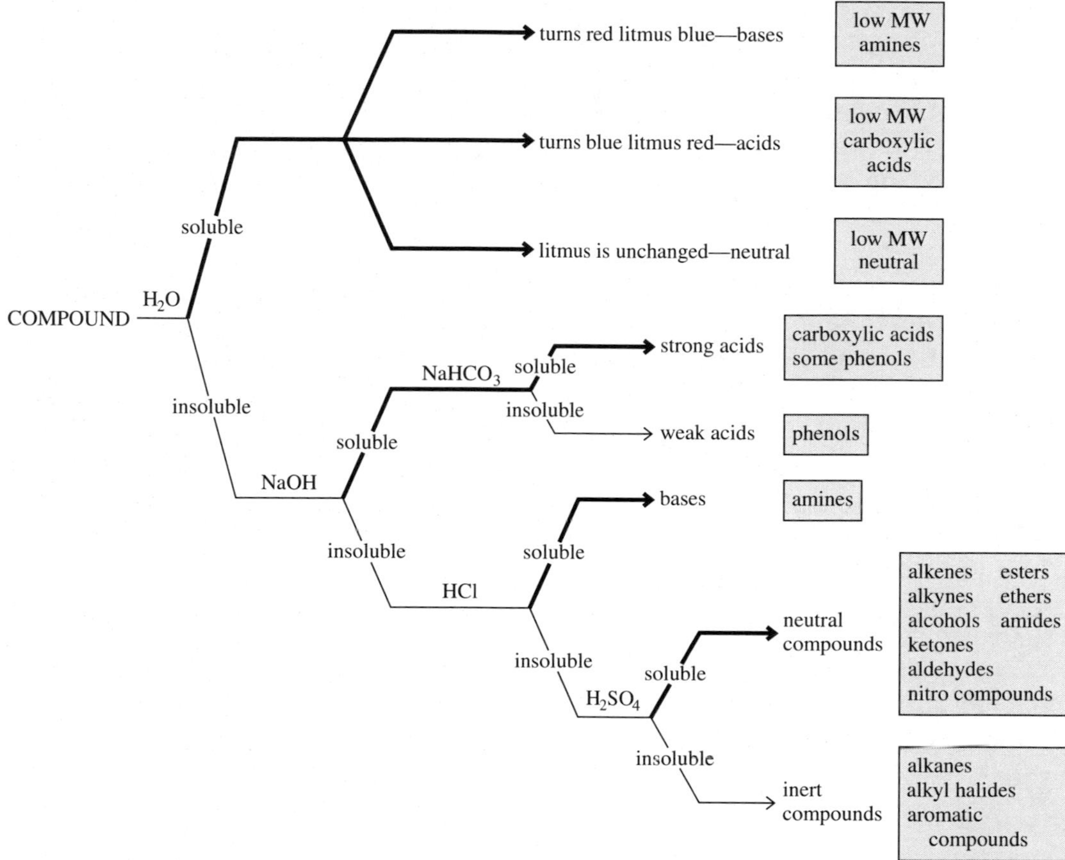

Solubility chart for compounds containing various functional groups.

Suggested Waste Disposal

Dispose of all aqueous solutions in the container designated for aqueous waste. Any remaining organic compounds must be disposed of in the appropriate organic waste container.

SOLUBILITY TESTS

Procedure. Place about 2 mL of the solvent in a small test tube. Add *1 drop* of an unknown liquid from a Pasteur pipet or a few crystals of an unknown solid from the end of a spatula, directly into the solvent. Gently tap the test tube with your finger to ensure mixing and then observe whether any mixing lines appear in the solution. The disappearance of the liquid or solid or the appearance of the mixing lines indicates that solution is taking place. Add several more drops of the liquid or a few more crystals of the solid to determine the extent of the compound's solubility. A common mistake in determining the solubility of a compound is testing with a quantity of the unknown too large to dissolve in the chosen solvent. Use small amounts. It may take several minutes to dissolve solids. Compounds in the form of large crystals need more time to dissolve than powders or very small crystals. In some cases, it is helpful to use a mortar and pestle to pulverize a compound with large crystals. Sometimes, gentle heating helps, but strong heating is discouraged, as it often leads to reaction. When colored compounds dissolve, the solution often assumes the color.

Using the preceding procedure, determine the solubility of the unknown in each of the following solvents: water, 5% HCl, 5% $NaHCO_3$, 5% NaOH, and concentrated H_2SO_4. With sulfuric acid, a color change may be observed rather than solution. A color change should be regarded as a positive solubility test. Solid unknowns that do not dissolve in any of the test solvents may be inorganic substances. To eliminate this possibility, determine the solubility of the unknown in several organic solvents, such as ether. If the compound is organic, a solvent that will dissolve it can usually be found.

If a compound is found to dissolve in water, the pH of the aqueous solution should be estimated with pH paper or litmus. Compounds soluble in water are usually soluble in *all* the aqueous solvents. If a compound is only slightly soluble in water, it may be *more* soluble in another aqueous solvent. For instance, a carboxylic acid may be only slightly soluble in water but very soluble in dilute base. It often will not be necessary to determine the solubility of the unknown in every solvent.

Test Compounds. Five solubility unknowns can be found on the supply shelf. The five unknowns include a base, a weak acid, a strong acid, a neutral substance with an oxygen-containing functional group, and a neutral substance that is inert. Using solubility tests, distinguish these unknowns by type. Verify your answer with the instructor. A general discussion of solubility behavior is provided in Technique 10, Section 10.2.

Discussion

Solubility in Water. Compounds that contain four or fewer carbons and also contain oxygen, nitrogen, or sulfur are often soluble in water. Almost any functional group containing these elements will lead to water solubility for low-molecular-weight (C_4) compounds. Compounds having five or six carbons and any of those elements are often insoluble in water or have borderline solubility. Branching of the alkyl chain in a compound lowers the intermolecular forces between its molecules. This is usually reflected in a lowered boiling point or melting point and a greater solubility in water for the branched compound than for the corresponding straight-chain compound. This occurs simply because the molecules of the branched compound are more easily separated from one another. Thus, *t*-butyl alcohol would be expected to be more soluble in water than *n*-butyl alcohol.

When the ratio of the oxygen, nitrogen, or sulfur atoms in a compound to the carbon atoms is increased, the solubility of that compound in water often increases. This is due to the increased number of polar functional groups. Thus, 1,5-pentanediol would be expected to be more soluble in water than 1-pentanol.

As the size of the alkyl chain of a compound is increased beyond about four carbons, the influence of a polar functional group is diminished, and the water solubility begins to decrease. A few examples of these generalizations are given here.

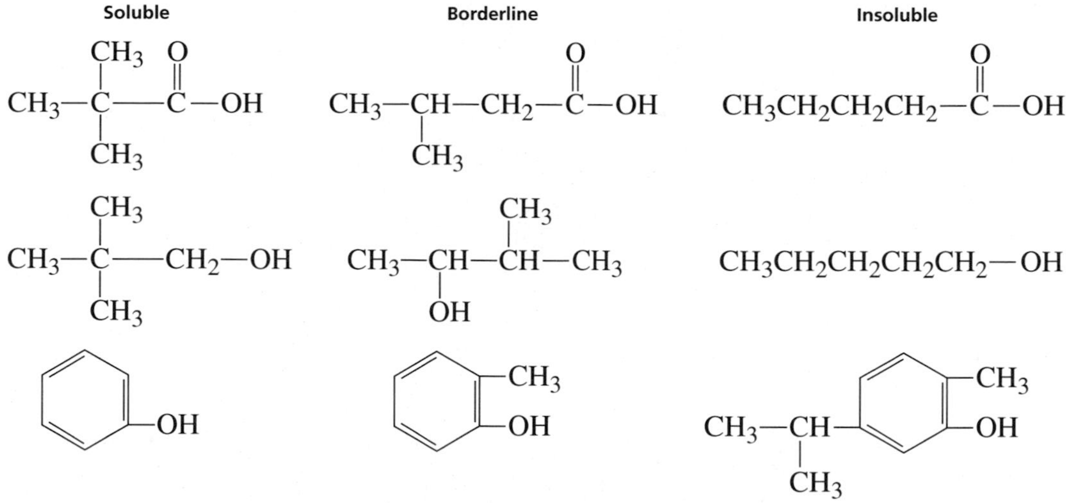

Soluble	Borderline	Insoluble
CH_3—C(CH_3)$_2$—C(=O)—OH	CH_3—CH(CH_3)—CH_2—C(=O)—OH	$CH_3CH_2CH_2CH_2$—C(=O)—OH
CH_3—C(CH_3)$_2$—CH_2—OH	CH_3—CH(OH)—CH(CH_3)—CH_3	$CH_3CH_2CH_2CH_2CH_2$—OH
phenol (benzene ring—OH)	o-cresol (benzene ring with —CH_3 and —OH)	CH_3—CH(CH_3)—benzene ring with —CH_3 and —OH

Solubility in 5% HCl. The possibility of an amine should be considered immediately if a compound is soluble in dilute acid (5% HCl). Aliphatic amines (RNH_2, R_2NH, R_3N) are basic compounds that readily dissolve in acid because they form hydrochloride salts that are soluble in the aqueous medium:

$$R—NH_2 + HCl \longrightarrow R—NH_3^+ + Cl^-$$

The substitution of an aromatic (benzene) ring Ar for an alkyl group R reduces the basicity of an amine somewhat, but the amine will still protonate, and it will still generally be soluble in dilute acid. The reduction in basicity in an aromatic amine is due to the resonance delocalization of the unshared electrons on the amino nitrogen of the free base. The delocalization is lost on protonation, a problem that does not exist for aliphatic amines. The substitution of two or three aromatic rings on an amine nitrogen reduces the basicity of the amine even further. Diaryl and triaryl amines do not dissolve in dilute HCl because they do not protonate easily. Thus, Ar_2NH and Ar_3N are insoluble in dilute acid. Some amines of very high molecular weight, such as tribromoaniline ($MW = 330$), may also be insoluble in dilute acid.

AROMATIC AMINE: [$\ddot{N}H_2$-benzene ⟷ $^+NH_2$ (ortho carbanion) ⟷ $^+NH_2$ (para carbanion) ⟷ $^+NH_2$ (ortho carbanion)] $\xrightarrow{H^+}$ NH_3^+-benzene

Delocalization — No delocalization

ALIPHATIC AMINE: $R—\ddot{N}H_2$ ⟶ $R—NH_3^+$

No delocalization — No delocalization

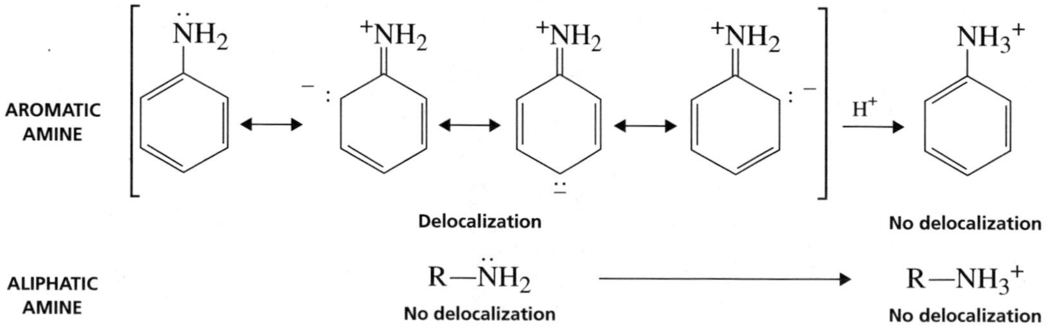

Solubility in 5% $NaHCO_3$ and 5% NaOH. Compounds that dissolve in sodium bicarbonate, a weak base, are strong acids. Compounds that dissolve in sodium hydroxide, a strong base, may be either strong or weak acids. Thus, one can distinguish weak and

strong acids by determining their solubility in both strong (NaOH) and weak ($NaHCO_3$) base. The classification of some functional groups as either weak or strong acids is given in the table below.

In this experiment, carboxylic acids (pK_a ~ 5) are generally indicated when a compound is soluble in both bases, and phenols (pK_a ~ 10) are indicated when it is soluble in NaOH only.

Compounds dissolve in base because they form sodium salts that are soluble in the aqueous medium. The salts of some high-molecular-weight compounds are not soluble, however, and precipitate. The salts of the long-chain carboxylic acids, such as myristic acid C_{14}, palmitic acid C_{16}, and stearic acid C_{18}, which form soaps, are in this category. Some phenols also produce insoluble sodium salts, and often these are colored due to resonance in the anion.

Strong Acids (soluble in both NaOH and $NaHCO_3$)		**Weak Acids (soluble in NaOH but not in $NaHCO_3$)**	
Sulfonic acids	RSO_3H	**Phenols**	ArOH
Carboxylic acids	RCOOH	**Nitroalkanes**	RCH_2NO_2 R_2CHNO_2
***ortho*- and *para*-substituted di- and trinitrophenols**	2,4-dinitrophenol (OH, NO_2, NO_2); 2,4,6-trinitrophenol (OH, NO_2, NO_2, NO_2)	**β-Diketones**	$R-C(=O)-CH_2-C(=O)-R$
		β-Diesters	$RO-C(=O)-CH_2-C(=O)-OR$
		Imides	$R-C(=O)-NH-C(=O)-R$
		Sulfonamides	$ArSO_2NH_2$ $ArSO_2NHR$

Both phenols and carboxylic acids produce resonance-stabilized conjugate bases. Thus, bases of the appropriate strength may easily remove their acidic protons to form the sodium salts.

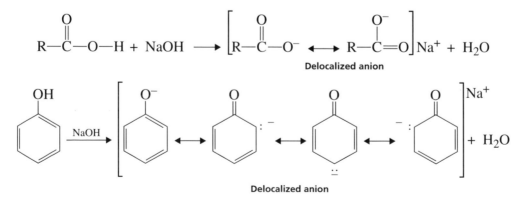

$$R-C(=O)-O-H + NaOH \longrightarrow \left[R-C(=O)-O^- \longleftrightarrow R-C(-O^-)=O\right]Na^+ + H_2O$$

Delocalized anion

$$C_6H_5OH \xrightarrow{NaOH} \left[C_6H_5O^- \longleftrightarrow \text{(ortho carbanion)} \longleftrightarrow \text{(para carbanion)} \longleftrightarrow \text{(ortho carbanion)}\right]Na^+ + H_2O$$

Delocalized anion

In phenols, substitution of nitro groups in the *ortho* and *para* positions of the ring increases the acidity. Nitro groups in these positions provide additional delocalization in the conjugate anion. Phenols that have two or three nitro groups in the *ortho* and *para* positions often dissolve in *both* sodium hydroxide and sodium bicarbonate solutions.

Solubility in Concentrated Sulfuric Acid. Many compounds are soluble in cold, concentrated sulfuric acid. Of the compounds included in this experiment, alcohols, ketones, aldehydes, and esters are in this category. These compounds are described as being "neutral." Other compounds that also dissolve include alkenes, alkynes, ethers, nitroaromatics, and amides. Because several different kinds of compounds are soluble in sulfuric acid, further chemical tests and spectroscopy will be needed to differentiate among them.

Compounds that are soluble in concentrated sulfuric acid but not in dilute acid are extremely weak bases. Almost any compound containing a nitrogen, an oxygen, or a sulfur atom can be protonated in concentrated sulfuric acid. The ions produced are soluble in the medium.

$$R{-}O{-}H + H_2SO_4 \longrightarrow R{-}\overset{+}{O}(H){-}H + HSO_4^- \longrightarrow R^+ + H_2O + HSO_4^-$$

$$R{-}C({=}O){-}R + H_2SO_4 \longrightarrow R{-}C({=}\overset{+}{O}{-}H){-}R + HSO_4^-$$

$$R{-}C({=}O){-}OR + H_2SO_4 \longrightarrow R{-}C({=}\overset{+}{O}{-}H){-}OR + HSO_4^-$$

$$R_2C{=}CR_2 + H_2SO_4 \longrightarrow R{-}C(R)(H){-}\overset{+}{C}(R){-}R + HSO_4^-$$

Inert Compounds. Compounds not soluble in concentrated sulfuric acid or any of the other solvents are said to be **inert.** Compounds not soluble in concentrated sulfuric acid include the alkanes, most simple aromatics, and the alkyl halides. Some examples of inert compounds are hexane, benzene, chlorobenzene, chlorohexane, and toluene.

EXPERIMENT 55B

Tests for the Elements (N, S, X)

—Br

—N— (with a third bond down) —C≡N

$—NO_2$

—Cl —I

S (with two bonds)

Except for amines (Experiment 55G), which are easily detected by their solubility behavior, all compounds issued in this experiment will contain heteroelements (N, S, Cl, Br, or I) only as *secondary* functional group. These will be subsidiary to some other important functional group. Thus, no alkyl or aryl halides, nitro compounds, thiols, or thioethers will be issued. However, some of the unknowns may contain a halogen or a nitro group. Less frequently, they may contain a sulfur atom or a cyano group.

Consider as an example *p*-bromobenzaldehyde, an **aldehyde** that contains bromine as a ring substituent. The identification of this compound would hinge on whether the investigator could identify it as an aldehyde. It could probably be identified *without* proving the existence of bromine in the molecule. That information, however, could make the identification easier. In this experiment, methods are given for identifying the presence of a halogen or a nitro group in an unknown compound. Also given is a general method (sodium fusion) for detecting the principal heteroelements that may exist in organic molecules.

Classification Tests

Halides	Nitro Groups	N, S, X (Cl, Br, I)
Beilstein test Silver nitrate Sodium iodide/acetone	Ferrous hydroxide	Sodium fusion

Suggested Waste Disposal

Dispose of all solutions containing silver into a waste container designated for this purpose. Any other aqueous solutions should be disposed of in the container designated for aqueous waste. Any remaining organic compounds must be disposed of in the appropriate organic waste container under the hood. This is particularly true of any solution containing benzyl bromide, which is a lachrymator.

Tests for a Halide

BEILSTEIN TEST

Procedure. Adjust the air and gas mixture so that the flame of a Bunsen burner or microburner is blue. Bend the end of a piece of copper wire so that a small closed loop is created. Heat the loop end of the wire in the flame until it glows brightly. After the wire has cooled, dip the wire directly into a sample of the unknown. If the unknown is a solid and won't adhere to the copper wire, place a small amount of the substance on a watch glass, wet the copper wire in distilled water, and place the wire into the sample on the watch glass. The solid should adhere to the wire. Now heat the wire in the Bunsen burner flame again. The compound will first burn. After the burning, a green flame will be produced if a halogen is present. You should hold the wire in flame either just above the tip of the flame or at its outside edge near the bottom of the flame. You will need to experiment to find the best position to hold the copper wire to obtain the best result.

Test Compounds. Try this test on bromobenzene and benzoic acid.

Discussion

Halogens can be detected easily and reliably by the Beilstein test. It is the simplest method for determining the presence of a halogen, but it does not differentiate among chlorine, bromine, and iodine, any one of which will give a positive test. However, when the identity of the unknown has been narrowed to two choices, of which one has a halogen and one does not, the Beilstein test will often be enough to distinguish between the two.

A positive Beilstein test results from the production of a volatile copper halide when an organic halide is heated with copper oxide. The copper halide imparts a blue green color to the flame.

This test can be very sensitive to small amounts of halide impurities in some compounds. Therefore, use caution in interpreting the results of the test if you obtain only a weak color.

SILVER NITRATE TEST

Procedure. Add 1 drop of a liquid or 5 drops of a concentrated ethanolic solution of a solid unknown to 2 mL of a 2% ethanolic silver nitrate solution. If no reaction is observed after 5 minutes at room temperature, heat the solution in a hot water bath at about 100°C and note whether a precipitate forms. If a precipitate forms, add 2 drops of 5% nitric acid and note whether the precipitate dissolves. Carboxylic acids give a false test by precipitating in silver nitrate, but they dissolve when nitric acid is added. Silver halides, in contrast, do not dissolve in nitric acid.

Test Compounds. Apply this test to benzyl bromide (α-bromotoluene) and bromobenzene. Discard all waste reagents in a suitable waste container in the hood, because benzyl bromide is a lachrymator.

Discussion

This test depends on the formation of a white or off-white precipitate of silver halide when silver nitrate is allowed to react with a sufficiently reactive halide.

$$RX + Ag^{+}NO_3^{-} \longrightarrow \underset{\text{Precipitate}}{\mathbf{AgX}} + R^{+}NO_3^{-} \xrightarrow{CH_3CH_2OH} R-O-CH_2CH_3$$

The test does not distinguish among chlorides, bromides, and iodides but does distinguish **labile** (reactive) halides from halides that are unreactive. Halides substituted on an aromatic ring will not usually give a positive silver nitrate test; however, alkyl halides of many types will give a positive test.

The most reactive compounds are those able to form stable carbocations in solution and those equipped with good leaving groups (X = I, Br, Cl). Benzyl, allyl, and tertiary halides react immediately with silver nitrate. Secondary and primary halides do not react at room temperature but react readily when heated. Aryl and vinyl halides do not react at all, even at elevated temperatures. This pattern of reactivity fits the stability order for various carbocations quite well. Compounds that produce stable carbocations react at higher rates than those that do not.

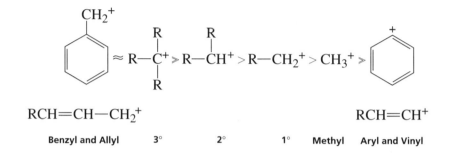

$$C_6H_5CH_2^+ \text{ or } RCH{=}CH{-}CH_2^+ \approx R_3C^+ > R_2CH^+ > RCH_2^+ > CH_3^+ > C_6H_5^+ \text{ or } RCH{=}CH^+$$

Benzyl and Allyl 3° 2° 1° Methyl Aryl and Vinyl

The fast reaction of benzylic and allylic halides is a result of the resonance stabilization that is available to the intermediate carbocations formed. Tertiary halides are more reactive than secondary halides, which are in turn more reactive than primary or methyl halides because alkyl substituents are able to stabilize the intermediate carbocations by an electron-releasing effect. The methyl carbocations have no alkyl groups and are the least stable of all carbocations mentioned thus far. Vinyl and aryl carbocations are extremely unstable because the charge is localized on an sp^2-hybridized carbon (double-bond carbon) rather than on one that is sp^3-hybridized.

SODIUM IODIDE IN ACETONE

Procedure. This test is described in Experiment 20.

Test Compounds. Apply this test to benzyl bromide (α-bromotoluene), bromobenzene, and 2-chloro-2-methylpropane (*tert*-butyl chloride).

Detection of Nitro Groups

Although nitro compounds will not be issued as distinct unknowns, many of the unknowns may have a nitro group as a secondary functional group. The presence of a nitro group, and hence nitrogen, in an unknown compound is determined most easily by infrared spectroscopy. However, many nitro compounds give a positive result in the following test. Unfortunately, functional groups other than the nitro group may also give a positive result. You should interpret the results of this test with caution.

FERROUS HYDROXIDE TEST

Procedure. Place 1.5 mL of freshly prepared 5% aqueous ferrous ammonium sulfate in a small test tube and add about 10 mg of a solid or 5 drops of a liquid compound. Mix the solution well and then add first 1 drop of 2 *M* sulfuric acid and then 1 mL of 2 *M* potassium hydroxide in methanol. Stopper the test tube and shake it vigorously. A positive test is indicated by the formation of a red brown precipitate, usually within 1 minute.

Test Compound. Apply this test to 2-nitrotoluene.

Discussion

Most nitro compounds oxidize ferrous hydroxide to ferric hydroxide, which is a red brown solid. A precipitate indicates a positive test.

$$R-NO_2 + 4H_2O + 6Fe(OH)_2 \longrightarrow R-NH_2 + 6Fe(OH)_3$$

INFRARED SPECTROSCOPY

The nitro group gives two strong bands near 1560 cm^{-1} and 1350 cm^{-1}. See Technique 25 for details.

Detection of a Cyano Group

Although nitriles will not be given as unknowns in this experiment, the cyano group may be a subsidiary functional group whose presence or absence is important to the final identification of an unknown compound. The cyano group can be hydrolyzed in a strong base, by heating vigorously, to give a carboxylic acid and ammonia gas:

$$R-C{\equiv}N + 2\,H_2O \xrightarrow[\Delta]{NaOH} R-COOH + NH_3$$

The ammonia can be detected by its odor or by moist pH paper. However, this method is somewhat difficult, and the presence of a nitrile group is confirmed most easily by infrared spectroscopy. No other functional groups (except some C≡C) absorb in the same region of the spectrum as C≡N.

INFRARED SPECTROSCOPY

C≡N stretch is a very sharp band of medium intensity near 2250 cm^{-1}. See Technique 25 for details.

Sodium Fusion Tests (Detection of N, S, and X) (Optional)

When an organic compound containing nitrogen, sulfur, or halide atoms is fused with sodium metal, there is a reductive decomposition of the compound, which converts these atoms to the sodium salts of the inorganic ions CN^-, S^{2-}, and X^-.

$$[N, S, X] \xrightarrow[\Delta]{Na} NaCN, Na_2S, NaX$$

When the fusion mixture is dissolved in distilled water, the cyanide, sulfide, and halide ions can be detected by standard qualitative inorganic tests.

> **Caution:** Always remember to manipulate the sodium metal with a knife or a forceps. Do not touch it with your fingers. Keep sodium away from water. Destroy all waste sodium with 1-butanol or ethanol. Wear safety glasses.

PREPARATION OF STOCK SOLUTION

General Method

Procedure. Using a forceps and a knife, take some sodium from the storage container, cut a small piece about the size of a small pea (3 mm on a side), and dry it on a paper towel. Place this small piece of sodium in a clean, dry small test tube (10 mm × 75 mm). Clamp the test tube to a ring stand and heat the bottom of the tube with a microburner until the sodium melts and its metallic vapor can be seen to rise about a third of the way up the tube. The bottom of the tube will probably have a dull red glow. Remove the burner and *immediately* drop the sample directly into the tube. Use about 10 mg of a solid placed on the end of a spatula or 2–3 drops of a liquid. Be sure to drop the sample directly down the center of the tube so that it touches the hot sodium metal and does not adhere to the side of the test tube. If the fusion is successful, there will usually be a flash or a small explosion. If the reaction is not successful, heat the tube to red heat for a few seconds to ensure complete reaction.

Allow the test tube to cool to room temperature and then carefully add 10 drops of methanol, a drop at a time, to the fusion mixture. Using a spatula or a long glass rod, reach into the test tube and stir the mixture to ensure complete reaction of any excess sodium metal. The fusion will have destroyed the test tube for other uses. Thus, the easiest way to recover the fusion mixture is to crush the test tube into a small beaker containing 5–10 mL of *distilled* water. The tube is easily crushed if it is placed in the angle of a clamp holder. Tighten the clamp until the tube is securely held near its bottom and then—standing back from the beaker and holding the clamp at its opposite end—continue tightening the clamp until the test tube breaks and the pieces fall into the beaker. Stir the solution well, heat it to boiling, and then filter it by gravity through a fluted filter (Figure 8.3, p. 648). Portions of this solution will be used for the tests to detect nitrogen, sulfur, and the halogens.

Alternative Method

Procedure. With some volatile liquids, the previous method will not work. The compounds volatilize before they reach the sodium vapors. For such compounds, place 4 or 5 drops of the pure liquid in the clean, dry test tube, clamp it, and cautiously add the small piece of sodium metal. If there is any reaction, wait until it subsides. Then heat the test tube to red heat and continue according to the instructions in the second paragraph of the preceding procedure.

NITROGEN TEST

Procedure. Using pH paper and a 10% sodium hydroxide solution, adjust the pH of about 1 mL of the stock solution to pH 13. Add 2 drops of saturated ferrous ammonium sulfate solution and 2 drops of 30% potassium fluoride solution. Boil the solution for about 30 seconds. Then acidify the hot solution by adding 30% sulfuric acid dropwise until the iron hydroxides dissolve. Avoid using excess acid. If nitrogen is present, a dark blue (not green) precipitate of Prussian blue $NaFe_2(CN)_6$ will form, or the solution will assume a dark blue color.

Reagents. Dissolve 5 g of ferrous ammonium sulfate in 100 mL of water. Dissolve 30 g of potassium fluoride in 100 mL of water.

SULFUR TEST

Procedure. Acidify about 1 mL of the test solution with acetic acid and add a few drops of a 1% lead acetate solution. The presence of sulfur is indicated by a black precipitate of lead sulfide PbS.

> **Caution:** Many compounds of lead(II) are suspected carcinogens (see p. 573) and should be handled with care. Avoid contact.

HALIDE TESTS

Procedure. Cyanide and sulfide ions interfere with the test for halides. If such ions are present, they must be removed. To accomplish this, acidify the solution with dilute nitric acid and boil it for about 2 minutes. This will drive off any HCN or H_2S that is formed. When the solution cools, add a few drops of a 5% silver nitrate solution. A *voluminous* precipitate indicates a halide. A faint turbidity *does not* mean a positive test. Silver chloride is white. Silver bromide is off-white. Silver iodide is yellow. Silver chloride will readily dissolve in concentrated ammonium hydroxide, whereas silver bromide is only slightly soluble.

DIFFERENTIATION OF CHLORIDE, BROMIDE, AND IODIDE

Procedure. Acidify 2 mL of the test solution with 10% sulfuric acid and boil it for about 2 minutes. Cool the solution and add about 0.5 mL of methylene chloride. Add a few drops of chlorine water or 2–4 mg of calcium hypochlorite.[1] Check to be sure that the solution is still acidic. Then stopper the tube, shake it vigorously, and set it aside to allow the layers to separate. An orange to brown color in the methylene chloride layer indicates bromine. Violet indicates iodine. No color or a *light* yellow indicates chlorine.

TECHNIQUE 25

Infrared Spectroscopy

Almost any compound having covalent bonds, whether organic or inorganic, will be found to absorb frequencies of electromagnetic radiation in the infrared region of the spectrum. The infrared region of the electromagnetic spectrum lies at wavelengths longer than those associated with visible light, which includes wavelengths from approximately 400 nm to 800 nm (1 nm = 10^{-9} m), but at wavelengths shorter than those associated with radio waves, which have wavelengths longer than 1 cm. For chemical purposes, we are interested in the *vibrational* portion of the infrared region. This portion includes radiations with wavelengths (λ) between 2.5 μm and 15 μm (1 μm = 10^{-6} m). The relation of the infrared region to other regions included in the electromagnetic spectrum is illustrated in Figure 25.1.

As with other types of energy absorption, molecules are excited to a higher energy state when they absorb infrared radiation. The absorption of the infrared radiation is, like other absorption processes, a quantized process. Only selected frequencies (energies) of infrared radiation are absorbed by a molecule. The absorption of infrared radiation corresponds to energy changes on the order of 8–40 kJ/mole (2–10 kcal/mole). Radiation in this energy range corresponds to the range encompassing the stretching and bending vibrational frequencies of the bonds in most covalent molecules. In the absorption process, those frequencies of infrared radiation that match the natural vibrational frequencies of the molecule in question are absorbed, and the energy absorbed increases the *amplitude* of the vibrational motions of the bonds in the molecule.

Most chemists refer to the radiation in the vibrational infrared region of the electromagnetic spectrum by units called **wavenumbers** ($\overline{\nu}$). Wavenumbers are expressed in reciprocal centimeters (cm^{-1}) and are easily computed by taking the reciprocal of the wavelength (λ) expressed in centimeters. This unit has the advantage, for those performing calculations, of being directly proportional to energy. Thus, the vibrational infrared region of the spectrum extends from about 4000 cm^{-1} to 650 cm^{-1} (or wavenumbers).

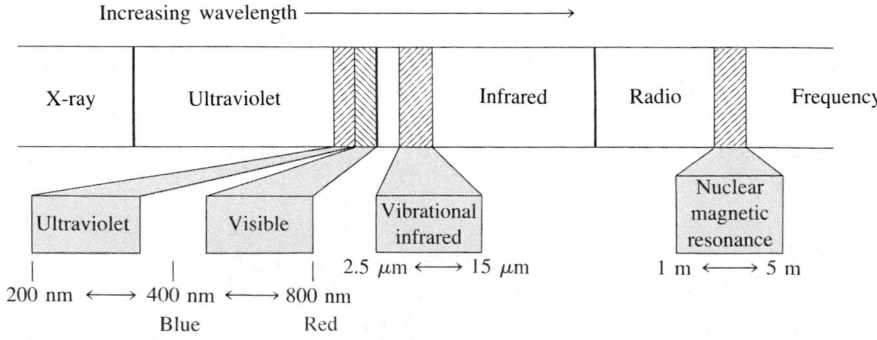

Figure 25.1 A portion of the electromagnetic spectrum showing the relation of vibrational infrared radiation to other types of radiation.

Wavelengths (μm) and wavenumbers (cm^{-1}) can be interconverted by the following relationships:

$$cm^{-1} = \frac{1}{(\mu m)} \times 10{,}000$$

$$\mu m = \frac{1}{(cm)^{-1}} \times 10{,}000$$

Part A. Sample Preparation and Recording the Spectrum

25.1 INTRODUCTION

To determine the infrared spectrum of the compound, one must place the compound in a sample holder or cell. In infrared spectroscopy, this immediately poses a problem. Glass, quartz, and plastics absorb strongly throughout the infrared region of the spectrum (any compound with covalent bonds usually absorbs) and cannot be used to construct sample cells. Ionic substances must be used in cell construction. Metal halides (sodium chloride, potassium bromide, silver chloride) are commonly used for this purpose.

Sodium Chloride Cells. Single crystals of sodium chloride are cut and polished to give plates that are transparent throughout the infrared region. These plates are then used to fabricate cells that can be used to hold *liquid* samples. Because sodium chloride is water soluble, samples must be *dry* before a spectrum can be obtained. In general, sodium chloride plates are preferred for most applications involving liquid samples. Potassium bromide plates may also be used in place of sodium chloride.

Silver Chloride Cells. Cells may be constructed of silver chloride. These plates may be used for *liquid* samples that contain small amounts of water, because silver chloride is water insoluble. However, because water absorbs in the infrared region, as much water as possible should be removed, even when using silver chloride. Silver chloride plates must be stored in the dark. They darken when exposed to light, and they cannot be used with compounds that have an amino functional group. Amines react with silver chloride.

Solid Samples. The easiest way to hold a *solid* sample in place is to dissolve the sample in a volatile organic solvent, place several drops of this solution on a salt plate, and allow the solvent to evaporate. This dry film method can be used only with modern FT-IR spectrometers. The other methods described here can be used with both FT-IR and dispersion spectrometers. A solid sample can also be held in place by making a potassium bromide pellet that contains a small amount of dispersed compound. A solid sample may also be suspended in mineral oil, which absorbs only in specific regions of the infrared spectrum. Another method is to dissolve the solid compound in an appropriate solvent and place the solution between two sodium chloride or silver chloride plates.

25.2 LIQUID SAMPLES—NaCl PLATES

The simplest method of preparing the sample, if it is a liquid, is to place a thin layer of the liquid between two sodium chloride plates that have been ground flat and polished. This is the method of choice when you need to determine the infrared spectrum of a pure liquid. A spectrum determined by this method is referred to as a **neat** spectrum. No solvent is used. The polished plates are expensive because they are cut from a large, single crystal of sodium chloride. Salt plates break easily, and they are water soluble.

Preparing the Sample. Obtain two sodium chloride plates and a holder from the desiccator where they are stored. Moisture from fingers will mar and occlude the polished surfaces. Samples that contain water will destroy the plates.

> **Note:** The plates should be touched only on their edges. Be certain to use a sample that is dry or free from water.

Add 1 or 2 drops of the liquid to the surface of one plate, and then place the second plate on top.[1] The pressure of this second plate causes the liquid to spread out and form a thin capillary film between the two plates. As shown in Figure 25.2, set the plates between

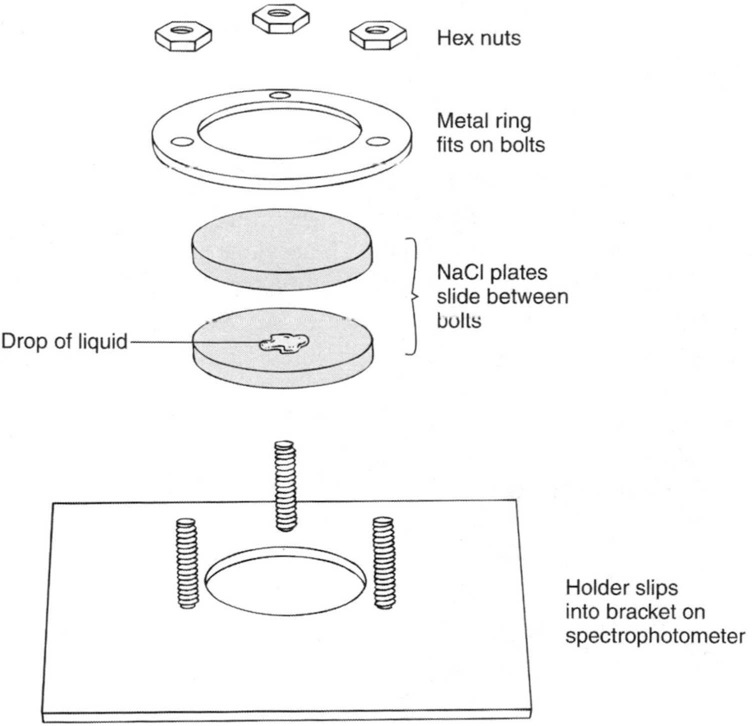

Figure 25.2 Salt plates and holder.

[1] Use a Pasteur pipet or a short length of microcapillary tubing. If you use the microcapillary tubing, it can be filled by touching it into the liquid sample. When you touch it (lightly) to the salt plate, it will empty. Be careful not to scratch the plate.

the bolts in a holder and place the metal ring carefully on the salt plates. Use the hex nuts to hold the salt plates in place.

Note: Do not overtighten the nuts, or the salt plates will cleave or split.

Tighten the nuts firmly, but do not use any force to turn them. Spin them with the fingers until they stop; then turn them just another fraction of a full turn, and they will be tight enough. If the nuts have been tightened carefully, you should observe a *transparent film of sample* (a uniform wetting of the surface). If a thin film has not been obtained, either loosen one or more of the hex nuts and adjust them so that a uniform film is obtained or add more sample.

The thickness of the film obtained between the two plates is a function of two factors: (1) the amount of liquid placed on the first plate (1 drop, 2 drops, and so on) and (2) the pressure used to hold the plates together. If more than 1 or 2 drops of liquid have been used, the amount will probably be too much, and the resulting spectrum will show strong absorptions that are off the scale of the chart paper. Only enough liquid to wet both surfaces is needed.

If the sample has a very low viscosity, the capillary film may be too thin to produce a good spectrum. Another problem you may find is that the liquid is so volatile that the sample evaporates before the spectrum can be determined. In these cases, you may need to use the silver chloride plates discussed in Section 25.3 or a solution cell described in Section 25.6. Often, you can obtain a reasonable spectrum by assembling the cell quickly and running the spectrum before the sample runs out of the salt plates or evaporates.

Determining the Infrared Spectrum. Slide the holder into the slot in the sample beam of the spectrophotometer. Determine the spectrum according to the instructions provided by your instructor. In some cases, your instructor may ask you to calibrate your spectrum. If this is the case, refer to Section 25.8.

Cleaning and Storing the Salt Plates. Once the spectrum has been determined, demount the holder and rinse the salt plates with methylene chloride (or *dry* acetone). (Keep the plates away from water!) Use a soft tissue, moistened with the solvent, to wipe the plates. If some of your compound remains on the plates, you may observe a shiny surface. Continue to clean the plates with solvent until no more compound remains on the surfaces of the plates.

Caution: Avoid direct contact with methylene chloride. Return the salt plates and holder to the desiccator for storage.

25.3 LIQUID SAMPLES—AgCl PLATES

The minicell shown in Figure 25.3 may also be used with liquids.[2] The cell assembly consists of a two-piece threaded body, an O-ring, and two silver chloride plates. The plates

[2]The Wilks Mini-Cell liquid sample holder is available from the Foxboro Company, 151 Woodward Avenue, South Norwalk, CT 06856. We recommend the AgCl cell windows with 0.10-mm depression rather than the 0.025-mm depression.

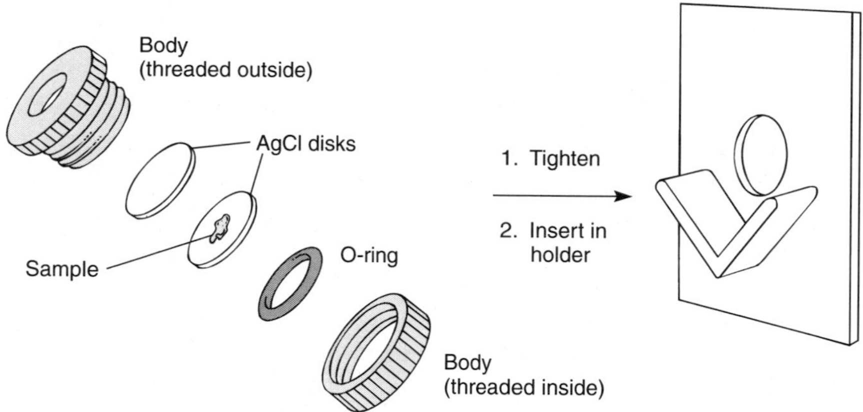

Figure 25.3 AgCl minicell liquid sample cell and V-mount holder.

are flat on one side, and there is a circular depression (0.025 mm or 0.10 mm deep) on the other side of the plate. An advantage of using silver chloride plates is that they may be used with wet samples or solutions. A disadvantage is that silver chloride darkens when exposed to light for extended periods. Silver chloride plates also scratch more easily than salt plates and react with amines.

Preparing the Sample. Silver chloride plates should be handled in the same way as salt plates. Unfortunately, they are smaller and thinner (about like a contact lens) than salt plates, and care must be taken not to lose them! Remove them from the light-tight container with care. It is difficult to tell which side of the plate has the slight circular depression. Your instructor may have etched a letter on each plate to indicate which side is the flat one. To determine the infrared spectrum of a pure liquid (neat spectrum), select the flat side of each silver chloride plate. Insert the O-ring into the cell body as shown in Figure 25.3, place the plate into the cell body with the flat surface up, and add 1 drop or less of liquid to the plate.

Note: Do not use amines with AgCl plates.

Place the second plate on top of the first with the flat side down. The orientation of the silver chloride plates is shown in Figure 25.4A. This arrangement is used to obtain a capillary film of your sample. Screw the top of the minicell into the body of the cell so that the silver chloride plates are held firmly together. A tight seal forms because AgCl deforms under pressure.

Other combinations may be used with these plates. For example, you may vary the sample path length by using the orientations shown in Figures 25.4B and C. If you add your

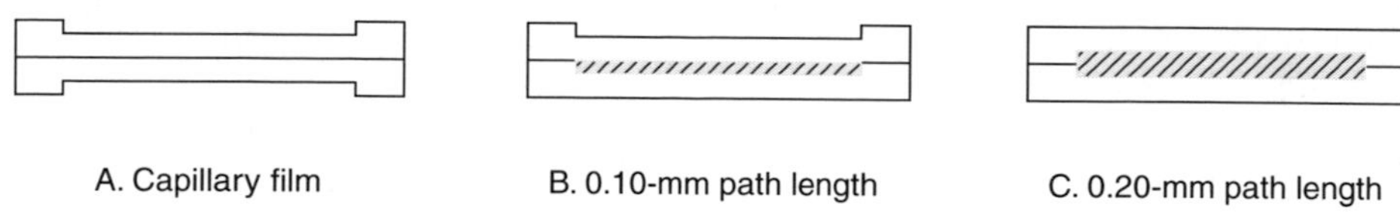

Figure 25.4 Path length variations for AgCl plates.

sample and the 0.10-mm depression of one plate and cover it with the flat side of the other one, you obtain a path length of 0.10 mm (Figure 25.4B). This arrangement is useful for analyzing volatile or low-viscosity liquids. Placement of the two plates with their depressions toward each other gives a path length of 0.20 mm (Figure 25.4C). This orientation may be used for a solution of a solid (or liquid) in carbon tetrachloride (Section 25.6B).

Determining the Spectrum. Slide the V-mount holder shown in Figure 25.3 into the slot on the infrared spectrophotometer. Set the cell assembly in the V-mount holder, and determine the infrared spectrum of the liquid.

Cleaning and Storing the AgCl Plates. Once the spectrum has been determined, the cell assembly holder should be demounted and the AgCl plates rinsed with methylene chloride or acetone. Do not use tissue to wipe the plates, as they scratch easily. AgCl plates are light sensitive. Store the plates in a light-tight container.

25.4 SOLID SAMPLES—DRY FILM

A simple method for determining the infrared spectrum of a solid sample is the **dry film** method. This method is easier than the other methods described here, it does not require any specialized equipment, and the spectra are excellent.[3] The disadvantage is that the dry film method can be used only with modern FT-IR spectrometers.

To use this method, place about 5 mg of your solid sample in a small, clean test tube. Add about 5 drops of methylene chloride (or diethyl ether or pentane), and stir the mixture to dissolve the solid. Using a Pasteur pipet (not a capillary tube), place several drops of the solution on the face of a salt plate. Allow the solvent to evaporate; a uniform deposit of your product will remain as a dry film coating the salt plate. Mount the salt plate on a V-shaped holder in the infrared beam. Note that only one salt plate is used; the second salt plate is not used to cover the first. Once the salt plate is positioned properly, you may determine the spectrum in the normal manner. With this method, it is *very important* that you clean your material off the salt plate. When you are finished, use methylene chloride or dry acetone to clean the salt plate.

25.5 SOLID SAMPLES—KBr PELLETS AND NUJOL MULLS

The methods described in this section can be used with both FT-IR and dispersion spectrometers.

A. KBr Pellets

One method of preparing a solid sample is to make a **potassium bromide (KBr) pellet.** When KBr is placed under pressure, it melts, flows, and seals the sample into a solid solution, or matrix. Because potassium bromide does not absorb in the infrared spectrum, a spectrum can be obtained on a sample without interference.

[3] P. L. Feist, *Journal of Chemical Education, 78* (2001): 351.

Preparing the Sample. Remove the agate mortar and pestle from the desiccator for use in preparing the sample. (Take care of them; they are expensive.) Grind 1 mg (0.001 g) of the solid sample for 1 minute in the agate mortar. At this point, the particle size will become so small that the surface of the solid appears shiny. Add 80 mg (0.080 g) of *powdered* potassium bromide and grind the mixture for about 30 seconds with the pestle. Scrape the mixture into the middle with a spatula and grind the mixture again for about 15 seconds. This grinding operation helps to mix the sample thoroughly with the KBr. You should work as rapidly as possible, because KBr absorbs water. The sample and KBr must be finely ground, or the mixture will scatter the infrared radiation excessively. Using your spatula, heap the mixture in the center of the mortar. Return the bottle of potassium bromide to the desiccator where it is stored when it is not in use.

The sample and potassium bromide should be weighed on an analytical balance the first few times that a pellet is prepared. After some experience, you can estimate these quantities quite accurately by eye.

Making a Pellet Using a KBr Handpress. Two methods are commonly used to prepare KBr pellets. The first method uses the handpress apparatus shown in Figure 25.5.[4]

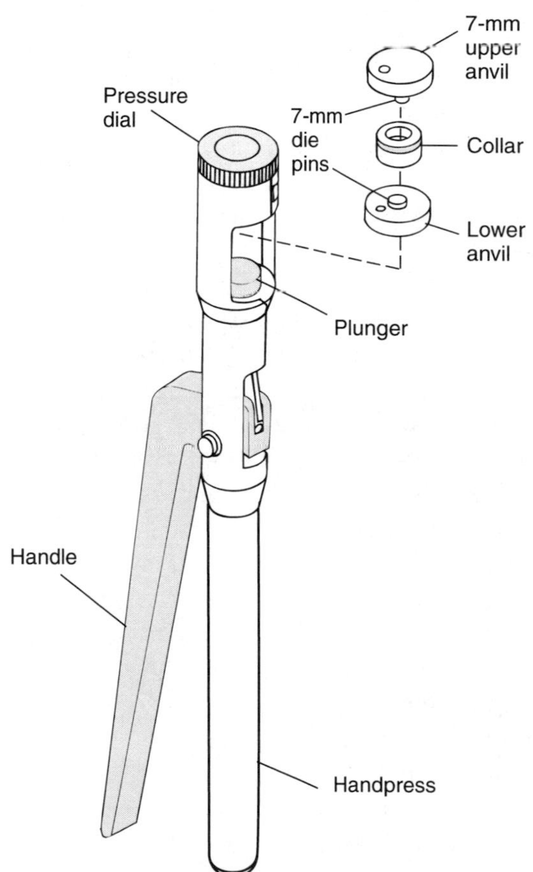

Figure 25.5 Making a KBr pellet with a handpress.

[4] KBr Quick Press unit is available from Wilmad Glass Company, Inc., Route 40 and Oak Road, Buena, NJ 08310.

Remove the die set from the storage container. Take extreme care to avoid scratching the polished surfaces of the die set. Place the anvil with the shorter die pin (lower anvil in Figure 25.5) on a bench. Slip the collar over the pin. Remove about one-fourth of your KBr mixture with a spatula and transfer it into the collar. The powder may not cover the head of the pin completely, but do not be concerned about this. Place the anvil with the longer die pin into the collar so that the die pin comes into contact with the sample. Never press the die set unless it contains a sample.

Lift the die set carefully by holding onto the lower anvil so that the collar stays in place. If you are careless with this operation, the collar may move enough to allow the powder to escape. Open the handle of the handpress slightly, tilt the press back a bit, and insert the die set into the press. Make sure that the die set is seated against the side wall of the chamber. Close the handle. It is imperative that the die set be seated against the side wall of the chamber so that the die is centered in the chamber. Pressing the die in an off-centered position can bend the anvil pins.

With the handle in the closed position, rotate the pressure dial so that the upper ram of the handpress just touches the upper anvil of the die assembly. Tilt the unit back so that the die set does not fall out of the handpress. Open the handle and rotate the pressure dial clockwise about one-half turn. Slowly compress the KBr mixture by closing the handle. The pressure should be no greater than that exerted by a very firm handshake. Do not apply excessive pressure, or the dies may be damaged. If in doubt, rotate the pressure dial counterclockwise to lower the pressure. If the handle closes too easily, open the handle, rotate the pressure dial clockwise, and compress the sample again. Compress the sample for about 60 seconds.

After this time, tilt the unit back so that the die set does not fall out of the handpress. Open the handle and carefully remove the die set from the unit. Turn the pressure dial counterclockwise about one full turn. Pull the die set apart and inspect the KBr pellet. Ideally, the pellet should appear clear like a piece of glass, but usually it will be translucent or somewhat opaque. There may be some cracks or holes in the pellet. The pellet will produce a good spectrum, even with imperfections, as long as light can travel through the pellet.

Making a Pellet with a KBr Minipress. The second method of preparing a pellet uses the minipress apparatus shown in Figure 25.6. Obtain a ground KBr mixture as described in "Preparing the Sample" and transfer a portion of the finely ground powder (usually not more than half) into a die that compresses it into a translucent pellet. As shown in Figure 25.6, the die consists of two stainless steel bolts and a threaded barrel. The bolts have their ends ground flat. To use this die, screw one of the bolts into the barrel, but not all the way; leave one or two turns. Carefully add the powder with a spatula into the open end of the partly assembled die and tap it lightly on the benchtop to give an even layer on the face of the bolt. While keeping the barrel upright, carefully screw the second bolt into the barrel until it is finger tight. Insert the head of the bottom bolt into the hexagonal hole in a plate bolted to the benchtop. This plate keeps the head of one bolt from turning. The top bolt is tightened with a torque wrench to compress the KBr mixture. Continue to turn the torque wrench until you hear a loud click (the ratchet mechanism makes softer clicks) or until you reach the appropriate torque value (20 ft-lb). If you tighten the bolt beyond this point, you may twist the head off one of the bolts. Leave the die under pressure for about 60 seconds; then reverse the ratchet on the torque wrench or pull the torque wrench in the opposite direction to open the assembly. When the two bolts are loose, hold the barrel horizontally and

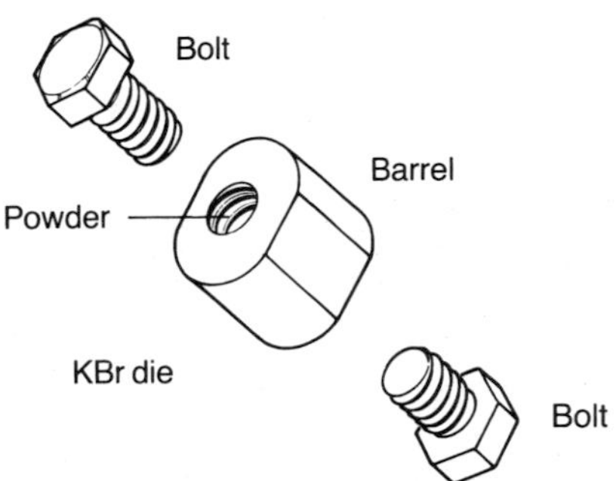

Figure 25.6 Making a KBr pellet with a minipress.

carefully remove the two bolts. You should observe a clear or translucent KBr pellet in the center of the barrel. Even if the pellet is not totally transparent, you should be able to obtain a satisfactory spectrum as long as light passes through the pellet.

Determining the Infrared Spectrum. To obtain the spectrum, slide the holder appropriate for the type of die that you are using into the slot on the infrared spectrophotometer. Set the die containing the pellet in the holder so that the sample is centered in the optical path. Obtain the infrared spectrum. If you are using a double-beam instrument, you may be able to compensate (at least partially) for a marginal pellet by placing a wire screen or attenuator in the reference beam, thereby balancing the lowered transmittance of the pellet. An FT-IR instrument will automatically deal with the low intensity if you select the "autoscale" option.

Problems with an Unsatisfactory Pellet. If the pellet is unsatisfactory (too cloudy to pass light), one of several things may have been wrong:

1. The KBr mixture may not have been ground finely enough, and the particle size may be too big. The large particle size creates too much light scattering.
2. The sample may not be dry.
3. Too much sample may have been used for the amount of KBr taken.
4. The pellet may be too thick; that is, too much of the powdered mixture was put into the die.
5. The KBr may have been "wet" or have acquired moisture from the air while the mixture was being ground in the mortar.
6. The sample may have a low melting point. Low-melting solids not only are difficult to dry but also melt under pressure. You may need to dissolve the compound in a solvent and run the spectrum in solution (Section 25.6).

Cleaning and Storing the Equipment. After you have determined the spectrum, punch the pellet out of the die with a wooden applicator stick (a spatula should not be used as it may scratch the dies). Remember that the polished faces of the die set must not be scratched, or they become useless. Pull a piece of Kimwipe through the die unit to remove all the sample. Also wipe any surfaces with a Kimwipe. *Do not wash the dies with water.* Check with your instructor to see if there are additional instructions for cleaning the die set. Return the dies to the storage container. Wash the mortar and pestle with water, dry them carefully with paper towels, and return them to the desiccator. Return the KBr powder to its desiccator.

B. Nujol Mulls

If an adequate KBr pellet cannot be obtained or if the solid is insoluble in a suitable solvent, the spectrum of a solid may be determined as a **Nujol mull.** In this method, finely grind about 5 mg of the solid sample in an agate mortar with a pestle. Then add 1 or 2 drops of Nujol mineral oil (white) and grind the mixture to a very fine dispersion. The solid is not dissolved in the Nujol; it is actually a suspension. This mull is then placed between two salt plates using a rubber policeman. Mount the salt plates in the holder in the same way as for liquid samples (Section 25.2).

Nujol is a mixture of high-molecular-weight hydrocarbons. Hence, it has absorptions in the C—H stretch and CH_2 and CH_3 bending regions of the spectrum (Figure 25.7). Clearly, if Nujol is used, no information can be obtained in these portions of the spectrum. In interpreting the spectrum, you must ignore these Nujol peaks. It is important to label the spectrum immediately after it was determined, noting that it was determined as a Nujol mull. Otherwise, you might forget that the C—H peaks belong to Nujol and not to the dispersed solid.

25.6 SOLID SAMPLES—SOLUTION SPECTRA

A. Method A—Solution between Salt (NaCl) Plates

For substances that are soluble in carbon tetrachloride, a quick and easy method for determining the spectra of solids is available. Dissolve as much solid as possible in 0.1 mL of carbon tetrachloride. Place 1 or 2 drops of the solution between sodium chloride plates in precisely the same manner as used for pure liquids (Section 25.2). The spectrum is determined as described for pure liquids using salt plates (Section 25.2). You should work as

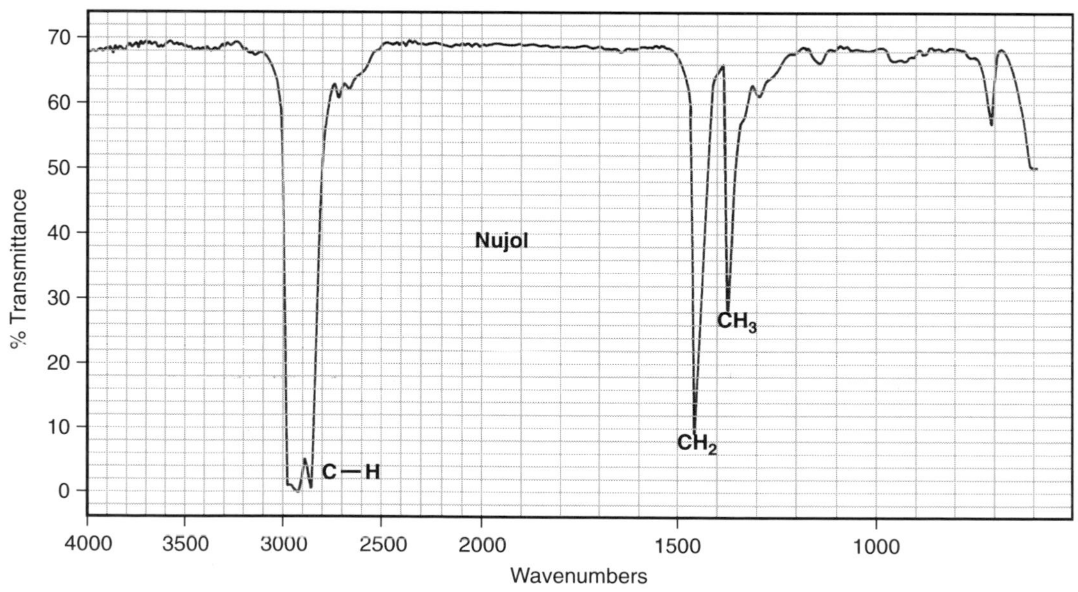

Figure 25.7 Infrared spectrum of Nujol (mineral oil).

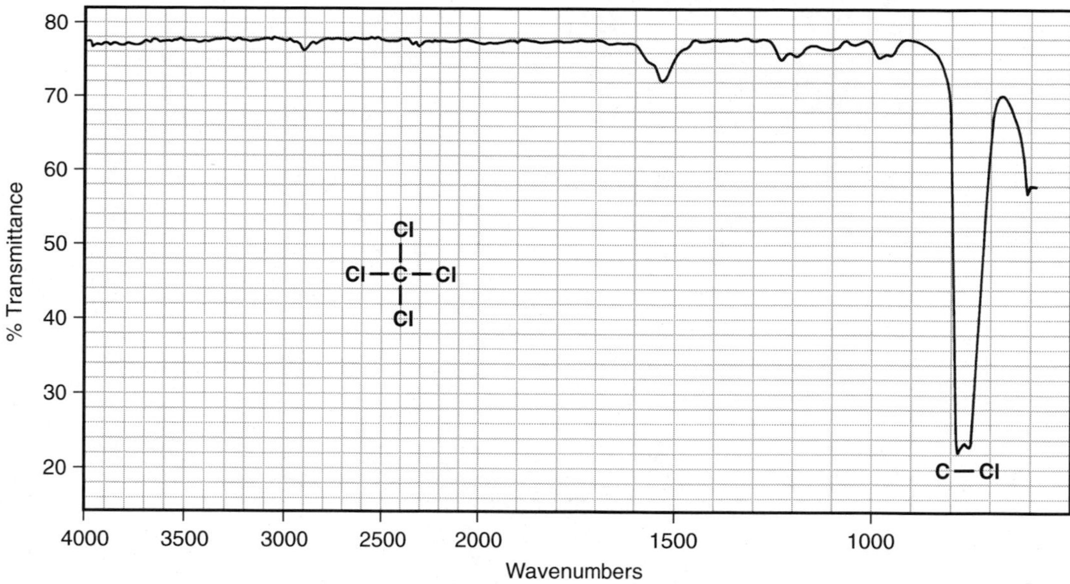

Figure 25.8 Infrared spectrum of carbon tetrachloride.

quickly as possible. If there is a delay, the solvent will evaporate from between the plates before the spectrum is recorded. Because the spectrum contains the absorptions of the solute superimposed on the absorptions of carbon tetrachloride, it is important to remember that any absorption that appears near 800 cm^{-1} may be due to the stretching of the C—Cl bond of the solvent. Information contained to the right of about 900 cm^{-1} is not usable in this method. There are no other interfering bands for this solvent (see Figure 25.8), and any other absorptions can be attributed to your sample. Chloroform solutions should not be studied by this method because the solvent has too many interfering absorptions (see Figure 25.9).

Caution: Carbon tetrachloride is a hazardous solvent. Work under the hood!

Carbon tetrachloride, besides being toxic, is suspected of being a carcinogen. In spite of the health problems associated with its use, there is no suitable alternative solvent for infrared spectroscopy. Other solvents have too many interfering infrared absorption bands. Handle carbon tetrachloride very carefully to minimize the adverse health effects. The spectroscopic-grade carbon tetrachloride should be stored in a glass-stoppered bottle in a hood. A Pasteur pipet should be attached to the bottle, possibly by storing it in a test tube taped to the side of the bottle. All sample preparation should be conducted in a hood. Rubber or plastic gloves should be worn. The cells should also be cleaned in the hood. All carbon tetrachloride used in preparing samples should be disposed of in an appropriately marked waste container.

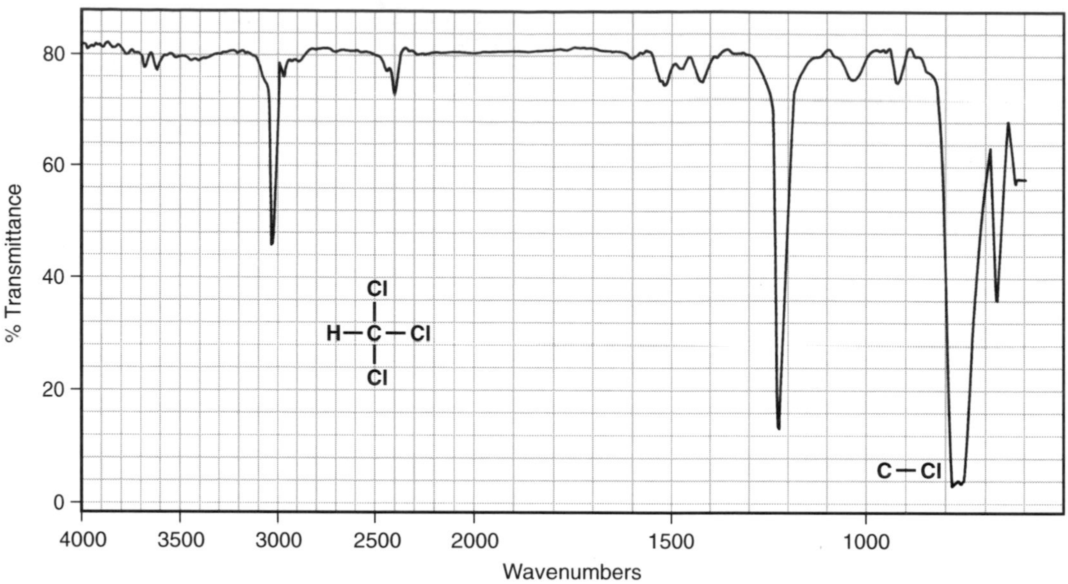

Figure 25.9 Infrared spectrum of chloroform.

B. Method B—AgCl Minicell

The AgCl minicell described in Section 25.3 may be used to determine the infrared spectrum of a solid dissolved in carbon tetrachloride. Prepare a 5–10% solution (5–10 mg in 0.1 mL) in carbon tetrachloride. If it is not possible to prepare a solution of this concentration because of low solubility, dissolve as much solid as possible in the solvent. Following the instructions given in Section 25.3, position the AgCl plates as shown in Figure 25.4C to obtain the maximum possible path length of 0.20 mm. When the cell is tightened firmly, the cell will not leak.

As indicated in method A, the spectrum will contain the absorptions of the dissolved solid superimposed on the absorptions of carbon tetrachloride. A strong absorption appears near 800 cm^{-1} for C—Cl stretch in the solvent. No useful information may be obtained for the sample to the right of about 900 cm^{-1}, but other bands that appear in the spectrum will belong to your sample. Read the safety material provided in method A. Carbon tetrachloride is toxic, and it should be used under a hood.

> **Note:** Care should be taken in cleaning the AgCl plates. Because AgCl plates scratch easily, they should not be wiped with tissue. Rinse them with methylene chloride and keep them in a dark place. Amines will destroy the plates.

C. Method C—Solution Cells (NaCl)

The spectra of solids may also be determined in a type of permanent sample cell called a **solution cell.** (The infrared spectra of liquids may also be determined in this cell.) The so-

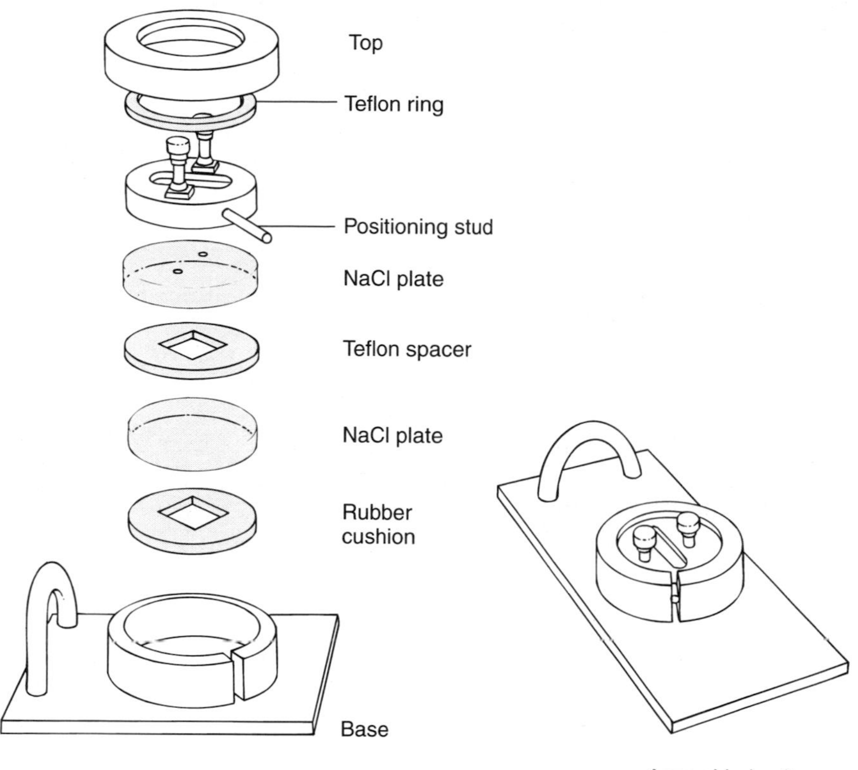

Figure 25.10 A solution cell.

lution cell, shown in Figure 25.10, is made from two salt plates, mounted with a Teflon spacer between them to control the thickness of the sample. The top sodium chloride plate has two holes drilled in it so that the sample can be introduced into the cavity between the two plates. These holes are extended through the face plate by two tubular extensions designed to hold Teflon plugs, which seal the internal chamber and prevent evaporation. The tubular extensions are tapered so that a syringe body (Luer lock without a needle) will fit snugly into them from the outside. The cells are thus filled from a syringe; usually, they are held upright and filled from the bottom entrance port.

These cells are very expensive, and you should try either method A or B before using solution cells. If you do need them, obtain your instructor's permission and receive instruction before using the cells. The cells are purchased in matched pairs, with identical path lengths. Dissolve a solid in a suitable solvent, usually carbon tetrachloride, and add the solution to one of the cells (**sample cell**) as described in the previous paragraph. The pure solvent, identical to that used to dissolve the solid, is placed in the other cell (**reference cell**). The spectrum of the solvent is subtracted from the spectrum of the solution (not always completely), and a spectrum of the solute is thus provided. For the solvent compensation to be as exact as possible and to avoid contamination of the reference cell, it is essential that one cell be used as a reference and that the other cell be used as a sample cell without ever being interchanged. After the spectrum is determined, it is important to clean the cells by flushing them with clean solvent. They should be dried by passing dry air through the cell.

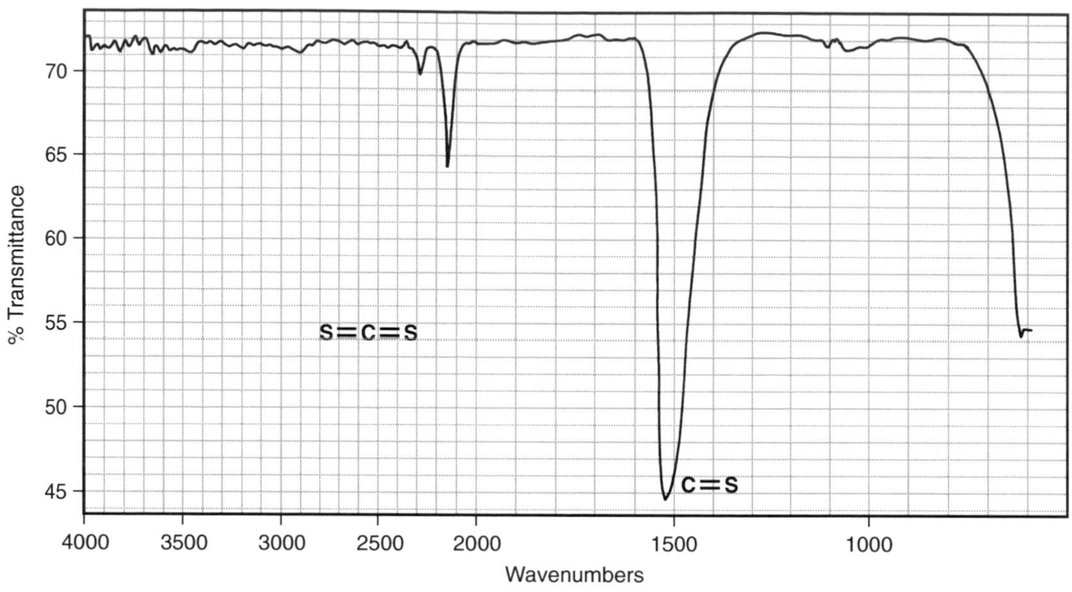

Figure 25.11 Infrared spectrum of carbon disulfide.

Solvents most often used in determining infrared spectra are carbon tetrachloride (Figure 25.8), chloroform (Figure 25.9), and carbon disulfide (Figure 25.11). A 5–10% solution of solid in one of these solvents usually gives a good spectrum. Carbon tetrachloride and chloroform are suspected carcinogens; however, because there are no suitable alternative solvents, these compounds must be used in infrared spectroscopy. The procedure outlined on page 883 for carbon tetrachloride should be followed. This procedure serves equally well for chloroform.

Note: Before you use the solution cells, you must obtain the instructor's permission and instruction on how to fill and clean the cells.

25.7 RECORDING THE SPECTRUM

The instructor will describe how to operate the infrared spectrophotometer, because the controls vary considerably, depending on the manufacturer, model of the instrument, and type. For example, some instruments involve pushing only a few buttons, whereas others use a more complicated computer interface system.

In all cases, it is important that the sample, the solvent, the type of cell or method used, and any other pertinent information be written on the spectrum immediately after the determination. This information may be important, and it is easily forgotten if not recorded. You may also need to calibrate the instrument (Section 25.8).

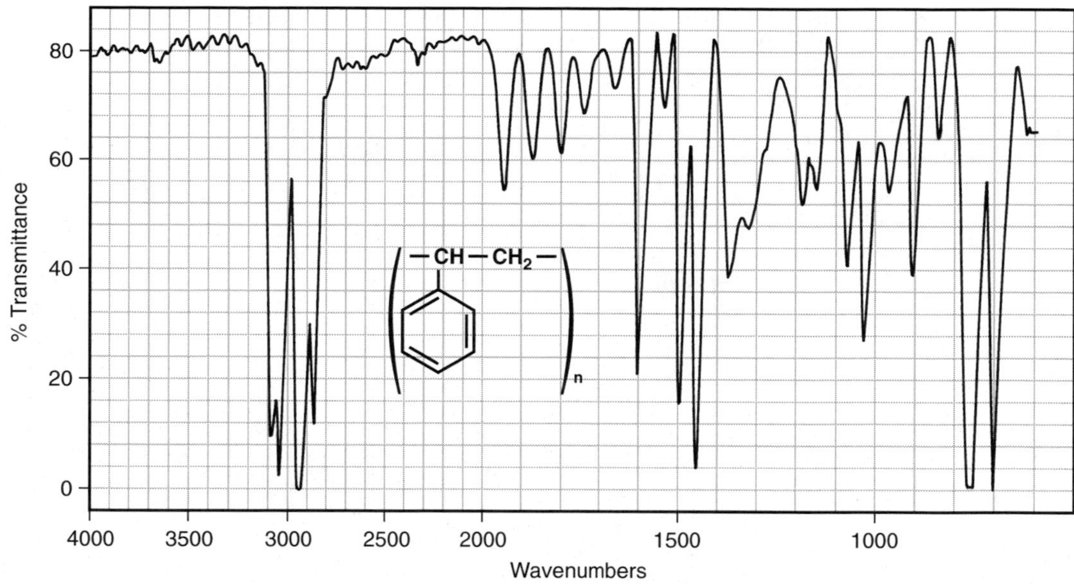

Figure 25.12 Infrared spectrum of polystyrene (thin film).

25.8 CALIBRATION

For some instruments, the frequency scale of the spectrum must be calibrated so that you know the position of each absorption peak precisely. You can recalibrate by recording a very small portion of the spectrum of polystyrene over the spectrum of your sample. The complete spectrum of polystyrene is shown in Figure 25.12. The most important of these peaks is at 1603 cm^{-1}; other useful peaks are at 2850 cm^{-1} and 906 cm^{-1}. After you record the spectrum of your sample, substitute a thin film of polystyrene for the sample cell and record the **tips** (not the entire spectrum) of the most important peaks over the sample spectrum.

It is always a good idea to calibrate a spectrum when the instrument uses chart paper with a preprinted scale. It is difficult to align the paper properly so that the scale matches the absorption lines precisely. You often need to know the precise values for certain functional groups (for example, the carbonyl group). Calibration is essential in these cases.

With computer-interfaced instruments, the instrument does not need to be calibrated. With this type of instrument, the spectrum and scale are printed on blank paper at the same time. The instrument has an internal calibration that ensures that the positions of the absorptions are known precisely and that they are placed at the proper positions on the scale. With this type of instrument, it is often possible to print a list of the locations of the major peaks as well as to obtain the complete spectrum of your compound.

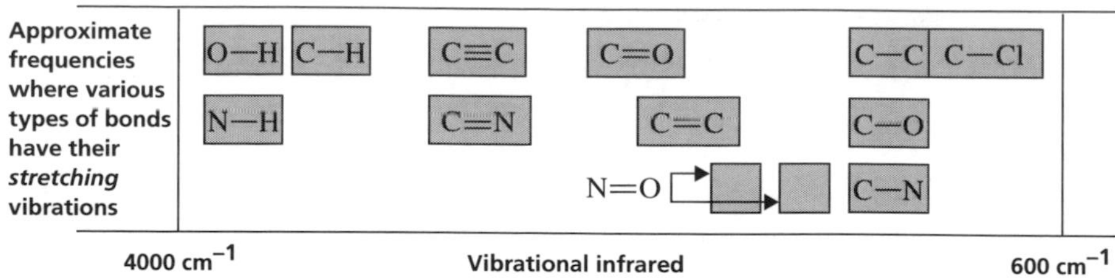

Figure 25.13 Approximate regions in which various common types of bonds absorb. (Bending, twisting, and other types of bond vibration have been omitted for clarity.)

Part B. Infrared Spectroscopy

25.9 USES OF THE INFRARED SPECTRUM

Because every type of bond has a different natural frequency of vibration and because the same type of bond in two different compounds is in a slightly different environment, no two molecules of different structure have exactly the same infrared absorption pattern, or **infrared spectrum.** Although some of the frequencies absorbed in the two cases might be the same, in no case of two different molecules will their infrared spectra (the patterns of absorption) be identical. Thus, the infrared spectrum can be used to identify molecules much as a fingerprint can be used to identify people. Comparing the infrared spectra of two substances thought to be identical will establish whether or not they are in fact identical. If the infrared spectra of two substances coincide peak for peak (absorption for absorption), in most cases, the substances are identical.

A second and more important use of the infrared spectrum is that it gives structural information about a molecule. The absorptions of each type of bond (N—H, C—H, O—H, C—X, C=O, C—O, C—C, C=C, C≡C, C≡N, and so on) are regularly found only in certain small portions of the vibrational infrared region. A small range of absorption can be defined for each type of bond. Outside this range, absorptions will normally be due to some other type of bond. Thus, for instance, any absorption in the range 3000 ± 150 cm^{-1} will almost always be due to the presence of a CH bond in the molecule; an absorption in the range 1700 ± 100 cm^{-1} will normally be due to the presence of a C=O bond (carbonyl group) in the molecule. The same type of range applies to each type of bond. The way these are spread out over the vibrational infrared is illustrated schematically in Figure 25.13. It is a good idea to remember this general scheme for future convenience.

25.10 MODES OF VIBRATION

The simplest types, or **modes,** of vibrational motion in a molecule that are **infrared active,** that is, give rise to absorptions, are the stretching and bending modes.

C—H   C(O)H

Stretching   Bending

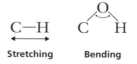

Other, more complex types of stretching and bending are also active, however. To introduce several words of terminology, the normal modes of vibration for a methylene group are shown below.

In any group of three or more atoms—at least two of which are identical—there are *two* modes of stretching or bending: the symmetric mode and asymmetric mode. Examples of such groupings are $—CH_3$, $—CH_2—$, $—NO_2$, $—NH_2$, and anhydrides $(CO)_2O$. For the anhydride, owing to asymmetric and symmetric modes of stretch, this functional group gives *two* absorptions in the C═O region. A similar phenomenon is seen for amino groups, where primary amines usually have *two* absorptions in the NH stretch region, whereas secondary amines R_2NH have only one absorption peak. Amides show similar bands. There are two strong N═O stretch peaks for a nitro group, which are caused by asymmetric and symmetric stretching modes.

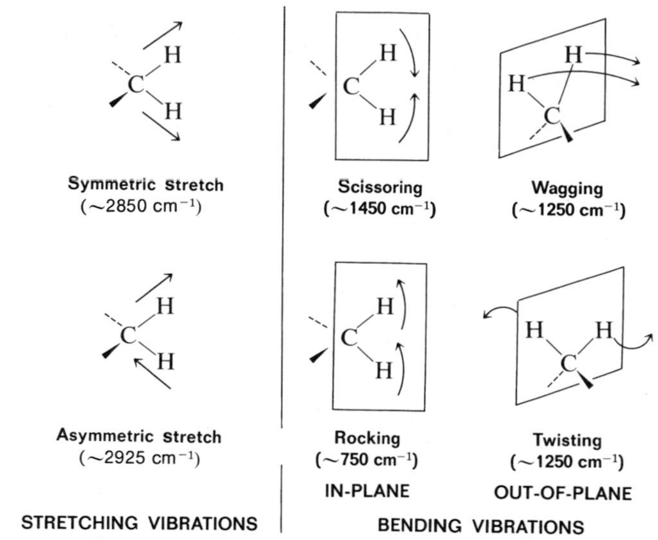

25.11 WHAT TO LOOK FOR IN EXAMINING INFRARED SPECTRA

The instrument that determines the absorption spectrum for a compound is called an **infrared spectrophotometer.** The spectrophotometer determines the relative strengths and positions of all the absorptions in the infrared region and plots this information on a piece of paper. This plot of absorption intensity versus wavenumber or wavelength is referred to as the **infrared spectrum** of the compound. A typical infrared spectrum, that of methyl isopropyl ketone, is shown in Figure 25.14.

The strong absorption in the middle of the spectrum corresponds to C═O, the carbonyl group. Note that the C═O peak is quite intense. In addition to the characteristic position of absorption, the **shape** and **intensity** of this peak are also unique to the C═O bond. This is true for almost every type of absorption peak; both shape and intensity characteristics can be described, and these characteristics often make it possible to distinguish the peak

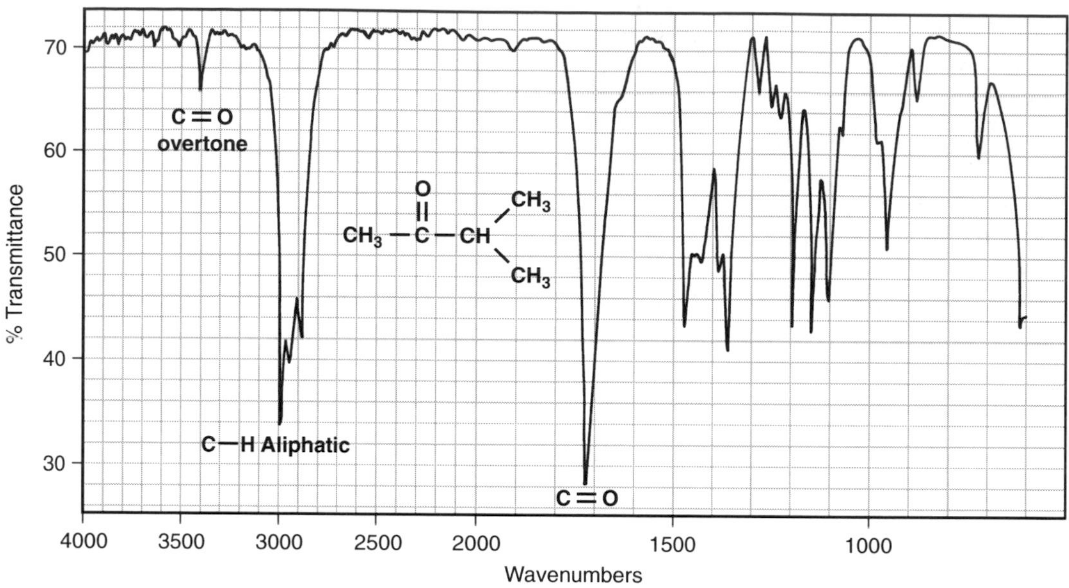

Figure 25.14 Infrared spectrum of methyl isopropyl ketone (neat liquid, salt plates).

in a confusing situation. For instance, to some extent both C=O and C=C bonds absorb in the same region of the infrared spectrum:

C=O 1850–1630 cm^{-1}
C=C 1680–1620 cm^{-1}

However, the C=O bond is a strong absorber, whereas the C=C bond generally absorbs only weakly. Hence, a trained observer would not normally interpret a strong peak at 1670 cm^{-1} to be a carbon–carbon double bond nor a weak absorption at this frequency to be due to a carbonyl group.

The shape of a peak often gives a clue to its identity as well. Thus, although the NH and OH regions of the infrared overlap,

OH 3650–3200 cm^{-1}
NH 3500–3300 cm^{-1}

NH usually gives a **sharp** absorption peak (absorbs a very narrow range of frequencies), and OH, when it is in the NH region, usually gives a **broad** absorption peak. Primary amines give *two* absorptions in this region, whereas alcohols give only one.

Therefore, while you are studying the sample spectra in the pages that follow, you should also notice shapes and intensities. They are as important as the frequency at which an absorption occurs, and you must train your eye to recognize these features. In the literature of organic chemistry, you will often find absorptions referred to as strong (s), medium (m), weak (w), broad, or sharp. The author is trying to convey some idea of what the peak looks like without actually drawing the spectrum. Although the intensity of an absorption often provides useful information about the identity of a peak, be aware that the relative intensities of all the peaks in the spectrum are dependent on the amount of sample that is used and the sensitivity setting of the instrument. Therefore, the *actual* intensity of a particular peak may vary from spectrum to spectrum, and you must pay attention to *relative* intensities.

25.12 CORRELATION CHARTS AND TABLES

To extract structural information from infrared spectra, you must know the frequencies or wavelengths at which various functional groups absorb. Infrared **correlation tables** present as much information as is known about where the various functional groups absorb. The books listed at the end of this chapter present extensive lists of correlation tables. Sometimes, the absorption information is given in a chart, called a **correlation chart.** A simplified correlation table is given in Table 25.1.

Although you may think assimilating the mass of data in Table 25.1 will be difficult, it is not if you make a modest start and then gradually increase your familiarity with the data. An ability to interpret the fine details of an infrared spectrum will follow. This is most easily accomplished by first establishing the broad visual patterns of Figure 25.13 firmly in mind. Then, as a second step, a "typical absorption value" can be memorized for each of the functional groups in this pattern. This value will be a single number that can be used as a pivot value for the memory. For instance, start with a simple aliphatic ketone as a model for all typical carbonyl compounds. The typical aliphatic ketone has carbonyl absorption of $1715 \pm 10\ cm^{-1}$. Without worrying about the variation, memorize $1715\ cm^{-1}$ as the base value for carbonyl absorption. Then learn the extent of the carbonyl range and the visual pattern of how the different kinds of carbonyl groups are arranged throughout this region. See, for instance, Figure 25.27 (page 902), which gives typical values for carbonyl compounds. Also learn how factors such as ring size (when the functional group is contained in a ring) and conjugation affect the base values (that is, in which direction the values are shifted). Learn the trends—always remembering the base value ($1715\ cm^{-1}$). It might prove useful as a beginning to memorize the base values in Table 25.2 for this approach. Notice that there are only eight values.

25.13 ANALYZING A SPECTRUM (OR WHAT YOU CAN TELL AT A GLANCE)

In analyzing the spectrum of an unknown, concentrate first on establishing the presence (or absence) of a few major functional groups. The most conspicuous peaks are C=O, O—H, N—H, C—O, C=C, C≡C, C≡N, and NO_2. If they are present, they give immediate structural information. Do not try to analyze in detail the CH absorptions near $3000\ cm^{-1}$; almost all compounds have these absorptions. Do not worry about subtleties of the exact type of environment in which the functional group is found. A checklist of the important gross features follows:

1. **Is a carbonyl group present?**
   The C=O group gives rise to a strong absorption in the region $1820–1600\ cm^{-1}$. The peak is often the strongest in the spectrum and of medium width. You can't miss it.
2. **If C=O is present, check the following types. (If it is absent, go to item 3.)**
   Acids   Is O—H also present?

TABLE 25.1 A Simplified Correlation Table

	Type of Vibration		Frequency (cm^{-1})	Intensity[a]
C—H	Alkanes	(stretch)	3000–2850	s
	—CH_3	(bend)	1450 and 1375	m
	—CH_2—	(bend)	1465	m
	Alkenes	(stretch)	3100–3000	m
		(bend)	1700–1000	s
	Aromatics	(stretch)	3150–3050	s
		(out-of-plane bend)	1000–700	s
	Alkyne	(stretch)	ca. 3300	s
	Aldehyde		2900–2800	w
			2800–2700	w
C—C	Alkane	Not interpretatively useful		
C=C	Alkene		1680–1600	m–w
	Aromatic		1600–1400	m–w
C≡C	Alkyne		2250–2100	m–w
C=O	Aldehyde		1740–1720	s
	Ketone (acyclic)		1725–1705	s
	Carboxylic acid		1725–1700	s
	Ester		1750–1730	s
	Amide		1700–1640	s
	Anhydride		ca. 1810	s
			ca. 1760	s
C—O	Alcohols, ethers, esters, carboxylic acids		1300–1000	s
O—H	Alcohol, phenols			
	Free		3650–3600	m
	H-Bonded		3400–3200	m
	Carboxylic acids		3300–2500	m
N—H	Primary and secondary amines		ca. 3500	m
C≡N	Nitriles		2260–2240	m
N=O	Nitro (R—NO_2)		1600–1500	s
			1400–1300	s
C—X	Fluoride		1400–1000	s
	Chloride		800–600	s
	Bromide, iodide		< 600	s

[a] s, strong; m, medium; w, weak.

TABLE 25.2 Base Values for Absorptions of Bonds

O—H	3400 cm^{-1}	C≡C	2150 cm^{-1}
N—H	3500 cm^{-1}	C=O	1715 cm^{-1}
C—H	3000 cm^{-1}	C=C	1650 cm^{-1}
C≡N	2250 cm^{-1}	C—O	1100 cm^{-1}

	Broad absorption near 3300–2500 cm^{-1} (usually overlaps C—H).
Amides	Is N—H also present?
	Medium absorption near 3500 cm^{-1}, sometimes a double peak, equivalent halves.
Esters	Is C—O also present?
	Medium intensity absorptions near 1300–1000 cm^{-1}.
Anhydrides	Have *two* C=O absorptions near 1810 and 1760 cm^{-1}.
Aldehydes	Is aldehyde C—H present?
	Two weak absorptions near 2850 cm^{-1} and 2750 cm^{-1} on the right side of C—H absorptions.
Ketones	The preceding five choices have been eliminated.

3. If C=O is absent

Alcohols or Phenols	Check for O—H.
	Broad absorption near 3600–3300 cm^{-1}.
	Confirm this by finding C—O near 1300–1000 cm^{-1}.
Amines	Check for N—H.
	Medium absorption(s) near 3500 cm^{-1}.
Ethers	Check for C—O (and absence of O—H) near 1300–1000 cm^{-1}.

4. Double bonds or aromatic rings or both

	C=C is a **weak** absorption near 1650 cm^{-1}.
	Medium to strong absorptions in the region 1650–1450 cm^{-1} often imply an aromatic ring.
	Confirm the above by consulting the C—H region.
	Aromatic and vinyl C—H occur to the left of 3000 cm^{-1} (aliphatic C—H occurs to the right of this value).
5. Triple bonds	C≡N is a medium, sharp absorption near 2250 cm^{-1}.
	C≡C is a weak but sharp absorption near 2150 cm^{-1}.
	Check also for acetylenic C—H near 3300 cm^{-1}.
6. Nitro groups	*Two* strong absorptions near 1600–1500 cm^{-1} and 1390–1300 cm^{-1}.
7. Hydrocarbons	None of the above is found.
	Main absorptions are in the C—H region near 3000 cm^{-1}.
	Very simple spectrum, only other absorptions are near 1450 cm^{-1} and 1375 cm^{-1}.

The beginning student should resist the idea of trying to assign or interpret *every* peak in the spectrum. You simply will not be able to do this. Concentrate first on learning the principal peaks and recognizing their presence or absence. This is best done by carefully studying the illustrative spectra in the section that follows.

> **Note:** In describing the shifts of absorption peaks or their relative positions, we have used the phrases "to the left" and "to the right." This was done to simplify descriptions of peak positions. The meaning is clear, because all spectra are conventionally presented left to right from 4000 to 600 cm^{-1}.

25.14 SURVEY OF THE IMPORTANT FUNCTIONAL GROUPS

A. Alkanes

The spectrum is usually simple, with a few peaks.

C—H Stretch occurs around 3000 cm^{-1}.

1. In alkanes (except strained ring compounds), absorption always occurs to the right of 3000 cm^{-1}.
2. If a compound has vinylic, aromatic, acetylenic, or cyclopropyl hydrogens, the CH absorption is to the left of 3000 cm^{-1}.

CH_2 Methylene groups have a characteristic absorption at approximately 1450 cm^{-1}.

CH_3 Methyl groups have a characteristic absorption at approximately 1375 cm^{-1}.

C—C Stretch—not interpretatively useful—has many peaks.

The spectrum of decane is shown in Figure 25.15.

B. Alkenes

=C—H Stretch occurs to the left of 3000 cm^{-1}.

=C—H Out-of-plane (oop) bending occurs at 1000–650 cm^{-1}.

The C—H out-of-plane absorptions often allow you to determine the type of substitution pattern on the double bond, according to the number of absorptions and their positions. The correlation chart in Figure 25.16 shows the positions of these bands.

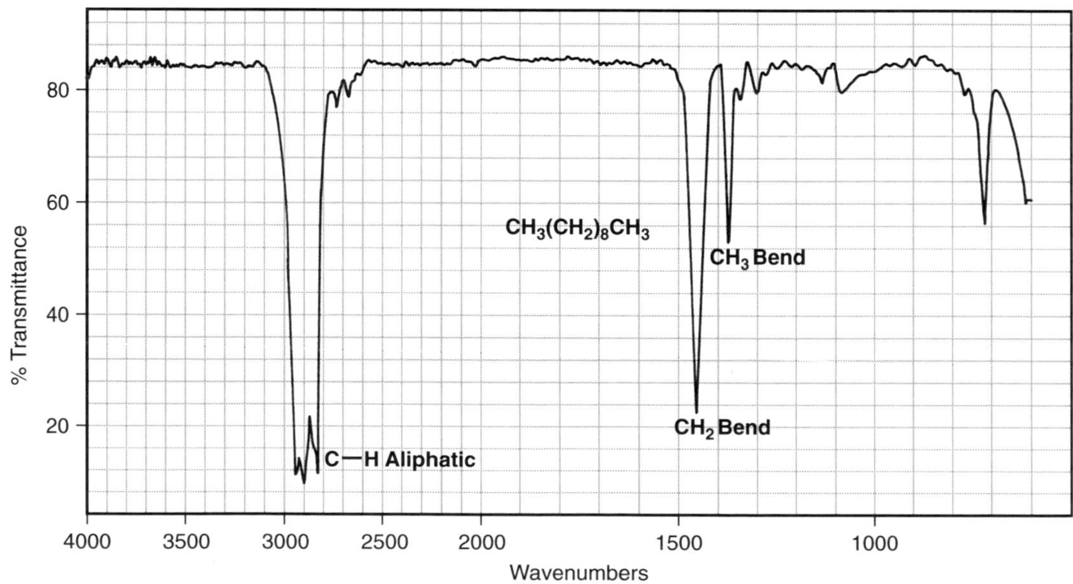

Figure 25.15 Infrared spectrum of decane (neat liquid, salt plates).

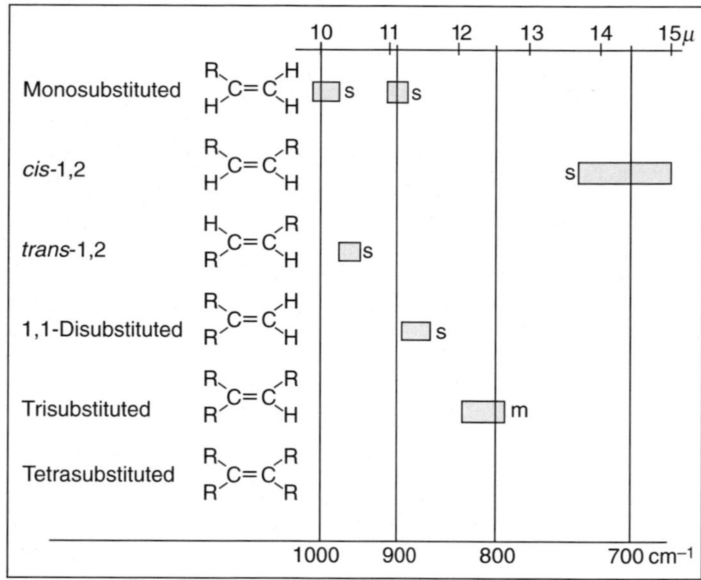

Figure 25.16 The C—H out-of-plane bending vibrations for substituted alkenes.

C═C Stretch 1675–1600cm^{-1}, often weak.
Conjugation moves C═C stretch to the right.
Symmetrically substituted bonds, as in 2,3-dimethyl-2-butene, do not absorb in the infrared region (no dipole change). Highly substituted double bonds are often vanishingly weak in absorption.

The spectra of 4-methylcyclohexene and styrene are shown in Figures 25.17 and 25.18.

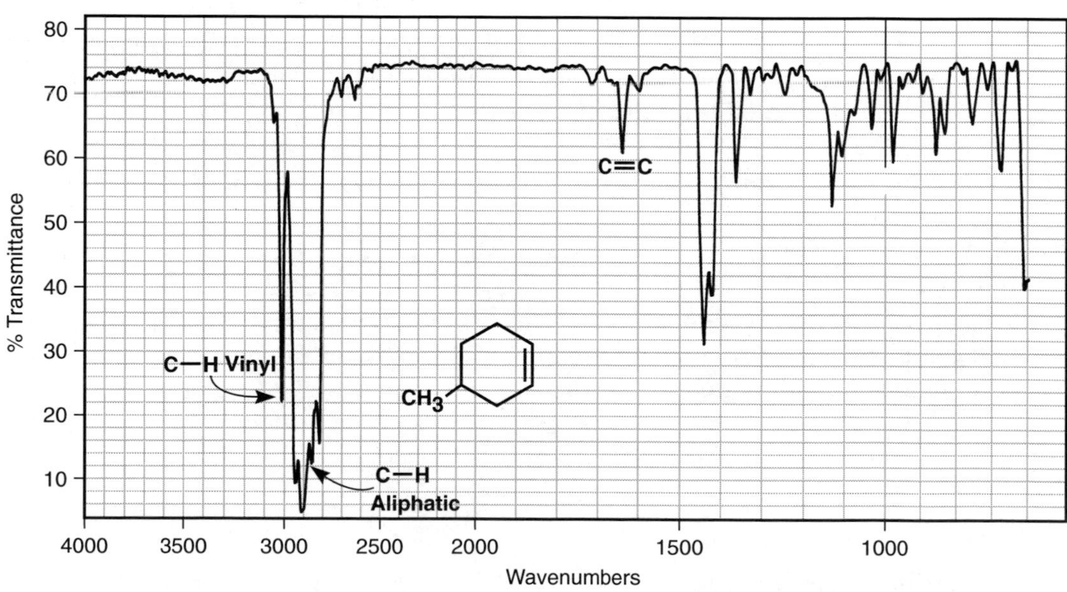

Figure 25.17 Infrared spectrum of 4-methylcyclohexene (neat liquid, salt plates).

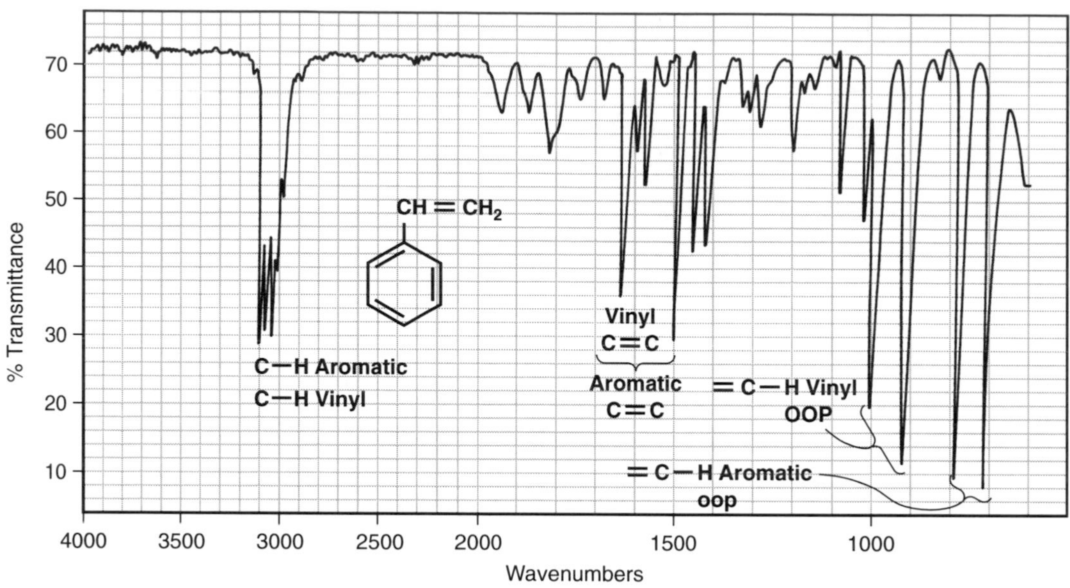

Figure 25.18 Infrared spectrum of styrene (neat liquid, salt plates).

C. Aromatic Rings

=C—H Stretch is always to the left of 3000 cm^{-1}.

=C—H Out-of-plane (oop) bending occurs at 900 to 690 cm^{-1}.

The C—H out-of-plane absorptions often allow you to determine the type of ring substitution by their numbers, intensities, and positions. The correlation chart in Figure 25.19A indicates the positions of these bands.

The patterns are generally reliable—they are most reliable for rings with alkyl substituents and least reliable for polar substituents.

Ring Absorptions (C=C). There are often four sharp absorptions that occur in pairs at 1600 cm^{-1} and 1450 cm^{-1} and are characteristic of an aromatic ring. See, for example, the spectra of anisole (Figure 25.23), benzonitrile (Figure 25.26), and methyl benzoate (Figure 25.35).

There are many weak combination and overtone absorptions that appear between 2000 cm^{-1} and 1667 cm^{-1}. The relative shapes and numbers of these peaks can be used to determine whether an aromatic ring is monosubstituted or di-, tri-, tetra-, penta-, or hexasubstituted. Positional isomers can also be distinguished. Because the absorptions are weak, these bands are best observed by using neat liquids or concentrated solutions. If the compound has a high-frequency carbonyl group, this absorption overlaps the weak overtone bands, so no useful information can be obtained from analyzing this region. The various patterns that are obtained in this region are shown in Figure 25.19B.

The spectra of styrene and *o*-dichlorobenzene are shown in Figures 25.18 and 25.20.

D. Alkynes

≡C—H Stretch is usually near 3300 cm^{-1}, sharp peak.

C≡C Stretch is near 2150 cm^{-1}, sharp peak.

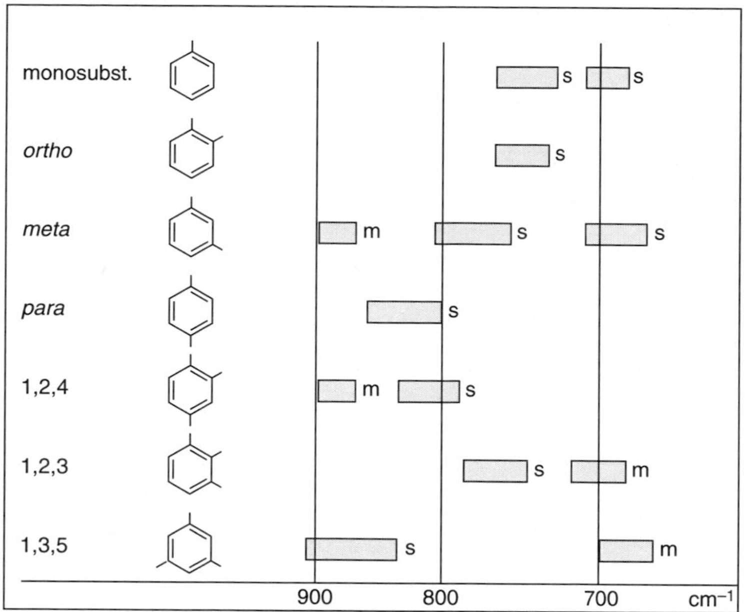

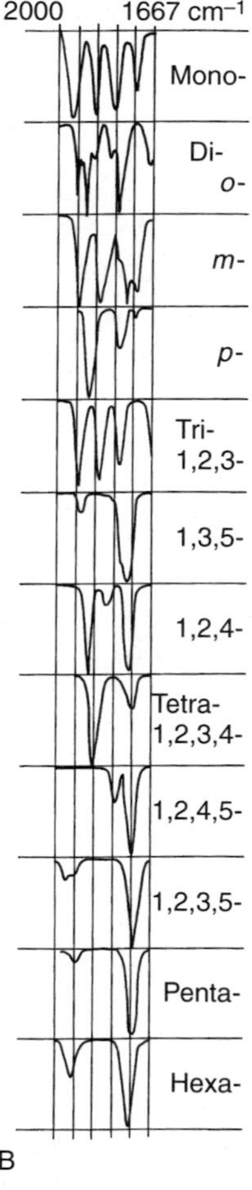

Figure 25.19 (A) The C—H out-of-plane bending vibrations for substituted benzenoid compounds. (B) The 2000–1667 cm-1 region for substituted benzenoid compounds. (From John R. Dyer, *Applications of Absorption Spectroscopy of Organic Compounds*, Englewood Cliffs, NJ: Prentice Hall, 1965.)

Conjugation moves C≡C stretch to the right.

Disubstituted or symmetrically substituted triple bonds give either no absorption or weak absorption.

E. Alcohols and Phenols

O—H Stretch is a sharp peak at 3650–3600 cm^{-1} if no hydrogen bonding takes place. (This is usually observed only in dilute solutions.)

If there is hydrogen bonding (usual in neat or concentrated solutions), the absorption is *broad* and occurs more to the right at 3500–3200 cm^{-1}, sometimes overlapping C—H stretch absorptions.

C—O Stretch is usually in the range of 1300–1000 cm^{-1}.

Phenols are like alcohols. The 2-naphthol shown in Figure 25.21 has some molecules hydrogen bonded and some free. The spectrum of

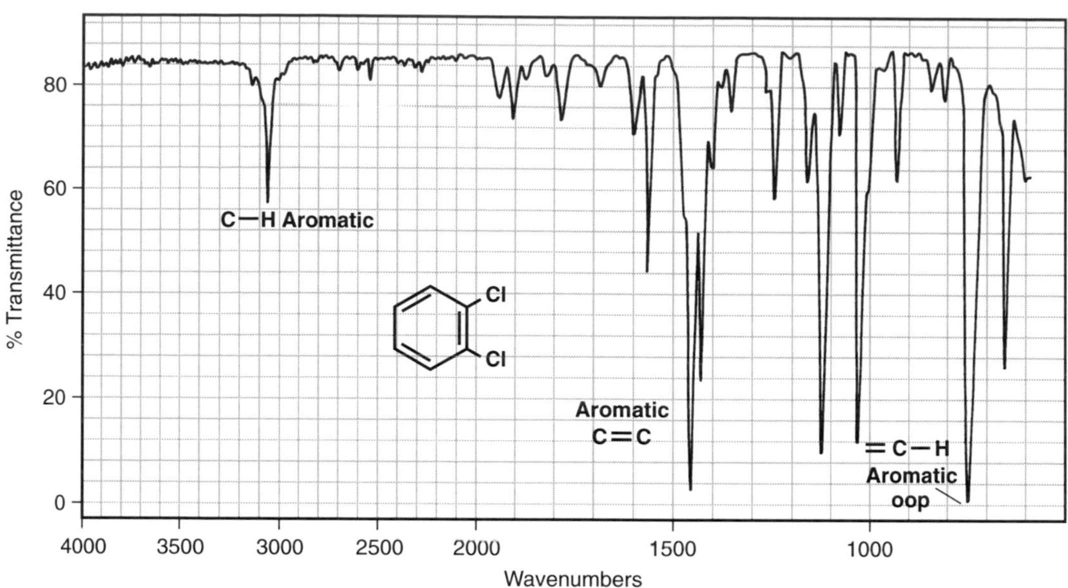

Figure 25.20 Infrared spectrum of *o*-dichlorobenzene (neat liquid, salt plates).

4-methylcyclohexanol is shown in Figure 25.22. This alcohol, which was determined neat, would also have had a free OH spike to the left of this hydrogen-bonded band if it had been determined in dilute solution.

F. Ethers

C—O The most prominent band is due to C—O stretch at 1300–1000 cm^{-1}. Absence of C=O and O—H bands is required to be sure C—O stretch is not due to an alcohol or ester. Phenyl and vinyl ethers are found in the left portion of the range, aliphatic ethers in the right. (Conjugation with the oxygen moves the absorption to the left.)

The spectrum of anisole is shown in Figure 25.23.

G. Amines

N—H Stretch occurs in the range of 3500–3300 cm^{-1}.
Primary amines have *two* bands typically 30 cm^{-1} apart.
Secondary amines have one band, often vanishingly weak.
Tertiary amines have no NH stretch.

C—N Stretch is weak and occurs in the range of 1350–1000 cm^{-1}.

N—H Scissoring bending mode occurs in the range of 1640–1560 cm^{-1} (broad).
An out-of-plane bending absorption can sometimes be observed at about 800 cm^{-1}.

The spectrum of *n*-butylamine is shown in Figure 25.24.

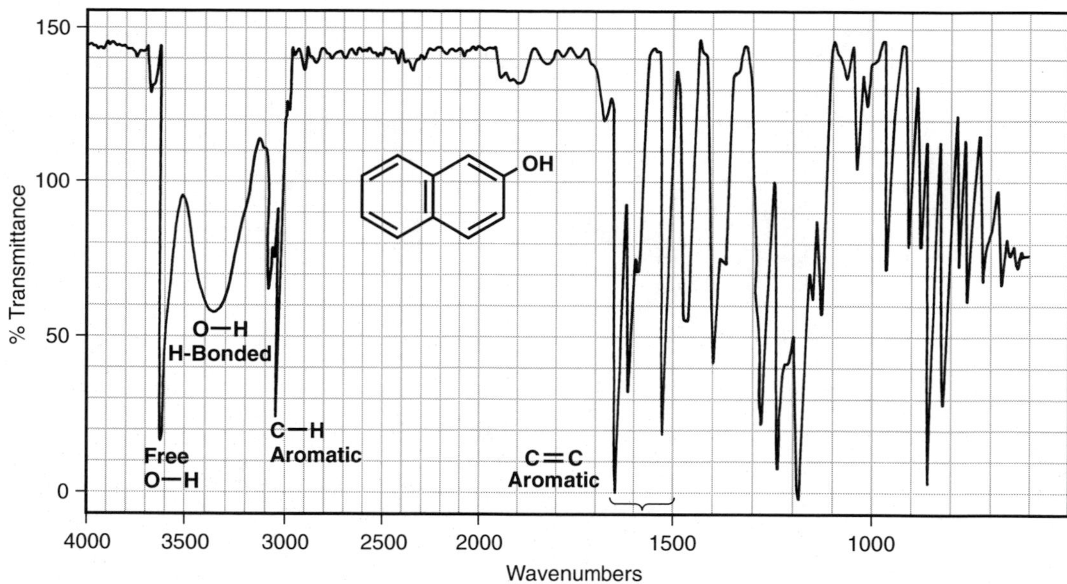

Figure 25.21 Infrared spectrum of 2-naphthol showing both free and hydrogen-bonded OH ($CHCl_3$ solution).

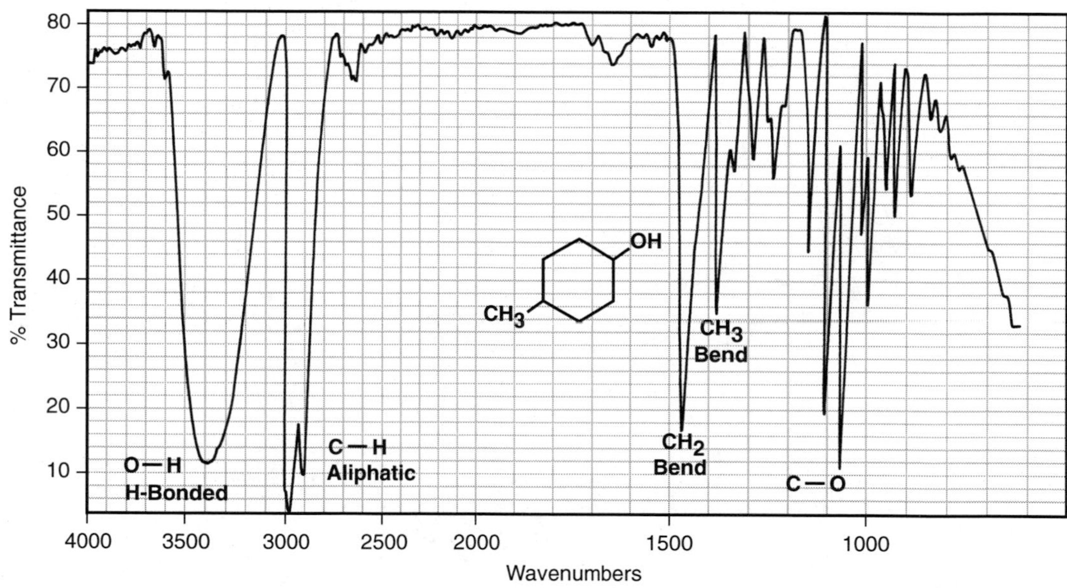

Figure 25.22 Infrared spectrum of 4-methylcyclohexanol (neat liquid, salt plates).

H. Nitro Compounds

N=O Stretch is usually two strong bands at 1600–1500 cm^{-1} and 1390–1300 cm^{-1}.

The spectrum of nitrobenzene is shown in Figure 25.25.

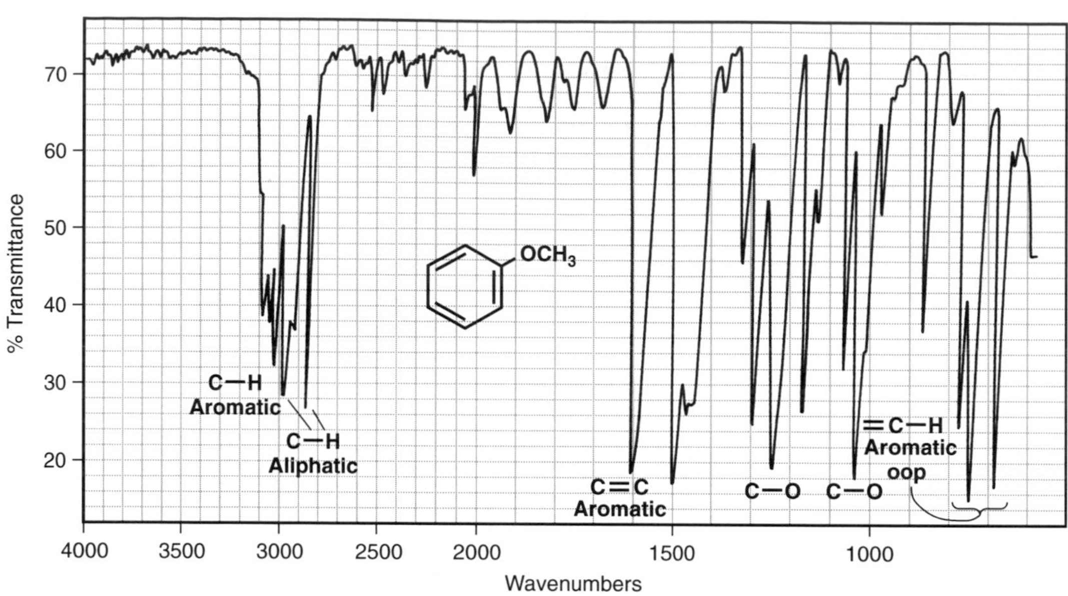

Figure 25.23 Infrared spectrum of anisole (neat liquid, salt plates).

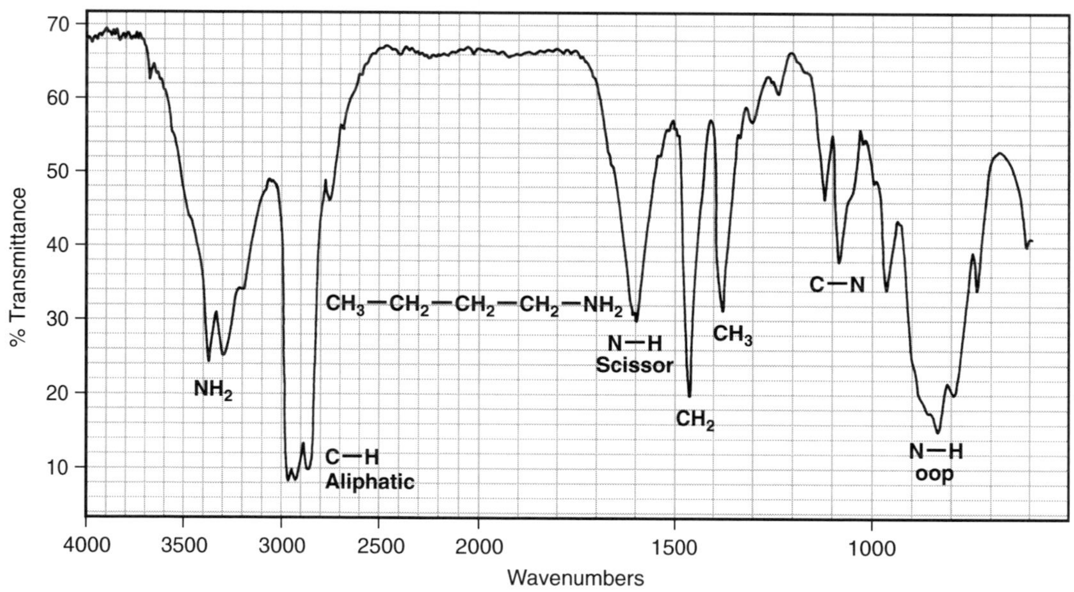

Figure 25.24 Infrared spectrum of *n*-butylamine (neat liquid, salt plates).

I. Nitriles

C≡N — Stretch is a sharp absorption near 2250 cm^{-1}.
Conjugation with double bonds or aromatic rings moves the absorption to the right.

The spectrum of benzonitrile is shown in Figure 25.26.

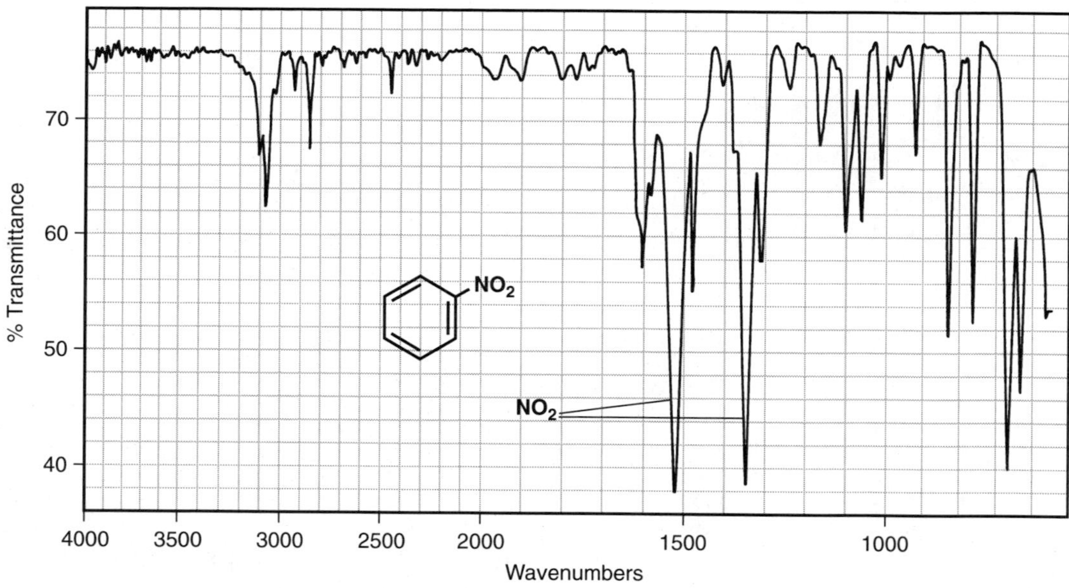

Figure 25.25 Infrared spectrum of nitrobenzene (neat liquid, salt plates).

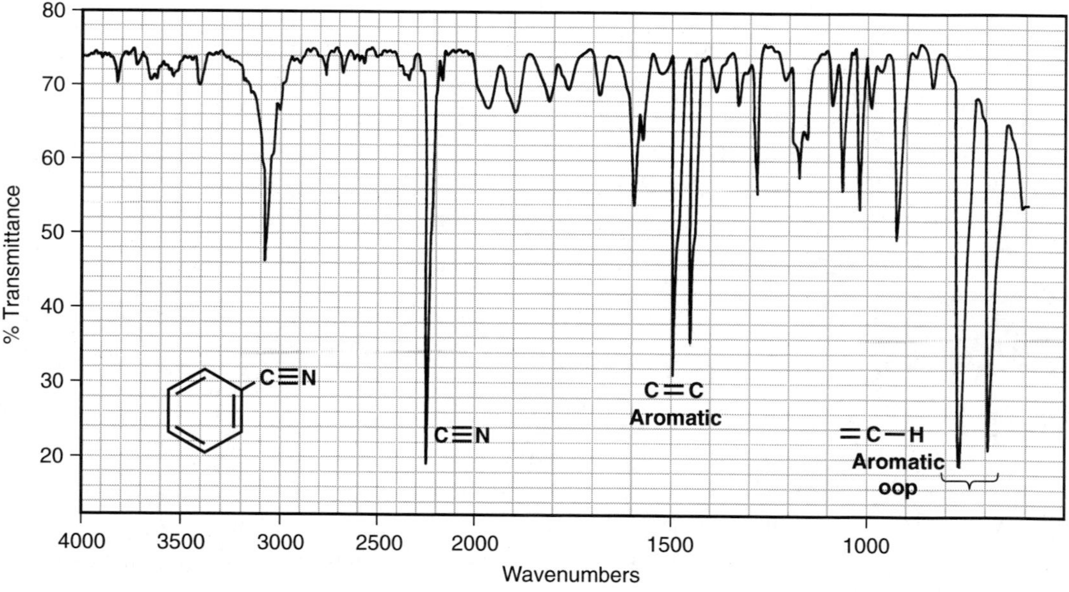

Figure 25.26 Infrared spectrum of benzonitrile (neat liquid, salt plates).

J. Carbonyl Compounds

The carbonyl group is one of the most strongly absorbing groups in the infrared region of the spectrum. This is mainly due to its large dipole moment. It absorbs in a variety of compounds (aldehydes, ketones, acids, esters, amides, anhydrides, and so on) in the range of 1850–1650 cm^{-1}. In Figure 25.27, the normal values for the various types of carbonyl groups are compared. In the sections that follow, each type is examined separately.

1810	1760	1735	1725	1715	1710	1690	cm^{-1}
Anhydride (Band 1)	Anhydride (Band 2)	Esters	Aldehydes	Ketones	Carboxylic acids	Amides	

Figure 25.27 Normal values (± 10 cm^{-1}) for various types of carbonyl groups.

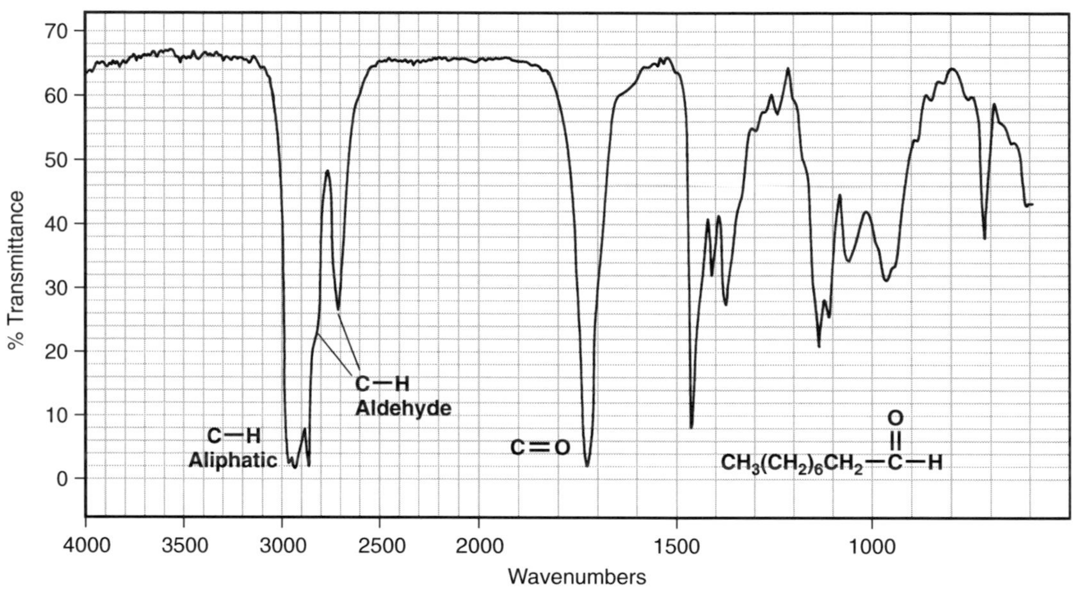

Figure 25.28 Infrared spectrum of nonanal (neat liquid, salt plates).

K. Aldehydes

C=O Stretch at approximately 1725 cm^{-1} is normal.
Aldehydes *seldom* absorb to the left of this value.
Conjugation moves the absorption to the right.

C—H Stretch, aldehyde hydrogen (—CHO), consists of *weak* bands at about 2750 cm^{-1} and 2850 cm^{-1}. Note that the CH stretch in alkyl chains does not usually extend this far to the right.

The spectrum of an unconjugated aldehyde, nonanal, is shown in Figure 25.28, and the conjugated aldehyde, benzaldehyde, is shown in Figure 25.29.

L. Ketones

C=O Stretch at approximately at 1715 cm^{-1} is normal.
Conjugation moves the absorption to the right.
Ring strain moves the absorption to the left in cyclic ketones. (See Figure 25.30.)

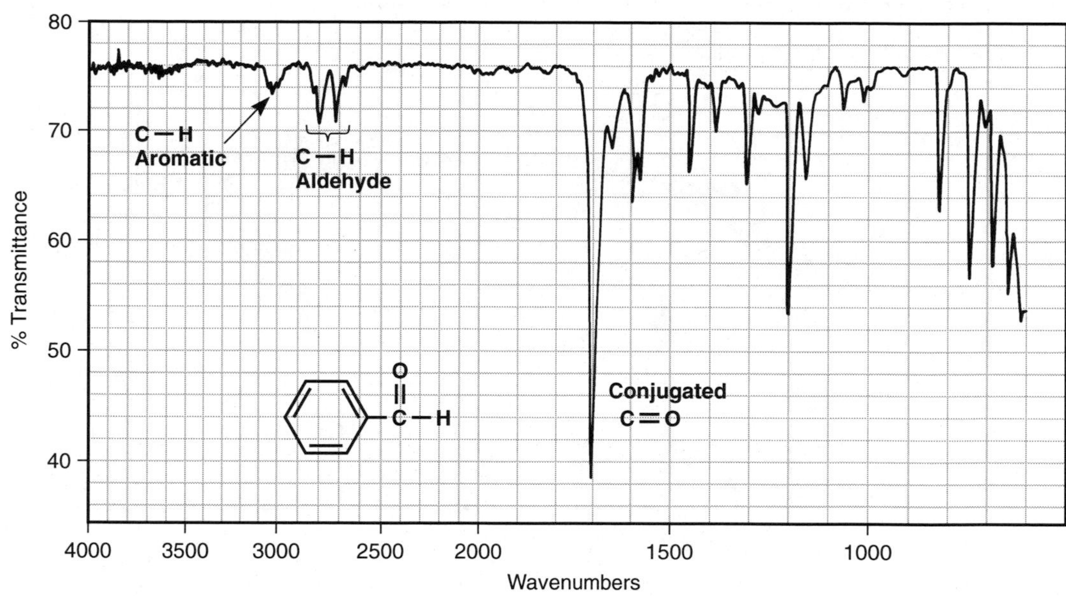

Figure 25.29 Infrared spectrum of benzaldehyde (neat liquid, salt plates).

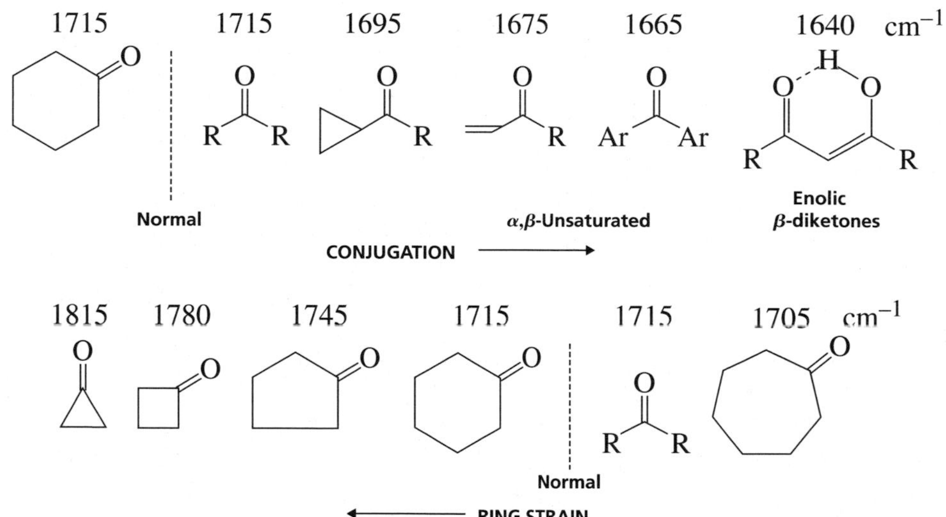

Figure 25.30 Effects of conjugation and ring strain on carbonyl frequencies in ketones.

The spectra of methyl isopropyl ketone and mesityl oxide are shown in Figures 25.14 and 25.31. The spectrum of camphor, shown in Figure 25.32, has a carbonyl group that has been shifted to a higher frequency because of ring strain (1745 cm^{-1}).

M. Acids

O—H Stretch, usually *very broad* (strongly hydrogen bonded) at 3300–2500 cm^{-1}, often interferes with C—H absorptions.

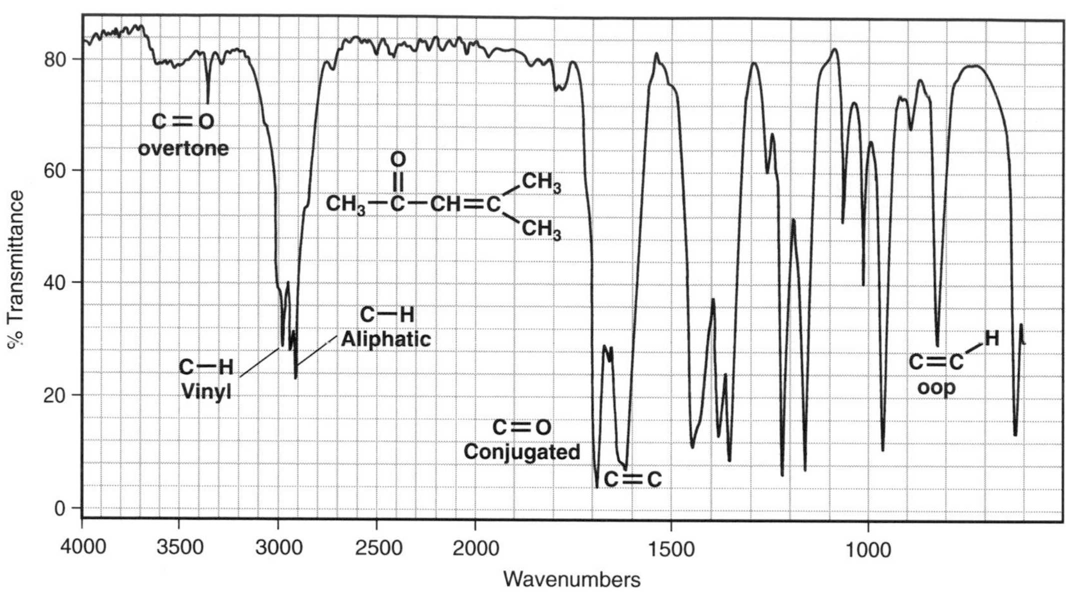

Figure 25.31 Infrared spectrum of mesityl oxide (neat liquid, salt plates).

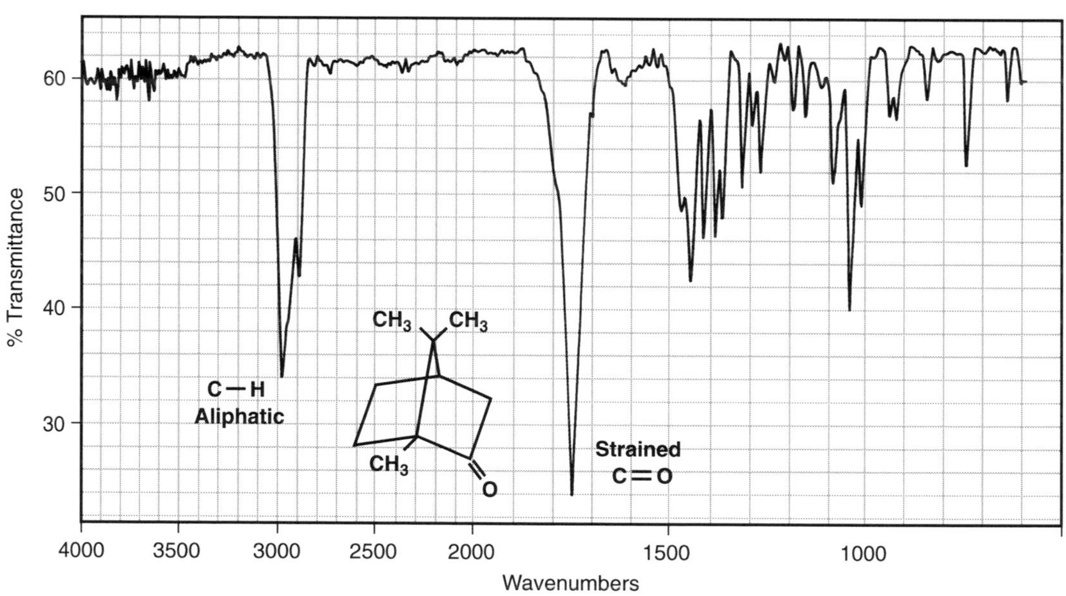

Figure 25.32 Infrared spectrum of camphor (KBr pellet).

C=O Stretch, broad, 1730–1700 cm^{-1}.
Conjugation moves the absorption to the right.

C—O Stretch, in the range of 1320–1210 cm^{-1}, is strong.

The spectrum of benzoic acid is shown in Figure 25.33.

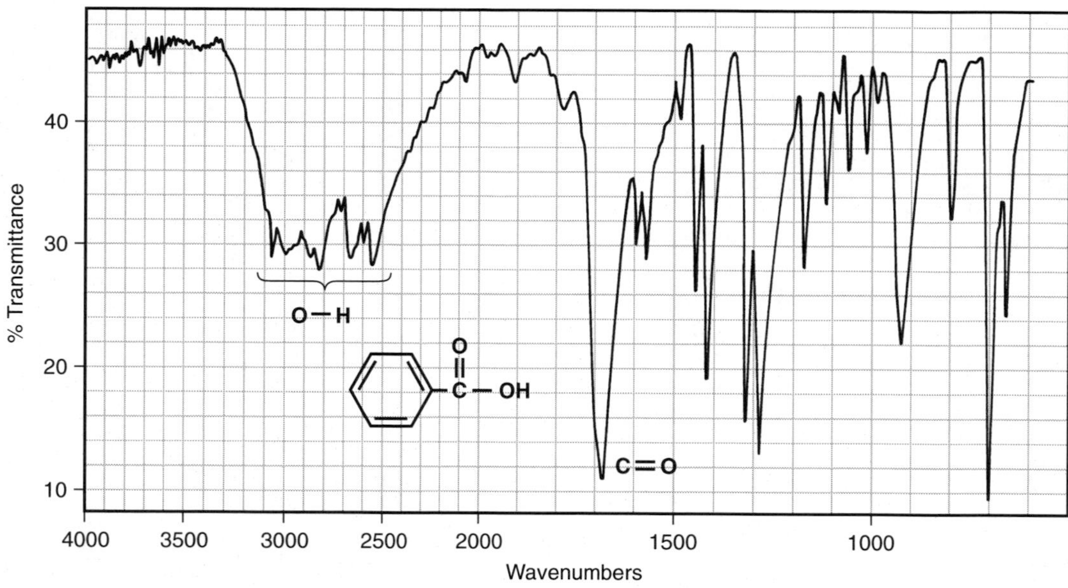

Figure 25.33 Infrared spectrum of benzoic acid (KBr pellet).

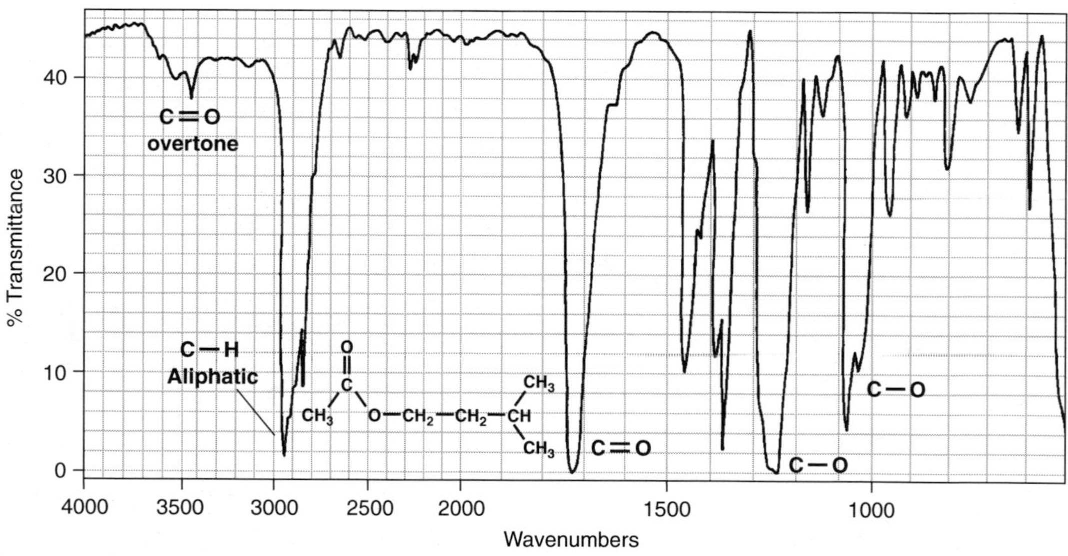

Figure 25.34 Infrared spectrum of isopentyl acetate (neat liquid, salt plates).

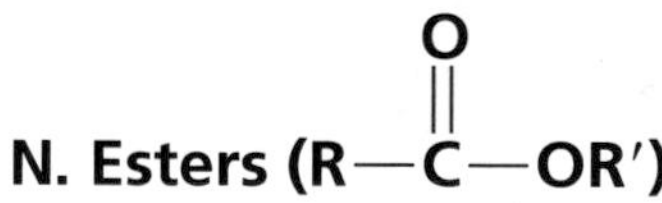

N. Esters (R—C(=O)—OR′)

C=O Stretch occurs at about 1735 cm^{-1} in normal esters.

1. Conjugation in the R part moves the absorption to the right.
2. Conjugation with the O in the R′ part moves the absorption to the left.
3. Ring strain (lactones) moves the absorption to the left.

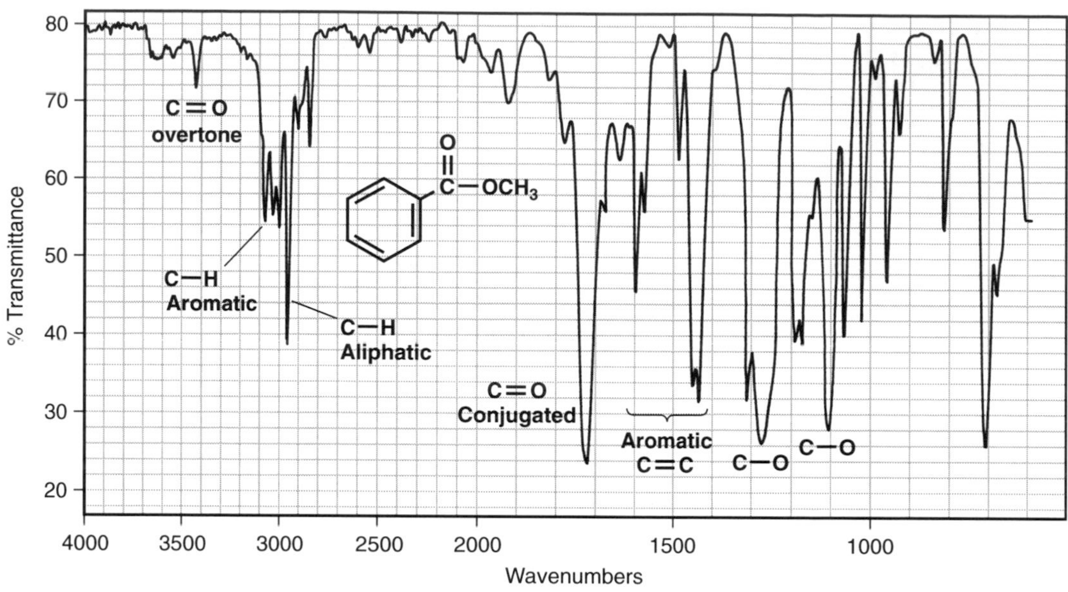

Figure 25.35 Infrared spectrum of methyl benzoate (neat liquid, salt plates).

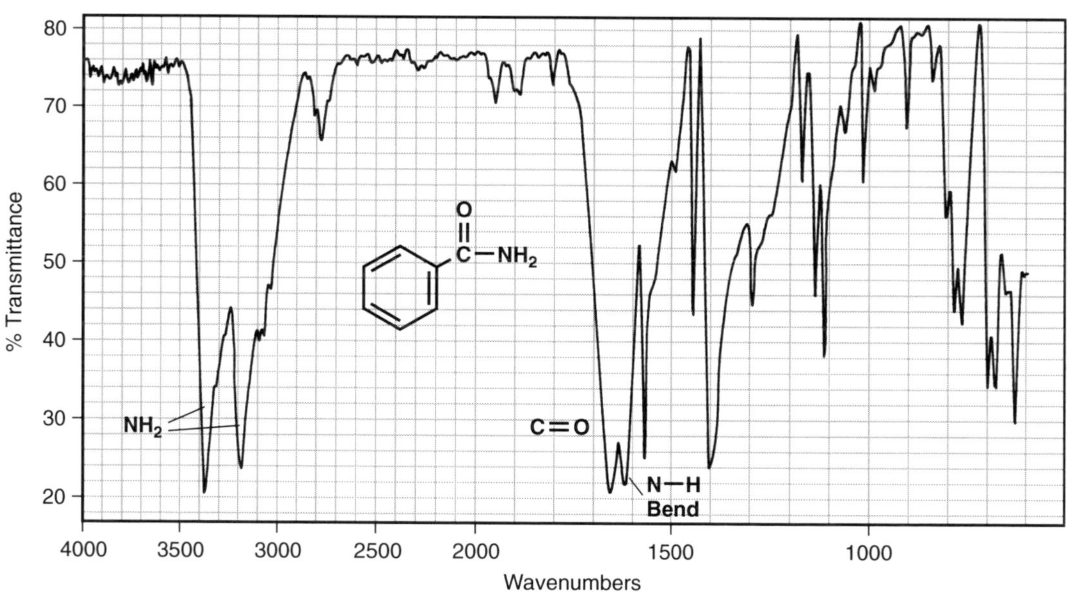

Figure 25.36 Infrared spectrum of benzamide (solid phase, KBr).

C—O Stretch, two bands or more, one stronger than the others, is in the range of 1300–1000 cm^{-1}.

The spectrum of an unconjugated ester, isopentyl acetate, is shown in Figure 25.34 (C=O appears at 1740 cm^{-1}). A conjugated ester, methyl benzoate, is shown in Figure 25.35 (C=O appears at 1720 cm^{-1}).

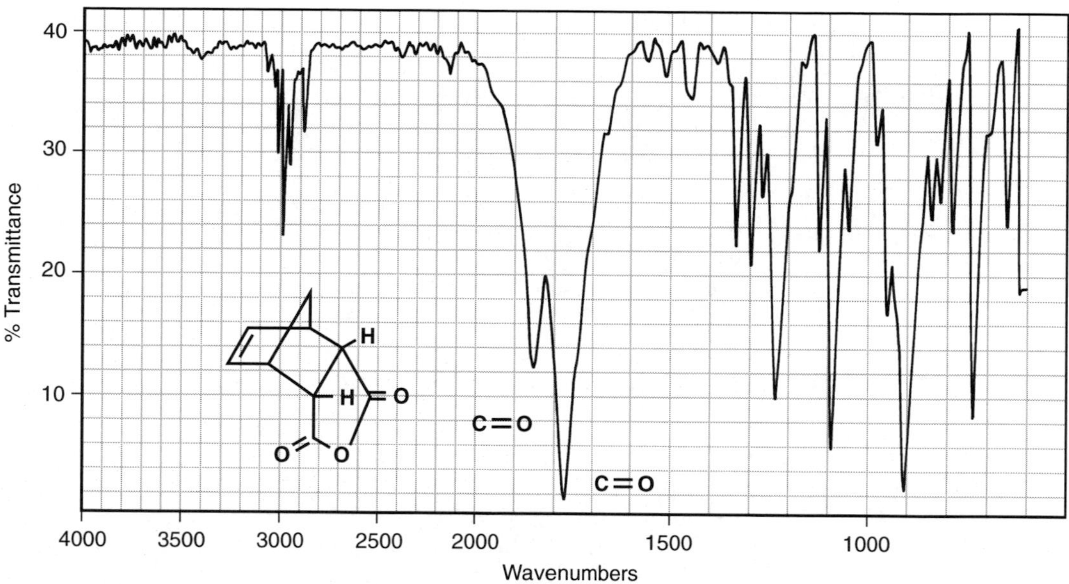

Figure 25.37 Infrared spectrum of *cis*-norbornene-5,6-*endo*-dicarboxylic anhydride (KBr pellet).

O. Amides

C=O Stretch is at approximately 1670–1640 cm^{-1}.
Conjugation and ring size (lactams) have the usual effects.

N—H Stretch (if monosubstituted or unsubstituted) is at 3500–3100 cm^{-1}.
Unsubstituted amides have two bands ($—NH_2$) in this region.

N—H Bending around 1640–1550 cm^{-1}.

The spectrum of benzamide is shown in Figure 25.36.

P. Anhydrides

C=O Stretch always has *two* bands: 1830–1800 cm^{-1} and 1775–1740 cm^{-1}.
Unsaturation moves the absorptions to the right.
Ring strain (cyclic anhydrides) moves the absorptions to the left.

C—O Stretch is at 1300–900 cm^{-1}. The spectrum of *cis*-norbornene-5,6-*endo*-dicarboxylic anhydride is shown in Figure 25.37.

Q. Halides

It is often difficult to determine either the presence or the absence of a halide in a compound by infrared spectroscopy. The absorption bands cannot be relied on, especially if the spectrum is being determined with the compound dissolved in CCl_4 or $CHCl_3$ solution.

C—F Stretch, 1350–960 cm^{-1}.

C—Cl Stretch, 850–500 cm^{-1}.

C—Br Stretch, to the right of 667 cm^{-1}.
C—I Stretch, to the right of 667 cm^{-1}.

The spectra of the solvents, carbon tetrachloride and chloroform, are shown in Figures 25.8 and 25.9, respectively.

REFERENCES

Bellamy, L. J. *The Infra-red Spectra of Complex Molecules,* 3rd ed. New York: Methuen, 1975.

Colthup, N. B., Daly, L. H., and Wiberly, S. E. *Introduction to Infrared and Raman Spectroscopy,* 3rd ed. San Diego, CA: Academic Press, 1990.

Dyer, J. R. *Applications of Absorption Spectroscopy of Organic Compounds.* Englewood Cliffs, NJ: Prentice-Hall, 1965.

Lin-Vien, D., Colthup, N. B., Fateley, W. G., and Grasselli, J. G. *Infrared and Raman Characteristic Frequencies of Organic Molecules.* San Diego, CA: Academic Press, 1991.

Nakanishi, K., and Soloman, P. H. *Infrared Absorption Spectroscopy,* 2nd ed. San Francisco: Holden-Day, 1977.

Pavia, D. L., Lampman, G. M., and Kriz, G. S. *Introduction to Spectroscopy: A Guide for Students of Organic Chemistry,* 3rd ed. Philadelphia: Saunders, 2001.

Silverstein, R. M., and Webster, F. X. *Spectrometric Identification of Organic Compounds,* 6th ed., New York: John Wiley & Sons, 1998.

PROBLEMS

1. Comment on the suitability of running the infrared spectrum under each of the following conditions. If there is a problem with the conditions given, provide a suitable alternative method.

- **a.** A neat spectrum of liquid with a boiling point of 150°C is determined using salt plates.
- **b.** A neat spectrum of a liquid with a boiling point of 35°C is determined using salt plates.
- **c.** A KBr pellet is prepared with a compound that melts at 200°C.
- **d.** A KBr pellet is prepared with a compound that melts at 30°C.
- **e.** A solid aliphatic hydrocarbon compound is determined as a Nujol mull.
- **f.** Silver chloride plates are used to determine the spectrum of aniline.
- **g.** Sodium chloride plates are selected to run the spectrum of a compound that contains some water.

2. Indicate how you could distinguish between the following pairs of compounds by using infrared spectroscopy.

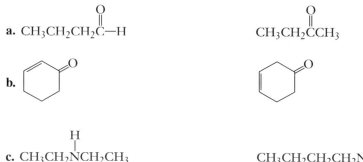

a. $CH_3CH_2CH_2C(=O)—H$ $CH_3CH_2C(=O)CH_3$

b. [cyclohex-2-enone] [cyclohex-3-enone]

c. $CH_3CH_2N(H)CH_2CH_3$ $CH_3CH_2CH_2CH_2NH_2$

d. $CH_3CH_2\overset{O}{\overset{\parallel}{C}}OCH_2CH_3$ $\qquad$ $CH_3CH_2\overset{O}{\overset{\parallel}{C}}CH_2OCH_3$

e. $CH_3CH_2\overset{O}{\overset{\parallel}{C}}OH$ $\qquad$ $CH_3CH_2CH_2OH$

f. CH_3 CH_3 $\qquad$ CH_3 CH_3

g. $CH_3CH_2CH{=}CH_2$ $\qquad$ $CH_3CH{=}CHCH_3$ (trans)

h. $CH_3CH_2CH_2C{\equiv}CH$ $\qquad$ $CH_3CH_2CH_2CH{=}CH_2$

i. CH_3 NH_2 $\qquad$ CH_3 NH_2

j. $CH_3CH_2CH_2CH_2\overset{O}{\overset{\parallel}{C}}{-}OH$ $\qquad$ $CH_3CH_2CH_2\overset{O}{\overset{\parallel}{C}}OCH_3$

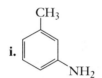

k. $CH_3CH_2CH_2CH_2CH_3$ $\qquad$ $CH_2{=}CHCH_2CH_2CH_2CH_3$

l. $CH_3CH_2CH_2CH_2C{\equiv}CH$ $\qquad$ $CH_3CH_2CH_2C{\equiv}CCH_3$

TECHNIQUE 26

Nuclear Magnetic Resonance Spectroscopy (Proton NMR)

Nuclear magnetic resonance (NMR) spectroscopy is an instrumental technique that allows the number, type, and relative positions of certain atoms in a molecule to be determined. This type of spectroscopy applies only to those atoms that have nuclear magnetic moments because of their nuclear spin properties. Although many atoms meet this requirement, hydrogen atoms (^1_1H) are of the greatest interest to the organic chemist. Atoms of the ordinary isotopes of carbon ($^{12}_{6}C$) and oxygen ($^{16}_{8}O$) do not have nuclear magnetic moments, and ordinary nitrogen atoms ($^{14}_{7}N$), although they do have magnetic moments, generally fail to show typical NMR behavior for other reasons. The same is true of the halogen atoms, except for fluorine ($^{19}_{9}F$), which does show active NMR behavior. Of the

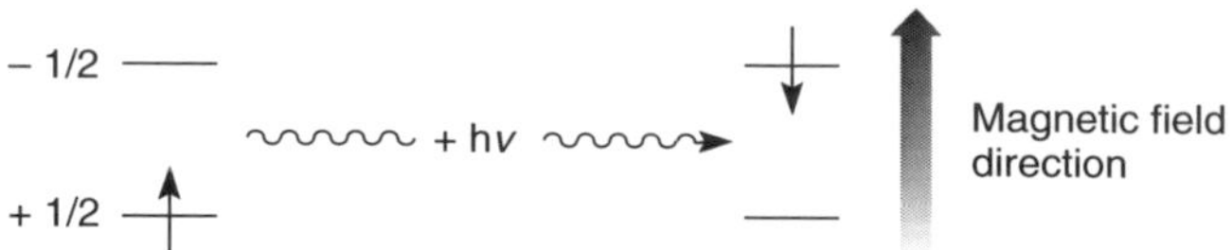

Figure 26.1 The NMR absorption process.

atoms mentioned here, the hydrogen nucleus ($^{1}_{1}H$) and carbon-13 nucleus ($^{13}_{6}C$) are the most important to organic chemists. Proton (^{1}H) NMR is discussed here and carbon (^{13}C) NMR is described in Technique 27.

Nuclei of NMR-active atoms placed in a magnetic field can be thought of as tiny bar magnets. In hydrogen, which has two allowed nuclear spin states (+½ and −½), either the nuclear magnets of individual atoms can be aligned with the magnetic field (spin +½) or they can be opposed to it (spin −½). A slight majority of the nuclei are aligned with the field, as this spin orientation constitutes a slightly lower-energy spin state. If radiofrequency waves of the appropriate energy are supplied, nuclei aligned with the field can absorb this radiation and reverse their direction of spin or become reoriented so that the nuclear magnet opposes the applied magnetic field (Figure 26.1).

The frequency of radiation required to induce spin conversion is a direct function of the strength of the applied magnetic field. When a spinning hydrogen nucleus is placed in a magnetic field, the nucleus begins to precess with angular frequency ω, much like a child's toy top. This precessional motion is depicted in Figure 26.2. The angular frequency of nuclear precession ω increases as the strength of the applied magnetic field is increased. The radiation that must be supplied to induce spin conversion in a hydrogen nucleus of spin +½ must have a frequency that just matches the angular precessional frequency ω. This is called the resonance condition, and spin conversion is said to be a resonance process.

For the average proton (hydrogen atom), if a magnetic field of approximately 1.4 tesla is applied, radio-frequency radiation of 60 MHz is required to induce a spin transition.[1] Fortunately, the magnetic field strength required to induce the various protons in a molecule to absorb 60-MHz radiation varies from proton to proton within the molecule and is a sensitive function of the immediate *electronic* environment of each proton. The proton nuclear magnetic resonance spectrometer supplies a basic radiofrequency radiation of 60 MHz to the sample being measured and *increases* the strength of the applied magnetic field over a range of several parts per million from the basic field strength. As the field increases, various protons come into resonance (absorb 60-MHz energy), and a resonance signal is generated for each proton. An NMR spectrum is a plot of the strength of the magnetic field versus the intensity of the absorptions. A typical 60-MHz NMR spectrum is shown in Figure 26.3.

Modern FT–NMR instruments produce the same type of NMR spectrum just described even though they do it by a different method. See your lecture textbook for a discussion of the differences between classic CW instruments and modern FT–NMR instruments. Fourier transform spectrometers operating at magnetic field strengths of at least 7.1 tesla and at spectrometer frequencies of 300 MHz and above allow chemists to obtain both the proton and carbon NMR spectra on the same sample.

[1] Most modern instruments (FT–NMR instruments) use higher fields than described here and operate differently. The classical 60-MHz continuous wave (CW) instrument is used here as a simple example.

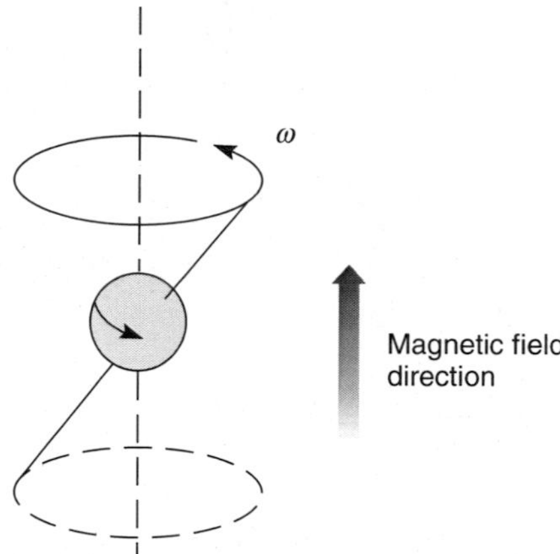

Figure 26.2 Precessional motion of a spinning nucleus in an applied magnetic field.

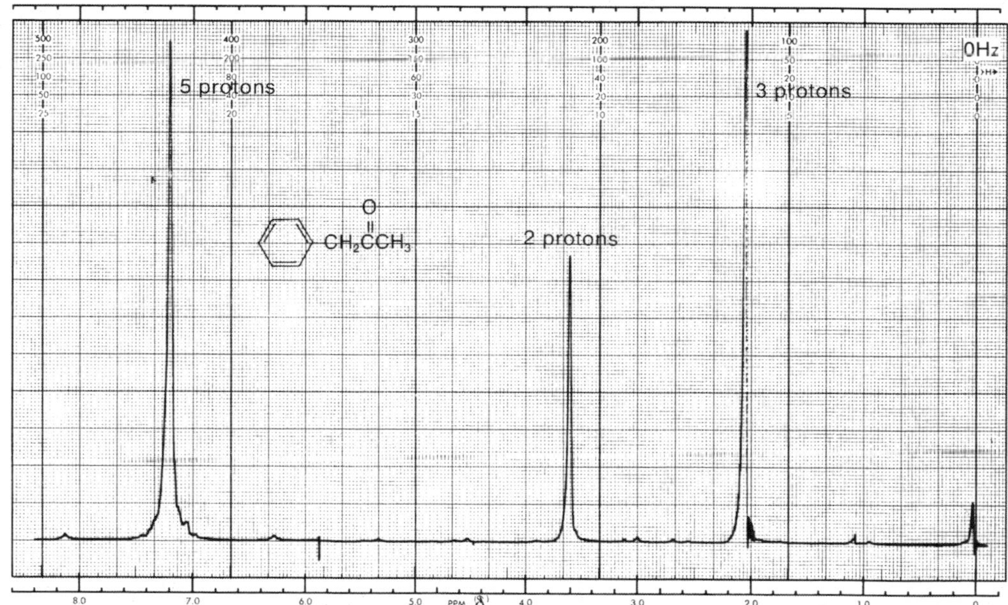

Figure 26.3 Nuclear magnetic resonance spectrum of phenylacetone (the absorption peak at the far right is caused by the added reference substance tetramethylsilane).

Part A. Preparing a Sample for NMR Spectroscopy

The NMR sample tubes used in most instruments are approximately 0.5 cm × 18 cm in overall dimension and are fabricated of uniformly thin glass tubing. These tubes are very fragile and expensive, so care must be taken to avoid breaking the tubes.

Caution: NMR tubes are made out of very thin glass and break easily. Never place the cap on tightly and take special care when removing it.

To prepare the solution, you must first choose the appropriate solvent. The solvent should not have NMR absorption peaks of its own, that is, it should contain no protons. Carbon tetrachloride (CCl_4) fits this requirement and can be used in some instruments. However, because FT–NMR spectrometers require deuterium to stabilize (lock) the field, organic chemists usually use deuterated chloroform ($CDCl_3$) as a solvent. This solvent dissolves most organic compounds and is relatively inexpensive. You can use this solvent with any NMR instrument. You should not use normal chloroform $CHCl_3$ because the solvent contains a proton. Deuterium ^2H does not absorb in the proton region and is thus "invisible," or not seen, in the proton NMR spectrum. Use deuterated chloroform to dissolve your sample unless you are instructed to use another solvent, such as deuterated derivatives of water, acetone, or dimethylsulfoxide.

26.1 ROUTINE SAMPLE PREPARATION USING DEUTERATED CHLOROFORM

1. Most organic liquids and low-melting solids will dissolve in deuterated chloroform. However, you should first determine if your sample will dissolve in ordinary $CHCl_3$ before using the deuterated solvent. If your sample does not dissolve in chloroform, consult your instructor about a possible alternative solvent, or consult Section 26.2.

Caution: Chloroform, deuterated chloroform, and carbon tetrachloride are all toxic solvents. In addition, they may be carcinogenic substances.

2. If you are using an FT–NMR spectrometer, add 30 mg (0.030 g) of your liquid or solid sample to a tared conical vial or test tube. Use a Pasteur pipet to transfer a liquid or a spatula to transfer a solid. Non-FT instruments usually require a more concentrated solution in order to obtain an adequate spectrum. Typically, a 10–30% sample concentration (weight/weight) is used.
3. Transfer about 0.5 mL of the deuterated chloroform with a *clean, dry Pasteur pipet* to your sample. Swirl the test tube or conical vial to help dissolve the sample. At this point, the sample should have completely dissolved. Add a little more solvent, if necessary, to dissolve the sample fully.
4. Transfer the solution to the NMR tube using a clean, dry Pasteur pipet. Be careful when transferring the solution to avoid breaking the edge of the fragile NMR tube. It is best to hold the NMR tube and the container with the solution in the same hand when making the transfer.

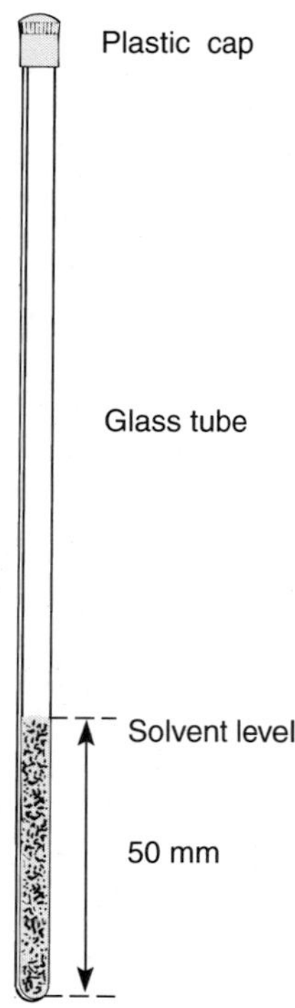

Figure 26.4 An NMR sample tube.

5. Once the solution has been transferred to the NMR tube, use a clean pipet to add enough deuterated chloroform to bring the total solution height to about 50 mm (Figure 26.4). In some cases, you will need to add a small amount of tetramethylsilane (TMS) as a **reference substance** (Section 26.3). Check with your instructor to see if you need to add TMS to your sample. Deuterated chloroform has a small amount of $CHCl_3$ impurity, which gives rise to a low-intensity peak in the NMR spectrum at 7.27 parts per million (ppm). This impurity may also help you to "reference" your spectrum.
6. Cap the NMR tube. Do this firmly but not too tightly. If you jam the cap on, you may have trouble removing it later without breaking the end off of the very thin glass tube. Make sure that the cap is on straight. Invert the NMR tube several times to mix the contents.
7. You are now ready to record the NMR spectrum of your sample. Insert the NMR tube into its holder and adjust its depth by using the gauge provided to you.

Cleaning the NMR Tube

1. Carefully uncap the tube so that you do not break it. Turn the tube upside down and hold it vertically over a beaker. Shake the tube up and down gently so that the contents of the tube empty into the beaker.
2. Partially refill the NMR tube with acetone using a Pasteur pipet. Carefully replace the cap and invert the tube several times to rinse it.

3. Remove the cap and drain the tube as before. Place the open tube upside down in a beaker with a Kimwipe or paper towel placed in the bottom of the beaker. Leave the tube standing in this position for at least one laboratory period so that the acetone completely evaporates. Alternatively, you may place the beaker and NMR tube in an oven for at least 2 hours. If you need to use the NMR tube before the acetone has fully evaporated, attach a piece of pressure tubing to the tube and pull a vacuum with an aspirator. After several minutes, the acetone should have fully evaporated. Because acetone contains protons, you must not use the NMR tube until the acetone has evaporated completely.[2]
4. Once the acetone is evaporated, place the clean tube and its cap (do not cap the tube) in its storage container and place it in your desk. The storage container will prevent the tube from being crushed.

Health Hazards Associated with NMR Solvents

Carbon tetrachloride, chloroform (and chloroform-d), and benzene (and benzene-d_6) are hazardous solvents. Besides being highly toxic, they are suspected carcinogens. In spite of these health problems, these solvents are commonly used in NMR spectroscopy because there are no suitable alternatives. These solvents are used because they contain no protons and are excellent solvents for most organic compounds. Therefore, you must learn to handle these solvents with great care to minimize the hazard. These solvents should be stored either under a hood or in septum-capped bottles. If the bottles have screw caps, a pipet should be attached to each bottle. A recommended way of attaching the pipet is to store it in a test tube taped to the side of the bottle. Septum-capped bottles can be used only by withdrawing the solvent with a hypodermic syringe that has been designated solely for this use. All samples should be prepared under a hood, and solutions should be disposed of in an appropriately designated waste container that is stored under the hood. Wear rubber or plastic gloves when preparing or discarding samples.

26.2 NONROUTINE SAMPLE PREPARATION

Some compounds do not dissolve readily in $CDCl_3$. A commercial solvent called **Unisol** will often dissolve the difficult cases. Unisol is a mixture of $CDCl_3$ and DMSO-d_6.

With highly polar substances, you may find that your sample will not dissolve in deuterated chloroform or Unisol. If this is the case, you may be able to dissolve the sample in deuterium oxide D_2O. Spectra determined in D_2O often show a small peak at about 5 ppm because of OH impurity. If the sample compound has acidic hydrogens, they may *exchange* with D_2O, leading to the appearance of an OH peak in the spectrum and the *loss* of the original absorption from the acidic proton, owing to the exchanged hydrogen. In many cases, this will also alter the splitting patterns of a compound.

Many solid carboxylic acids do not dissolve in $CDCl_3$ or even D_2O. In such cases, add a small piece of sodium metal to about 1 mL of D_2O. The acid is then dissolved in this so-

[2] If you can't wait to be sure all of the acetone has evaporated, you may rinse the tube once or twice with a *very small* amount of $CDCl_3$ before using it.

$$R{-}C(=O){-}O{-}H + D_2O \rightleftharpoons R{-}C(=O){-}O{-}D + D{-}OH$$

~12.0 ppm; becomes invisible; OH peak appears

$$CH_3{-}C(=O){-}CH_3 + D_2O \rightleftharpoons D{-}CH_2{-}C(=O){-}CH_3 + D{-}OH$$

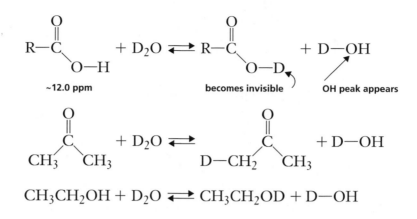

$$CH_3CH_2OH + D_2O \rightleftharpoons CH_3CH_2OD + D{-}OH$$

lution. The resulting basic solution enhances the solubility of the carboxylic acid. In such a case, the hydroxyl proton of the carboxylic acid cannot be observed in the NMR spectrum because it exchanges with the solvent. A large DOH peak is observed, however, due to the exchange and the H_2O impurity in the D_2O solvent.

When the above solvents fail, other special solvents can be used. Acetone, acetonitrile, dimethylsulfoxide, pyridine, benzene, and dimethylformamide can be used if you are not interested in the region or regions of the NMR spectrum in which they give rise to absorption. The deuterated (but expensive) analogs of these compounds are also used in special instances (for example, acetone-d_6, dimethylsulfoxide-d_6, dimethylformamide-d_7, and benzene-d_6). If the sample is not sensitive to acid, trifluoroacetic acid (which has no protons with $\delta < 12$) can be used. You must be aware that these solvents often lead to chemical shift values different from those determined in CCl_4 or $CDCl_3$. Variations of as much as 0.5–1.0 ppm have been observed. In fact, it is sometimes possible, by switching to pyridine, benzene, acetone, or dimethylsulfoxide as solvents, to separate peaks that overlap when CCl_4 or $CDCl_3$ solutions are used.

26.3 REFERENCE SUBSTANCES

To provide the internal reference standard, tetramethylsilane (TMS) must be added to the sample solution. This substance has the formula $(CH_3)_4Si$. By universal convention, the chemical shifts of the protons in this substance are defined as 0.00 ppm. The spectrum should be shifted so that the TMS signal appears at this position on precalibrated paper.

The concentration of TMS in the sample should range from 1% to 3%. Some people prefer to add 1 to 2 drops of TMS to the sample just before determining the spectrum. Because TMS has 12 equivalent protons, not much of it needs to be added. A Pasteur pipet or a syringe may be used for the addition. It is far easier to have available in the laboratory a prepared solvent that already contains TMS. Deuterated chloroform and carbon tetrachloride often have TMS added to them. Because TMS is highly volatile (bp 26.5°C), such solutions should be stored, tightly stoppered, in a refrigerator. Tetramethylsilane itself is best stored in a refrigerator as well.

Tetramethylsilane does not dissolve in D_2O. For spectra determined in D_2O, a different internal standard, sodium 2,2-dimethyl-2-silapentane-5-sulfonate, must be used. This standard is water soluble and gives a resonance peak at 0.00 ppm.

$$\begin{array}{c} \quad CH_3 \\ \quad | \\ CH_3{-}\overset{}{Si}{-}CH_2{-}CH_2{-}CH_2{-}SO_3^-Na^+ \\ \quad | \\ \quad CH_3 \end{array}$$

Sodium 2,2-dimethyl-2-silapentane-5-sulfonate (DSS)

Part B. Nuclear Magnetic Resonance (^{1}H NMR)

26.4 THE CHEMICAL SHIFT

The differences in the applied field strengths at which the various protons in a molecule absorb 60-MHz radiation are extremely small. The different absorption positions amount to a difference of only a few parts per million (ppm) in the magnetic field strength. Because it is experimentally difficult to measure the precise field strength at which each proton absorbs to less than one part in a million, a technique has been developed whereby the *difference* between two absorption positions is measured directly. A standard reference substance is used to achieve this measurement and the positions of the absorptions of all other protons are measured relative to the values for the reference substance. The reference substance that has been universally accepted is **tetramethylsilane** $(CH_3)_4Si$, which is also called **TMS.** The proton resonances in this molecule appear at a higher field strength than the proton resonances in most other molecules, and all the protons of TMS have resonance at the same field strength.

To give the position of absorption of a proton, a quantitative measurement, a parameter called the **chemical shift** (δ), has been defined. One δ unit corresponds to a one-ppm change in the magnetic field strength. To determine the chemical shift value for the various protons in a molecule, the operator determines an NMR spectrum of the molecule with a small quantity of TMS added directly to the sample. That is, both spectra are determined *simultaneously.* The TMS absorption is adjusted to correspond to the $\delta = 0$ ppm position on the recording chart, which is calibrated in δ units, and the δ values of the absorption peaks for all other protons can be read directly from the chart.

Because the NMR spectrometer increases the magnetic field as the pen moves from left to right on the chart, the TMS absorption appears at the extreme right edge of the spectrum ($\delta = 0$ ppm) or at the *upfield* end of the spectrum. The chart is calibrated in δ units (or ppm), and most other protons absorb at a lower field strength (or *downfield*) from TMS.

The shift from TMS for a given proton depends on the strength of the applied magnetic field. In an applied field of 1.41 tesla the resonance of a proton is approximately 60 MHz, whereas in an applied field of 2.35 tesla, (23,500 gauss), the resonance appears at approximately 100 MHz. The ratio of the resonance frequencies is the same as the ratio of the two field strengths:

$$\frac{100 \text{ MHz}}{60 \text{ MHz}} = \frac{2.35 \text{ Tesla}}{1.41 \text{ Tesla}} = \frac{23{,}500 \text{ Gauss}}{14{,}100 \text{ Gauss}} = \frac{5}{3}$$

Hence, for a given proton, the shift (in hertz) from TMS is five-thirds larger in the 100-MHz range than in the 60-MHz range. This can be confusing for workers trying to compare data if they have spectrometers that differ in the strength of the applied magnetic field. The confusion is easily overcome by defining a new parameter that is independent of field strength—for instance, by dividing the shift in hertz of a given proton by the frequency in megahertz of the spectrometer with which the shift value was obtained. In this manner, a field-independent measure called the **chemical shift** (δ) is obtained

$$\delta = \frac{\text{(shift in Hz)}}{\text{(spectrometer frequency in MHz)}} \tag{1}$$

The chemical shift in δ units expresses the amount by which a proton resonance is shifted from TMS, in parts per million (ppm), of the spectrometer's basic operating frequency. Values of δ for a given proton are always the same irrespective of whether the measurement was made at 60 MHz, 100 MHz, or 300 MHz. For instance, at 60 MHz, the shift of the protons in CH_3Br is 162 Hz from TMS; at 100 MHz, the shift is 270 Hz; and at 300 MHz, the shift is 810 Hz. However, all three correspond to the same value of $\delta = 2.70$ ppm:

$$\delta = \frac{162\text{ Hz}}{60\text{ MHz}} = \frac{270\text{ Hz}}{100\text{ MHz}} = \frac{810\text{ Hz}}{300\text{ MHz}} = 2.70\text{ ppm}$$

26.5 CHEMICAL EQUIVALENCE—INTEGRALS

All the protons in a molecule that are in chemically identical environments often exhibit the same chemical shift. Thus, all the protons in TMS or all the protons in benzene, cyclopentane, or acetone have their own respective resonance values all at the same δ value. Each compound gives rise to a single absorption peak in its NMR spectrum. The protons are said to be **chemically equivalent.** On the other hand, molecules that have sets of protons that are chemically distinct from one another may give rise to an absorption peak from each set.

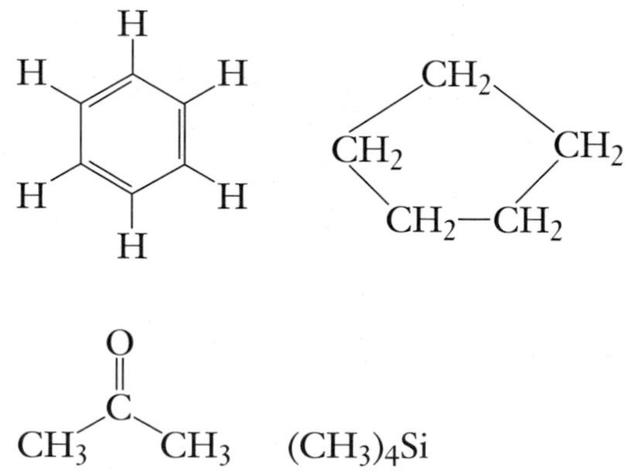

CH_3COCH_3 $(CH_3)_4Si$

Molecules giving rise to one NMR absorption peak—all protons chemically equivalent

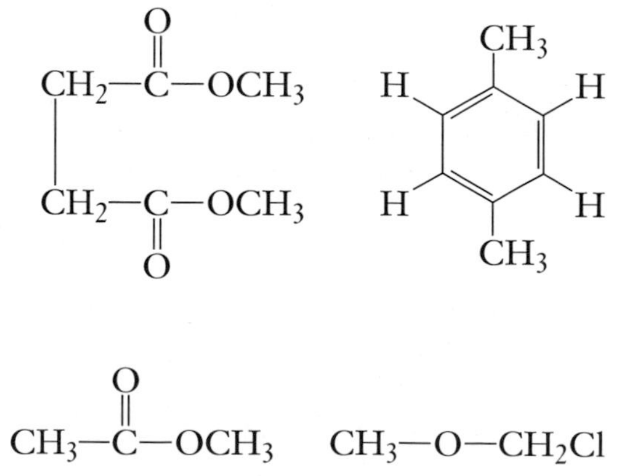

$CH_3—CO—OCH_3$ $CH_3—O—CH_2Cl$

Molecules giving rise to two NMR absorption peaks—two different sets of chemically equivalent protons

The NMR spectrum given in Figure 26.3 is that of phenylacetone, a compound having *three* chemically distinct types of protons:

$C_6H_5-CH_2-C(=O)-CH_3$

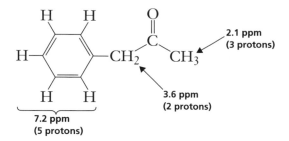

2.1 ppm (3 protons)
3.6 ppm (2 protons)
7.2 ppm (5 protons)

You can immediately see that the NMR spectrum furnishes valuable information on this basis alone. In fact, the NMR spectrum not only can distinguish how many types of protons a molecule has but also can reveal *how many* of each type are contained within the molecule.

In the NMR spectrum, the area under each peak is proportional to the number of hydrogens generating that peak. Hence, in the case of phenylacetone, the area ratio of the three peaks is 5:2:3, the same as the ratio of the numbers of each type of hydrogen. The NMR spectrometer can electronically "integrate" the area under each peak. It does this by tracing over each peak a vertically rising line, which rises in height by an amount proportional to the area under the peak. Shown in Figure 26.5 is an NMR spectrum of benzyl acetate, with each of the peaks integrated in this way.

It is important to note that the height of the integral line does not give the absolute number of hydrogens; it gives the *relative* numbers of each type of hydrogen. For a given

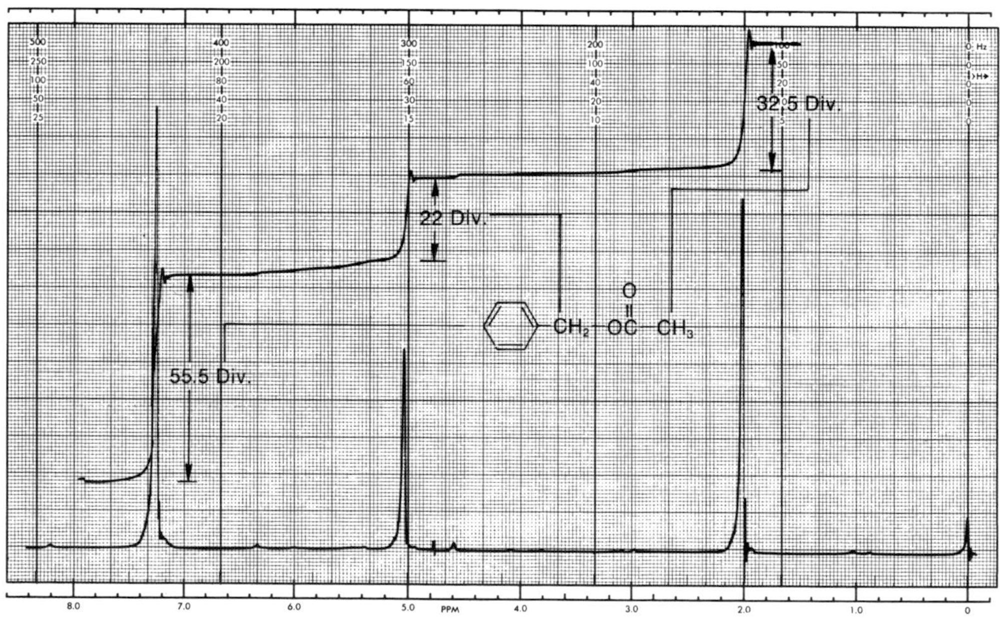

Figure 26.5 Determination of the integral ratios for benzyl acetate.

integral to be of any use, there must be a second integral to which it is referred. The benzyl acetate case provides a good example of this. The first integral rises for 55.5 divisions on the chart paper, the second for 22.0 divisions, and the third for 32.5 divisions. These numbers are relative and give the *ratios* of the various types of protons. You can find these ratios by dividing each of the larger numbers by the smallest number:

$$\frac{55.5 \text{ div}}{22.0 \text{ div}} = 2.52 \qquad \frac{22.0 \text{ div}}{22.0 \text{ div}} = 1.00 \qquad \frac{32.5 \text{ div}}{22.0 \text{ div}} = 1.48$$

Thus, the number ratio of the protons of each type is 2.52:1.00:1.48. If you assume that the peak at 5.1 ppm is really caused by two hydrogens and that the integrals are slightly in error (this can be as much as 10%), then you can arrive at the true ratios by multiplying each figure by 2 and rounding off; we then get 5:2:3. Clearly, the peak at 7.3 ppm, which integrates for 5, arises from the resonance of the aromatic ring protons, and the peak at 2.0 ppm, which integrates for 3, is caused by the methyl protons. The two-proton resonance at 5.1 ppm arises from the benzyl protons. Notice then that the integrals give the simplest ratios, but not necessarily the true ratios, of the number of protons in each type.

In addition to the rising integral line, modern instruments usually give digitized numerical values for the integrals. Like the heights of the integral lines, these digitized integral values are not absolute but relative, and they should be treated as explained in the preceding paragraph. These digital values are also not exact; like the integral lines, they have the potential for a small degree of error (up to 10%). Figure 26.6 is an example of an integrated spectrum of benzyl acetate determined on a 300-MHz pulsed FT–NMR instrument. The digitized values of the integrals appear under the peaks.

26.6 CHEMICAL ENVIRONMENT AND CHEMICAL SHIFT

If the resonance frequencies of all protons in a molecule were the same, NMR would be of little use to the organic chemist. However, not only do different types of protons have different chemical shifts but they also have a value of chemical shift that characterizes the type of proton they represent. Every type of proton has only a limited range of δ values over which it gives resonance. Hence, the numerical value of the chemical shift for a proton indicates the *type of proton* originating the signal, just as the infrared frequency suggests the type of bond or functional group. Notice, for instance, that the aromatic protons of both phenylacetone (Figure 26.3) and benzyl acetate (Figure 26.5) have resonance near 7.3 ppm and that both methyl groups attached directly to a carbonyl group have a resonance of approximately 2.1 ppm. Aromatic protons characteristically have resonance near 7–8 ppm, and acetyl groups (the methyl protons) have their resonance near 2 ppm. These values of chemical shift are diagnostic. Notice also how the resonance of the benzyl (—CH_2—) protons comes at a higher value of chemical shift (5.1 ppm) in benzyl acetate than in phenylacetone (3.6 ppm). Being attached to the electronegative element, oxygen, these protons are more deshielded (see Section 26.7) than the protons in phenylacetone. A trained chemist would have readily recognized the probable presence of the oxygen by the chemical shift shown by these protons.

It is important to learn the ranges of chemical shifts over which the most common

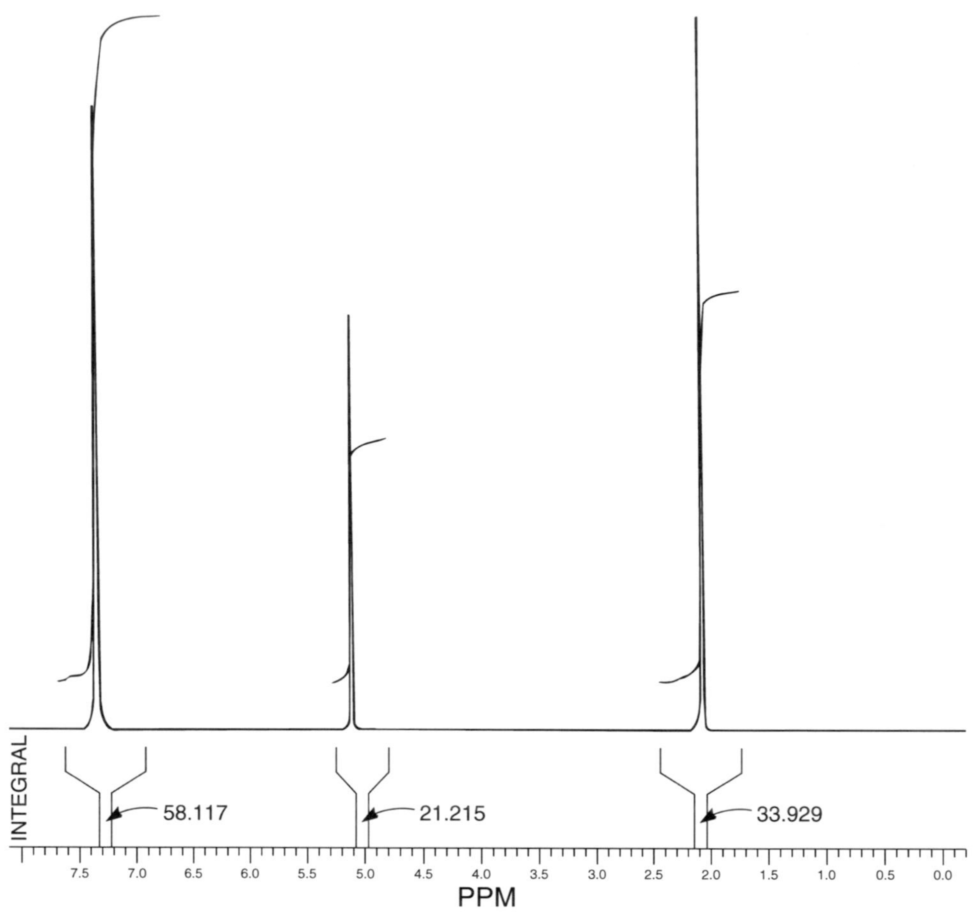

Figure 26.6 An integrated spectrum of benzyl acetate determined on a 300-MHz FT-NMR.

types of protons have resonance. Figure 26.7 is a correlation chart that contains the most essential and frequently encountered types of protons. Table 26.1 lists the chemical shift ranges for selected types of protons. For the beginner, it is often difficult to memorize a large body of numbers relating to chemical shifts and proton types. However, this needs to be done only crudely. It is more important to "get a feel" for the regions and the types of protons than to know a string of actual numbers. To do this, study Figure 26.7 carefully.

The values of chemical shift given in Figure 26.7 and in Table 26.1 can be easily understood in terms of two factors: local diamagnetic shielding and anisotropy. These two factors are discussed in Sections 26.7 and 26.8.

26.7 LOCAL DIAMAGNETIC SHIELDING

The trend of chemical shifts that is easiest to explain is that involving electronegative elements substituted on the same carbon to which the protons of interest are attached. The chemical shift simply increases as the electronegativity of the attached element increases. This is illustrated in Table 26.2 for several compounds of the type CH_3X.

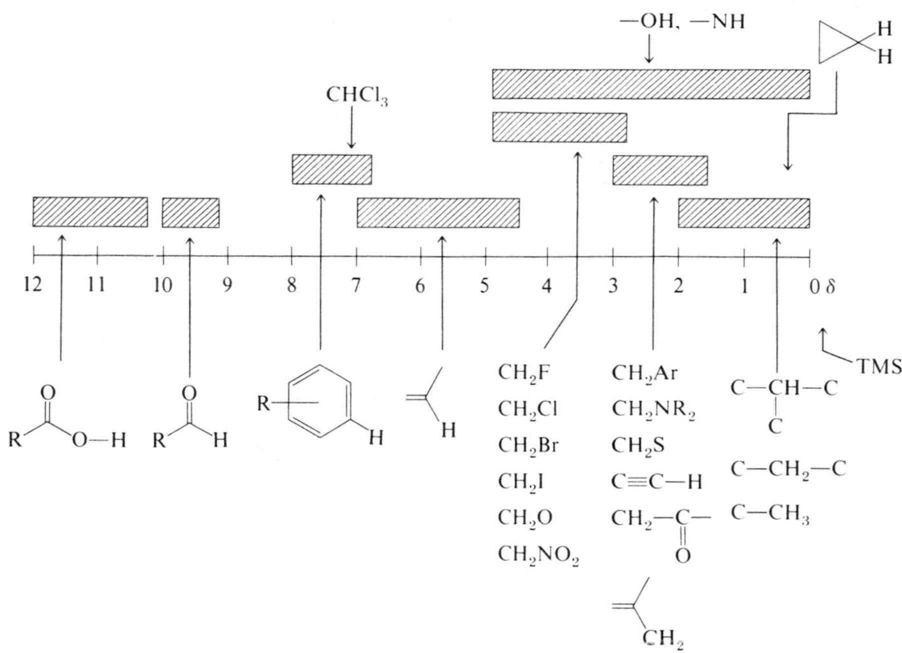

Figure 26.7 A simplified correlation chart for proton chemical shift values.

Multiple substituents have a stronger effect than a single substituent. The influence of the substituent drops off rapidly with distance. An electronegative element has little effect on protons that are more than three carbons away from it. These effects are illustrated in Table 26.3.

Electronegative substituents attached to a carbon atom, because of their electron-withdrawing effects, reduce the valence electron density around the protons attached to that carbon. These electrons *shield* the proton from the applied magnetic field. This effect, called **local diamagnetic shielding,** occurs because the applied magnetic field induces the valence electrons to circulate. This circulation generates an induced magnetic field, which *opposes* the applied field. This is illustrated in Figure 26.8. Electronegative substituents on carbon reduce the local diamagnetic shielding in the vicinity of the attached protons because they reduce the electron density around those protons. Substituents that produce this effect are said to *deshield* the proton. The greater the electronegativity of the substituent, the more the deshielding of the protons and, hence, the greater the chemical shift of those protons.

26.8 ANISOTROPY

Figure 26.7 clearly shows that several types of protons have chemical shifts not easily explained by a simple consideration of the electronegativity of the attached groups. Consider, for instance, the protons of benzene or other aromatic systems. Aryl protons generally have a chemical shift that is as large as that for the proton of chloroform. Alkenes, alkynes, and aldehydes also have protons whose resonance values are not in line with the expected magnitude of any electron-withdrawing effects. In each of these cases, the effect is due to the presence of an unsaturated system (π electrons) in the vicinity of the proton in question. In

TABLE 26.1 Approximate Chemical Shift Ranges (ppm) for Selected Types of Protons

Type of proton		Shift (ppm)
R–CH_3		0.7–1.3
R–CH_2–R		1.2–1.4
R_3CH		1.4–1.7
R–C=C–C–**H**		1.6 – 2.6
R–C(=O)–C–**H**, H–C(=O)–C–**H**		2.1 – 2.4
RO–C(=O)–C–**H**, HO–C(=O)–C–**H**		2.1 – 2.5
N≡C–C–**H**		2.1 – 3.0
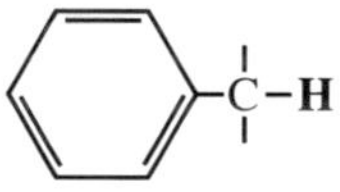 ⌬–C–**H**		2.3 – 2.7
R–C≡C–**H**		1.7 – 2.7
R–S–**H**	var	1.0 – 4.0[a]
R–N–**H**	var	0.5 – 4.0[a]
R–O–**H**	var	0.5 – 5.0[a]
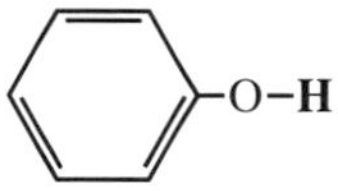 ⌬–O–**H**	var	4.0 – 7.0[a]
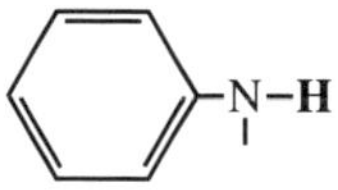 ⌬–N–**H**	var	3.0 – 5.0[a]
R–C(=O)–N–**H**	var	5.0 – 9.0[a]

Type of proton	Shift (ppm)
R–N–C–**H**	2.2–2.9
R–S–C–**H**	2.0–3.0
I–C–**H**	2.0–4.0
Br–C–**H**	2.7–4.1
Cl–C–**H**	3.1–4.1
R–S(=O)(=O)–O–C–**H**	ca. 3.0
RO–C–**H**, HO–C–**H**	3.2–3.8
R–C(=O)–O–C–**H**	3.5–4.8
O_2N–C–**H**	4.1–4.3
F–C–**H**	4.2–4.8
R–C=C–**H**	4.5–6.5
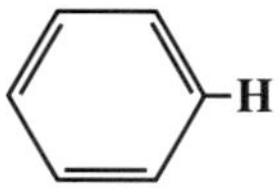 ⌬–**H**	6.5–8.0
R–C(=O)–**H**	9.0–10.0
R–C(=O)–OH	11.0–12.0

Note: For those hydrogens shown as —C—H, if that hydrogen is part of a methyl group (CH_3) the shift is generally at the low end of the range given; if the hydrogen is in a methylene group (—CH_2—) the shift is intermediate; and if the hydrogen is in a methine group (—CH—), the shift is typically at the high end of the range given.

[a]The chemical shift of these groups is variable, depending on the chemical environment in the molecule and on concentration, temperature, and solvent.

TABLE 26.2 Dependence of Chemical Shift of CH_3X on the Element X

Compound CH_3X	CH_3F	CH_3OH	CH_3Cl	CH_3Br	CH_3I	CH_4	$(CH_3)_4Si$
Element X	F	O	Cl	Br	I	H	Si
Electronegativity of X	4.0	3.5	3.1	2.8	2.5	2.1	1.8
Chemical shift (ppm)	4.26	3.40	3.05	2.68	2.16	0.23	0

TABLE 26.3 Substitution Effects

	$\mathbf{C\underline{H}Cl_3}$	$\mathbf{C\underline{H}_2Cl_2}$	$\mathbf{C\underline{H}_3Cl}$	$\mathbf{—C\underline{H}_2Br}$	$\mathbf{—C\underline{H}_2—CH_2Br}$	$\mathbf{—C\underline{H}_2—CH_2CH_2Br}$
δ (ppm)	7.27	5.30	3.05	3.3	1.69	1.25

Note: Values apply to underlined hydrogens.

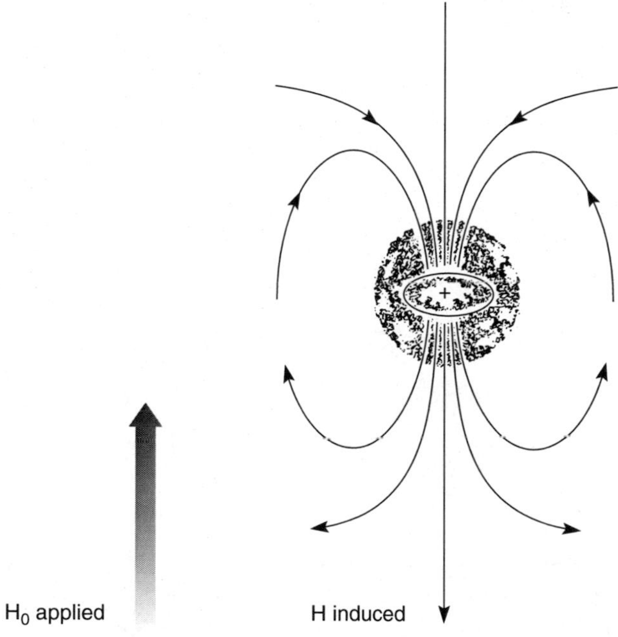

Figure 26.8 Local diamagnetic shielding of a proton due to its valence electrons.

benzene, for example, when the π electrons in the aromatic ring system are placed in a magnetic field, they are induced to circulate around the ring. This circulation is called a **ring current.** Moving electrons (the ring current) generate a magnetic field much like that generated in a loop of wire through which a current is induced to flow. The magnetic field covers a spatial volume large enough to influence the shielding of the benzene hydrogens. This is illustrated in Figure 26.9. The benzene hydrogens are deshielded by the **diamagnetic anisotropy** of the ring. An applied magnetic field is nonuniform (anisotropic) in the vicinity of a benzene molecule because of the labile electrons in the ring that interact with the ap-

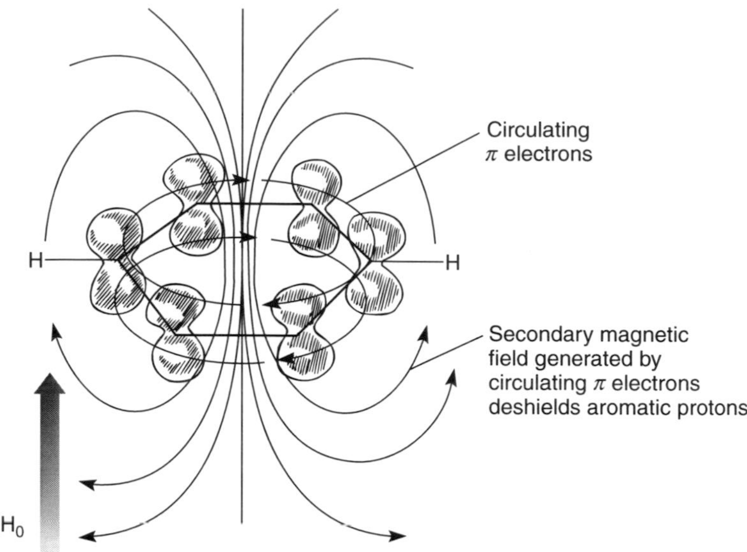

Figure 26.9 Diamagnetic anisotropy in benzene.

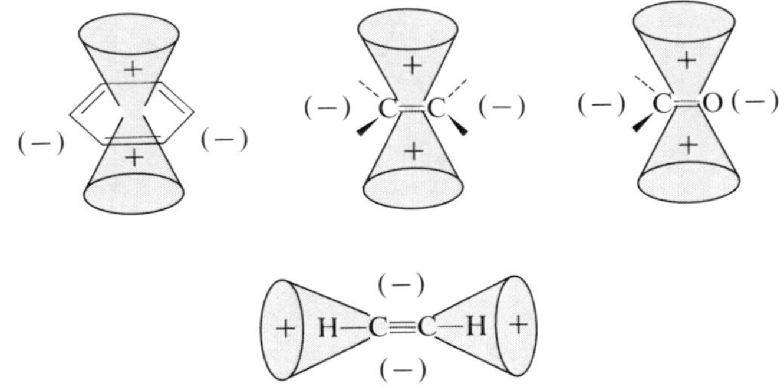

Figure 26.10 Anisotropy caused by the presence of π electrons in some common multiple-bond systems.

plied field. Thus, a proton attached to a benzene ring is influenced by *three* magnetic fields: the strong magnetic field applied by the magnets of the NMR spectrometer and two weaker fields, one due to the usual shielding by the valence electrons around the proton and the other due to the anisotropy generated by the ring system electrons. It is this anisotropic effect that gives the benzene protons a greater chemical shift than is expected. These protons just happen to lie in a **deshielding** region of this anisotropic field. If a proton were placed in the center of the ring rather than on its periphery, the proton would be shielded, because the field lines would have the opposite direction.

All groups in a molecule that have π electrons generate secondary anisotropic fields. In acetylene, the magnetic field generated by induced circulation of π electrons has a geometry such that the acetylene hydrogens are **shielded.** Hence, acetylenic hydrogens come at a higher field than expected. The shielding and deshielding regions due to the various π electron functional groups have characteristic shapes and directions; they are illustrated in

Figure 26.10. Protons falling within the cones are shielded, and those falling outside the conical areas are deshielded. Because the magnitude of the anisotropic field diminishes with distance, beyond a certain distance anisotropy has essentially no effect.

26.9 SPIN–SPIN SPLITTING (n + 1 RULE)

We have already considered how the chemical shift and the integral (peak area) can give information about the numbers and types of hydrogens contained in a molecule. A third type of information available from the NMR spectrum is derived from spin–spin splitting. Even in simple molecules, each type of proton rarely gives a single resonance peak. For instance, in 1,1,2-trichloroethane there are two chemically distinct types of hydrogen:

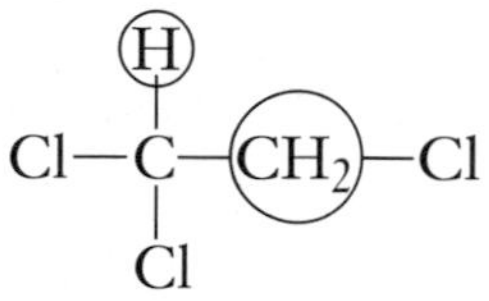

From information given thus far, you would predict *two* resonance peaks in the NMR spectrum of 1,1,2-trichloroethane with an area ratio (integral ratio) of 2:1. In fact, the NMR spectrum of this compound has *five* peaks. A group of three peaks (called a **triplet**) exists at 5.77 ppm, and a group of two peaks (called a **doublet**) is found at 3.95 ppm. The spectrum is shown in Figure 26.11. The methine (CH) resonance (5.77 ppm) is split into a triplet, and the methylene resonance (3.95 ppm) is split into a doublet. The area under the three triplet peaks is *one,* relative to an area of *two* under the two doublet peaks.

This phenomenon is called **spin–spin splitting.** Empirically, spin–spin splitting can be explained by the "$n + 1$ rule." Each type of proton "senses" the number of equivalent protons (n) on the carbon atom or atoms next to the one to which it is bonded, and its resonance peak is split into $n + 1$ components.

Let's examine the case at hand, 1,1,2-trichloroethane, using the $n + 1$ rule. First, the lone methine hydrogen is situated next to a carbon bearing two methylene protons. According to the rule, it has two equivalent neighbors ($n = 2$) and is split into $n + 1 = 3$ peaks (a triplet). The methylene protons are situated next to a carbon bearing only one methine hydrogen. According to the rule, they have one neighbor ($n = 1$) and are split into $n + 1 = 2$ peaks (a doublet).

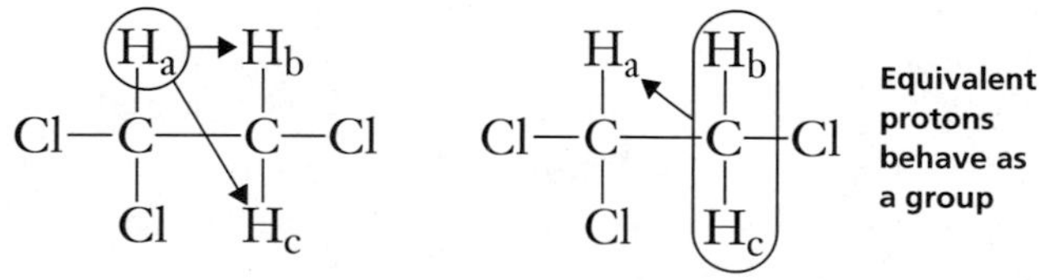

Two neighbors give a triplet ($n + 1 = 3$) (area = 1)

One neighbor gives a doublet ($n + 1 = 2$) (area = 2)

Equivalent protons behave as a group

The spectrum of 1,1,2-trichloroethane can be explained easily by the interaction, or coupling, of the spins of protons on adjacent carbon atoms. The position of absorption of

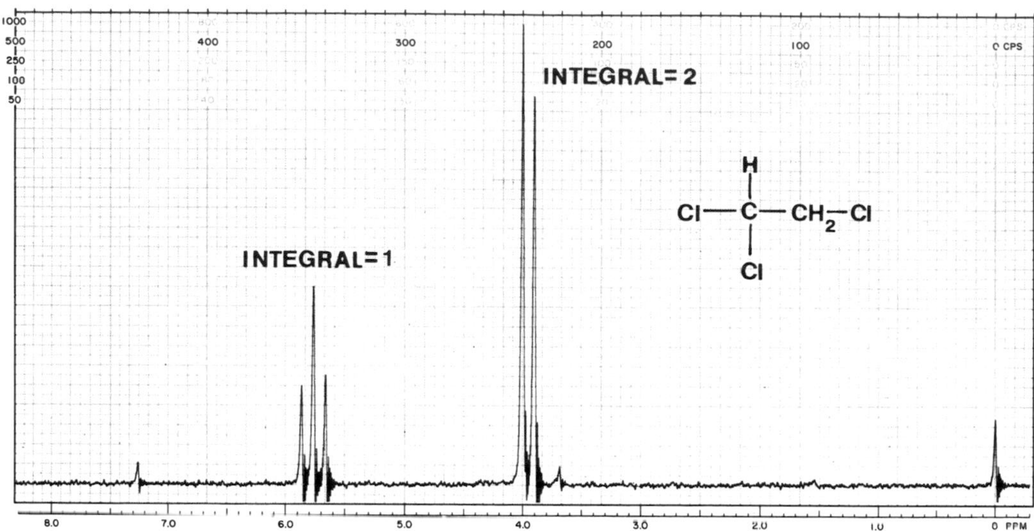

Figure 26.11 NMR spectrum of 1,1,2-trichloroethane. (Courtesy of Varian Associates.)

proton H_a is affected by the spins of protons H_b and H_c attached to the neighboring (adjacent) carbon atom. If the spins of these protons are aligned with the applied magnetic field, the small magnetic field generated by their nuclear spin properties will augment the strength of the field experienced by the first-mentioned proton H_a. The proton H_a will thus be *deshielded.* If the spins of H_b and H_c are opposed to the applied field, they will decrease the field experienced by proton H_a. It will then be *shielded.* In each of these situations, the absorption position of H_a will be altered. Among the many molecules in the solution, you will find all the various possible spin combinations for H_b and H_c; hence, the NMR spectrum of the molecular solution will give *three* absorption peaks (a triplet) for H_a because H_b and H_c have three different possible spin combinations (Figure 26.12). By a similar analysis, it can be seen that protons H_b and H_c should appear as a doublet.

Some common splitting patterns that can be predicted by the $n + 1$ rule and that are frequently observed in a number of molecules are shown in Figure 26.13. Notice particularly the last entry, where *both* methyl groups (six protons in all) function as a unit and split the methine proton into a septet ($6 + 1 = 7$).

26.10 THE COUPLING CONSTANT

The quantitative amount of spin–spin interaction between two protons can be defined by the **coupling constant.** The spacing between the component peaks in a single multiplet is called the coupling constant *J*. This distance is measured on the same scale as the chemical shift and is expressed in hertz (Hz).

Coupling constants for protons on adjacent carbon atoms have magnitudes of from about 6 Hz to 8 Hz (see Table 26.4). You should expect to see a coupling constant in this range for compounds where there is free rotation about a single bond. Because three bonds separate protons from each other on adjacent carbon atoms, we label these coupling constants as ^3J. For example, the coupling constant for the compound shown in Figure 26.11

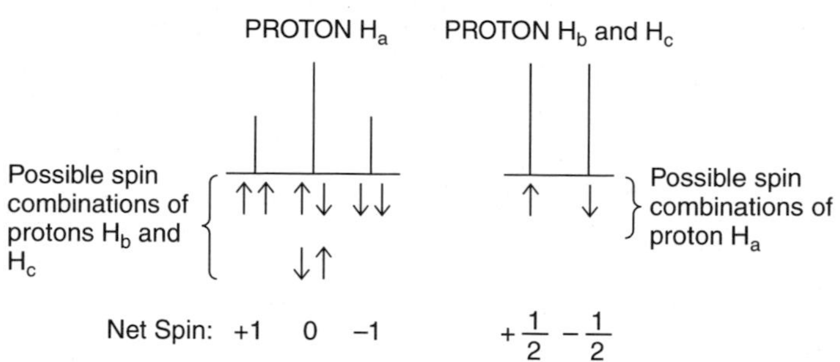

Figure 26.12 Analysis of spin–spin splitting pattern for 1,1,2-trichloroethane.

TABLE 26.4 Representative Coupling Constants and Approximate Values (Hz)

Structure	Coupling	Value
H—C—C—H	^3J	6 – 8
	$^3J_{trans}$	11 – 18
	$^3J_{cis}$	6 – 15
	$^2J_{gem}$	0 – 5
	^3J	4 – 10
H—C=C—C—H	^4J	0 – 3

Structure	Coupling		Value
	^3J	*ortho*	6 – 10
	^4J	*meta*	1 – 4
	^5J	*para*	≈ 0
	^3J		8 – 11

Structure	Coupling		Value
	^3J	a,a	8 – 14
		a,e	0 – 7
		e,e	0 – 5
	^3J	*cis*	6 – 12
		trans	4 – 8
O	^3J	*cis*	2 – 5
		trans	1 – 3
	^3J		5 – 7

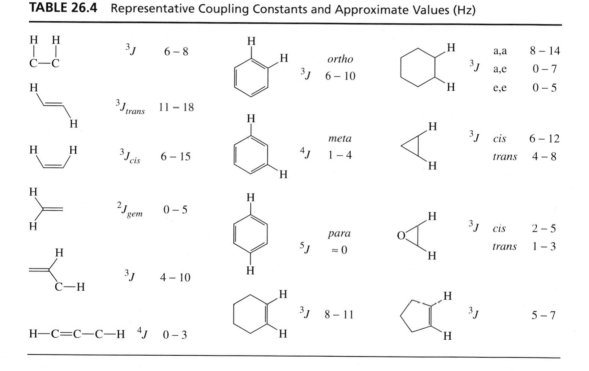

would be written as ^3J = 6 Hz. The boldfaced lines in the following diagram show how the protons on adjacent carbon atoms are three bonds away from each other.

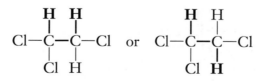

H H / Cl—**C—C**—Cl / Cl H or H H / Cl—**C—C**—Cl / Cl **H**

In compounds where there is a C=C double bond, free rotation is restricted. In compounds of this kind, we often find two types of ^3J coupling constants; $^3J_{trans}$ and $^3J_{cis}$. These coupling constants vary in value as shown in Table 26.4, but $^3J_{trans}$ is almost always larger than $^3J_{cis}$. The magnitudes of these ^3Js often provide important structural clues. You can dis-

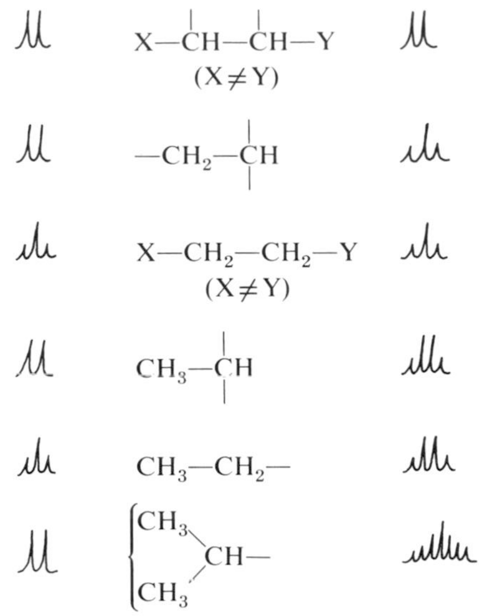

X—CH—CH—Y (X≠Y)

—CH_2—CH

X—CH_2—CH_2—Y (X≠Y)

CH_3—CH

CH_3—CH_2—

CH_3 / CH_3 CH—

Figure 26.13 Some common splitting patterns.

tinguish, for example, between a *cis* alkene and a *trans* alkene on the basis of the observed coupling constants for the two vinyl protons on disubstituted alkenes. Most of the coupling constants shown in the first column of Table 26.4 are three bond couplings, but you will notice that there is a two-bond (^2J) coupling constant listed. These protons that are bonded to a common carbon atom are often referred to as *geminal* protons and can be labeled as $^2J_{gem}$. Notice that the coupling constants for *geminal* protons are quite small for alkenes. The ^2J couplings are observed only when the protons on a methylene group are in a different environment (see Section 26.11). The following structure shows the various types of couplings that you observe for protons on a C=C double bond in a typical alkene, vinyl acetate. The spectrum for this compound is described in detail in Section 26.11.

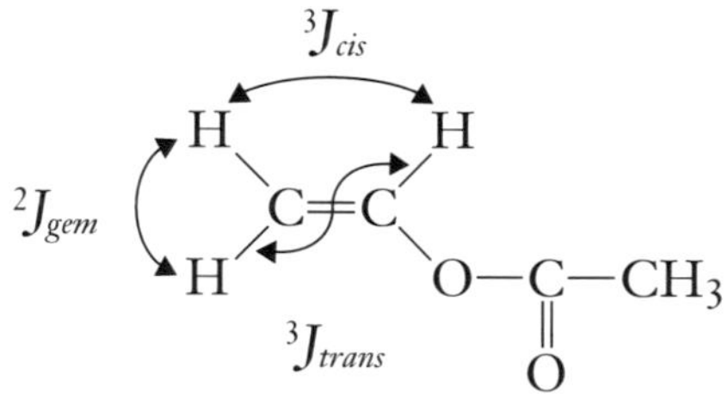

$^3J_{cis}$ $^2J_{gem}$ $^3J_{trans}$

H, H, C=C, H, O—C(=O)—CH_3

Vinyl acetate

Longer-range couplings that occur over four or more bonds are observed in some alkenes and also in aromatic compounds. Thus, in Table 26.4, we see that it is possible to observe a small H—H coupling (^4J = 0–3 Hz) occurring over four bonds in an alkene. In an aromatic compound, you often observe a small but measurable coupling between *meta* protons that are four bonds away from each other (^4J = 1–4 Hz). Couplings over five bonds are usually quite small, with values close to 0 Hz. The long-range couplings are usually observed only in *unsaturated* compounds. The spectra of saturated compounds are often more easily interpreted because they usually have only three bond couplings. Aromatic compounds are discussed in detail in Section 26.13.

26.11 MAGNETIC EQUIVALENCE

In the example of spin–spin splitting in 1,1,2-trichloroethane (Figure 26.11), notice that the two protons H_b and H_c, which are attached to the same carbon atom, do not split one another. They behave as an integral group. Actually, the two protons H_b and H_c *are* coupled to one another; however, for reasons we cannot explain fully here, protons that are attached to the same carbon and both of which have the *same chemical shift* do not show spin–spin splitting. Another way of stating this is that protons coupled to the same extent to *all* other protons in a molecule do not show spin–spin splitting. Protons that have the same chemical shift and are coupled equivalently to all other protons are *magnetically equivalent* and do not show spin–spin splitting. Thus, in 1,1,2-trichloroethane, protons H_b and H_c have the same value of δ and are coupled by the same value of J to proton H_a. They are magnetically equivalent, and ${}^2J_{gem} = 0$.

It is important to differentiate magnetic equivalence and chemical equivalence. Note the following two compounds.

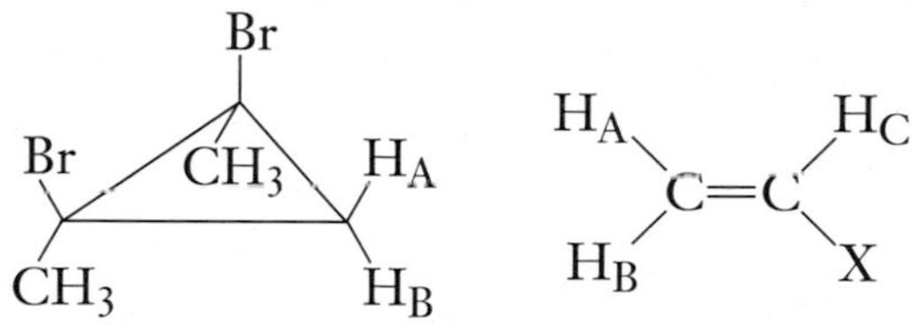

In the cycloproprane compound, the two geminal hydrogens H_A and H_B are chemically equivalent; however, they are not magnetically equivalent. Proton H_A is on the same side of the ring as the two halogens. Proton H_B is on the same side of the ring as the two methyl groups. Protons H_A and H_B will have different chemical shifts, will couple to one another, and will show spin–spin splitting. Two doublets will be seen for H_A and H_B. For cyclopropane rings, ${}^2J_{gem}$ is usually around 5 Hz.

The general vinyl structure (alkene) shown in the previous figure and the specific example of vinyl acetate shown in Figure 26.14 are examples of cases in which the methylene protons H_A and H_B are nonequivalent. They appear at different chemical shift values and will split each other. This coupling constant, ${}^2J_{gem}$, is usually small with vinyl compounds (about 2 Hz).

The spectrum of vinyl acetate is shown in Figure 26.14. H_C appears downfield at about 7.3 ppm because of the electronegativity of the attached oxygen atom. This proton is split by H_B into a doublet (${}^3J_{trans} = {}^3J_{BC} = 15$ Hz), and then each leg of the doublet is split by H_A into a doublet (${}^3J_{cis} = {}^3J_{AC} = 7$ Hz). Notice that the $n + 1$ rule is applied individually to each adjacent proton. The pattern that results is usually referred to as a doublet of doublets (dd). The graphic analysis shown in Figure 26.15 should help you understand the pattern obtained for proton H_C.

Now look at the pattern shown in Figure 26.14 for proton H_B at 4.85 ppm. It is also a doublet of doublets. Proton H_B is split by proton H_C into a doublet (${}^3J_{trans} = {}^3J_{BC} = 15$ Hz), and then each leg of the doublet is split by the geminal proton H_A into doublets (${}^2J_{gem} = {}^2J_{AB} = 2$ Hz).

Proton H_A shown in Figure 26.14 appears at 4.55 ppm. This pattern is also a doublet of doublets. Proton H_A is split by proton H_C into a doublet (${}^3J_{cis} = {}^3J_{AC} = 7$ Hz), and then each leg of the doublet is split by the geminal proton H_B into doublets (${}^2J_{gem} = {}^2J_{AB} = 2$ Hz).

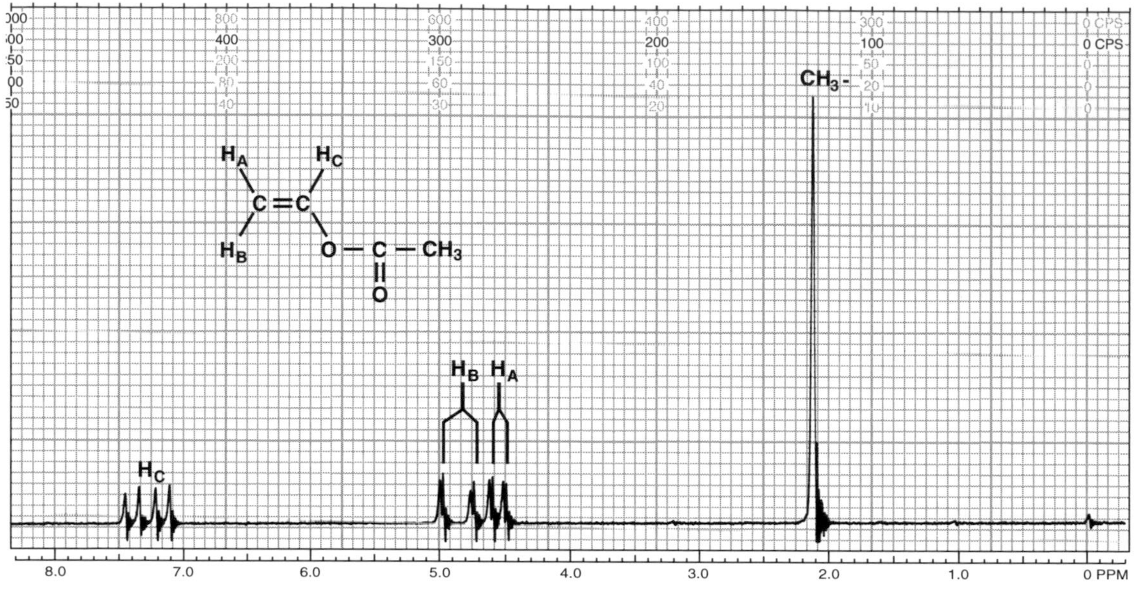

Figure 26.14 NMR spectrum of vinyl acetate. (Courtesy of Varian Associates.)

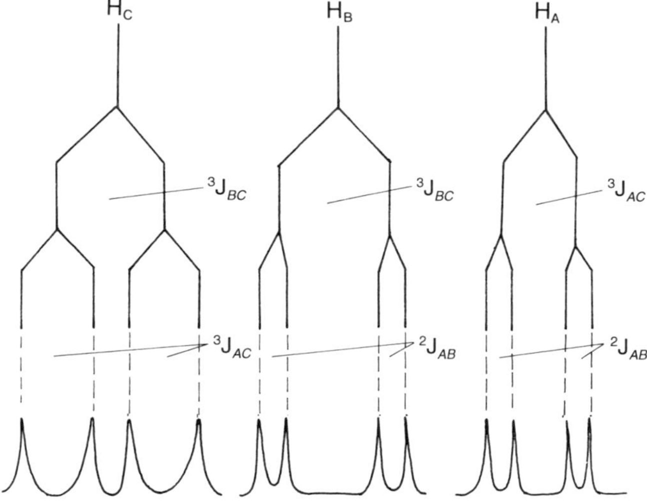

Figure 26.15 Analysis of the splittings in vinyl acetate.

For each proton shown in Figure 26.14, the NMR spectrum must be analyzed graphically, splitting by splitting. This complete graphic analysis is shown in Figure 26.15.

26.12 SPECTRA AT HIGHER FIELD STRENGTH

Occasionally, the 60-MHz spectrum of an organic compound, or a portion of it, is almost undecipherable because the chemical shifts of several groups of protons are all very similar. In these cases, all the proton resonances occur in the same area of the spectrum, and peaks often overlap so extensively that individual peaks and splittings cannot be extracted. One way to simplify such a situation is to use a spectrometer that operates at a higher frequency. Although both 60-MHz and 100-MHz instruments are still in use, it is becoming increasingly common to find instruments operating at much higher fields and with spectrometer frequencies 300, 400, or 500 MHz.

Although NMR coupling constants do not depend on the frequency or the field strength of operation of the NMR spectrometer, chemical shifts in hertz depend on these parameters. This circumstance can often be used to simplify an otherwise undecipherable spectrum. Suppose, for instance, that a compound contained three multiplets derived from groups of protons with very similar chemical shifts. At 60 MHz, these peaks might overlap, as illustrated in Figure 26.16, and simply give an unresolved envelope of absorption. It turns out that the $n + 1$ rule fails to make the proper predictions when chemical shifts are similar for the protons in a molecule. The spectral patterns that result are said to be **second order,** and what you end up seeing is an amorphous blob of unrecognizable patterns!

Figure 26.16 also shows the spectrum of the same compound at two higher frequencies (100 MHz and 300 MHz). When the spectrum is redetermined at a higher frequency, the coupling constants *(J)* do not change, but the chemical shifts in *hertz* (not ppm) of the proton groups (H_A, H_B, H_C) responsible for the multiplets do increase. It is important to realize, however, that the chemical shift in *ppm* is a constant, and it will not change when the frequency of the spectrometer is increased (see equation 1 on p. 917).

Notice that at 300 MHz, the individual multiplets are cleanly separated and resolved. At high frequency, the chemical shift differences of each proton increase, resulting in more clearly recognizable patterns (that is, triplets, quartets, and so on) and less overlap of proton patterns in the spectrum. At high frequency, the chemical shift differences are large, and

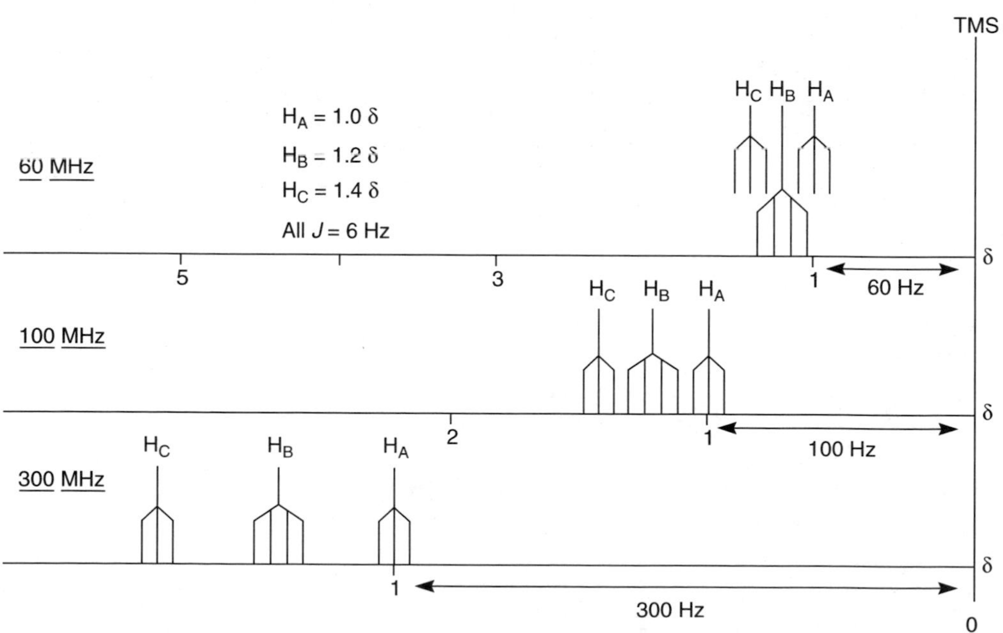

Figure 26.16 A comparison of the spectrum of a compound with overlapping multiplets at 60 MHz, with spectra of the same compound also determined at 100 MHz and 300 MHz.

the $n + 1$ rule will more likely correctly predict the patterns. Thus, it is a clear advantage to use NMR spectrometers operating at high frequency (300 MHz or above) because the resulting spectra are more likely to provide nonoverlapped and well-resolved peaks. When the protons in a spectrum follow the $n + 1$ rule, the spectrum is said to be **first order.** The result is that you will obtain a spectrum with much more recognizable patterns, as shown in Figure 26.16.

26.13 AROMATIC COMPOUNDS—SUBSTITUTED BENZENE RINGS

Phenyl rings are so common in organic compounds that it is important to know a few facts about NMR absorptions in compounds that contain them. In general, the ring protons of a benzenoid system have resonance near 7.3 ppm; however, electron-withdrawing ring substituents (for example, nitro, cyano, carboxyl, or carbonyl) move the resonance of these protons downfield (larger ppm values), and electron-donating ring substituents (for example, methoxy or amino) move the resonance of these protons upfield (smaller ppm values). Table 26.5 shows these trends for a series of symmetrically *p*-disubstituted benzene compounds. The *p*-disubstituted compounds were chosen because their two planes of symmetry render all of the hydrogens equivalent. Each compound gives only one aromatic peak (a singlet) in the proton NMR spectrum. Later, you will see that some positions are affected more strongly than others in systems with substitution patterns different from this one.

In the sections that follow, we will attempt to cover some of the most important types of benzene ring substitution. In some cases, it will be necessary to examine sample spectra taken at both 60 MHz and 300 MHz. Many benzenoid rings show second-order splittings at 60 MHz but are essentially first order at 300 MHz.

A. Monosubstituted Rings

Alkylbenzenes. In monosubstituted benzenes in which the substituent is neither a strongly electron-withdrawing nor a strongly electron-donating group, all the ring protons

TABLE 26.5 Proton Chemical Shifts in *p*-Disubstituted Benzene Compounds

Substituent X	δ (ppm)	
—OCH_3	6.80	Electron donating (shielding)
—OH	6.60	
—NH_2	6.36	
—CH_3	7.05	
—H	7.32	
—COOH	8.20	Electron withdrawing (deshielding)
—NO_2	8.48	

give rise to what appears to be a *single resonance* when the spectrum is determined at 60 MHz. This is a particularly common occurrence in alkyl-substituted benzenes. Although the protons *ortho, meta,* and *para* to the substituent are not chemically equivalent, they generally give rise to a single unresolved absorption peak. A possible explanation is that the chemical shift differences, which should be small in any event, are somehow eliminated by the presence of the ring current, which tends to equalize them. All of the protons are nearly equivalent under these conditions. The NMR spectra of the aromatic portions of alkylbenzene compounds are good examples of this type of circumstance. Figure 26.17A is the 60-MHz ^{1}H spectrum of ethylbenzene.

The 300-MHz spectrum of ethylbenzene, shown in Figure 26.17B, presents quite a different picture. With the increased frequency shifts at 300 MHz, the nearly equivalent (at 60 MHz) protons are neatly separated into two groups. The *ortho* and *para* protons appear upfield from the *meta* protons. The splitting pattern is clearly second order.

Electron-Donating Groups. When electron-donating groups are attached to the ring, the ring protons are not equivalent, even at 60 MHz. A highly activating substituent such as methoxy clearly increases the electron density at the *ortho* and *para* positions of the ring (by resonance) and helps to give these protons greater shielding than those in the *meta* positions and, thus, a substantially different chemical shift.

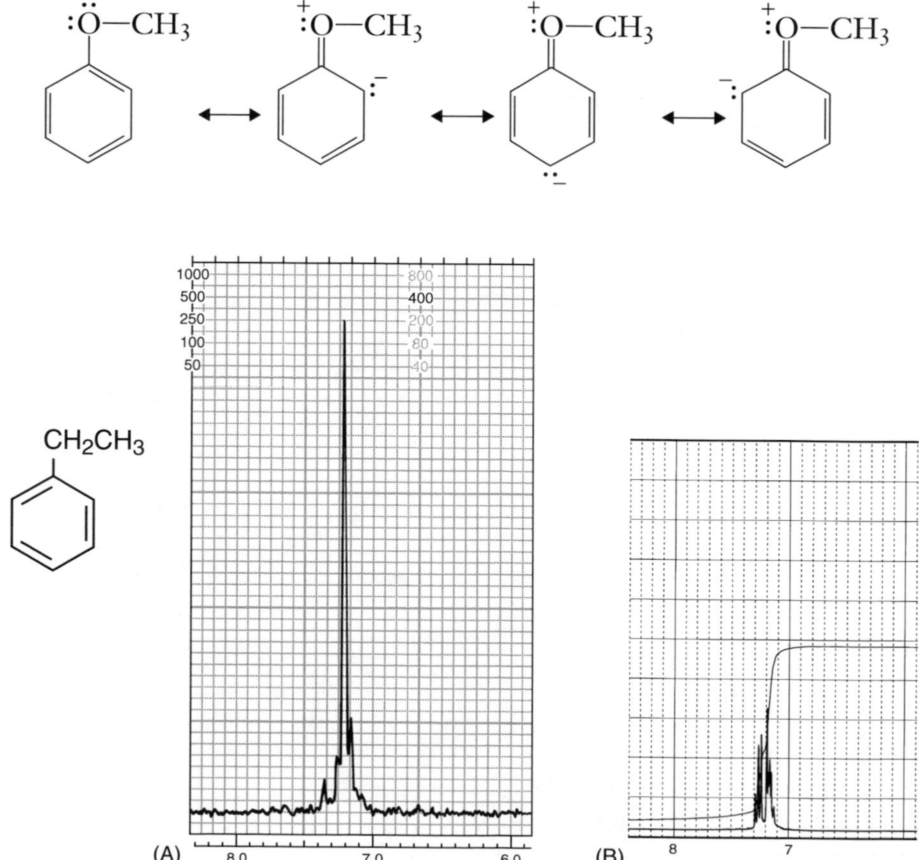

Figure 26.17 The aromatic ring portions of the ^{1}H NMR spectra of ethylbenzene at (A) 60 MHz and (B) 300 MHz.

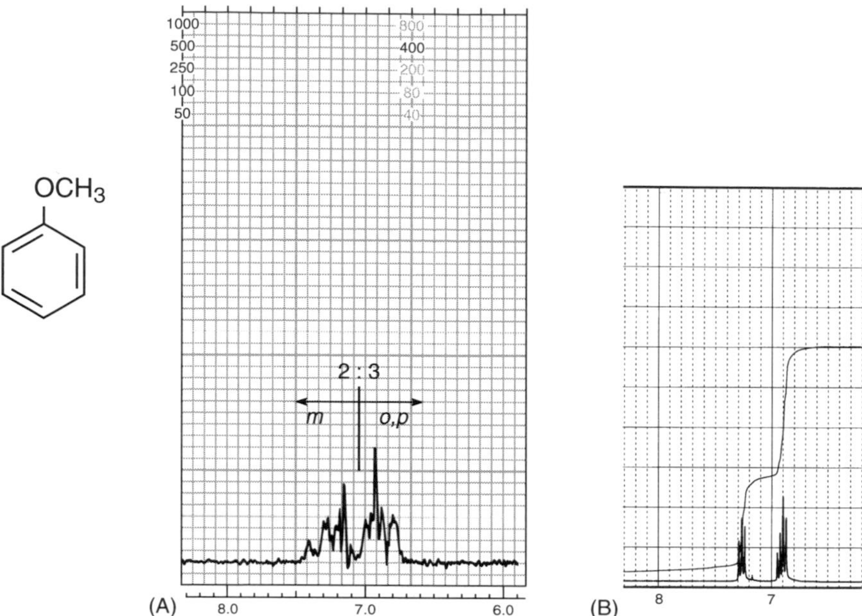

Figure 26.18 The aromatic ring portions of the ^{1}H NMR spectra of anisole at (A) 60 MHz and (B) 300 MHz.

At 60 MHz, this chemical shift difference results in a complicated second-order splitting pattern for anisole (methoxybenzene), but the protons do fall clearly into two groups, the *ortho/para* protons and the *meta* protons. The 60-MHz NMR spectrum of the aromatic portion of anisole (Figure 26.18A) has a complex multiplet for the *o,p,* protons (integrating for three protons) that is upfield from the *meta* protons (integrating for two protons), with a clear distinction (gap) between the two types. Aniline (aminobenzene) provides a similar spectrum, also with a 3:2 split, owing to the electron-releasing effect of the amino group.

The 300-MHz spectrum of anisole (Figure 26.18B) shows the same separation between the *ortho/para* hydrogens (upfield) and the *meta* hydrogens (downfield). However, because the actual shift in hertz between the two types of hydrogens is greater, there is less second-order interaction, and the lines in the pattern are sharper at 300 MHz. In fact, it might be tempting to try to interpret the observed pattern as if it were first order, a triplet at 7.25 ppm (*meta,* 2H) and an overlapping triplet (*para,* 1 H) with a doublet (*ortho,* 2 H) at about 6.9 ppm.

Anisotropy—Electron-Withdrawing Groups. A carbonyl or a nitro group would be expected to show (aside from anisotropy effects) a reverse effect, because these groups are electron withdrawing. It would be expected that the group would act to decrease the electron density around the *ortho* and *para* positions, thus deshielding the *ortho* and *para* hydrogens and providing a pattern exactly the reverse of the one shown for anisole (3:2 ratio, downfield:upfield). Convince yourself of this by drawing resonance structures. Nevertheless, the actual NMR spectra of nitrobenzene and benzaldehyde do not have the appearances that would be predicted on the basis of resonance structures. Instead, the *ortho* protons are much more deshielded than the *meta* and *para* protons, due to the magnetic anisotropy of the π bonds in these groups.

Anisotropy is observed when a substituent group bonds a carbonyl group directly to the benzene ring (Figure 26.19). Once again, the ring protons fall into two groups, with the *ortho* protons downfield from the *meta/para* protons. Benzaldehyde (Figure 26.20) and acetophenone both show this effect in their NMR spectra. A similar effect is sometimes observed when a carbon–carbon double bond is attached to the ring. The 300-MHz spectrum of benzaldehyde (Figure 26.20b) is a nearly first-order spectrum and shows a doublet (H_C, 2 H), a triplet (H_B, 1 H), and a triplet (H_A, 2 H). It can be analyzed by the $n + 1$ rule.

B. *para*-Disubstituted Rings

Of the possible substitution patterns of a benzene ring, some are easily recognized. One of these is the *para*-disubstituted benzene ring. Examine anethole (Figure 26.21) as a first example.

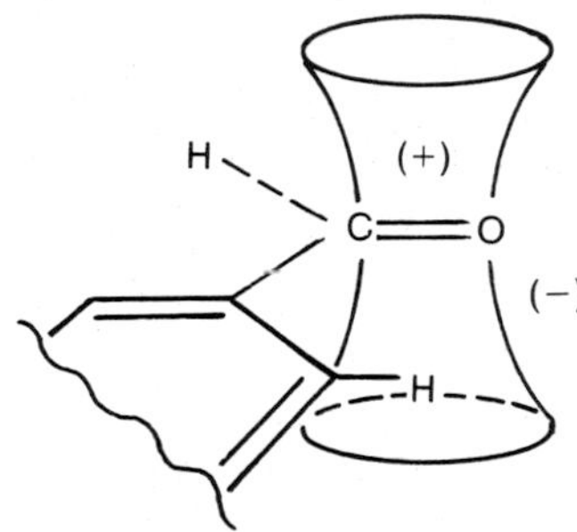

Figure 26.19 Anisotropic deshielding of the *ortho* protons of benzaldehyde.

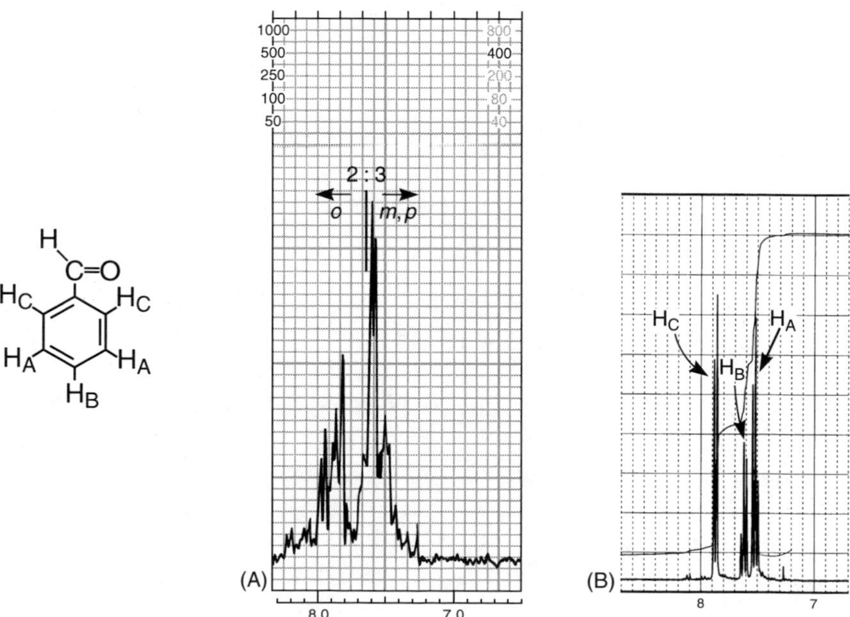

Figure 26.20 The aromatic ring portions of the ¹H NMR spectra of benzaldehyde at (A) 60 MHz and (B) 300 MHz.

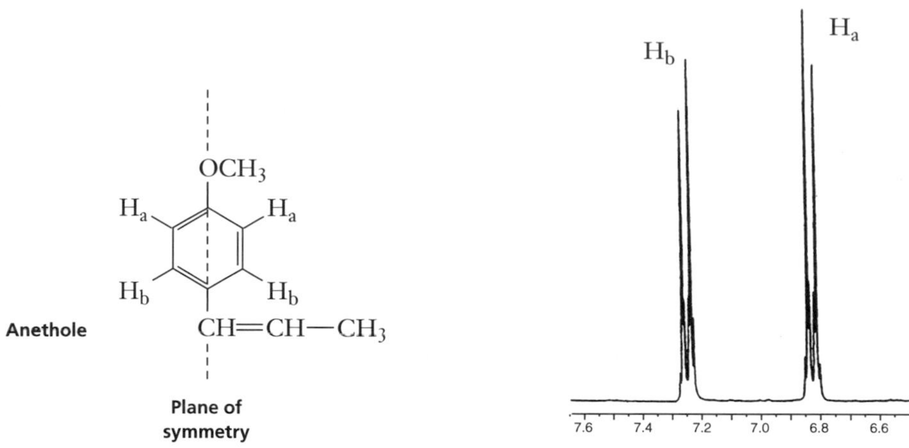

Figure 26.21 The aromatic ring protons of the 300-MHz ^{1}H NMR spectrum of anethole showing a *para*-disubstituted pattern.

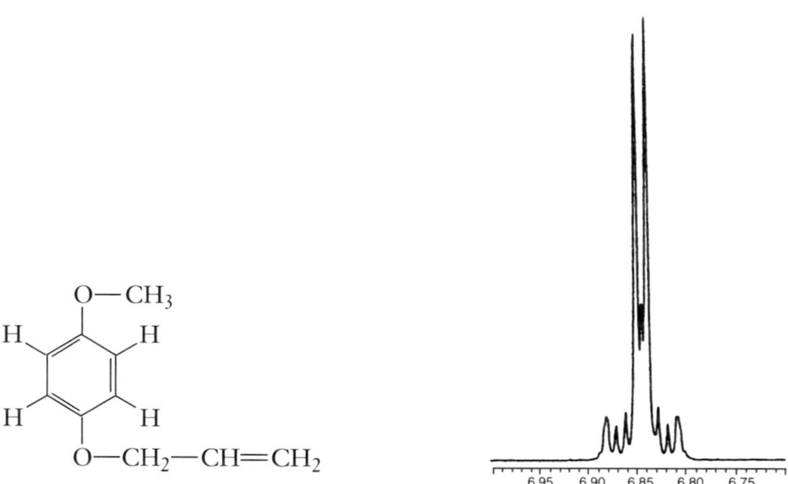

Figure 26.22 The aromatic ring protons of the 300-MHz ^{1}H NMR spectrum of 4-allyloxyanisole.

On one side of the anethole ring shown in Figure 26.21, proton H_a is coupled to H_b, $^3J = 8$ Hz, resulting in a doublet at about 6.80 ppm in the spectrum. Proton H_a appears upfield (smaller ppm value) relative to H_b because of shielding by the electron-releasing effect of the methoxy group (see p. 933). Likewise, H_b is coupled to H_a, $^3J = 8$ Hz, producing another doublet at 7.25 ppm for this proton. Because of the plane of symmetry, both halves of the ring are equivalent. Thus, H_a and H_b on the other side of the ring also appear at 6.80 ppm and 7.25 ppm, respectively. Each doublet, therefore, integrates for two protons each. A *para*-disubstituted ring, with two different substituents attached, is easily recognized by the appearance of two doublets, each integrating for two protons each.

As the chemical shifts of H_a and H_b approach each other in value, the *para*-disubstituted pattern becomes similar to that of 4-allyloxyanisole (Figure 26.22). The inner peaks move closer together, and the outer ones become smaller or even disappear. Ultimately, when H_a and H_b approach each other closely enough in chemical shift, the outer peaks disappear, and the two inner peaks merge into a *singlet;* 1,4-dimethylbenzene (*para*-xylene), for instance, gives a singlet at 7.05 ppm. Hence, a single aromatic resonance integrating for four protons could easily represent a *para*-disubstituted ring, but the substituents would obviously be either identical or very similar.

C. Other Substitution

Figure 26.23 shows the 300-MHz ^{1}H spectra of the aromatic ring portions of 2-, 3-, and 4-nitroaniline (the *ortho, meta,* and *para* isomers). The characteristic pattern of a *para*-disubstituted ring, with its pair of doublets, makes it easy to recognize 4-nitroaniline. The splitting patterns for 2- and 3-nitroaniline are first order, and they can be analyzed by the $n + 1$ rule. As an exercise, see if you can analyze these patterns, assigning the multiplets to specific protons on the ring. Use the indicated multiplicities (s, d, t) and expected chemical shifts to help your assignments. Remember that the amino group releases electrons by resonance, and the nitro group shows a significant anisotropy toward *ortho* protons. You may ignore any *meta* and *para* couplings, remembering that these long-range couplings will be too small in magnitude to be observed on the scale on which these figures are presented. If the spectra were expanded, you would be able to observe ^4J couplings.

The spectrum shown in Figure 26.24 is of 2-nitrophenol. It is helpful to look also at the coupling constants for the benzene ring found in Table 26.4. Because the spectrum is expanded, it is now possible to see ^3J couplings (about 8 Hz) as well as ^4J couplings (about 1.5 Hz). ^5J couplings are not observed ($^5J \approx 0$). Each of the protons on this com-

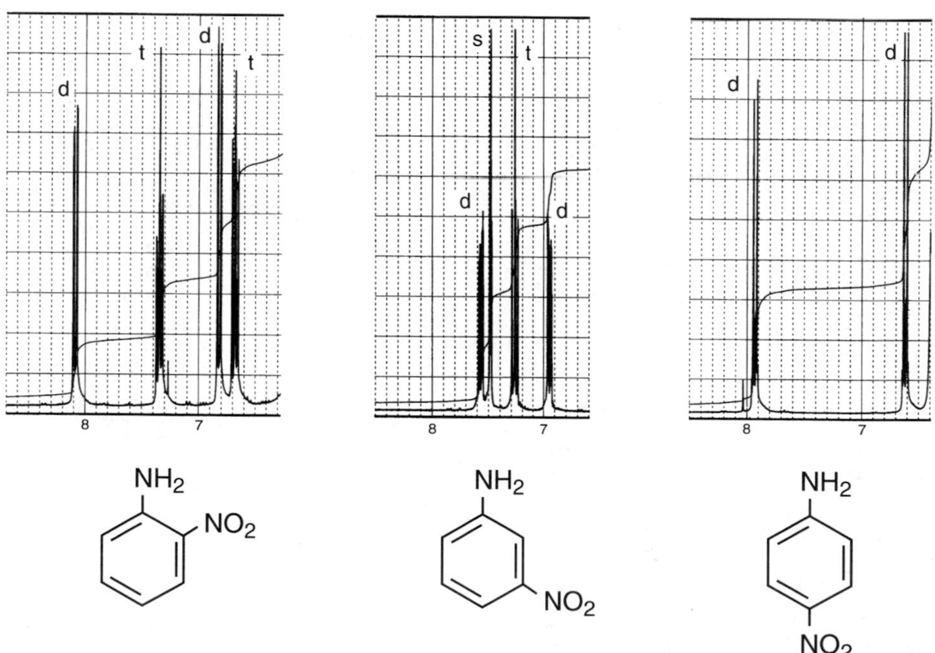

Figure 26.23 The 300-MHz ^{1}H NMR spectra of the aromatic ring portions of 2-, 3-, and 4-nitroaniline. (s, singlet; d, doublet; t, triplet).

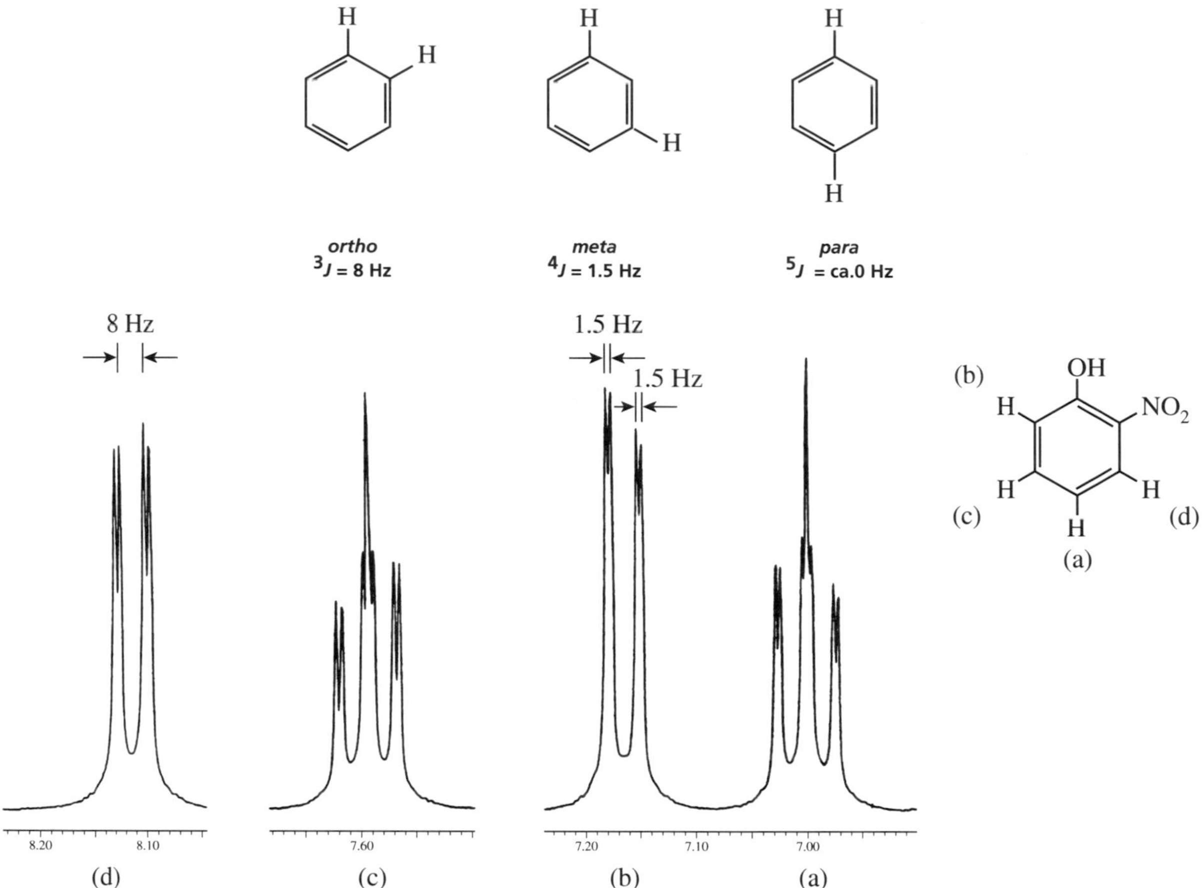

Figure 26.24 Expansions of the aromatic ring proton multiplets from the 300-MHz ^{1}H spectrum of 2-nitrophenol. The accompanying hydroxyl absorption (OH) is not shown. Coupling constants are indicated on some of the peaks of the spectrum to give an idea of scale.

pound is assigned on the spectrum. Proton H_d appears downfield at 8.11 ppm as a doublet of doublets ($^3J_{ad}$ = 8 Hz and $^4J_{cd}$ = 1.5 Hz); H_c appears at 7.6 ppm as a triplet of doublets ($^3J_{ac}$ = $^3J_{bc}$ = 8 Hz and $^4J_{cd}$ = 1.5 Hz); H_b appears at 7.17 ppm as a doublet of doublets ($^3J_{bc}$ = 8 Hz and $^4J_{ab}$ = 1.5 Hz); and H_a appears at 7.0 ppm as a triplet of doublets ($^3J_{ac}$ = $^3J_{ad}$ = 8 Hz and $^4J_{ab}$ = 1.5 Hz). H_d appears the furthest downfield because of the anisotropy of the nitro group. H_a and H_b are relatively shielded because of the resonance-releasing effect of the hydroxyl group, which shields these two protons. H_c is assigned by a process of elimination in the absence of these two effects.

26.14 PROTONS ATTACHED TO ATOMS OTHER THAN CARBON

Protons attached to atoms other than carbon often have a widely variable range of absorptions. Several of these groups are tabulated in Table 26.6. In addition, under the usual conditions of determining an NMR spectrum, protons on heteroelements normally do not

TABLE 26.6 Typical Ranges for Groups with Variable Chemical Shift

Acids	RCOOH	10.5–12.0 ppm
Phenols	ArOH	4.0–7.0
Alcohols	ROH	0.5–5.0
Amines	RNH_2	0.5–5.0
Amides	$RCONH_2$	5.0–8.0
Enols	CH=CH—OH	≥ 15

couple with protons on adjacent carbon atoms to give spin–spin splitting. The primary reason is that such protons often exchange very rapidly with those of the solvent medium. The absorption position is variable because these groups also undergo varying degrees of hydrogen bonding in solutions of different concentrations. The amount of hydrogen bonding that occurs with a proton radically affects the valence electron density around that proton and produces correspondingly large changes in the chemical shift. The absorption peaks for protons that have hydrogen bonding or are undergoing exchange are frequently broad relative to other singlets and can often be recognized on that basis. For a different reason, called **quadrupole broadening,** protons attached to nitrogen atoms often show an extremely broad resonance peak, often almost indistinguishable from the baseline.

26.15 CHEMICAL SHIFT REAGENTS

Researchers have known for some time that interactions between molecules and solvents, such as those due to hydrogen bonding, can cause large changes in the resonance positions of certain types of protons (for example, hydroxyl and amino). They have also known that the resonance positions of some groups of protons can be greatly affected by changing from the usual NMR solvents such as CCl_4 and $CDCl_3$ to solvents such as benzene, which impose local anisotropic effects on surrounding molecules. In many cases, it is possible to resolve partially overlapping multiplets by such a solvent change. The use of **chemical shift reagents** for this purpose dates from about 1969. Most of these chemical shift reagents are organic complexes of paramagnetic rare earth metals from the lanthanide series of elements. When these metal complexes are added to the compound whose spectrum is being determined, profound shifts in the resonance positions of the various groups of protons are observed. The direction of the shift (upfield or downfield) depends primarily on which metal is being used. Complexes of europium, erbium, thulium, and ytterbium shift resonances to lower field; complexes of cerium, praseodymium, neodymium, samarium, terbium, and holmium generally shift resonances to higher field. The advantage of using such reagents is that shifts similar to those observed at higher field can be induced without the purchase of an expensive higher-field instrument.

Of the lanthanides, europium is probably the most commonly used metal. Two of its widely used complexes are *tris*-(dipivalomethanato)europium and *tris*-(6,6,7,7,8,8,8-heptafluoro-2,2-dimethyl-3,5-octanedionato)europium. These are frequently abbreviated $Eu(dpm)_3$ and $Eu(fod)_3$, respectively.

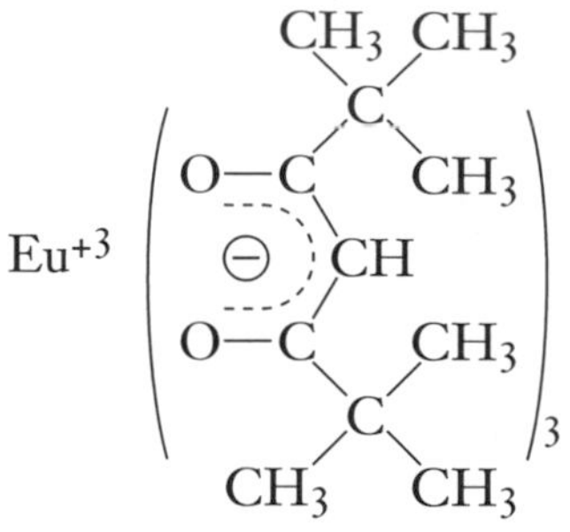

$$Eu^{+3}\left(\begin{array}{c} (CH_3)_3C-C(-O)=CH-C(-O)-C(CH_3)_3 \end{array}\right)_3$$

$Eu(dpm)_3$ or $Eu(thd)_3$

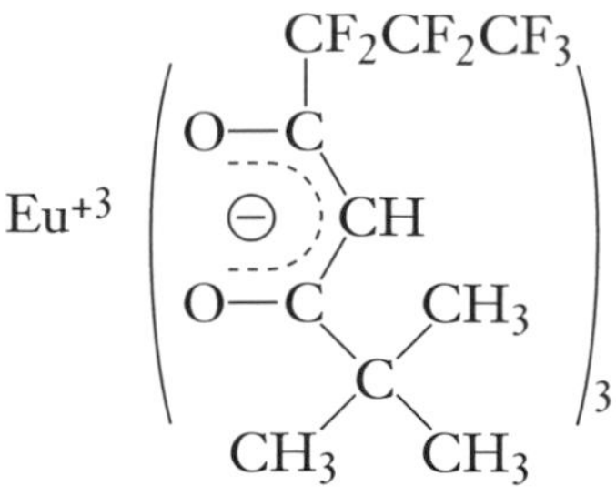

$$Eu^{+3}\left(\begin{array}{c} CF_2CF_2CF_3-C(-O)=CH-C(-O)-C(CH_3)_3 \end{array}\right)_3$$

$Eu(fod)_3$

These lanthanide complexes produce spectral simplifications in the NMR spectrum of any compound that has a relatively basic pair of electrons (unshared pair) that can coordinate with Eu^{3+}. Typically, aldehydes, ketones, alcohols, thiols, ethers, and amines will all interact:

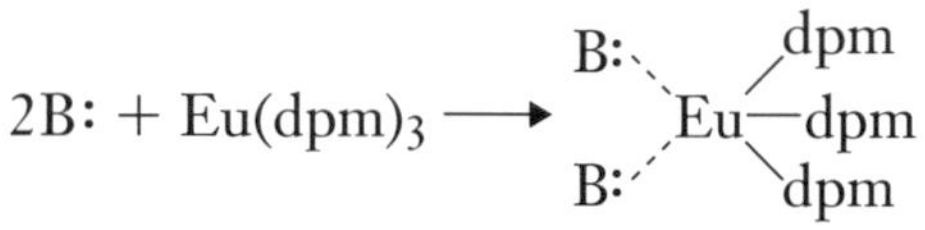

$$2B\!: + Eu(dpm)_3 \longrightarrow (B\!:)_2Eu(dpm)_3$$

The amount of shift that a given group of protons will experience depends (1) on the distance separating the metal (Eu^{3+}) and that group of protons, and (2) on the concentration of the shift reagent in the solution. Because of the latter dependence, it is necessary when reporting a lanthanide-shifted spectrum to report the number of mole equivalents of shift reagent used or its molar concentration.

The distance factor is illustrated in the spectra of hexanol, which are given in Figures 26.25 and 26.26. In the absence of shift reagent, the normal spectrum is obtained (Figure 26.25). Only the triplet of the terminal methyl group and the triplet of the methylene group next to the hydroxyl are resolved in the spectrum. The other protons (aside from OH) are found together in a broad unresolved group. With shift reagent added (Figure 26.26), each of the methylene groups is clearly separated and resolved into the proper multiplet structure. The spectrum is first order and simplified; all the splittings are explained by the $n + 1$ rule.

One final consequence of using a shift reagent should be noted. Notice in Figure 26.26 that the multiplets are not as nicely resolved into sharp peaks as you might expect. This is due to the fact that shift reagents cause a small amount of peak broadening. At high-shift reagent concentrations, this problem becomes serious, but at most useful concentrations the amount of broadening experienced is tolerable.

REFERENCES

Textbooks

Friebolin, H. *Basic One- and Two-Dimensional NMR Spectroscopy,* 2nd ed. New York: VCH Publishers, 1993.

Gunther, H. *NMR Spectroscopy,* 2nd ed. New York: John Wiley & Sons, 1995.

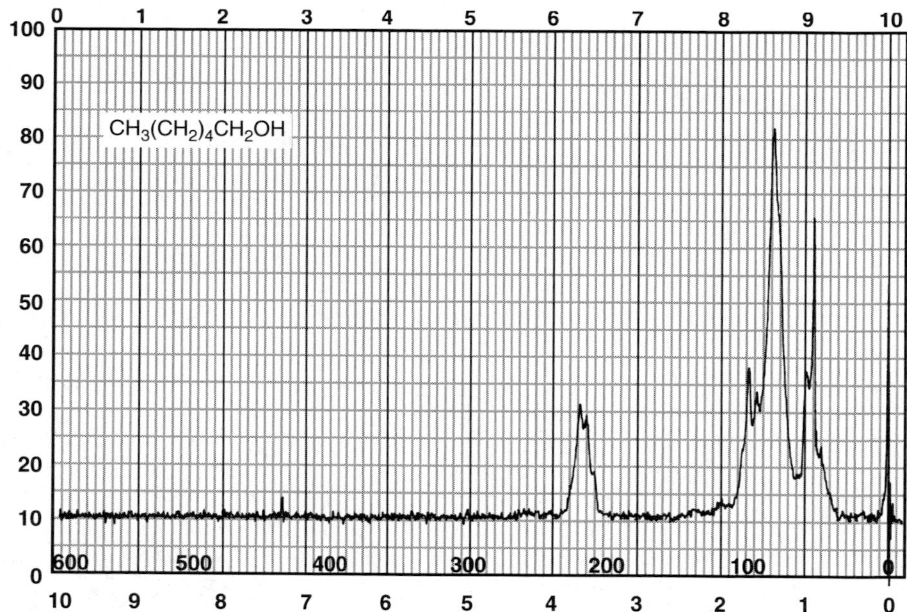

Figure 26.25 The normal 60-MHz ^1H NMR spectrum of hexanol. (Courtesy of Aldrich Chemical Co.)

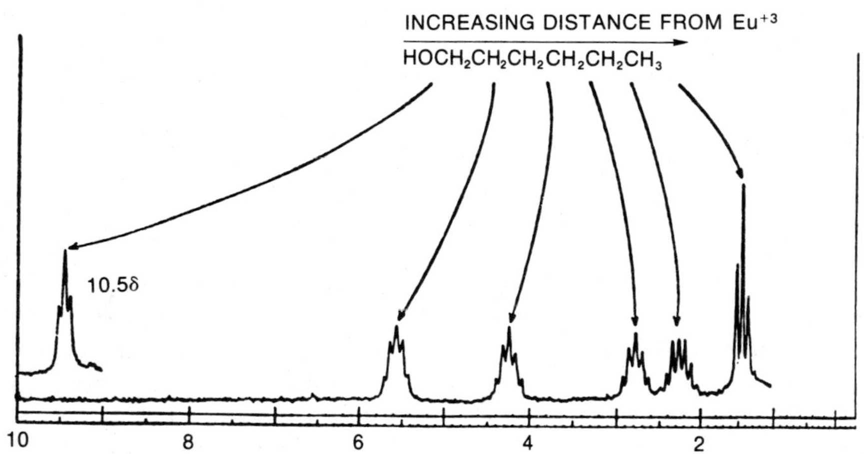

Figure 26.26 The 100-MHz ^1H NMR spectrum of hexanol with 0.29 mole equivalents of $Eu(dpm)_3$ added. From J. K. M. Sanders and D. H. Williams, Chemical Communications, (1970): 422. Reproduced by permission of The Royal Society of Chemistry.

Jackman, L. M., and Sternhell, S. *Nuclear Magnetic Resonance Spectroscopy in Organic Chemistry,* 2nd ed. New York: Pergamon Press, 1969.

Macomber, R. S. *A Complete Introduction to Modern NMR Spectroscopy.* New York: John Wiley & Sons, 1997.

Macomber, R. S. *NMR Spectroscopy: Essential Theory and Practice.* New York: College Outline Series, Harcourt Brace Jovanovich, 1988.

Pavia, D. L., Lampman, G. M., and Kriz, G. S. *Introduction to Spectroscopy,* 3rd ed. Philadelphia: Harcourt College Publishers, 2001.

Sanders, J. K. M., and Hunter, B. K. *Modern NMR Spectroscopy—a Guide for Chemists,* 2nd ed. Oxford: Oxford University Press, 1993.

Silverstein, R. M., and Webster, F. X. *Spectrometric Identification of Organic Compounds,* 6th ed. New York: John Wiley & Sons, 1998.

Williams, D. H., and Fleming, I. *Spectroscopic Methods in Organic Chemistry,* 4th ed. London–New York: McGraw-Hill, 1987.

Compilations of Spectra

Pouchert, C. J. *The Aldrich Library of NMR Spectra, 60 MHz,* 2nd ed. Milwaukee, WI: Aldrich Chemical Company, 1983.

Pouchert, C. J., and Behnke, J. *The Aldrich Library of ^{13}C and ^{1}H FT–NMR Spectra, 300 MHz.* Milwaukee, WI: Aldrich Chemical Company, 1993.

Pretsch, E., Clerc, T., Seibl, J., and Simon, W. *Tables of Spectral Data for Structure Determination of Organic Compounds,* 2nd ed. Berlin and New York: Springer-Verlag, 1989. Translated from the German by K. Biemann.

Web Sites

http://www.aist.go.jp/RIODB/SDBS/menu-e.html

Integrated Spectral DataBase System for Organic Compounds, National Institute of Materials and Chemical Research, Tsukuba, Ibaraki 305-8565, Japan. This database includes infrared, mass spectra, and NMR data (proton and carbon-13) for a large number of compounds.

http://www.chem.ucla.edu/~webspectra/

UCLA Department of Chemistry and Biochemistry in connection with Cambridge University Isotope Laboratories maintains a Web site, WebSpectra, that provides NMR and IR spectroscopy problems for students to interpret. They provide links to other sites with problems for students to solve.

PROBLEMS

1. Describe the method that you should use to determine the proton NMR spectrum of a carboxylic acid, which is insoluble in *all* the common organic solvents that your instructor is likely to make available.

2. To save money, a student uses chloroform instead of deuterated chloroform to run a carbon-13 NMR spectrum. Is this a good idea?

3. Look up the solubilities for the following compounds and decide whether you would select deuterated chloroform or deuterated water to dissolve the substances for NMR spectroscopy.

- **a.** Glycerol (1,2,3-propanetriol)
- **b.** 1,4-Diethoxybenzene
- **c.** Propyl pentanoate (propyl ester of pentanoic acid)

4. Assign each of the proton patterns in the spectra of 2-, 3-, and 4-nitroaniline as shown in Figure 26.23.

5. The following compounds are isomeric esters derived from acetic acid, each with formula $C_5H_{10}O_2$. The peaks of the spectrum have been labeled to indicate the degrees of splitting. With the first spectrum as an example, use the integral curve traced on the spectrum to calculate the number of hydrogens represented in each multiplet. The multiplets appear both on the spectrum and in the first column of the following table. The second column is obtained by dividing through by the lowest number (1.7 div). The third column is obtained by multiplying by 2 and rounding off the values. Notice that the sum of the numbers in the third column equals the number of hydrogen atoms (10) present in the formula. Often one can inspect the spectrum and visually approximate the relative numbers of hydrogen atoms, thus avoiding the more mathematical approach demonstrated in the following table. Using either method, the second spectrum yields a ratio of 1:3:6. What are the structures of the two esters?

1.7 div	1.0	2 H
2.5 div	1.47	3 H
1.7 div	1.0	2 H
2.5 div	1.47	3 H

a.

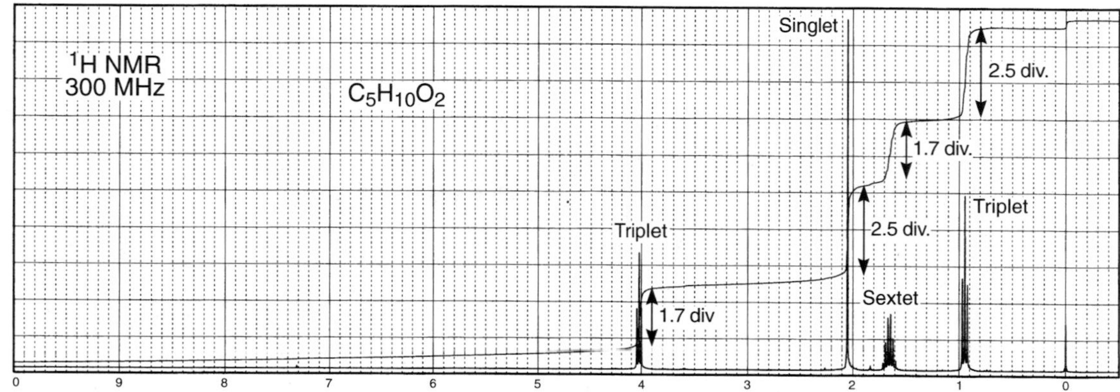

b.

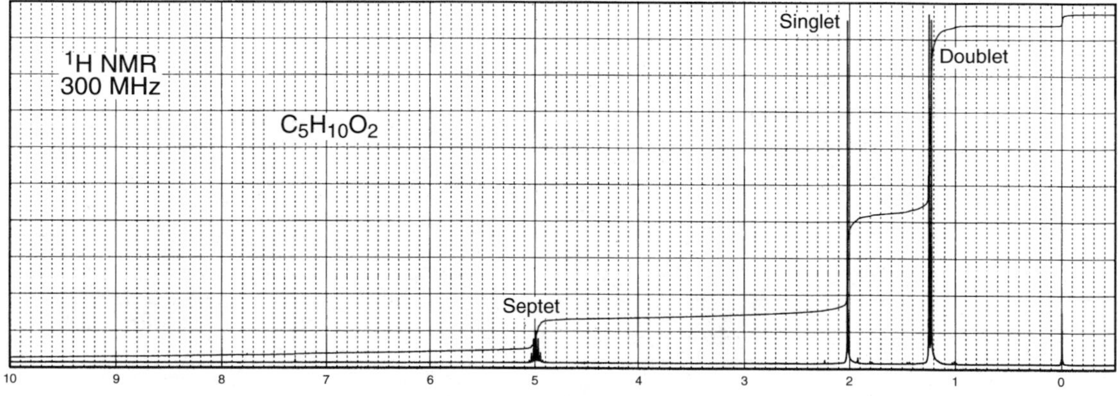

6. The compound that gives the following NMR spectrum has the formula $C_3H_6Br_2$. Draw the structure.

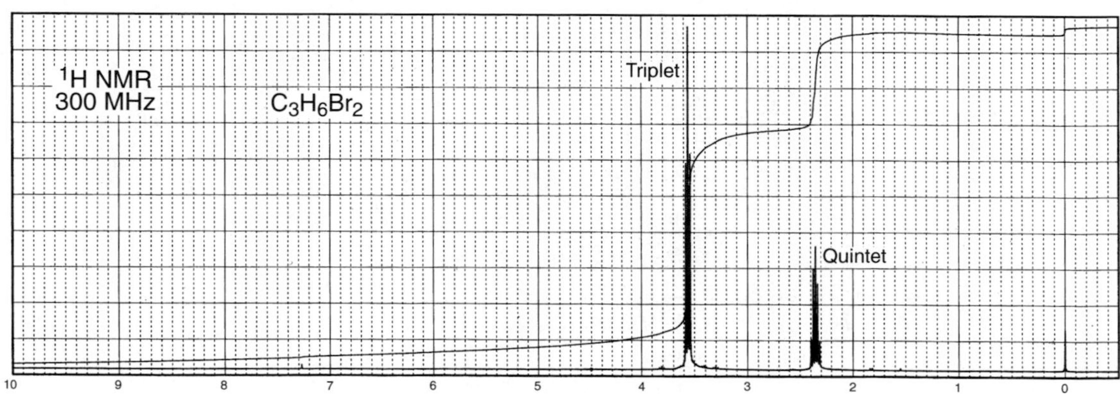

7. Draw the structure of an ether with formula $C_5H_{12}O_2$ that fits the following NMR spectrum.

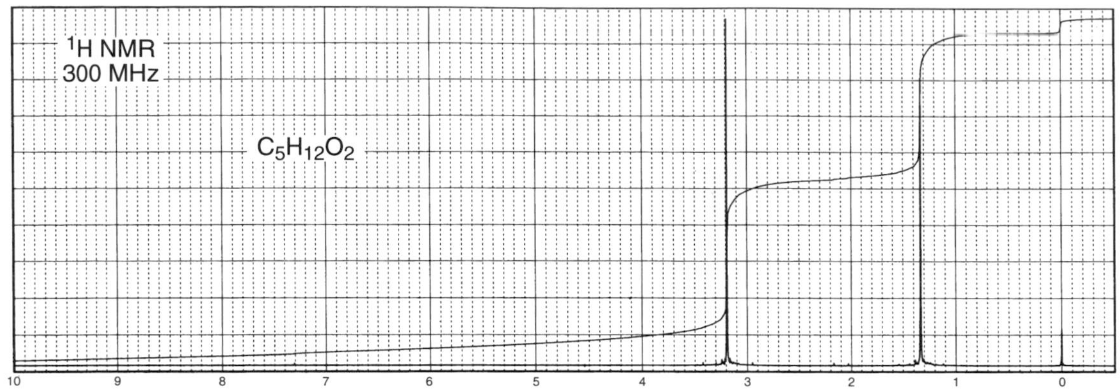

8. Following are the NMR spectra of three isomeric esters with the formula $C_7H_{14}O_2$, all derived from propanoic acid. Provide a structure for each.

a.

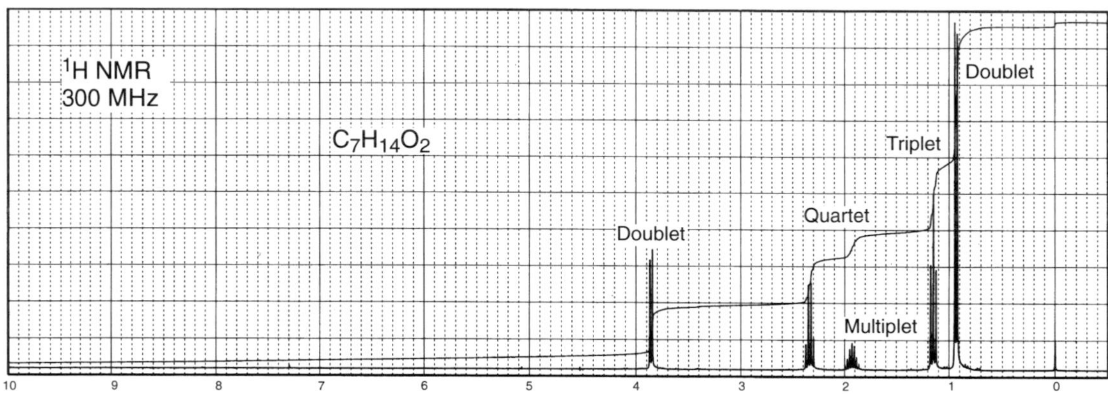

b.

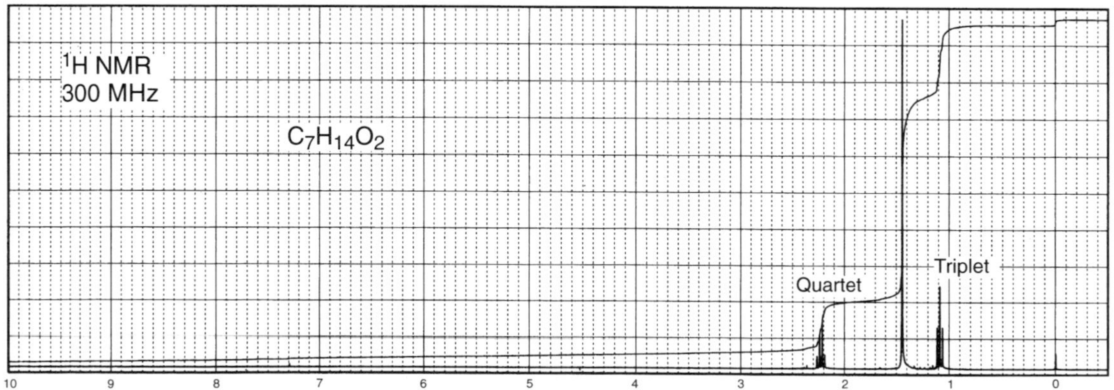

c.

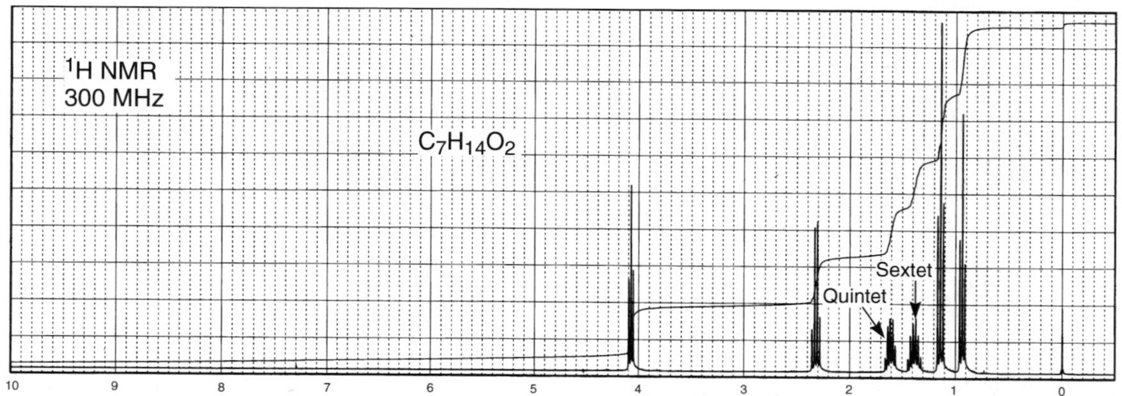

9. The two isomeric carboxylic acids that give the following NMR spectra both have the formula $C_3H_5ClO_2$. Draw their structures.

a.

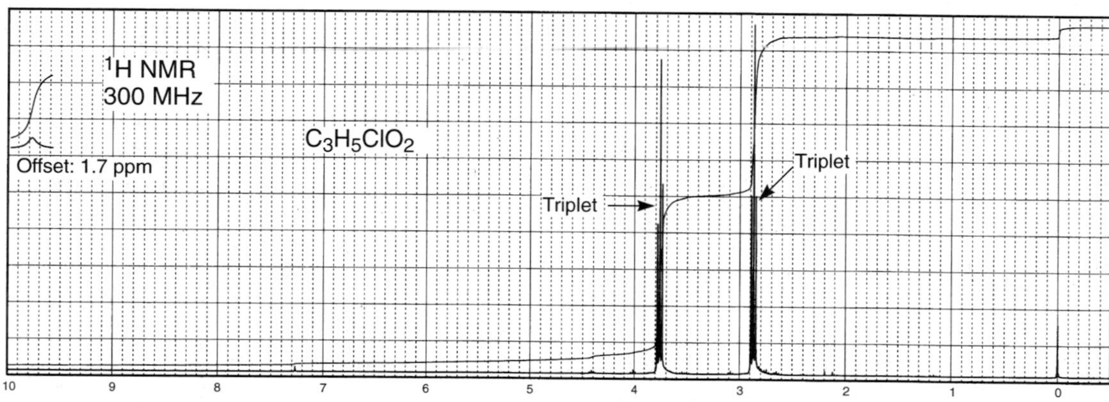

b.

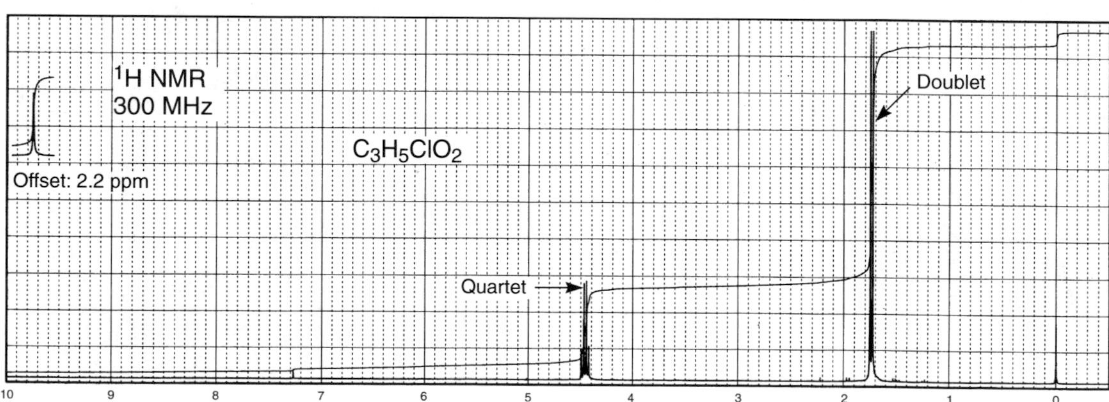

10. The following compounds are isomers with formula $C_{10}H_{12}O$. Their infrared spectra show strong bands near 1715 cm^{-1} and in the range from 1600 cm^{-1} to 1450 cm^{-1}. Draw their structures.

a.

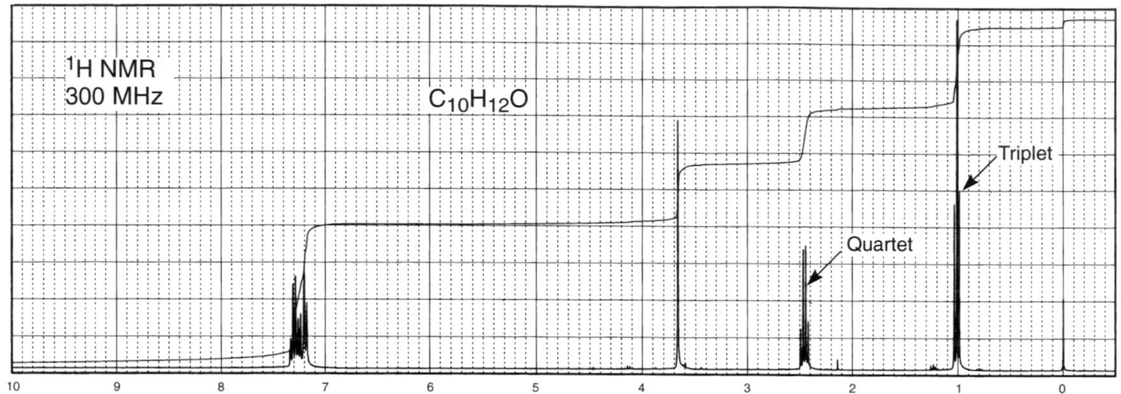

b.

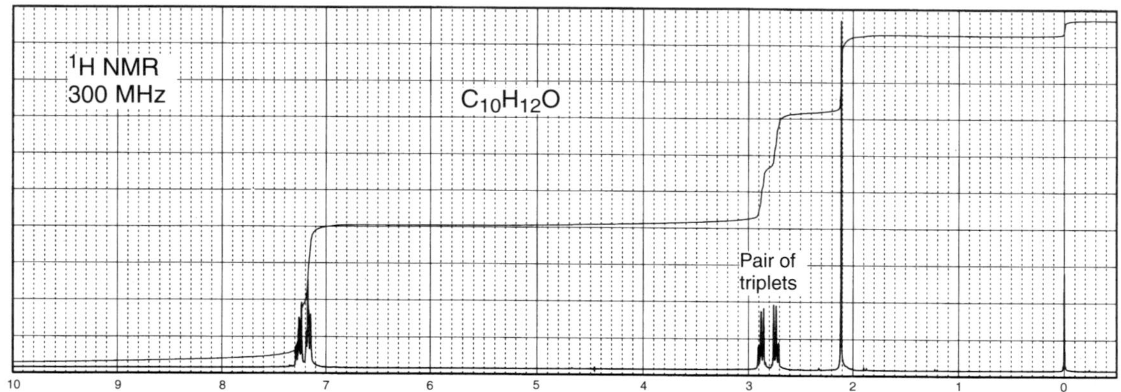

TECHNIQUE 19

Column Chromatography

The most modern and sophisticated methods of separating mixtures available to the organic chemist all involve **chromatography.** Chromatography is defined as the separation of a mixture of two or more different compounds or ions by distribution between two phases, one of which is stationary and the other of which is moving. Various types of chromatography are possible, depending on the nature of the two phases involved: **solid–liquid** (column, thin-layer, and paper), **liquid–liquid** (high-performance liquid), and **gas–liquid** (vapor-phase) chromatographic methods are common.

All chromatography works on much the same principle as solvent extraction (Technique 12). Basically, the methods depend on the differential solubilities or adsorptivities of the substances to be separated relative to the two phases between which they are to be partitioned. Here, column chromatography, a solid–liquid method, is considered. Thin-layer chromatography is examined in Technique 20; high-performance liquid chromatography is discussed in Technique 21; and gas chromatography, a gas–liquid method, is discussed in Technique 22.

19.1 ADSORBENTS

Column chromatography is a technique based on both adsorptivity and solubility. It is a solid–liquid phase-partitioning technique. The solid may be almost any material that does not dissolve in the associated liquid phase; the solids used most commonly are silica gel $SiO_2 \cdot xH_2O$, also called silicic acid, and alumina $Al_2O_3 \cdot xH_2O$. These compounds are used in their powdered or finely ground forms (usually 200–400 mesh).[1]

Most alumina used for chromatography is prepared from the impure ore bauxite $Al_2O_3 \cdot xH_2O + Fe_2O_3$. The bauxite is dissolved in hot sodium hydroxide and filtered to remove the insoluble iron oxides; the alumina in the ore forms the soluble amphoteric hydroxide $Al(OH)_4^-$. The hydroxide is precipitated by CO_2, which reduces the pH, as $Al(OH)_3$. When heated, the $Al(OH)_3$ loses water to form pure alumina Al_2O_3.

$$\text{Bauxite (crude)} \xrightarrow{\text{hot NaOH}} Al(OH)_4^-(aq) + Fe_2O_3\ \text{(insoluble)}$$

$$Al(OH)_4^-(aq) + CO_2 \longrightarrow Al(OH)_3 + HCO_3^-$$

$$2Al(OH)_3 \xrightarrow{\text{heat}} Al_2O_3\ (s) + 3H_2O$$

Alumina prepared in this way is called **basic alumina** because it still contains some hydroxides. Basic alumina cannot be used for chromatography of compounds that are base sensitive. Therefore, it is washed with acid to neutralize the base, giving **acid-washed alumina.** This material is unsatisfactory unless it has been washed with enough water to remove *all* the acid; on being so washed, it becomes the best chromatographic material, called **neutral alumina.** If a compound is acid sensitive, either basic or neutral alumina must be used. You should be careful to ascertain what type of alumina is being used for chromatography. Silica gel is not available in any form other than that suitable for chromatography.

19.2 INTERACTIONS

If powdered or finely ground alumina (or silica gel) is added to a solution containing an organic compound, some of the organic compound will **adsorb** onto or adhere to the fine particles of alumina. Many kinds of intermolecular forces cause organic molecules to bind to alumina. These forces vary in strength according to their type. Nonpolar compounds bind to the alumina using only van der Waals forces. These are weak forces, and nonpolar molecules do not bind strongly unless they have extremely high molecular weights. The most important interactions are those typical of polar organic compounds. Either these forces are of the dipole–dipole type or they involve some direct interaction (coordination, hydrogen bonding, or salt formation). These types of interactions are illustrated in Figure 19.1, which for convenience shows only a portion of the alumina structure. Similar interactions occur with silica gel. The strengths of such interactions vary in the following approximate order:

---

[1] The term "mesh" refers to the number of openings per linear inch found in a screen. A large number refers to a fine screen (finer wires more closely spaced). When particles are sieved through a series of these screens, they are classified by the smallest mesh screen that they will pass through. Mesh 5 would represent a coarse gravel, and mesh 800 would be a fine powder.

Salt formation > coordination > hydrogen bonding > dipole–dipole > van der Waals

Strength of interaction varies among compounds. For instance, a strongly basic amine would bind more strongly than a weakly basic one (by coordination). In fact, strong bases and strong acids often interact so strongly that they **dissolve** alumina to some extent. You can use the following rule of thumb:

> The more polar the functional group, the stronger the bond to alumina (or silica gel).

A similar rule holds for solubility. Polar solvents dissolve polar compounds more effectively than nonpolar solvents do; nonpolar compounds are dissolved best by nonpolar solvents. Thus, the extent to which any given solvent can wash an adsorbed compound from alumina depends almost directly on the relative polarity of the solvent. For example, although a ketone adsorbed on alumina might not be removed by hexane, it might be removed completely by chloroform. For any adsorbed material, a kind of **distribution** equilibrium can be envisioned between the adsorbent material and the solvent. This is illustrated in Figure 19.2.

The distribution equilibrium is **dynamic,** with molecules constantly **adsorbing** from the solution and **desorbing** into it. The average number of molecules remaining adsorbed on the solid particles at equilibrium depends both on the particular molecule (RX) involved and the dissolving power of the solvent with which the adsorbent must compete.

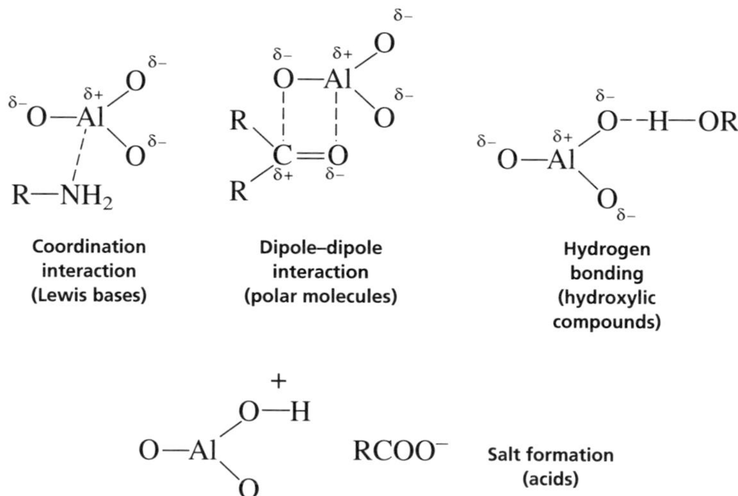

Figure 19.1 Possible interactions of organic compounds with alumina.

19.3 PRINCIPLE OF COLUMN CHROMATOGRAPHIC SEPARATION

The dynamic equilibrium mentioned previously and the variations in the extent to which different compounds adsorb on alumina or silica gel underlie a versatile and ingen-

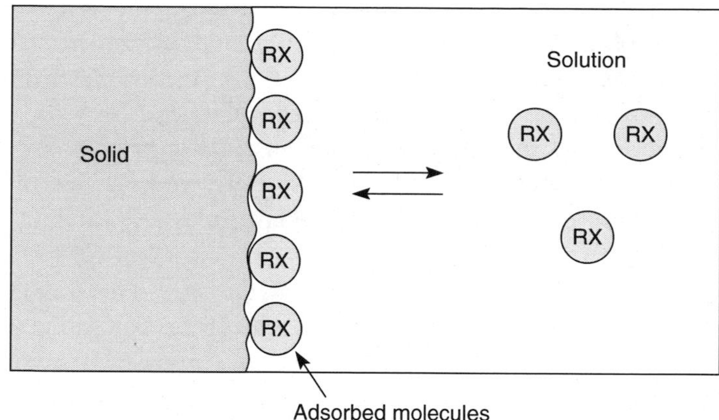

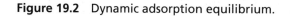

Figure 19.2 Dynamic adsorption equilibrium.

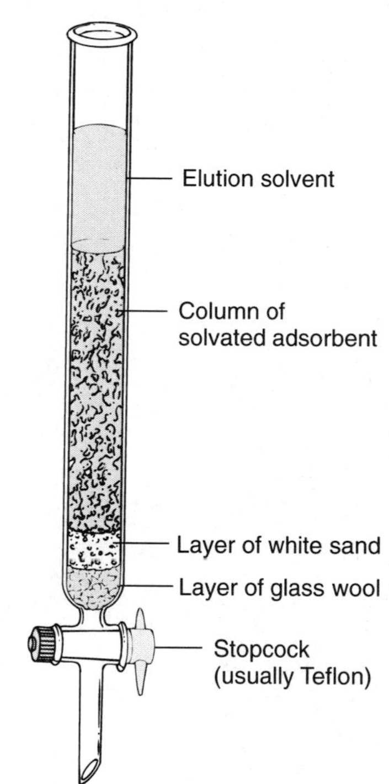

Figure 19.3 A chromatographic column.

ious method for **separating** mixtures of organic compounds. In this method, the mixture of compounds to be separated is introduced onto the top of a cylindrical glass column (Figure 19.3) **packed** or filled with fine alumina particles (stationary solid phase). The adsorbent is continuously washed by a flow of solvent (moving phase) passing through the column.

Initially, the components of the mixture adsorb onto the alumina particles at the top of the column. The continuous flow of solvent through the column **elutes,** or washes, the solutes off the alumina and sweeps them down the column. The solutes (or materials to be separated) are called **eluates** or **elutants,** and the solvents are called **eluents.** As the solutes pass down the column to fresh alumina, new equilibria are established among the adsorbent, the solutes, and the solvent. The constant equilibration means that different compounds will move down at differing rates depending on their relative affinity for the adsorbent on the one hand, and for the solvent on the other. Because the number of alumina particles is large, because they are closely packed, and because fresh solvent is being added continuously, the number of equilibrations between adsorbent and solvent that the solutes experience is enormous.

As the components of the mixture are separated, they begin to form moving bands (or zones), with each band containing a single component. If the column is long enough and the other parameters (column diameter, adsorbent, solvent, and flow rate) are correctly chosen, the bands separate from one another, leaving gaps of pure solvent in between. As each band (solvent and solute) passes out from the bottom of the column, it can be collected before the next band arrives. If the parameters mentioned are poorly chosen, the various bands either overlap or coincide, in which case either a poor separation or no separation is the result. A successful chromatographic separation is illustrated in Figure 19.4.

19.4 PARAMETERS AFFECTING SEPARATION

The versatility of column chromatography results from the many factors that can be adjusted. These include

1. Adsorbent chosen
2. Polarity of the solvents chosen
3. Size of the column (both length and diameter) relative to the amount of material to be chromatographed
4. Rate of elution (or flow)

If the conditions are carefully chosen, almost any mixture can be separated. This technique has even been used to separate optical isomers. An optically active solid-phase adsorbent was used to separate the enantiomers.

Two fundamental choices for anyone attempting a chromatographic separation are the kind of adsorbent and the solvent system. In general, nonpolar compounds pass through the column faster than polar compounds, because they have a smaller affinity for the adsorbent. If the adsorbent chosen binds all the solute molecules (both polar and nonpolar) strongly, they will not move down the column. On the other hand, if too polar a solvent is chosen, all the solutes (polar and nonpolar) may simply be washed through the column, with no separation taking place. The adsorbent and the solvent should be chosen so that neither is favored excessively in the equilibrium competition for solute molecules.[2]

[2] Often, the chemist uses thin-layer chromatography (TLC), which is described in Technique 20, to arrive at the best choices of solvents and adsorbents for the best separation. The TLC experimentation can be performed quickly and with extremely small amounts (microgram quantities) of the mixture to be separated. This saves significant time and materials. Technique 20, Section 20.10, describes this use of TLC.

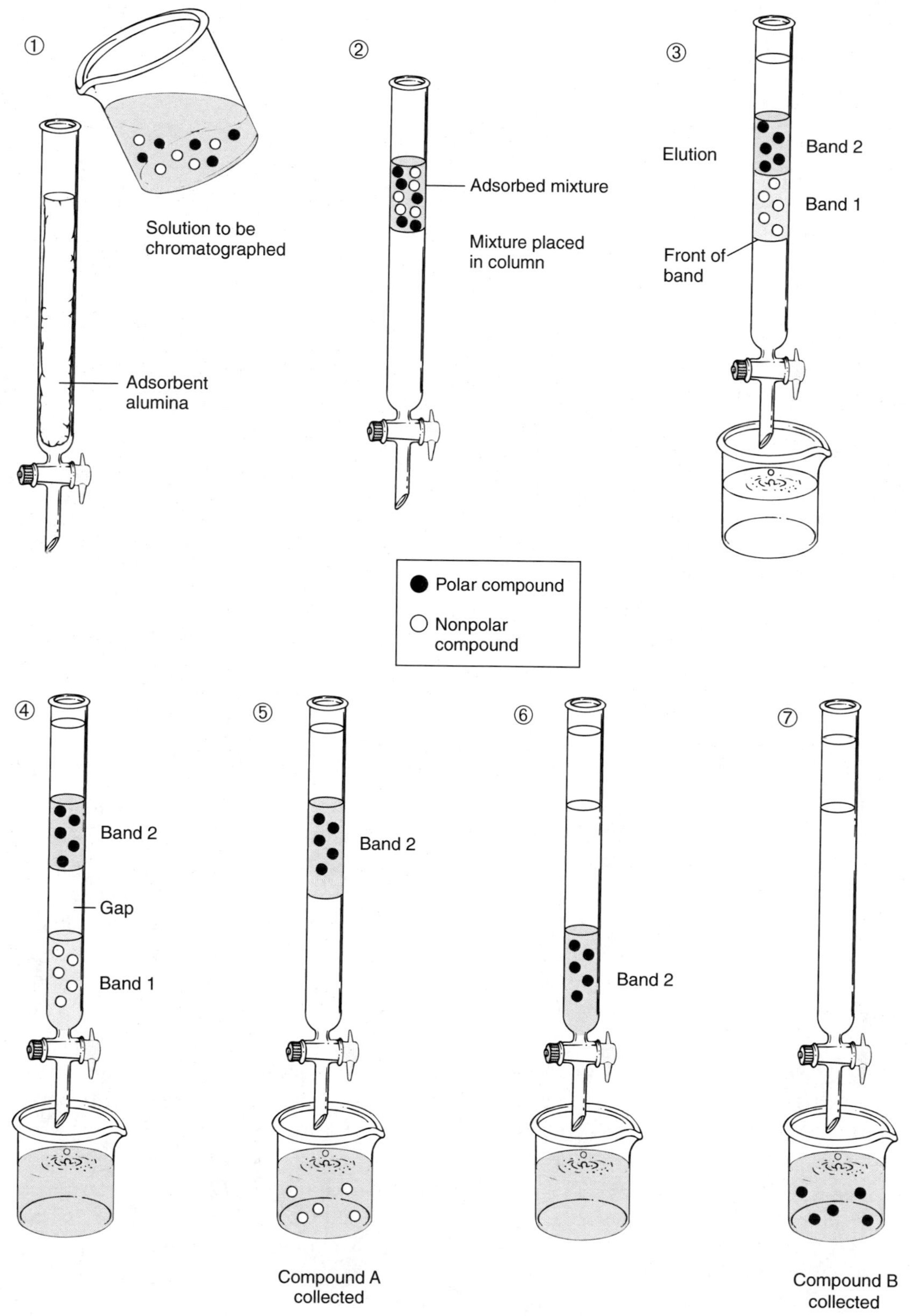

Figure 19.4 Sequence of steps in a chromatographic separation.

TABLE 19.1 Solid Adsorbents for Column Chromatography

Adsorbent	
Paper	Increasing strength of binding interactions toward polar compounds (↓)
Cellulose	
Starch	
Sugars	
Magnesium silicate	
Calcium sulfate	
Silicic acid	
Florisil	
Magnesium oxide	
Aluminum oxide (alumina)[a]	
Activated charcoal (Norit)	

[a]Basic, acid washed, and neutral.

A. Adsorbents

In Table 19.1, various kinds of adsorbents (solid phases) used in column chromatography are listed. The choice of adsorbent often depends on the types of compounds to be separated. Cellulose, starch, and sugars are used for polyfunctional plant and animal materials (natural products) that are very sensitive to acid–base interactions. Magnesium silicate is often used for separating acetylated sugars, steroids, and essential oils. Silica gel and Florisil are relatively mild toward most compounds and are widely used for a variety of functional groups—hydrocarbons, alcohols, ketones, esters, acids, azo compounds, and amines. Alumina is the most widely used adsorbent and is obtained in the three forms mentioned in Section 19.1: acidic, basic, and neutral. The pH of acidic or acid-washed alumina is approximately 4. This adsorbent is particularly useful for separating acidic materials such as carboxylic acids and amino acids. Basic alumina has a pH of 10 and is useful in separating amines. Neutral alumina can be used to separate a variety of nonacidic and nonbasic materials.

The approximate strength of the various adsorbents listed in Table 19.1 is also given. The order is only approximate, and therefore it may vary. For instance, the strength, or separating abilities, of alumina and silica gel largely depends on the amount of water present. Water binds very tightly to either adsorbent, taking up sites on the particles that could otherwise be used for equilibration with solute molecules. If water is added to the adsorbent, it is said to have been **deactivated.** Anhydrous alumina or silica gel is said to be highly **activated.** High activity is usually avoided with these adsorbents. Use of the highly active forms of either alumina or silica gel, or of the acidic or basic forms of alumina, can often lead to molecular rearrangement or decomposition in certain types of solute compounds.

The chemist can select the degree of activity that is appropriate to carry out a particular separation. To accomplish this, highly activated alumina is mixed thoroughly with a precisely measured quantity of water. The water partially hydrates the alumina and thus reduces its activity. By carefully determining the amount of water required, the chemist can have available an entire spectrum of possible activities.

TABLE 19.2 Solvents (Eluents) for Chromatography

Solvent	
Petroleum ether	↓ Increasing polarity and "solvent power" toward polar functional groups
Cyclohexane	
Carbon tetrachloride[a]	
Toluene	
Chloroform[a]	
Methylene chloride	
Diethyl ether	
Ethyl acetate	
Acetone	
Pyridine	
Ethanol	
Methanol	
Water	
Acetic acid	

[a]Suspected carcinogens.

TABLE 19.3 Elution Sequence for Compounds

Compound	
Hydrocarbons	Fastest (will elute with nonpolar solvent)
Olefins	
Ethers	
Halocarbons	
Aromatics	
Ketones	Order of elution ↓
Aldehydes	
Esters	
Alcohols	
Amines	
Acids, strong bases	Slowest (needs a polar solvent)

B. Solvents

In Table 19.2, some common chromatographic solvents are listed along with their relative ability to dissolve polar compounds. Sometimes a single solvent can be found that will separate all the components of a mixture. Sometimes a mixture of solvents can be found that will achieve separation. More often you must start elution with a nonpolar solvent to remove relatively nonpolar compounds from the column and then gradually increase the solvent polarity to force compounds of greater polarity to come down the column, or to elute. The approximate order in which various classes of compounds elute by this procedure is given in Table 19.3. In general, nonpolar compounds travel through the column faster (elute first), and polar compounds travel more slowly (elute last). However, molecular weight is also a factor in determining the order of elution. A nonpolar compound of high molecular weight travels more slowly than a nonpolar compound of low molecular weight, and it may even be passed by some polar compounds.

Solvent polarity functions in two ways in column chromatography. First, a polar solvent will better dissolve a polar compound and move it down the column faster. Therefore, as already mentioned, the polarity of the solvent is usually increased during column chromatography to wash down compounds of increasing polarity. Second, as the polarity of the solvent increases, the solvent itself will displace adsorbed molecules from the alumina or silica and take their place on the column. Because of this second effect, a polar solvent will move **all types of compounds,** both polar and nonpolar, down the column at a faster rate than a nonpolar solvent will.

When the polarity of the solvent has to be changed during a chromatographic separation, some precautions must be taken. Rapid changes from one solvent to another are to be avoided (especially when silica gel or alumina is involved). Usually, small percentages of a new solvent are mixed slowly into the one in use until the percentage reaches the desired level. If this is not done, the column packing often "cracks" as a result of the heat liberated when alumina or silica gel is mixed with a solvent. The solvent solvates the adsorbent, and the formation of a weak bond generates heat.

$$\text{Solvent} + \text{alumina} \longrightarrow (\text{alumina} \cdot \text{solvent}) + \text{heat}$$

Often, enough heat is generated locally to evaporate the solvent. The formation of vapor creates bubbles, which forces a separation of the column packing; this is called **cracking.** A cracked column does not produce a good separation because it has discontinuities in the packing. The way in which a column is packed or filled is also very important in preventing cracking.

Certain solvents should be avoided with alumina or silica gel, especially with the acidic, basic, and highly active forms. For instance, with any of these adsorbents, acetone dimerizes via an aldol condensation to give diacetone alcohol. Mixtures of esters **transesterify** (exchange their alcoholic portions) when ethyl acetate or an alcohol is the eluent. Finally, the most active solvents (pyridine, methanol, water, and acetic acid) dissolve and elute some of the adsorbent itself. Generally, try to avoid solvents more polar than diethyl ether or methylene chloride in the eluent series (Table 19.2).

C. Column Size and Adsorbent Quantity

The column size and the amount of adsorbent must also be selected correctly to separate a given amount of sample well. As a rule of thumb, the amount of adsorbent should be 25 to 30 times, by weight, the amount of material to be separated by chromatography. Furthermore, the column should have a height-to-diameter ratio of about 8:1. Some typical relations of this sort are given in Table 19.4.

Note, as a caution, that the difficulty of the separation is also a factor in determining the size and length of the column to be used and the amount of adsorbent needed. Compounds that do not separate easily may require longer columns and more adsorbent than specified in Table 19.4. For easily separated compounds, a shorter column and less adsorbent may suffice.

TABLE 19.4 Size of Column and Amount of Adsorbent for Typical Sample Sizes

Amount of Sample (g)	Amount of Adsorbent (g)	Column Diameter (mm)	Column Height (mm)
0.01	0.3	3.5	30
0.10	3.0	7.5	60
1.00	30.0	16.0	130
10.00	300.0	35.0	280

D. Flow Rate

The rate at which solvent flows through the column is also significant in the effectiveness of a separation. In general, the time the mixture to be separated remains on the column is directly proportional to the extent of equilibration between stationary and moving phases. Thus, similar compounds eventually separate if they remain on the column long enough. The time a material remains on the column depends on the flow rate of the solvent. If the flow is too slow, however, the dissolved substances in the mixture may diffuse faster than the rate at which they move down the column. Then the bands grow wider and more diffuse, and the separation becomes poor.

19.5 PACKING THE COLUMN: TYPICAL PROBLEMS

The most critical operation in column chromatography is packing (filling) the column with adsorbent. The **column packing** must be evenly packed and free of irregularities, air bubbles, and gaps. As a compound travels down the column, it moves in an advancing zone, or **band.** It is important that the leading edge, or **front,** of this band be horizontal, or perpendicular to the long axis of the column. If two bands are close together and do not have horizontal band fronts, it is impossible to collect one band while completely excluding the other. The leading edge of the second band begins to elute before the first band has finished eluting. This condition can be seen in Figure 19.5. There are two main reasons for this problem. First, if the top surface edge of the adsorbent packing is not level, nonhorizontal bands result. Second, bands may be nonhorizontal if the column is not held in an exactly vertical position in both planes (front to back and side to side). When preparing a column, you must watch both these factors carefully.

Another phenomenon, called **streaming** or **channeling,** occurs when part of the band front advances ahead of the major part of the band. Channeling occurs if there are any cracks or irregularities in the adsorbent surface or any irregularities caused by air bubbles in the packing. A part of the advancing front moves ahead of the rest of the band by flowing through the channel. Two examples of channeling are shown in Figure 19.6.

The methods outlined in Sections 19.6, 19.7, and 19.8 are used to avoid problems resulting from uneven packing and column irregularities. These procedures should be fol-

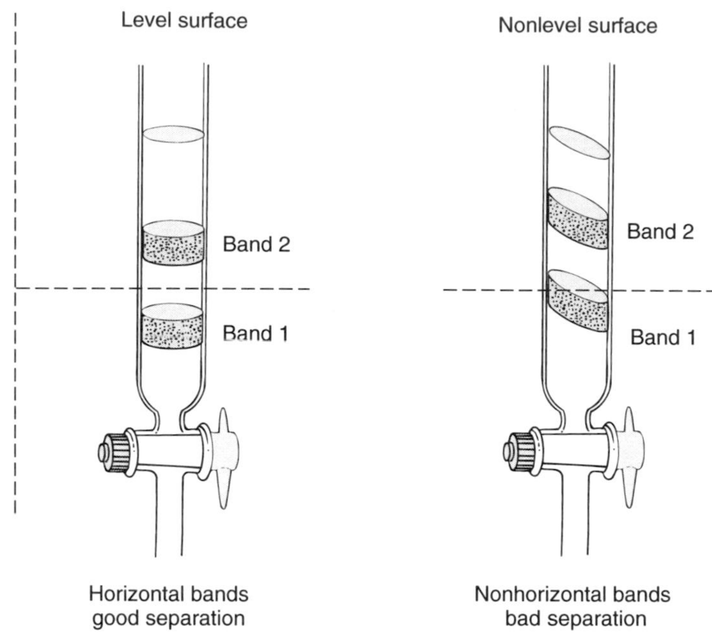

Figure 19.5 Comparison of horizontal and nonhorizontal band fronts.

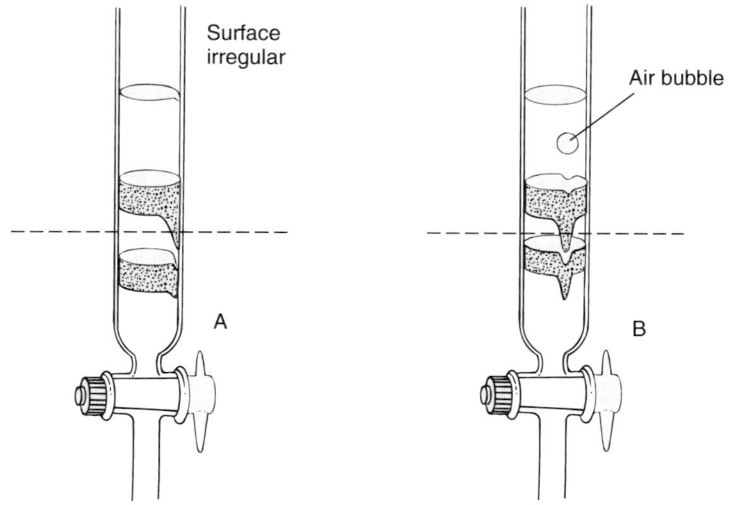

Figure 19.6 Channeling complications.

lowed carefully in preparing a chromatography column. Failure to pay close attention to the preparation of the column may affect the quality of the separation.

19.6 PACKING THE COLUMN: PREPARING THE SUPPORT BASE

Preparation of a column involves two distinct stages. In the first stage, a support base on which the packing will rest is prepared. This must be done so that the packing, a finely

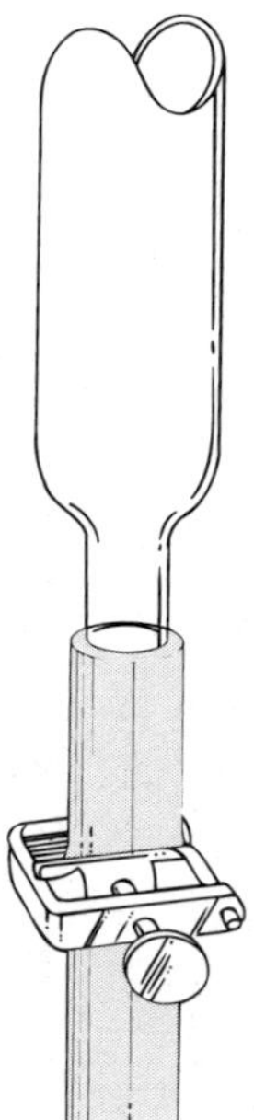

Figure 19.7 Tubing with screw clamp to regulate solvent flow on a chromatography column.

divided material, does not wash out of the bottom of the column. In the second stage, the column of adsorbent is deposited on top of the supporting base.

A. Macroscale Columns

For large-scale applications, a chromatography column is clamped upright (vertically). The column (Figure 19.3) is a piece of cylindrical glass tubing with a stopcock attached at one end. The stopcock usually has a Teflon plug, because stopcock grease (used on glass plugs) dissolves in many of the organic solvents used as eluents. Stopcock grease in the eluent will contaminate the eluates.

Instead of a stopcock, a piece of flexible tubing may be attached to the bottom of the column, with a screw clamp used to stop or regulate the flow (Figure 19.7). When a screw clamp is used, care must be taken that the tubing used is not dissolved by the solvents that will pass through the column during the experiment. Rubber, for instance, dissolves in chloroform, benzene, methylene chloride, toluene, or tetrahydrofuran (THF). Tygon tubing dissolves (actually, the plasticizer is removed) in many solvents, including benzene, methylene chloride, chloroform, ether, ethyl acetate, toluene, and THF. Polyethylene tubing is the best choice for use at the end of a column because it is inert with most solvents.

Next, the column is partially filled with a quantity of solvent, usually a nonpolar solvent such as hexane, and a support for the finely divided adsorbent is prepared in the following way. A loose plug of glass wool is tamped down into the bottom of the column with a long glass rod until all entrapped air is forced out as bubbles. Take care not to plug the column totally by tamping the glass wool too hard. A small layer of clean, white sand is formed on top of the glass wool by pouring sand into the column. The column is tapped to level the surface of the sand. Any sand adhering to the side of the column is washed down with a small quantity of solvent. The sand forms a base that supports the column of adsorbent and prevents it from washing through the stopcock. The column is packed in one of two ways: by the slurry method (Section 9.8) or by the dry pack method (Section 9.7).

B. Semi-microscale Columns

An alternative apparatus for macroscale column chromatography on a smaller scale is a commercial column, such as the one shown in Figure 19.8. This type of column is made of glass and has a solvent-resistant plastic stopcock at the bottom.[3] The stopcock assembly contains a filter disc to support the adsorbent column. An optional upper fitting, also made of solvent-resistant plastic, serves as a solvent reservoir. The column shown in Figure 19.8 is equipped with the solvent reservoir. This type of column is available in a variety of lengths, ranging from 100 mm to 300 mm. Because the column has a built-in filter disc, it is not necessary to prepare a support base before the adsorbent is added.

C. Microscale Columns

For microscale applications, a Pasteur pipet (5¾-inch) is used; it is clamped upright (vertically). To reduce the amount of solvent needed to fill the column, you may break off most of the tip of the pipet. A small ball of cotton is placed in the pipet and tamped into position using a glass rod or a piece of wire. Take care not to plug the column totally by tamping the cotton too hard. The correct position of the cotton is shown in Figure 19.9. A microscale chromatography column is packed by one of the dry pack methods described in Section 19.7.

19.7 PACKING THE COLUMN: DEPOSITING THE ADSORBENT—DRY PACK METHODS

A. Dry Pack Method 1

Macroscale Columns. In the first of the dry pack methods introduced here, the column is filled with solvent and allowed to drain *slowly*. The dry adsorbent is added, a little at a time, while the column is tapped gently with a pencil, finger, or glass rod.

A plug of cotton is placed at the base of the column, and an even layer of sand is formed on top (see p. 805). The column is filled about half-full with solvent, and the solid adsorbent is added carefully from a beaker while the solvent is allowed to flow slowly from the column. As the solid is added, the column is tapped as described for the slurry method (see p. 809) to ensure that the column is packed evenly. When the column has the desired length, no more adsorbent is added. This method produces an evenly packed column. Solvent should be cycled through this column (for macroscale applications) sev-

[3]Note to the instructor: With certain organic solvents, we have found that the "solvent-resistant" plastic stopcock may tend to dissolve! We recommend that instructors test their equipment with the solvent that they intend to use before the start of the laboratory class.

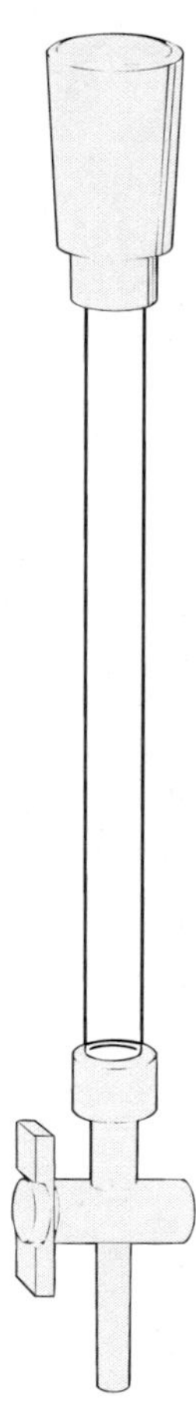

Figure 19.8 A commercial semi-microscale chromatography column. (The column shown is equipped with an optional solvent reservoir.)

eral times before each use. The same portion of solvent that has drained from the column during the packing is used to cycle through the column.

Semi-microscale Columns. The procedure to fill a commercial semi-microscale column is essentially the same as that used to fill a Pasteur pipet (see the following paragraph). The commercial column has the advantage that it is much easier to control the flow of solvent from the column during the filling process, because the stopcock can be adjusted appropriately. It is not necessary to use a cotton plug or to deposit a layer of sand before adding the adsorbent. The presence of the fritted disc at the base of the column prevents adsorbent from escaping from the column.

Microscale Columns. To fill a microscale column, fill the Pasteur pipet (with the cotton plug, prepared as described in Section 19.6) about half full with solvent. Using a microspatula, add the solid adsorbent slowly to the solvent in the column. As you add the solid, tap the column *gently* with a pencil, a finger, or a glass rod. The tapping promotes even settling and mixing and gives an evenly packed column free of air bubbles. As the adsorbent is added, solvent flows out of the Pasteur pipet. Because the adsorbent must not be allowed to dry during the packing process, you must use a means of controlling the solvent flow. If a piece of small-diameter plastic tubing is available, it can be fitted over the narrow

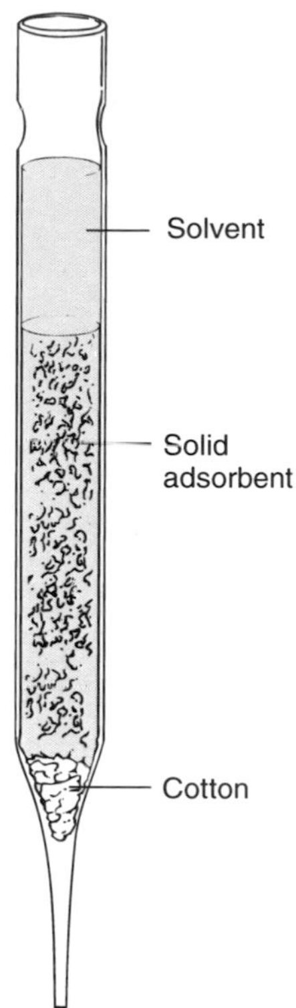

Figure 19.9 A microscale chromatography column.

tip of the Pasteur pipet. The flow rate can then be controlled using a screw clamp. A simple approach to controlling the flow rate is to use a finger over the top of the Pasteur pipet, much as you control the flow of liquid in a volumetric pipet. Continue adding the adsorbent slowly, with constant tapping, until the adsorbent has reached the desired level. As you pack the column, be careful not to let the column run dry. The final column should appear as shown in Figure 19.9.

B. Dry Pack Method 2

Macroscale Columns. Macroscale columns can also be packed by a dry pack method that is commonly used in the packing of microscale columns (see "Microscale Columns," following). In this method, the column is filled with dry adsorbent without any solvent. When the desired amount of adsorbent has been added, solvent is allowed to percolate through the column. The disadvantages described for the microscale method also apply to the macroscale method. This method is not recommended for use with silica gel or alumina because the combination leads to uneven packing, air bubbles, and cracking, especially if a solvent that has a highly exothermic heat of solvation is used.

Semi-microscale Columns. The dry pack method 2 for semi-microscale columns is similar to that described for Pasteur pipets (see next paragraph), except that the plug of cotton is not required. The flow rate of solvent through the column can be controlled using the stopcock, which is part of the column assembly (see Figure 19.8).

Microscale Columns. An alternative dry pack method for microscale columns is to fill the Pasteur pipet with *dry* adsorbent, without any solvent. Position a plug of cotton in the bottom of the Pasteur pipet. The desired amount of adsorbent is added slowly, and the pipet is tapped constantly until the level of adsorbent has reached the desired height. Figure 19.9 can be used as a guide to judge the correct height of the column of adsorbent. When the column is packed, added solvent is allowed to percolate through the adsorbent until the entire column is moistened. The solvent is not added until just before the column is to be used.

This method is useful when the adsorbent is alumina, but it does not produce satisfactory results with silica gel. Even with alumina, poor separations can arise due to uneven packing, air bubbles, and cracking, especially if a solvent that has a highly exothermic heat of solvation is used.

19.8 PACKING THE COLUMN: DEPOSITING THE ADSORBENT—THE SLURRY METHOD

The slurry method is not recommended as a microscale method for use with Pasteur pipets. On a very small scale, it is too difficult to pack the column with the slurry without losing the solvent before the packing has been completed. Microscale columns should be packed by one of the dry pack methods, as described in Section 19.7.

In the slurry method, the adsorbent is packed into the column as a mixture of a solvent and an undissolved solid. The slurry is prepared in a separate container (Erlenmeyer flask) by adding the solid adsorbent, a little at a time, to a quantity of the solvent. This order of addition (adsorbent added to solvent) should be followed strictly, because the adsorbent solvates and liberates heat. If the solvent is added to the adsorbent, it may boil away almost as fast as it is added due to heat evolved. This will be especially true if ether or another low-boiling solvent is used. When this happens, the final mixture will be uneven and lumpy. Enough adsorbent is added to the solvent, and mixed by swirling the container, to form a thick, but flowing, slurry. The container should be swirled until the mixture is homogeneous and relatively free of entrapped air bubbles.

For a macroscale column, the procedure is as follows. When the slurry has been prepared, the column is filled about half full with solvent, and the stopcock is opened to allow solvent to drain slowly into a large beaker. The slurry is mixed by swirling and is then poured in portions into the top of the draining column (a wide-necked funnel may be useful here). Be sure to swirl the slurry thoroughly before each addition to the column. The column is tapped constantly and *gently* on the side during the pouring operation, with the fingers or with a pencil fitted with a rubber stopper. A short piece of large-diameter pressure tubing may also be used for tapping. The tapping promotes even settling and mixing and gives an evenly packed column free of air bubbles. Tapping is continued until all the material has settled, showing a well-defined level at the top of the column. Solvent from the collecting beaker may be readded to the slurry if it becomes too thick to be poured into the column at one time. In fact, the collected solvent should be cycled through the column several times to ensure that settling is complete and that the column is firmly packed. The downward flow of solvent tends to compact the adsorbent. Take care never to let the column "run dry" during packing. There should always be solvent on top of the absorbent column.

19.9 APPLYING THE SAMPLE TO THE COLUMN

The solvent (or solvent mixture) used to pack the column is normally the least polar elution solvent that can be used during chromatography. The compounds to be chromatographed are not highly soluble in the solvent. If they were, they would probably have a greater affinity for the solvent than for the adsorbent and would pass right through the column without equilibrating with the stationary phase.

The first elution solvent, however, is generally not a good solvent to use in preparing the sample to be placed on the column. Because the compounds are not highly soluble in nonpolar solvents, it takes a large amount of the initial solvent to dissolve the compounds, and it is difficult to get the mixture to form a narrow band on top of the column. A narrow band is ideal for an optimum separation of components. For the best separation, therefore, the compound is applied to the top of the column undiluted if it is a liquid, or in a *very small* amount of polar solvent if it is a solid. Water must not be used to dissolve the initial sample being chromatographed because it reacts with the column packing.

In adding the sample to the column, use the following procedure. Lower the solvent level to the top of the adsorbent column by draining the solvent from the column. Add the sample (either a pure liquid or a solution) to form a small layer on top of the adsorbent. A Pasteur pipet is convenient for adding the sample to the column. Take care not to disturb the surface of the adsorbent. This is best accomplished by touching the pipet to the inside of the glass column and slowly draining it to allow the sample to spread into a thin film, which slowly descends to cover the entire adsorbent surface. Drain the pipet close to the surface of the adsorbent. When all the sample has been added, drain this small layer of liquid into the column until the top surface of the column *just begins* to dry. Then add a small layer of the chromatographic solvent carefully with a Pasteur pipet, again being careful not to disturb the surface. Drain this small layer of solvent into the column until the top surface of the column just dries. Add another small layer of fresh solvent, if necessary, and repeat the process until it is clear that the sample is strongly adsorbed on the top of the column. If the sample is colored and the fresh layer of solvent acquires some of this color, the sample has not been properly adsorbed. Once the sample has been properly applied, you can protect the level surface of the adsorbent by carefully filling the top of the column with solvent and sprinkling clean, white sand into the column to form a small protective layer on top of the adsorbent. For microscale applications, this layer of sand is not required.

Separations are often better if the sample is allowed to stand a short time on the column before elution. This allows a true equilibrium to be established. In columns that stand for too long, however, the adsorbent often compacts or even swells, and the flow can become annoyingly slow. Diffusion of the sample to widen the bands also becomes a problem if a column is allowed to stand over an extended period. For small-scale chromatography using Pasteur pipets, there is no stopcock, and it is not possible to stop the flow. In this case, it is not necessary to allow the column to stand.

19.10 ELUTION TECHNIQUES

Solvents for analytical and preparative chromatography should be pure reagents. Commercial-grade solvents often contain small amounts of residue, which remain when the solvent is evaporated. For routine work and for relatively easy separations that take only small amounts of solvent, the residue usually presents few problems. For large-scale work, commercial-grade solvents may have to be redistilled before use. This is especially true for hydrocarbon solvents, which tend to have more residue than other solvent types.

Elution of the products is usually begun with a nonpolar solvent, such as hexane or petroleum ether. The polarity of the elution solvent can be increased gradually by adding successively greater percentages of ether or toluene (for instance, 1, 2, 5, 10, 15, 25, 50, or 100%) or some other solvent of greater solvent power (polarity) than hexane. The transition from one solvent to another should not be too rapid in most solvent changes. If the two solvents to be changed differ greatly in their heats of solvation in binding to the adsorbent, enough heat can be generated to crack the column. Ether is especially troublesome in this respect, as it has both a low boiling point and a relatively high heat of solvation. Most organic compounds can be separated on silica gel or alumina using hexane–ether or hexane–toluene combinations for elution, and following these by pure methylene chloride. Solvents of greater polarity are usually avoided for the various reasons mentioned previously. In microscale work, the usual procedure is to use only one solvent for the chromatography.

The flow of solvent through the column should not be too rapid, or the solutes will not have time to equilibrate with the adsorbent as they pass down the column. If the rate of flow is too low or stopped for a period, diffusion can become a problem—the solute band will diffuse, or spread out, in all directions. In either of these cases, separation will be poor. As a general rule (and only an approximate one), most macroscale columns are run with flow rates ranging from 5 to 50 drops of effluent per minute; a steady flow of solvent is usually avoided. Microscale columns made from Pasteur pipets do not have a means of controlling the solvent flow rate, but commercial microscale columns are equipped with stopcocks. The solvent flow rate in this type of column can be adjusted in a manner similar to that used with larger columns. To avoid diffusion of the bands, do not stop the column, and do not set it aside overnight.

In some cases, the chromatography may proceed too slowly; the rate of solvent flow can be accelerated by attaching a rubber dropper bulb to the top of the Pasteur pipet column and squeezing *gently.* The additional air pressure forces the solvent through the column more rapidly. If this technique is used, however, care must be taken to remove the rubber bulb from the column before releasing it. Otherwise, air may be drawn up through the bottom of the column, destroying the column packing.

19.11 RESERVOIRS

When large quantities of solvent are used in a chromatographic separation, it is often convenient to use a solvent reservoir to forestall having to add small portions of fresh solvent continually. The simplest type of reservoir, a feature of many columns, is created by fusing the top of the column to a round-bottom flask (Figure 19.10A). If the column has a standard-taper joint at its top, a reservoir can be created by joining a standard-taper separatory funnel to the column (Figure 19.10B). In this arrangement, the stopcock is left open, and no stopper is placed in the top of the separatory funnel. A third common arrangement is shown in Figure 19.10C. A separatory funnel is filled with solvent; its stopper is wetted with solvent and put *firmly* in place. The funnel is inserted into the empty filling space at the top of the chromatographic column, and the stopcock is opened. Solvent flows out of the funnel, filling the space at the top of the column until the solvent level is well above the

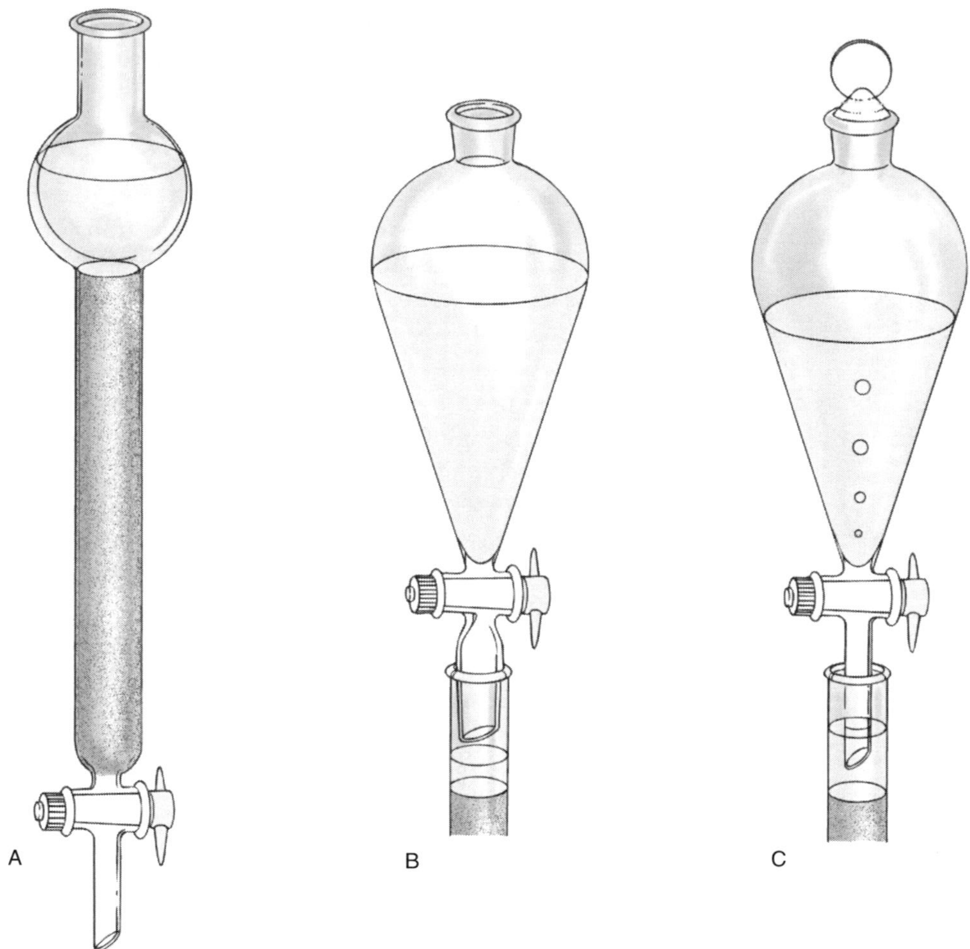

Figure 19.10 Various types of solvent-reservoir arrangements for chromatographic columns.

outlet of the separatory funnel. As solvent drains from the column, this arrangement automatically refills the space at the top of the column by allowing air to enter through the stem of the separatory funnel.

Some semi-microscale columns, such as that shown in Figure 19.8, are equipped with a solvent reservoir that fits onto the top of the column. It functions just as the reservoirs do that are described in this section.

For a microscale chromatography, the portion of the Pasteur pipet above the adsorbent is used as a reservoir of solvent. Fresh solvent, as needed, is added by means of another Pasteur pipet. When it is necessary to change solvent, the new solvent is also added in this manner.

19.12 MONITORING THE COLUMN

It is a lucky circumstance when the compounds to be separated are colored. The separation can then be followed visually and the various bands collected separately as they elute

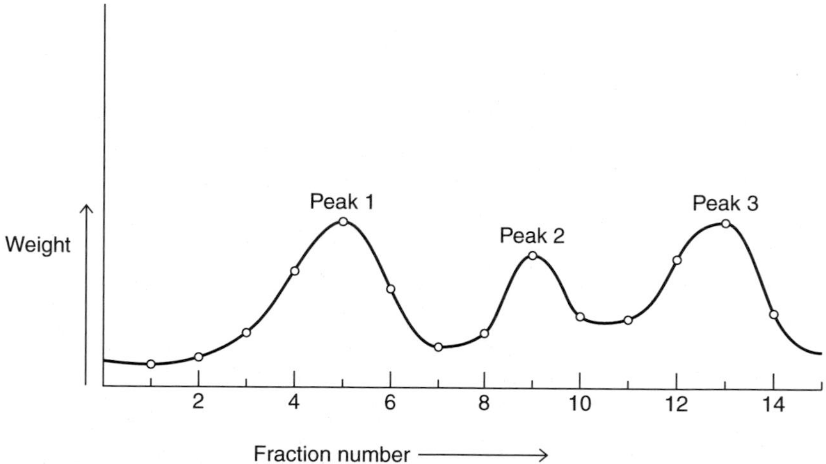

Figure 19.11 A typical elution graph.

from the column. For the majority of organic compounds, however, this lucky circumstance does not exist, and other methods must be used to determine the positions of the bands. The most common method of following a separation of colorless compounds is to collect *fractions* of constant volume in preweighed flasks or test tubes, to evaporate the solvent from each fraction, and to reweigh the container plus any residue. A plot of fraction number versus the weight of the residues after evaporation of solvent gives a plot similar to that in Figure 19.11. Clearly, fractions 2 through 7 (peak 1) may be combined as a single compound, and so can fractions 8 through 11 (peak 2) and 12 through 15 (peak 3). The size of the fractions collected (1, 10, 100, or 500 mL) depends on the size of the column and the ease of separation.

Another common method of monitoring the column is to mix an inorganic phosphor into the adsorbent used to pack the column. When the column is illuminated with an ultraviolet light, the adsorbent treated in this way fluoresces. However, many solutes have the ability to **quench** the fluorescence of the indicator phosphor. In areas in which solutes are present, the adsorbent does not fluoresce, and a dark band is visible. In this type of column, the separation can also be followed visually.

Thin-layer chromatography is often used to monitor a column. This method is described in Technique 20 (Section 20.10, p. 828). Several sophisticated instrumental and spectroscopic methods, which we shall not detail, can also monitor a chromatographic separation.

19.13 TAILING

When a single solvent is used for elution, an elution curve (weight versus fraction) such as that shown as a solid line in Figure 19.12 is often observed. An ideal elution curve is shown by dashed lines. In the nonideal curve, the compound is said to be **tailing.** Tailing can interfere with the beginning of a curve or a peak of a second component and lead to a poor separation. One way to avoid this is to increase the polarity of the solvent constantly while eluting. In this way, at the tail of the peak, where the

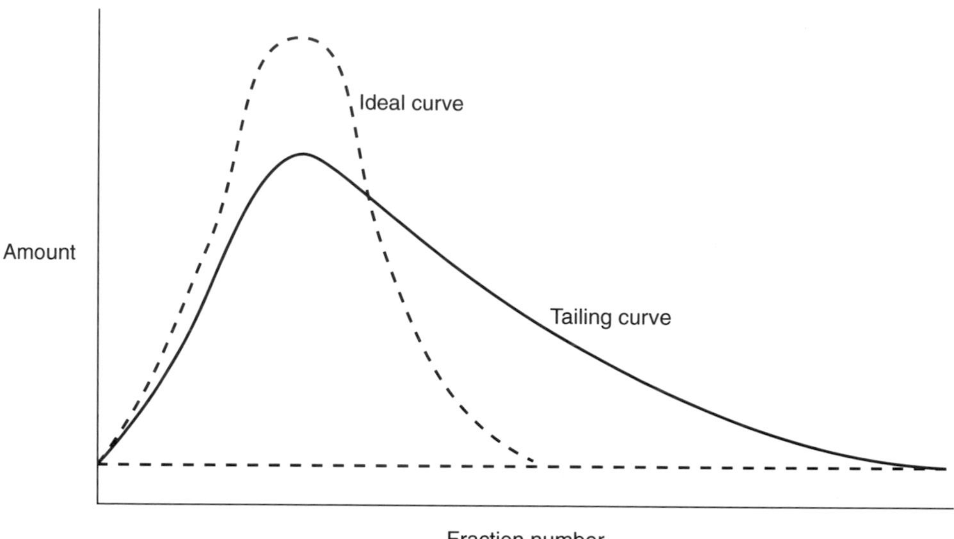

Figure 19.12 Elution curves: one ideal and one that "tails."

solvent polarity is increasing, the compound will move slightly faster than at the front and allow the tail to squeeze forward, forming a more nearly ideal band.

19.14 RECOVERING THE SEPARATED COMPOUNDS

In recovering each of the separated compounds of a chromatographic separation when they are solids, the various correct fractions are combined and evaporated. If the combined fractions contain sufficient material, they may be purified by recrystallization. If the compounds are liquids, the correct fractions are combined, and the solvent is evaporated. If sufficient material has been collected, liquid samples can be purified by distillation. The combination of chromatography–crystallization or chromatography–distillation usually yields very pure compounds. For microscale applications, the amount of sample collected is too small to allow a purification by crystallization or distillation. The samples that are obtained after the solvent has been evaporated are considered to be sufficiently pure, and no additional purification is attempted.

EXPERIMENT 24

4-Methylcyclohexene

Preparation of an alkene
Dehydration of an alcohol
Distillation
Bromine and permanganate tests for unsaturation

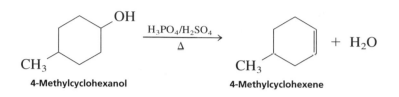

$$\text{4-Methylcyclohexanol} \xrightarrow[\Delta]{H_3PO_4/H_2SO_4} \text{4-Methylcyclohexene} + H_2O$$

4-Methylcyclohexanol 4-Methylcyclohexene

Alcohol dehydration is an acid-catalyzed reaction performed by strong, concentrated mineral acids such as sulfuric and phosphoric acids. The acid protonates the alcoholic hydroxyl group, permitting it to dissociate as water. Loss of a proton from the intermediate (elimination) brings about an alkene. Because sulfuric acid often causes extensive charring in this reaction, phosphoric acid, which is comparatively free of this problem, is a better choice. In order to make the reaction proceed faster, however, you will also use a minimal amount of sulfuric acid.

The equilibrium that attends this reaction will be shifted in favor of the product by distilling it from the reaction mixture as it is formed. The 4-methylcyclohexene (bp 101–102°C) will codistill with the water that is also formed. By continuously removing the products, you can obtain a high yield of 4-methylcyclohexene. Because the starting material, 4-methylcyclohexanol, also has a somewhat low boiling point (bp 171–173°C), the distillation must be done carefully so that the alcohol does not also distill.

Unavoidably, a small amount of phosphoric acid codistills with the product. It is removed by washing the distillate mixture with a saturated sodium chloride solution. This step also partially removes the water from the 4-methylcyclohexene layer; the drying process will be completed by allowing the product to stand over anhydrous sodium sulfate.

Compounds containing double bonds react with a bromine solution (red) to decolorize it. Similarly, they react with a solution of potassium permanganate (purple) to discharge its color and produce a brown precipitate (MnO_2). These reactions are often used as qualitative tests to determine the presence of a double bond in an organic molecule (see Experiment 55). Both tests will be performed on the 4-methylcyclohexene formed in this experiment.

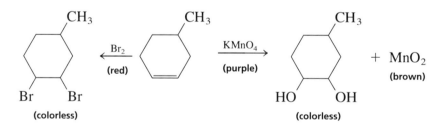

$$\text{dibromide (colorless)} \xleftarrow[\text{(red)}]{Br_2} \text{4-methylcyclohexene} \xrightarrow[\text{(purple)}]{KMnO_4} \text{diol (colorless)} + MnO_2 \text{ (brown)}$$

CH$_3$, Br, Br (colorless) — CH$_3$, HO, OH (colorless)

Required Reading

Review: Techniques 5 and 6
Technique 12 Extractions, Separations, and Drying Agents, Sections 12.7, 12.8, and 12.9

New: Technique 14 Simple Distillation

If performing the optional infrared spectroscopy, also read
Technique 25 Infrared Spectroscopy

Special Instructions

Phosphoric and sulfuric acids are very corrosive. Do not allow either acid to touch your skin.

Suggested Waste Disposal

Dispose of aqueous wastes by pouring them into the container designated for aqueous wastes. Residues that remain after the first distillation may also be placed in the aqueous waste container. Discard the solutions that remain after the bromine test for unsaturation in an organic waste container designated for the disposal of *halogenated* wastes. The solutions that remain after the potassium permanganate test should be discarded into a waste container specifically marked for the disposal of potassium permanganate waste.

Procedure

Apparatus Assembly. Place 7.5 mL of 4-methylcyclohexanol ($MW = 114.2$) in a tared 50-mL round-bottom flask and reweigh the flask to determine an accurate weight for the alcohol. Add 2.0 mL of 85% phosphoric acid and 30 drops (0.40 mL) of concentrated sulfuric acid to the flask. Mix the liquids thoroughly using a glass stirring rod and add a boiling stone. Assemble a distillation apparatus as shown in Technique 14, Figure 14.1, p. 734 (omit the condenser), using a 25-mL flask as a receiver. Immerse the receiving flask in an ice-water bath to minimize the possibility that 4-methylcyclohexene vapors will escape into the laboratory.

Dehydration. Start circulating the cooling water in the condenser and heat the mixture with a heating mantle until the product begins to distill and collect in the receiver. The heating should be regulated so that the distillation requires about 30 minutes. Too rapid distillation leads to incomplete reaction and isolation of the starting material, 4-methylcyclohexanol. Continue the distillation until no more liquid is collected. The distillate contains 4-methylcyclohexene as well as water.

Isolation and Drying of the Product. Transfer the distillate to a centrifuge tube with the aid of 1 or 2 mL of saturated sodium chloride solution. Allow the layers to separate and remove the bottom aqueous layer with a Pasteur pipet (discard it). Using a dry Pasteur pipet, transfer the organic layer remaining in the centrifuge tube to an Erlenmeyer flask containing a small amount of granular anhydrous sodium sulfate. Place a stopper in the flask and set it aside for 10–15 minutes to remove the last traces of water. During this time, wash and dry the distillation apparatus, using small amounts of acetone and an air stream to aid the drying process.

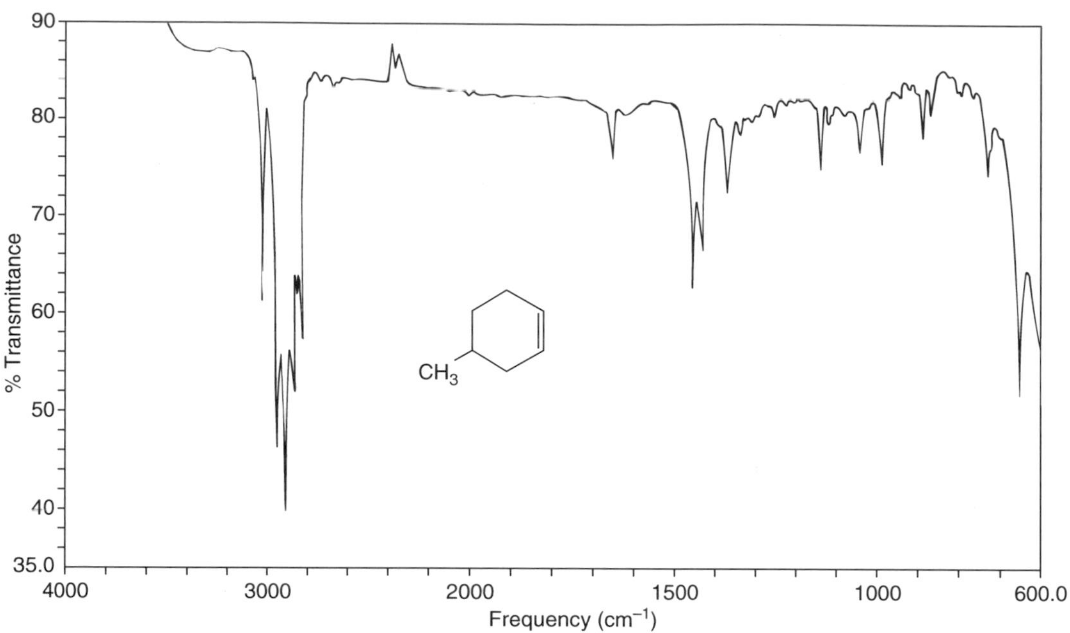

Infrared spectrum of 4-methylcyclohexene (neat).

Distillation. Transfer as much of the dried liquid as possible to the clean, dry 50-mL round-bottom flask, being careful to leave as much of the solid drying agent behind as possible. Add a boiling stone to the flask and assemble the distillation apparatus as before, using a *preweighed* 25-mL receiving flask. Because 4-methylcyclohexene is so volatile, you will recover more product if you cool the receiver in an ice-water bath. Using a heating mantle, distill the 4-methylcyclohexene, collecting the material that boils over the range 100–105°C. Record your observed boiling-point range in your notebook. There will be little or no forerun, and very little liquid will remain in the distilling flask at the end of the distillation. Reweigh the receiving flask to determine how much 4-methylcyclohexene you prepared. Calculate the percentage yield of 4-methylcyclohexene ($MW = 96.2$).

Spectroscopy. At the instructor's option, obtain the infrared spectrum of 4-methylcyclohexene (Technique 25, Section 25.2, p. 875, or 25.3, p. 876). Because 4-methylcyclohexene is so volatile, you must work quickly to obtain a good spectrum using sodium chloride plates. Compare the spectrum with the one shown in this experiment. After performing the following tests, submit your sample, along with the report, to the instructor.[1]

UNSATURATION TESTS

Place 4–5 drops of 4-methylcyclohexanol in each of two small test tubes. In each of another pair of small test tubes, place 4–5 drops of the 4-methylcyclohexene you

[1] The product of the distillation may also be analyzed by gas chromatography. We have found that when using gas chromatography–mass spectrometry to analyze the products of this reaction, it is possible to observe the presence of isomeric methylcyclohexenes. These isomers arise from rearrangement reactions that occur during the dehydration.

prepared. Do not confuse the test tubes. Take one test tube from each group and add a solution of bromine in carbon tetrachloride or methylene chloride, drop by drop, to the contents of the test tube until the red color is no longer discharged. Record the result in each case, including the number of drops required. Test the remaining two test tubes in a similar fashion with a solution of potassium permanganate. Because aqueous potassium permanganate is not miscible with organic compounds, you will have to add about 0.3 mL of 1,2-dimethoxyethane to each test tube before making the test. Record your results and explain them.

QUESTIONS

1. Outline a mechanism for the dehydration of 4-methylcyclohexanol catalyzed by phosphoric acid.

2. What major alkene product is produced by the dehydration of the following alcohols?

- **a.** Cyclohexanol
- **b.** 1-Methylcyclohexanol
- **c.** 2-Methylcyclohexanol
- **d.** 2,2-Dimethylcyclohexanol
- **e.** 1,2-Cyclohexanediol (*Hint:* Consider keto-enol tautomerism.)

3. Compare and interpret the infrared spectra of 4-methylcyclohexene and 4-methylcyclohexanol.

4. Identify the C—H out-of-plane bending vibrations in the infrared spectrum of 4-methylcyclohexene. What structural information can be obtained from these bands?

5. In this experiment, 1–2 mL of saturated sodium chloride is used to transfer the crude product after the initial distillation. Why is saturated sodium chloride, rather than pure water, used for this procedure?

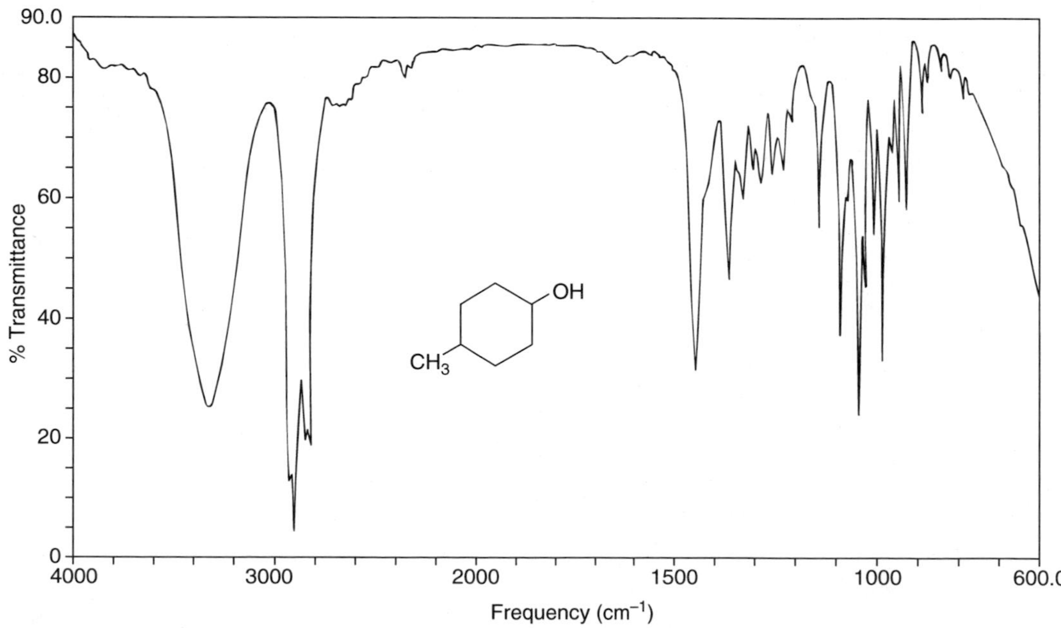

Infrared spectrum of 4-methylcyclohexanol (neat).

TECHNIQUE 22

Gas Chromatography

Gas chromatography is one of the most useful instrumental tools for separating and analyzing organic compounds that can be vaporized without decomposition. Common uses include testing the purity of a substance and separating the components of a mixture. The relative amounts of the components in a mixture may also be determined. In some cases, gas chromatography can be used to identify a compound. In microscale work, it can also be used as a preparative method to isolate pure compounds from a small amount of a mixture.

Gas chromatography resembles column chromatography in principle, but it differs in three respects. First, the partitioning processes for the compounds to be separated are carried out between a **moving gas phase** and a **stationary liquid phase.** (Recall that in column chromatography, the moving phase is a liquid, and the stationary phase is a solid adsorbent.) Second, the temperature of the gas system can be controlled, because the column is contained in an insulated oven. And third, the concentration of any given compound in the gas phase is a function of its vapor pressure only. Because gas chromatography separates the components of a mixture primarily on the basis of their vapor pressures (or boiling points), this technique is also similar in principle to fractional distillation. In microscale work, it is sometimes used to separate and isolate compounds from a mixture; fractional distillation would normally be used with larger amounts of material.

Gas chromatography (GC) is also known as vapor-phase chromatography (VPC) and as gas–liquid partition chromatography (GLPC). All three names, as well as their indicated abbreviations, are often found in the literature of organic chemistry. In reference to the technique, the last term, GLPC, is the most strictly correct and is preferred by most authors.

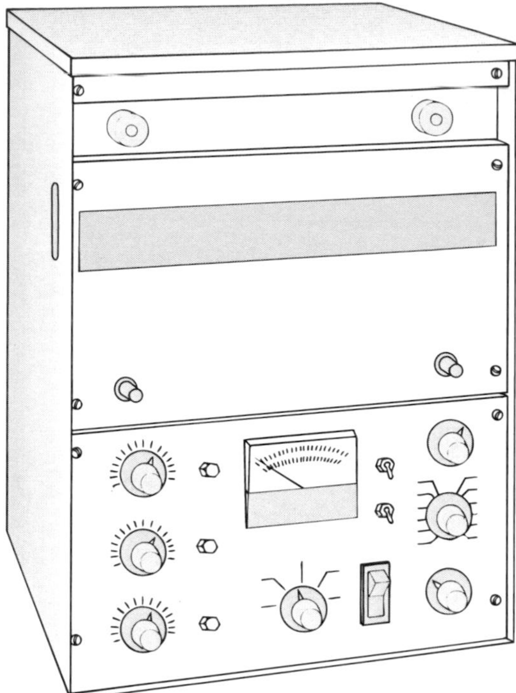

Figure 22.1 A gas chromatograph.

22.1 THE GAS CHROMATOGRAPH

The apparatus used to carry out a gas–liquid chromatographic separation is generally called a **gas chromatograph.** A typical student-model gas chromatograph, the GOW-MAC model 69-350, is illustrated in Figure 22.1. A schematic block diagram of a basic gas chromatograph is shown in Figure 22.2. The basic elements of the apparatus are apparent. The sample is injected into the chromatograph, and it is immediately vaporized in a heated injection chamber and introduced into a moving stream of gas, called the **carrier gas.** The vaporized sample is then swept into a column filled with particles coated with a liquid adsorbent. The column is contained in a temperature-controlled oven. As the sample passes through the column, it is subjected to many gas–liquid partitioning processes, and the components are separated. As each component leaves the column, its presence is detected by an electrical detector that generates a signal that is recorded on a strip chart recorder.

Many modern instruments are also equipped with a microprocessor, which can be programmed to change parameters, such as the temperature of the oven, while a mixture is being separated on a column. With this capability, it is possible to optimize the separation of components and to complete a run in a relatively short time.

22.2 THE COLUMN

The heart of the gas chromatograph is the packed column. This column is usually made of copper or stainless steel tubing, but sometimes glass is used. The most common di-

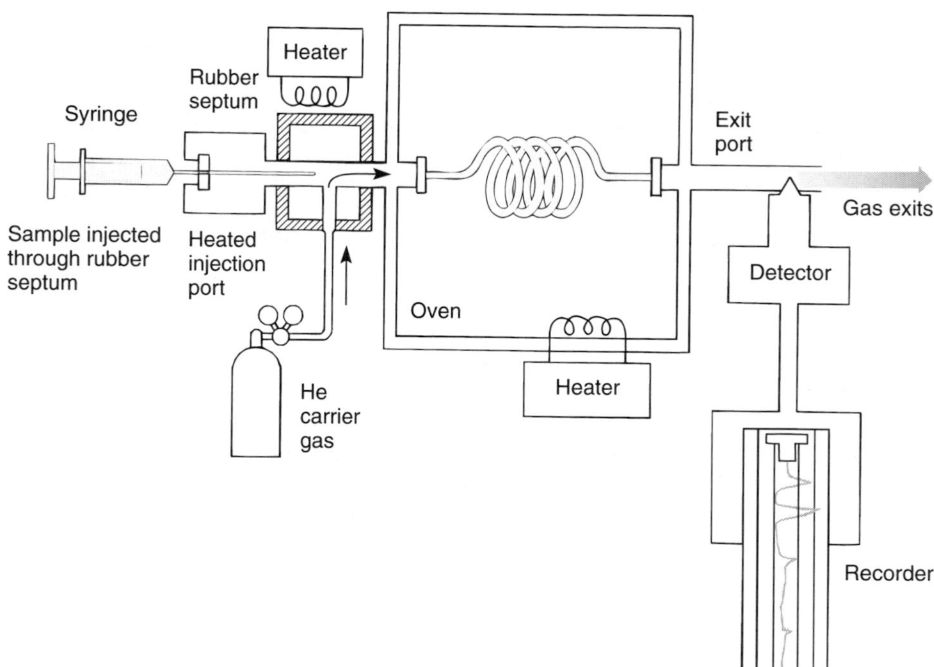

Figure 22.2 A schematic diagram of a gas chromatograph.

ameters of tubing are ⅛ inch (3 mm) and ¼ inch (6 mm). To construct a column, cut a piece of tubing to the desired length and attach the proper fittings on each of the two ends to connect to the apparatus. The most common length is 4–12 feet, but some columns may be up to 50 feet in length.

The tubing (column) is then packed with the **stationary phase.** The material chosen for the stationary phase is usually a liquid, a wax, or a low-melting solid. This material should be relatively nonvolatile; that is, it should have a low vapor pressure and a high boiling point. Liquids commonly used are high-boiling hydrocarbons, silicone oils, waxes, and polymeric esters, ethers, and amides. Some typical substances are listed in Table 22.1.

The liquid phase is usually coated onto a **support material.** A common support material is crushed firebrick. Many methods exist for coating the high-boiling liquid phase onto the support particles. The easiest is to dissolve the liquid (or low-melting wax or solid) in a volatile solvent such as methylene chloride (bp 40°C). The firebrick (or other support) is added to this solution, which is then slowly evaporated (rotary evaporator) so as to leave each particle of support material evenly coated. Other support materials are listed in Table 22.2.

In the final step, the liquid-phase-coated support material is packed into the tubing as evenly as possible. The tubing is bent or coiled so that it fits into the oven of the gas chromatograph with its two ends connected to the gas entrance and exit ports.

Selection of a liquid phase usually revolves about two factors. First, most liquid phases have an upper temperature limit above which they cannot be used. Above the specified limit of temperature, the liquid phase itself will begin to "bleed" off the column. Second, the materials to be separated must be considered. For polar samples, it is usually best to use a polar liquid phase; for nonpolar samples, a nonpolar liquid phase is indicated. The liquid phase performs best when the substances to be separated *dissolve* in it.

TABLE 22.1 Typical Liquid Phases

		Type	Composition	Maximum Temperature (°C)	Typical Use
Increasing polarity ↓	Apiezons (L, M, N, etc.)	Hydrocarbon greases (varying MW)	Hydrocarbon mixtures	250–300	Hydrocarbons
	SE-30	Methyl silicone rubber	Like silicone oil, but cross-linked	350	General applications
	DC-200	Silicone oil ($R = CH_3$)	$R_3Si{-}O{-}\left[\begin{matrix}R\\ \vert\\ Si{-}O\\ \vert\\ R\end{matrix}\right]_n{-}SiR_3$	225	Aldehydes, ketones, halocarbons
	DC-710	Silicone oil ($R = CH_3$) ($R' = C_6H_5$)	$\left[\begin{matrix}R'\\ \vert\\ Si{-}O\\ \vert\\ R\end{matrix}\right]_n{-}$	300	General applications
	Carbowaxes (400–20M)	Polyethylene glycols (varying chain lengths)	Polyether $HO{-}(CH_2CH_2{-}O)n{-}CH_2CH_2OH$	Up to 250	Alcohols, ethers, halocarbons
	DEGS	Diethylene glycol succinate	Polyester $\left(CH_2CH_2{-}O{-}\underset{\Vert\atop O}{C}{-}(CH_2)_2{-}\underset{\Vert\atop C}{C}{-}O\right)_n$	200	General applications

TABLE 22.2 Typical Solid Supports

Crushed firebrick	Chromosorb T (Teflon beads)
Nylon beads	Chromosorb P (pink diatomaceous earth, highly absorptive, pH 6–7)
Glass beads	Chromosorb W (white diatomaceous earth, medium absorptivity, pH 8–10)
Silica	Chromosorb G (like the above, low absorptivity, pH 8.5)
Alumina	
Charcoal	
Molecular sieves	

Most researchers today buy packed columns from commercial sources rather than pack their own. A wide variety of types and lengths is available.

Alternatives to packed columns are Golay or glass capillary columns of diameters 0.1–0.2 mm. With these columns, no solid support is required, and the liquid is coated directly on the inner walls of the tubing. Liquid phases commonly used in glass capillary columns are similar in composition to those used in packed columns. They include DB-1 (similar to SE-30), DB-17 (similar to DC-710), and DB-WAX (similar to Carbowax 20M). The length of a capillary column is usually very long, typically 50–100 feet. Because of the length and small diameter, there is increased interaction between the sample and the stationary phase. Gas chromatographs equipped with these small-diameter columns are able to separate components more effectively than instruments using larger packed columns.

22.3 PRINCIPLES OF SEPARATION

After a column is selected, packed, and installed, the **carrier gas** (usually helium, argon, or nitrogen) is allowed to flow through the column supporting the liquid phase. The mixture of compounds to be separated is introduced into the carrier gas stream, where its components are equilibrated (or partitioned) between the moving gas phase and the stationary liquid phase (Figure 22.3). The latter is held stationary because it is adsorbed onto the surfaces of the support material.

The sample is introduced into the gas chromatograph by a microliter syringe. It is injected as a liquid or as a solution through a rubber septum into a heated chamber, called the **injection port,** where it is vaporized and mixed with the carrier gas. As this mixture reaches the column, which is heated in a controlled oven, it begins to equilibrate between the liquid and gas phases. The length of time required for a sample to move through the column is a function of how much time the sample spends in the vapor phase and how much time it spends in the liquid phase. The more time the sample spends in the vapor phase, the faster it gets to the end of the column. In most separations, the components of a sample have similar solubilities in the liquid phase. Therefore, the time the different compounds spend in the vapor phase is primarily a function of the vapor pressure of the compounds, and the

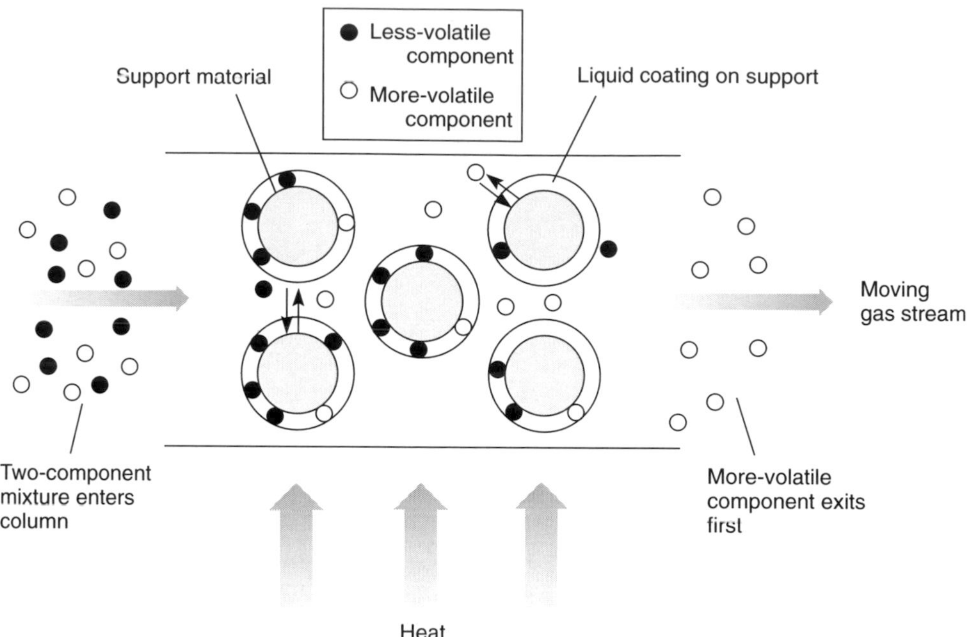

Figure 22.3 The separation process.

more-volatile component arrives at the end of the column first, as illustrated in Figure 22.3. When the correct temperature of the oven and the correct liquid phase have been selected, the compounds in the injected mixture travel through the column at different rates and are separated.

22.4 FACTORS AFFECTING SEPARATION

Several factors determine the rate at which a given compound travels through a gas chromatograph. First, compounds with low boiling points will generally travel through the gas chromatograph faster than compounds with higher boiling points. The reason is that the column is heated, and low-boiling compounds always have higher vapor pressures than higher-boiling compounds. In general, therefore, for compounds with the same functional group, the higher the molecular weight, the longer the retention time. For most molecules, the boiling point increases as the molecular weight increases. If the column is heated to a temperature that is too high, however, the entire mixture to be separated is flushed through the column at the same rate as the carrier gas, and no equilibration takes place with the liquid phase. On the other hand, at too low a temperature, the mixture dissolves in the liquid phase and never revaporizes. Thus, it is retained on the column.

The second factor is the rate of flow of the carrier gas. The carrier gas must not move so rapidly that molecules of the sample in the vapor phase cannot equilibrate with those dissolved in the liquid phase. This may result in poor separation between components in the injected mixture. If the rate of flow is too slow, however, the bands broaden significantly, leading to poor resolution (see Section 22.8).

The third factor is the choice of liquid phase used in the column. The molecular weights, functional groups, and polarities of the component molecules in the mixture to be separated must be considered when a liquid phase is being chosen. A different type of material is generally used for hydrocarbons, for instance, than for esters. The materials to be separated should dissolve in the liquid. The useful temperature limit of the liquid phase selected must also be considered.

The fourth factor is the length of the column. Compounds that resemble one another closely, in general, require longer columns than dissimilar compounds. Many kinds of isomeric mixtures fit into the "difficult" category. The components of isomeric mixtures are so much alike that they travel through the column at very similar rates. You need a longer column, therefore, to take advantage of any differences that may exist.

22.5 ADVANTAGES OF GAS CHROMATOGRAPHY

All factors that have been mentioned must be adjusted by the chemist for any mixture to be separated. Considerable preliminary investigation is often required before a mixture can be separated successfully into its components by gas chromatography. Nevertheless, the advantages of the technique are many.

First, many mixtures can be separated by this technique when no other method is adequate. Second, as little as 1–10 μL (1 μL = 10^{-6}L) of a mixture can be separated by this technique. This advantage is particularly important when working at the microscale level. Third, when gas chromatography is coupled with an electronic recording device (see following discussion), the amount of each component present in the separated mixture can be estimated quantitatively.

The range of compounds that can be separated by gas chromatography extends from gases, such as oxygen (bp –183°C) and nitrogen (bp –196°C), to organic compounds with boiling points over 400°C. The only requirement for the compounds to be separated is that they have an appreciable vapor pressure at a temperature at which they can be separated and that they be thermally stable at this temperature.

22.6 MONITORING THE COLUMN (THE DETECTOR)

To follow the separation of the mixture injected into the gas chromatograph, it is necessary to use an electrical device called a **detector.** Two types of detectors in common use are the **thermal conductivity detector (TCD)** and the **flame-ionization detector (FID).**

The thermal conductivity detector is simply a hot wire placed in the gas stream at the column exit. The wire is heated by constant electrical voltage. When a steady stream of carrier gas passes over this wire, the rate at which it loses heat and its electrical conductance have constant values. When the composition of the vapor stream changes, the rate of heat flow from the wire, and hence its resistance, changes. Helium, which has a thermal conductivity higher than that of most organic substances, is a common carrier gas. Thus, when a substance elutes in the vapor stream, the thermal conductivity of the moving gases will be lower than with helium alone. The wire then heats up, and its resistance decreases.

A typical TCD operates by difference. Two detectors are used: one exposed to the ac-

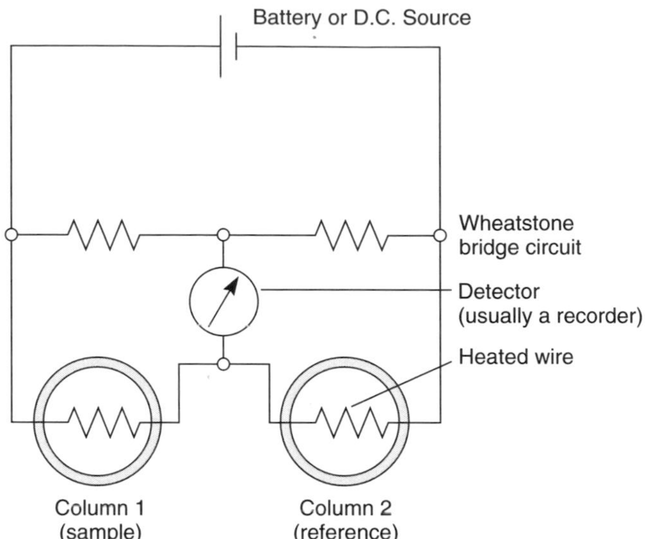

Figure 22.4 A typical thermal conductivity detector.

tual effluent gas and the other exposed to a reference flow of carrier gas only. To achieve this situation, a portion of the carrier gas stream is diverted before it enters the injection port. The diverted gas is routed through a reference column into which no sample has been admitted. The detectors mounted in the sample and reference columns are arranged to form the arms of a Wheatstone bridge circuit, as shown in Figure 22.4. As long as the carrier gas alone flows over both detectors, the circuit is in balance. However, when a sample elutes from the sample column, the bridge circuit becomes unbalanced, creating an electrical signal. This signal can be amplified and used to activate a strip chart recorder. The recorder is an instrument that plots, by means of a moving pen, the unbalanced bridge current versus time on a continuously moving roll of chart paper. This record of detector response (current) versus time is called a **chromatogram.** A typical gas chromatogram is illustrated in Figure 22.5. Deflections of the pen are called **peaks.**

When a sample is injected, some air (CO_2, H_2O, N_2, and O_2) is introduced along with the sample. The air travels through the column almost as rapidly as the carrier gas; as air passes the detector, it causes a small pen response, thereby giving a peak, called the **air peak.** At later times (t_1, t_2, t_3), the components also give rise to peaks on the chromatogram as they pass out of the column and past the detector.

In a flame-ionization detector, the effluent from the column is directed into a flame produced by the combustion of hydrogen, as illustrated in Figure 22.6. As organic compounds burn in the flame, ion fragments are produced and collect on the ring above the flame. The resulting electrical signal is amplified and sent to a recorder in a manner similar to that for a TCD, except that an FID does not produce an air peak. The main advantage of the FID is that it is more sensitive and can be used to analyze smaller quantities of sample. Also, because an FID does not respond to water, a gas chromatograph with this detector can be used to analyze aqueous solutions. Two disadvantages are that it is more difficult to operate and the detection process destroys the sample. Therefore, an FID gas chromatograph cannot be used to do preparative work.

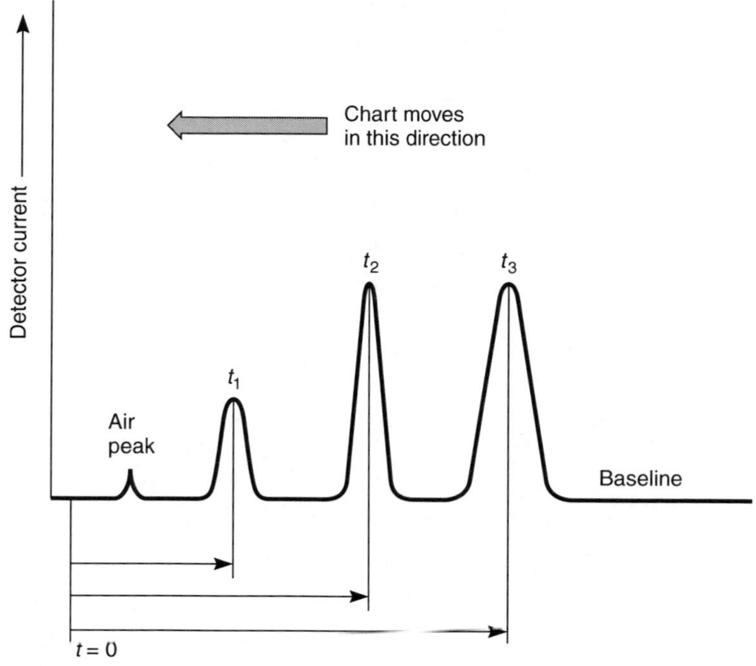

Figure 22.5 A typical gas chromatograph.

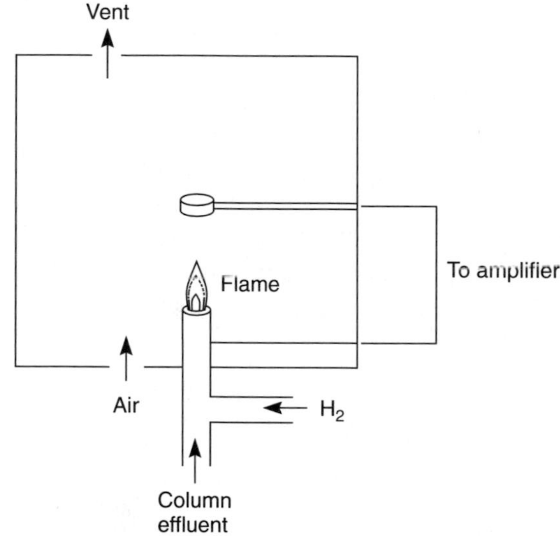

Figure 22.6 A flame-ionization detector.

22.7 RETENTION TIME

The period following injection that is required for a compound to pass through the column is called the **retention time** of that compound. For a given set of constant conditions (flow rate of carrier gas, column temperature, column length, liquid phase, injection port temperature, carrier), the retention time of any compound is always constant (much like the

R_f value in thin-layer chromatography, as described in Technique 20, Section 20.9, p. 827). The retention time is measured from the time of injection to the time of maximum pen deflection (detector current) for the component being observed. This value, when obtained under controlled conditions, can identify a compound by a direct comparison of it with values for known compounds determined under the same conditions. For easier measurement of retention times, most strip chart recorders are adjusted to move the paper at a rate that corresponds to time divisions calibrated on the chart paper. The retention times (t_1, t_2, t_3) are indicated in Figure 22.5 for the three peaks illustrated.

Most modern gas chromatographs are attached to a "data station," which uses a computer or a microprocessor to process the data. With these instruments, the chart often does not have divisions. Instead, the computer prints the retention time, usually to the nearest 0.01 minute, above each peak. A more complete discussion of the results obtained from a modern data station and how these data are treated may be found in Section 22.12.

22.8 POOR RESOLUTION AND TAILING

The peaks in Figure 22.5 are well **resolved.** That is, the peaks are separated from one another, and between each pair of adjacent peaks the tracing returns to the baseline. In Figure 22.7, the peaks overlap, and the resolution is not good. Poor resolution is often caused by using too much sample; by a column that is too short, has too high a temperature, or has too large a diameter; by a liquid phase that does not discriminate well between the two components; or, in short, by almost any wrongly adjusted parameter. When peaks are poorly resolved, it is more difficult to determine the relative amount of each component. Methods for determining the relative percentages of each component are given in Section 22.11.

Another desirable feature illustrated by the chromatogram in Figure 22.5 is that each peak is symmetrical. A common example of an unsymmetrical peak is one in which **tailing** has occurred, as shown in Figure 22.8. Tailing usually results from injecting too much sample into the gas chromatograph. Another cause of tailing occurs with polar compounds, such as alcohols and aldehydes. These compounds may be temporarily adsorbed on column walls or areas of the support material that are not adequately coated by the liquid phase. Therefore, they do not leave in a band, and tailing results.

22.9 QUALITATIVE ANALYSIS

A disadvantage of the gas chromatograph is that it gives no information about the identities of the substances it has separated. The little information it does provide is given

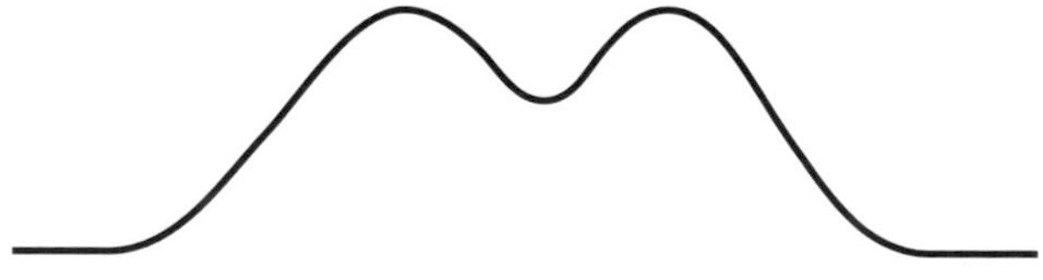

Figure 22.7 Poor resolution, or peaks overlap.

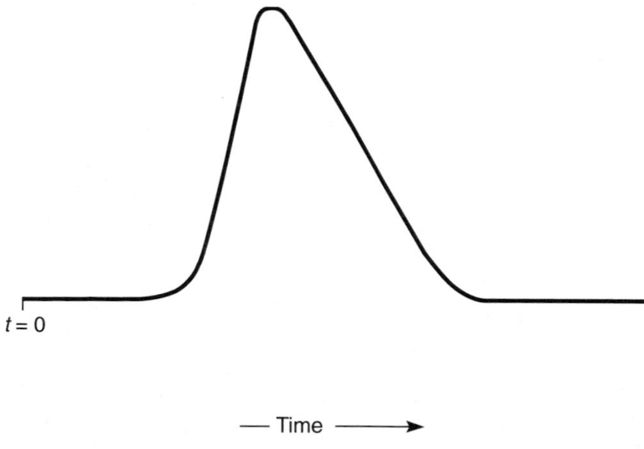

Figure 22.8 Tailing.

by the retention time. It is hard to reproduce this quantity from day to day, however, and exact duplications of separations performed last month may be difficult to make this month. It is usually necessary to **calibrate** the column each time it is used. That is, you must run pure samples of all known and suspected components of a mixture individually, just before chromatographing the mixture, to obtain the retention time of each known compound. As an alternative, each suspected component can be added, one by one, to the unknown mixture while the operator looks to see which peak has its intensity increased relative to the unmodified mixture. Another solution is to collect the components individually as they emerge from the gas chromatograph. Each component can then be identified by other means, such as by infrared or nuclear magnetic resonance spectroscopy or by mass spectrometry.

22.10 COLLECTING THE SAMPLE

For gas chromatographs with a thermal conductivity detector, it is possible to collect samples that have passed through the column. One method uses a gas collection tube (see Figure 22.9), which is included in most microscale glassware kits. A collection tube is joined to the exit port of the column by inserting the ₸ 5/5 inner joint into a metal adapter, which is connected to the exit port. When a sample is eluted from the column in the vapor state, it is cooled by the connecting adapter and the gas collection tube and condenses in the collection tube. The gas collection tube is removed from the adapter when the recorder indicates that the desired sample has completely passed through the column. After the first sample has been collected, the process can be repeated with another gas collection tube.

To isolate the liquid, insert the tapered joint of the collection tube into a 0.1-mL conical vial, which has a ₸ 5/5 outer joint. Place the assembly into a test tube, as illustrated in Figure 22.10. During centrifugation, the sample is forced into the bottom of the conical vial. After disassembling the apparatus, the liquid can be removed from the vial with a syringe for a boiling-point determination or analysis by infrared spectroscopy. If a determination of the sample weight is desired, the empty conical vial and cap should be tared and reweighed after the liquid has been collected. It is advisable to dry the gas collection tube and the con-

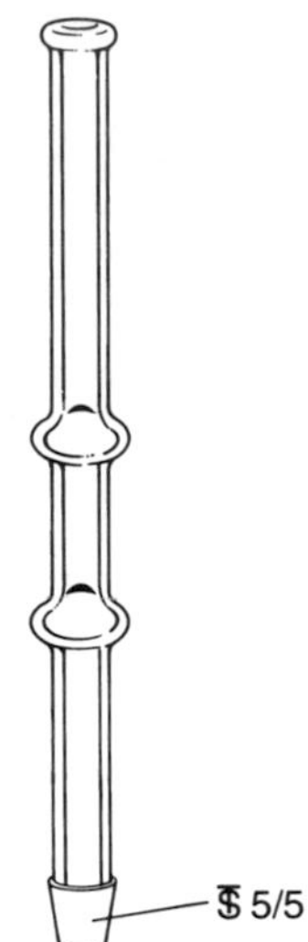

Figure 22.9 A gas chromatography collection tube.

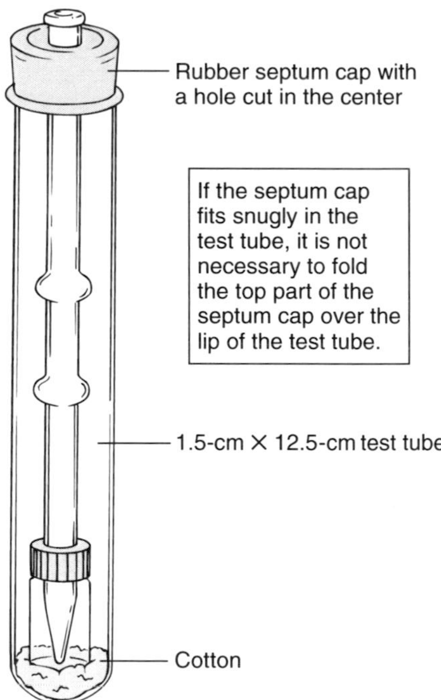

Figure 22.10 A gas chromatography collection tube and a 0.1-mL conical vial.

ical vial in an oven before use to prevent contamination by water or other solvents used in cleaning this glassware.

Another method for collecting samples is to connect a cooled trap to the exit port of the column. A simple trap, suitable for microscale work, is illustrated in Figure 22.11. Suitable coolants include ice water, liquid nitrogen, or dry ice–acetone. For instance, if the

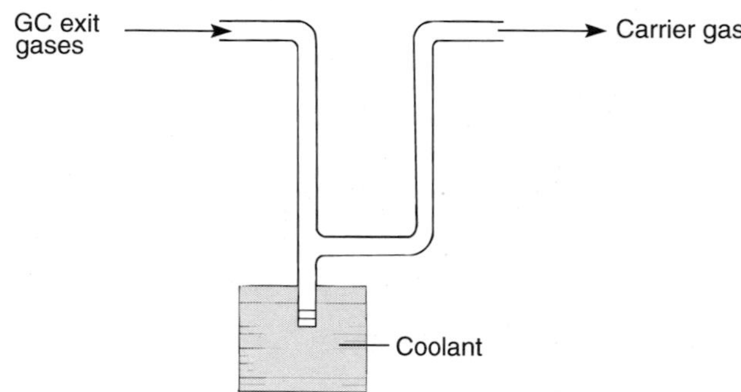

Figure 22.11 A collection trap.

coolant is liquid nitrogen (bp –196°C) and the carrier gas is helium (bp –269°C), compounds boiling above the temperature of liquid nitrogen generally are condensed or trapped in the small tube at the bottom of the U-shaped tube. The small tube is scored with a file just below the point at which it is connected to the larger tube, the tube is broken off, and the sample is removed for analysis. To collect each component of the mixture, you must change the trap after each sample is collected.

22.11 QUANTITATIVE ANALYSIS

The area under a gas chromatograph peak is proportional to the amount (moles) of compound eluted. Hence, the molar percentage composition of a mixture can be approximated by comparing relative peak areas. This method of analysis assumes that the detector is equally sensitive to all compounds eluted and that it gives a linear response with respect to amount. Nevertheless, it gives reasonably accurate results.

The simplest method of measuring the area of a peak is by geometric approximation, or triangulation. In this method, you multiply the height h of the peak above the baseline of the chromatogram by the width of the peak at half of its height $w_{1/2}$. This is illustrated in Figure 22.12. The baseline is approximated by drawing a line between the two sidearms of the peak. This method works well only if the peak is symmetrical. If the peak has tailed or is unsymmetrical, it is best to cut out the peaks with scissors and weigh the pieces of paper on an **analytical balance.** Because the weight per area of a piece of good chart paper is reasonably constant from place to place, the ratio of the areas is the same as the ratio of the weights. To obtain a percentage composition for the mixture, first add all the peak areas (weights). Then, to calculate the percentage of any component in the mixture, divide its individual area by the total area and multiply the result by 100. A sample calculation is illustrated in Figure 22.13. If peaks overlap (see Figure 22.7), either the gas chromatographic conditions must be readjusted to achieve better resolution of the peaks or the peak shape must be estimated.

There are various instrumental means, which are built into recorders, of detecting the amounts of each sample automatically. One method uses a separate pen that produces a trace that integrates the area under each peak. Another method employs an electronic device that automatically prints out the area under each peak and the percentage composition of the sample.

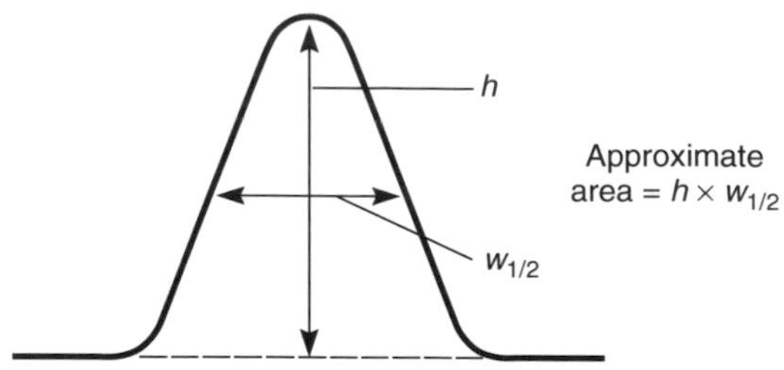

Figure 22.12 Triangulation of a peak.

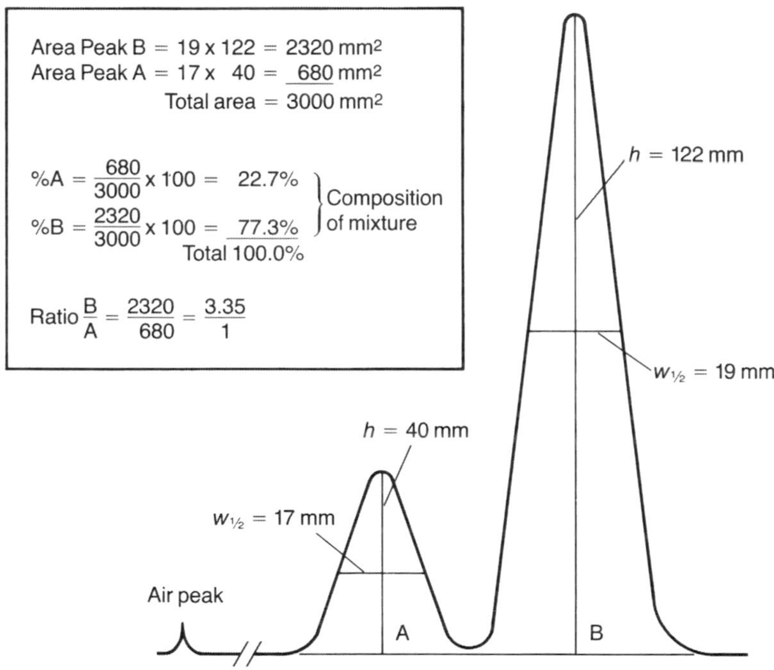

Figure 22.13 Sample percentage composition calculation.

Most modern data stations (see Section 22.12) label the top of each peak with its retention time in minutes. When the trace is completed, the computer prints a table of all the peaks with their retention times, areas, and the percentage of the total area (sum of all the peaks) that each peak represents. Some caution should be used with these results because the computer often does not include smaller peaks and occasionally does not resolve narrow peaks that are so close together that they overlap. If the trace has several peaks and you would like the ratio of only two of them, you will have to determine their percentages yourself using only their two areas or instruct the instrument to integrate only these two peaks.

For many applications, one assumes that the detector is equally sensitive to all compounds eluted. Compounds with different functional groups or with widely varying molecular weights, however, produce different responses with both TCD and FID gas chromatographs. With a TCD, the responses are different because not all compounds have the same thermal conductivity. Different compounds analyzed with an FID gas chromatograph also give different responses because the detector response varies with the type of ions produced. For both types of detectors, it is possible to calculate a **response factor** for each compound in a mixture. Response factors are usually determined by making up an equimolar mixture of two compounds, one of which is considered to be the reference. The mixture is separated on a gas chromatograph, and the relative percentages are calculated using one of the methods described previously. From these percentages, you can determine a response factor for the compound being compared to the reference. If you do this for all the components in a mixture, you can then use these correction factors to make more accurate calculations of the relative percentages for the compounds in the mixture.

To illustrate how response factors are determined, consider the following example. An equimolar mixture of benzene, hexane, and ethyl acetate is prepared and analyzed using a flame-ionization gas chromatograph. The peak areas obtained are

Hexane	831158
Ethyl acetate	1449695
Benzene	966463

In most cases, benzene is taken as the standard, and its response factor is defined to be equal to 1.00. Calculation of the response factors for the other components of the test mixture proceeds as follows:

Hexane	831158/966463 = 0.86
Ethyl acetate	1449695/966463 = 1.50
Benzene	966463/966463 = 1.00 (by definition)

Notice that the response factors calculated in this example are molar response factors. It is necessary to correct these values by the relative molecular weights of each substance to obtain weight response factors.

When you use a flame-ionization gas chromatograph for quantitative analysis, it is first necessary to determine the response factors for each component of the mixture being analyzed, as just shown. For a quantitative analysis, it is likely that you will have to convert molar response factors into weight response factors. Next, the chromatography experiment using the unknown samples is performed. The observed peak areas for each component are corrected using the response factors in order to arrive at the correct weight percentage of each component in the sample. The application of response factors to correct the original results of a quantitative analysis will be illustrated in the following section.

22.12 TREATMENT OF DATA: CHROMATOGRAMS PRODUCED BY MODERN DATA STATIONS

A. Gas Chromatograms and Data Tables

Most modern gas chromatography instruments are equipped with computer-based data stations. Interfacing the instrument with a computer allows the operator to display and manipulate the results in whatever manner might be desired. The operator thus can view the output in a convenient form. The computer can both display the actual gas chromatogram and display the integration results. It can even display the result of two experiments simultaneously, making a comparison of parallel experiments convenient.

Figure 22.14 shows a gas chromatogram of a mixture of hexane, ethyl acetate, and benzene. The peaks corresponding to each peak can be seen; the peaks are labeled with their respective retention times:

	Retention Time (minutes)
Hexane	2.959
Ethyl acetate	3.160
Benzene	3.960

We can also see that there is a very small amount of an unspecified impurity, with a retention time of about 3.4 minutes.

Figure 22.15 shows part of the printed output that accompanies the gas chromatogram. It is this information that is used in the quantitative analysis of the mixture. According to the printout, the first peak has a retention time of 2.954 minutes (the difference between the retention times that appear as labels on the graph and those that appear in the data table are not significant). The computer has also determined the area under this peak (422373 counts). Finally, the computer has calculated the percentage of the first substance (hexane) by determining the total area of all the peaks in the chromatogram (1227054 counts) and dividing that into the area for the hexane peak. The result is displayed as 34.4217%. In a similar manner, the data table shows the retention times and peak areas for the other two peaks in the sample, along with a determination of the percentage of each substance in the mixture.

B. Application of Response Factors

If the detector responded with equal sensitivity to each of the components of the mixture, the data table shown in Figure 22.15 would contain the complete quantitative analysis of the sample. Unfortunately, as we have seen (Section 22.11), gas chromatography detectors respond more sensitively to some substances than they do to others. To correct for this discrepancy, it is necessary to apply corrections that are based on the **response factors** for each component of the mixture.

The method for determining the response factors was introduced in Section 22.11. In this section we will see how this information is applied in order to obtain a correct analysis. This example should serve to demonstrate the procedure for correcting raw gas chromatography results when response factors are known. According to the data table, the reported peak area for the first (hexane) peak is 422373 counts. The response factor for hexane was previously determined to be 0.86. The area of the hexane peak is thus corrected as follows:

$$422373/0.86 = 491000$$

Notice that the calculated result has been adjusted to reflect a reasonable number of significant figures.

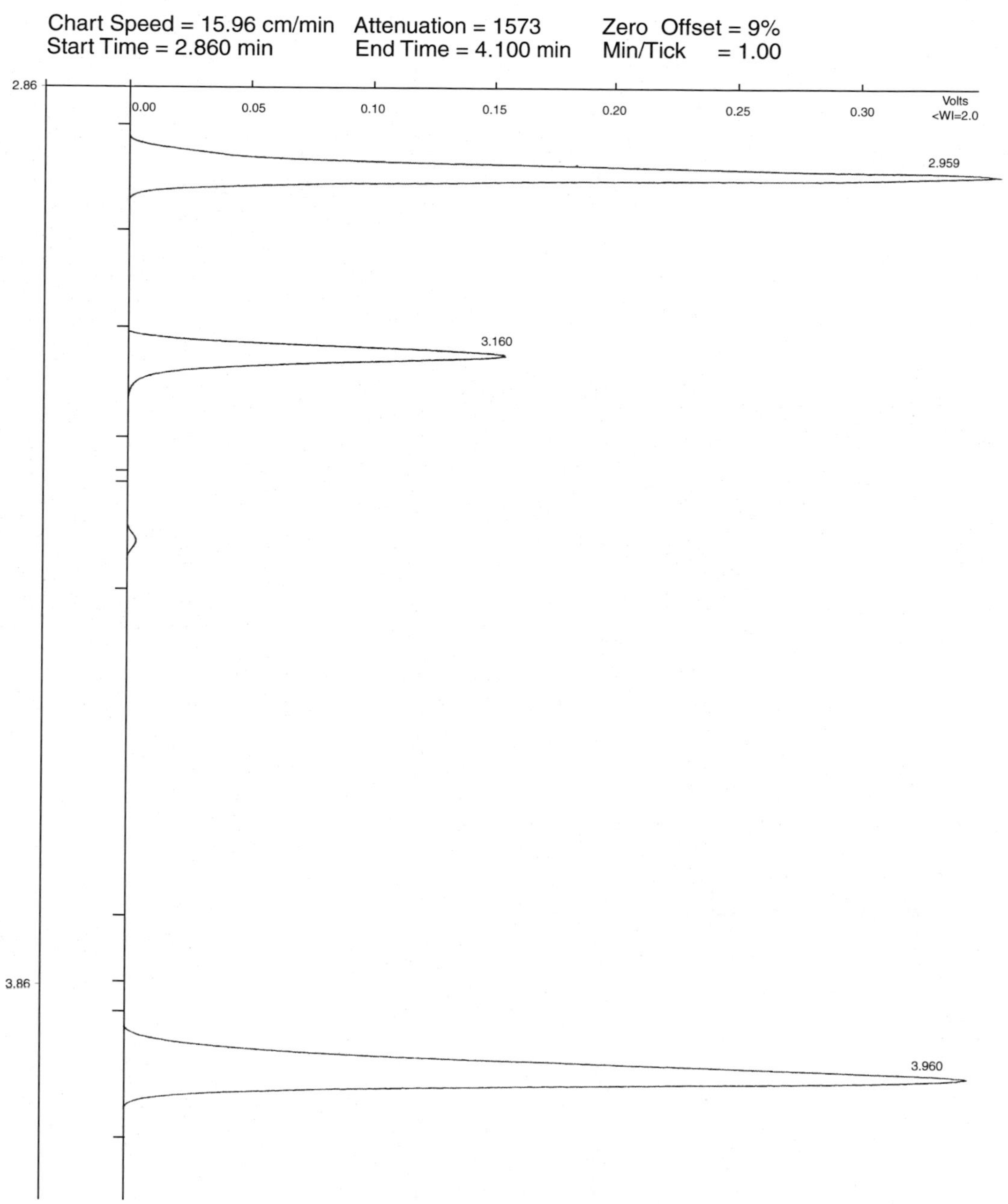

Figure 22.14 A sample gas chromatogram obtained from a data station.

```
Run Mode         : Analysis
Peak Measurement: Peak Area
Calculation Type: Percent
```

Peak No.	Peak Name	Result ()	Ret. Time (min)	Time Offset (min)	Area (counts)	Sep. Code	Width 1/2 (sec)	Status Codes
1		34.4217	2.954	0.000	422373	BB	1.0	
2		16.6599	3.155	0.000	204426	BB	1.2	
3		48.9184	3.954	0.000	600255	BB	1.6	
	Totals:	100.0000		0.000	1227054			

```
Total Unidentified Counts :    1227054 counts

Detected Peaks: 8          Rejected Peaks: 5       Identified Peaks: 0

Multiplier: 1          Divisor: 1          Unidentified Peak Factor: 0

Baseline Offset: 1 microVolts

Noise (used): 28 microVolts — monitored before this run

Manual injection

*****************************************************************************
```

Figure 22.15 A data table to accompany the gas chromatogram shown in Figure 22.14.

The areas for the other peaks in the gas chromatogram are corrected in a similar manner:

Hexane	422373/0.86 =	491000
Ethyl acetate	204426/1.50 =	136000
Benzene	600255/1.00 =	600000
Total peak area		1227000

Using these corrected areas, the true percentages of each component can be easily determined:

		Composition
Hexane	491000/1227000	40.0%
Ethyl acetate	136000/1227000	11.1%
Benzene	600000/1227000	48.9%
Total		100.0%

C. Determination of Relative Percentages of Components in a Complex Mixture

In some circumstances, one may wish to determine the relative percentages of two components when the mixture being analyzed may be more complex and may contain more than two components. Examples of this situation might include the analysis of a reaction product where the laboratory worker might be interested in the relative percentages of two isomeric products when the sample might also contain peaks arising from the solvent, unreacted starting material, or some other product or impurity.

The example provided in Figures 22.14 and 22.15 can be used to illustrate the method of determining the relative percentages of some, but not all, of the components in the sample. Assume we are interested in the relative percentages of hexane and ethyl acetate in the sample but not in the percentage of benzene, which may be a solvent or an impurity. We know from the previous discussion that the *corrected* relative areas of the two peaks of interest are as follows:

	Relative Area
Hexane	491000
Ethyl acetate	136000
Total	627000

We can determine the relative percentages of the two components simply by dividing the area of each peak by the total area of the two peaks:

		Percentage
Hexane	491000/627000	78.3%
Ethyl acetate	136000/627000	21.7%
Total		100.0%

22.13 GAS CHROMATOGRAPHY–MASS SPECTROMETRY (GC–MS)

A recently developed variation on gas chromatography is **gas chromatography–mass spectrometry,** also known as **GC–MS.** In this technique, a gas chromatograph is coupled to a mass spectrometer (see Technique 28). In effect, the mass spectrometer acts as a detector. The gas stream emerging from the gas chromatograph is admitted through a valve into a tube, where it passes over the sample inlet system of the mass spectrometer. Some of the gas stream is thus admitted into the ionization chamber of the mass spectrometer.

The molecules in the gas stream are converted into ions in the ionization chamber, and thus the gas chromatogram is actually a plot of time versus **ion current,** a measure of the number of ions produced. At the same time that the molecules are converted into ions, they are also accelerated and passed through the **mass analyzer** of the instrument. The instrument, therefore, determines the mass spectrum of each fraction eluting from the gas chromatography column.

A drawback of this method involves the need for rapid scanning by the mass spectrometer. The instrument must determine the mass spectrum of each component in the mixture before the next component exits from the column so that the spectrum of one substance is not contaminated by the spectrum of the next fraction.

Because high-efficiency capillary columns are used in the gas chromatograph, in most cases compounds are completely separated before the gas stream is analyzed. The typical GC–MS instrument has the capability of obtaining at least one scan per second in the range of 10–300 amu. Even more scans are possible if a narrow range of masses is analyzed. Using capillary columns, however, requires the user to take particular care to ensure that the sample does not contain any particles that might obstruct the flow of gases through the column. For this reason, the sample is carefully filtered through a very fine filter before the sample is injected into the chromatograph.

With a GC–MS system, a mixture can be analyzed and results obtained that resemble very closely those shown in Figures 22.14 and 22.15. A library search on each component of the mixture can also be conducted. The data stations of most instruments contain a library of standard mass spectra in their computer memory. If the components are known compounds, they can be identified tentatively by a comparison of their mass spectrum with the spectra of compounds found in the computer library. In this way, a "hit list" can be generated that reports on the probability that the compound in the library matches the known substance. A typical printout from a GC–MS instrument will list probable compounds that fit the mass spectrum of the component, the names of the compounds, their CAS Nos. (see Technique 29, Section 29.11, p. 993), and a "quality" or "confidence" number. This last number provides an estimate of how closely the mass spectrum of the component matches the mass spectrum of the substance in the computer library.

A variation on the GC–MS technique includes coupling a Fourier-transform infrared spectrometer (FT–IR) to a gas chromatograph. The substances that elute from the gas chromatograph are detected by determining their infrared spectra rather than their mass spectra. A new technique that also resembles GC–MS is **high-performance liquid chromatography–mass spectrometry (HPLC–MS).** An HPLC instrument is coupled through a special interface to a mass spectrometer. The substances that elute from the HPLC column are detected by the mass spectrometer, and their mass spectra can be displayed, analyzed, and compared with standard spectra found in the computer library built into the instrument.

PROBLEMS

1. a. A sample consisting of 1-bromopropane and 1-chloropropane is injected into a gas chromatograph equipped with a nonpolar column. Which compound has the shorter retention time? Explain your answer.

b. If the same sample were run several days later with the conditions as nearly the same as possible, would you expect the retention times to be identical to those obtained the first time? Explain.

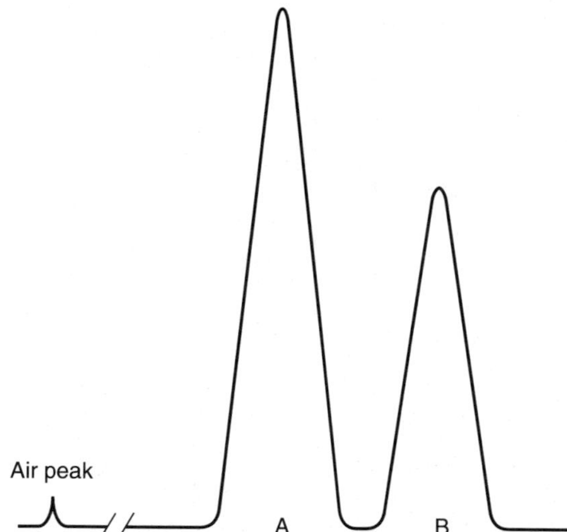

Figure 22.16 A chromatogram for problem 2.

2. Using triangulation, calculate the percentage of each component in a mixture composed of two substances, A and B. The chromatogram is shown in Figure 22.16.

3. Make a photocopy of the chromatogram in Figure 22.16. Cut out the peaks and weigh them on an analytical balance. Use the weights to calculate the percentage of each component in the mixture. Compare your answer to what you calculated in problem 2.

4. What would happen to the retention time of a compound if the following changes were made?

- **a.** Decrease the flow rate of the carrier gas
- **b.** Increase the temperature of the column
- **c.** Increase the length of the column

TECHNIQUE 18

Steam Distillation

The simple, fractional, and vacuum distillations described in Techniques 14, 15, and 16 are applicable to completely soluble (miscible) mixtures only. When liquids are *not* mutually soluble (immiscible), they can also be distilled but with a somewhat different result. A mixture of immiscible liquids will boil at a lower temperature than the boiling points of any of the separate components as pure compounds. When steam is used to provide one of the immiscible phases, the process is called **steam distillation.** The advantage of this technique is that the desired material distills at a temperature below 100°C. Thus, if unstable or very high-boiling substances are to be removed from a mixture, decomposition is avoided. Because all gases mix, the two substances can mix in the vapor and codistill. Once the distillate is cooled, the desired component, which is not miscible, separates from the water. Steam distillation is used widely in isolating liquids from natural sources. It is also used in removing a reaction product from a tarry reaction mixture.

Part A. Theory

18.1 DIFFERENCES BETWEEN DISTILLATION OF MISCIBLE AND IMMISCIBLE MIXTURES

$$\text{Miscible liquids} \qquad P_{\text{total}} = P_{\text{A}}^{0}N_{\text{A}} + P_{\text{B}}^{0}N_{\text{B}} \tag{1}$$

Two liquids A and B that are mutually soluble (miscible) and that do not interact form an ideal solution and follow Raoult's Law, as shown in equation 1. Note that the vapor pressures of pure liquids P_{A}^{0} and P_{B}^{0} are not added directly to give the total pressure P_{total} but are reduced by the respective mole fractions N_{A} and N_{B}. The total pressure above a miscible or homogeneous solution will depend on P_{A}^{0} and P_{B}^{0} and also on N_{A} and N_{B}. Thus, the composition of the vapor will depend on *both* the vapor pressures and the mole fractions of each component.

$$\text{Immiscible liquids} \qquad P_{\text{total}} = P_{\text{A}}^{0} + P_{\text{B}}^{0} \tag{2}$$

In contrast, when two mutually insoluble (immiscible) liquids are "mixed" to give a heterogeneous mixture, each exerts its own vapor pressure, independently of the other, as shown in equation 2. The mole fraction term does not appear in this equation, because the compounds are not miscible. You simply add the vapor pressures of the pure liquids P_{A}^{0} and P_{B}^{0} at a given temperature to obtain the total pressure above the mixture. When the total pressure equals 760 mmHg, the mixture boils. The composition of the vapor from an immiscible mixture, in contrast to that of the miscible mixture, is determined only by the vapor pressures of the two substances codistilling. Equation 3 defines the composition of the vapor from an immiscible mixture. Calculations involving this equation are given in Section 18.2.

$$\frac{\text{Moles A}}{\text{Moles B}} = \frac{P_{\text{A}}^{0}}{P_{\text{B}}^{0}} \tag{3}$$

A mixture of two immiscible liquids boils at a lower temperature than the boiling points of either component. The explanation for this behavior is similar to that given for minimum-boiling-point azeotropes (Technique 15, Section 15.7). Immiscible liquids behave as they do because an extreme incompatibility between the two liquids leads to higher combined vapor pressure than Raoult's Law would predict. The higher combined vapor pressures cause a lower boiling point for the mixture than for either single component. Thus, you may think of steam distillation as a special type of azeotropic distillation in which the substance is completely insoluble in water.

The differences in behavior of miscible and immiscible liquids, where it is assumed that P_{A}^{0} equals P_{B}^{0}, are shown in Figure 18.1. Note that with miscible liquids, the composition of the vapor depends on the relative amounts of A and B present (Figure 18.1A). Thus, the composition of the vapor must change during a distillation. In contrast, the composition of the vapor with immiscible liquids is independent of the amounts of A and B present (Figure 18.1B). Hence, the vapor composition must remain *constant* during the distillation of

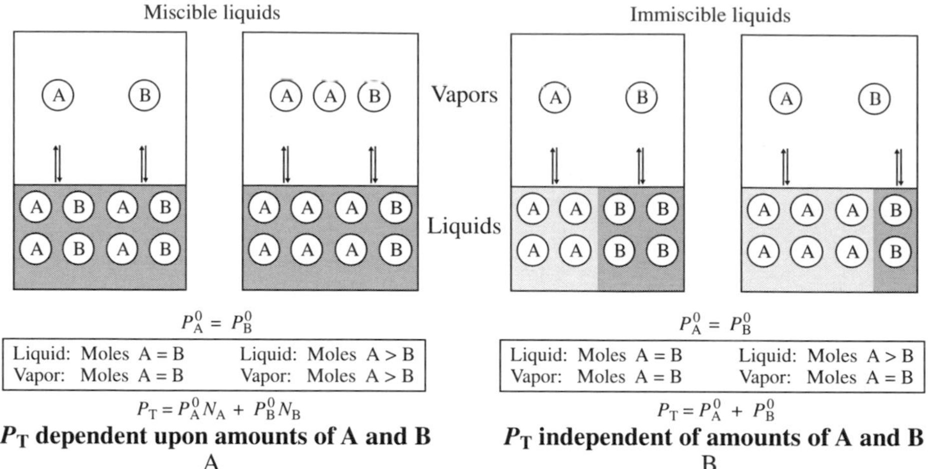

Figure 18.1 Total pressure behavior for miscible and immiscible liquids. (A) Ideal miscible liquids follow Raoult's Law: P_T depends on the mole fractions and vapor pressures of A and B. (B) Immiscible liquids do not follow Raoult's Law: P_T depends only on the vapor pressures of A and B.

such liquids, as predicted by equation 3. Immiscible liquids act as if they were being distilled simultaneously from separate compartments, as shown in Figure 18.1B, even though in practice they are "mixed" during a steam distillation. Because all gases mix, they do give rise to a homogeneous vapor and codistill.

18.2 IMMISCIBLE MIXTURES: CALCULATIONS

The composition of the distillate is constant during a steam distillation, as is the boiling point of the mixture. The boiling points of steam-distilled mixtures will always be below the boiling point of water (bp 100°C) as well as the boiling point of any of the other substances distilled. Some representative boiling points and compositions of steam distillates are given in Table 18.1. Note that the higher the boiling point of a pure substance, the more closely the temperature of the steam distillate approaches, but does not exceed, 100°C. This is a reasonably low temperature, and it avoids the decomposition that might result at high temperatures with a simple distillation.

For immiscible liquids, the molar proportions of two components in a distillate equal the ratio of their vapor pressures in the boiling mixture, as given in equation 3. When equation 3 is rewritten for an immiscible mixture involving water, equation 4 results. Equation 4 can be modified by substituting the relation moles = (weight/molecular weight) to give equation 5.

$$\frac{\text{Moles substance}}{\text{Moles water}} = \frac{P^0_{\text{substance}}}{P^0_{\text{water}}} \qquad (4)$$

TABLE 18.1 Boiling Points and Compositions of Steam Distillates

Mixture	Boiling Point of Pure Substance (°C)	Boiling Point of Mixture (°C)	Composition (% water)
Benzene–water	80.1	69.4	8.9%
Toluene–water	110.6	85.0	20.2%
Hexane–water	69.0	61.6	5.6%
Heptane–water	98.4	79.2	12.9%
Octane–water	125.7	89.6	25.5%
Nonane–water	150.8	95.0	39.8%
1-Octanol–water	195.0	99.4	90.0%

TABLE 18.2 Sample Calculations for a Steam Distillation

Problem: How many grams of water must be distilled to steam distill 1.55 g of 1-octanol from an aqueous solution? What will be the composition (wt%) of the distillate? The mixture distills at 99.4°C.

Answer: The vapor pressure of water at 99.4°C must be obtained from the CRC Handbook (= 744 mmHg).

a. Obtain the partial pressure of 1-octanol.

$$P^{\circ}_{\text{1-octanol}} = P_{\text{total}} - P^{\circ}_{\text{water}}$$

$$P^{\circ}_{\text{1-octanol}} = (760 - 744) = 16 \text{ mmHg}$$

b. Obtain the composition of the distillate.

$$\frac{\text{wt 1-octanol}}{\text{wt water}} = \frac{(16)(130)}{(744)(18)} = 0.155 \text{ g/g-water}$$

c. Clearly, 10 g of water must be distilled.

$$(0.155 \text{ g/g-water})(10 \text{ g-water}) = 1.55 \text{ g 1-octanol}$$

d. Calculate the weight percentages.

$$\text{1-octanol} = 1.55 \text{ g}/(10 \text{ g} + 1.55 \text{ g}) = 13.4\%$$

$$\text{water} = 10 \text{ g}/(10 \text{ g} + 1.55 \text{ g}) = 86.6\%$$

$$\frac{\text{Wt substance}}{\text{Wt water}} = \frac{(P^0_{\text{substance}})(\text{Molecular weight}_{\text{substance}})}{(P^0_{\text{water}})(\text{Molecular weight}_{\text{water}})} \qquad (5)$$

A sample calculation using this equation is given in Table 18.2. Notice that the result of this calculation is very close to the experimental value given in Table 18.1.

Part B. Macroscale Distillation

18.3 STEAM DISTILLATION—MACROSCALE METHODS

Two methods for steam distillation are in general use in the laboratory: the **direct method** and the **live steam method.** In the first method, steam is generated *in situ* (in place) by heating a distillation flask containing the compound and water. In the second method, steam is generated outside and is passed into the distillation flask using an inlet tube.

A. Direct Method

A macroscale direct method steam distillation is illustrated in Figure 18.2. Although a heating mantle may be used, it is probably best to use a flame with this method, because a large volume of water must be heated rapidly. A boiling stone must be used to prevent bumping. The separatory funnel allows more water to be added during the course of the distillation.

Distillate is collected as long as it is either cloudy or milky white in appearance. Cloudiness indicates that an immiscible liquid is separating. When the distillate runs clear

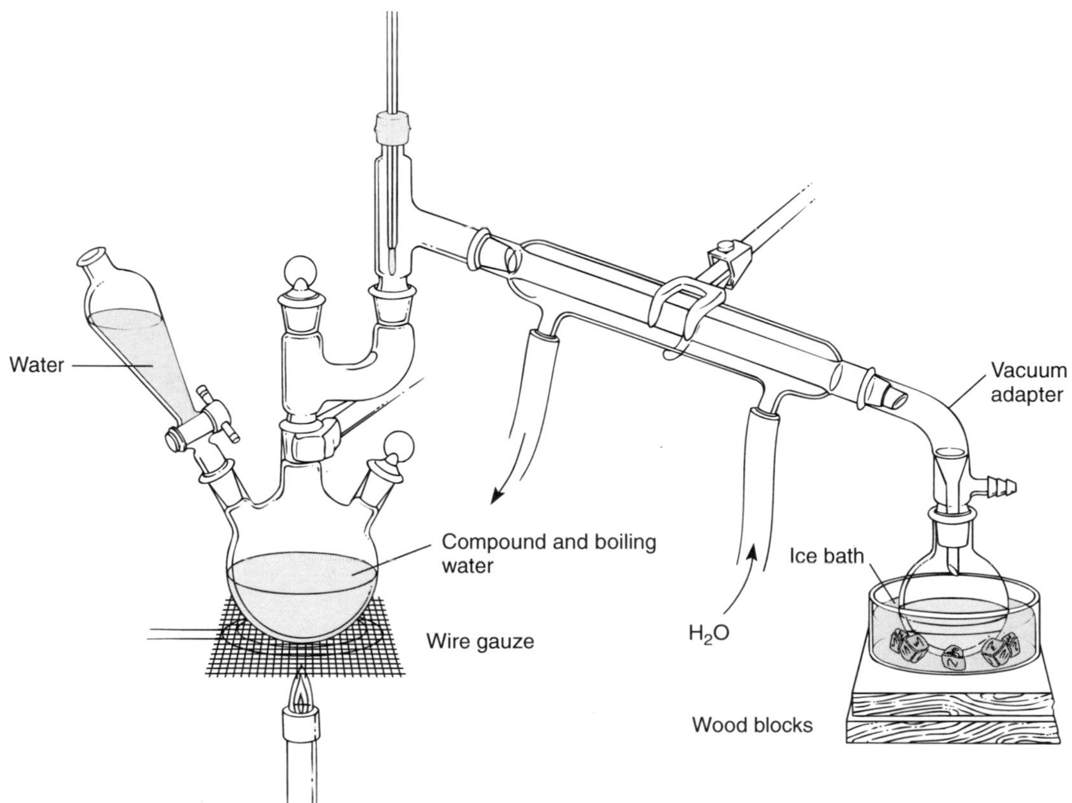

Figure 18.2 A macroscale direct method steam distillation.

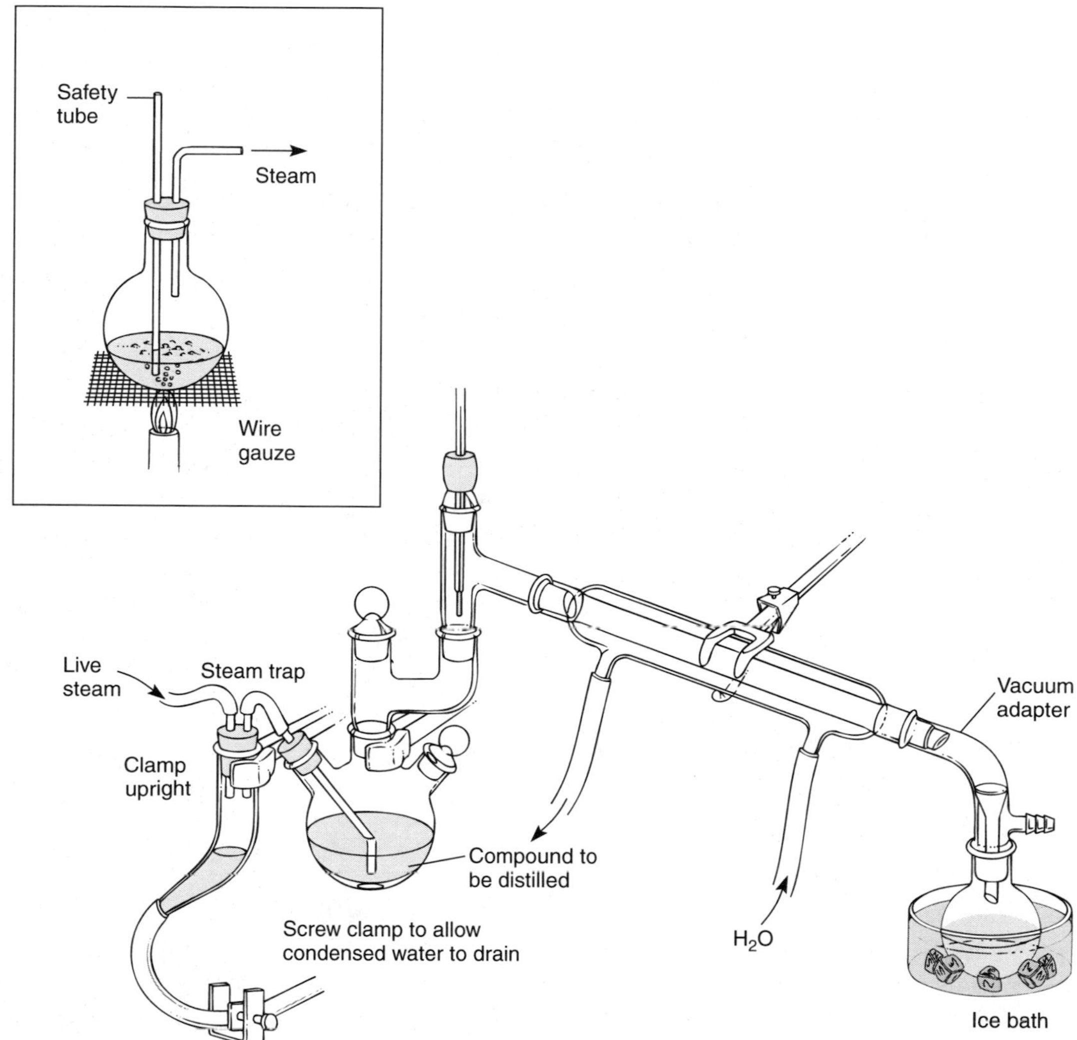

Figure 18.3 A macroscale steam distillation using live steam.

in the distillation, it is usually a sign that only water is distilling. However, there are some steam distillations where the distillate is never cloudy, even though material has codistilled. You must observe carefully, and be sure to collect enough distillate so that all of the organic material codistills.

B. Live Steam Method

A macroscale steam distillation using the live steam method is shown in Figure 18.3. If steam lines are available in the laboratory, they may be attached directly to the steam trap (purge them first to drain water). If steam lines are not available, an external steam generator (see inset) must be prepared. The external generator usually will require a flame to produce steam at a rate fast enough for the distillation. When the distillation is first started, the clamp at the bottom of the steam trap is left open. The steam lines will have a large quantity of condensed water in them until they are well heated. When the lines become hot and condensation of steam ceases, the clamp may be closed. Occasionally, the clamp will have to be reopened to remove condensate. In this method, the steam agitates the mixture as it enters the bottom of the flask, and a stirrer or boiling stone is not required.

Caution: Hot steam can produce very severe burns.

Sometimes it is helpful to heat the three-necked distilling flask with a heating mantle (or flame) to prevent excessive condensation at that point. Steam must be admitted at a fast enough rate for you to see the distillate condensing as a milky white fluid in the condenser. The vapors that codistill will separate on cooling to give this cloudiness. When the condensate becomes clear, the distillation is near the end. The flow of water through the condenser should be faster than in other types of distillation to help cool the vapors. Make sure the vacuum adapter remains cool to the touch. An ice bath may be used to cool the receiving flask if desired. When the distillation is to be stopped, the screw clamp on the steam trap should be opened, and the steam inlet tube must be removed from the three-necked flask. If this is not done, liquid will back up into the tube and steam trap.

Part C. Microscale Distillation

18.4 STEAM DISTILLATION—MICROSCALE METHODS

The direct method of steam distillation is the only one suitable for microscale experiments. Steam is produced in the conical vial or distillation flask (*in situ*) by heating water to its boiling point in the presence of the compound to be distilled. This method works well for small amounts of materials. A microscale steam distillation apparatus is shown in Figure 18.4. Water and the compound to be distilled are placed in the flask and heated. A stirring bar or a boiling stone should be used to prevent bumping. The vapors of the water and the desired compound codistill when they are heated. They are condensed and collect in the Hickman head. When the Hickman head fills, the distillate is removed with a Pasteur pipet and placed in another vial for storage. For the typical microscale experiment, it will be necessary to fill the well and remove the distillate three or four times. All of these distillate fractions are placed in the same storage container. The efficiency in collecting the distillate can sometimes be improved if the inside walls of the Hickman head are rinsed several times into the well. A Pasteur pipet is used to perform the rinsing. Distillate is withdrawn from the well, and then it is used to wash the walls of the Hickman head all the way around the head. After the walls have been washed and when the well is full, the distillate can be withdrawn and transferred to the storage container. It may be necessary to add more water during the course of the distillation. More water is added (remove the condenser if used) through the center of the Hickman head by using a Pasteur pipet.

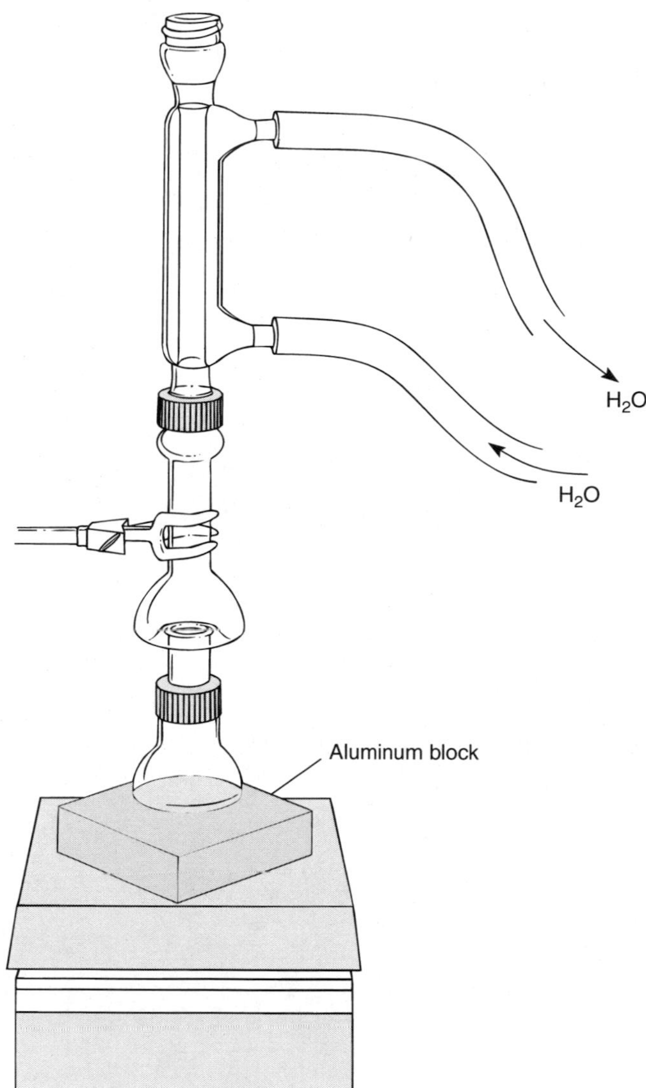

Figure 18.4 Microscale steam distillation.

Part D. Semi-microscale Distillation

18.5 STEAM DISTILLATION—SEMI-MICROSCALE METHODS

The apparatus shown in Figure 14.5, p. 741, may also be used to perform a steam distillation at the microscale level or slightly above. This apparatus avoids the need to empty the collected distillate during the course of the distillation as is required when a Hickman head is used.

PROBLEMS

1. Calculate the weight of benzene codistilled with each gram of water and the percentage composition of the vapor produced during a steam distillation. The boiling point of the mixture is 69.4°C. The vapor pressure of water at 69.4°C is 227.7 mmHg. Compare the result with the data in Table 18.1.

2. Calculate the approximate boiling point of a mixture of bromobenzene and water at atmospheric pressure. A table of vapor pressure of water and bromobenzene at various temperatures is given.

	Vapor Pressures (mmHg)	
Temperature (°C)	**Water**	**Bromobenzene**
93	588	110
94	611	114
95	634	118
96	657	122
97	682	127
98	707	131
99	733	136

3. Calculate the weight of nitrobenzene that codistills (bp 99°C of mixture) with each gram of water during a steam distillation. You may need the data given in problem 2.

4. A mixture of *p*-nitrophenol and *o*-nitrophenol can be separated by steam distillation. The *o*-nitrophenol is steam volatile, and the *para* isomer is not volatile. Explain. Base your answer on the ability of the isomers to form hydrogen bonds internally.

EXPERIMENT 23

Synthesis of *n*-Butyl Bromide and *t*-Pentyl Chloride

Synthesis of alkyl halides
Extraction
Simple distillation

The synthesis of two alkyl halides from alcohols is the basis for these experiments. In the first experiment, a primary alkyl halide *n*-butyl bromide is prepared as shown in equation 1.

$$\underset{n\text{-Butyl alcohol}}{CH_3\text{-}CH_2\text{-}CH_2\text{-}CH_2\text{-}OH} + NaBr + H_2SO_4 \longrightarrow \underset{n\text{-Butyl bromide}}{CH_3\text{-}CH_2\text{-}CH_2\text{-}CH_2\text{-}Br} + NaHSO_4 + H_2O \qquad (1)$$

In the second experiment, a tertiary alkyl halide *t*-pentyl chloride is prepared as shown in equation 2.

$$\underset{t\text{-Pentyl alcohol}}{CH_3{-}CH_2{-}\overset{\displaystyle CH_3}{\underset{\displaystyle OH}{C}}{-}CH_3} + HCl \longrightarrow \underset{t\text{-Pentyl chloride}}{CH_3{-}CH_2{-}\overset{\displaystyle CH_3}{\underset{\displaystyle Cl}{C}}{-}CH_3} + H_2O \qquad (2)$$

These reactions provide an interesting contrast in mechanisms. The *n*-butyl bromide synthesis proceeds by an S_N2 mechanism, while *t*-pentyl chloride is prepared by an S_N1 reaction.

n-BUTYL BROMIDE

The primary alkyl halide *n*-butyl bromide can be prepared easily by allowing *n*-butyl alcohol to react with sodium bromide and sulfuric acid by equation 1. The sodium bromide reacts with sulfuric acid to produce hydrobromic acid.

$$2\ NaBr + H_2SO_4 \longrightarrow 2\ HBr + Na_2SO_4$$

Excess sulfuric acid serves to shift the equilibrium and thus to speed the reaction by producing a higher concentration of hydrobromic acid. The sulfuric acid also protonates the hydroxyl group of *n*-butyl alcohol so that water is displaced rather than the hydroxide ion OH^-. The acid also protonates the water as it is produced in the reaction and deactivates it as a nucleophile. Deactivation of water keeps the alkyl halide from being converted back to the alcohol by nucleophilic attack of water. The reaction of the primary substrate proceeds via an S_N2 mechanism.

$$CH_3{-}CH_2{-}CH_2{-}CH_2{-}O{-}H + H^+ \xrightarrow{\text{fast}} CH_3{-}CH_2{-}CH_2{-}CH_2{-}\overset{+}{O}(H){-}H$$

$$CH_3{-}CH_2{-}CH_2{-}CH_2{-}\overset{+}{O}(H){-}H + Br^- \xrightarrow[S_N2]{\text{slow}} CH_3{-}CH_2{-}CH_2{-}CH_2{-}Br + H_2O$$

During the isolation of the *n*-butyl bromide, the crude product is washed with sulfuric acid, water, and sodium bicarbonate to remove any remaining acid or *n*-butyl alcohol.

t-PENTYL CHLORIDE

The tertiary alkyl halide can be prepared by allowing *t*-pentyl alcohol to react with concentrated hydrochloric acid according to equation 2. The reaction is accomplished simply by shaking the two reagents in a separatory funnel. As the reaction proceeds, the insoluble alkyl halide product forms an upper phase. The reaction of the tertiary substrate occurs via an S_N1 mechanism.

$$CH_3{-}CH_2{-}C(CH_3)(OH){-}CH_3 + H^+ \xrightarrow{\text{fast}} CH_3{-}CH_2{-}C(CH_3)(\overset{+}{O}H_2){-}CH_3$$

$$CH_3{-}CH_2{-}C(CH_3)(\overset{+}{O}H_2){-}CH_3 \xrightarrow{\text{slow}} CH_3{-}CH_2{-}\overset{+}{C}(CH_3){-}CH_3 + H_2O$$

$$CH_3{-}CH_2{-}\overset{+}{C}(CH_3){-}CH_3 + Cl^- \xrightarrow{\text{fast}} CH_3{-}CH_2{-}C(CH_3)(Cl){-}CH_3$$

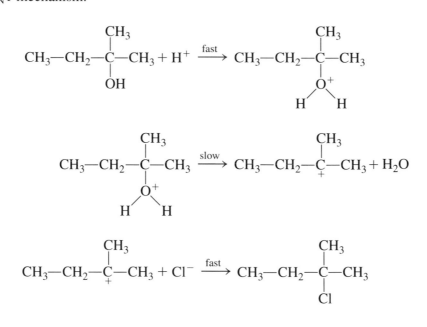

A small amount of alkene, 2-methyl-2-butene, is produced as a by-product in this reaction. If sulfuric acid had been used as it was for *n*-butyl bromide, a much larger amount of this alkene would have been produced.

Required Reading

Review: Techniques 5, 6, 7, 12, and 14

Special Instructions

Caution: Take special care with concentrated sulfuric acid; it causes severe burns.

As your instructor indicates, perform either the *n*-butyl bromide or the *t*-pentyl chloride procedure, or both.

Suggested Waste Disposal

Dispose of all aqueous solutions produced in this experiment in the container marked for the disposal of aqueous waste. If your instructor asks you to dispose of your alkyl halide product, dispose of it in the container marked for the disposal of alkyl halides. Note that your instructor may have specific instructions for the disposal of wastes that differ from the instructions given here.

EXPERIMENT 23A

n-Butyl Bromide

Procedure

Preparation of *n*-Butyl Bromide. Place 17.0 g of sodium bromide in a 100-mL round-bottom flask and add 17 mL of water and 10.0 mL of *n*-butyl alcohol (1-butanol, $MW = 74.1$, $d = 0.81$ g/mL). Cool the mixture in an ice bath and slowly add 14 mL of concentrated sulfuric acid with continuous swirling in the ice bath. Add several boiling stones to the mixture and assemble the reflux apparatus and trap shown in the figure. The trap absorbs the hydrogen bromide gas evolved during the reaction period. Heat the mixture to a gentle boil for 60–75 minutes.

Extraction. Remove the heat source and allow the apparatus to cool until you can disconnect the round-bottom flask without burning your fingers.

Note: Do not allow the reaction mixture to cool to room temperature. Complete the operations in this paragraph as quickly as possible. Otherwise, salts may precipitate, making this procedure more difficult to perform.

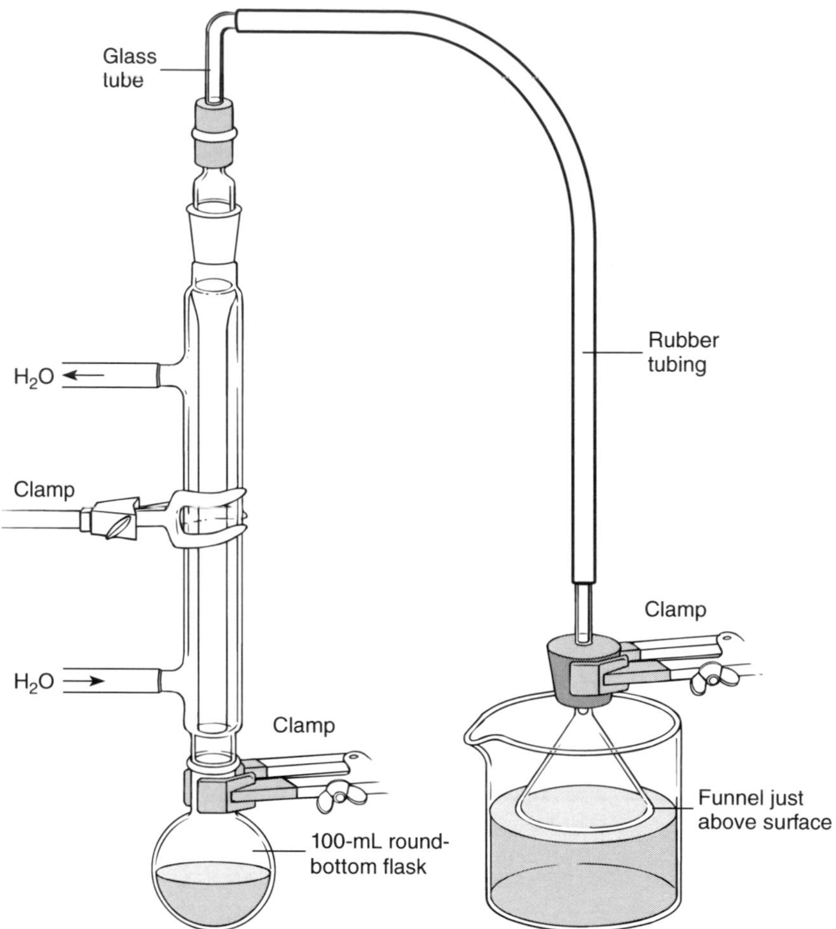

Apparatus for preparing *n*-butyl bromide.

Disconnect the round-bottom flask and carefully pour the reaction mixture into a 125-mL separatory funnel. The *n*-butyl bromide layer should be on top. If the reaction is not yet complete, the remaining *n*-butyl alcohol will sometimes form a *second organic layer* on top of the *n*-butyl bromide layer. Treat both organic layers as if they were one. Drain the lower aqueous layer from the funnel.

The organic and aqueous layers should separate as described in the following instructions. However, to make sure that you do not discard the wrong layer, it would be a good idea to add a drop of water to any aqueous layer you plan to discard. If a drop of water dissolves in the liquid, you can be confident that it is an aqueous layer. Add 14 mL of 9 *M* H_2SO_4 to the separatory funnel and shake the mixture (Technique 12, Section 12.4, p. 704). Allow the layers to separate. Because any remaining *n*-butyl alcohol is extracted by the H_2SO_4 solution, there should now be only one organic layer. The organic layer should be the top layer. Drain and discard the lower aqueous layer.

Add 14 mL H_2O to the separatory funnel. Stopper the funnel and shake it, venting occasionally. Allow the layers to separate. Drain the lower layer, which contains *n*-butyl bromide (d = 1.27 g/mL), into a small beaker. Discard the aqueous layer after making certain the correct layer has been saved. Return the alkyl halide to the funnel. Add 14 mL of saturated aqueous sodium bicarbonate, a little at a time, while swirling. Stopper the funnel and shake it for 1 minute, venting frequently to relieve any pressure that is produced. Drain the lower alkyl halide layer into a dry Erlenmeyer flask. Add 1.0 g of anhydrous calcium chloride to dry the solution Technique 12, Section 12.9, p. 713). Stopper the flask and swirl the contents until the liquid is *clear.* The drying process can be accelerated by gently warming the mixture on a steam bath.

Distillation. Transfer the clear liquid to a *dry* 25-mL round-bottom flask using a Pasteur pipet. Add a boiling stone and distill the crude *n*-butyl bromide in a *dry* apparatus (Technique 14, Section 14.1, Figure 14.1, p. 734). Collect the material that boils between 94°C and 102°C. Weigh the product, calculate the percentage yield, and determine a microscale boiling point. Determine the infrared spectrum of the product using salt plates (Technique 25, Section 25.2, p. 875). Submit the remainder of your sample in a properly labeled vial, along with the infrared spectrum, when you submit your report to the instructor.

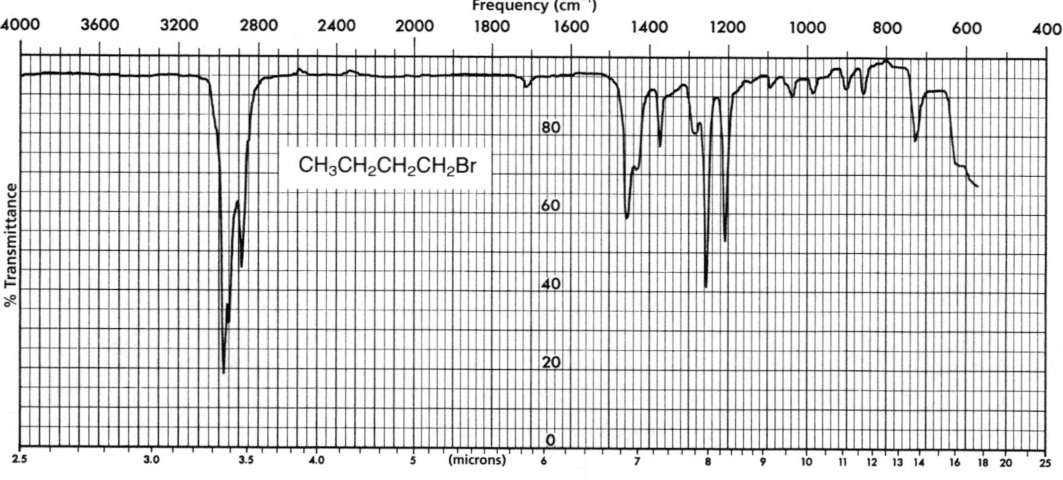

Infrared spectrum of *n*-butyl bromide (neat).

EXPERIMENT 23B

t-Pentyl Chloride

Procedure

Preparation of *t*-Pentyl Chloride. In a 125-mL separatory funnel, place 10.0 mL of *t*-pentyl alcohol (2-methyl-2-butanol, *MW* = 88.2, *d* = 0.805 g/mL) and 25 mL of concentrated hydrochloric acid (*d* = 1.18 g/mL). Do not stopper the funnel. Gently swirl the mixture in the separatory funnel for about 1 minute. After this period of swirling, stopper the separatory funnel and carefully invert it. Without shaking the separatory funnel, immediately open the stopcock to release the pressure. Close the stopcock, shake the funnel several times, and again release the pressure through the stopcock (Technique 12, Section 12.4, p. 704). Shake the funnel for 2–3 minutes, with occasional venting. Allow the mixture to stand in the separatory funnel until the two layers have completely separated. The *t*-pentyl chloride (d = 0.865 g/mL) should be the top layer, but be sure to verify this by adding a few drops of water. The water should dissolve in the lower (aqueous) layer. Drain and discard the lower layer.

Extraction. The operations in this paragraph should be done as rapidly as possible, because the *t*-pentyl chloride is unstable in water and sodium bicarbonate solution. It is easily hydrolyzed back to the alcohol. In each of the following steps, the organic layer should be on top; however, you should add a few drops of water to make sure. Wash (swirl and shake) the organic layer with 10 mL of water. Separate the layers and discard the aqueous phase after making certain that the proper layer has been saved. Add a 10-mL portion of 5% aqueous sodium bicarbonate to the separatory funnel. Gently swirl the funnel (unstoppered) until the contents are thoroughly mixed. Stopper the funnel and carefully invert it. Release the excess pressure through the stopcock. Gently shake the separatory funnel, with frequent release of pressure. Following this, vigorously shake the funnel, again with release of pressure, for about 1 minute. Allow the layers to separate and drain the lower aqueous layer. Wash (swirl and shake) the organic layer with one 10-mL portion of water and again drain the lower aqueous layer.

Transfer the organic layer to a small, dry Erlenmeyer flask by pouring it from the top of the separatory funnel. Dry the crude *t*-pentyl chloride over 1.0 g of anhydrous calcium chloride until it is clear (Technique 12, Section 12.9, p. 713). Swirl the alkyl halide with the drying agent to aid the drying.

Distillation. Transfer the clear liquid to a dry 25-mL round-bottom flask using a Pasteur pipet. Add a boiling stone and distill the crude *t*-pentyl chloride in a dry apparatus (Technique 14, Section 14.1, Figure 14.1, p. 734). Collect the pure *t*-pentyl chloride in a receiver cooled in ice. Collect the material that boils between 78°C and 84°C.

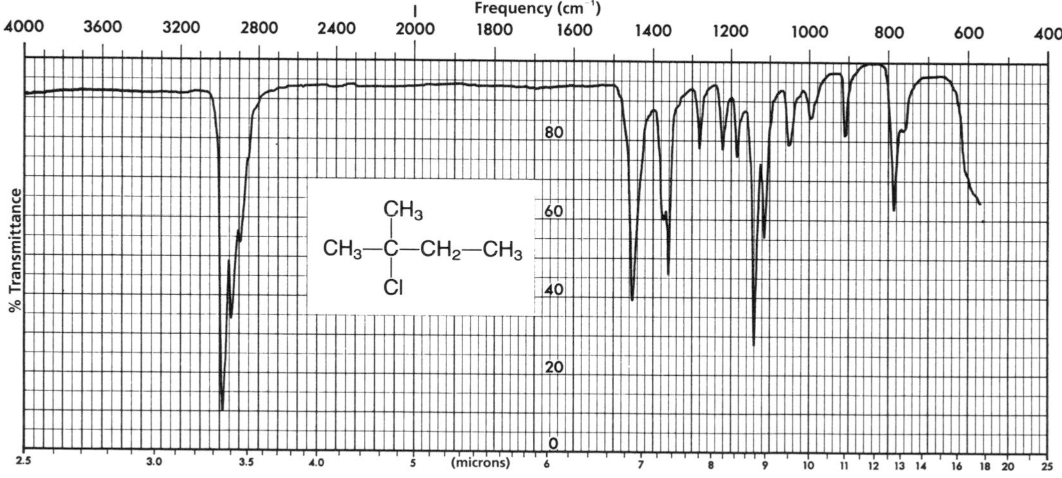

Infrared spectrum of *t*-pentyl chloride (neat).

Weigh the product, calculate the percentage yield, and determine the boiling point (Technique 13, Section 13.3 or 13.4, pp. 727–731). Determine the infrared spectrum of the product using salt plates (Technique 25, Section 25.2, p. 875). Submit the remainder of your sample in a properly labeled vial, along with the infrared spectrum, when you submit your report to the instructor.

QUESTIONS

n-Butyl Bromide

1. What are the formulas of the salts that may precipitate when the reaction mixture is cooled?

2. Why does the alkyl halide layer switch from the top layer to the bottom layer at the point where water is used to extract the organic layer?

3. An ether and an alkene are formed as by-products in this reaction. Draw the structures of these by-products and give mechanisms for their formation.

4. Aqueous sodium bicarbonate was used to wash the crude *n*-butyl bromide.

  a. What was the purpose of this wash? Give equations.

  b. Why would it be undesirable to wash the crude halide with aqueous sodium hydroxide?

5. Look up the density of *n*-butyl chloride (1-chlorobutane). Assume that this alkyl halide was prepared instead of the bromide. Decide whether the alkyl chloride would appear as the upper or lower phase at each stage of the separation procedure: after the reflux, after the addition of water, and after the addition of sodium bicarbonate.

6. Why must the alkyl halide product be dried carefully with anhydrous calcium chloride before the distillation? (*Hint:* See Technique 15, Section 15.8.)

t-Pentyl Chloride

1. Aqueous sodium bicarbonate was used to wash the crude *t*-pentyl chloride.

  a. What was the purpose of this wash? Give equations.

  b. Why would it be undesirable to wash the crude halide with aqueous sodium hydroxide?

2. Some 2-methyl-2-butene may be produced in the reaction as a by-product. Give a mechanism for its production.

3. How is unreacted *t*-pentyl alcohol removed in this experiment? Look up the solubility of the alcohol and the alkyl halide in water.

4. Why must the alkyl halide product be dried carefully with anhydrous calcium chloride before the distillation? (*Hint:* See Technique 15, Section 15.8.)

5. Will *t*-pentyl chloride (2-chloro-2-methylbutane) float on the surface of water? Look up its density in a handbook.

EXPERIMENT 20

Reactivities of Some Alkyl Halides

S_N1/S_N2 reactions
Relative rates
Reactivities

The reactivities of alkyl halides in nucleophilic substitution reactions depend on two important factors: reaction conditions and substrate structure. The reactivities of several substrate types will be examined under both S_N1 and S_N2 reaction conditions in this experiment.

SODIUM IODIDE OR POTASSIUM IODIDE IN ACETONE

A reagent composed of sodium iodide or potassium iodide dissolved in acetone is useful in classifying alkyl halides according to their reactivity in an S_N2 reaction. Iodide ion is an excellent nucleophile, and acetone is a nonpolar solvent. The tendency to form a precipitate increases the completeness of the reaction. Sodium iodide and potassium iodide are soluble in acetone, but the corresponding bromides and chlorides are not soluble. Consequently, as bromide ion or chloride ion is produced, the ion is precipitated from the solution. According to LeChâtelier's Principle, the precipitation of a product from the reaction solution drives the equilibrium toward the right; such is the case in the reaction described here:

$$R{-}Cl + Na^+I^- \longrightarrow RI + NaCl\downarrow$$

$$R{-}Br + Na^+I^- \longrightarrow RI + NaBr\downarrow$$

SILVER NITRATE IN ETHANOL

A reagent composed of silver nitrate dissolved in ethanol is useful in classifying alkyl halides according to their reactivity in an S_N1 reaction. Nitrate ion is a poor nucleophile, and ethanol is a moderately powerful ionizing solvent. The silver ion, because of its ability to coordinate the leaving halide ion to form a silver halide precipitate, greatly assists the ionization of the alkyl halide. Again, a precipitate as one of the reaction products also enhances the reaction.

$$R{-}Cl \longrightarrow \begin{matrix} R^+ \xrightarrow{C_2H_5OH} R{-}OC_2H_5 \\ + \\ Cl^- \xrightarrow{Ag^+} AgCl\downarrow \end{matrix}$$

$$R{-}Br \longrightarrow R^+ + Br^- ; \quad R^+ \xrightarrow{C_2H_5OH} R{-}OC_2H_5 ; \quad Br^- \xrightarrow{Ag^+} AgBr\downarrow$$

Required Reading

Before this experiment, review the chapters dealing with nucleophilic substitution in your lecture textbook.

Special Instructions

Some compounds used in this experiment, particularly crotyl chloride and benzyl chloride, are powerful lachrymators. **Lachrymators** cause eye irritation and the formation of tears.

> **Caution:** Because some of these compounds are lachrymators, perform these tests in a hood. Be careful to dispose of the test solutions in a waste container marked for halogenated organic waste. After testing, rinse the test tubes with acetone and pour the contents into the same waste container.

Suggested Waste Disposal

Dispose of all the halide wastes into the container marked for the disposal of these solutions. Any acetone washings should also be placed in the same container. Any leftover sodium iodide-in-acetone or silver nitrate–in-ethanol solutions should be discarded in specially marked waste containers. Note that your instructor may choose to establish a different method of collecting wastes.

Notes to the Instructor

Each of the halides should be checked with NaI/acetone and $AgNO_3$/ethanol to test for their purity before the class performs this experiment.

Procedure

PART A. SODIUM IODIDE IN ACETONE

The Experiment. Label a series of 10 clean, dry test tubes (10-mm × 75-mm test tubes may be used) from 1 to 10. In each test tube, add 2 mL of a 15% NaI-in-acetone solution. Now add 4 drops of one of the following halides to the appropriate test tube: (1) 2-chlorobutane, (2) 2-bromobutane, (3) 1-chlorobutane, (4) 1-bromobutane, (5) 2-chloro-2-methylpropane (*t*-butyl chloride), (6) crotyl chloride $CH_3CH{=}CHCH_2Cl$ (see Special Instructions), (7) benzyl chloride (α-chlorotoluene) (see Special Instructions), (8) bromobenzene, (9) bromocyclohexane, and (10) bromocyclopentane. Make certain that you return the dropper to the proper container to avoid cross-contamination of these halides.

Reaction at Room Temperature. After adding the halide, shake the test tube well to ensure adequate mixing of the alkyl halide and the solvent. Record the times needed for any precipitate or cloudiness to form.

Reaction at Elevated Temperature. After about 5 minutes, place any test tubes that do not contain a precipitate in a 50°C water bath. Be careful not to allow the temperature of the water bath to exceed 50°C, because the acetone will evaporate or boil out of the test tube. After about 1 minute of heating, cool the test tubes to room temperature and note whether a reaction has occurred. Record the results.

Observations. Generally, reactive halides give a precipitate within 3 minutes at room temperature, moderately reactive halides give a precipitate when heated, and unreactive halides do not give a precipitate even after being heated. Ignore any color changes.

Report. Record your results in tabular form in your notebook. Explain why each compound has the reactivity that you observed. Explain the reactivities in terms of structure.

PART B. SILVER NITRATE IN ETHANOL

The Experiment. Label a series of 10 clean, dry test tubes from 1 to 10, as described in the previous section. Add 2 mL of a 1% ethanolic silver nitrate solution to each test tube. Now add 4 drops of the appropriate halide to each test tube, using the same numbering scheme indicated for the sodium iodide test. Return the dropper to the proper container to avoid cross-contamination of these halides.

Reaction at Room Temperature. After adding the halide, shake the test tube well to ensure adequate mixing of the alkyl halide and the solvent. After thoroughly mixing the samples, record the times needed for any precipitate or cloudiness to form. Record your results as dense precipitate, cloudiness, or no precipitate/cloudiness.

Reaction at Elevated Temperature. After about 5 minutes, place any test tubes that do not contain a precipitate or cloudiness in a hot water bath at about 100°C. After about 1 minute of heating, cool the test tubes to room temperature and note whether a reaction has occurred. Record your results as dense precipitate, cloudiness, or no precipitate/cloudiness.

Observations. Reactive halides give a precipitate (or cloudiness) within 3 minutes at room temperature, moderately reactive halides give a precipitate (or cloudiness) when heated, and unreactive halides do not give a precipitate even after being heated. Ignore any color changes.

Report. Record your results in tabular form in your notebook. Explain why each compound has the reactivity that you observed. Explain the reactivities in terms of structure. Compare relative reactivities for compounds with similar structures.

QUESTIONS

1. In the tests with sodium iodide in acetone and silver nitrate in ethanol, why should 2-bromobutane react faster than 2-chlorobutane?
2. Why is benzyl chloride reactive in both tests, but bromobenzene is unreactive?
3. When treated with sodium iodide in acetone, benzyl chloride reacts much faster than 1-chlorobutane, even though both compounds are primary alkyl chlorides. Explain this rate difference.
4. 2-Chlorobutane reacts much more slowly than 2-chloro-2-methylpropane in the silver nitrate test. Explain this difference in reactivity.
5. Bromocyclopentane is more reactive than bromocyclohexane when heated with sodium iodide in acetone. Explain this difference in reactivity.
6. How do you expect the following series of compounds to compare in behavior in the two tests?

$CH_3-CH=CH-CH_2-Br$ $\quad$ $CH_3-C(Br)=CH-CH_3$ $\quad$ $CH_3-CH_2-CH_2-CH_2-Br$

ESSAY

Aspirin

Aspirin is one of the most popular cure-alls of modern life. Even though its curious history began over 200 years ago, we still have much to learn about this enigmatic remedy. No one yet knows exactly how or why it works, yet more than 15 billion aspirin tablets are consumed each year in the United States.

The history of aspirin began on June 2, 1763, when Edward Stone, a clergyman, read a paper to the Royal Society of London entitled "An Account of the Success of the Bark of the Willow in the Cure of Agues." By *ague,* Stone was referring to what we now call malaria, but his use of the word *cure* was optimistic; what his extract of willow bark actually did was to reduce the feverish symptoms of the disease. Almost a century later, a Scottish physician was to find that extracts of willow bark would also alleviate the symptoms of acute rheumatism. This extract was ultimately found to be a powerful **analgesic** (pain reliever), **antipyretic** (fever reducer), and **anti-inflammatory** (reduces swelling) drug.

Soon thereafter, organic chemists working with willow bark extract and flowers of the meadowsweet plant (which gave a similar compound) isolated and identified the active ingredient as salicylic acid (from *salix,* the Latin name for the willow tree). The substance could then be chemically produced in large quantities for medical use. It soon became apparent that using salicylic acid as a remedy was severely limited by its acidic properties. The substance irritated the mucous membranes lining the mouth, gullet, and stomach. The first attempts at circumventing this problem by using the less acidic sodium salt (sodium salicylate) were only partially successful. This substance was less irritating but had such an objectionable sweetish taste that most people could not be induced to take it. The breakthrough came at the turn of the century (1893) when Felix Hofmann, a chemist for the German firm of Bayer, devised a practical route for synthesizing acetylsalicylic acid, which was found to have all the same medicinal properties without the highly objectionable taste or the high degree of mucosal-membrane irritation. Bayer called its new product "aspirin," a name derived from *a-* for acetyl, and the root *-spir,* from the Latin name for the meadowsweet plant, *spirea.*

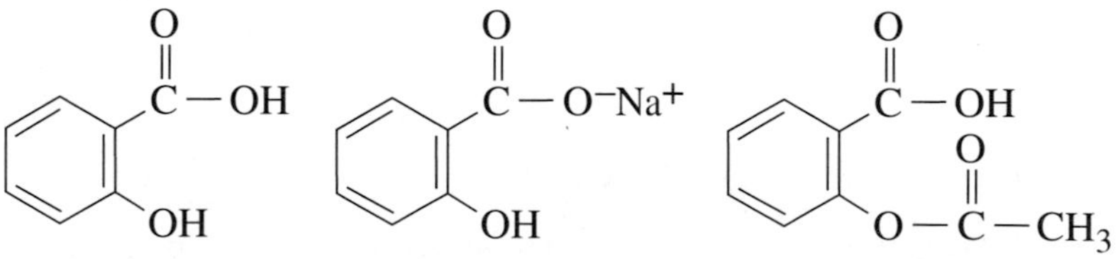

Salicylic acid | Sodium salicylate | Acetylsalicylic acid (aspirin)

The history of aspirin is typical of many of the medicinal substances in current use. Many began as crude plant extracts or folk remedies whose active ingredients were isolated and their structure was determined by chemists, who then improved on the original.

In the last few years, the mode of action of aspirin has just begun to be explained. A whole new class of compounds, called **prostaglandins,** has been found to be involved in the body's immune responses. Their synthesis is provoked by interference with the body's normal functioning by foreign substances or unaccustomed stimuli.

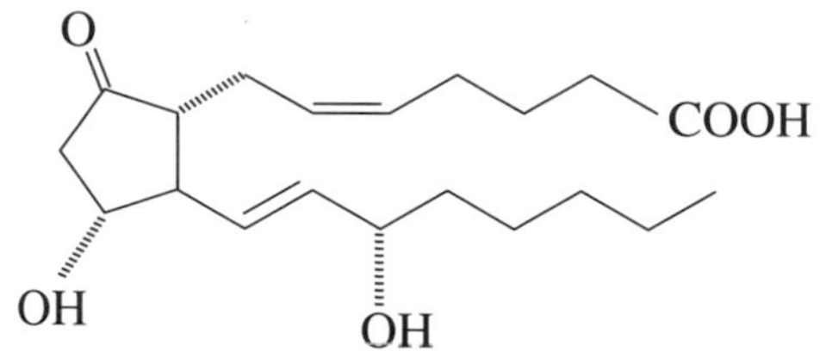

Prostaglandin E_2

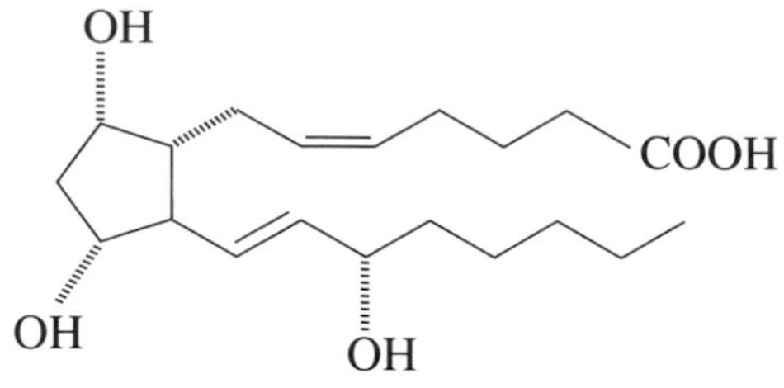

Prostaglandin $F_{2\alpha}$

These substances are involved in a wide variety of physiological processes and are thought to be responsible for evoking pain, fever, and local inflammation. Aspirin has recently been shown to prevent bodily synthesis of prostaglandins and thus to alleviate the symptomatic portion (fever, pain, inflammation, menstrual cramps) of the body's immune responses (that is, the ones that let you know something is wrong). One report suggests that aspirin may inactivate one of the enzymes responsible for the synthesis of prostaglandins. The natural precursor for prostaglandin synthesis is **arachidonic acid.** This substance is converted to a peroxide intermediate by an enzyme called **cyclo-oxygenase,** or prostaglandin synthase. This intermediate is converted further to prostaglandin. The apparent role of aspirin is to attach an acetyl group to the active site of cyclo-oxygenase, thus rendering it unable to convert arachidonic acid to the peroxide intermediate. In this way, prostaglandin synthesis is blocked.

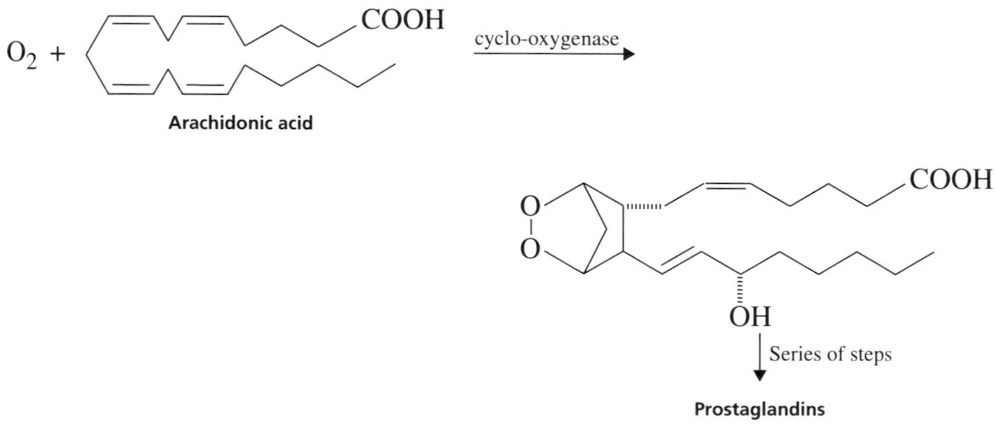

O_2 + Arachidonic acid —cyclo-oxygenase→ (peroxide intermediate) —Series of steps→ Prostaglandins

Arachidonic acid

Prostaglandins

Aspirin tablets (5-grain size) are usually compounded of about 0.32 g of acetylsalicylic acid pressed together with a small amount of starch, which binds the ingredients. Buffered aspirin usually contains a basic buffering agent to reduce the acidic irritation of mucous membranes in the stomach, because the acetylated product is not totally free of this irritating effect. Bufferin contains 0.325 g of aspirin together with calcium carbonate, magnesium oxide, and magnesium carbonate as buffering agents. Combination pain relievers usually contain aspirin, acetaminophen, and caffeine. Extra-Strength Excedrin, for instance, contains 0.250 g aspirin, 0.250 g acetaminophen, and 0.065 g caffeine.

REFERENCES

"Aspirin Cuts Deaths after Heart Attacks." *New Scientist,* 118 (April 7, 1988): 22.

Collier, H. O. J. "Aspirin." *Scientific American,* 209 (November 1963): 96.

Collier, H. O. J. "Prostaglandins and Aspirin." *Nature,* 232 (July 2, 1971): 17.

Disla, E., Rhim, H. R., Reddy, A., and Taranta, A. "Aspirin on Trial as HIV Treatment." *Nature,* 366 (November 18, 1993): 198.

Kingman, S. "Will an Aspirin a Day Keep the Doctor Away?" *New Scientist,* 117 (February 11, 1988): 26.

Kolata, G. "Study of Reye's–Aspirin Link Raises Concerns." *Science,* 227 (January 25, 1985): 391.

Macilwain, C. "Aspirin on Trial as HIV Treatment." *Nature,* 364 (July 29, 1993): 369.

Nelson, N. A., Kelly, R. C., and Johnson, R. A. "Prostaglandins and the Arachidonic Acid Cascade." *Chemical and Engineering News* (August 16, 1982): 30.

Pike, J. E. "Prostaglandins." *Scientific American,* 225 (November 1971): 84.

Roth, G. J., Stanford, N., and Majerus, P. W. "Acetylation of Prostaglandin Synthase by Aspirin." *Proceedings of the National Academy of Science of the U.S.A.,* 72 (1975): 3073.

Street, K. W. "Method Development for Analysis of Aspirin Tablets." *Journal of Chemical Education,* 65 (October 1988): 914.

Vane, J. R. "Inhibition of Prostaglandin Synthesis as a Mechanism of Action for Aspirin-Like Drugs." *Nature New Biology,* 231 (June 23, 1971): 232.

Weissmann, G. "Aspirin." *Scientific American,* 264 (January 1991): 84.

EXPERIMENT 7

Acetylsalicylic Acid

Crystallization
Vacuum filtration
Melting point
Esterification

Aspirin (acetylsalicylic acid) can be prepared by the reaction between salicylic acid and acetic anhydride:

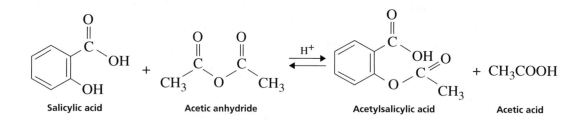

$$\text{Salicylic acid} + (CH_3CO)_2O \underset{}{\overset{H^+}{\rightleftharpoons}} \text{Acetylsalicylic acid} + CH_3COOH$$

Salicylic acid   Acetic anhydride   Acetylsalicylic acid   Acetic acid

In this reaction, the **hydroxyl group** (—OH) on the benzene ring in salicylic acid reacts with acetic anhydride to form an **ester** functional group. Thus, the formation of acetylsalicylic acid is referred to as an **esterification** reaction. This reaction requires the presence of an acid catalyst, indicated by the H^+ above the equilibrium arrows.

When the reaction is complete, some unreacted salicylic acid and acetic anhydride will be present along with acetylsalicylic acid, acetic acid, and the catalyst. The technique used to purify the acetylsalicylic acid from the other substances is called **crystallization.** The basic principle is quite simple. At the end of this reaction, the reaction mixture will be hot, and all substances will be in solution. As the solution is allowed to cool, the solubility of acetylsalicylic acid will decrease, and it will gradually come out of solution, or crystallize. Because the other substances are either liquids at room temperature or are present in much smaller amounts, the crystals formed will be composed mainly of acetylsalicylic acid. Thus, a separation of acetylsalicylic acid from the other materials will have been accomplished. The purification process is facilitated by the addition of water after the crystals have formed. The water decreases the solubility of acetylsalicylic acid and dissolves some of the impurities.

To purify thc product even more, a recrystallization procedure will also be performed. In order to prevent the decomposition of acetylsalicylic acid, ethyl acetate, rather than water, will be used as the solvent for recrystallization.

The most likely impurity in the product after purification is salicylic acid itself, which can arise from incomplete reaction of the starting materials or from **hydrolysis** (reaction with water) of the product during the isolation steps. The hydrolysis reaction of acetylsalicylic acid produces salicylic acid. Salicylic acid and other compounds that contain a hydroxyl group on the benzene ring are referred to as **phenols.** Phenols form a highly colored complex with ferric chloride (Fe^{3+} ion). Aspirin is not a phenol, because it does not possess a hydroxyl group directly attached to the ring. Because aspirin will not give the color reaction with ferric chloride, the presence of salicylic acid in the final product is easily detected. The purity of your product will also be determined by obtaining the melting point.

Required Reading

Review:	Technique 8	Filtration, Sections 8.1–8.6
	Technique 9	Physical Constants of Solids: The Melting Point
New:	Technique 5	Measurement of Volume and Weight
	Technique 6	Heating and Cooling Methods
	Technique 7	Reaction Methods, Sections 7.1, 7.4–7.6
	Technique 11	Crystallization: Purification of Solids
	Essay	Aspirin

Special Instructions

This experiment involves concentrated sulfuric acid, which is highly corrosive. It will cause burns if it is spilled on the skin. Exercise care in handling it.

Suggested Waste Disposal

Dispose of the aqueous filtrate in the container for aqueous waste. The filtrate from the recrystallization in ethyl acetate should be disposed of in the container for nonhalogenated organic waste.

Procedure

Preparation of Acetylsalicylic Acid (Aspirin). Weigh 2.0 g of salicyclic acid ($MW = 138.1$) and place this in a 125-mL Erlenmeyer flask. Add 5.0 mL of acetic anhydride ($MW = 102.1$, $d = 1.08$ g/mL), followed by 5 drops of concentrated sulfuric acid,

> **Caution:** Concentrated sulfuric acid is highly corrosive. You must handle it with great care.

and swirl the flask gently until the salicylic acid dissolves. Heat the flask gently on the steam bath or in a hot water bath at about 50°C (see Technique 6, Figure 6.4, p. 616) for at least 10 minutes. Allow the flask to cool to room temperature, during which time the acetylsalicylic acid should begin to crystallize from the reaction mixture. If it does not, scratch the walls of the flask with a glass rod and cool the mixture slightly in an ice bath until crystallization has occurred. After crystal formation is complete (usually when the product appears as a solid mass), add 50 mL of water and cool the mixture in an ice bath.

Vacuum Filtration. Collect the product by vacuum filtration on a Büchner funnel (see Technique 8, Section 8.3, p. 651, and Figure 8.5, p. 652). A small amount of additional cold water can be used to aid in the transfer of crystals to the funnel. Rinse the crystals several times with small portions of cold water. Continue drawing air through the crystals on the Büchner funnel by suction until the crystals are free of solvent (5–10 minutes). Remove the crystals for air drying. Weigh the crude product, which may contain some unreacted salicylic acid, and calculate the percentage yield of crude acetylsalicylic acid ($MW = 180.2$).

Ferric Chloride Test for Purity. You can perform this test on a sample of your product that is not completely dry. To determine if there is any salicylic acid remaining in your product, carry out the following procedure. Obtain three small test tubes. Add 0.5 mL of water to each test tube. Dissolve a small amount of salicylic acid in the first tube. Add a similar amount of your product to the second tube. The third test tube, which contains only solvent, will serve as the control. Add one drop of 1% ferric chloride solution to each tube and note the color after shaking. Formation of an iron–phenol complex with Fe(III) gives a definite color ranging from red to violet, depending on the particular phenol present.

Optional Exercise: Recrystallization.[1] Water is not a suitable solvent for crystallization because aspirin will partially decompose when heated in water. Follow the general instructions described in Technique 11, Section 11.3, page 682, and Figure 11.4, page 683. Dissolve the product in a minimum of hot ethyl acetate (no more than 2–3 mL) in a 25-mL Erlenmeyer flask, while gently and continuously heating the mixture on a steam bath or a hot plate.[2]

When the mixture cools to room temperature, the aspirin should crystallize. If it does not, evaporate some of the ethyl acetate solvent to concentrate the solution and cool the solution in ice water while scratching the inside of the flask with a glass rod (not a fire-polished one). Collect the product by vacuum filtration, using a Büchner funnel. Any remaining material can be rinsed out of the flask with a few milliliters of cold petroleum ether. Dispose of the residual solvents in the waste container for nonhalogenated organic waste. Test the aspirin for purity with ferric chloride as described on page 59. Determine the melting point of your product (see Technique 9, Sections 9.5–9.8, pp. 662–667). The melting point must be obtained with a completely dried sample. Pure aspirin has a melting point of 135–136°C.

Place your product in a small vial, label it properly (p. 583), and submit it to your instructor.

ASPIRIN TABLETS

Aspirin tablets are acetylsalicylic acid pressed together with a small amount of inert binding material. Common binding substances include starch, methylcellulose, and microcrystalline cellulose. You can test for the presence of starch by boiling approximately one-fourth of an aspirin tablet with 2 mL of water. Cool the liquid and add a drop of iodine solution. If starch is present, it will form a complex with the iodine. The starch–iodine complex is deep blue violet. Repeat this test with a commercial aspirin tablet and with the acetylsalicylic acid prepared in this experiment.

QUESTIONS

1. What is the purpose of the concentrated sulfuric acid used in the first step?
2. What would happen if the sulfuric acid were left out?
3. If you used 5.0 g of salicylic acid and excess acetic anhydride in the preceding synthesis of aspirin, what would be the theoretical yield of acetylsalicylic acid in moles? in grams?
4. What is the equation for the decomposition reaction that can occur with aspirin?
5. Most aspirin tablets contain five grains of acetylsalicylic acid. How many milligrams is this?
6. A student performed the reaction in this experiment using a water bath at 90°C instead of 50°C. The final product was tested for the presence of phenols with ferric chloride. This test was negative

[1] Crystallization is not necessary. The crude product is quite pure and is sometimes degraded by the crystallization (as judged by $FeCl_3$).

[2] It will usually not be necessary to filter the hot mixture. If an appreciable amount of solid material remains, add 5 mL of additional ethyl acetate, heat the solution to boiling, and filter the hot solution by gravity into an Erlenmeyer flask through a fluted filter. Be sure to preheat the short-stemmed funnel by pouring hot ethyl acetate through it (see Technique 8, Section 8.1, p. 645, and Technique 11, Section 11.3, p. 682). Reduce the volume until crystals appear. Add a minimum additional amount of hot ethyl acetate until the crystals dissolve. Let the filtered solution stand.

ESSAY

Local Anesthetics

Local anesthetics, or "painkillers," are a well-studied class of compounds. Chemists have shown their ability to study the essential features of a naturally occurring drug and to improve on them by substituting totally new, synthetic surrogates. Often such substitutes are superior in desired medical effects and have fewer unwanted side effects or hazards.

The coca shrub (*Erythroxylon coca*) grows wild in Peru, specifically in the Andes Mountains, at elevations of 1,500 to 6,000 ft above sea level. The natives of South America have long chewed these leaves for their stimulant effects. Leaves of the coca shrub have even been found in pre-Inca Peruvian burial urns. Chewing the leaves brings about a definite sense of mental and physical well-being and the power to increase endurance. For chewing, the Indians smear the coca leaves with lime and roll them. The lime, $Ca(OH)_2$, apparently releases the free alkaloid components; it is remarkable that the Indians learned this subtlety long ago by some empirical means. The pure alkaloid responsible for the properties of the coca leaves is **cocaine.**

The amounts of cocaine the Indians consume in this way are extremely small. Without such a crutch of central-nervous-system stimulation, the natives of the Andes would probably find it more difficult to perform the nearly Herculean tasks of their daily lives, such as carrying heavy loads over the rugged mountainous terrain. Unfortunately, overindulgence can lead to mental and physical deterioration and eventually an unpleasant death.

The pure alkaloid in large quantities is a common drug of addiction. Sigmund Freud first made a detailed study of cocaine in 1884. He was particularly impressed by the ability of the drug to stimulate the central nervous system, and he used it as a replacement drug to wean one of his addicted colleagues from morphine. This attempt was successful, but unhappily, the colleague became the world's first known cocaine addict.

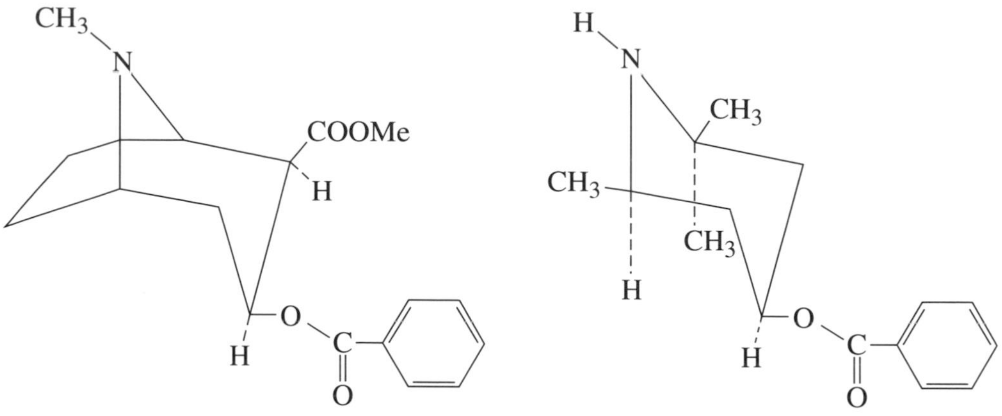

Cocaine

Eucaine

An extract from coca leaves was one of the original ingredients in Coca-Cola. However, early in the present century, government officials, with much legal difficulty, forced the manufacturer to omit coca from its beverage. The company has managed to this day to maintain the *coca* in its trademarked title, even though "Coke" contains none.

Our interest in cocaine lies in its anesthetic properties. The pure alkaloid was isolated in 1862 by Niemann, who noted that it had a bitter taste and produced a queer numbing sensation on the tongue, rendering it almost devoid of sensation. (Oh, those brave, but foolish chemists of yore who used to taste everything!) In 1880, Von Anrep found that the skin was made numb and insensitive to the prick of a pin when cocaine was injected subcutaneously. Freud and his assistant Karl Koller, having failed at attempts to rehabilitate morphine addicts, turned to a study of the anesthetizing properties of cocaine. Eye surgery is made difficult by involuntary reflex movements of the eye in response to even the slightest touch. Koller found that a few drops of a solution of cocaine would overcome this problem. Not only can cocaine serve as a local anesthetic but it can also be used to produce **mydriasis** (dilation of the pupil). The ability of cocaine to block signal conduction in nerves (particularly of pain) led to its rapid medical use in spite of its dangers. It soon found use as a "local" in both dentistry (1884) and in surgery (1885). In this type of application, it was injected directly into the particular nerves it was intended to deaden.

Soon after the structure of cocaine was established, chemists began to search for a substitute. Cocaine has several drawbacks for wide medical use as an anesthetic. In eye surgery, it also produces mydriasis. It can also become a drug of addiction. Finally, it has a dangerous effect on the central nervous system.

The first totally synthetic substitute was eucaine. It was synthesized by Harries in 1918 and retains many of the essential skeletal features of the cocaine molecule. The development of this new anesthetic partly confirmed the portion of the cocaine structure essential for local anesthetic action. The advantage of eucaine over cocaine is that it does not produce mydriasis and is not habit forming. Unfortunately, it is highly toxic.

A further attempt at simplification led to piperocaine. The molecular portion common to cocaine and eucaine is outlined by dotted lines in the structure shown on page 359. Piperocaine is only a third as toxic as cocaine itself.

The most successful synthetic for many years was the drug procaine, known more commonly by its trade name Novocain (see table). Novocain is only a fourth as toxic as co-

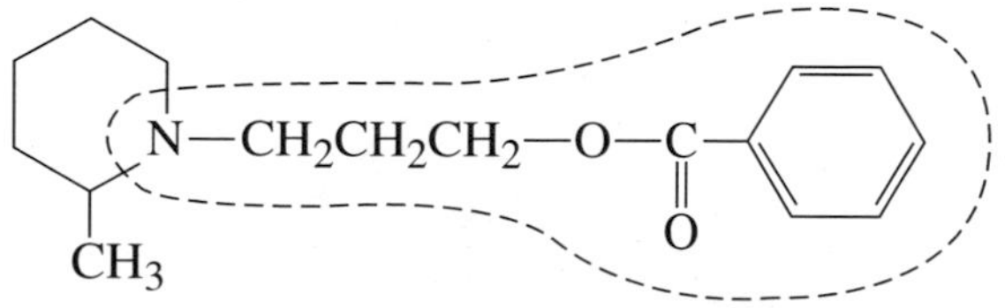

$$\text{Piperocaine: (2-methylpiperidino)}-CH_2CH_2CH_2-O-C(=O)-C_6H_5$$

Piperocaine

caine, giving a better margin of safety in its use. The toxic dose is almost 10 times the effective amount, and it is not a habit-forming drug.

Over the years, hundreds of new local anesthetics have been synthesized and tested. For one reason or another, most have not come into general use. The search for the perfect local anesthetic is still under way. All the drugs found to be active have certain structural features in common. At one end of the molecule is an aromatic ring. At the other is a secondary or tertiary amine. These two essential features are separated by a central chain of atoms usually one to four units long. The aromatic part is usually an ester of an aromatic acid. The ester group is important to the bodily detoxification of these compounds. The first step in deactivating them is a hydrolysis of this ester linkage, a process that occurs in the bloodstream. Compounds that do not have the ester link are both longer lasting in their effects and generally more toxic. An exception is lidocaine, which is an amide. The tertiary amino group is apparently necessary to enhance the solubility of the compounds in the injection solvent. Most of these compounds are used in their hydrochloride salt forms, which can be dissolved in water for injection.

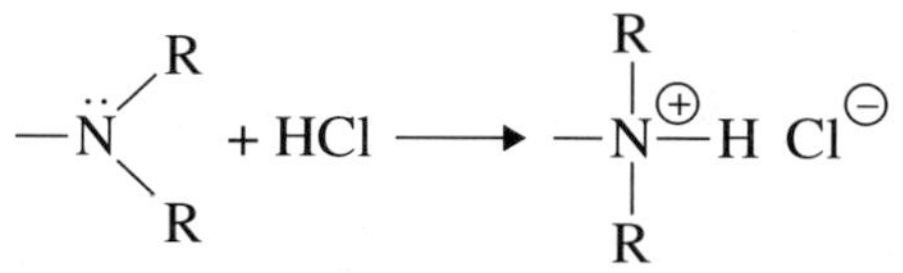

$$-\ddot{N}R_2 + HCl \longrightarrow -\overset{\oplus}{N}R_2-H \; Cl^{\ominus}$$

Benzocaine, in contrast, is active as a local anesthetic but is not used for injection. It does not suffuse well into tissue and is not water soluble. It is used primarily in skin preparations, in which it can be included in an ointment or salve for direct application. It is an ingredient of many sunburn-relief preparations.

How these drugs act to stop pain conduction is not well understood. Their main site of action is at the nerve membrane. They seem to compete with calcium at some receptor site, altering the permeability of the membrane and keeping the nerve slightly depolarized electrically.

REFERENCES

Doerge, R. F. "Local Anesthetic Agents." Chap. 22 in C. O. Wilson, O. Gisvold, and R. F. Doerge, eds., *Textbook of Organic Medicinal and Pharmaceutical Chemistry,* 6th ed. Philadelphia: J. B. Lippincott, 1971.

Foye, W. O. "Local Anesthetics." Chap. 14 in *Principles of Medicinal Chemistry.* Philadelphia: Lea & Febiger, 1974.

Ray, O. S. "Stimulants and Depressants." Chap. 11 in *Drugs, Society, and Human Behavior,* 3rd ed. St. Louis: C. V. Mosby, 1983.

Ritchie, J. M., et al. "Cocaine, Procaine and Other Synthetic Local Anesthetics." Chap. 15 in L. S.

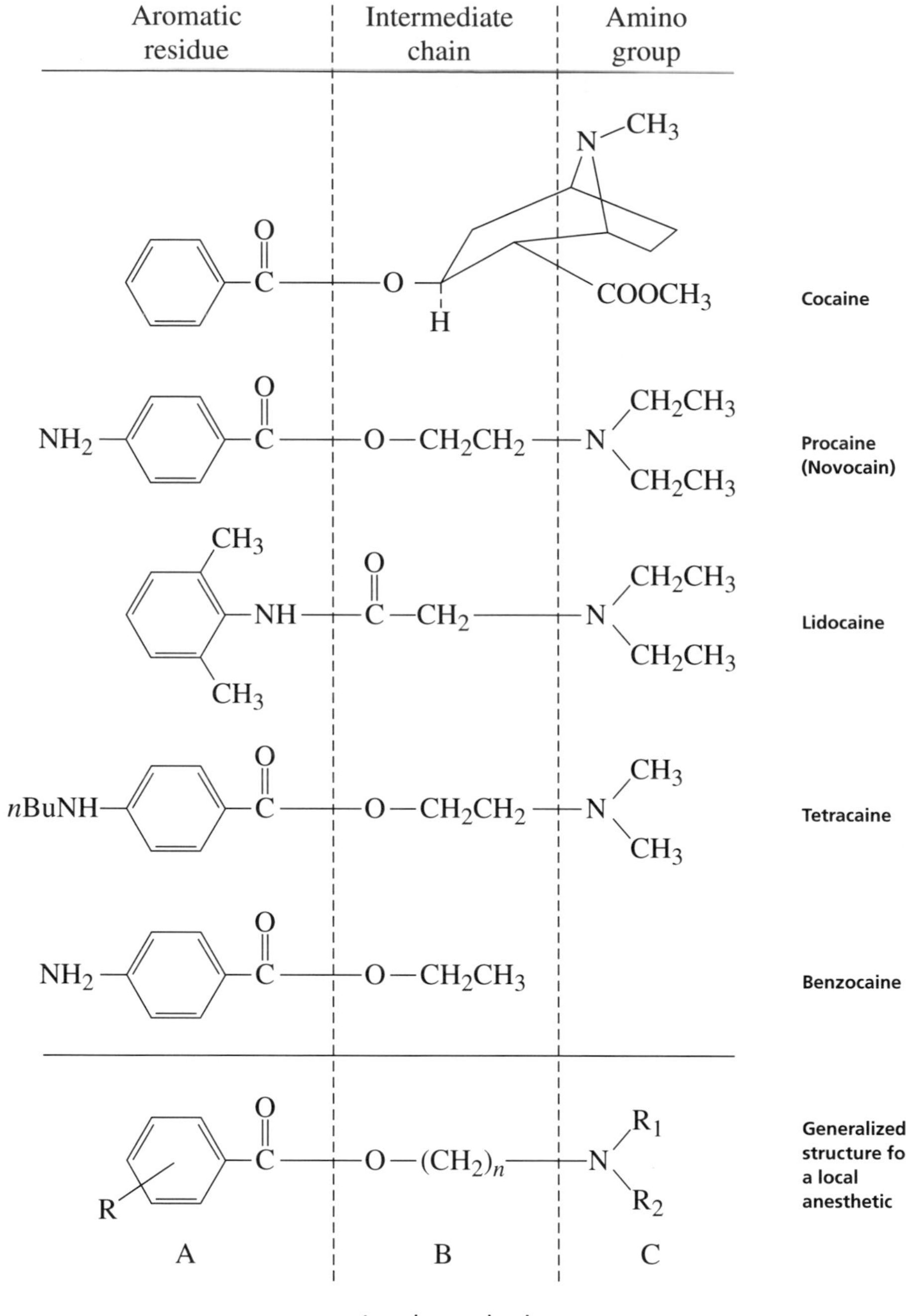

Local anesthetics.

Goodman and A. Gilman, eds., *The Pharmacological Basis of Therapeutics,* 8th ed. New York: Pergamon Press, 1990.

Snyder, S. H. "The Brain's Own Opiates." *Chemical and Engineering News* (November 28, 1977): 26–35.

Taylor, N. *Plant Drugs That Changed the World.* New York: Dodd, Mead, 1965. Pp. 14–18.

Taylor, N. "The Divine Plant of the Incas." Chap. 3 in *Narcotics: Nature's Dangerous Gifts.* New York: Dell, 1970. (Paperbound revision of *Flight from Reality.*)

EXPERIMENT 36

Triphenylmethanol and Benzoic Acid

Grignard reaction
Extraction
Crystallization

In this experiment, you will prepare a Grignard reagent, or organomagnesium reagent. The reagent is phenylmagnesium bromide.

$$C_6H_5{-}Br + Mg \xrightarrow{\text{ether}} C_6H_5{-}MgBr$$

Bromobenzene **Phenylmagnesium bromide**

This reagent will be converted to a tertiary alcohol or a carboxylic acid, depending on the experiment selected.

EXPERIMENT 36A

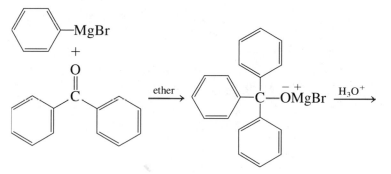

$$C_6H_5{-}MgBr + (C_6H_5)_2C{=}O \xrightarrow{\text{ether}} (C_6H_5)_3C{-}\overset{-}{O}\overset{+}{M}gBr \xrightarrow{H_3O^+} (C_6H_5)_3C{-}OH + MgBr(OH)$$

Benzophenone

Triphenylmethanol

EXPERIMENT 36B

$$C_6H_5\text{—MgBr} + CO_2 \xrightarrow{\text{ether}} C_6H_5\text{—}\overset{\overset{\displaystyle O}{\|}}{C}\text{—}\overset{-}{O}\overset{+}{Mg}Br^{+} \xrightarrow{H_3O^+}$$

$$C_6H_5\text{—}\overset{\overset{\displaystyle O}{\|}}{C}\text{—OH} + \text{MgBr(OH)}$$

Benzoic acid

The alkyl portion of the Grignard reagent behaves as if it had the characteristics of a **carbanion.** We may write the structure of the reagent as a partially ionic compound:

$$\overset{\delta-}{R}\cdots\overset{\delta+}{MgX}$$

This partially bonded carbanion is a Lewis base. It reacts with strong acids, as you would expect, to give an alkane:

$$\overset{\delta-}{R}\cdots\overset{\delta+}{MgX} + HX \longrightarrow R\text{—}H + MgX_2$$

Any compound with a suitably acidic hydrogen will donate a proton to destroy the reagent. Water, alcohols, terminal acetylenes, phenols, and carboxylic acids are all acidic enough to bring about this reaction.

The Grignard reagent also functions as a good nucleophile in nucleophilic addition reactions of the carbonyl group. The carbonyl group has electrophilic character at its carbon atom (due to resonance), and a good nucleophile seeks out this center for addition.

$$\left[\;\overset{\ddot{O}}{\underset{\diagup C \diagdown}{\|}} \longleftrightarrow \overset{:\ddot{O}:^{-}}{\underset{\diagup \overset{+}{C} \diagdown}{|}}\;\right] \qquad \overset{\delta+}{C}=\overset{\delta-}{\ddot{O}}$$

The magnesium salts produced form a complex with the addition product, an alkoxide salt. In a second step of the reaction, these must be hydrolyzed (protonated) by addition of dilute aqueous acid:

$$\overset{\overset{\displaystyle O}{\|}}{\diagup C \diagdown} + RMgX \longrightarrow \text{—}\overset{\overset{\displaystyle O\text{—MgX}}{|}}{\underset{\underset{\displaystyle R}{|}}{C}}\text{—} \xrightarrow[H_2O]{HX} \text{—}\overset{\overset{\displaystyle OH}{|}}{\underset{\underset{\displaystyle R}{|}}{C}}\text{—} + MgX_2$$

Step 1 **Step 2**

The Grignard reaction is used synthetically to prepare secondary alcohols from aldehydes and tertiary alcohols from ketones. The Grignard reagent will react with esters twice to give tertiary alcohols. Synthetically, it also can be allowed to react with carbon dioxide to give carboxylic acids and with oxygen to give hydroperoxides:

$$\text{RMgX} + \text{O}{=}\text{C}{=}\text{O} \longrightarrow \text{R}{-}\overset{\overset{\displaystyle \text{O}}{\|}}{\text{C}}{-}\text{OMgX} \xrightarrow[\text{H}_2\text{O}]{\text{HX}} \text{R}{-}\overset{\overset{\displaystyle \text{O}}{\|}}{\text{C}}{-}\text{OH}$$

Carboxylic acid

$$\text{RMgX} + \text{O}_2 \longrightarrow \text{ROOMgX} \xrightarrow[\text{H}_2\text{O}]{\text{HX}} \text{ROOH}$$

Hydroperoxide

Because the Grignard reagent reacts with water, carbon dioxide, and oxygen, it must be protected from air and moisture when it is used. The apparatus in which the reaction is to be conducted must be scrupulously dry (recall that 18 mL of H_2O is 1 mole), and the solvent must be free of water, or anhydrous. During the reaction, the flask must be protected by a calcium chloride drying tube. Oxygen should also be excluded. In practice, this can be done by allowing the solvent ether to reflux. This blanket of solvent vapor keeps air from the surface of the reaction mixture.

In the experiment described here, the principal impurity is **biphenyl,** which is formed by a heat- or light-catalyzed coupling reaction of the Grignard reagent and unreacted bromobenzene. A high reaction temperature favors the formation of this product. Biphenyl is highly soluble in petroleum ether, and it is easily separated from triphenylmethanol. Biphenyl can be separated from benzoic acid by extraction.

$$\text{C}_6\text{H}_5\text{MgBr} + \text{C}_6\text{H}_5\text{Br} \longrightarrow \text{C}_6\text{H}_5{-}\text{C}_6\text{H}_5 + \text{MgBr}_2$$

Required Reading

Review:	Technique 8	Filtration, Section 8.3
	Technique 11	Crystallization: Purification of Solids, Section 11.3
	Technique 12	Extractions, Separations, and Drying Agents, Sections 12.4, 12.5, 12.8, and 12.10
	Technique 25	Infrared Spectroscopy, Section 25.5

Special Instructions

This experiment must be conducted in one laboratory period either to the point after which benzophenone is added (Experiment 36A) or to the point after which the Grignard reagent is poured over dry ice (Experiment 36B). The Grignard reagent cannot be stored;

you must react it before stopping. This experiment uses diethyl ether, which is extremely flammable. Be certain that no open flames are in your vicinity when you are using ether.

During this experiment, you will need to use *anhydrous* diethyl ether, which is usually contained in metal cans with a screw cap. You are instructed in the experiment to transfer a small portion of this solvent to a stoppered Erlenmeyer flask. Be certain to minimize exposure to atmospheric water during this transfer. Always recap the ether container after use. Do not use solvent-grade ether because it may contain some water.

All students will prepare the same Grignard reagent, phenylmagnesium bromide. At the option of the instructor, you should then proceed to either Experiment 36A (triphenylmethanol) or Experiment 36B (benzoic acid) when your reagent is ready.

Suggested Waste Disposal

All aqueous solutions should be placed in a container designated for aqueous waste. Be sure to decant these solutions away from any magnesium chips before placing them in the waste container. The unreacted magnesium chips that you separate should be placed in a solid waste container designated for that purpose. Place all ether solutions in the container for nonhalogenated liquid wastes. Likewise, the mother liquor from the crystallization using isopropyl alcohol (Experiment 36A) should also be placed in the container for nonhalogenated liquid wastes.

Notes to the Instructor

Whenever possible, you should require that your class wash and dry the necessary glassware *the period before this experiment is scheduled.* It is not a good idea to use glassware that has been washed earlier in the same period, even if it has been dried in the oven. When drying, be certain that no Teflon stopcocks, plastic stoppers, or plastic clips are placed in the oven.

Procedure

$$C_6H_5\text{—Br} + \text{Mg} \xrightarrow{\text{ether}} C_6H_5\text{—MgBr}$$

PREPARATION OF THE GRIGNARD REAGENT: PHENYLMAGNESIUM BROMIDE

Glassware. The following glassware is used:

100-mL round-bottom flask	Claisen head
125-mL separatory funnel	water-jacketed condenser
$CaCl_2$ drying tubes (2)	50-mL Erlenmeyer flasks (2)
10-mL graduated cylinder	

Preparation of Glassware. If necessary, dry all the pieces of *glassware* (no plastic parts) in the previous list in an oven at 110°C for at least 30 minutes. This step can be omitted if your glassware is clean and has been unused in your drawer for at least two to three days. Otherwise, all glassware used in your Grignard reaction must be scrupulously dried. Surprisingly large amounts of water adhere to the walls of glassware, even when it is apparently dry. Glassware washed and dried the same day it is to be used can still give problems in starting a Grignard reaction.

Apparatus. Add a clean, dry stirring bar to the 100-mL round-bottom flask and assemble the apparatus as shown in the figure. Place drying tubes (filled with fresh calcium chloride) on both the separatory funnel and on the top of the condenser. A

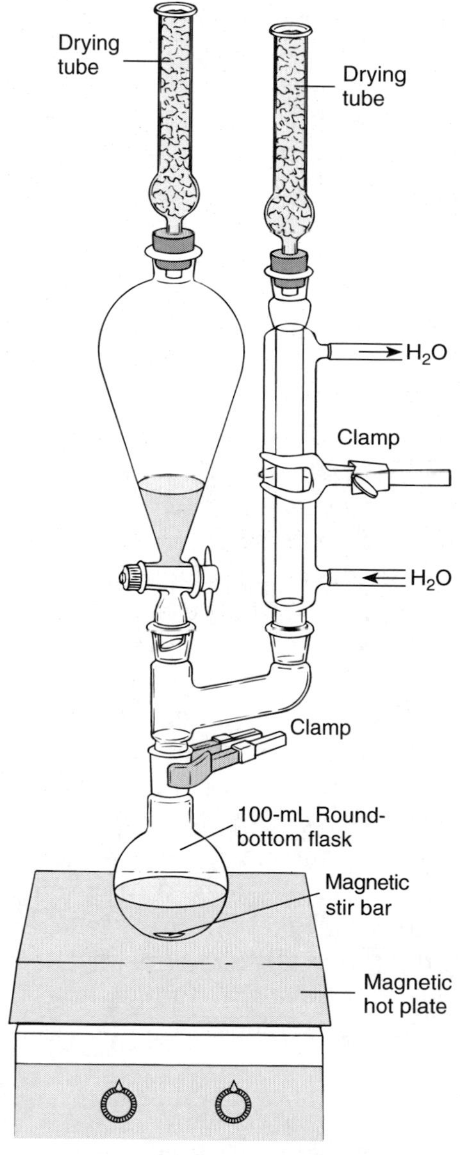

Apparatus for Grignard reactions.

Caution: Do not place any plasticware, plastic connectors, or Teflon stoppers in the oven as they may melt, burn, or soften. Check with your instructor if in doubt.

stirring hotplate will be used to stir and heat the reaction.[1] Make sure that the apparatus can be moved up and down easily on the ring stand. Movement up and down relative to the hot plate will be used to control the amount of heat applied to the reaction.

Formation of the Grignard Reagent. Using smooth paper or a small beaker, weigh about 0.5 g of magnesium turnings ($AW = 24.3$) and place them in the 100-mL round-bottom flask. Using a preweighed 10-mL graduated cylinder, measure approximately 2.1 mL of bromobenzene ($MW = 157.0$) and reweigh the cylinder to determine the exact mass of the bromobenzene. Transfer the bromobenzene to a stoppered 50-mL Erlenmeyer flask. Without cleaning the graduated cylinder, measure a 10-mL portion of anhydrous ether and transfer it to the same 50-mL Erlenmeyer flask containing the bromobenzene. Mix the solution (swirl) and then, using a dry, disposable Pasteur pipet, transfer about half of it into the round-bottom flask containing the magnesium turnings. Add the remainder of the solution to the 125-mL separatory funnel. Then add an additional 7.0 mL of anhydrous ether to the bromobenzene solution in the separatory funnel. At this point, make sure all joints are sealed and that the drying tubes are in place.

Position the apparatus just above the hot plate and stir the mixture *gently* to avoid throwing the magnesium out of the solution and onto the side of the flask. You should begin to notice the evolution of bubbles from the surface of the metal, which signals that the reaction is starting. It will probably be necessary to heat the mixture using your hot plate to start the reaction. The hot plate should be adjusted to its lowest setting. Because ether has a low boiling point (35°C), it should be sufficient to heat the reaction by placing the round-bottom flask just above the hot plate. Once the ether is boiling, check to see if the bubbling action continues after the apparatus is lifted above the hot plate. If the reaction continues to bubble without heating, the magnesium is reacting. You may have to repeat the heating several times to successfully start the reaction. After you have made several tries at heating, the reaction should start, but if you are still experiencing difficulty, proceed to the next paragraph.

Optional Steps. You may need to employ one or more of the following procedures if heating fails to start the reaction. If you are experiencing difficulty, remove the separatory funnel. Place a long, *dry* glass stirring rod into the flask and gently twist the stirring rod to crush the magnesium against the glass surface. *Be careful not to poke a hole in the bottom of the flask; do this gently!* Reattach the separatory funnel and heat the mixture again. Repeat the crushing procedure several times, if necessary, to start the reaction. If the crushing procedure fails to start the reaction, then

[1] A steam bath or steam cone may be used, but you will probably have to forgo any stirring and use a boiling stone instead of a spin bar. A heating mantle could be used to heat the reaction. With a heating mantle, it is probably best to clamp the apparatus securely and to support the heating mantle under the reaction flask with wooden blocks that can be added or removed. When the blocks are removed, the heating mantle can be lowered away from the flask.

add one small crystal of iodine to the flask. Again, heat the mixture *gently.* The most drastic action, other than starting the experiment over again, is to prepare a small sample of the Grignard reagent *externally* in a test tube. When this external reaction starts, add it to the main reaction mixture. This "booster shot" will react with any water that is present in the mixture and allow the reaction to get started.

Completing the Grignard Preparation. When the reaction has started, you should observe the formation of a brownish gray, cloudy solution. Add the remaining solution of bromobenzene slowly over a period of 5 minutes at a rate that keeps the solution boiling gently. If the boiling stops, add more bromobenzene. It may be necessary to heat the mixture occasionally with the hot plate during the addition. If the reaction becomes too vigorous, slow the addition of the bromobenzene solution and raise the apparatus higher above the hot plate. Ideally, the mixture will boil without the application of external heat. *It is important that you heat the mixture if the reflux slows or stops.* As the reaction proceeds, you should observe the gradual disintegration of the magnesium metal. When all the bromobenzene has been added, place an additional 1.0 mL of *anhydrous* ether in the separatory funnel to rinse it and add it to the reaction mixture. Remove the separatory funnel after making this addition and replace it with a stopper. Heat the solution under gentle reflux until most of the remaining magnesium dissolves (don't worry about a few small pieces). This should require about 15 minutes. Note the level of the solution in the flask. You should add additional anhydrous ether to replace any that is lost during the reflux period. During this reflux period, you can prepare any solutions needed for Experiment 36A or Experiment 36B. When the reflux is complete, allow the mixture to cool to room temperature. As your instructor designates, go on to either Experiment 36A or Experiment 36B.

EXPERIMENT 36A

Triphenylmethanol

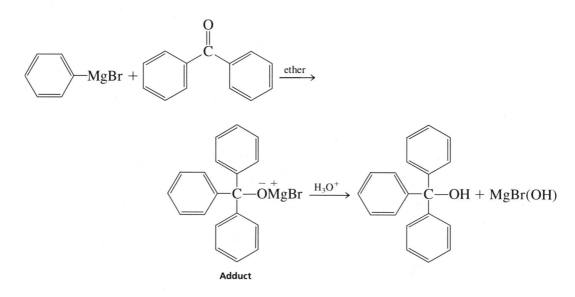

$$C_6H_5\text{—MgBr} + C_6H_5\text{—}\overset{\displaystyle O}{\overset{\|}{C}}\text{—}C_6H_5 \xrightarrow{\text{ether}}$$

$$(C_6H_5)_3C\text{—}\overset{-}{O}\overset{+}{M}gBr \xrightarrow{H_3O^+} (C_6H_5)_3C\text{—OH} + \text{MgBr(OH)}$$

Adduct

Procedure

Addition of Benzophenone. While the phenylmagnesium bromide solution is being heated and stirred under reflux, make a solution of 2.4 g benzophenone in 9.0 mL of *anhydrous* ether in a 50-mL Erlenmeyer flask. Stopper the flask until the reflux period is over. Once the Grignard reagent is cooled to room temperature, reattach the separatory funnel and transfer the benzophenone solution into it. Add this solution as rapidly as possible to the stirred Grignard reagent, but at such a rate that the solution does not reflux too vigorously. Rinse the Erlenmeyer flask that contained the benzophenone solution with about 5.0 mL of anhydrous ether and add it to the mixture. Once the addition has been completed, allow the mixture to cool to room temperature. The solution turns a rose color and then gradually solidifies as the adduct is formed. When magnetic stirring is no longer effective, stir the mixture with a spatula. Remove the reaction flask from the apparatus and stopper it. Occasionally, stir the contents of the flask. The adduct should be fully formed after about 15 minutes. You may stop here.

Hydrolysis. Add enough 6 *M* hydrochloric acid (*dropwise at first*) to neutralize the reaction mixture (approximately 7.0 mL). Enough acid has been added when the lower aqueous layer turns blue litmus paper red. The acid converts the adduct to triphenylmethanol and inorganic compounds (MgX_2). Eventually, you should obtain two distinct phases: the upper ether layer will contain triphenylmethanol; the lower aqueous hydrochloric acid layer will contain the inorganic compounds. Use a spatula to break up the solid during the addition of hydrochloric acid. Swirl the flask occasionally to assure thorough mixing. Because the neutralization procedure evolves heat, some ether will be lost due to evaporation. You should add enough ether to maintain a 5- to 10-mL volume in the upper organic phase. Make sure that you have two distinct liquid phases before proceeding to separate the layers. More ether or hydrochloric acid may be added, if necessary, to dissolve any remaining solid.[2]

If some material stubbornly remains undissolved or if there are three layers, transfer all the liquids to a 250-mL Erlenmeyer flask. Add more ether and more hydrochloric acid to the flask and swirl it to mix the contents. Continue adding small portions of ether and hydrochloric acid to the flask and swirl it until everything dissolves. At this point, you should have two clear layers.

Separation and Drying. Transfer your mixture to a 125-mL separatory funnel, but avoid transferring the spin bar (or boiling stone). Shake and vent the mixture and then allow the layers to separate. If any unreacted magnesium metal is present, you will observe bubbles of hydrogen being formed. You may remove the aqueous layer even though the magnesium is still producing hydrogen. Drain off the lower aqueous phase and place it in a beaker for storage. Next, *save the upper ether layer* in an Erlenmeyer flask; it contains the triphenylmethanol product. Reextract the saved aqueous phase with 5.0 mL of ether. Remove the lower aqueous phase and discard it. Combine the remaining ether phase with the first ether extract. Transfer the combined ether layers to a dry Erlenmeyer flask and add about 1.0 g of granular anhydrous sodium sulfate to dry the solution. Add more drying agent if necessary.

---

[2] In some cases, it may be necessary to add additional water instead of more hydrochloric acid.

Evaporation. Decant the dried ether solution from the drying agent into a small Erlenmeyer flask and rinse the drying agent with more diethyl ether. Evaporate the ether solvent in a hood by heating the flask in a warm water bath. Evaporation will occur more quickly if a stream of nitrogen or air is directed into the flask. You should be left with a mixture that varies from a brown oil to a colored solid mixed with an oil. This crude mixture contains the desired triphenylmethanol and the by-product biphenyl. Most of the biphenyl can be removed by adding about 10 mL of petroleum ether (bp 30–60°C). Petroleum ether is a mixture of hydrocarbons that easily dissolves the hydrocarbon biphenyl and leaves behind the alcohol triphenylmethanol. Do not confuse this solvent with diethyl ether ("ether"). Heat the mixture slightly, stir it, and then cool the mixture to room temperature. Collect the triphenylmethanol by vacuum filtration on a small Büchner funnel and rinse it with small portions of petroleum ether (Technique 8, Section 8.3, p. 651, and Figure 8.5, p. 652). Air-dry the solid, weigh it, and calculate the percentage yield of the crude triphenylmethanol ($MW = 260.3$).

Crystallization. Crystallize all your product from hot isopropyl alcohol and collect the crystals using a Büchner funnel (Technique 11, Section 11.3, p. 862, and Fig-

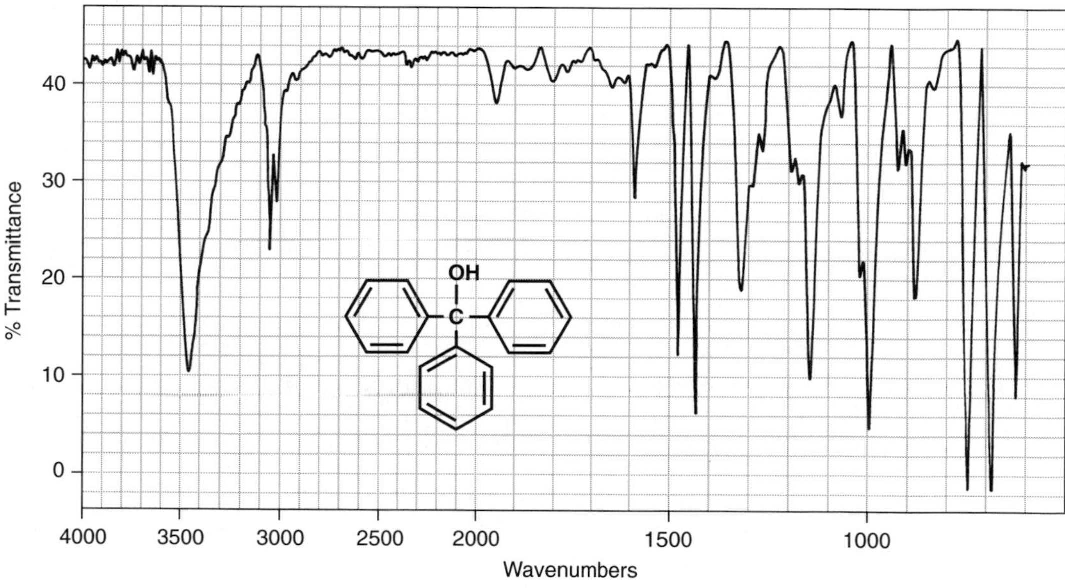

Infrared spectrum of triphenylmethanol, KBr.

ure 11.4, p. 683). Step 2 in Figure 11.4 (removal of insoluble impurities) should not be required in this crystallization. Set the crystals aside to air-dry. Report the melting point of the purified triphenylmethanol (literature value, 162°C) and the recovered yield in grams. Submit the sample to the instructor.

Spectroscopy. At the option of the instructor, determine the infrared spectrum of the purified material in a KBr pellet (Technique 25, Section 25.5, p. 878). Your instructor may assign certain tests on the product you prepared. These tests are described in the Instructor's Manual.

EXPERIMENT 36B

Benzoic Acid

$$C_6H_5MgBr + CO_2 \xrightarrow{\text{ether}} C_6H_5\text{—}\overset{O}{\overset{\|}{C}}\text{—}\overset{-}{O}\overset{+}{Mg}Br \xrightarrow{H_3O^+} C_6H_5\text{—}\overset{O}{\overset{\|}{C}}\text{—}OH + MgBr(OH)$$

Benzoic acid

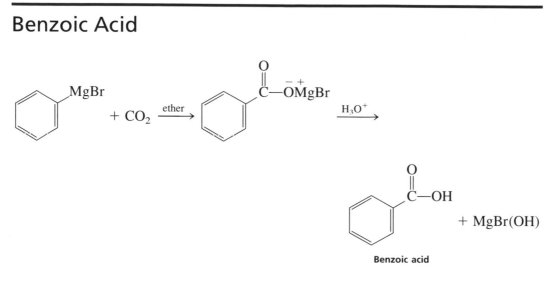

Procedure

Addition of Dry Ice. When the phenylmagnesium bromide solution has cooled to room temperature, pour it as quickly as possible onto 10 g of crushed dry ice contained in a 250-mL beaker. The dry ice should be weighed as quickly as possible to avoid contact with atmospheric moisture. It need not be weighed precisely. Rinse the flask in which the phenylmagnesium bromide was prepared with 2 mL of anhydrous ether and add it to the beaker.

> **Caution:** Exercise caution in handling dry ice. Contact with the skin can cause severe frostbite. Always use gloves or tongs. The dry ice is best crushed by wrapping large pieces in a clean, dry towel and striking them with a hammer or a wooden block. It should be used as soon as possible after crushing it to avoid contact with atmospheric water.

Cover the reaction mixture with a watch glass and allow it to stand until the excess dry ice has completely sublimed. The Grignard addition compound will appear as a viscous, glassy mass.

Hydrolysis. Hydrolyze the Grignard adduct by slowly adding approximately 8 mL of 6 *M* hydrochloric acid to the beaker and stirring the mixture with a glass rod or spatula. Any remaining magnesium chips will react with acid to evolve hydrogen. At this point, you should have two distinct liquid phases in the beaker. If you have solid present (other than magnesium), try adding a little more ether. If the solid is insoluble in ether, try adding a little more 6 *M* hydrochloric acid solution or water. Benzoic acid is soluble in ether, and inorganic compounds (MgX_2) are soluble in the aqueous acid solution. Transfer the liquid phases to an Erlenmeyer flask, leaving behind any residual magnesium. Add more ether to the beaker to rinse it, and add this additional ether to the Erlenmeyer flask. You may stop here. Stopper the flask with a cork and continue with the experiment during the next laboratory period.

Isolation of the Product. If you stored your product and the ether layer evaporated, add several milliliters of ether. If the solids do not dissolve on stirring or if no water layer is apparent, try adding some water. Transfer your mixture to a 125-mL separatory funnel. If some material remains undissolved or if there are three layers, add more ether and hydrochloric acid to the separatory funnel, stopper it, shake it, and allow the layers to separate. Continue adding small portions of ether and hydrochloric acid to the separatory funnel and shake it until everything dissolves. After layers have been separated, remove the lower aqueous layer. The aqueous phase contains inorganic salts and may be discarded. The ether layer contains the product benzoic acid and the by-product biphenyl. Add 5.0 mL of 5% sodium hydroxide solution, restopper the funnel, and shake it. Allow the layers to separate, *remove the lower aqueous layer, and save this layer in a beaker.* This extraction removes benzoic acid from the ether layer by converting it to the water-soluble sodium benzoate. The by-product biphenyl stays in the ether layer along with some remaining benzoic acid. Again, shake the remaining ether phase in the separatory funnel with a second 5.0-mL portion of 5% sodium hydroxide and transfer the lower aqueous layer into the beaker with the first extract. Repeat the extraction process with a third portion (5.0 mL) of 5% sodium hydroxide and save the aqueous layer, as before. Discard the ether layer, which contains the biphenyl impurity, into the waste container designated for nonhalogenated organic wastes.

Heat the combined basic extracts while stirring on a hot plate (100–120°C) for about 5 minutes to remove any ether that may be dissolved in this aqueous phase. Ether is soluble in water to the extent of 7%. During this heating period, you may ob-

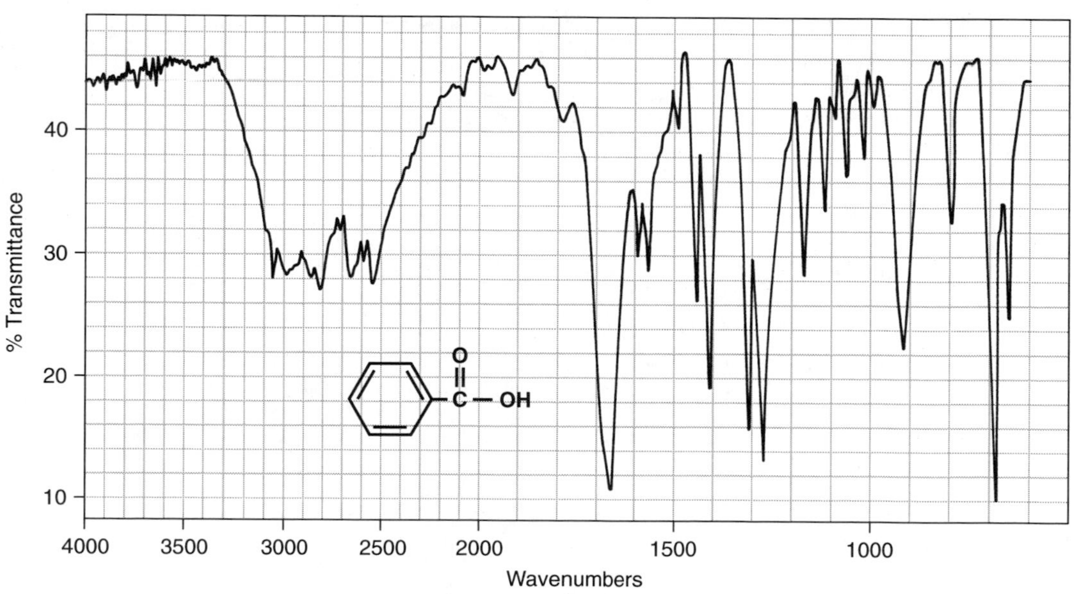

Infrared spectrum of benzoic acid, KBr.

serve slight bubbling, but the volume of liquid *will not decrease* substantially. Unless the ether is removed before the benzoic acid is precipitated, the product may appear as a waxy solid instead of crystals.

Cool the alkaline solution and precipitate the benzoic acid by adding 10.0 mL of 6 *M* hydrochloric acid, while stirring. Cool the mixture in an ice bath. Collect the solid by vacuum filtration on a Büchner funnel (Technique 8, Section 8.3, p. 651, and Figure 8.5, p. 652). The transfer may be aided and the solid washed with several small portions of cold water. Allow the crystals to dry thoroughly at room temperature at least overnight. Weigh the solid and calculate the percentage yield of benzoic acid ($MW = 122.1$).

Crystallization. Crystallize your product from hot water using a Büchner funnel to collect the product by vacuum filtration (Technique 11, Section 11.3, p. 682, and Figure 11.4, p. 683). Step 2 in Figure 11.4 (removal of insoluble impurities) should not be required in this crystallization. Set the crystals aside to air-dry at room temperature before determining the melting point of the purified benzoic acid (literature value, 122°C) and the recovered yield in grams.[3] Submit your product to your instructor in a properly labeled vial.

Spectroscopy. At the option of the instructor, determine the infrared spectrum of the purified material in a KBr pellet (Technique 25, Section 25.5, p. 878). Your instructor may assign certain tests on the product you prepared. These tests are described in the Instructor's Manual.

QUESTIONS

1. Benzene is often produced as a side product during Grignard reactions using phenylmagnesium bromide. How can its formation be explained? Give a balanced equation for its formation.

2. Write a balanced equation for the reaction of benzoic acid with hydroxide ion. Why is it necessary to extract the ether layer with sodium hydroxide?

3. Interpret the principal peaks in the infrared spectrum of either triphenylmethanol or benzoic acid, depending on the procedure used in this experiment.

4. Outline a separation scheme for isolating either triphenylmethanol or benzoic acid from the reaction mixture, depending on the procedure used in this experiment.

5. Provide methods for preparing the following compounds by the Grignard method:

(a) $CH_3CH_2CH(OH)CH_2CH_3$

(b) $CH_3CH_2-C(CH_3)(OH)-CH_2CH_3$

(c) $CH_3CH_2CH_2CH_2CH_2-C(=O)-OH$

(d) $C_6H_5-CH(OH)-CH_2CH_3$

[3]If necessary, the crystals may be dried in a low temperature (ca. 50°C) oven for a short period of time. Be warned that benzoic acid sublimes, and heating it for a long time at elevated temperatures could result in loss of your product.

EXPERIMENT 50

Photoreduction of Benzophenone and Rearrangement of Benzpinacol to Benzopinacolone

Photochemistry
Photoreduction
Energy transfer
Pinacol rearrangement

This experiment consists of two parts. In the first part (Experiment 50A), benzophenone will be subjected to **photoreduction,** a dimerization brought about by exposing a solution of benzophenone in isopropyl alcohol to natural sunlight. The product of this photoreaction is benzpinacol. In the second part (Experiment 50B), benzpinacol will be induced to undergo an acid-catalyzed rearrangement called the **pinacol rearrangement.** The product of the rearrangement is benzopinacolone.

EXPERIMENT 50A

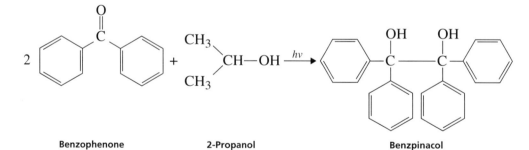

2 Benzophenone + 2-Propanol $\xrightarrow{h\nu}$ Benzpinacol

EXPERIMENT 50B

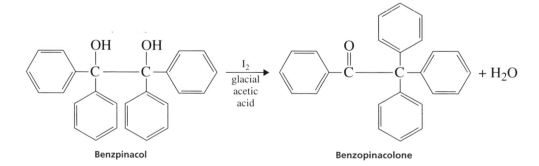

Benzpinacol $\xrightarrow[\text{glacial acetic acid}]{I_2}$ Benzopinacolone $+ H_2O$

EXPERIMENT 50A

Photoreduction of Benzophenone

The photoreduction of benzophenone is one of the oldest and most thoroughly studied photochemical reactions. Early in the history of photochemistry, it was discovered that solutions of benzophenone are unstable in light when certain solvents are used. If benzophenone is dissolved in a "hydrogen-donor" solvent, such as 2-propanol, and exposed to ultraviolet light, hν, an insoluble dimeric product, benzpinacol, will form.

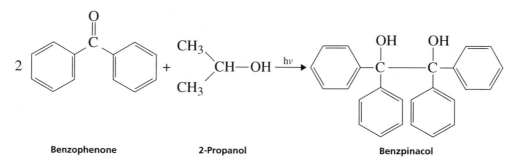

2 Benzophenone + 2-Propanol $\xrightarrow{h\nu}$ Benzpinacol

Benzophenone **2-Propanol** **Benzpinacol**

To understand this reaction, let's review some simple photochemistry as it relates to aromatic ketones. In the typical organic molecule, all the electrons are paired in the occupied orbitals. When such a molecule absorbs ultraviolet light of the appropriate wavelength, an electron from one of the occupied orbitals, usually the one of highest energy, is excited to an unoccupied molecular orbital, usually to the one of lowest energy. During this transition, the electron must retain its spin value, because during an electronic transition a change of spin is forbidden by the laws of quantum mechanics. Therefore, just as the two electrons in the highest occupied orbital of the molecule originally had their spins paired (opposite), so they will retain paired spins in the first electronically excited state of the molecule. This is true even though the two electrons will be in *different* orbitals after the transition. This first excited state of a molecule is called a **singlet state** (S_1) because its spin multiplicity ($2S + 1$) is 1. The original unexcited state of the molecule is also a singlet state because its electrons are paired, and it is called the **ground-state** singlet state (S_0) of the molecule.

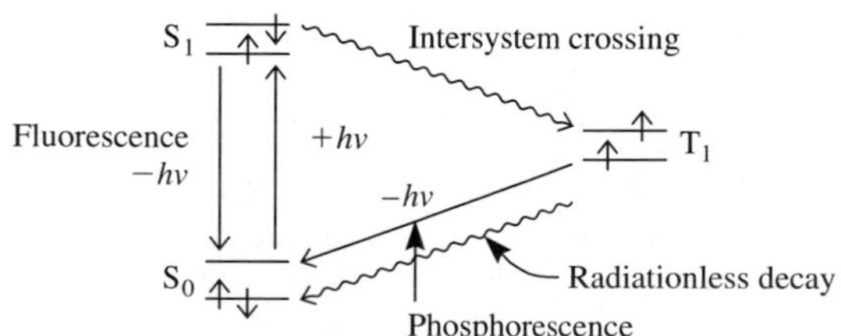

Electronic states of a typical molecule and the possible interconversions. In each state (S_0, S_1, T_1), the lower line represents the highest occupied orbital, and the upper line represents the lowest unoccupied orbital of the unexcited molecule. Straight lines represent processes in which a photon is absorbed or emitted. Wavy lines represent radiationless processes—those that occur without emission or absorption of a photon.

The excited state singlet S_1 may return to the ground state S_0 by reemission of the absorbed photon of energy. This process is called **fluorescence.** Alternatively, the excited electron may undergo a change of spin to give a state of higher multiplicity, the excited **triplet state,** so called because its spin multiplicity ($2S + 1$) is 3. The conversion from the first excited singlet state to the triplet state is called **intersystem crossing.** Because the triplet state has a higher multiplicity, it inevitably has a lower energy state than the excited singlet state (Hund's Rule). Normally, this change of spin (intersystem crossing) is a process forbidden by quantum mechanics, just as a direct excitation of the ground state (S_0) to the triplet state (T_1) is forbidden. However, in those molecules in which the singlet and triplet states lie close to one another in energy, the two states inevitably have several overlapping vibrational states—that is, states in common—a situation that allows the "forbidden" transition to occur. In many molecules in which S_1 and T_1 have similar energy ($\Delta E < 10$ Kcal/mole), intersystem crossing occurs faster than fluorescence, and the molecule is rapidly converted from its excited singlet state to its triplet state. In benzophenone, S_1 undergoes intersystem crossing to T_1 with a rate of $k_{isc} = 10^{10}$ sec^{-1}, meaning that the lifetime of S_1 is only 10^{-10} second. The rate of fluorescence for benzophenone is $k_f = 10^6$ sec^{-1}, meaning that intersystem crossing occurs at a rate that is 10^4 times faster than fluorescence. Thus, the conversion of S_1 to T_1 in benzophenone is essentially a quantitative process. In molecules that have a wide energy gap between S_1 and T_1, this situation would be reversed. As you will see shortly, the naphthalene molecule presents a reversed situation.

Because the excited triplet state is lower in energy than the excited singlet state, the molecule cannot easily return to the excited singlet state. Nor can it easily return to the ground state by returning the excited electron to its original orbital. Once again, the transition $T_1 \rightarrow S_0$ would require a change of spin for the electron, and this is a forbidden process. Hence, the triplet excited state usually has a long lifetime (relative to other excited states) because it generally has nowhere to which it can easily go. Even though the process is forbidden, the triplet T_1 may eventually return to the ground state (S_0) by a process called a **radiationless transition.** In this process, the excess energy of the triplet is lost to the surrounding solution as heat, thereby "relaxing" the triplet back to the ground state (S_0). This process is the study of much current research and is not well understood. In the second process, in which a triplet state may revert to the ground state, **phosphorescence,** the excited triplet emits a photon to dissipate the excess energy and returns directly to the ground state. Although this process is "forbidden," it nevertheless occurs when there is no other open pathway by which the molecule can dissipate its excess energy. In benzophenone, radiationless decay is the faster process, with rate $k_d = 10^5$ sec^{-1}, and phosphorescence, which is not observed, has a lower rate of $k_p = 10^2$ sec^{-1}.

Benzophenone is a ketone. Ketones have *two* possible excited singlet states and, consequently, two excited triplet states as well. This occurs because two relatively low-energy transitions are possible in benzophenone. It is possible to excite one of the π electrons in the carbonyl π bond to the lowest-energy unoccupied orbital, a π^* orbital. It is also possible to excite one of the unbonded or n electrons on oxygen to the same orbital. The first type of transition is called a π–π^* transition, whereas the second is called an n–π^* transition. In the figure, these transitions and the states that result are illustrated pictorially.

Spectroscopic studies show that for benzophenone and most other ketones, the n–π^*

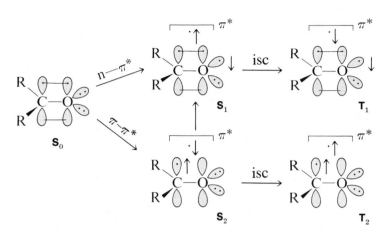

n–π* and π–π* transitions for ketones.

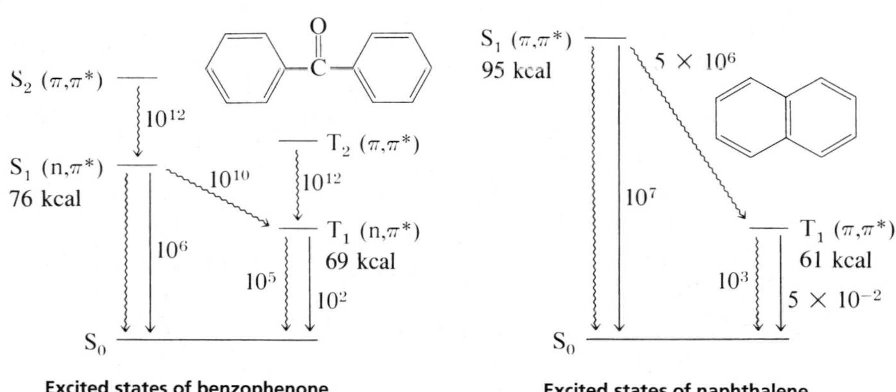

Excited energy states of benzophenone and naphthalene.

excited states S_1 and T_1 are of lower energy than the π–π^* excited states. An energy diagram depicting the excited states of benzophenone (along with one that depicts those of naphthalene) is shown.

It is now known that the photoreduction of benzophenone is a reaction of the n–π^* triplet state (T_1) of benzophenone. The n–π^* excited states have radical character at the carbonyl oxygen atom because of the unpaired electron in the nonbonding orbital. Thus, the radical-like and energetic T_1 excited-state species can abstract a hydrogen atom from a suitable donor molecule to form the diphenylhydroxymethyl radical. Two of these radicals, once formed, may couple to form benzpinacol. The complete mechanism for photoreduction is outlined in the steps that follow.

$$Ph_2C{=}O \xrightarrow{h\nu} Ph_2\dot{C}{-}O\cdot(S_1)$$

$$Ph_2\dot{C}{-}O\cdot(S_1) \xrightarrow{isc} Ph_2\dot{C}{-}O\cdot(T_1)$$

$$\underset{(T_1)}{Ph_2\dot{C}{-}O\cdot} \;\; H{-}\underset{CH_3}{\overset{CH_3}{C}}{-}OH \longrightarrow Ph_2\dot{C}{-}OH + \cdot\underset{CH_3}{\overset{CH_3}{C}}{-}OH$$

$$\underset{(T_1)}{Ph_2\dot{C}{-}O\cdot} \;\; HO{-}\underset{CH_3}{\overset{CH_3}{C}}\cdot \longrightarrow Ph_2\dot{C}{-}OH + O{=}C(CH_3)_2$$

$$2\ Ph_2\dot{C}{-}OH \longrightarrow Ph{-}\underset{Ph}{\overset{OH}{C}}{-}\underset{Ph}{\overset{OH}{C}}{-}Ph$$

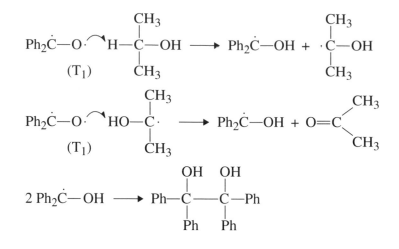

Many photochemical reactions must be carried out in a quartz apparatus because they require ultraviolet radiation of shorter wavelengths (higher energy) than the wavelengths that can pass through Pyrex. Benzophenone, however, requires radiation of approximately 350 nm to become excited to its n–π^* singlet state S_1, a wavelength that readily passes through Pyrex. In the figure shown below, the ultraviolet absorption spectra of benzophenone and naphthalene are given. Superimposed on their spectra are two curves, which show the wavelengths that can be transmitted by Pyrex and quartz, respectively. Pyrex will not allow any radiation of wavelength shorter than approximately 300 nm to pass, whereas quartz allows wavelengths as short as 200 nm to pass. Thus, when benzophenone is placed in a Pyrex flask, the only electronic transition possible is the n–π^* transition, which occurs at 350 nm.

However, even if it were possible to supply benzophenone with radiation of the appropriate wavelength to produce the second excited singlet state of the molecule, this singlet would rapidly convert to the lowest singlet state (S_1). The state S_2 has a lifetime of less than 10^{-12} second. The conversion process $S_2 \rightarrow S_1$ is called an **internal conversion.** Internal conversions are processes of conversion between excited states of the same multiplicity (singlet–singlet or triplet–triplet), and they usually are very rapid. Thus, when an S_2 or T_2 is formed, it readily converts to S_1 or T_1, respectively. As a consequence of their very short lifetimes, very little is known about the properties or the exact energies of S_2 and T_2 of benzophenone.

ENERGY TRANSFER

Using a simple **energy-transfer** experiment, one can show that the photoreduction of benzophenone proceeds via the T_1 excited state of benzophenone rather than the S_1 excited state. If naphthalene is added to the reaction, the photoreduction is stopped because the excitation energy of the benzophenone triplet is transferred to naphthalene. The naphthalene is said to have **quenched** the reaction. This occurs in the following way.

When the excited states of molecules have long enough lifetimes, they often can transfer their excitation energy to another molecule. The mechanisms of these transfers are complex and cannot be explained here; however, the essential requirements can be outlined. First, for two molecules to exchange their respective states of excitation, the process must

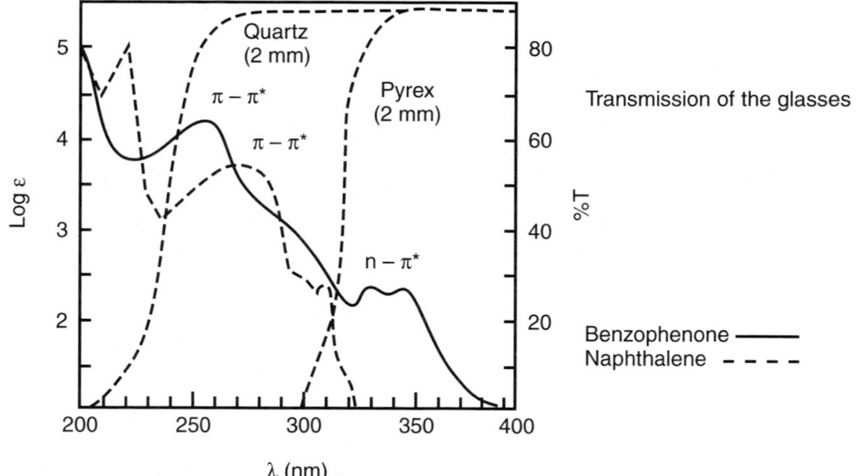

Ultraviolet absorption spectra for benzophenone and naphthalene.

occur with an overall decrease in energy. Second, the spin multiplicity of the total system must not change. These two features can be illustrated by the two most common examples of energy transfer—singlet transfer and triplet transfer. In these two examples, the superscript 1 denotes an excited singlet state, the superscript 3 denotes a triplet state, and the subscript 0 denotes a ground-state molecule. The designations A and B represent different molecules.

$$A^1 + B_0 \longrightarrow B^1 + A_0 \qquad \text{Singlet energy transfer}$$

$$A^3 + B_0 \longrightarrow B^3 + A_0 \qquad \text{Triplet energy transfer}$$

In singlet energy transfer, excitation energy is transferred from the excited singlet state of A to a ground-state molecule of B, converting B to its excited singlet state and returning A to its ground state. In triplet energy transfer, there is a similar interconversion of excited state and ground state. Singlet energy is transferred through space by a dipole–dipole coupling mechanism, but triplet energy transfer requires the two molecules involved in the transfer to collide. In the usual organic medium, about 10^9 collisions occur per second. Thus, if a triplet state A^3 has a lifetime longer than 10^{-9} second, and if an acceptor molecule B_0, which has a lower triplet energy than that of A^3, is available, energy transfer can be expected. If the triplet A^3 undergoes a reaction (such as photoreduction) at a rate lower than the rate of collisions in the solution, and if an acceptor molecule is added to the solution, the reaction can be *quenched.* The acceptor molecule, which is called a **quencher,** deactivates, or "quenches," the triplet before it has a chance to react. Naphthalene has the ability to quench benzophenone triplets in this way and to stop the photoreduction.

Naphthalene cannot quench the excited-state singlet S_1 of benzophenone because its own singlet has an energy (95 kcal/mol) that is higher than the energy of benzophenone (76 kcal/mol). In addition, the conversion $S_1 \rightarrow T_1$ is very rapid (10^{-10} second) in benzophenone. Thus, naphthalene can intercept only the triplet state of benzophenone. The triplet excitation energy of benzophenone (69 kcal/mol) is transferred to naphthalene

(T_1 = 61 kcal/mol) in an exothermic collision. Finally, the naphthalene molecule does not absorb light of the wavelengths transmitted by Pyrex (see spectra, p. 427); therefore, benzophenone is not inhibited from absorbing energy when naphthalene is present in solution. Thus, because naphthalene quenches the photoreduction reaction of benzophenone, we can infer that this reaction proceeds via the triplet state T_1 of benzophenone. If naphthalene did not quench the reaction, the singlet state of benzophenone would be indicated as the reactive intermediate. In the following experiment, the photoreduction of benzophenone is attempted both in the presence and in the absence of added naphthalene.

Required Reading

Review: Technique 8 Filtration, Section 8.3

Special Instructions

This experiment may be performed concurrently with some other experiment. It requires only 15 minutes during the first laboratory period and only about 15 minutes in a subsequent laboratory period about 1 week later (or at the end of the laboratory period if you use a sunlamp).

Using Direct Sunlight. It is important that the reaction mixture be left where it will receive direct sunlight. If it does not, the reaction will be slow and may need more than 1 week for completion. It is also important that the room temperature not be too low, or the benzophenone will precipitate. If you perform this experiment in the winter and the laboratory is not heated at night, you must shake the solutions every morning to redissolve the benzophenone. Benzpinacol should not redissolve easily.

Using a Sunlamp. If you wish, you may use a 275-W sunlamp instead of direct sunlight. Place the lamp in a hood that has had its window covered with aluminum foil (shiny side in). The lamp (or lamps) should be mounted in a ceramic socket attached to a ring stand with a three-pronged clamp.

> **Caution:** The purpose of the aluminum foil is to protect the eyes of people in the laboratory. You should not view a sunlamp directly, or damage to the eyes may result. Take all possible viewing precautions.

Attach samples to a ring stand placed at least 18 inches from the sunlamp. Placing them at this distance will avoid their being heated by the lamp. Heating may cause loss of the solvent. It is a good idea to agitate the samples every 30 minutes. With a sunlamp, the reaction will be complete in 3–4 hours.

Suggested Waste Disposal

Dispose of the filtrate from the vacuum filtration procedure in the container designated for nonhalogenated organic wastes.

Procedure

Label two 13-mm × 100-mm test tubes near the top of the tubes. The labels should have your name and "No. 1" and "No. 2" written on them. Place 0.50 g of benzophenone in the first tube. Place 0.50 g of benzophenone and 0.05 g of naphthalene in the second tube. Add about 2 mL of 2-propanol (isopropyl alcohol) to each tube and warm them in a beaker of warm water to dissolve the solids. When the solids have dissolved, add one small drop (Pasteur pipet) of glacial acetic acid to each tube and then fill each tube nearly to the top with more 2-propanol. Stopper the tubes tightly with rubber stoppers, shake them well, and place them in a beaker on a windowsill where they will receive direct sunlight.

> **Note:** You may be directed by your instructor to use a sunlamp instead of direct sunlight (see Special Instructions).

The reaction requires about 1 week for completion (3 hours with a sunlamp). If the reaction has occurred during this period, the product will have crystallized from the solution. Observe the result in each test tube. Collect the product by vacuum filtration using a small Büchner or Hirsch funnel (Technique 8, Section 8.3, p. 651) and allow it to dry. Weigh the product and determine its melting point and percentage yield. At the option of the instructor, obtain the infrared spectrum using the dry film method (Technique 25, Section 25.4, p. 878) or as a KBr pellet (Technique 25, Section 25.5, p. 878). Submit the product to the instructor in a labeled vial along with the report.

REFERENCE

Vogler, A., and Kunkely, H. "Photochemistry and Beer." *Journal of Chemical Education, 59* (January 1982): 25.

EXPERIMENT 50B

Synthesis of β-Benzopinacolone: The Acid-Catalyzed Rearrangement of Benzpinacol

The ability of carbocations to rearrange represents an important concept in organic chemistry. In this experiment, the benzpinacol, prepared in Experiment 50A, will rearrange to **benzopinacolone (2,2,2-triphenylacetophenone)** under the influence of iodine in glacial acetic acid.

OH OH
C—C
I_2
glacial acetic acid
O
C—C
+ H_2O

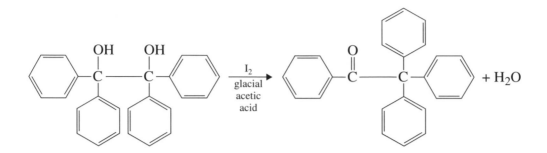

The product is isolated as a crystalline white solid. Benzopinacolone is known to crystallize in two different crystalline forms, each with a different melting point. The **alpha** form has a melting point of 206–207°C, whereas the **beta** form melts at 182°C. The product formed in this experiment is the β-benzopinacolone.

Required Reading

Review:	Technique 7	Reaction Methods, Section 7.2
	Technique 11	Crystallization: Purification of Solids, Section 11.3
	Technique 25	Infrared Spectroscopy, Part B
	Technique 26	Nuclear Magnetic Resonance Spectroscopy, Part B

Before beginning this experiment, you should read the material dealing with carbocation rearrangements in your lecture textbook.

Special Instructions

This experiment requires very little time and can be coscheduled with another short experiment.

Suggested Waste Disposal

All organic residues must be placed in the appropriate container for nonhalogenated organic waste.

Procedure

In a 25-mL round-bottom flask, add 5 mL of a 0.015 *M* solution of iodine dissolved in glacial acetic acid. Add 1 g of benzpinacol and attach a water-cooled condenser. Using a small heating mantle, allow the solution to heat under reflux for 5 minutes. Crystals may begin to appear from the solution during this heating period.

Remove the heat source and allow the solution to cool slowly. The product will crystallize from the solution as it cools. When the solution has cooled to room temperature, collect the crystals by vacuum filtration using a small Büchner funnel. Rinse the crystals with three 2-mL portions of cold, glacial acetic acid. Allow the crystals to dry in the air overnight. Weigh the dried product and determine its melting point. Pure β-benzopinacolone melts at 182°C. Obtain the infrared spectrum using the dry film method (Technique 25, Section 25.4, p. 878) or as a KBr pellet (Technique 25, Section 25.5, p. 878) and the NMR spectrum in carbon tetrachloride or $CDCl_3$ (Technique 26, Section 26.1, p. 912).

Calculate the percentage yield. Submit the product to your instructor in a labeled vial, along with your spectra. Interpret your spectra, showing how they are consistent with the rearranged structure of the product.

QUESTIONS

1. Can you think of a way to produce the benzophenone n–π^* triplet T_1 *without* having benzophenone pass through its first singlet state? Explain.

2. A reaction similar to the one described here occurs when benzophenone is treated with the metal magnesium (pinacol reduction).

$$2\ Ph_2C{=}O \xrightarrow{Mg} Ph_2\overset{\displaystyle OH}{\overset{|}{C}}-\overset{\displaystyle OH}{\overset{|}{C}}Ph_2$$

Compare the mechanism of this reaction with the photoreduction mechanism. What are the differences?

3. Which of the following molecules do you expect would be useful in quenching benzophenone photoreduction? Explain.

Oxygen	(S_1 = 22 kcal/mol)
9,10-Diphenylanthracene	(T_1 = 42 kcal/mol)
trans-1,3-Pentadiene	(T_1 = 59 kcal/mol)
Naphthalene	(T_1 = 61 kcal/mol)
Biphenyl	(T_1 = 66 kcal/mol)
Toluene	(T_1 = 83 kcal/mol)
Benzene	(T_1 = 84 kcal/mol)

ESSAY

Fireflies and Photochemistry

The production of light as a result of a chemical reaction is called **chemiluminescence.** A chemiluminescent reaction generally produces one of the product molecules in an electronically excited state. The excited state emits a photon, and light is produced. If a reaction that produces light is biochemical, occurring in a living organism, the phenomenon is called **bioluminescence.**

The light produced by fireflies and other bioluminescent organisms has fascinated observers for many years. Many different organisms have developed the ability to emit light. They include bacteria, fungi, protozoans, hydras, marine worms, sponges, corals, jellyfish, crustaceans, clams, snails, squids, fish, and insects. Curiously, among the higher forms of life, only fish are included on the list. Amphibians, reptiles, birds, mammals, and the higher plants are excluded. Among the marine species, none is a freshwater organism. The excellent *Scientific American* article by McElroy and Seliger (see References) delineates the natural history, characteristics, and habits of many bioluminescent organisms.

The first significant studies of a bioluminescent organism were performed by the French physiologist Raphael Dubois in 1887. He studied the mollusk *Pholas dactylis,* a bioluminescent clam indigenous to the Mediterranean Sea. Dubois found that a cold-water extract of the clam was able to emit light for several minutes following the extraction. When the light emission ceased, it could be restored, he found, by a material extracted from the clam by hot water. A hot-water extract of the clam alone did not produce the luminescence. Reasoning carefully, Dubois concluded that there was an enzyme in the cold-water extract that was destroyed in hot water. The luminescent compound, however, could be extracted without destruction in either hot or cold water. He called the luminescent material **luciferin,** and the enzyme that induced it to emit light, **luciferase;** both names were derived from *Lucifer,* a Latin name meaning "bearer of light." Today the luminescent materials from all organisms are called *luciferins,* and the associated enzymes are called *luciferases.*

The most extensively studied bioluminescent organism is the firefly. Fireflies are found in many parts of the world and probably represent the most familiar example of bioluminescence. In such areas, on a typical summer evening, fireflies, or "lightning bugs," can frequently be seen to emit flashes of light as they cavort over the lawn or in the garden. It is now universally accepted that the luminescence of fireflies is a mating device. The male firefly flies about 2 feet above the ground and emits flashes of light at regular intervals. The female, who remains stationary on the ground, waits a characteristic interval and then flashes a response. In return, the male reorients his direction of flight toward her and flashes a signal once again. The entire cycle is rarely repeated more than 5 to 10 times before the male reaches the female. Fireflies of different species can recognize one another by their flash patterns, which vary in number, rate, and duration among species.

Although the total structure of the luciferase enzyme of the American firefly *Photinus pyralis* is unknown, the structure of the luciferin has been established. In spite of a large amount of experimental work, however, the complete nature of the chemical reactions that produce the light is still subject to some controversy. It is possible, nevertheless, to outline the most salient details of the reaction.

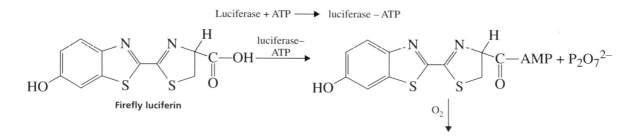

Luciferase + ATP ⟶ luciferase – ATP

Firefly luciferin (HO–benzothiazolyl–thiazoline–CH–C(=O)–OH) $\xrightarrow{\text{luciferase–ATP}}$ HO–benzothiazolyl–thiazoline–CH–C(=O)–AMP + $P_2O_7^{2-}$

Firefly luciferin

$\downarrow O_2$

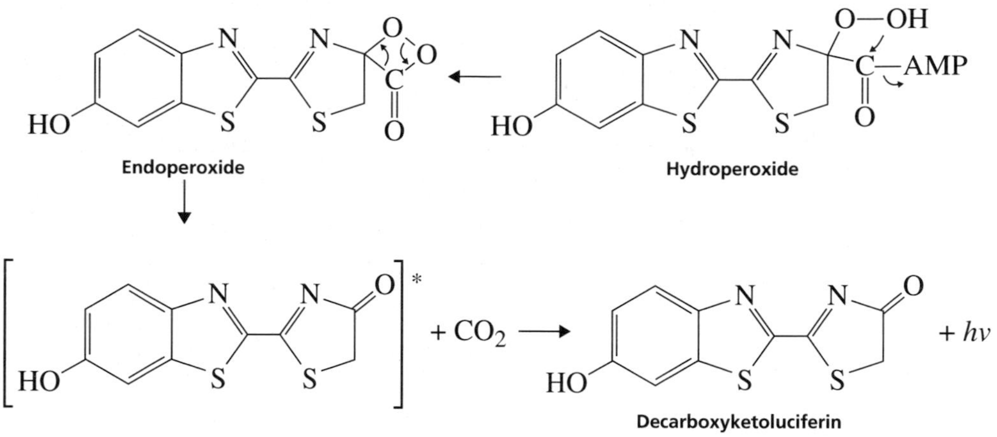

Endoperoxide

Hydroperoxide

$+ CO_2 \longrightarrow$ $+ h\nu$

Decarboxyketoluciferin

Besides the luciferin and the luciferase, other substances—magnesium(II), ATP (adenosine triphosphate), and molecular oxygen—are needed to produce the luminescence. In the postulated first step of the reaction, the luciferase complexes with an ATP molecule. In the second step, the luciferin binds to the luciferase and reacts with the already bound ATP molecule to become "primed." In this reaction, pyrophosphate ion is expelled, and AMP (adenosine monophosphate) becomes attached to the carboxyl group of the luciferin. In the third step, the luciferin–AMP complex is oxidized by molecular oxygen to form a hydroperoxide; this cyclizes with the carboxyl group, expelling AMP and forming the cyclic endoperoxide. This reaction would be difficult if the carboxyl group of the luciferin had not been primed with ATP. The endoperoxide is unstable and readily decarboxylates, producing decarboxyketoluciferin in an *electronically excited state,* which is deactivated by the emission of a photon (fluorescence). Thus, it is the cleavage of the four-membered-ring endoperoxide that leads to the electronically excited molecule and hence the bioluminescence.

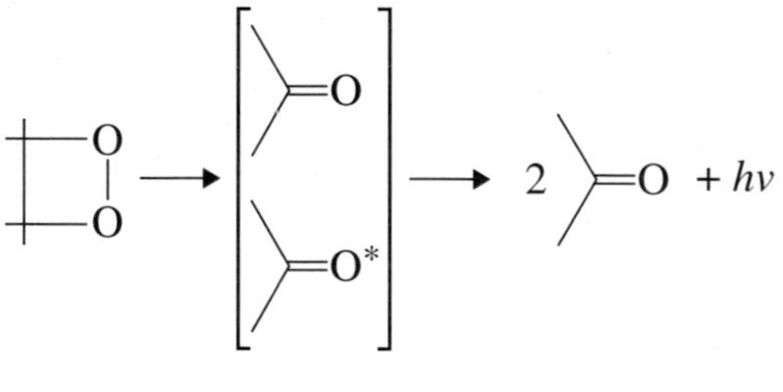

$\longrightarrow 2 \; \rangle\!=\!O + h\nu$

That one of the two carbonyl groups, either that of the decarboxyketoluciferin or that of the carbon dioxide, should be formed in an excited state can be readily predicted from the orbital symmetry conservation principles of Woodward and Hoffmann. This reaction is formally like the decomposition of a cyclobutane ring and yields two ethylene molecules. In analyzing the forward course of that reaction, that is, 2 ethylene $\rightarrow$ cyclobutane, one can easily show that the reaction, which involves four π electrons, is forbidden for two ground-state ethylenes but allowed for only one ethylene in the ground state and the other in an excited state. This suggests that, in the reverse process, one of the ethylene molecules should be formed in an excited state. Extending these arguments to the endoperoxide also suggests that one of the two carbonyl groups should be formed in its excited state.

The emitting molecule, decarboxyketoluciferin, has been isolated and synthesized. When it is excited photochemically by photon absorption in basic solution (pH $>$ 7.5–8.0), it fluoresces, giving a fluorescence emission spectrum that is identical to the emission spectrum produced by the interaction of firefly luciferin and firefly luciferase. The emitting form of decarboxyketoluciferin has thus been identified as the **enol dianion.** In neutral or acidic solution, the emission spectrum of decarboxyketoluciferin does not match the emission spectrum of the bioluminescent system.

The exact function of the enzyme firefly luciferase is not yet known, but it is clear that all these reactions occur while luciferin is bound to the enzyme as a substrate. Also, because the enzyme undoubtedly has several basic groups ($-COO^-$, $-NH_2$, and so on), the buffering action of those groups would easily explain why the enol dianion is also the emitting form of decarboxyketoluciferin in the biological system.

Decarboxyketoluciferin $\xrightarrow{-2H^+}$

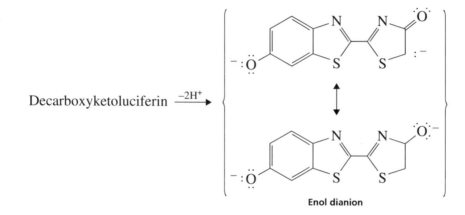

Enol dianion

Most chemiluminescent and bioluminescent reactions require oxygen. Likewise, most produce an electronically excited emitting species through the decomposition of a **peroxide** of one sort or another. In the experiment that follows, a **chemiluminescent** reaction that involves the decomposition of a peroxide intermediate is described.

REFERENCES

Clayton, R. K. "The Luminescence of Fireflies and Other Living Things." Chap. 6 in *Light and Living Matter.* Vol. 2: *The Biological Part.* New York: McGraw-Hill, 1971.

Fox, J. L. "Theory May Explain Firefly Luminescence." *Chemical and Engineering News, 56* (March 6, 1978): 17.

Harvey, E. N. *Bioluminescence.* New York: Academic Press, 1952.

Hastings, J. W. "Bioluminescence." *Annual Review of Biochemistry, 37* (1968): 597.

McCapra, F. "Chemical Mechanisms in Bioluminescence." *Accounts of Chemical Research, 9* (1976): 201.

McElroy, W. D., and Seliger, H. H. "Biological Luminescence." *Scientific American, 207* (December 1962): 76.

McElroy, W. D., Seliger, H. H., and White, E. H. "Mechanism of Bioluminescence, Chemiluminescence and Enzyme Function in the Oxidation of Firefly Luciferin." *Photochemistry and Photobiology, 10* (1969): 153.

Seliger, H. H., and McElroy, W. D. *Light: Physical and Biological Action.* New York: Academic Press, 1965.

EXPERIMENT 51

Luminol

Chemiluminescence
Energy transfer
Reduction of a nitro group
Amide formation

In this experiment, the chemiluminescent compound **luminol,** or **5-amino-phthalhydrazide,** will be synthesized from 3-nitrophthalic acid.

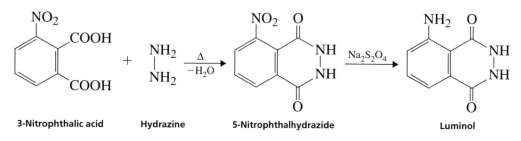

3-Nitrophthalic acid + Hydrazine $\xrightarrow[-H_2O]{\Delta}$ 5-Nitrophthalhydrazide $\xrightarrow{Na_2S_2O_4}$ Luminol

The first step of the synthesis is the simple formation of a cyclic diamide, 5-nitrophthalhydrazide, by reaction of 3-nitrophthalic acid with hydrazine. Reduction of the nitro group with sodium dithionite affords luminol.

In neutral solution, luminol exists largely as a dipolar anion (zwitterion). This dipolar ion exhibits a weak blue fluorescence after being exposed to light. However, in alkaline solution, luminol is converted to its dianion, which may be oxidized by molecular oxygen to give an intermediate that is chemiluminescent. The reaction is thought to have the following sequence:

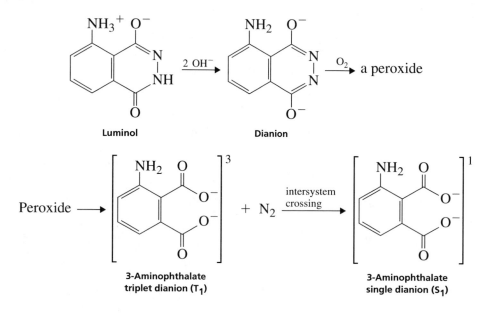

Luminol $\xrightarrow{2\ OH^-}$ Dianion $\xrightarrow{O_2}$ a peroxide

Peroxide $\longrightarrow$ 3-Aminophthalate triplet dianion (T_1) + N_2 $\xrightarrow{\text{intersystem crossing}}$ 3-Aminophthalate single dianion (S_1)

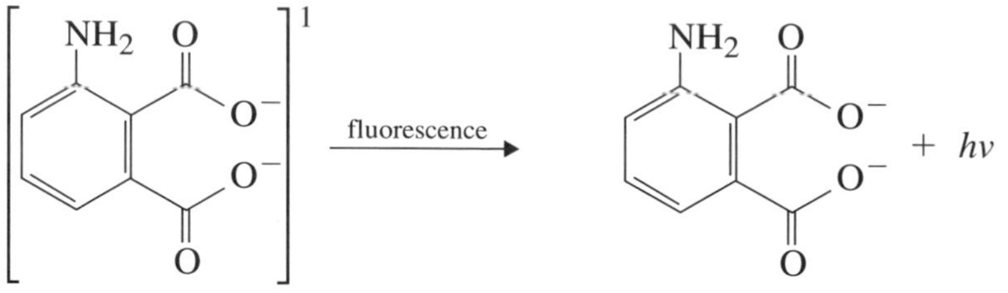

S_1

fluorescence

3-Aminophthalate ground-state dianion, S_0

The dianion of luminol undergoes a reaction with molecular oxygen to form a peroxide of unknown structure. This peroxide is unstable and decomposes with the evolution of nitrogen gas, producing the 3-aminophthalate dianion in an electronically excited state. The excited dianion emits a photon that is visible as light. One very attractive hypothesis for the structure of the peroxide postulates a cyclic endoperoxide that decomposes by the following mechanism:

A postulate

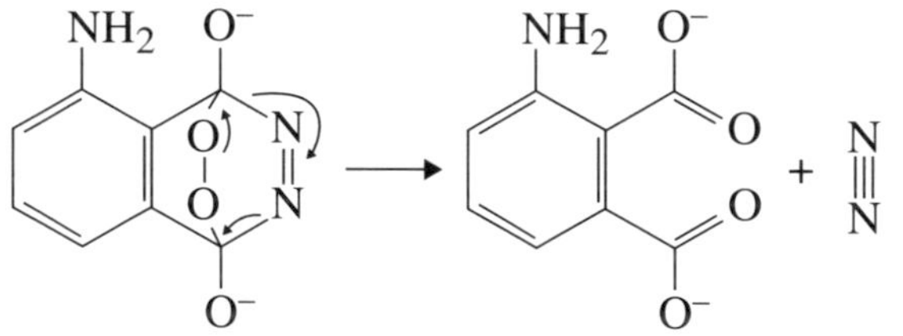

Certain experimental facts argue against this intermediate, however. For instance, certain acyclic hydrazides that cannot form a similar intermediate have also been found to be chemiluminescent.

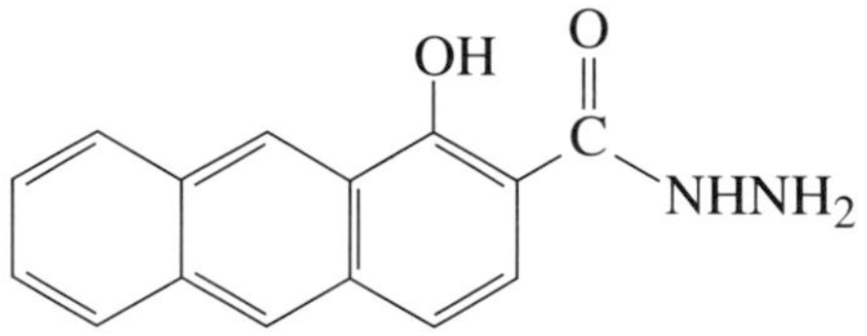

1-Hydroxy-2-anthroic acid hydrazide (chemiluminescent)

Although the nature of the peroxide is still debatable, the remainder of the reaction is well understood. The chemical products of the reaction have been shown to be the 3-aminophthalate dianion and molecular nitrogen. The intermediate that emits light has been identified definitely as the *excited-state singlet* of the 3-aminophthalate dianion.[1] Thus, the fluorescence emission spectrum of the 3-aminophthalate dianion (produced by photon absorption) is identical to the spectrum of the light emitted from the chemiluminescent reaction. However, for numerous complicated reasons, it is believed that the 3-aminophthalate

[1] The terms *singlet, triplet, intersystem crossing, energy transfer,* and *quenching* are explained in Experiment 50.

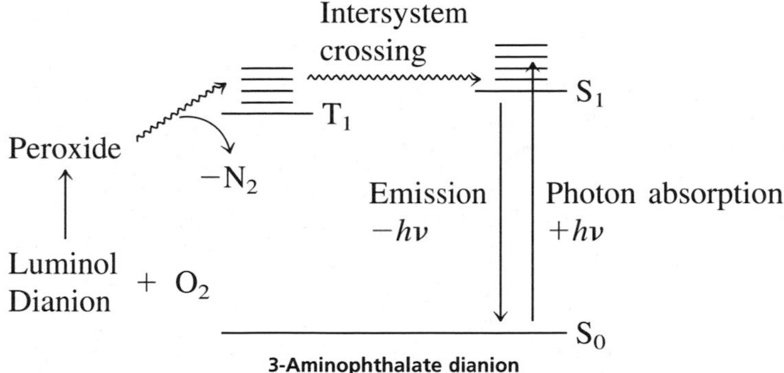

Fluorescence emission spectrum of the 3-aminophthalate dianion.

dianion is formed first as a vibrationally excited triplet state molecule, which makes the intersystem crossing to the singlet state before emission of a photon.

The excited state of the 3-aminophthalate dianion may be quenched by suitable acceptor molecules, or the energy (about 50–80 Kcal/mol) may be transferred to give emission from the acceptor molecules. Several such experiments are described in the following procedure.

The system chosen for the chemiluminescence studies of luminol in this experiment uses dimethylsulfoxide $(CH_3)_2SO$ as the solvent, potassium hydroxide as the base required for the formation of the dianion of luminol, and molecular oxygen. Several alternative systems have been used, substituting hydrogen peroxide and an oxidizing agent for molecular oxygen. An aqueous system using potassium ferricyanide and hydrogen peroxide is an alternative system used frequently.

References

Rahaut, M. M. "Chemiluminescence from Concerted Peroxide Decomposition Reactions." *Accounts of Chemical Research, 2* (1969): 80.

White, E. H., and Roswell, D. F. "The Chemiluminescence of Organic Hydrazides." *Accounts of Chemical Research, 3* (1970): 54.

Required Reading

Review:	Technique 7	Reaction Methods, Section 7.9
New:	Essay	Fireflies and Photochemistry

Special Instructions

This entire experiment can be completed in about 1 hour. When you are working with hydrazine, you should remember that it is toxic and should not be spilled on the skin. It is also a suspected carcinogen. Dimethylsulfoxide may also be toxic; avoid breathing the vapors or spilling it on your skin.

A darkened room is required to observe adequately the chemiluminescence of luminol. A darkened hood that has had its window covered with butcher paper or aluminum foil also works well. Other fluorescent dyes besides those mentioned (for instance, 9,10-diphenylanthracene) can also be used for the energy-transfer experiments. The dyes selected may depend on what is immediately available. The instructor may have each student use one dye for the energy-transfer experiments, with one student making a comparison experiment without a dye.

Suggested Waste Disposal

Dispose of the filtrate from the vacuum filtration of 5-nitrophthalhydrazide in the container designated for nonhalogenated organic solvents. The filtrate from the vacuum filtration of 5-aminophthalhydrazide may be diluted with water and poured into the waste container designated for aqueous waste. The mixture containing potassium hydroxide, dimethylsulfoxide, and luminol should be placed in the special container designated for this material.

Procedure

PART A. 3-NITROPHTHALHYDRAZIDE

Place 0.60 g of 3-nitrophthalic acid and 0.8 mL of a 10% aqueous solution of hydrazine (use gloves) in a small (15-mm × 125-mm) sidearm test tube.[2] At the same time, heat 8 mL of water in a beaker on a hot plate to about 80°C. Heat the test tube over a microburner until the solid dissolves. Add 1.6 mL of triethylene glycol and clamp the test tube in an upright position on a ring stand. Place a thermometer (do not seal the system) and a boiling stone in the test tube and attach a piece of pressure tubing to the sidearm. Connect this tubing to an aspirator (use a trap). The thermometer bulb should be in the liquid as much as possible. Heat the solution with a microburner until the liquid boils vigorously and the refluxing water vapor is drawn away by the aspirator vacuum (the temperature will rise to about 120°C). Continue heating and allow the temperature to increase rapidly until it rises just above 200°C. This heating requires 2–3 minutes, and you must watch the temperature closely to avoid heating the mixture well above 200°C. Remove the burner briefly when this temperature has been achieved and then resume gentle heating to maintain a fairly constant temperature of 220–230°C for about 3 minutes. Allow the test tube to cool to about 100°C, add the 8 mL of hot water that was prepared previously, and cool the test tube to

[2]A 10% aqueous solution of hydrazine can be prepared by diluting 15.6 g of a commercial 64% hydrazine solution to a volume of 100 mL using water.

room temperature by allowing tap water to flow over the outside of the test tube. Collect the brown crystals of 5-nitrophthalhydrazide by vacuum filtration, using a small Hirsch funnel. It is not necessary to dry the product before you go on with the next reaction step.

PART B. LUMINOL (5-AMINOPHTHALHYDRAZIDE)

Transfer the moist 5-nitrophthalhydrazide to a 20-mm × 150-mm test tube. Add 2.6 mL of a 10% sodium hydroxide solution and agitate the mixture until the hydrazide dissolves. Add 1.6 g of sodium dithionite dihydrate (sodium hydrosulfite dihydrate, $Na_2S_2O_4 \cdot 2\,H_2O$). Using a Pasteur pipet, add 2–4 mL of water to wash the solid from the walls of the test tube. Add a boiling stone to the test tube. Heat the test tube until the solution boils. Agitate the solution and maintain the boiling, continuing the agitation for at least 5 minutes. Add 1.0 mL of glacial acetic acid and cool the test tube to room temperature by allowing tap water to flow over the outside of it. Agitate the mixture during the cooling step. Collect the light yellow or gold crystals of luminol by vacuum filtration, using a small Hirsch funnel. Save a small sample of this product, allow it to dry overnight, and determine its melting point (mp 319–320°C). The remainder of the luminol may be used without drying for the chemiluminescence experiments. When drying the luminol, it is best to use a vacuum desiccator charged with calcium sulfate drying agent.

PART C. CHEMILUMINESCENCE EXPERIMENTS

Caution: Be careful not to allow any of the mixture to touch your skin while shaking the flask. Hold the stopper securely.

Cover the bottom of a 10-mL Erlenmeyer flask with a layer of potassium hydroxide pellets. Add enough dimethylsulfoxide to cover the pellets. Add about 0.025 g of the moist luminol to the flask, stopper it, and shake it vigorously to mix air into the solution.[3] In a dark room, a faint glow of bluish white light will be visible. The intensity of the glow will increase with continued shaking of the flask and occasional removal of the stopper to admit more air.

To observe energy transfer to a fluorescent dye, dissolve 1 or 2 crystals of the indicator dye in about 0.25 mL of water. Add the dye solution to the dimethylsulfoxide solution of luminol, stopper the flask, and shake the mixture vigorously. Observe the intensity and the color of the light produced.

A table of some dyes and the colors produced when they are mixed with luminol follows. Other dyes not included on this list may also be tested in this experiment.

---

[3] An alternative method for demonstrating chemiluminescence, using potassium ferricyanide and hydrogen peroxide as oxidizing agents, is described in E. H. Huntress, L. N. Stanley, and A. S. Parker, *Journal of Chemical Education, 11* (1934): 142.

Fluorescent Dye	Color
No dye	Faint bluish white
2,6-Dichloroindophenol	Blue
9-Aminoacridine	Blue green
Eosin	Salmon pink
Fluorescein	Yellow green
Dichlorofluorescein	Yellow orange
Rhodamine B	Green
Phenolphthalein	Purple

ESSAY

Polymers and Plastics

Chemically, plastics are composed of chainlike molecules of high molecular weight called **polymers.** Polymers have been built up from simpler chemicals called **monomers.** The word *poly* is defined as "many," *mono* means "one," and *mer* indicates "units." Thus, many monomers are combined to give a polymer. A different monomer or combination of monomers is used to manufacture each type or family of polymers. There are two broad classes of polymers: addition and condensation. Both types are described here.

Many polymers (plastics) produced in the past were of such low quality that they gained a bad reputation. The plastics industry now produces high-quality materials that are increasingly replacing metals in many applications. They are used in many products such as clothes, toys, furniture, machine components, paints, boats, automobile parts, and even artificial organs. In the automobile industry, metals have been replaced with plastics to help reduce the overall weight of the car and to help reduce corrosion. This reduction in weight helps improve gas mileage. Epoxy resins can even replace metal in engine parts.

CHEMICAL STRUCTURES OF POLYMERS

Basically, a polymer is made up of many repeating molecular units formed by sequential addition of monomer molecules to one another. Many monomer molecules of A, say 1,000 to 1 million, can be linked to form a gigantic polymeric molecule:

[3] See footnote 1, page 391.

$$\underset{\text{Monomer molecules}}{\text{Many A}} \longrightarrow \text{etc.} \; \underset{\text{Polymer molecule}}{\text{— A-A-A-A-A —}} \; \text{etc.} \quad \text{or} \quad \left(\text{A} \right)_n$$

Monomers that are different can also be linked to form a polymer with an alternating structure. This type of polymer is called a **copolymer.**

$$\underset{\text{Monomer molecules}}{\text{Many A + many B}} \longrightarrow \text{etc.} \; \underset{\text{Polymer molecule}}{\text{— A-B-A-B-A-B —}} \; \text{etc.} \quad \text{or} \quad \left(\text{A-B} \right)_n$$

TYPES OF POLYMERS

For convenience, chemists classify polymers in several main groups, depending on the method of synthesis.

1. **Addition polymers** are formed by a reaction in which monomer units simply add to one another to form a long-chain (generally linear or branched) polymer. The monomers usually contain carbon–carbon double bonds. Examples of synthetic addition polymers include polystyrene (Styrofoam), polytetrafluoroethylene (Teflon), polyethylene, polypropylene, polyacrylonitrile (Orlon, Acrilan, Creslan), poly(vinyl chloride) (PVC), and poly(methyl methacrylate) (Lucite, Plexiglas). The process can be represented as follows:

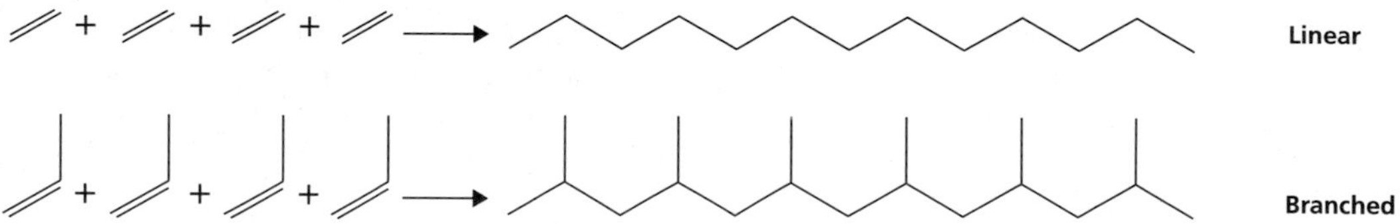

2. **Condensation polymers** are formed by the reaction of bifunctional or polyfunctional molecules, with the elimination of some small molecule (such as water, ammonia, or hydrogen chloride) as a by-product. Familiar examples of synthetic condensation polymers include polyesters (Dacron, Mylar), polyamides (nylon), polyurethanes, and epoxy resin. Natural condensation polymers include polyamino acids (protein), cellulose, and starch. The process can be represented as follows:

$$\text{H}-\boxed{}-\text{X} + \text{H}-\boxed{}-\text{X} \longrightarrow \text{H}-\boxed{}-\boxed{}-\text{X} + \text{HX}$$

3. **Cross-linked polymers** are formed when long chains are linked in one gigantic, three-dimensional structure with tremendous rigidity. Addition and condensation polymers can exist with a cross-linked network, depending on the monomers used

in the synthesis. Familiar examples of cross-linked polymers are Bakelite, rubber, and casting (boat) resin. The process can be represented as follows:

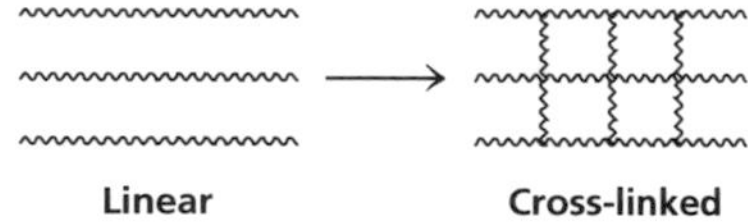

Linear and crossed-linked polymers.

THERMAL CLASSIFICATION OF POLYMERS

Industrialists and technologists often classify polymers as either thermoplastics or thermoset plastics rather than as addition or condensation polymers. This classification takes into account their thermal properties.

1. **Thermal properties of thermoplastics.** Most addition polymers and many condensation polymers can be softened (melted) by heat and re-formed (molded) into other shapes. Industrialists and technologists often refer to these types of polymers as **thermoplastics.** Weaker, noncovalent bonds (dipole–dipole and London dispersion) are broken during the heating. Technically, thermoplastics are the materials we call plastics. Thermoplastics may be repeatedly melted and recast into new shapes. They may be recycled as long as degradation does not occur during reprocessing.

   Some addition polymers, such as poly(vinyl chloride), are difficult to melt and process. Liquids with high boiling points, such as dibutyl phthalate, are added to the polymer to separate the chains from each other. These compounds are called **plasticizers.** In effect, they act as lubricants that neutralize the attractions that exist between chains. As a result, the polymer can be melted at a lower temperature to aid in processing. In addition, the polymer becomes more flexible at room temperature. By varying the amount of plasticizer, poly(vinyl chloride) can range from a very flexible, rubberlike material to a very hard substance.

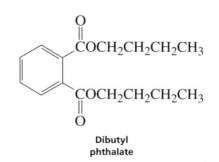

   $$\text{C}_6\text{H}_4\left(\overset{\text{O}}{\overset{\|}{\text{C}}}\text{OCH}_2\text{CH}_2\text{CH}_2\text{CH}_3\right)_2$$

   Dibutyl phthalate

   Phthalate plasticizers are volatile compounds of low molecular weight. Part of the new car smell comes from the odor of these materials as they evaporate from the vinyl upholstery. The vapor often condenses on the windshield as an oily film. After some time, the vinyl material may lose enough plasticizer to cause it to crack.

2. **Thermal properties of thermoset plastics.** Industrialists use the term **thermoset** plastics to describe materials that melt initially but on further heating become permanently hardened. Once formed, thermoset materials cannot be softened and re-

molded without destruction of the polymer, because covalent bonds are broken. Thermoset plastics cannot be recycled. Chemically, thermoset plastics are cross-linked polymers. They are formed when long chains are linked in one gigantic, three-dimensional structure with tremendous rigidity.

Polymers can also be classified in other ways; for example, many varieties of rubber are often referred to as *elastomers,* Dacron is a fiber, and poly(vinyl acetate) is an adhesive. The addition and condensation classifications are used in this essay.

ADDITION POLYMERS

By volume, most of the polymers prepared in industry are of the addition type. The monomers generally contain a carbon–carbon double bond. The most important example of an addition polymer is the well-known polyethylene, for which the monomer is ethylene. Countless numbers (n) of ethylene molecules are linked in long-chain polymeric molecules by breaking the pi bond and creating two new single bonds between the monomer units. The number of recurring units may be large or small, depending on the polymerization conditions.

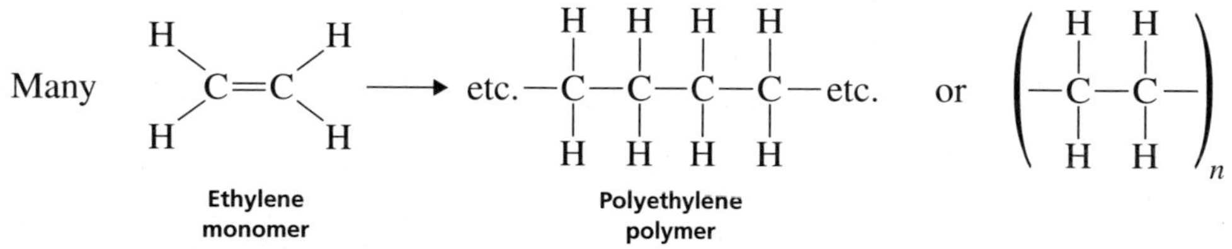

$$\text{Many}\quad H_2C{=}CH_2 \longrightarrow \text{etc.}{-}CH_2{-}CH_2{-}CH_2{-}CH_2{-}\text{etc.} \quad \text{or} \quad \left({-}CH_2{-}CH_2{-}\right)_n$$

Ethylene monomer

Polyethylene polymer

This reaction can be promoted by heat, pressure, and a chemical catalyst. The molecules produced in a typical reaction vary in the number of carbon atoms in their chains. In other words, a mixture of polymers of varying length, rather than a pure compound, is produced.

Polyethylenes with linear structures can pack together easily and are referred to as high-density polyethylenes. They are fairly rigid materials. Low-density polyethylenes consist of branched-chain molecules, with some cross-linking in the chains. They are more flexible than the high-density polyethylenes. The reaction conditions and the catalysts that produce polyethylenes of low and high density are quite different. The monomer, however, is the same in each case.

Another example of an addition polymer is polypropylene. In this case, the monomer is propylene. The polymer that results has a branched methyl on alternate carbon atoms of the chain.

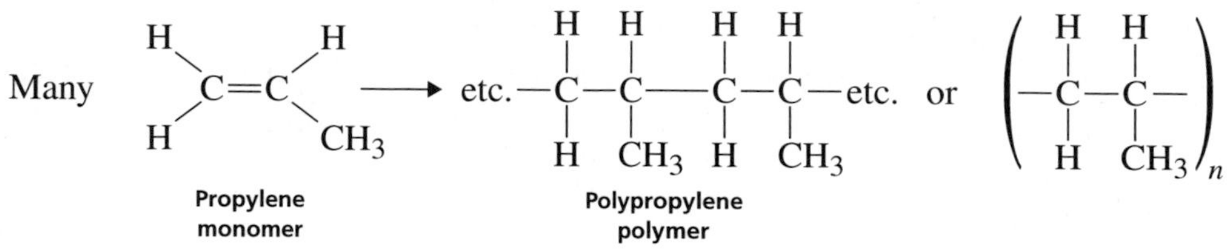

$$\text{Many}\quad H_2C{=}CH(CH_3) \longrightarrow \text{etc.}{-}CH_2{-}CH(CH_3){-}CH_2{-}CH(CH_3){-}\text{etc.} \quad \text{or} \quad \left({-}CH_2{-}CH(CH_3){-}\right)_n$$

Propylene monomer

Polypropylene polymer

A number of common addition polymers are shown in Table One. Some of their principal uses are also listed. The last three entries in the table all have a carbon–carbon double bond remaining after the polymer is formed. These bonds activate or participate in a further reaction to form cross-linked polymers called *elastomers;* this term is almost synonymous with *rubber,* because elastomers are materials with common characteristics.

CONDENSATION POLYMERS

Condensation polymers, for which the monomers contain more than one type of functional group, are more complex than addition polymers. In addition, most condensation polymers are copolymers made from more than one type of monomer. Recall that addition polymers, in contrast, are all prepared from substituted ethylene molecules. The single functional group in each case is one or more double bonds, and a single type of monomer is generally used.

Dacron, a polyester, can be prepared by causing a dicarboxylic acid to react with a bifunctional alcohol (a diol):

$$\text{HO—}\overset{\text{O}}{\overset{\|}{\text{C}}}\text{—}C_6H_4\text{—}\overset{\text{O}}{\overset{\|}{\text{C}}}\text{—}\boxed{\text{OH H}}\text{—}OCH_2CH_2OH \longrightarrow$$

Terephthalic acid — Ethylene glycol

$$\text{—}\overset{\text{O}}{\overset{\|}{\text{C}}}\text{—}C_6H_4\text{—}\overset{\text{O}}{\overset{\|}{\text{C}}}\text{—}OCH_2CH_2\text{—O—} \quad + H_2O$$

Dacron

Nylon 6-6, a polyamide, can be prepared by causing a dicarboxylic acid to react with a bifunctional amine.

$$\text{HO—}\overset{\text{O}}{\overset{\|}{\text{C}}}(CH_2)_4\overset{\text{O}}{\overset{\|}{\text{C}}}\text{—}\boxed{\text{OH H}}\text{—}\overset{\text{H}}{\overset{|}{\text{N}}}(CH_2)_6\overset{\text{H}}{\overset{|}{\text{N}}}\text{H} \longrightarrow \text{—}\overset{\text{O}}{\overset{\|}{\text{C}}}(CH_2)_4\overset{\text{O}}{\overset{\|}{\text{C}}}\text{—}\underset{\text{H}}{\underset{|}{\text{N}}}(CH_2)_6\underset{\text{H}}{\underset{|}{\text{N}}}\text{—} \quad + H_2O$$

Adipic acid — Hexamethylene-diamine — Nylon

Notice, in each case, that a small molecule, water, is eliminated as a product of the reaction. Several other condensation polymers are listed in Table Two. Linear (or branched) chain polymers as well as cross-linked polymers are produced in condensation reactions.

The nylon structure contains the amide linkage at regular intervals:

$$\text{—}\overset{\text{O}}{\overset{\|}{\text{C}}}\text{—}\overset{\text{H}}{\overset{|}{\text{N}}}\text{—}$$

TABLE ONE Addition Polymers

Example	Monomer(s)	Polymer	Uses
Polyethylene	$CH_2{=}CH_2$	$—CH_2—CH_2—$	Most common and important polymer; bags, insulation for wires, squeeze bottles
Polypropylene	$CH_2{=}CH(CH_3)$	$—CH_2—CH(CH_3)—$	Fibers, indoor–outdoor carpets, bottles
Polystyrene	$CH_2{=}CH(C_6H_5)$	$—CH_2—CH(C_6H_5)—$	Styrofoam, inexpensive household goods, inexpensive molded objects
Poly(vinyl chloride) (PVC)	$CH_2{=}CH(Cl)$	$—CH_2—CH(Cl)—$	Synthetic leather, clear bottles, floor covering, phonograph records, water pipe
Polytetrafluoroethylene (Teflon)	$CF_2{=}CF_2$	$—CF_2—CF_2—$	Nonstick surfaces, chemically resistant films
Poly(methyl methacrylate) (Lucite, Plexiglas)	$CH_2{=}C(CO_2CH_3)(CH_3)$	$—CH_2—C(CO_2CH_3)(CH_3)—$	Unbreakable "glass," latex paints
Polyacrylonitrile (Orlon, Acrilan, Creslan)	$CH_2{=}CH(CN)$	$—CH_2—CH(CN)—$	Fiber used in sweaters, blankets, carpets
Poly(vinyl acetate) (PVA)	$CH_2{=}CH(OCCH_3)$ with C=O	$—CH_2—CH(OCCH_3)—$ with C=O	Adhesives, latex paints, chewing gum, textile coatings
Natural rubber	$CH_2{=}C(CH_3)CH{=}CH_2$	$—CH_2—C(CH_3){=}CH—CH_2—$	Polymer cross-linked with sulfur (vulcanization)
Polychloroprene (neoprene rubber)	$CH_2{=}C(Cl)CH{=}CH_2$	$—CH_2—C(Cl){=}CH—CH_2—$	Cross-linked with ZnO; resistant to oil and gasoline
Styrene butadiene rubber (SBR)	$CH_2{=}CH(C_6H_5)$ $CH_2{=}CHCH{=}CH_2$	$—CH_2CH(C_6H_5)—CH_2CH{=}CHCH_2—$	Cross-linked with peroxides; most common rubber; used for tires; 25% styrene, 75% butadiene

TABLE TWO Condensation Polymers

Example	Monomers	Polymer	Uses
Polyamides (nylon)	$HOC(=O)(CH_2)_nC(=O)OH$ $H_2N(CH_2)_nNH_2$	$-C(=O)(CH_2)_nC(=O)-NH(CH_2)_nNH-$	Fibers, molded objects
Polyesters (Dacron, Mylar, Fortrel)	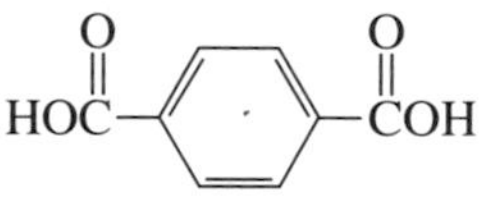 $HOC(=O)-C_6H_4-C(=O)OH$ $HO(CH_2)_nOH$	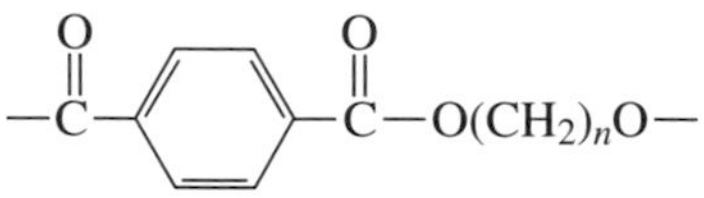 $-C(=O)-C_6H_4-C(=O)-O(CH_2)_nO-$	Linear polyesters, fibers, recording tape
Polyesters (Glyptal resin)	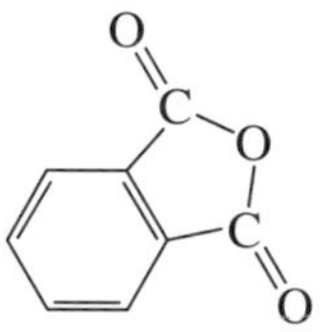 Phthalic anhydride $HOCH_2CH(OH)CH_2OH$	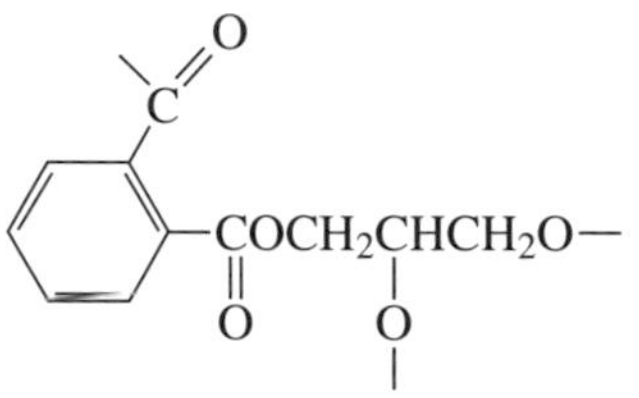 $C_6H_4(-C(=O)-)(-C(=O)OCH_2CH(O-)CH_2O-)$	Cross-linked polyester, paints
Polyesters (casting resin)	$HOC(=O)CH{=}CHC(=O)OH$ $HO(CH_2)_nOH$	$-C(=O)CH{=}CHC(=O)-O(CH_2)_nO-$	Cross-linked with styrene and peroxide, fiberglass boat resin
Phenol-formaldehyde resin (Bakelite)	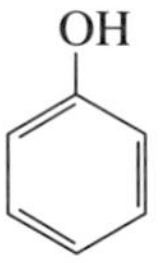 C_6H_5OH (phenol) $CH_2{=}O$	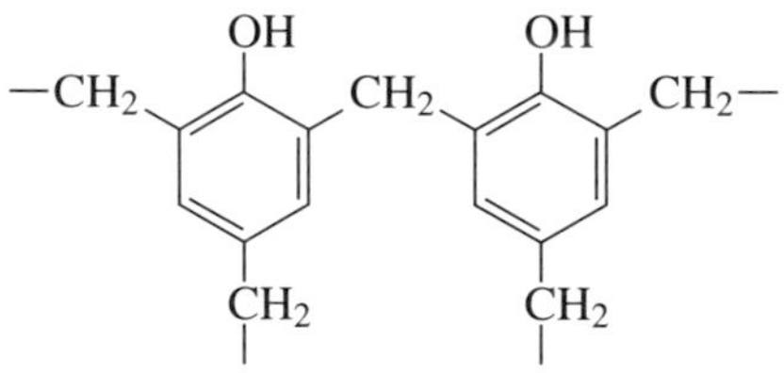 $-CH_2-C_6H_2(OH)(CH_2-)-CH_2-C_6H_2(OH)(CH_2-)-CH_2-$	Mixed with fillers, molded electrical goods, adhesives, laminates, varnishes
Cellulose acetate*	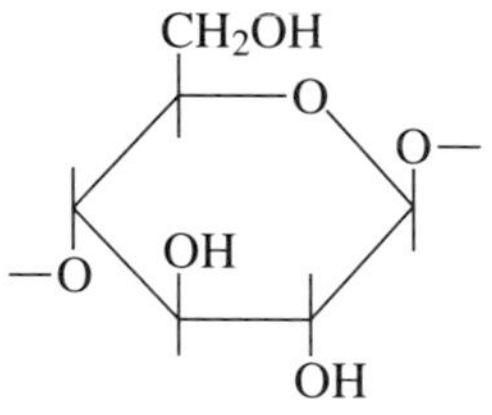 Glucose unit (CH_2OH, OH, OH; $-O-$ links) CH_3COOH	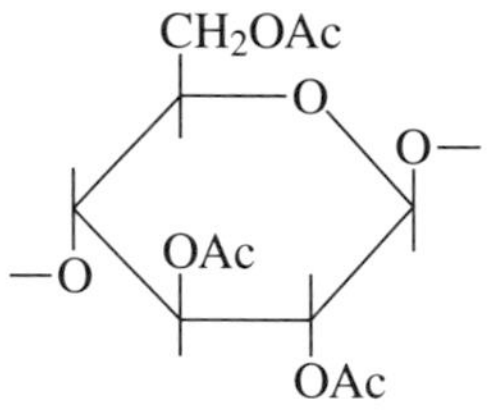 Glucose unit (CH_2OAc, OAc, OAc; $-O-$ links)	Photographic film
Silicones	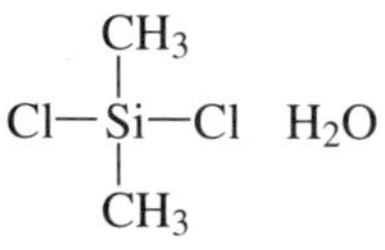 $Cl-Si(CH_3)_2-Cl$ $\quad H_2O$	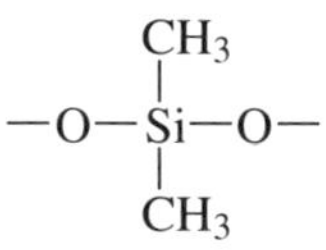 $-O-Si(CH_3)_2-O-$	Water-repellent coatings, temperature-resistant fluids and rubbers (CH_3SiCl_3 cross-links in water)
Polyurethanes	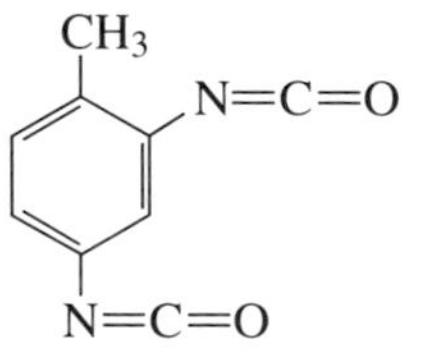 $CH_3C_6H_3(N{=}C{=}O)_2$ $HO(CH_2)_nOH$	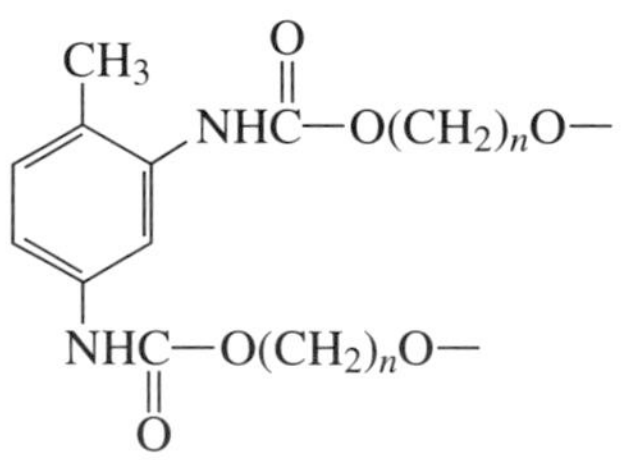 $CH_3C_6H_3(NHC(=O)-O(CH_2)_nO-)_2$	Rigid and flexible foams, fibers

*Cellulose, a polymer of glucose, is used as the monomer.

This type of linkage is extremely important in nature because of its presence in proteins and polypeptides. Proteins are gigantic polymeric substances made up of monomer units of amino acids. They are linked by the peptide (amide) bond.

Other important natural condensation polymers are starch and cellulose. They are polymeric materials made up of the sugar monomer glucose. Another important natural condensation polymer is the DNA molecule. A DNA molecule is made up of the sugar deoxyribose linked with phosphates to form the backbone of the molecule.

DISPOSABILITY PROBLEMS

What do we do with all our wastes? Currently, the most popular method is to bury our garbage in sanitary landfills. However, as we run out of good places to bury our garbage, incineration has become a more attractive method for solving the solid waste problem. Plastics, which compose about 2% of our garbage, burn readily. The new high-temperature incinerators are extremely efficient and can be operated with very little air pollution. It should also be possible to burn our garbage and generate electrical power from it.

Ideally, we should either recycle all our wastes or not produce the waste in the first place. Plastic waste consists of about 55% polyethylene and polypropylene, 20% polystyrene, and 11% PVC. All these polymers are thermoplastics and can be recycled. They can be resoftened and remolded into new goods. Unfortunately, thermosetting plastics (cross-linked polymers) cannot be remelted. They decompose on high-temperature heating. Thus, thermosetting plastics should not be used for "disposable" purposes. To recycle plastics effectively, we must sort the materials according to the various types. The plastics industry has introduced a code system consisting of seven categories for the common plastics used in packaging. The code is conveniently stamped on the bottom of the container. Using these codes, consumers can separate the plastics into groups for recycling purposes. These codes are listed in Table Three, together with the most common uses around the home. Notice that the seventh category is a miscellaneous one, called "Other."

It is quite amazing that so few different plastics are used in packaging. The most common ones are polyethylene (low and high density), polypropylene, polystyrene, and poly(ethylene terephthlate). All these materials can easily be recycled because they are thermoplastics. Incidently, vinyls (polyvinyl chloride) are becoming less common in packaging. The "Other" category, Code 7, is virtually nonexistent and usually consists of packaging where the top is made of a material different from that of the bottom. This dilemma should be easy to solve by placing the appropriate code on each part of the container.

Polymers, if they are well made, will not corrode or rust, and they last almost indefinitely. Unfortunately, these desirable properties also lead to a problem when plastics are buried in a landfill or thrown on the landscape—they do not decompose. Research is being undertaken to discover plastics that are biodegradable or photodegradable so that either microorganisms or light from the sun can decompose our litter and garbage. Although there are some advantages to this approach, it is probably better to eliminate packaging at the source or to engage in an effective recycling program. We must learn to use plastics wisely.

TABLE THREE Code System for Plastic Materials

Code	Polymer	Uses
1 PETE	Poly(ethylene terephthlate) (PET) $-O-CH_2-CH_2-O-C(=O)-C_6H_4-C(=O)-$	Soft-drink bottles
2 HDPE	High-density polyethylene $-CH_2-CH_2-CH_2-CH_2-$	Milk and beverage containers, products in squeeze bottles
3 V	Vinyl/poly(vinyl chloride) (PVC) $-CH_2-CH(Cl)-CH_2-CH(Cl)-$	Some shampoo containers, bottles with cleaning materials in them
4 LDPE	Low-density polyethylene $-CH_2-CH_2-CH_2-CH_2-$ with some branches	Thin plastic bags, some plastic wrap
5 PP	Polypropylene $-CH_2-CH(CH_3)-CH_2-CH(CH_3)-$	Heavy-duty, microwaveable containers used in kitchens
6 PS	Polystyrene $-CH_2-CH(C_6H_5)-CH_2-CH(C_6H_5)-$	Beverage/foam cups, window in envelopes
7 Other	All other resins, layered multimaterials, containers made of different materials	Some ketchup bottles, snack packs, mixture where top differs from bottom

REFERENCES

Ainsworth, S. J. "Plastics Additives." *Chemical and Engineering News, 70* (August 31, 1992): 34–55.

Burfield, D. R. "Polymer Glass Transition Temperatures." *Journal of Chemical Education, 64* (1987): 875.

Carraher, C. E., Jr., Hess, G., and Sperling, L. H. "Polymer Nomenclature—or What's in a Name?" *Journal of Chemical Education, 64* (1987): 36.

Carraher, C. E., Jr., and Seymour, R. B. "Physical Aspects of Polymer Structure: A Dictionary of Terms." *Journal of Chemical Education, 63* (1986): 418.

Carraher, C. E., Jr., and Seymour, R. B. "Polymer Properties and Testing—Definitions." *Journal of Chemical Education, 64* (1987): 866.

Carraher, C. E., Jr., and Seymour, R. B. "Polymer Structure—Organic Aspects (Definitions)." *Journal of Chemical Education, 65* (1988): 314.

Fried, J. R. "The Polymers of Commercial Plastics." *Plastics Engineering* (June 1982): 49–55.

Fried, J. R. "Polymer Properties in the Solid State." *Plastics Engineering* (July 1982): 27–37.

Fried, J. R. "Molecular Weight and Its Relation to Properties." *Plastics Engineering* (August 1982): 27–33.

Fried, J. R. "Elastomers and Thermosets." *Plastics Engineering* (March 1983): 67–73.

Fried, J. R., and Yeh, E. B. "Polymers and Computer Alchemy." *Chemtech, 23* (March 1993): 35–40.

Goodall, B. L. "The History and Current State of the Art of Propylene Polymerization Catalysts." *Journal of Chemical Education, 63* (1986): 191.

Harris, F. W., et al. "State of the Art: Polymer Chemistry." *Journal of Chemical Education, 58* (November 1981). (This issue contains 17 papers on polymer chemistry. The series covers structures, properties, mechanisms of formation, methods of preparation, stereochemistry, molecular weight distribution, rheological behavior of polymer melts, mechanical properties, rubber elasticity, block and graft copolymers, organometallic polymers, fibers, ionic polymers, and polymer compatibility.)

Jordan, R. F. "Cationic Metal–Alkyl Olefin Polymerization Catalysts." *Journal of Chemical Education, 65* (1988): 285.

Kauffman, G. B. "Wallace Hume Carothers and Nylon, the First Completely Synthetic Fiber." *Journal of Chemical Education, 65* (1988): 803.

Kauffman, G. B. "Rayon: The First Semi-Synthetic Fiber Product." *Journal of Chemical Education, 70* (1993): 887.

Kauffman, G. B., and Seymour, R. B. "Elastomers I. Natural Rubber." *Journal of Chemical Education, 67* (1990): 422.

Kauffman, G. B., and Seymour, R. B. "Elastomers II. Synthetic Rubbers." *Journal of Chemical Education, 68* (1991): 217.

Morse, P. M. "New Catalysts Renew Polyolefins." *Chemical and Engineering News, 76* (July 6, 1998): 11–16.

Seymour, R. B. "Polymers Are Everywhere." *Journal of Chemical Education, 65* (1988): 327.

Seymour, R. B. "Alkenes and Their Derivatives: The Alchemists' Dream Come True." *Journal of Chemical Education, 66* (1989): 670.

Seymour, R. B., and Kauffman, G. B. "Polymer Blends: Superior Products from Inferior Materials." *Journal of Chemical Education, 69* (1992): 646.

Seymour, R. B., and Kauffman, G. B. "Polyurethanes: A Class of Modern Versatile Materials." *Journal of Chemical Education, 69* (1992): 909.

Seymour, R. B., and Kauffman, G. B. "The Rise and Fall of Celluloid." *Journal of Chemical Education, 69* (1992): 311.

Seymour, R. B., and Kauffman, G. B. "Thermoplastic Elastomers." *Journal of Chemical Education, 69* (1992): 967.

Stevens, M. P. "Polymer Additives: Chemical and Aesthetic Property Modifiers." *Journal of Chemical Education, 70* (1993): 535.

Stevens, M. P. "Polymer Additives: Mechanical Property Modifiers." *Journal of Chemical Education, 70* (1993): 444.

Stevens, M. P. "Polymer Additives: Surface Property and Processing Modifiers." *Journal of Chemical Education, 70* (1993): 713.

Thayer, A. M. "Metallocene Catalysts Initiate New Era in Polymer Synthesis." *Chemical and Engineering News, 73* (September 11, 1995): 15–20.
Waller, F. J. "Fluoropolymers." *Journal of Chemical Education, 66* (1989): 487.
Webster, O. W. "Living Polymerization Methods." *Science, 251* (1991): 887.

EXPERIMENT 48

Preparation and Properties of Polymers: Polyester, Nylon, and Polystyrene

Condensation polymers
Addition polymers
Cross-linked polymers
Infrared spectroscopy

In this experiment, the syntheses of two polyesters (Experiment 48A), nylon (Experiment 48B), and polystyrene (Experiment 48C) will be described. These polymers represent important commercial plastics. They also represent the main classes of polymers: condensation (linear polyester, nylon), addition (polystyrene), and cross-linked (Glyptal polyester). Infrared spectroscopy is used in Experiment 48D to determine the structure of polymers.

Required Reading

Review:	Technique 25	Infrared Spectroscopy, Section 25B
New:	Essay	Polymers and Plastics

Special Instructions

Experiments 48A, 48B, and 48C all involve toxic vapors. Each experiment should be conducted in a good hood. The styrene used in Experiment 48C irritates the skin and eyes. Avoid breathing its vapors. Styrene must be dispensed and stored in a hood. Benzoyl peroxide is flammable and may detonate on impact or on heating.

Suggested Waste Disposal

The test tubes containing the polyester polymers from Experiment 48A should be placed in a box designated for disposal of these samples. The nylon from Experiment 48B should be washed thoroughly with water and placed in a waste basket. The liquid wastes from Experiment 48B (nylon) should be poured into a container designated for disposal of these wastes. The polystyrene prepared in Experiment 48C should be placed in the container designated for solid wastes.

EXPERIMENT 48A

Polyesters

Linear and cross-linked polyesters will be prepared in this experiment. Both are examples of condensation polymers. The linear polyester is prepared as follows:

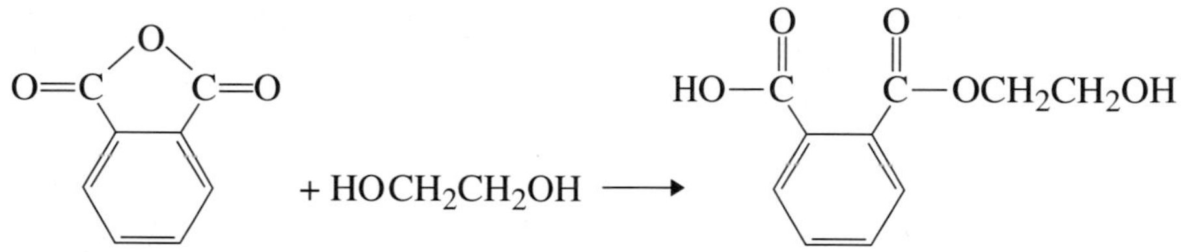

O=C C=O (O bridging) + $HOCH_2CH_2OH$ ⟶ HO—C(=O) C(=O)—OCH_2CH_2OH

Phthalic anhydride

Ethylene glycol (a diol)

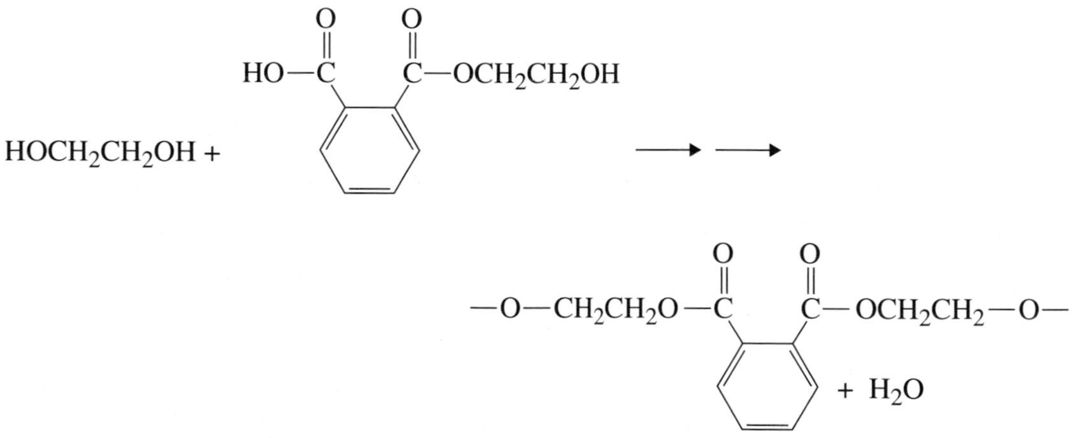

$HOCH_2CH_2OH$ + HO—C(=O) C(=O)—OCH_2CH_2OH ⟶ ⟶

—O—CH_2CH_2O—C(=O) C(=O)—OCH_2CH_2—O— + H_2O

Linear polyester

This linear polyester is isomeric with Dacron, which is prepared from terephthalic acid and ethylene glycol (see the preceding essay). Dacron and the linear polyester made in this experiment are both thermoplastics.

If more than two functional groups are present in one of the monomers, the polymer chains can be linked to one another (cross-linked) to form a three-dimensional network. Such structures are usually more rigid than linear structures and are useful in making paints and coatings. They may be classified as thermosetting plastics. The polyester Glyptal is prepared as follows:

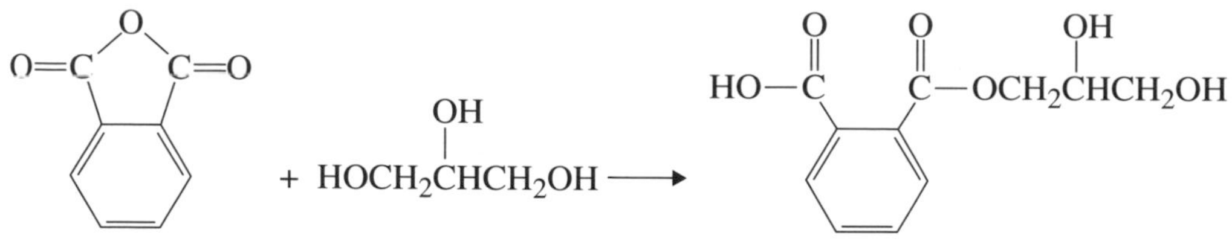

$$\text{Phthalic anhydride} + HOCH_2CH(OH)CH_2OH \longrightarrow HO{-}C(=O){-}C_6H_4{-}C(=O){-}OCH_2CH(OH)CH_2OH$$

Phthalic anhydride

Glycerol (a triol)

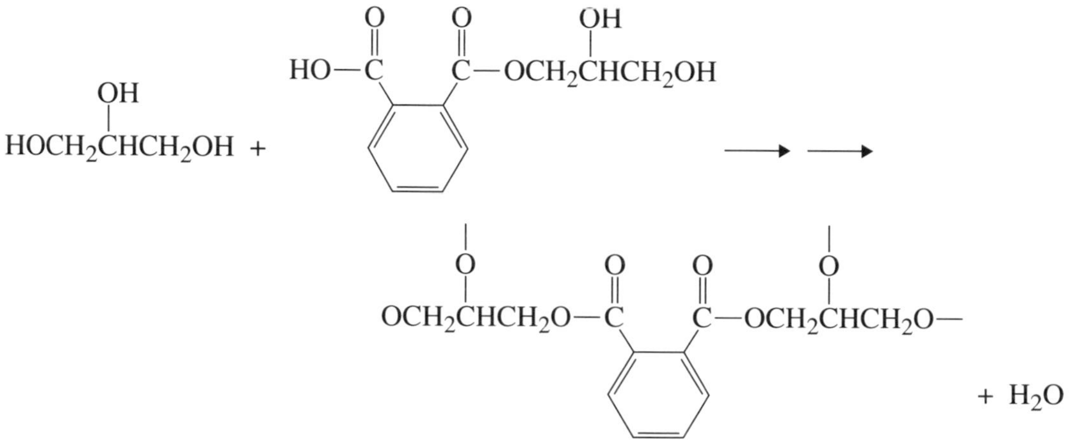

$$HOCH_2CH(OH)CH_2OH + HO{-}C(=O){-}C_6H_4{-}C(=O){-}OCH_2CH(OH)CH_2OH \longrightarrow \longrightarrow$$

$$OCH_2CH(O{-})CH_2O{-}C(=O){-}C_6H_4{-}C(=O){-}OCH_2CH(O{-})CH_2O{-} \quad + H_2O$$

Cross-linked polyester (Glyptal resin)

The reaction of phthalic anhydride with a diol (ethylene glycol) is described in the procedure. This linear polyester is compared with the cross-linked polyester (Glyptal) prepared from phthalic anhydride and a triol (glycerol).

Procedure

Place 1 g of phthalic anhydride and 0.05 g of sodium acetate in each of two test tubes. To one tube, add 0.4 mL of ethylene glycol and to the other, add 0.4 mL of glycerol. Clamp both tubes so that they can be heated simultaneously with a flame. Heat the tubes gently until the solutions appear to boil (water is eliminated during the esterification); then continue heating for 5 minutes.

If you are performing the optional infrared analysis of the polymer, immediately save a sample of the polymer formed from ethylene glycol only. After removing a sample for infrared spectroscopy, allow the two test tubes to cool and compare the viscosity and brittleness of the two polymers. The test tubes cannot be cleaned.

Optional Exercise: Infrared Spectroscopy. Lightly coat a watch glass with stopcock grease. Pour some of the *hot* polymer from the tube containing ethylene glycol; use a wooden applicator stick to spread the polymer on the surface to create a thin film of the polymer. Remove the polymer from the watch glass and save it for Experiment 48D.

EXPERIMENT 48B

Polyamide (Nylon)

Reaction of a dicarboxylic acid, or one of its derivatives, with a diamine leads to a linear polyamide through a condensation reaction. Commercially, nylon 6-6 (so called because

$$Cl{-}\overset{\overset{\displaystyle O}{\|}}{C}CH_2CH_2CH_2CH_2\overset{\overset{\displaystyle O}{\|}}{C}{-}Cl + H{-}\overset{\overset{\displaystyle H}{|}}{N}CH_2CH_2CH_2CH_2CH_2CH_2\overset{\overset{\displaystyle H}{|}}{N}{-}H \longrightarrow$$

Adipoyl chloride Hexamethylenediamine

$${-}\overset{\overset{\displaystyle O}{\|}}{C}CH_2CH_2CH_2CH_2\overset{\overset{\displaystyle O}{\|}}{C}{-}\overset{\overset{\displaystyle H}{|}}{N}CH_2CH_2CH_2CH_2CH_2CH_2\overset{\overset{\displaystyle H}{|}}{N}{-}$$

Nylon 6-6

each monomer has six carbons) is made from adipic acid and hexamethylenediamine. In this experiment, you will use the acid chloride instead of adipic acid. The acid chloride is dissolved in cyclohexane, and this is added *carefully* to hexamethylenediamine dissolved in water. These liquids do not mix, so two layers will form. The polymer can then be drawn

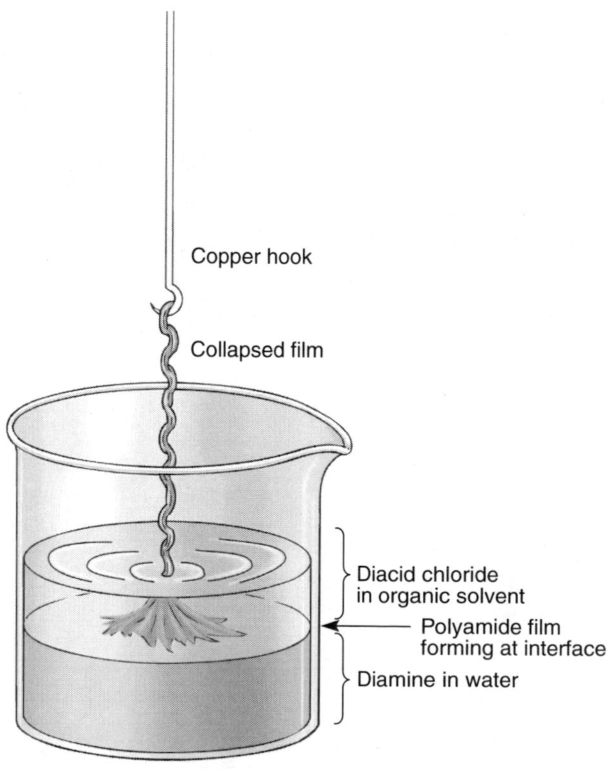

Preparation of nylon.

out continuously to form a long strand of nylon. Imagine how many molecules have been linked in this long strand! It is a fantastic number.

Procedure

Pour 10 mL of a 5% aqueous solution of hexamethylenediamine (1,6-hexanediamine) into a 50-mL beaker. Add 10 drops of 20% sodium hydroxide solution. Carefully add 10 mL of a 5% solution of adipoyl chloride in cyclohexane to the solution by pouring it down the wall of the slightly tilted beaker. Two layers will form (see figure), and there will be an immediate formation of a polymer film at the liquid–liquid interface. Using a copper-wire hook (a 6-inch piece of wire bent at one end), gently free the walls of the beaker from polymer strings. Then hook the mass at the center and slowly raise the wire so that polyamide forms continuously, producing a rope that can be drawn out for many feet. The strand can be broken by pulling it faster. Rinse the rope several times with water and lay it on a paper towel to dry. With the piece of wire, vigorously stir the remainder of the two-phase system to form additional polymer. Decant the liquid and wash the polymer thoroughly with water. Allow the polymer to dry. Do not discard the nylon in the sink; use a waste container.

EXPERIMENT 48C

Polystyrene

An addition polymer, polystyrene, will be prepared in this experiment. Reaction can be brought about by free-radical, cationic, or anionic catalysts (initiators), the first of these being the most common. In this experiment, polystyrene is prepared by free-radical-initiated polymerization.

The reaction is initiated by a free-radical source. The initiator will be benzoyl peroxide, a relatively unstable molecule, which at 80–90°C decomposes with homolytic cleavage of the oxygen–oxygen bond:

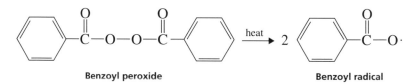

$$C_6H_5-\overset{O}{\overset{\|}{C}}-O-O-\overset{O}{\overset{\|}{C}}-C_6H_5 \xrightarrow{\text{heat}} 2\ C_6H_5-\overset{O}{\overset{\|}{C}}-O\cdot$$

Benzoyl peroxide **Benzoyl radical**

If an unsaturated monomer is present, the radical adds to it, initiating a chain reaction by producing a new free radical. If we let R stand for the initiator radical, the reaction with styrene can be represented as

$$R\cdot + CH_2{=}CH(C_6H_5) \longrightarrow R-CH_2-CH(C_6H_5)\cdot$$

The chain continues to grow:

$$R{-}CH_2{-}\underset{\displaystyle C_6H_5}{CH\cdot} \;+\; CH_2{=}\underset{\displaystyle C_6H_5}{CH} \longrightarrow R{-}CH_2{-}\underset{\displaystyle C_6H_5}{CH}{-}CH_2{-}\underset{\displaystyle C_6H_5}{CH\cdot}\text{, etc.}$$

The chain can be terminated by causing two radicals to combine (either both polymer radicals or one polymer radical and one initiator radical) or by causing a hydrogen atom to become abstracted from another molecule.

Procedure

Because it is difficult to clean the glassware, this experiment is best performed by the laboratory instructor. One large batch should be made for the entire class (at least 10 times the amounts given). After the polystyrene is prepared, a small amount will be dispensed to each student. The students will provide their own watch glass for this purpose. Perform the experiment in a hood. Place several thicknesses of newspaper in the hood.

> **Caution:** Styrene vapor is very irritating to the eyes, mucous membranes, and upper respiratory tract. Do not breathe the vapor and do not get it on your skin. Exposure can cause nausea and headaches. All operations with styrene must be conducted in a hood.
>
> Benzoyl peroxide is flammable and may detonate on impact or on heating (or grinding). It should be weighed on glassine (glazed, not ordinary) paper. Clean all spills with water. Wash the glassine paper with water before discarding it.

Place 12–15 mL of styrene monomer in a 100-mL beaker and add 0.35 g of benzoyl peroxide. Heat the mixture on a hot plate until the mixture turns yellow. When the color disappears and bubbles begin to appear, immediately take the beaker of styrene off the hot plate because the reaction is exothermic (use tongs or an insulated glove). After the reaction subsides, put the beaker of styrene back on the hot plate and continue heating it until the liquid becomes very syrupy. With a stirring rod, draw out a long filament of material from the beaker. If this filament can be cleanly snapped after a few seconds of cooling, the polystyrene is ready to be poured. If the filament does not break, continue heating the mixture and repeat this process until the filament breaks easily.

If you are performing the optional infrared analysis of the polymer, immediately save a sample of the polymer. After removing a sample for infrared spectroscopy, pour the remainder of the syrupy liquid on a watch glass that has been lightly coated with stopcock grease. After being cooled, the polystyrene can be lifted from the glass surface by gently prying with a spatula.

Optional Exercise: Infrared Spectroscopy. Pour a small amount of the *hot* polymer from the beaker onto a warm watch glass (no grease) and spread the polymer with a wooden applicator stick to create a thin film of the polymer. Peel the polymer from the watch glass and save it for Experiment 48D.

ESSAY

Sulfa Drugs

The history of chemotherapy extends as far back as 1909 when Paul Ehrlich first used the term. Although Ehrlich's original definition of chemotherapy was limited, he is recognized as one of the giants of medicinal chemistry. **Chemotherapy** might be defined as "the treatment of disease by chemical reagents." It is preferable that these chemical reagents exhibit a toxicity toward only the pathogenic organism and not toward both the organism and the host. A chemotherapeutic agent would not be useful if it poisoned the patient at the same time that it cured the patient's disease!

In 1932, the German dye manufacturing firm I. G. Farbenindustrie patented a new drug, Prontosil. Prontosil is a red azo dye, and it was first prepared for its dye properties. Remarkably, it was discovered that Prontosil showed antibacterial action when it was used to dye wool. This discovery led to studies of Prontosil as a drug capable of inhibiting the growth of bacteria. The following year, Prontosil was successfully used against staphylococcal septicemia, a blood infection. In 1935, Gerhard Domagk published the results of his research, which indicated that Prontosil was capable of curing streptococcal infections of

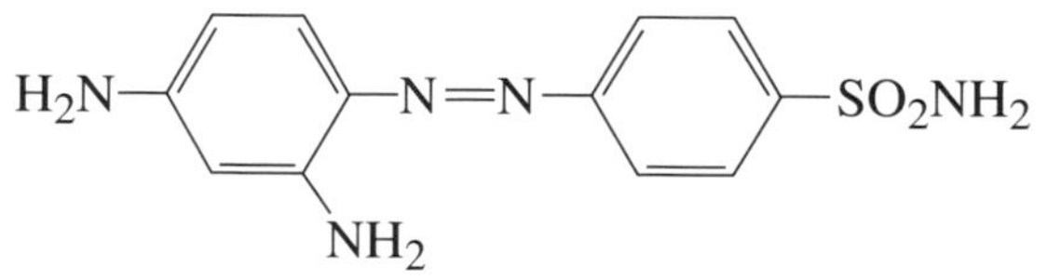

H_2N–$C_6H_3(NH_2)$–N=N–C_6H_4–SO_2NH_2

Prontosil

H_2N–C_6H_4–SO_2NH_2

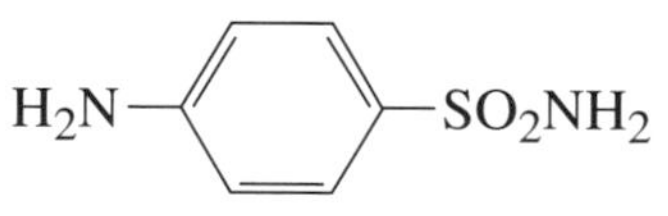

Sulfanilamide

mice and rabbits. Prontosil was shown to be active against a wide variety of bacteria in later work. This important discovery, which paved the way for a tremendous amount of research on the chemotherapy of bacterial infections, earned for Domagk the 1939 Nobel Prize in medicine, but an order from Hitler prevented Domagk from accepting the honor.

Prontosil is an effective antibacterial substance **in vivo,** that is, when injected into a living animal. Prontosil is not medicinally active when the drug is tested **in vitro,** that is, on a bacterial culture grown in the laboratory. In 1935, the research group at the Pasteur Institute in Paris headed by J. Tréfouël learned that Prontosil is metabolized in animals to **sulfanilamide.** Sulfanilamide had been known since 1908. Experiments with sulfanilamide showed that it had the same action as Prontosil in vivo and that it was also active in vitro, where Prontosil was known to be inactive. It was concluded that the active portion of the Prontosil molecule was the sulfanilamide moiety. This discovery led to an explosion of interest in sulfonamide derivatives. Well over a thousand sulfonamide substances were prepared within a few years of these discoveries.

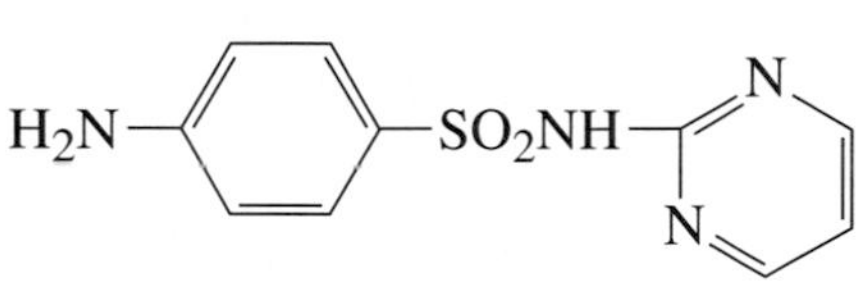

Sulfadiazine

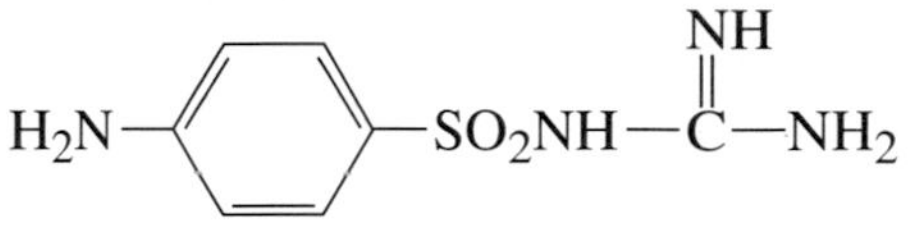

Sulfaguanidine

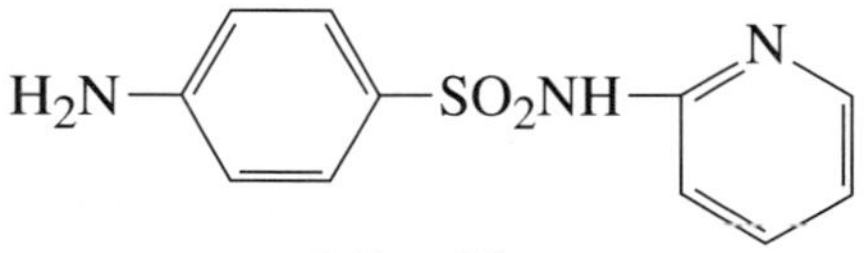

Sulfapyridine

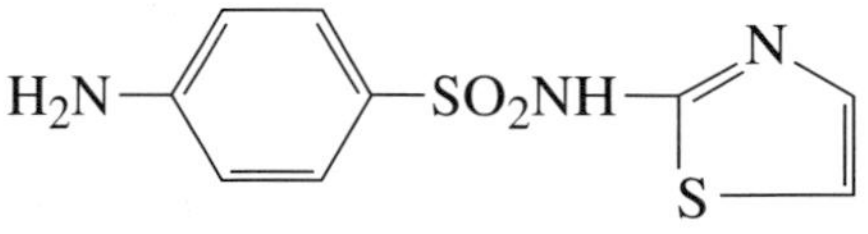

Sulfathiazole

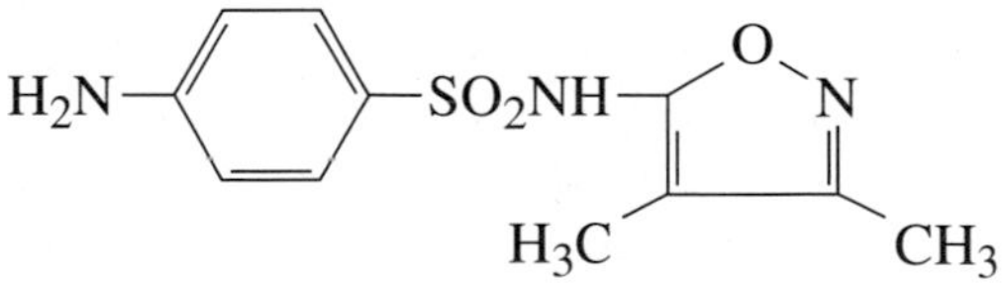

Sulfisoxazole

Although many sulfonamide compounds were prepared, only a relative few showed useful antibacterial properties. As the first useful antibacterial drugs, these few medicinally active sulfonamides, or **sulfa drugs,** became the wonder drugs of their day. An antibacterial drug may be either **bacteriostatic** or **bactericidal.** A bacteriostatic drug suppresses the growth of bacteria; a bactericidal drug kills bacteria. Strictly speaking, the sulfa drugs are bacteriostatic. The structures of some of the most common sulfa drugs are shown here. These more complex sulfa drugs have various important applications. Although they do not have the simple structure characteristic of sulfanilamide, they tend to be less toxic than the simpler compound.

Sulfa drugs began to lose their importance as generalized antibacterial agents when production of antibiotics in large quantity began. In 1929, Sir Alexander Fleming made his famous discovery of **penicillin.** In 1941, penicillin was first used successfully on humans.

Since that time, the study of antibiotics has spread to molecules that bear little or no structural similarity to the sulfonamides. Besides penicillin derivatives, antibiotics that are derivatives of **tetracycline,** including Aureomycin and Terramycin, were also discovered. These newer antibiotics have high activity against bacteria, and they do not usually have the severe unpleasant side effects of many of the sulfa drugs. Nevertheless, the sulfa drugs are still widely used in treating malaria, tuberculosis, leprosy, meningitis, pneumonia, scarlet fever, plague, respiratory infections, and infections of the intestinal and urinary tracts.

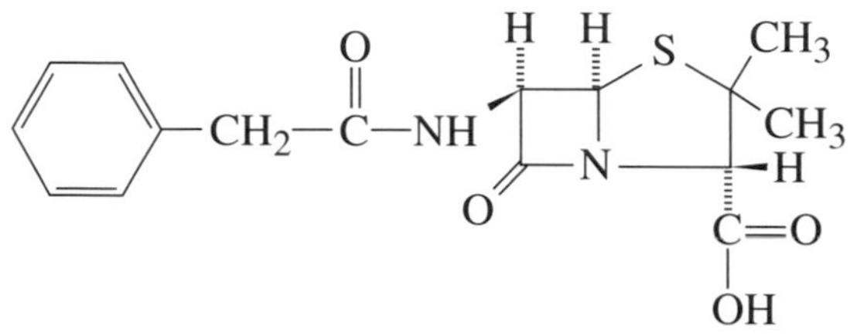

Penicillin G 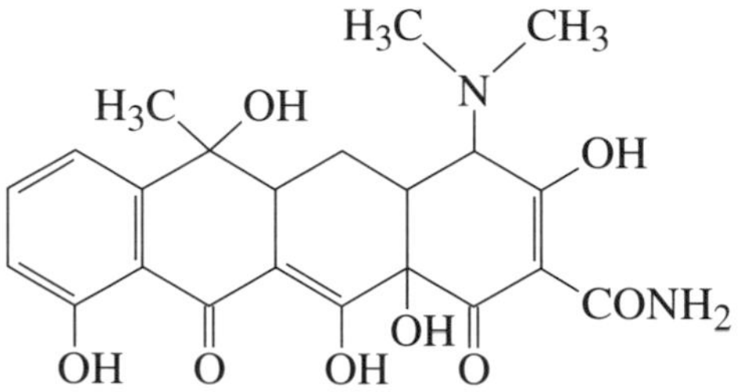 **Tetracycline**

Even though the importance of sulfa drugs has declined, studies of how these materials act provide very interesting insights into how chemotherapeutic substances might behave. In 1940, Woods and Fildes discovered that *p*-aminobenzoic acid (PABA) inhibits the action of sulfanilamide. They concluded that sulfanilamide and PABA, because of their structural similarity, must compete with each other within the organism even though they cannot carry out the same chemical function. Further studies indicated that sulfanilamide does not kill bacteria but inhibits their growth. In order to grow, bacteria require an enzyme-catalyzed reaction that uses **folic acid** as a cofactor. Bacteria synthesize folic acid, using PABA as one of the components. When sulfanilamide is introduced into the bacterial cell, it competes with PABA for the active site of the enzyme that carries out the incorporation of PABA into the molecule of folic acid. Because sulfanilamide and PABA compete for an active site due to their structural similarity and because sulfanilamide cannot carry out the chemical transformations characteristic of PABA once it has formed a complex with the enzyme, sulfanilamide is called a **competitive inhibitor** of the enzyme. The enzyme, once it has formed a complex with sulfanilamide, is incapable of catalyzing the reaction required for the synthesis of folic acid. Without folic acid, the bacteria cannot synthesize the nucleic acids required for growth. As a result, bacterial growth is arrested until the body's immune system can respond and kill the bacteria.

One might well ask the question "Why, when someone takes sulfanilamide as a drug, doesn't it inhibit the growth of *all* cells, bacterial and human alike?" The answer is simple. Animal cells cannot synthesize folic acid. Folic acid must be a part of the diet of animals and is therefore an essential vitamin. Because animal cells receive their fully synthesized folic acid molecules through the diet, only the bacterial cells are affected by the sulfanilamide, and only their growth is inhibited.

For most drugs, a detailed picture of their mechanism of action is unavailable. The sulfa drugs, however, provide a rare example from which we can theorize how other therapeutic agents carry out their medicinal activity.

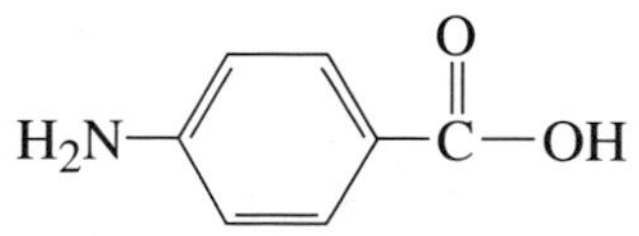

p-Aminobenzoic acid (PABA)

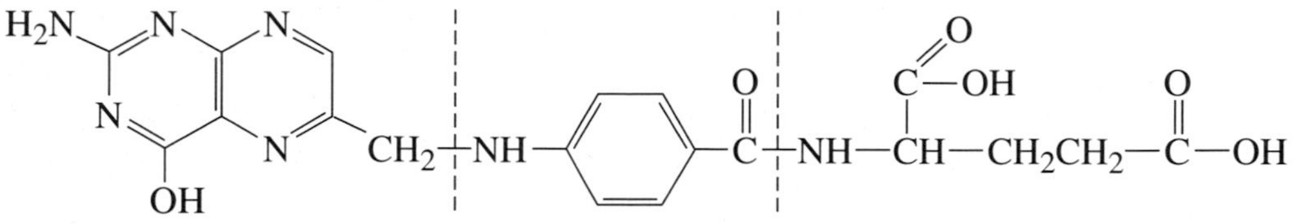

PABA residue (Folic acid)

REFERENCES

Amundsen, L. H. "Sulfanilamide and Related Chemotherapeutic Agents." *Journal of Chemical Education, 19* (1942): 167.

Evans, R. M. *The Chemistry of Antibiotics Used in Medicine.* London: Pergamon Press, 1965.

Fieser, L. F., and Fieser, M. "Chemotherapy." Chap. 7 in *Topics in Organic Chemistry.* New York: Reinhold, 1963.

Garrod, L. P., and O'Grady, F. *Antibiotic and Chemotherapy.* Edinburgh: E. and S. Livingstone, Ltd., 1968.

Mandell, G. L., and Sande, M. A. "The Sulfonamides." Chap. 45 in L. S. Goodman and A. Gilman, eds., *The Pharmacological Basis of Therapeutics,* 8th ed. New York: Pergamon Press, 1990.

Sementsov, A. "The Medical Heritage from Dyes." *Chemistry, 39* (November 1966): 20.

Zahner, H., and Maas, W. K. *Biology of Antibiotics.* Berlin: Springer-Verlag, 1972.

EXPERIMENT 46

Sulfa Drugs: Preparation of Sulfanilamide

Crystallization
Protecting groups
Testing the action of drugs on bacteria
Preparation of a sulfonamide
Aromatic substitution

In this experiment, you will prepare the sulfa drug sulfanilamide by the following synthetic scheme. The synthesis involves converting acetanilide to the intermediate *p*-acetamidobenzenesulfonyl chloride in step 1. This intermediate is converted to sulfanilamide by way of *p*-acetamidobenzenesulfonamide in step 2.

HOSO$_2$Cl (1)

Acetanilide

p-Acetamidobenzenesulfonyl chloride

NH_3 ammonia; (1) HCl, H_2O (2) $NaHCO_3$ (2)

p-Acetamidobenzene-sulfonamide

Sulfanilamide

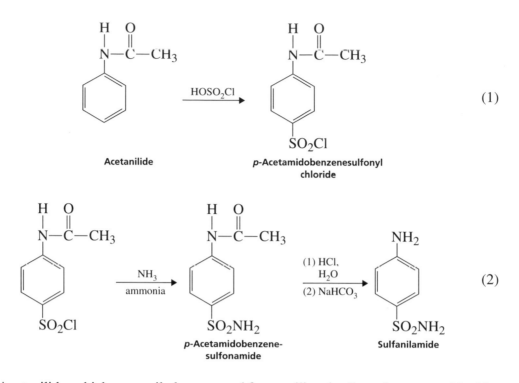

Acetanilide, which can easily be prepared from aniline, is allowed to react with chlorosulfonic acid to yield *p*-acetamidobenzenesulfonyl chloride. The acetamido group directs substitution almost totally to the *para* position. The reaction is an example of an electrophilic aromatic substitution reaction. Two problems would result if aniline itself were used in the reaction. First, the amino group in aniline would be protonated in strong acid to become a *meta* director; and, second, the chlorosulfonic acid would react with the amino group rather than with the ring, to give $C_6H_5—NHSO_3H$. For these reasons, the amino group has been "protected" by acetylation. The acetyl group will be removed in the final step, after it is no longer needed, to regenerate the free amino group present in sulfanilamide.

p-Acetamidobenzenesulfonyl chloride is isolated by adding the reaction mixture to ice water, which decomposes the excess chlorosulfonic acid. This intermediate is fairly stable in water; nevertheless, it is converted slowly to the corresponding sulfonic acid ($Ar—SO_3H$). Thus, it should be isolated as soon as possible from the aqueous medium by filtration.

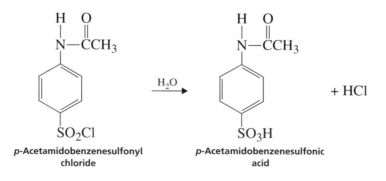

H_2O + HCl

p-Acetamidobenzenesulfonyl chloride

p-Acetamidobenzenesulfonic acid

The intermediate sulfonyl chloride is converted to *p*-acetamidobenzenesulfonamide by a reaction with aqueous ammonia (step 2). Excess ammonia neutralizes the hydrogen chloride produced. The only side reaction is the hydrolysis of the sulfonyl chloride to *p*-acetamidobenzenesulfonic acid.

The protecting acetyl group is removed by acid-catalyzed hydrolysis to generate the hydrochloride salt of the product, sulfanilamide. Note that of the two amide linkages present, only the carboxylic acid amide (acetamido group) was cleaved, not the sulfonic acid amide (sulfonamide). The salt of the sulfa drug is converted to sulfanilamide when the base, sodium bicarbonate, is added.

H O
N—C—CH_3 (ring) SO_2NH_2 $\xrightarrow[H_2O]{HCl}$ $^+NH_3Cl^-$ (ring) SO_2NH_2 + CH_3—C(=O)—OH $\xrightarrow{NaHCO_3}$ NH_2 (ring) SO_2NH_2 + CH_3C(=O)—O^-

p-Acetamidobenzene-sulfonamide **Sulfanilamide**

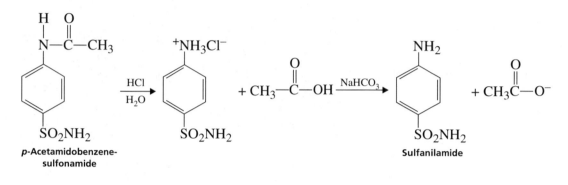

Required Reading

Review:	Technique 7	Reaction Methods, Sections 7.2 and 7.8A
	Technique 8	Filtration, Section 8.3
	Technique 11	Crystallization: Purification of Solids, Section 11.3
	Technique 25	Infrared Spectroscopy, Sections 25.4 and 25.5
New:	Essay	Sulfa Drugs

Special Instructions

If possible, all of this experiment should be completed in a fume hood. Otherwise, a hood must be used where indicated in the procedure.

Chlorosulfonic acid must be handled with care because it is a corrosive liquid and reacts violently with water. Be very careful when washing any glassware that has come in contact with chlorosulfonic acid. Even a small amount of the acid will react vigorously with water.

The *p*-acetamidobenzenesulfonyl chloride should be used during the same laboratory period in which it is prepared. It is unstable and will not survive long storage. The sulfa drug may be tested on several kinds of bacteria (see Instructor's Manual).

Suggested Waste Disposal

Dispose of all aqueous filtrates in the container for aqueous waste. Place organic wastes in the nonhalogenated organic waste container. Place the glass wool that has been moistened with 0.1 *M* sodium hydroxide into the container designated for this material.

Procedure

PART A. *p*-ACETAMIDOBENZENESULFONYL CHLORIDE

The Reaction Apparatus. Assemble the apparatus as shown in the figure. Prepare the sidearm test tube for use as a gas trap by packing the tube loosely with dry glass wool wrapped around the glass tube. Add about 2.5 mL of 0.1 *M* sodium hydroxide dropwise to the glass wool until it is moistened but not soaked. This apparatus will capture any hydrogen chloride that is evolved in the reaction. Attach the Erlenmeyer flask after the acetanilide and chlorosulfonic acid have been added, as directed in the following paragraph.

Reaction of Acetanilide with Chlorosulfonic Acid. Place 1.80 g of acetanilide in the *dry* 50-mL Erlenmeyer flask. Melt the acetanilide (mp 113°C) by heating gently with a flame. Remove the flask from the heat and swirl the heavy oil so that it is deposited uniformly on the lower wall and bottom of the flask. Allow the flask to cool to room temperature and then cool it further in an ice-water bath. Keep the flask in the ice bath until you are instructed to remove it.

Caution: Chlorosulfonic acid is an extremely noxious and corrosive chemical and should be handled with care. Use only dry glassware with this reagent. Should the chlorosulfonic acid be spilled on your skin, wash it off immediately with water. Be very careful when washing any glassware that has come in contact with chlorosulfonic acid. Even a small amount of the acid will react vigorously with water and may splatter. Wear safety glasses.

In a hood, transfer 5.0 mL of chlorosulfonic acid, $ClSO_2OH$ ($MW = 116.5$, $d =$ 1.77 g/mL), to the acetanilide in the flask. Attach the trap to the flask at your laboratory bench, remove the flask from the ice bath, and swirl it. Hydrogen chloride gas is evolved vigorously, so be certain that the rubber stopper is securely placed in the neck of the flask. The reaction mixture usually will not have to be cooled. If the reaction becomes too vigorous, however, slight cooling may be necessary. After 10 minutes, the reaction should have subsided, and only a small amount of acetanilide should remain. Heat the flask for an additional 10 minutes on the steam bath or in a hot water bath at 70°C to complete the reaction (continue to use the trap). After this time, remove the trap assembly and cool the flask in an ice bath.

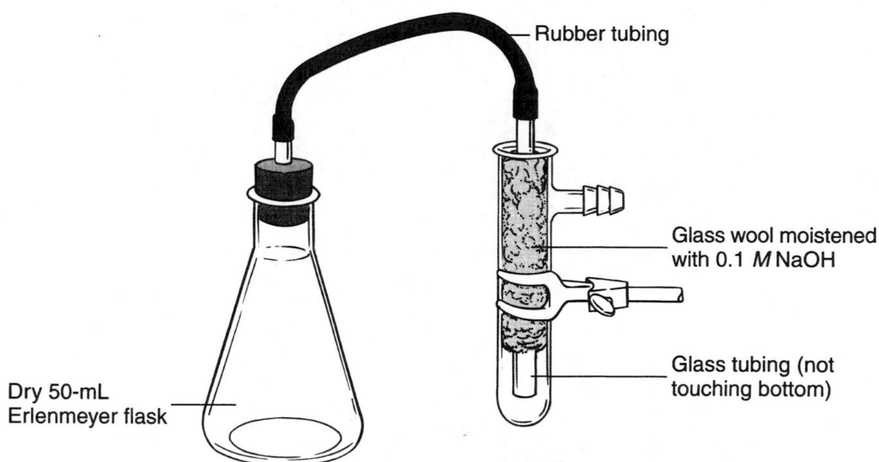

Apparatus for making *p*-acetamidobenzenesulfonyl chloride.

Isolation of *p*-Acetamidobenzenesulfonyl Chloride. The operations described in this paragraph should be conducted as rapidly as possible because the *p*-acetamidobenzenesulfonyl chloride reacts with water. Add 30 g of crushed ice to a 250-mL beaker. In a hood, transfer the cooled reaction mixture slowly (it may splatter somewhat) with a Pasteur pipet onto the ice while stirring the mixture with a glass stirring rod. (The remaining operations in this paragraph may be completed at your laboratory bench.) Rinse the flask with 5 mL of cold water and transfer the contents to the beaker containing the ice. Stir the precipitate to break up the lumps and then filter the *p*-acetamidobenzenesulfonyl chloride on a Büchner funnel (Technique 8, Section 8.3, p. 651, and Figure 8.5, p. 652). Rinse the flask and beaker with two 5-mL portions of ice water. Use the rinse water to wash the crude product on the funnel. Do not stop here. Convert the solid into *p*-acetamidobenzenesulfonamide in the same laboratory period.

PART B. SULFANILAMIDE

Preparation of *p*-Acetamidobenzenesulfonamide. In a hood, prepare a hot water bath at 70°C using a 250-mL beaker. Place the crude *p*-acetamidobenzenesulfonyl chloride into a 50-mL Erlenmeyer flask and add 11 mL of dilute ammonium hydroxide solution.[1] Stir the mixture well with a stirring rod to break up the lumps. Heat the mixture in the hot water bath for 10 minutes, stirring occasionally. Allow the flask to cool to the touch and place it in an ice-water bath for several minutes. The remainder of this experiment may be completed at your laboratory bench. Collect the *p*-acetamidobenzenesulfonamide on a Büchner funnel and rinse the flask and product with about 10 mL of ice water. You may stop here.

---

[1] Solution prepared by mixing 110 mL of concentrated ammonium hydroxide with 110 mL of water.

Hydrolysis of *p*-Acetamidobenzenesulfonamide. Transfer the solid into a 25-mL round-bottom flask and add 5.3 mL of dilute hydrochloric acid solution and a boiling stone.[2] Attach a reflux condenser to the flask. Using a heating mantle, heat the mixture under reflux until the solid has dissolved (about 10 minutes) and then reflux for an additional 5 minutes. Allow the mixture to cool to room temperature. If a solid (unreacted starting material) appears, bring the mixture to a boil again for several minutes. When the flask has cooled to room temperature, no further solids should appear.

Isolation of Sulfanilamide. With a Pasteur pipet, transfer the solution to a 100-mL beaker. While stirring with a glass rod, cautiously add dropwise a slurry of 5 g of sodium bicarbonate in about 10 mL of water to the mixture in the beaker. Foaming will occur after each addition of the bicarbonate mixture because of carbon dioxide evolution. Allow gas evolution to cease before making the next addition. Eventually, sulfanilamide will begin to precipitate. At this point, begin to check the pH of the solution. Add the aqueous sodium bicarbonate until the pH of the solution is between 4 and 6. Cool the mixture thoroughly in an ice-water bath. Collect the sulfanilamide on a Büchner funnel and rinse the beaker and solid with about 5 mL of cold water. Allow the solid to air dry on the Büchner funnel for several minutes using suction.

Crystallization of Sulfanilamide. Weigh the crude product and crystallize it from hot water, using about 10–12 mL water per gram of crude product. Allow the purified product to dry until the next laboratory period.

Yield Calculation, Melting Point, and Infrared Spectrum. Weigh the dry sulfanilamide and calculate the percentage yield (*MW* = 172.2). Determine the melting point (pure sulfanilamide melts at 163–164°C). At the option of the instructor, obtain the infrared spectrum using the dry film method (Technique 25, Section 25.4, p. 878) or as a KBr pellet (Technique 25, Section 25.5, p. 878). Compare your infrared spectrum with the one reproduced here. Submit the sulfanilamide to the instructor in a labeled vial or save it for the tests with bacteria (see Instructor's Manual).

QUESTIONS

1. Write an equation showing how excess chlorosulfonic acid is decomposed in water.

2. In the preparation of sulfanilamide, why was aqueous sodium bicarbonate, rather than aqueous sodium hydroxide, used to neutralize the solution in the final step?

3. At first glance, it might seem possible to prepare sulfanilamide from sulfanilic acid by the set of reactions shown here.

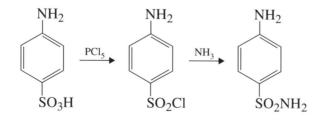

$$H_2N\text{-}C_6H_4\text{-}SO_3H \xrightarrow{PCl_5} H_2N\text{-}C_6H_4\text{-}SO_2Cl \xrightarrow{NH_3} H_2N\text{-}C_6H_4\text{-}SO_2NH_2$$

[2] Solution prepared by mixing 70 mL of water with 36 mL of concentrated hydrochloric acid.

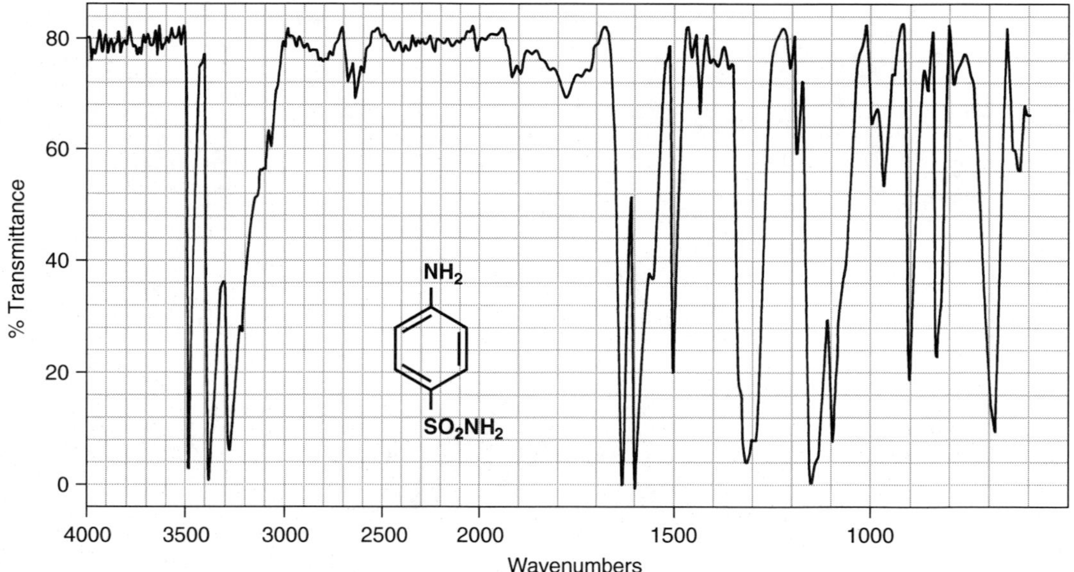

Infrared spectrum of sulfanilamide, KBr.

When the reaction is conducted in this way, however, a polymeric product is produced after step 1. What is the structure of the polymer? Why does *p*-acetamidobenzenesulfonyl chloride not produce a polymer?

EXPERIMENT 34

Multistep Reaction Sequences: The Conversion of Benzaldehyde to Benzilic Acid

Green chemistry
Multistep reactions
Thiamine catalyzed reaction
Oxidation with nitric acid
Rearrangement
Crystallization
Computational chemistry (optional)

The experiment demonstrates multistep synthesis of benzilic acid starting from benzaldehyde. In Experiment 34A, benzaldehyde is converted to benzoin using a thiamine-catalyzed reaction. This part of the experiment demonstrates how a "green" reagent can be utilized in organic chemistry. In Experiment 34B, nitric acid oxidizes benzoin to benzil. Finally, in Experiment 34C, benzil is rearranged to benzilic acid. The scheme on p. 288 shows the reactions.

Required Reading

Review:	Technique 6	Heating and Cooling Methods, Sections 6.1–6.3
	Technique 7	Reaction Methods, Sections 7.1–7.4
	Technique 8	Filtration, Section 8.3

Technique 9	Physical Constants of Solids: The Melting Point, Sections 9.7 and 9.8
Technique 11	Crystallization: Purification of Solids, Section 11.3
Technique 12	Extractions, Separations, and Drying Agents, Section 12.4
Technique 25	Infrared Spectroscopy, Section 25.4

New: Essay and Experiment 19 Computational Chemistry (Optional)

Notes to the Instructor

Although this experiment is intended to illustrate a multistep synthesis to the students, each part may be done separately, or two out of the three reactions can be linked together. The sections on Special Instructions and Waste Disposal are included in each part of this experiment. You may also create another multistep synthesis by linking together benzoin (Experiment 34A), benzil (Experiment 34B) and tetraphenylcyclopentadienone (Experiment 35).

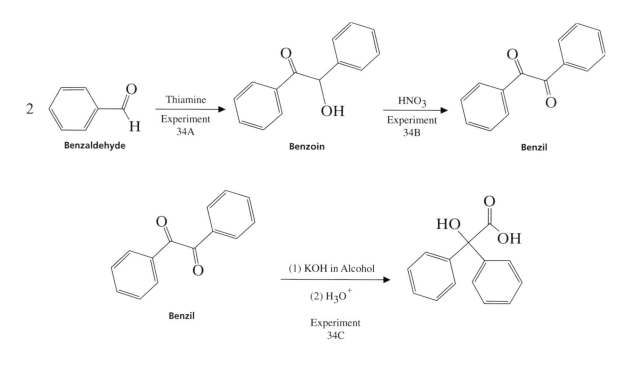

2 Benzaldehyde —Thiamine / Experiment 34A→ Benzoin —HNO_3 / Experiment 34B→ Benzil

Benzil —(1) KOH in Alcohol (2) H_3O^+ / Experiment 34C→ HO, OH

EXPERIMENT 34A

Preparation of Benzoin by Thiamine Catalysis

In this experiment, two molecules of benzaldehyde will be converted to benzoin using the catalyst thiamine hydrochloride. This reaction is known as a benzoin condensation reaction:

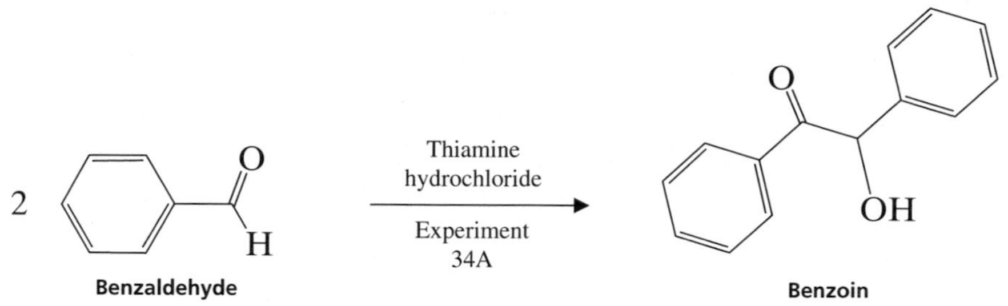

2 Benzaldehyde —(Thiamine hydrochloride; Experiment 34A)→ Benzoin

Thiamine hydrochloride is structurally similar to thiamine pyrophosphate (TPP). TPP is a coenzyme universally present in all living systems. It catalyzes several biochemical reactions in natural systems. It was originally discovered as a required nutritional factor (vitamin) in humans by its link with the disease beriberi. **Beriberi** is a disease of the peripheral nervous system caused by a deficiency of Vitamin B_1 in the diet. Symptoms include pain and paralysis of the extremities, emaciation, and swelling of the body. The disease is most common in Asia.

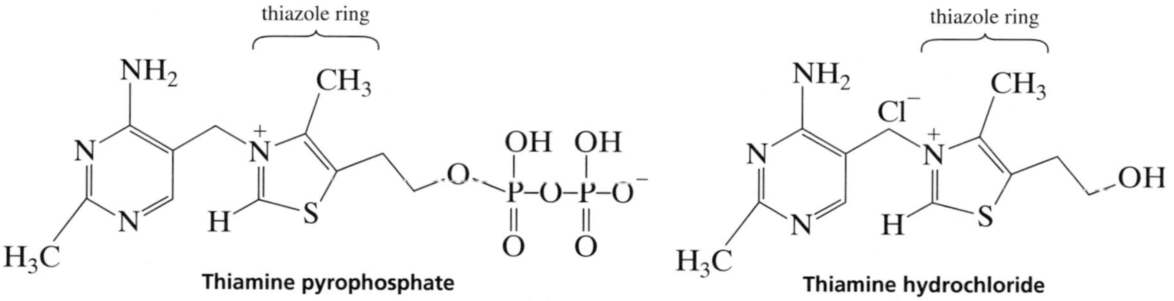

thiazole ring

Thiamine pyrophosphate

thiazole ring

Thiamine hydrochloride

Thiamine binds to an enzyme before the enzyme is activated. The enzyme also binds to the substrate (a large protein). Without the coenzyme thiamine, no chemical reaction would occur. The coenzyme is the *chemical reagent.* The protein molecule (the enzyme) helps and mediates the reaction by controlling stereochemical, energetic, and entropic factors, but it is nonessential to the overall course of reactions that its catalyzes. A special name, vitamins, is given to coenzymes that are essential to the nutrition of the organism.

The most important part of the entire thiamine molecule is the central ring, the thiazole ring, which contains nitrogen and sulfur. This ring constitutes the *reagent* portion of the coenzyme. Experiments with the model compound 3,4-dimethylthiazolium bromide have explained how thiamine-catalyzed reactions work. It was found that this model thiazolium compound rapidly exchanged the C-2 proton for deuterium in D_2O solution. At a pD of 7 (no pH here), this proton was completely exchanged in seconds!

This indicates that the C-2 proton is more acidic than one would have expected. It is apparently easily removed because the conjugate base is a highly stabilized ylide. An **ylide** is a compound or intermediate with positive and negative formal charges on adjacent atoms.

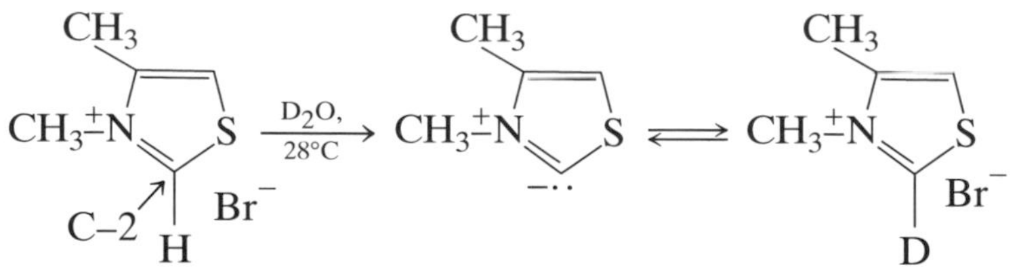

3,4-Dimethylthiazolium bromide **Ylide**

The sulfur atom plays an important role in stabilizing this ylide. This was shown by comparing the rate of exchange of 1,3-dimethyl-imidazolium ion with the rate for the thiazolium compound shown in the previous equation. The dinitrogen compound exchanged its C-2 proton more slowly than the sulfur-containing ion. Sulfur, being in the third row of the periodic chart, has *d* orbitals available for bonding to adjacent atoms. Thus, it has fewer geometrical restrictions than carbon and nitrogen atoms do and can form carbon–sulfur multiple bonds in situations in which carbon and nitrogen normally would not.

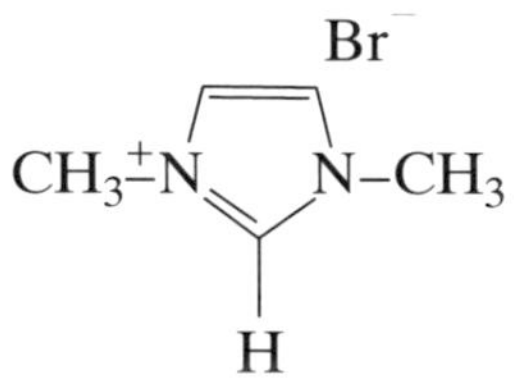

1,3-Dimethylimidazolium bromide

In Experiment 34A, we will utilize thiamine hydrochloride rather than thiamine pyrophosphate (TPP) to catalyze the benzoin condensation. The mechanism is shown on pages 290–291. For simplicity, only the thiazole ring is shown.

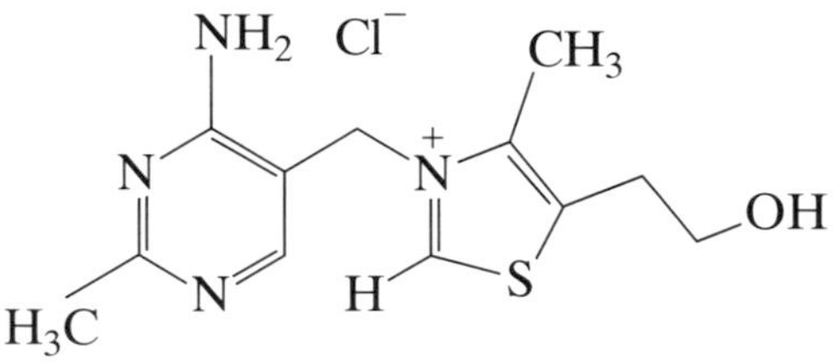

Thiamine hydrochloride 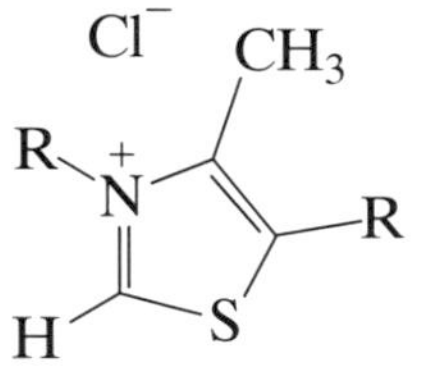 **Thiazole ring in thiamine hydrochloride**

The mechanism involves the removal of the proton at C-2 from the thiazole ring with a weak base to give the ylide (step 1). The ylide acts as a nucleophile that adds to the carbonyl group of benzaldehyde forming an intermediate (step 2). A proton is removed to yield a new intermediate with a double bond (step 3). Notice that the nitrogen atom helps to increase the acidity of that proton. This intermediate can now react with a second benzaldehyde molecule to yield a new intermediate (step 4). A base removes a proton to produce benzoin and also regenerates the ylide (step 5). The ylide reenters the mechanism to form more benzoin by the condensation of two more molecules of benzaldehyde.

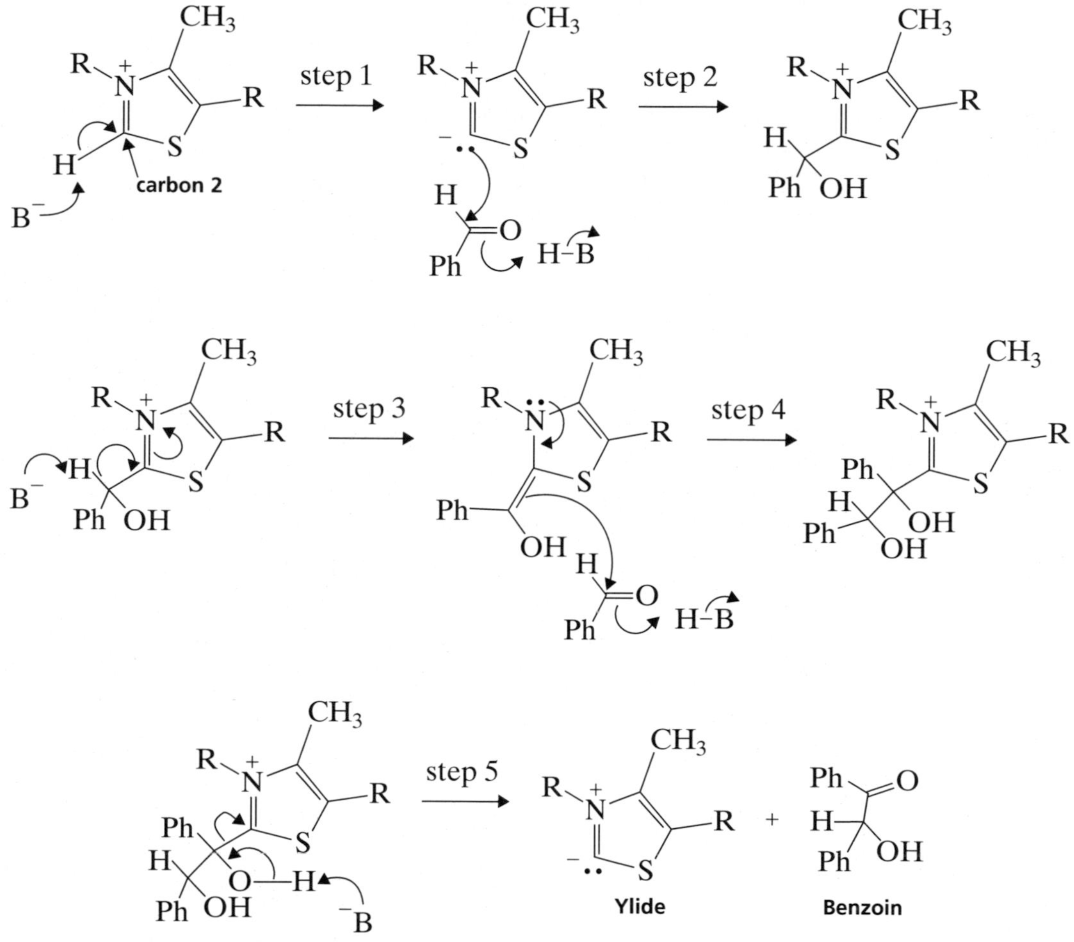

Special Instructions

This experiment may be conducted concurrently with another experiment. It involves a few minutes at the beginning of a laboratory period for mixing reagents. The remaining portion of the period may be used for another experiment.

Suggested Waste Disposal

Pour all of the aqueous solutions produced in this experiment into a waste container designated for aqueous waste. The ethanolic mixtures obtained from the crystallization of crude benzoin should be poured into a waste container designated for nonhalogenated waste.

Notes to the Instructor

It is essential that the benzaldehyde used in this experiment be *pure.* Benzaldehyde is easily oxidized in air to benzoic acid. Even when benzaldehyde *appears* free of benzoic acid by infrared spectroscopy, you should check the purity of your benzaldehyde and thiamine by following the instructions given in the first paragraph of the Procedure ("Reaction Mixture"). When the benzaldehyde is pure, the solution will be nearly filled with solid benzoin after 2 days (you may need to scratch the inside of the flask to induce crystallization). If no solid appears, or very little appears, then there is a problem with the purity of the benzaldehyde. If possible, use a newly opened bottle that has been purchased recently. *However, it is essential that you check both the old and new benzaldehyde before doing the laboratory experiment.*

We have found that the following procedure does an adequate job of purifying benzaldehyde. The procedure does not require distillation of benzaldehyde. Shake the benzaldehyde in a separatory funnel with an equal volume of 5% aqueous sodium carbonate solution. Shake gently and occasionally open the stopcock of the funnel to vent carbon dioxide gas. An emulsion forms that may take 2–3 hours to separate. It is helpful to stir the mixture occasionally during this period to help break the emulsion. Remove the lower sodium carbonate layer, including any remaining emulsion. Add about ¼ volume of water to the benzaldehyde and shake the mixture gently to avoid an emulsion. Remove the cloudy *lower* organic layer and dry the benzaldehyde with calcium chloride until the next day. Any remaining cloudiness is removed by gravity filtration through fluted filter paper. The resulting *clear,* purified benzaldehyde should be suitable for this experiment without vacuum distillation. *You must check the purified benzaldehyde to see if it is suitable for the experiment by following the instructions in the first paragraph of the Procedure.*

It is advisable to use a fresh bottle of thiamine hydrochloride, which should be stored in the refrigerator. Fresh thiamine does not seem to be as important as pure benzaldehyde for success in this experiment.

Procedure

Reaction Mixture. Add 1.5 g thiamine hydrochloride to a 50-mL Erlenmeyer flask. Dissolve the solid in 2 mL of water by swirling the flask. Add 15 mL of 95% ethanol and swirl the solution until it is homogeneous. To this solution, add 4.5 mL of an aqueous sodium hydroxide solution and swirl the flask until the bright yellow color fades to a pale yellow color.[1] Carefully measure 4.5 mL of pure benzaldehyde (density = 1.04 g/mL) and add it to the flask. Swirl the contents of the flask until they are homogeneous. Stopper the flask and allow it to stand in a dark place for at least 2 days.

Isolation of Crude Benzoin. If crystals have not formed after 2 days, initiate crystallization by scratching the inside of the flask with a glass stirring rod. Allow about 5 minutes for the crystals of benzoin to form fully. Place the flask, with crystals, into an ice bath for 5–10 minutes.

If for some reason the product separates as an oil, it may be helpful to scratch the flask with a glass rod or seed the mixture by allowing a small amount of solution to dry on the end of a glass rod and then placing this into the mixture. Cool the mixture in an ice bath before filtering.

[1] Dissolve 40 g of NaOH in 500 mL water.

Break up the crystalline mass with a spatula, swirl the flask rapidly, and quickly transfer the benzoin to a Büchner funnel under vacuum (Technique 8, Section 8.3, and Figure 8.5, p. 651). Wash the crystals with two 5-mL portions of ice-cold water. Allow the benzoin to dry in the Büchner funnel by drawing air through the crystals for about 5 minutes. Transfer the benzoin to a watch glass and allow it to dry in air until the next laboratory period. The product may also be dried in a few minutes in an oven set at about 100°C.

Yield Calculation and Melting-Point Determination. Weigh the benzoin and calculate the percentage yield based on the amount of benzaldehyde used initially. Determine the melting point (pure benzoin melts between 134°C and 135°C). Because your crude benzoin will normally melt between 129°C and 132°C, the benzoin should be crystallized before the conversion to benzil (Experiment 34B).

Crystallization of Benzoin. Purify the crude benzoin by crystallization from hot 95% ethanol (use 8 mL of alcohol/g of crude benzoin) using an Erlenmeyer flask for the crystallization (Technique 11, Section 11.3, p. 682; omit step 2 shown in Figure 11.4). After the crystals have cooled in an ice bath, collect the crystals on a Büchner funnel. The product may be dried in a few minutes in an oven set at about 100°C. Determine the melting point of the purified benzoin. If you are not scheduled to perform Experiment 34B, submit the sample of benzoin, along with your report, to the instructor.

Spectroscopy. Determine the infrared spectrum of the benzoin by the dry film method (Technique 25, Section 25.4, p. 878). A spectrum is shown here for comparison.

QUESTIONS

1. The infrared spectrum of benzoin and benzaldehyde are given in this experiment. Interpret the principal peaks in the spectra.

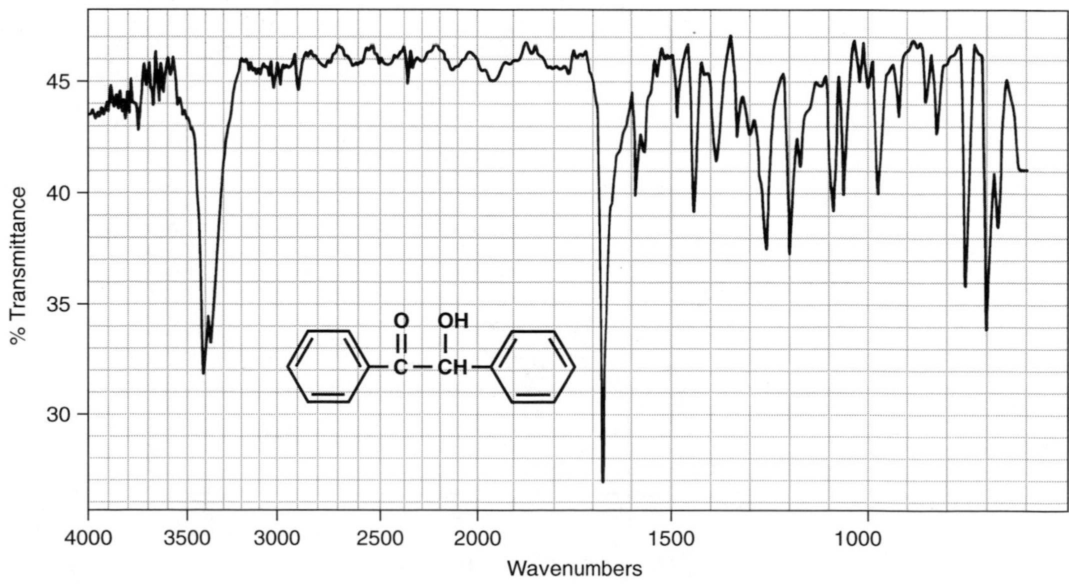

Infrared spectrum of benzoin, KBr.

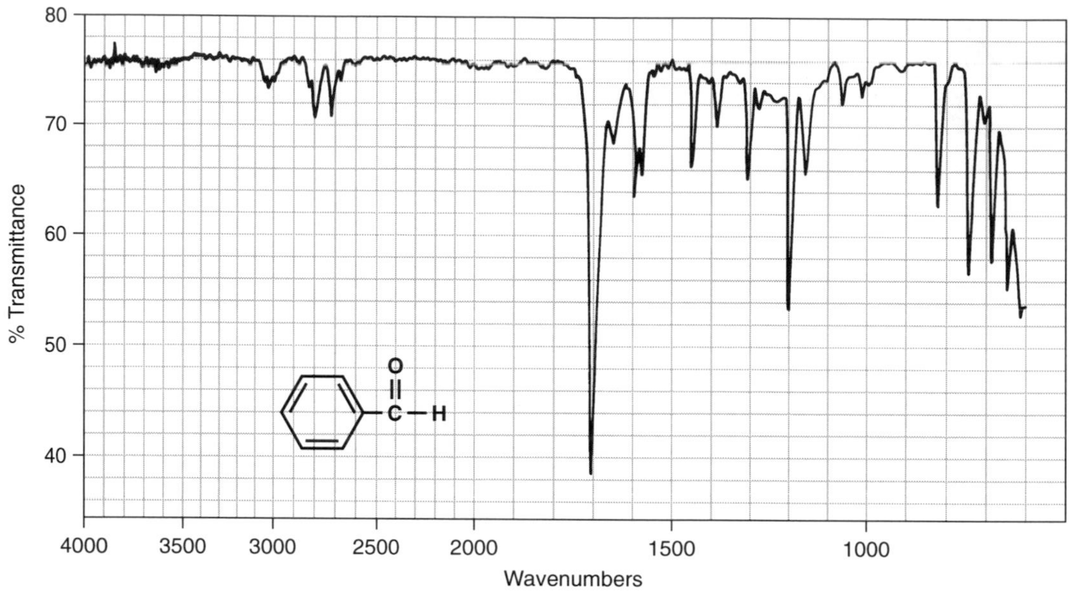

Infrared spectrum of benzaldehyde (neat).

2. How do you think the appropriate enzyme would have affected the reaction (degree of completion, yield, stereochemistry)?

3. What modifications of conditions would be appropriate if the enzyme were to be used?

4. Draw a mechanism for the cyanide-catalyzed conversion of benzaldehyde to benzoin. The intermediate, shown in brackets, is thought to be involved in the mechanism.

$$2\, C_6H_5\text{—CHO} \xrightarrow{:\bar{C}{\equiv}N:} C_6H_5\text{—}\overset{O}{\overset{\|}{C}}\text{—}\overset{OH}{\overset{|}{C}H}\text{—}C_6H_5$$

Benzaldehyde **Benzoin**

$$\left[C_6H_5\text{—}\overset{OH}{\overset{|}{\underset{C\equiv N}{\underset{|}{C}}}}\!:^{-} \right]$$

ESSAY

Polymers and Plastics

Chemically, plastics are composed of chainlike molecules of high molecular weight called **polymers.** Polymers have been built up from simpler chemicals called **monomers.** The word *poly* is defined as "many," *mono* means "one," and *mer* indicates "units." Thus, many monomers are combined to give a polymer. A different monomer or combination of monomers is used to manufacture each type or family of polymers. There are two broad classes of polymers: addition and condensation. Both types are described here.

Many polymers (plastics) produced in the past were of such low quality that they gained a bad reputation. The plastics industry now produces high-quality materials that are increasingly replacing metals in many applications. They are used in many products such as clothes, toys, furniture, machine components, paints, boats, automobile parts, and even artificial organs. In the automobile industry, metals have been replaced with plastics to help reduce the overall weight of the car and to help reduce corrosion. This reduction in weight helps improve gas mileage. Epoxy resins can even replace metal in engine parts.

CHEMICAL STRUCTURES OF POLYMERS

Basically, a polymer is made up of many repeating molecular units formed by sequential addition of monomer molecules to one another. Many monomer molecules of A, say 1,000 to 1 million, can be linked to form a gigantic polymeric molecule:

---

[3]See footnote 1, page 391.

$$\text{Many A} \longrightarrow \text{etc.} — \text{A-A-A-A-A} — \text{etc.} \quad \text{or} \quad -\!(\text{A})\!-_n$$

Monomer molecules — Polymer molecule

Monomers that are different can also be linked to form a polymer with an alternating structure. This type of polymer is called a **copolymer.**

$$\text{Many A} + \text{many B} \longrightarrow \text{etc.} — \text{A-B-A-B-A-B} — \text{etc.} \quad \text{or} \quad -\!(\text{A-B})\!-_n$$

Monomer molecules — Polymer molecule

TYPES OF POLYMERS

For convenience, chemists classify polymers in several main groups, depending on the method of synthesis.

1. **Addition polymers** are formed by a reaction in which monomer units simply add to one another to form a long-chain (generally linear or branched) polymer. The monomers usually contain carbon–carbon double bonds. Examples of synthetic addition polymers include polystyrene (Styrofoam), polytetrafluoroethylene (Teflon), polyethylene, polypropylene, polyacrylonitrile (Orlon, Acrilan, Creslan), poly(vinyl chloride) (PVC), and poly(methyl methacrylate) (Lucite, Plexiglas). The process can be represented as follows:

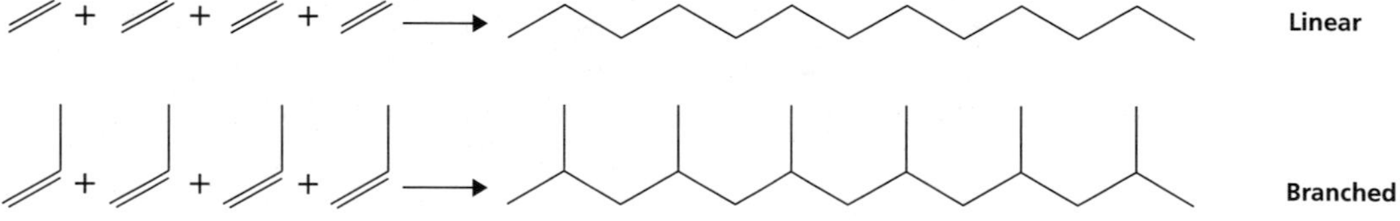

2. **Condensation polymers** are formed by the reaction of bifunctional or polyfunctional molecules, with the elimination of some small molecule (such as water, ammonia, or hydrogen chloride) as a by-product. Familiar examples of synthetic condensation polymers include polyesters (Dacron, Mylar), polyamides (nylon), polyurethanes, and epoxy resin. Natural condensation polymers include polyamino acids (protein), cellulose, and starch. The process can be represented as follows:

$$\text{H}-\square-\text{X} + \text{H}-\square-\text{X} \longrightarrow \text{H}-\square-\square-\text{X} + \text{HX}$$

3. **Cross-linked polymers** are formed when long chains are linked in one gigantic, three-dimensional structure with tremendous rigidity. Addition and condensation polymers can exist with a cross-linked network, depending on the monomers used

in the synthesis. Familiar examples of cross-linked polymers are Bakelite, rubber, and casting (boat) resin. The process can be represented as follows:

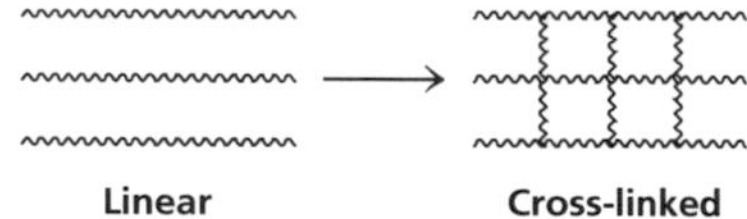

Linear and crossed-linked polymers.

THERMAL CLASSIFICATION OF POLYMERS

Industrialists and technologists often classify polymers as either thermoplastics or thermoset plastics rather than as addition or condensation polymers. This classification takes into account their thermal properties.

1. **Thermal properties of thermoplastics.** Most addition polymers and many condensation polymers can be softened (melted) by heat and re-formed (molded) into other shapes. Industrialists and technologists often refer to these types of polymers as **thermoplastics.** Weaker, noncovalent bonds (dipole–dipole and London dispersion) are broken during the heating. Technically, thermoplastics are the materials we call plastics. Thermoplastics may be repeatedly melted and recast into new shapes. They may be recycled as long as degradation does not occur during reprocessing.

   Some addition polymers, such as poly(vinyl chloride), are difficult to melt and process. Liquids with high boiling points, such as dibutyl phthalate, are added to the polymer to separate the chains from each other. These compounds are called **plasticizers.** In effect, they act as lubricants that neutralize the attractions that exist between chains. As a result, the polymer can be melted at a lower temperature to aid in processing. In addition, the polymer becomes more flexible at room temperature. By varying the amount of plasticizer, poly(vinyl chloride) can range from a very flexible, rubberlike material to a very hard substance.

   $$C_6H_4(COOCH_2CH_2CH_2CH_3)_2$$

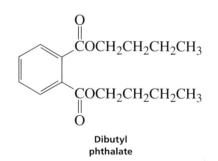

   Dibutyl phthalate

   Phthalate plasticizers are volatile compounds of low molecular weight. Part of the new car smell comes from the odor of these materials as they evaporate from the vinyl upholstery. The vapor often condenses on the windshield as an oily film. After some time, the vinyl material may lose enough plasticizer to cause it to crack.

2. **Thermal properties of thermoset plastics.** Industrialists use the term **thermoset** plastics to describe materials that melt initially but on further heating become permanently hardened. Once formed, thermoset materials cannot be softened and re-

molded without destruction of the polymer, because covalent bonds are broken. Thermoset plastics cannot be recycled. Chemically, thermoset plastics are cross-linked polymers. They are formed when long chains are linked in one gigantic, three-dimensional structure with tremendous rigidity.

Polymers can also be classified in other ways; for example, many varieties of rubber are often referred to as *elastomers,* Dacron is a fiber, and poly(vinyl acetate) is an adhesive. The addition and condensation classifications are used in this essay.

ADDITION POLYMERS

By volume, most of the polymers prepared in industry are of the addition type. The monomers generally contain a carbon–carbon double bond. The most important example of an addition polymer is the well-known polyethylene, for which the monomer is ethylene. Countless numbers (*n*) of ethylene molecules are linked in long-chain polymeric molecules by breaking the pi bond and creating two new single bonds between the monomer units. The number of recurring units may be large or small, depending on the polymerization conditions.

$$\text{Many}\quad \mathrm{H_2C{=}CH_2} \longrightarrow \text{etc.}{-}\mathrm{CH_2{-}CH_2{-}CH_2{-}CH_2}{-}\text{etc.} \quad \text{or} \quad \left(\mathrm{{-}CH_2{-}CH_2{-}}\right)_n$$

Ethylene monomer — Polyethylene polymer

This reaction can be promoted by heat, pressure, and a chemical catalyst. The molecules produced in a typical reaction vary in the number of carbon atoms in their chains. In other words, a mixture of polymers of varying length, rather than a pure compound, is produced.

Polyethylenes with linear structures can pack together easily and are referred to as high-density polyethylenes. They are fairly rigid materials. Low-density polyethylenes consist of branched-chain molecules, with some cross-linking in the chains. They are more flexible than the high-density polyethylenes. The reaction conditions and the catalysts that produce polyethylenes of low and high density are quite different. The monomer, however, is the same in each case.

Another example of an addition polymer is polypropylene. In this case, the monomer is propylene. The polymer that results has a branched methyl on alternate carbon atoms of the chain.

$$\text{Many}\quad \mathrm{H_2C{=}CH(CH_3)} \longrightarrow \text{etc.}{-}\mathrm{CH_2{-}CH(CH_3){-}CH_2{-}CH(CH_3)}{-}\text{etc.} \quad \text{or} \quad \left(\mathrm{{-}CH_2{-}CH(CH_3){-}}\right)_n$$

Propylene monomer — Polypropylene polymer

A number of common addition polymers are shown in Table One. Some of their principal uses are also listed. The last three entries in the table all have a carbon–carbon double bond remaining after the polymer is formed. These bonds activate or participate in a further reaction to form cross-linked polymers called *elastomers;* this term is almost synonymous with *rubber,* because elastomers are materials with common characteristics.

CONDENSATION POLYMERS

Condensation polymers, for which the monomers contain more than one type of functional group, are more complex than addition polymers. In addition, most condensation polymers are copolymers made from more than one type of monomer. Recall that addition polymers, in contrast, are all prepared from substituted ethylene molecules. The single functional group in each case is one or more double bonds, and a single type of monomer is generally used.

Dacron, a polyester, can be prepared by causing a dicarboxylic acid to react with a bifunctional alcohol (a diol):

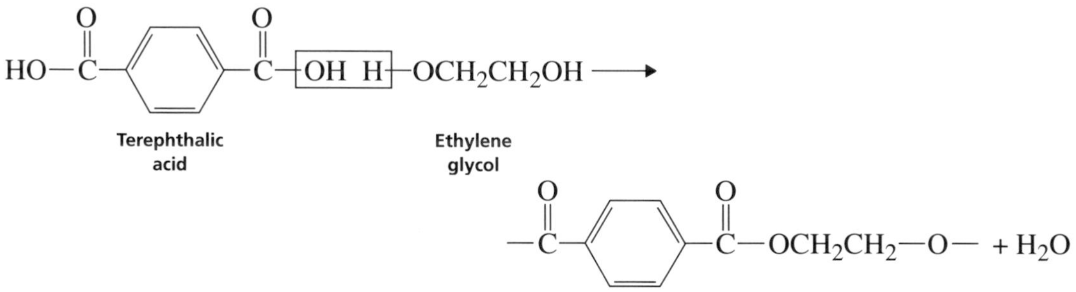

$$HO-\overset{O}{\overset{\|}{C}}-C_6H_4-\overset{O}{\overset{\|}{C}}-\boxed{OH\ H}-OCH_2CH_2OH \longrightarrow$$

Terephthalic acid   Ethylene glycol

$$-\overset{O}{\overset{\|}{C}}-C_6H_4-\overset{O}{\overset{\|}{C}}-OCH_2CH_2-O- \quad + H_2O$$

Dacron

Nylon 6-6, a polyamide, can be prepared by causing a dicarboxylic acid to react with a bifunctional amine.

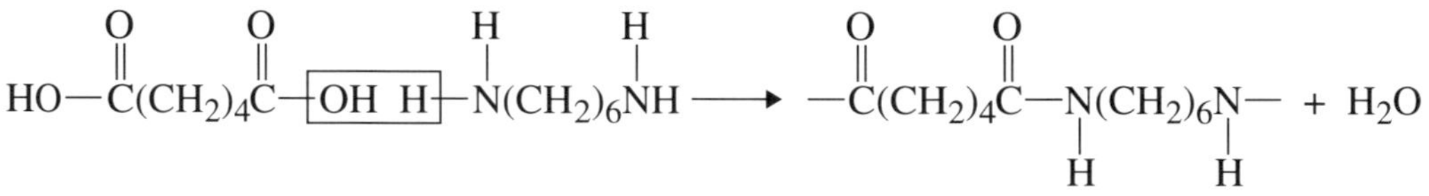

$$HO-\overset{O}{\overset{\|}{C}}(CH_2)_4\overset{O}{\overset{\|}{C}}-\boxed{OH\ H}-\overset{H}{\overset{|}{N}}(CH_2)_6\overset{H}{\overset{|}{N}}H \longrightarrow -\overset{O}{\overset{\|}{C}}(CH_2)_4\overset{O}{\overset{\|}{C}}-\underset{H}{\underset{|}{N}}(CH_2)_6\underset{H}{\underset{|}{N}}- \quad + H_2O$$

Adipic acid   Hexamethylene-diamine   Nylon

Notice, in each case, that a small molecule, water, is eliminated as a product of the reaction. Several other condensation polymers are listed in Table Two. Linear (or branched) chain polymers as well as cross-linked polymers are produced in condensation reactions.

The nylon structure contains the amide linkage at regular intervals:

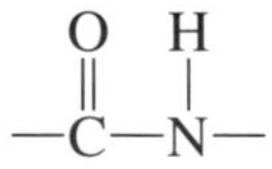

$$-\overset{O}{\overset{\|}{C}}-\overset{H}{\overset{|}{N}}-$$

TABLE ONE Addition Polymers

Example	Monomer(s)	Polymer	Uses
Polyethylene	$CH_2{=}CH_2$	$-CH_2-CH_2-$	Most common and important polymer; bags, insulation for wires, squeeze bottles
Polypropylene	$CH_2{=}CH(CH_3)$	$-CH_2-CH(CH_3)-$	Fibers, indoor–outdoor carpets, bottles
Polystyrene	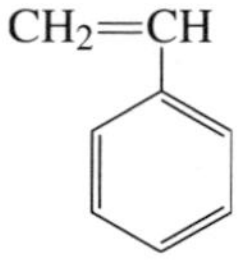 $CH_2{=}CH(C_6H_5)$	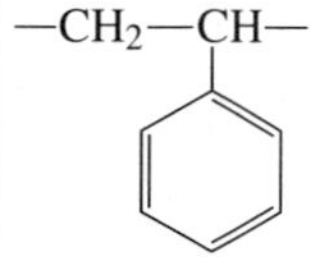 $-CH_2-CH(C_6H_5)-$	Styrofoam, inexpensive household goods, inexpensive molded objects
Poly(vinyl chloride) (PVC)	$CH_2{=}CH(Cl)$	$-CH_2-CH(Cl)-$	Synthetic leather, clear bottles, floor covering, phonograph records, water pipe
Polytetrafluoroethylene (Teflon)	$CF_2{=}CF_2$	$-CF_2-CF_2-$	Nonstick surfaces, chemically resistant films
Poly(methyl methacrylate) (Lucite, Plexiglas)	$CH_2{=}C(CO_2CH_3)(CH_3)$	$-CH_2-C(CO_2CH_3)(CH_3)-$	Unbreakable "glass," latex paints
Polyacrylonitrile (Orlon, Acrilan, Creslan)	$CH_2{=}CH(CN)$	$-CH_2-CH(CN)-$	Fiber used in sweaters, blankets, carpets
Poly(vinyl acetate) (PVA)	$CH_2{=}CH(OCCH_3)$, C=O	$-CH_2-CH(OCCH_3)-$, C=O	Adhesives, latex paints, chewing gum, textile coatings
Natural rubber	$CH_2{=}C(CH_3)CH{=}CH_2$	$-CH_2-C(CH_3){=}CH-CH_2-$	Polymer cross-linked with sulfur (vulcanization)
Polychloroprene (neoprene rubber)	$CH_2{=}C(Cl)CH{=}CH_2$	$-CH_2-C(Cl){=}CH-CH_2-$	Cross-linked with ZnO; resistant to oil and gasoline
Styrene butadiene rubber (SBR)	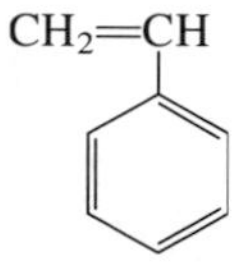 $CH_2{=}CH(C_6H_5)$; $CH_2{=}CHCH{=}CH_2$	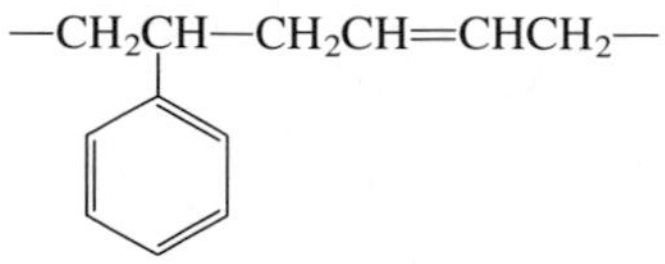 $-CH_2CH(C_6H_5)-CH_2CH{=}CHCH_2-$	Cross-linked with peroxides; most common rubber; used for tires; 25% styrene, 75% butadiene

TABLE TWO Condensation Polymers

Example	Monomers	Polymer	Uses
Polyamides (nylon)	$HOC(=O)(CH_2)_nC(=O)OH$ $H_2N(CH_2)_nNH_2$	$-C(=O)(CH_2)_nC(=O)-NH(CH_2)_nNH-$	Fibers, molded objects
Polyesters (Dacron, Mylar, Fortrel)	$HOC(=O)-C_6H_4-C(=O)OH$ $HO(CH_2)_nOH$	$-C(=O)-C_6H_4-C(=O)-O(CH_2)_nO-$	Linear polyesters, fibers, recording tape
Polyesters (Glyptal resin)	phthalic anhydride $HOCH_2CH(OH)CH_2OH$	$-C(=O)-C_6H_4-C(=O)OCH_2CH(O-)CH_2O-$	Cross-linked polyester, paints
Polyesters (casting resin)	$HOC(=O)CH{=}CHC(=O)OH$ $HO(CH_2)_nOH$	$-C(=O)CH{=}CHC(=O)-O(CH_2)_nO-$	Cross-linked with styrene and peroxide, fiberglass boat resin
Phenol-formaldehyde resin (Bakelite)	C_6H_5OH $CH_2{=}O$	$-CH_2-C_6H_2(OH)(CH_2-)-CH_2-C_6H_2(OH)(CH_2-)-CH_2-$	Mixed with fillers, molded electrical goods, adhesives, laminates, varnishes
Cellulose acetate*	glucose unit (CH_2OH, OH, OH; $-O-$ links) CH_3COOH	glucose unit (CH_2OAc, OAc, OAc; $-O-$ links)	Photographic film
Silicones	$Cl-Si(CH_3)_2-Cl$ H_2O	$-O-Si(CH_3)_2-O-$	Water-repellent coatings, temperature-resistant fluids and rubbers (CH_3SiCl_3 cross-links in water)
Polyurethanes	$CH_3C_6H_3(N{=}C{=}O)_2$ $HO(CH_2)_nOH$	$CH_3C_6H_3[NHC(=O)-O(CH_2)_nO-]_2$	Rigid and flexible foams, fibers

*Cellulose, a polymer of glucose, is used as the monomer.

This type of linkage is extremely important in nature because of its presence in proteins and polypeptides. Proteins are gigantic polymeric substances made up of monomer units of amino acids. They are linked by the peptide (amide) bond.

Other important natural condensation polymers are starch and cellulose. They are polymeric materials made up of the sugar monomer glucose. Another important natural condensation polymer is the DNA molecule. A DNA molecule is made up of the sugar deoxyribose linked with phosphates to form the backbone of the molecule.

DISPOSABILITY PROBLEMS

What do we do with all our wastes? Currently, the most popular method is to bury our garbage in sanitary landfills. However, as we run out of good places to bury our garbage, incineration has become a more attractive method for solving the solid waste problem. Plastics, which compose about 2% of our garbage, burn readily. The new high-temperature incinerators are extremely efficient and can be operated with very little air pollution. It should also be possible to burn our garbage and generate electrical power from it.

Ideally, we should either recycle all our wastes or not produce the waste in the first place. Plastic waste consists of about 55% polyethylene and polypropylene, 20% polystyrene, and 11% PVC. All these polymers are thermoplastics and can be recycled. They can be resoftened and remolded into new goods. Unfortunately, thermosetting plastics (cross-linked polymers) cannot be remelted. They decompose on high-temperature heating. Thus, thermosetting plastics should not be used for "disposable" purposes. To recycle plastics effectively, we must sort the materials according to the various types. The plastics industry has introduced a code system consisting of seven categories for the common plastics used in packaging. The code is conveniently stamped on the bottom of the container. Using these codes, consumers can separate the plastics into groups for recycling purposes. These codes are listed in Table Three, together with the most common uses around the home. Notice that the seventh category is a miscellaneous one, called "Other."

It is quite amazing that so few different plastics are used in packaging. The most common ones are polyethylene (low and high density), polypropylene, polystyrene, and poly(ethylene terephthlate). All these materials can easily be recycled because they are thermoplastics. Incidently, vinyls (polyvinyl chloride) are becoming less common in packaging. The "Other" category, Code 7, is virtually nonexistent and usually consists of packaging where the top is made of a material different from that of the bottom. This dilemma should be easy to solve by placing the appropriate code on each part of the container.

Polymers, if they are well made, will not corrode or rust, and they last almost indefinitely. Unfortunately, these desirable properties also lead to a problem when plastics are buried in a landfill or thrown on the landscape—they do not decompose. Research is being undertaken to discover plastics that are biodegradable or photodegradable so that either microorganisms or light from the sun can decompose our litter and garbage. Although there are some advantages to this approach, it is probably better to eliminate packaging at the source or to engage in an effective recycling program. We must learn to use plastics wisely.

TABLE THREE Code System for Plastic Materials

Code	Polymer	Uses
1 PETE	Poly(ethylene terephthlate) (PET) —O—CH_2—CH_2—O—C(=O)—C_6H_4—C(=O)—	Soft-drink bottles
2 HDPE	High-density polyethylene —CH_2—CH_2—CH_2—CH_2—	Milk and beverage containers, products in squeeze bottles
3 V	Vinyl/poly(vinyl chloride) (PVC) —CH_2—CH(Cl)—CH_2—CH(Cl)—	Some shampoo containers, bottles with cleaning materials in them
4 LDPE	Low-density polyethylene —CH_2—CH_2—CH_2—CH_2— with some branches	Thin plastic bags, some plastic wrap
5 PP	Polypropylene —CH_2—CH(CH_3)—CH_2—CH(CH_3)—	Heavy-duty, microwaveable containers used in kitchens
6 PS	Polystyrene —CH_2—CH(C_6H_5)—CH_2—CH(C_6H_5)—	Beverage/foam cups, window in envelopes
7 Other	All other resins, layered multimaterials, containers made of different materials	Some ketchup bottles, snack packs, mixture where top differs from bottom

REFERENCES

Ainsworth, S. J. "Plastics Additives." *Chemical and Engineering News, 70* (August 31, 1992): 34–55.

Burfield, D. R. "Polymer Glass Transition Temperatures." *Journal of Chemical Education, 64* (1987): 875.

Carraher, C. E., Jr., Hess, G., and Sperling, L. H. "Polymer Nomenclature—or What's in a Name?" *Journal of Chemical Education, 64* (1987): 36.

Carraher, C. E., Jr., and Seymour, R. B. "Physical Aspects of Polymer Structure: A Dictionary of Terms." *Journal of Chemical Education, 63* (1986): 418.

Carraher, C. E., Jr., and Seymour, R. B. "Polymer Properties and Testing—Definitions." *Journal of Chemical Education, 64* (1987): 866.

Carraher, C. E., Jr., and Seymour, R. B. "Polymer Structure—Organic Aspects (Definitions)." *Journal of Chemical Education, 65* (1988): 314.

Fried, J. R. "The Polymers of Commercial Plastics." *Plastics Engineering* (June 1982): 49–55.

Fried, J. R. "Polymer Properties in the Solid State." *Plastics Engineering* (July 1982): 27–37.

Fried, J. R. "Molecular Weight and Its Relation to Properties." *Plastics Engineering* (August 1982): 27–33.

Fried, J. R. "Elastomers and Thermosets." *Plastics Engineering* (March 1983): 67–73.

Fried, J. R., and Yeh, E. B. "Polymers and Computer Alchemy." *Chemtech, 23* (March 1993): 35–40.

Goodall, B. L. "The History and Current State of the Art of Propylene Polymerization Catalysts." *Journal of Chemical Education, 63* (1986): 191.

Harris, F. W., et al. "State of the Art: Polymer Chemistry." *Journal of Chemical Education, 58* (November 1981). (This issue contains 17 papers on polymer chemistry. The series covers structures, properties, mechanisms of formation, methods of preparation, stereochemistry, molecular weight distribution, rheological behavior of polymer melts, mechanical properties, rubber elasticity, block and graft copolymers, organometallic polymers, fibers, ionic polymers, and polymer compatibility.)

Jordan, R. F. "Cationic Metal–Alkyl Olefin Polymerization Catalysts." *Journal of Chemical Education, 65* (1988): 285.

Kauffman, G. B. "Wallace Hume Carothers and Nylon, the First Completely Synthetic Fiber." *Journal of Chemical Education, 65* (1988): 803.

Kauffman, G. B. "Rayon: The First Semi-Synthetic Fiber Product." *Journal of Chemical Education, 70* (1993): 887.

Kauffman, G. B., and Seymour, R. B. "Elastomers I. Natural Rubber." *Journal of Chemical Education, 67* (1990): 422.

Kauffman, G. B., and Seymour, R. B. "Elastomers II. Synthetic Rubbers." *Journal of Chemical Education, 68* (1991): 217.

Morse, P. M. "New Catalysts Renew Polyolefins." *Chemical and Engineering News, 76* (July 6, 1998): 11–16.

Seymour, R. B. "Polymers Are Everywhere." *Journal of Chemical Education, 65* (1988): 327.

Seymour, R. B. "Alkenes and Their Derivatives: The Alchemists' Dream Come True." *Journal of Chemical Education, 66* (1989): 670.

Seymour, R. B., and Kauffman, G. B. "Polymer Blends: Superior Products from Inferior Materials." *Journal of Chemical Education, 69* (1992): 646.

Seymour, R. B., and Kauffman, G. B. "Polyurethanes: A Class of Modern Versatile Materials." *Journal of Chemical Education, 69* (1992): 909.

Seymour, R. B., and Kauffman, G. B. "The Rise and Fall of Celluloid." *Journal of Chemical Education, 69* (1992): 311.

Seymour, R. B., and Kauffman, G. B. "Thermoplastic Elastomers." *Journal of Chemical Education, 69* (1992): 967.

Stevens, M. P. "Polymer Additives: Chemical and Aesthetic Property Modifiers." *Journal of Chemical Education, 70* (1993): 535.

Stevens, M. P. "Polymer Additives: Mechanical Property Modifiers." *Journal of Chemical Education, 70* (1993): 444.

Stevens, M. P. "Polymer Additives: Surface Property and Processing Modifiers." *Journal of Chemical Education, 70* (1993): 713.

Thayer, A. M. "Metallocene Catalysts Initiate New Era in Polymer Synthesis." *Chemical and Engineering News, 73* (September 11, 1995): 15–20.
Waller, F. J. "Fluoropolymers." *Journal of Chemical Education, 66* (1989): 487.
Webster, O. W. "Living Polymerization Methods." *Science, 251* (1991): 887.

ESSAY

Chemistry of Milk

Milk is a food of exceptional interest. Not only is milk an excellent food for the very young but humans have also adopted milk, specifically cow's milk, as a food substance for persons of all ages. Many specialized milk products, such as cheese, yogurt, butter, and ice cream, are staples of our diet.

Milk is probably the most nutritionally complete food that can be found in nature. This property is important for milk, because it is the only food young mammals consume in the nutritionally significant weeks following birth. Whole milk contains vitamins (principally thiamine, riboflavin, pantothenic acid, and vitamins A, D, and K), minerals (calcium, potassium, sodium, phosphorus, and trace metals), proteins (which include all the essential amino acids), carbohydrates (chiefly lactose), and lipids (fats). The only important elements in which milk is seriously deficient are iron and Vitamin C. Infants are usually born with a storage supply of iron large enough to meet their needs for several weeks. Vitamin C is easily secured through an orange juice supplement. The average composition of the milk of each of several mammals follows.

Average Percentage Composition of Milk from Various Mammals

	Cow	Human	Goat	Sheep	Horse
Water	87.1	87.4	87.0	82.6	90.6
Protein	3.4	1.4	3.3	5.5	2.0
Fats	3.9	4.0	4.2	6.5	1.1
Carbohydrates	4.9	7.0	4.8	4.5	5.9
Minerals	0.7	0.2	0.7	0.9	0.4

FATS

Whole milk is an oil–water type of emulsion, containing about 4% fat dispersed as very small (5–10 microns in diameter) globules. The globules are so small that a drop of milk contains about a million of them. Because the fat in milk is so finely dispersed, it is digested more easily than fat from any other source. The fat emulsion is stabilized to some extent by complex phospholipids and proteins that are absorbed on the surfaces of the globules. The fat globules, which are lighter than water, coalesce on standing and eventually rise to the surface of the milk, forming a layer of **cream.** Because Vitamins A and D are fat-soluble vitamins, they are carried to the surface with the cream. Commercially, the cream is often removed by centrifugation and skimming and is either diluted to form coffee cream ("half and half"), sold as **whipping cream,** converted to **butter,** or converted to **ice cream.** The milk that remains is called **skimmed milk.** Skimmed milk, except for lacking the fats and Vitamins A and D, has approximately the same composition as whole milk. If milk is **homogenized,** its fatty content will not separate. Milk is homogenized by forcing it through a small hole. This breaks up the fat globules and reduces their size to about 1–2 μ in diameter.

The structure of fats and oils is discussed in the essay that precedes Experiment 26. The fats in milk are primarily triglycerides. For the saturated fatty acids, the following percentages have been reported:

C_2 (3%)	C_8 (2.7%)	C_{14} (25.3%)	$> C_{18}$ (~5%)
C_4 (1.4%)	C_{10} (3.7%)	C_{16} (9.2%)	
C_6 (1.5%)	C_{12} (12.1%)	C_{18} (1.3%)	

Thus, about two-thirds of all the fatty acids in milk are saturated, and about one-third are unsaturated. Milk is unusual in that about 12% of the fatty acids are *short*-chain fatty acids (C_2–C_{10}), such as butyric, caproic, and caprylic acids.

Additional lipids (fats and oils) in milk include small amounts of cholesterol, phospholipids, and lecithins (phospholipids conjugated with choline). The structures of phospholipids and lecithins are shown. The phospholipids help to stabilize the whole-milk emulsion; the phosphate groups help to achieve partial water solubility for the fat globules. All the fat can be removed from milk by extraction with petroleum ether or a similar organic solvent.

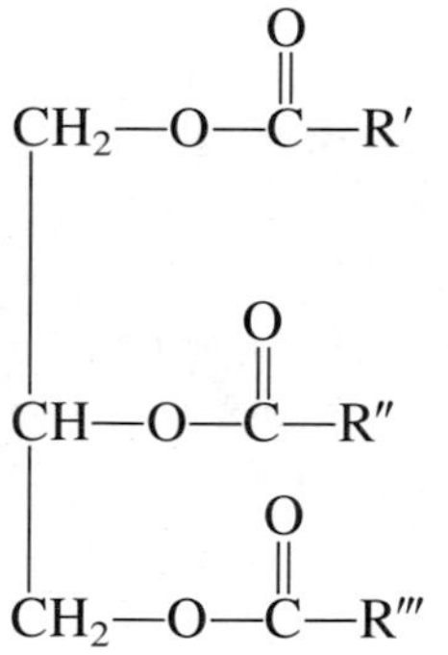

$$\begin{array}{l} CH_2-O-C(=O)-R' \\ | \\ CH-O-C(=O)-R'' \\ | \\ CH_2-O-C(=O)-R''' \end{array}$$

A triglyceride

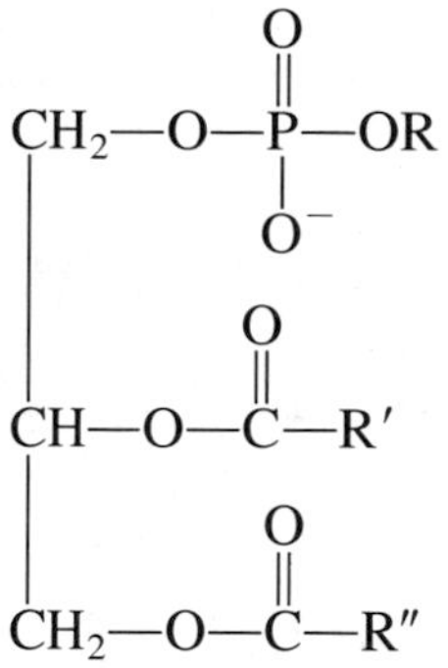

$$\begin{array}{l} CH_2-O-P(=O)(O^-)-OR \\ | \\ CH-O-C(=O)-R' \\ | \\ CH_2-O-C(=O)-R'' \end{array}$$

A phospholipid

$$\begin{array}{l} CH_2-O-P(=O)(O^-)-O-CH_2CH_2-N(CH_3)_3^+ \\ | \\ CH-O-C(=O)-R' \\ | \\ CH_2-O-C(=O)-R'' \end{array}$$

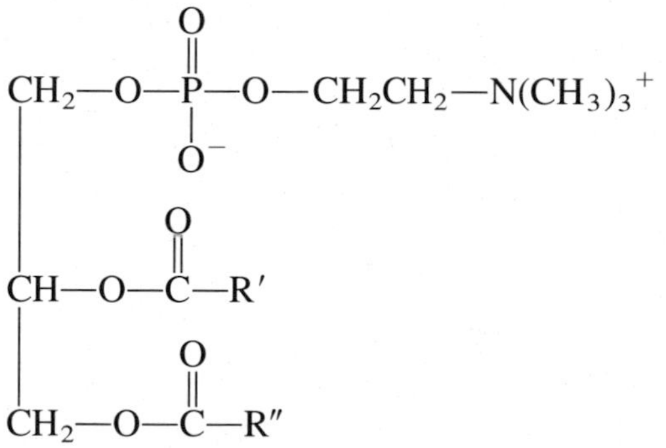

A lecithin

PROTEINS

Proteins may be classified broadly in two general categories: globular and fibrous. Globular proteins are those that tend to fold back on themselves into compact units that approach nearly spheroidal shapes. These types of proteins do not form intermolecular interactions between protein units (hydrogen bonds and so on) as fibrous proteins do, and they are more easily solubilized as colloidal suspensions. There are three kinds of proteins in milk: **caseins, lactalbumins,** and **lactoglobulins.** All are globular.

Casein is a phosphoprotein, meaning that phosphate groups are attached to some of the amino acid side chains. These are attached mainly to the hydroxyl groups of the serine and threonine moieties. Actually, casein is a mixture of at least three similar proteins, prin-

Casein	MW	Phosphate Groups/Molecule
α	27,300	~9
β	24,100	~4–5
κ	~8,000	~1.5

cipally α, β, and κ caseins. These three proteins differ primarily in molecular weight and amount of phosphorus they contain (number of phosphate groups).

Casein exists in milk as the calcium salt **calcium caseinate.** This salt has a complex structure. It is composed of α, β, and κ caseins, which form a **micelle,** or a solubilized unit. Neither the α nor the β casein is soluble in milk, and neither is soluble either singly or in combination. If κ casein is added to either one or to a combination of the two, however, the result is a casein complex that is soluble owing to the formation of the micelle.

A structure proposed for the casein micelle is shown in the figure below. The κ casein is thought to stabilize the micelle. Because both α and β casein are phosphoproteins, they are precipitated by calcium ions. Recall that $Ca_3(PO_4)_2$ is fairly insoluble.

$$\boxed{\text{PROTEIN}}-O-\overset{\displaystyle O}{\overset{\|}{\underset{\underset{\displaystyle O^-}{|}}{P}}}-O^- + Ca^{2+} \longrightarrow \boxed{\text{PROTEIN}}-O-\overset{\displaystyle O}{\overset{\|}{\underset{\underset{\displaystyle O^-}{|}}{P}}}-O^-Ca^{2+}\downarrow$$

Insoluble

The κ casein protein, however, has fewer phosphate groups and a high content of carbohydrate bound to it. It is also thought to have all its serine and threonine residues (which have hydroxyl groups), as well as its bound carbohydrates, on only one side of its outer surfaces. This portion of its outer surface is easily solubilized in water because these polar groups are present. The other portion of its surface binds well to the water-insoluble α and β caseins and solubilizes them by forming a protective colloid or micelle around them. Because the entire outer surface of the micelle can be solubilized in water, the unit is solubilized *as a whole,* thus bringing the α and β caseins, as well as κ casein, into solution.

Calcium caseinate has its isoelectric (neutrality) point at pH 4.6. Therefore, it is insoluble in solutions of pH less than 4.6. The pH of milk is about 6.6; therefore, casein has a negative charge at this pH and is solubilized as a salt. If acid is added to milk, the negative charges on the outer surface of the micelle are neutralized (the phosphate groups are protonated), and the neutral protein precipitates:

$$Ca^{2+}\ \text{Caseinate} + 2\ HCl \longrightarrow \text{Casein}\downarrow + CaCl_2$$

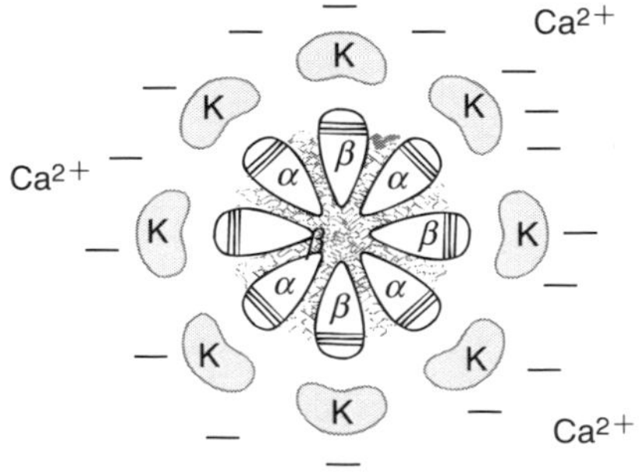

A casein micelle (average diameter, 1200 Å).

The calcium ions remain in solution. When milk sours, lactic acid is produced by bacterial action (see equations on p. 460), and the consequent lowering of the pH causes the same *clotting* reaction. The isolation of casein from milk is described in Experiment 54.

The casein in milk can also be clotted by the action of an enzyme called **rennin.** Rennin is found in the fourth stomach of young calves. However, both the nature of the clot and the mechanism of clotting differ when rennin is used. The clot formed using rennin, **calcium paracaseinate,** contains calcium.

$$\text{Ca}^{2+}\ \text{Caseinate} \xrightarrow{\text{rennin}} \text{Ca}^{2+}\ \text{Paracaseinate} + \text{a small peptide}$$

Rennin is a hydrolytic enzyme (peptidase) and acts specifically to cleave peptide bonds between phenylalanine and methionine residues. It attacks the κ casein, breaking the peptide chain to release a small segment of it. This destroys the water-solubilizing surface of the κ casein, which protects the inner α and κ caseins, and causes the entire micelle to precipitate as calcium paracaseinate. Milk can be decalcified by treatment with oxalate ion, which forms an insoluble calcium salt. If the calcium ions are removed from milk, a clot will not be formed when the milk is treated with rennin.

The clot, or **curd,** formed by the action of rennin is sold commercially as **cottage cheese.** The liquid remaining is called the **whey.** The curd can also be used in producing various types of **cheese.** It is washed, pressed to remove any excess whey, and chopped. After this treatment, it is melted, hardened, and ground. The ground curd is then salted, pressed into molds, and set aside to age.

Albumins are globular proteins that are soluble in water and in dilute salt solutions. They are, however, denatured and coagulated by heat. The second most abundant protein types in milk are the **lactalbumins.** Once the caseins have been removed and the solution has been made acidic, the lactalbumins can be isolated by heating the mixture to precipitate them. The typical albumin has a molecular weight of about 41,000.

A third type of protein in milk is the **lactoglobulins.** They are present in smaller amounts than the albumins and generally denature and precipitate under the same conditions as the albumins. The lactoglobulins carry the immunological properties of milk. They protect the young mammal until its own immune systems have developed.

CARBOHYDRATES

When the fats and the proteins have been removed from milk, the carbohydrates remain, as they are soluble in aqueous solution. The main carbohydrate in milk is lactose.

Lactose, a disaccharide, is the *only* carbohydrate that mammals synthesize. Hydrolyzed, it yields one molecule of D-glucose and one of D-galactose. It is synthesized in the mammary glands. In this process, one molecule of glucose is converted to galactose and joined to another of glucose. The galactose is apparently needed by the developing infant to build brain and nervous tissue. Brain cells contain **glycolipids** as a part of their structure. A glycolipid is a triglyceride in which one of the fatty acid groups has been replaced by a sugar, in this case galactose. Galactose is more stable (to metabolic oxidation) than glucose and affords a better material for forming structural units in cells.

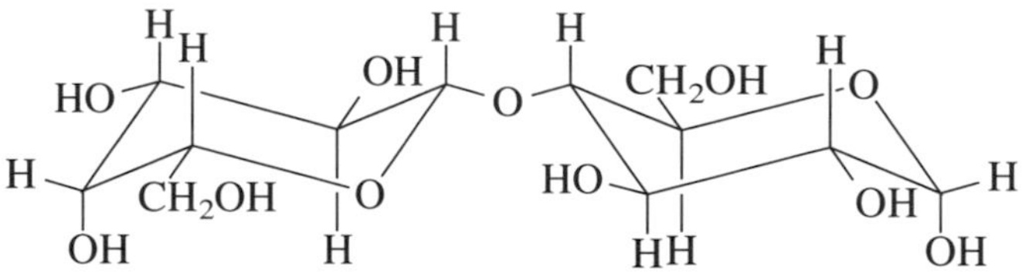

Lactose
D-Galactose + D-Glucose

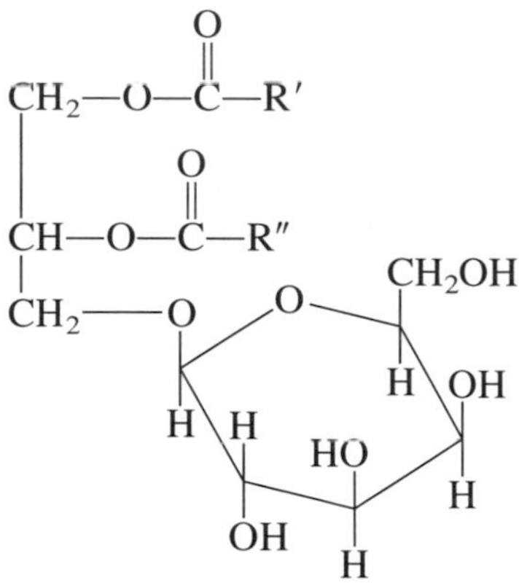

A glycolipid

Although almost all human infants can digest lactose, some adults lose this ability on reaching maturity, because milk is no longer an important part of their diet. An enzyme called **lactase** is necessary to digest lactose. Lactase is secreted by the cells of the small intestine, and it cleaves lactose into its two component sugars, which are easily digested. Persons lacking the enzyme lactase do not digest lactose properly. Because it is poorly absorbed by the small intestine, it remains in the digestive tract, where its osmotic potential causes an influx of water. This results in cramps and diarrhea for the affected individual. Persons with a lactase deficiency cannot tolerate more than one glass of milk a day. The deficiency is most common among blacks, but it is also quite common among older Caucasians.

Lactose can be removed from whey by adding ethanol. Lactose is insoluble in ethanol, and when the ethanol is mixed with the aqueous solution, the lactose is forced to crystallize. The isolation of lactose from milk is described in Experiment 54.

When milk is allowed to stand at room temperature, it sours. Many bacteria are present in milk, particularly **lactobacilli.** These bacteria act on the lactose in milk to produce the sour **lactic acid.** These microorganisms actually **hydrolyze** lactose and produce lactic acid only from the galactose portion of the lactose. Since the production of the lactic acid also lowers the pH of the milk, the milk clots when it sours:

$$\underset{\text{Lactose}}{C_{12}H_{22}O_{11}} + H_2O \longrightarrow \underset{\text{Galactose}}{C_6H_{12}O_6} + \underset{\text{Glucose}}{C_6H_{12}O_6}$$

$$\underset{\text{Galactose}}{C_6H_{12}O_6} \xrightarrow{\text{lactobacilli}} \underset{\text{Lactic acid}}{CH_3-\underset{\displaystyle OH}{\underset{|}{CH}}-COOH}$$

Many "cultured" milk products are manufactured by allowing milk to sour before it is processed. For instance, milk or cream is usually allowed to sour somewhat by lactic acid bacteria before it is churned to make butter. The fluid left after the milk is churned is sour and is called **buttermilk.** Other cultured milk products include sour cream, yogurt, and certain types of cheese.

REFERENCES

Boyer, R. F. "Purification of Milk Whey α-Lactalbumin by Immobilized Metal-Ion Affinity Chromatography." *Journal of Chemical Education, 68* (May 1991): 430.

Fox, B. A., and Cameron, A. G. "Oils, Fats, and Colloids." Chap. 6 in *Food Science—a Chemical Approach.* New York: Crane, Russak, 1973.

Kleiner, I. S., and Orten, J. M. "Milk." Chap. 7 in *Biochemistry.* 7th ed. St. Louis: C. V. Mosby, 1966.

McKenzie, H. A., ed. *Milk Proteins,* 2 vols. New York: Academic Press, 1970.

Oberg, C. J. "Curdling Chemistry—Coagulated Milk Products." *Journal of Chemical Education, 63* (September 1986): 770.

EXPERIMENT 54

Isolation of Casein and Lactose from Milk

Isolation of a protein
Isolation of a sugar

In this experiment, you will isolate several of the chemical substances found in milk. First, you will isolate a phosphorus-containing protein, casein (Experiment 54A). The remaining milk mixture will then be used as a source of a sugar, α-lactose (Experiment 54B). After you isolate the milk sugar, you will make several chemical tests on this material. Fats, which are present in whole milk, are not isolated in this experiment because powdered nonfat milk is used.

Here is the procedure you will follow. First, the casein is precipitated by warming the powdered milk and adding dilute acetic acid. It is important that the heating not be excessive or the acid too strong, because these conditions also hydrolyze lactose into its components, glucose and galactose. After the casein has been removed, the excess acetic acid is neutralized with calcium carbonate, and the solution is heated to its boiling point to precipitate the initially soluble protein, albumin. The liquid containing the lactose is poured away from the albumin. Alcohol is added to the solution, and any remaining protein is removed by centrifugation. α-Lactose crystallizes on cooling.

Lactose is an example of a disaccharide. It is made up of two sugar molecules: galactose and glucose. In the preceding structures, the galactose portion is on the left, and glucose is on the right. Galactose is bonded through an acetal linkage to glucose.

Notice that the glucose portion can exist in one of two isomeric hemiacetal structures: α-lactose and β-lactose. Glucose can also exist in a free aldehyde form. This aldehyde form (open form) is an intermediate in the equilibration (interconversion) of α- and β-lactose. Very little of this free aldehyde form exists in the equilibrium mixture. The isomeric α- and β-lactose are diastereomers because they differ in the configuration at one carbon atom, called the anomeric carbon atom.

The sugar α-lactose is easily obtainable by crystallization from a water–ethanol mixture at room temperature. However, β-lactose must be obtained by a more difficult process, which involves crystallization from a concentrated solution of lactose at temperatures about

93.5°C. In the present experiment, α-lactose is isolated because the experimental procedure is easier.

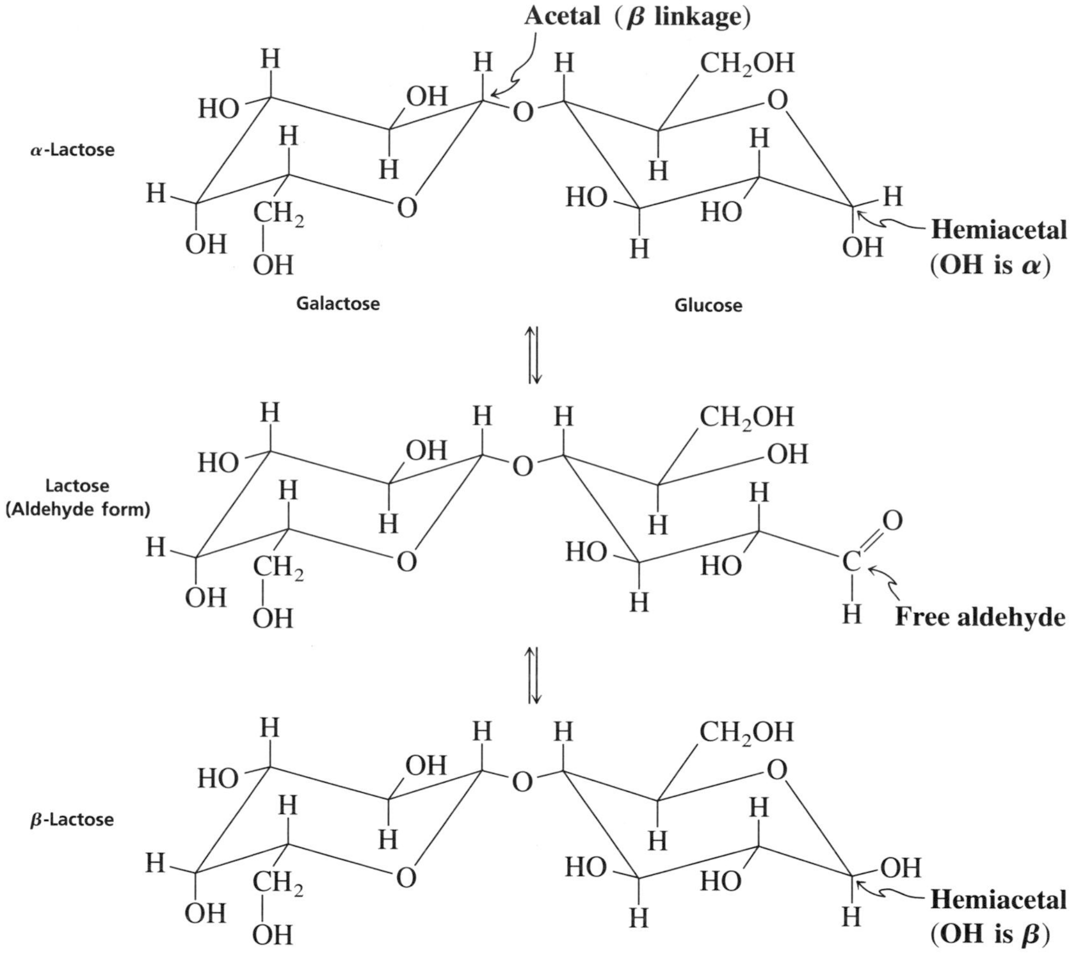

Acetal (β linkage)

α-Lactose

Galactose

Glucose

Hemiacetal (OH is α)

Lactose (Aldehyde form)

Free aldehyde

β-Lactose

Hemiacetal (OH is β)

α-Lactose undergoes numerous interesting reactions. First, α-lactose interconverts, via the free aldehyde form, to a large extent, to the β-isomer in aqueous solution. This causes a change in the rotation of polarized light from +92.6° to +52.3° with increasing time. The process that causes the change in optical rotation with time is called **mutarotation.**

A second reaction of lactose is the oxidation of the free aldehyde form by Benedict's reagent. Lactose is referred to as a reducing sugar because it reduces Benedict's reagent (copper[II] ion to copper[I] ion) and produces a red precipitate (Cu_2O). In the process, the aldehyde group is oxidized to a carboxyl group. The reaction that takes place in Benedict's test is

$$R{-}CHO + 2\,Cu^{2+} + 4\,OH^- \longrightarrow RCOOH + Cu_2O + 2\,H_2O$$

A third reaction of lactose is the oxidation of the galactose part by the mucic acid test. In this test, the acetal linkage between galactose and glucose units is cleaved by the acidic